RAJIV GANDHI

His Mind And Ideology

RAJIV GANDHI

HIS MIND AND IDEOLOGY

Attar Chand

Foreword by

Dr. Shankar Dayal Sharma
Vice-President of India,

GIAN PUBLISHING HOUSE

NEW DELHI-110002

GIAN PUBLISHING HOUSE
5, Ansari Road,
New Delhi-110002

ISBN 81-312-0397-X

PRINTED IN INDIA

Published by Mrs Gayatri Garg, for Gian Publishing House
New Delhi 110002
Typesetting by Creative Typesetters, New Delhi
Printed by Goyal Offset Works, Delhi

CONTENTS

FOREWORD
RAJIV - A LEADER OF VISION

I remember coming to Teen Murti House in 1952; Rajiv was than a Child of eight years. Today when I offered flower petals (at his photograph) it struck me it would have been more appropriate had he been paying homage to me.

The sense of benumbment is very much with us all to mourn the passing away from our midst. of a world statesman, a leader of vision with a position of deep significance in the ethos of India, a very appealing attractive and warm personality.

Rajiv owed much to Pandit Jawaharlal Nehru, who moulded his life and was his mentor and guide in every way, and Indira Gandhi with whom he worked closely. I was always touched by the unfailing consideration and regard Rajiv showed me-perhaps even more so after he became the Prime Minister.

Rajiv was a wonderfully fine human being, who courageously picked up the gauntlet and faced awesome challenges on behalf of the people of India, being intersely devoted to their well-being and future in a rapidly changing world.

Rajiv, stood for national unity, secularism, peace, brotherhood and progress. He had a vision of the growth of India and the rest of the world, he appreciated the role of science and technology.....he was engaged in a valiant struggle at one time on a large number of fronts.

I never imagined that in my lifetime a day would dawn of India without Rajiv. The world is proper... Rajiv always talked of taking the country into the 21st century, and it is a tragedy that his life was taken on May 21.

It was incumbent upon all to perservere in the tasks Rajiv had initiated and to face boldly, fearlessly, unitedly the challenges that threaten not just the country but us timeless ethos of pluralism and oneness, an ethos of growing significance for the good of the whole world.

We owe it to Rajiv as we did to Indira, Nehru, and Bapu (Mahatma Gandhi) to be resolute and devoted in the service of the people of India for a better future for all.

Dr. Shankar Dayal Sharma
Vice-President of India,

May 25, 1991.
New Delhi.

ACKNOWLEDGEMENTS

The present study could not have reached fruition without the encouragement of my we-wishers, who suggested sundry improvements and provided nourishing guidance and inspiration. I am much obliged to my fellow writers, journalists, academicians and professors whose writings I have consulted and taken notes, in parts or in full, in writing this book of global interest.

Delhi Attar Chand

1
PREFACE : THE RAJIV YEARS

The assassination of Rajiv Gandhi has stunned the entire nation because he was snatched away from the Indian people at a time when he was engaged in a grim political battle to defend the secular edifice of the country with a crusader's zeal. The upper- most question in the minds of the people is: Why was he physically liquidated and that too at a time when he was rousing the people to defend the democratic and secular political structure of the country by exercising their right to elect a government of their choice at the Centre? Was it because he had unleashed a new popular upsurge among the secular-minded people throughout the country? Was it due to the fact that this upsurge had begun to transform itself into a silent pro-Congress wave? Is it a fact that by rousing the secular and democratic instincts of the people, he slowly but surely, was putting brakes on the rise of the monster of communalism and forces of internal and external subversion? No one can answer these questions at this stage, because the whole sequence of developments which led to his assassination is still a mystery; and, perhaps, this mystery will never be unmasked. In a shot span of a decade, from an obscure life of a pilot, he became an outstanding national leader. Born at Bombay on August 20, 1944 and educated at Doon School and Trinity College, Cambridge, Rajiv Gandhi was not interested in active politics. Soft-spoken and mild-mannered, Rajiv was pushed into politics by circumstances beyond his control, particularly after the death of his younger brother Sanjay Gandhi.[1]

Assassination of his mother, Indira Gandhi, in the last week of October, 1984 marked the beginning of a new phase in his political life. He became the Prime Minister of India and after the election to the Lok Sabha in 1984, he again became the Prime Minister in 1984, a post which he held till 1989, when the Congress was defeated at the polls.

Twice the death came knocking at his door, and returned. The third time, Rajiv Gandhi was unlucky.

Two unsuccessful attempts were made on Rajiv Gandhi's life when he was the Prime Minister. The first one occurred on Oct. 2, 1986, when he went to offer prayers at Rajghat on the 117th birth anniversary of Mahatma Gandhi. He was walking down to the memorial along with his wife when a Punjab terrorist, Karamjit Singh, took a pot shot at him. He escaped, as it was found later, only because the 12 bore pistol of Karamjit Singh developed a fault. Hardly eight months later on July

1. V.D. Chopra. Rajiv Gandhi. *Patriot*, 23 May 1991.

20, 1987, when Rajiv Gandhi went to Colombo to sign the historic Indo-Sri Lanka Accord, a Sri Lankan soldier swung his rifle at his head. Rajiv Gandhi, who saw the rifle butt moving in the air in the nick of the time, ducked and escaped with minor injuries on his left shoulder and neck.

For a man who became the electioned elected head of the largest democracy in the world at the age of 40. Rajiv Gandhi, in a short span of time, came to be widely regarded as the pivot around which India's destiny would revolve. His promise of a brave new world, unfettered by dogmas, enthused millions in this country. And just at a time when he was about to recapture the magic of his earlier days as Prime Minister and had acquired the reflectiveness which comes with passing years, the cruel hands of destiny have snatched him away from our midst. For a man who became the seventh Prime Minister of the country at the bidding of his party, on the morrow of his mother. Indira Gandhi's assassination, Rajiv Gandhi had slowly but surely come to grips with the byzantine ways of Indian politics. And at a time when the country was sought to be divided on religious and communal lines by his arch adversaries, he rose above the temptation of a populist appeal to capture votes in the ongoing elections and painstakingly strove for a Nehruvian consensus to settle the ills plauging India's polity. His recent style of campaigning was indicative of the new approach which Rajiv Gandhi would have adopted as the new incumbent of South Block. In his election meetings, he invariably brake the security cordon, to mix with the crowd and inquire about their well being. Truely, the scion of the oldest and most famous political dynasty in India had emerged as a leader of Jawaharlal mould in the recent weeks. Drawing upon his earlier avocation as a pilot, Rajiv had begun to mix the preciseness associated with the aviator with the realpolitik of a public man. He joined politics in 1981 after his younger brother. Sanjay, died, in an air crash. He emerged as a hands down winner in the by-election from the Amethi constituency, represented by his brother, the same year. Subsequently, Rajiv became a general secretary of the All India Congress Committee. The former Indian Airline pilot earned his political and electoral spurs when he led the Congress to a thumping victory in the December 1984 elections, bagging 415 of the 452 seats in the eighty Lok Sabha.

The first signs of Rajiv's strong, Charismatic personality was revealed to the Indian people in his campaign for the by- elections to Amethi Lok Sabha seat which he contested at the age of 36 in 1981.

Rajiv began his tenure as Prime Minister as a leader who projected an image of modernity and new blood in Indian politics. He appeared as an incorruptible and straightforward politician who was honest and sincere about implementing the policies of his party.

Rajiv, who began to be called "Mr Clean", became synonymous with a new style of government and condemned outmoded techniques and wanted to use technology for the advancement of the nation. The assassination of his mother and his sudden propulson to power was a traumatic experience for the young-leader. He barely had time to absorb his grief and his responsibilities as Prime Minister took all his time. He was constantly under threat during his five-year term in office in spite of high security ring around him and his family. There was an assassination attempt on him on October 2, 1986, at Rajghat where he had gone to pay respect to Mahatma Gandhi, the Father of the Nation. He emerged from the assassination bid calm and unperturbed. He also appeared to have taken in his stride another attempt on his life in Sri Lanka in 1987. During his tenure, he signed the historic Punjab and Assam accords in 1985, the Indo-Sri Lanka peace accord in 1987 and sent emergency aid to the Maldives in 1988. He also formalised bilateral trade treaties with Pakistan and China and thawed the ice in the Sino-Indian relations with his Beijing visit in 1988. Back home, Rajiv introduced the Jawahar Rozgar Yojna and Panchayati Raj Institution Bill for the uplift of the poor in 1989. He, however, lost power in 1989 elections fighting a united opposition led by the National Front which projected the Bofors and other Corruption-related charges as a Major campaign plank against Mr. Gandhi. Born on August 20, 1944,. Rajiv was the eldest son of Indira Gandhi and Feroz Gandhi. His grandfather, Jawaharlal Nehru, was India's first Premier. He spent his early childhood under the care of a Danish governess named Anna Ornsholt. Rajiv was shy, well behaved and courteous. He talked little and in a low voice, but was considered by his mother as having more self confidence than his younger brother.

In the fifties, Rajiv attended the prestigious Doon School, where his teacher felt frustrated because his above-average intelligence was not revealed in his examinations. A month after Rajiv turned 16, his father Feroz Gandhi, died. Later, Rajiv attended Imperial College in London, where he studied mechanical engineering in Trinity College.

He worked part-time, shopped at discount sales and sharped shared cramped accommodation with fellow students. He met Sonia Maino, his future wife, at Cambridge, When he was 20, Jawaharlal Nehru died, and two years later, his mother became Prime Minister. Rajiv showed no interest in politics while living with his mother, wife and two children-Priyanka and Rahul-and continued to be quiet and unassuming. He trained to become a pilot and later worked for Indian Air lines, earning a reputation for being a stickler for mechanical detail and receiving an above-average rating.

In 1982, Rajiv Gandhi played an instrumental role in organising the Asian Games in New Delhi. At the same time, as general secretary of Congress, he managed party affairs with diligence.

Indira Gandhi told how Nehru had a first glimpse of his grandson. Rajiv's parents had heard that Nehru was moving prisons and might spend the night at Allahabad's Naini Jail. Their information was correct and, as he entered the prison late at night, they held seven-month-old Rajiv up for his grandfather's inspection. "Under a very dim roadside light, my father peered at him," Indira wrote. Prior to that, Nehru had been sent photographs of his grandson, which elicited the comment: "the forehead seems to be rather like Feroze's." Indira also told how Nehru had selected his grandson's names from lists she and Feroze sent to him in jail. Rajiv was chosen because in Sanskrit it means 'lotus' - as does Kamala, the name of Nehru's wife who had died eight years earlier. Though he had has always been called Rajiv, his full name is Rajivaratna, Ratns means "jewel", which is one of the meanings of Jawahar; so he inherited names from both his maternal grandparents.[2]

Speaking of the influence his father had on his upbringing, Rajiv talks with obvious approval of 'the way he acted in Parliament, independent and a little outspoken, without caring too much for the consequences." Feroze had been a bit of a revolutionary in his student days, and was once briefly arrested for taking part in a leftist demonstration in Paris. Rajiv likes to think he has inherited something of his father's leftist streak, though he has never really demonstrated it.[3]

Rajiv Gandhi belonged to the category of boys for whom childhood is but a fleeting halt in the journey of life. Rajiv Gandhi was only 16 when lost his father Feroze Gandhi. He was still in school when he and younger brother Sanjay received the news of their father's passing away on September 8, 1960. That day Rajiv Gandhi became a man - and a friend and companion to his mother Indira Gandhi and a father figure to young Sanjay. Jawaharlal Nehru was still around. So Rajiv Gandhi was spared the responsibility of running the family. But the war with China made Nehru lose his usual poise and confidence and two years later, on May 27, 1964, he became a valuable chapter of the contemporary history of India. Being the eldest male in the family Rajiv Gandhi was asked to light the pyre of his grandfather.

2. Nicholas Nugent. *Rajiv Gandhi.* London, BBC, 1990. See also *The Sunday Observer,* 26 May, 1991.
3. *Ibid.*

That day, at the age of 20, even before he could earn the right to vote, he became the head of the Nehru-Gandhi family. The next 16 years were spent in relative peace. He went to Cambridge and found himself an Italian for a wife, returned home and planned a quiet private life for his family while Sanjay Gandhi found the turbulance of politics more attractive. Rajiv and Sonia and their two children and Sanjay and Maneka with Indira Gandhi at the head of the table - it was such a happy family. Came 1980 and the picture of a happy Nehru-Gandhi family began to develop cracks. It all happended so suddenly. The Congress (I) had returned to power and Indira Gandhi was Prime Minister again. Sanjay Gandhi was rearing to go. Then came the news that Sanjay had died in an air crash while on a joy ride. Rajiv Gandhi was all alone as the only adult male member of the family. On a hot June day he lit a pyre for the third time to say goodbye to his younger brother. A few months later Maneka Gandhi walked out of 1-Safdarjung Road. And then there was just Indira Gandhi, Rajiv, Sonia, Priyanka and Rahul at the dinner table. Rajiv Gandhi made a reluctant entry into politics and retained the Amethi Lok Sabha seat won earlier by Sanjay. Destiny did not allow him sufficient time to learn the basics of Indian politics. On October 31, 1984, Indira Gandhi was assassinated by her own bodyguards. Such were the exigencies of politics that President Zail Singh did not allow him "time out" to help him get over the shock of his mother's death. This time it was as Prime Minister of India that he lit the fourth pyre - that of the woman who had given him birth.[4]

Now Rajiv Gandhi was the sole surviving adult member of the Nehru-Gandhi clan. There were only four members of the happy family of the early eighties at the breakfast table. It is tragically strange but true that the *bahus* of the family have nerves of steel and carry on "manfully" in spite of losing their partners fairly early in life. Neither Feroze Gandhi nor Rajiv and Sanjay had the satisfaction of seeking seeing their children settled in life. In fact Sanjay's son Feroze Varun Gandhi is posthumous child.

Rajiv Gandhi, who took over as prime minister in 1984 at the age of 40, was one of the youngest elected heads of state worldwide.

He became the country's seventh prime minister hours after the assassination of Indira Gandhi by her bodyguards on October 30, 1984.

A pilot with Indian Airlines, Rajiv Gandhi was a late and reluctant entrant in politics, joining at the behest of his mother after the death of his brother Sanjay in an air crash in 1980.

4. L.H. Naqvi. Tragedy of Being Nehru-Gandhi. The Tribune, 25 May, 1991.

He contested the Amethi byelection in 1981 and was subsequently appointed AICC general secretary.

The sympathy wave generated for the Congress after Indira Gandhi's assassination helped the Congress to a thumping victory bagging 415 of the 542 seats in eighth Lok Sabha in the December 1984 elections under Rajiv Gandhi's stewardship.

During his tenure, he signed the historic Punjab and Assam accords in 1985, the Indo-Sri Lanka peace accord in 1987 and sent emergency aid to the Maldives in 1988.

He also formalised bilateral trade treaties with Pakistan and China and thawed the ice in the Sino-Indian relations with his Beijing visit in 1988.

Back home, Rajiv Gandhi introduced the Jawahar Rozagar Yojna and panchayati raj institution bill for the uplift of the poor in 1989.

He, however, lost power in the 1989 elections fighting a united opposition-led by the National Front which projected the Bofors and other corruption-related charges as a major campaign plank against Mr. Gandhi.

Born on August 20, 1944, Rajiv Gandhi went to Doon School and Trintiy College, Cambridge, and did a course in mechanical engineering. As a Young man, he was not interested in politics and his bookshelves were stacked with volumes on science and engineering and not politics.

He liked western and Hindustani classical music and was keenly interested in photography and amateur radio.

His greatest passion, however, was flying. Soon after his return from England, he obtained a commercial pilot's licence and joined Indian Airlines.

In 1968, he married Sonia Maino, the Italian student he had met at Cambridge. They had two children: son Rahul and daughter Priyanka.

In 1982, Rajiv Gandhi played an instrumental role in organising the Asian Games in New Delhi.

At the same time, as general secretary of Congress (I), he managed party affairs with diligence.

He took over as prime minister and president of the party in October 1984 with Indira Gandhi's assassination.

In the general elections that followed two months later, he spearheaded his party to a massive win bagging nearly 50 per cent of the votes polled.

In the next elections in 1989, his party though short of majority, was still the largest single party in the House.

During the 1991 elections Rajiv Gandhi as Congress - I president has been on an intensive tour of the country, often ignoring manadatory security requirements.

During the five years that he was prime minister, he conducted himself with aplomb and poise. No one would have wished such a violent and tragic end to his brief political carrer. His assassination raises issues that are of grave concern. The most important of these is the use of violence to settle political scores. Indira Gandhi was assassinated in 1984 for the same reason. The killing of candidates in Punjab and the violence during polling underscore the increasing brutalisation of Indian politics.

Another cause for concern is the growing dominance of caste and religion in elections. If elections are fought around emotional issues like case and religion, we will be confronted with increasing mayhem and turmoil. The important issues that should concern us, like inflation, population control, unemployment, poverty alleviation, balance of payments and technological progress do not figure at all in the election campaign. We are proud of being the world's largest democracy. It is time we also tried to become the best democracy by avoiding resort to violence and terrorism to solve problems.[5]

May 21, 1991 was perhaps the saddest day in the life of the nation. Rajiv Gandhi, the illustrious son of India and beloved of millions of Indians was done to death by a dastardly and cowardly act of an assassin hired by the enemies of the country. I blame his death directly to the security lapses despite the denials of Chandra Shekhar. An energetic, Young and charismatic leader who would have taken India to her glorious future and into the twenty first century had his dreams.

During his five years' of prime ministership he had already achieved so much nationally and internationally.

He saved Sri Lanka and Maldives from disintegration by quick despatch of Indian troops. At the same time he started the process of improving and stengthening good neighbourly relations specially with China and Pakistan. NAM and SAARC received his special attention. Someone has said that "show me a man a who says he is not affraid of death and I would say there goes the biggest liar," Rajiv was an exception. Despite perpetual threat to his life he went about the whole business with dangers, a trait of the Nehru family who were taught to shun fears altogether in pursuit of their ideals. Rajiv surpassed each

5. Billu. Rajiv Gandhi. *The Business and Political Observer*, 31 May 1991.

one of them by making a supreme sacrifice of his beloved country and the secular idealism. He has amply discharged his debt that he owed to his country. The pall of gloom that descended the whole country was unbelievable. He was holding no governmental office when the cruel death snatched him away. The whole country was plunged into darkness. "No man is an island upto himeself. Each man's death diminishes me," very well said. He was the brightest jewel in India's crown. In this hour of Nation's profound and everlasting grief our heart reaches out to his beloved wife Sonia Gandhi and his two adorable children, Rahul and Priyanka. Their stoic sangfroid and dignified composure at their irreparable loss drew the applause and admiration from the Heads of various countries and dignitaries who were present at the funeral to pay their last tearful tribute to Rajiv.

It is my prayer that if there is a God watching the affairs of men, no harm should come to this bereaved family anymore.

No man is indispensable but for India Rajiv was. Now in his death a little of each one of us has also died. His death is highly regrettable. What is more regrettable is the end of his vision which he had chartered in his mind to take India into the twenty first century; a nation so strong dynamic and powerful as to be the envy of the whole world. But alas; I, at this juncture, cannot think of any other person doing just that. My fear is that the professional politicians after the elections will drag this country to pits for their own selfish motives and personal aggrandisement.[6]

The assassination of the Rajiv Gandhi, in the midst of the tenth elections of a new Parliament was a dagger thurst in the heart of secular Indian democracy. So was the assassination of the Mahatma Gandhi by the bullets of Nathuram Godse after Independence. The same process got Indira Gandhi killed by her own bodygurds so that India was drowned into the chaos and anarchy.[7]

Rajiv Gandhi was inspired by the nobel vision of making India great and powerful nation and his contribution to bringing the cold war to an end and strengthening the global movement for nuclear disarmament was invaluable.

It was one of the most distressing ironies of our time that Rajiv Gandhi who took the historic initiative to build a world free of violence and strife have met such a brutal end. By his contribution to the modernisation of India, his steadfast fight against divisive forces harmony in the forces and strengthening peace and harmony in the world,

6. Shiv Rai. Rajiv Gandhi. *National Herald*, 31 May 1991.
7. R.K. Garg. The President's Responsibility. *National Herald* 26 May 1991.

Rajiv Gandhi has carved for himself an unforgettable place in the history of our times.

Terrorism and assassinations are by no means specific to any region or country. There are few leaders who have not been the target of an assassination threat or attempt. In India, Mahatma Gandhi, Pratap Singh Kairon, L.N. Mishra, Indira Gandhi, General A.S. Vaidya, and now Rajiv Gandhi have been felled by the assassins' bullets.

In fact, violence, political or otherwise, is today locked in a hand-to-hand combat with peace. Never before has it's presence been so pervasive, it's threat so real, it's glare so garish. Ideally, a political killing is more serious business, or at any rate should be, considering how much is at stake, and how much damage it can cause to a nation's soul. Much more thought needs to go into it. Violence is an essential component of all political struggle, whether it is to secede from the state, or establish a Marxisit/Fascist one in its place. That is why all it's principal votaries have carefully considered the circumstances under which it can be let loose. It's final goal paradoxically has always been the betterment of people in general, as against a section's. Even anarchism's appeal lay in how it's propounders Godwin, Produhon, Saint Simon and Comte attacked a 'tentacular' nation state, and aimed at a classless society possessed of modern technology in which the ills of capitalism could be countered. But it isn't enough to seek the success of a 'just' movement through violent means. Equally crucial is to assess the degree of success any such action can bring in its wake. Is the basic framework workable? What is the extent of mass support it can garner? Most important, what is the stature and maturity of its leader. Does their hectoring have any intellectual content, or are they mere rabble-rousers making mountains out of molehills?[8]

Terrorism in Jammu and Kashmir is a more recent phenomenon, of the late 1980s. There is a common pattern in both even if their forms are different. It is the systematic use of murder and destruction (random killings in Punjab and attack on property and installations) or terrorising individuals, communities and governments into conceding their political demands. It is one of the oldest techniques of psychological warfare. As Bakunin called it, it is the propaganda of the deed. A Primary target of terrorisation is chosen, the objective or message to be conveyed is determined and credibilyt is established by convinving the target that the threat can be actually carried out. Illustratively, the Srinagar station director of Doordarshan was killed to convey a message to the government. Similarly late last year, when the Khalisatni

8. Sudhir K. Singh. And a Murder Most Foul. *The Business and Political Observer*, 28 May 1991.

militants wanted to enforce their Panthic Code for the media, an AIR official was killed to get the message across. The propagnda of the deed has no meaning unless the target audience identifies the deed with a particular cause. Before the emergence of terrorism in Jammu and Kashmir, every bomb explosion, act of sabotage or killing in Pubjab and even outside the state was attributed to the Khalistani militants. Even if none of the groups claimed responsibility for them.

But there is a great deal of ambiguity now. For instance those arrested in New Delhi in connection with the recent bomb explosions in the city have been identified as belonging to one of the Jammu and Kashmir militant groups. With groups representing different causes extending their activities beyond their usual domain, it is logical to expect a group responsible for an act to own it up. In the case of Rajiv Gandhi's assassination, no group has claimed responsibility while the LTTE (from its London office) and the Jammu and Kashmir Liberation Front (From Rawalpindi, in Pakistan) have disowned the Sriperambudur explosion. If the LTTE is treated as a non-Indian group, there are several groups of Khalistani and Jammu and Kashmir militants active outside Punjab and Jammu and Kashmir.

Terrorists can shift their operations easily from one state to another within the country. They can move rapidly to and from their targets or even in and out of the country. Complex and costly technological systems of society - power plants, nuclear research centres, airports and aircrafts have become sitting targets for sabotage and destruction. Khalistani militants have hijacked Indian Airlines's planes thrice. Terrorists the world over are acquiring sophisticated technology which is easily available. If it is not a government interested in helping a cause, private arms dealers and mercenaries are willing to oblige. Terrorist groups can train their own experts. Groups from Ulster are known to have designed bombs with novel anti-handling devices that could be a challenge even to the most experienced bomb disposal squads. The bomb used at Sriperambudur eluded the security net and forensic experts are baffled by the sophistication of the device and manner of its activation. The investigating agencies must be even more baffled that no one has claimed responsibility yet for the act.[9]

The mortal remains of Rajiv Gandhi were consigned to flames in the evening by the banks of the river Yamuna, close to the memorial of his mother Indira Gandhi.

9. Mohan Ram. The Echoes of Terrorism. *The Independent*, 26 May, 1991.

As the pyre was lit by Rahul, Rajiv Gandhi's son, thousands of people sobbed uncontrollably in the midst of chanting of scriptures. Sonia Gandhi and daughter Priyanka stood in sombre silence as the flames engulfed the body immersed in a heap of sandalwood.

Minutes before Rahul went around the mortal remains of his father to lit the pyre, the army buglers sounded the Last Post followed by the Rouse. A galaxy of world leaders, Governors, Ministers and other dignitaries stood up in silence to pay their last tribute to the man of peace who had laboured relentlessly for the well- being of mankind.

Cries of 'Rajiv Gandhi Amar Rahe' rent the air as family members and close friends of the former Prime Minister put flowers and sandalwood over the pyre.

The whole atmosphere was charged with heightened emotions with many world leaders wiping their eyes.

The President and the Vice-President along with their wives came near the specially creacted platform to console the grieving members of Rajiv family as the flames leapt from all sides.

President R. Venkataraman, looking in deep shock, hugged Rahul as he came down to meet with family friends.

Suddenly hundreds of Rajiv admirers broke the police cordon to reach the pyre and shower flowers and incense. The wailing and slogan-shouting crowds went around the burning pyre to pay respects to the departed leader who had guided the destiny of the nation for over five years as Prime Minister.

Braving the scorching heat of the blazing summer sun, the world leaders and other dignitaries sat through the funeral ceremony in calm composure. Except for a few umbrellas, they braved it in open.

The mortal remains of Rajiv Gandhi were carried on a gun carriage in a procession from Teen Murti, New Delhi where it lay in state since May 22, escorted by five platoons of 33 soldires each both in the front and in the rear, the cortege carried by pall-bearers reached Shakti Sthal by around 4.35 p.m.

Congress-I leaders Ghulam Nabi Azad, Moopanar, M.J. Akbar and Narasimha Rao were the first to enter the cremation site. Then followed the bier with Mrs. Sonia Gandhi, Rahul, Priyanka and Amitabh Bachchan walking by the side of the pallbearers.

The body was then taken to the specially erected platform supporting the funeral pyre. The National Flag covering the body was removed as the guard commander ordered 'present arms' and 'rest on your arms reversed.' The chief pundit in attendance then helped the close family members unite the 'thread knots.' Pieces of sandalwood were then placed around the body by Rahul, Priyanka, Sonia Gandhi and Gautam Kaul, cousin of the late Prime Minister.

The body was covered with 'havan Samagri' (mix of ritualistic offerings) and incense. Rajiv's close friend, Amitabh Bachchan, was present all through the funeral rites. While the priests chanted hymns from the religious scriptures, a Parsi priest extended help in the completion of the cremation ceremony.

A round piece of threat was passed on by Sonia Gandhi to her son, to be placed over the head of the body.

All through, commandoes stood in alert all around the cremation-site. A helicopter made rounds, showering flowers and also helping in the beefing up of the security vigil.

As the chief pall-bearers moved to their positions, three volleys were fired before the sounding of the 'Last Post'. It was followed by the Rouse-symbolising the continuity of life.

Everybody including the dignitaries stood in silence in homage to the departed leader while the firing party presented arms. Officers from the three services stood in salute throughout the calls.

The pyre was lit by Rahul from the right-hand side of the bier with the help of a small Piece of burning wood. Inflammable material in the form of 'ghee' was poured as Rahul took ritualistic' rounds of the pyre.

Finally, the pyre got transformed into a blazing heap of wood. The cremation ceremony was completed with Rahul pushing the head of his father with a long piece of wood. Rahul was helped by the Chief priest in the last instalment of 'funeral rites.'

The mourners including a large number of women and children waited patiently for hours in stunned silence, many wiping their tears.

Braving the hot summer sun, thousands of people lined up on both sides of the 11 km. long funeral procesion route from Teen Murti House to Shakti Sthal.

Loudspeakers played hymns and devotional songs around the historic India Gate adding to the sombre atmosphere.

A large number of security personel comprising men of the Army and para-military forces and the police were deployed at all the roundabouts and strategic points.

About 10 quintals of wood, including four quintals of sandalwood, were used for the cremation of Rajiv Gandhi.

Priests at the cremation site said about 20 kg. of ghee were also used.

The "havan samagri" (offering for the pyre) weighed about 50 kg.

Rajiv Gandhi's departure leaves a big gap in the Indian political equilibrium and suddenly unleashes new forces in the national polity. In the flash-floods that have followed no one is sure of even the safety and survival of the values and norms. The last hope lies in the common sense of ordinary Indian citizens. However, the ultimate steps that translate public pressures for change into system, reality are the ones those in power can take. It is generally said that the history of politics in India is a story of tragedy that began in hope. The challenge today is far more grim since we are called upon to overcome the tragedy and work to build a stronger and united India. The mess has been created by politicians and it is for the people to make them behave not like lumpen elements but as honourable citizens of an ancient civiliasation. Perhaps it will take a number of elections before the message goes home and India is rescued from the clutches of vested interests. The continuing violence in the country has shown that the basic Indian ethos of peaceful co- existence has been mythicized. There is no sign of healthy politics, tasteful political slogans. This time the election had simply been a matter of image killing; issues hardly entered the arena.

The President's role is also to be seen at the post-Rajiv era. The request for National Government, or even later the framing of new Govt. will definitetely make President's role a tough one.[10]

A curious aspect of the situation is that no one seems to be really outraged at a proposal that amounts to surreptitiously aborting the democratic process. True, the Congress (I), the Janata Dal and SJP have all turned it down but not in particularly emphatic terms. The comments of the CPI(M) and CPI seem to indicate that the objection is less to the principle than to the likely constituents, while the BJP is considering the matter this weekend. If the suggestion is inappropriate at this stage, it was improper for a BJP vice-president to make public what was obviously a confidential conversation, especially since he himself admits that the President may only have been "thinking aloud". The difference with the decorum and restraint dispalyed by more conventional politicians may be one more pointer to the quick-profit, fly-by-night style of the BJP's second and third rungs. But this is a minor point. What matters now is how the Congress(I) comports itself. It can seestablish itself as the party of national consensus; it can assert a far more vigorous role as the vehicle of secular democracy; it can preside over the evolution of a genuine federalism in which the relationship between the Centre and the States is not only that between the high command and its branch offices, the latter paying in obedience for favours received from the former. Nor can changes in personnel be

10. Democratic World, 26 May, 1991

ruled out for some of the politicians who have fallen out with the Nehru-Gandhis over the years, and yet professed loyalty to the original Congress creed, may now try to return to the fold. They will want to fill the vacuum at the top. There may be turmoil and splits, anguish and confusion as the party tries at last to stand on its own feet. But out of it something good may come. What would be fatal, sealing the doom of the party's legacy, is for Congressmen to do nothing except try to preserve the old forms, the old style and the old connections. That would be shirking the chance that fate has tossed it in such admittedly cruel circumstances. The slate has been wiped clean for the Congress what the party writes on the blank space, and how, will determine its right to claim to be the Indian National Congress's true and only heir.[11]

Those who wish to have an idea of what such a government will be like need look no further than the Janta Dal Government of V.P. Singh. Propped up as it was by the Left, on the one side, and the BJP, on the other, with the limited aim of getting the Congress out of power - strains that would have been a good deal more apparent had not the antics of Devi Lal and Chandra Shekhar hogged the limelight. Thus, few even got to know that the V.P. Singh Government was forced to give up its all- important pledge to hold elections to the state Assembly in Punjab in February 1990 because both the BJP and the CPI(M) stiffly opposed it and the former threatened to withdraw support to the Government if it went ahead. The BJP, for its part, felt increasingly threatened by its continued association with the National Front Government as time went by and the VHP continued to make inroads into its traditional vote banks. It would have been saved from its dilemma only if V.P. Singh had succeeded in persuading the Muslim leaders to agree to the relocation of the mosque. But when he was unable to do so and, instead, announced a gazetted holiday for Muslims on the Prophet's birthday, its position with its own rank and file and its committed electorate became untenable and its embarked on a course that was calculated to consolidate its vote and put an end to the 'friendly alliance.' There is a built-in mechanism in the political system that will ensure that when India completes the transition, it will end up with a two - and not multi-party system (or two stable combines of national and regional parties). That mechanism is the simple majority voting system.

Our electoral system invariably exaggerates the largest party's share of seats in relation to its share of the vote. But precisely because it does so, it also reduce the smaller parties share of seats in relation to their votes. The disproportion grows progressively larger as the party grows smaller. Thus over time smaller parties wither away as their supporters

11. Sunanda K. Datta-Ray. No End to Politics. *Statesman*, 27 May 1991.

realise that they are only wasting their vote and large parties have to accommodate as many interest groups as possible and woo the uncommitted middle vote to grow even larger. The only way in which a small party can survive under the simple majority voting system is by building a strong local or regional base in which it is the largest or the second largest party. But it too comes under pressure over time to build lasting relationships with other regional or national parties. The enduring relationship between the Congress(I) and the AIADMK and the solidifying relationship between the constitutents of the National Front are cases in point. It is too early to predict with any degree of accuracy what the shape of the Indian polity will be when the transition is complete, but it seems more and more likely that two opposing combines will coalesce around the BJP and the Janata Dal-National Front. Should this happen, both will be changed beyond recognition by their need to widen their appeal and compete for the uncommitted middle vote. The end product will most likely be two pragmatic middle of the road parties with left and right-of-centre casts in their eye, the that respect the basic features of Constitution, and strive to give a stable government. When that transition is completed India's '*agnipareeksha*' will be over.[12]

Rajiv Gandhi's sacrifice will have been in vain if Congressman do not engage themselves seriously in restoring the national consesnsus, the disruption of which caused his death in the first place. In his death-he has intervened on a scale reserved for epics in the caste and communal strife that was the stuff of the elections being contested. It develoves on his partymen to further arrest the nosedive and recover the middle-ground that once belonged to the Congress. This will be a suitable tribute to Rajiv Gandhi. How should Congressmen address themselves to this task?

The Year 1967 was the first assault on the Congress monolith. That year began the authoritarian phase in Congress rule when Indira Gandhi split the party and centralized authority. Part of the subsequent history consisted in ex-congressmen regrouping with Lohia socialists on the one hand and the Jana Sangh on the other, (with the CPI-M often finding itself in this company because of its compulsions in Kerala and west Bengal to attack the Congress citadel). Over a period of time, the anti-Congress stance of this opposition transformed itself into exasperation with the stronge hold of the Nehru Gandhi dynasty on both the Congress and the Delhi '*gaddi*'. We were a feudal as well as a Hindu society. We were comfortable with dynasties and we deified our leaders, placed them on a pedestal from which they could not be

12. Prem Shankar Jha. Mirage of Stability, National Govt. *The Hindu*, 29 May, 1991.

dislodged. It was the ingenuity of the anti-Congress mind that brought to the centre stage a retiring Jayapraksh Narayan to counter Mrs. Gandhi's charisma. J.P. has renounced power and renunciation was the stuff for deification. It was in the crucible of the Bihar Movement that the Janata Party was forged. Pressure was applied on Mrs. Gandhi. She blundered in with the emergency, paving the way for the Janata victory in 1977. Since the welding was imperfect, the Janata Party broke up and Indiara Gandhi regained power from 1980 until her assassination in 1984. Two important trends emerged, which Congressmen would do well to bear in mind:

a) Indira Gandhi's national coalition consisted of a sprinking of Brahmins at the apex with Harijans, backwards, minorities and other castes forming the bulk of this coalition.
b) That only Andhra Pradesh and Karanataka were able to withstand the anti-Congress wave in 1977. And both these States were under non-Brahimin leaders-Vengala Rao and Devraj Urs.[13]

When Rajiv Gandhi conceded power to V.P. Singh in 1989, the tradition of the Brhim Brahmin-led Central coalition was broken.

This nasty business of caste being an essential ingredient of political discourse became all the more pronounced after V.P. Singh embarked on Mandal.

Unfortunately, it was not Mandal as much as the extreme reaction to it that resulted in a caste Hindu consolidation away from V.P. Singh's Janata Dal.

The Mandir agitation attracted this polarized bulk in favour of the BJP, as the trend in UP undoubtedly showed. The beneficiaries of a reaction to this trend were the Janata Dal and the Bahujan Samaj Party, not the Congress. The Congress, in other words, was losing at the top to the BJP and below to the Janata Dal and the BJP. In popular perception, the Congress was acquiring an upper caste image and the upper caste vote was, ironically, shifting to the BJP:

This is the situation that Congressmen have to contend with. What is called for at this stage is an act of overt symbolism. This is not time for sophistication and subtlety. Men like P.V. Narasimha Rao and Narain Dutt Tewari are known for their secularism and experience. But any hurried decision to confer the party's leadership on these gentlmen will be misunderstood by the party rank and file in states like Maharashtra, Karnataka and Andhra Pradesh, where the party is holding its ground.[14]

13. Saeed Naqvi. Time for Congress for Overt *Symbolism*. *Patriot*, 23 May, 1991.
14. Ibid.

Rajiv Gandhi lived a dangerous life while he worked ardently for peace at home and abroad. His efforts for international peace and disarmament set off a move to nominate him for Nobel Peace Prize four years back in 1987.

His last peace mission was an air dash to Moscow and Teheran in February, 1991 as a last-ditch effort to end the Gulf war.

Rajiv Gandhi in his commitment to settle the Tamil problem despatched Indian troops to Sri Lanka - an unprecedented step.

He also sent forces to the Maldives to crush a coup against President M. Abdul Gayoom in 1988.

As the peace-keeping role in Sri Lanka floundered, he signed an accord with President Junius Jayewardene to end the ethnic conflict.

He survived two assassination attempts, one at home and the other in Colombo. He had a providential escape when a naval rating tried to hit him with a rifle butt as he was about to leave the Sri Lankan Capital for home.

Rajiv Gandhi's visit to China in December 1988 was recognised as an event of major importance and historic significance.

During his visit, the two countries besides signing agreements to promote cooperation in the fields of science and technology and civil aviation set up a joint working group to settle the boundary question.

The group, at the foreign secretary level, is addressing the question of an overall boundary settlement.

India's traditionally close relations with the Soviet Union were strengthened during his stewardship exchange of high-level visits added stimulus and provided greater content to India's bilateral economic and cultural ties with Moscow.

We did not know much about democracy just around two hundred years ago. Today, we consider it at as the most pious system of governance. What an irony of our fate is that one country that is in the forefront in advocating democracy for all the countries of the world, would be the last one to have the democracy extended to the central world body (UNO) since her own supremacy in wealth. Armament and political doninance over the rest of the world is at stake. She has taken upon herself to be the sole salvator of humanity and under the process looks like caplor of the rest of the world. Regional and ethnic aspirations for autonomy and territorial boundaries are the major cause of conflict in the world. Why all such cases are decided only through bloodbath? Why a peaceloving smaller nation should remain shadowed by a powerful neighbour for all time to come? India is the largest democracy of the world. Today Indian election process is being keenly watched by all eyes of the world. We produced saints and seers that have been the greatest pioneers of peace in the world. This brings us to a crucial point. All that we have got today, was conceived by our fore-runners.[15]

Rajiv Gandhi's grotesque assassination provides us a fresh start. We have twenty-one days to get organized. Already, it is clear who the human beings are and who the political beasts. And the catankerous braying of most other politicians in response to the sound suggestions by the President that this is a time to bury old rivalries and word together is equally shameless. The only three leaders who count on the national level - judging from the humaneness of their behaviour - are Jyoti Basu, Chandra Shekhar and Atal Behari Vajpayee. No doubt there are others, perhaps somewhat less in stature in the nation's eye-Sharad Pawar, for one. And, of course, there are the 844 million of us. The world stands ready to embrace us-the shocking quality of Rajiv Gandhi's death ensures that. The IMF and the World Bank have sent messages of condolence. They are not as heartless as some would like to believe. And we need the money now. It is time for each of us to strengthen the President's hands so that he keeps pushing for some form of a genuine democratic (meaning not dependent on political parties) government, perhaps he aded by the triumvirate listed above.[16]

Rajiv was not unduly pertrubed when security was beefed up five years ago following an assassination attempt at Rajghat. "I remember he went about his work that day as if nothing had happened," says an officer. The protection shields had increased but for Rajiv it was as if they were never there.

He had once remarks to a senior SPG officer that he was like a caged prisoner, with all the fencing done at his Race Course Road residence. But he had no say in the matter - a year later, the road was closed to traffice. Officers responsible for Rajiv's security cover maintain that his fondness for his personal security officers (PSOs) always stood out. He was warm and cordial to them and would often make personal enquiries. Ravi and Mahinder, two SPG guards who formed a part of the close proximity group for four years when Rajiv was in power, were indebted to him for his concern for them. Ravi, in fact, chose to resign from the Delhi Police and join Rajiv, when he ceased to be the PM. Similar was the case with Pradip Gupta, the PSo who died in the bomb blast at Sriperumbudur. He was hand-picked from among hundreds of other sub-inspectors in the police force for the simple reason that his superiors thought he had a mindest which would suit Rajiv's style of

15. Avtar Singh. Democracy. *National Herald*, 24 May 1991
16. *The Independent*, 25May, 1991

functioning. It proved right - Rajiv took an instant liking to the quick-witted Gupta. In the 16 months that Gupta worked with Rajiv's a strong bond of friendship developed between the two. A case in point was when Rajiv left for Namibia last year to participate in the country's celebration of independence. No sanction had been granted for Gupta's inclusion in the entourage. It was finally decided that the Congress party would finance his air passage. On another occasion, when Rajiv was in transit at Heathrow airport in London, he found that he had ample time at his disposal. He asked Gupta to look around in the duty free shop. Pradip expressed his desire to buy a pair of Raybans sunglasses, similar to Rajiv's. He bought one for $ 50. It was only on arrival at Delhi did Rajiv discover that the steep price Gupta had fished out for the sunglasses and chided the PSo for readily paying so much. His own sunglasses, he told Gupta, came from Palika Bazaar for just Rs. 500.

A month ago when Gupta sprained his ankle it was Rajiv who applied the pain-killing spray for him. Even while he stayed at 10, Janpath, security officials always found that he functioned like a Prime Minister. He had a far greater number of guests than both Chandrashekhar and V.P. Singh, they say. And sometimes in the middle of the night he would get into his car and go for a spin with son Rahul. When it was pointed out that his impromptu departures were causing some concern, Rajiv would remark, "You are trained to be faster than me."[17]

When US Secret Service agents are trained, their instructors tell them one thing: "You cannot stop the first bullet from an assassin's gun. But the second should hit you, not the President. Come between the assassin and the President." Unlike in India, this instruction is complied with blindly in the US. It's a part of the Secret Service agent's drill. When Lee Harvey Oswald shot John Kennedy in 1963. Vice-President Lyndon Johnson was travelling in the third car behind kennedy. The moment the first shot rang out, Johnson's agent pushed him to the floor of the limousine and covered Jonson's body with his own. One security problem in India is that our security men are too intimidated by their charge. In the US, if danger threatens the President, the Secret Service agents take charge instantly, they do not consult him. Like lightning, they form a human wall around him.

But our Black Casts are not so professional. In early 1987, for instance. I remember that Rajiv Gandhi, on impulse, decided to para-sail in New Delhi. His securitymen did not object. Another time while

17. Murali Krishnan. The Shadow of Danger. *The Sunday Observer*, 26 May, 1991.

going in a cavalcade, Mr. Gandhi slipped behind the steering-wheel of a Mercedes-Benz that was carrying him and pulled away from the escort cars. In the US, it would be unimaginable for President Bush to drive like this.

Many times in recent months, Rajiv Gandhi did most of the driving himself though he would have been far less exposed to an assassin's bullet if he had sat behind between two security men.[18]

It is a matter of utmost regret that the BJP leader, L.K. Advani, has refused the services of the National Security Guards (Black Cats) who are assigned for his security. Advani undoubtedly had his compulsions- the need to interact freely with his party members and ordinary voters- but he should have been mindful of the fact that these are very dangerous times, and that even a stray incident can escalate into a turmoil. There are too many people and powers who have a vested interest in further vitiating the political process and unsetting Indian democracy. The best efforts have to be made to prevent them from succeeding. If this involves senior politicians curbing their natural flamboyance, it is a small price to pay for the larger national interest. The brutal assassination of Rajiv Gandhi has driven home the point that an understandable desire to reach out to the people can prove woefully counter-productive and, indeed, dangerous if security is compromised. For the sake of Indian democracy, Advani must shed his inhibitions and allow the professionals to do their job effectively.[19]

The need for adequate security for senior politicians is all the more in view of the disturbing rumors that are gaining currency each day. Chandra Shekhar was right in scotching all "anti- national" speculation over an imposition of the Emergency. Unfortunately, others have not proved all that circumspect. Subodh kant Sahay's plea for a government of "stalwarts" and the talk, emanating from the highest quarters, of a national government have merely added to fears that powerful lobby is working overtime to short-circuit the political process. Nor does Sidhartha Shankar Ray's irresponsible utterances against Jyoti Basu help matters. To this can be added the prophecies of doom of the band of itinerant *jyotishis*; who thrive in a climate of uncertainty. If normalcy is to be restored and the people reassured, it is incumbent that all politicians act with the utmost restraint and responsibility. This may, arguably, prove difficult at election time when national issues are debated with customary passion and zeal. However, when the entire future of democracy is at stake, it is necessary that minor compromises are made. The political class must realise that the very survival of the

18. Arvind Kala. Protecting VIPs from Terrorists. *Indian Express*, 30 May 1991.
19. *The Times of India*, 30 May, 1991.

democratic system is more important than petty considerations of electoral one upmanship. If India passes this litmus test, there will be many more occasions for scoring debating points. The political process need not be derailed, but subliminal passions must certainly be curbed.

To pre-empt unhealthy speculation about the conspiracy behind Rajiv Gandhi's murder, and the levelling of charges and counter-charges among political parties competing in the election, the Government must immediately make public the two probe reports dealing with the violent deaths of the late Sanjay Gandhi and Indira Gandhi. It is only in the light of those two reports that the proposed commission of inquiry investigating the murder of Rajiv Gandhi will be able to conduct its affairs with requisite credibility. Otherwise, there is danger that ill-informed public speculation about a larger conspiracy behind the assassination of Rajiv Gandhi could continue to haunt the country, and succeed in creating violent and fatal divisions in society.[20]

India has recently gone through a lot of political experiments. This has brought about immense uncertainity in the minds of peoples both at home and abroad. We are on the brink of both political and economic disaster. Our spirit of national independence seems to be threatened. Today, this does not mean the annexation of territory. It means the freedom to profess our will as a nation-politically, economically and socially. Our political leaders seem to have forgotten the task of nation- building. They are concentrating their energy to stay in power. They have explored people's sentiments on religion and revived the forgotten caste and creed differences. This itself goes against the fundamental issue of our Constitution to build India, into a secular state and a casteless society. The law and order situation is sacrificed by succumbing to terrorist demands and infiltration of wrong elements in the political set-up of our country. Today 100 criminals have been given tickets to stand for election. This only encourages disruptive tendencies in the states of our Republic.[21]

The untimely assassination of Rajiv Gandhi has dramatically altered the political equations at the Centre. It now appears that all the three major political groupings, the BJP/Shiv Sena, National Front and Congress/allies have an equal chance to come to power.

The Congress and its allies, with a suitable leader at, the helm, could hope to ride the sympathy wave and emerge victorious by cornering from the majority of the seats to which elections will shortly be held. The BJP (and its allies)can now exploit the "stability plank" by project

20. Rajinder Puri. Inquiries or Futile Rituals? Sunday Mail, 26 May, 1991
21. Asha Modi. Priorities for New Govt. The Hindustan Times, 27 May 1991.

ing itself as the only organisation equipped to take over the Congress's mantle in the changed ciurcumstances. The National Front, was till now was in the third place in the electoral battle because of the division of the Hindu votes among the three political groupings and of minority votes between itself, the Congress and a lesser extent the BJP. The Front can now claim the lion's share of the Muslim votes. But this can happen only if the Congress is unable to elect a dynamic leader.[22]

In any case the process of ascertaining the wishes of the people must be completed. Only when their decision is known can it be decided as to who should rule the country, whether it is to be one political party or some combination. The people must not be denied their right to choose their own government under the pretext of a national government. All those who value the values advocated by Rajiv Gandhi must put their heads toghther to continue the light for a stable, secular, self-sustaining. democratically developing and non, aligned India willing to work for the cause of world peace and yet not prepared for surrendering to the dictate of others.[23]

Where do we go from here? The political churning process will continue, as it must, and the venality of our politicians will ensure that our journey to a brighter future will be set with much violence and many uncertainties. By sacrificing his life, Rajiv Gandhi may have served the purpose of giving the country a much-needed jolt in taking stock of its failling and the correctives necessary for making the ride to the future less bumpy.[24]

The assassination of Rajiv Gandhi may see the end of the Nehru-Gandhi hegemony over the Congress party. That is certain to bring in its wake a radical transformation of Indian polity itself as the Country's biggest political organisation struggles to overcome factionalism and present a united face in the absence of a supreme leader. This is no mean task, for over the years the principle of dynastic succession has come to be firmly established and accepted in this 106-year-old organisation whether there can be life for the Congress outside the ambit of the Gandhi family.

And India, remember, is an enduring sort of place. There was a time when it seemed that the southern states wanted to break away from the Hindi-speaking belt along the Ganges in the north. It didn't happen. There was a time when the Ganges belt seemed to be in revolution against Rajiv Gandhi's mother, in one of her dictatorial moods. It faded

22. Apoorv Pandey. In Memoriam. *The Times of India*, 31 May, 1991.
23. V.P. Dutt. The Assassination and After. *Nation Herald*, 29 May 1991
24. S. Nihal Singh. *Will the Country Now Take Stock of its Failing? The Telegraph*. 24 May 1991.

away. For people in Western countries, to whom a shared language is part of the badge of identity, it is hard to realize the sense of Indians that still holds most of multi-language, multi-religion India together. What will not hold it together is the exahausted, panic-stricked Congress party that in the past few days has been trying to shove poor Rajiv's shy widow Sonia into its leadership, just so that it could still have the name Gandhi on its banner. India deserves a new pattern of politics.[25]

The Congress Party on May 31, 1991 alleged that there was "a clear political motive" behind Rajiv Gandhi's assassination. Those who did not want him to become the Prime Minister were behind the conspiracy.

H.K.L. Bhagat, AICC general secretary, charged that Rajiv Gandhi was eliminated because he was "the tallest leader" in the country and could have provided a stable government.

Bhagat accused the BJP and the Janata Dal of taking advantage of the assassination of Rajiv Gandhi by attempting to project that the Congress was in disarray.

Referring to the smooth and unanimous election of P.V. Narasimha Rao as the Congress president, Bhagat said the Congress Working Committee had sent a clear signal to the nation: the Congress stood united.

That in the midst of the election to the tenth Lok Sabha, Rajiv has been assassinated has once again brought into sharp focus how organised political terrorism has begun to destablise and disintegrate our ancient country with renewed vigour. Rajiv Gandhi was not only the leader of the biggest political party of the country but an outstanding international leader on his own right. If one looks at the Indian polity from any angle, the conclusion is inevitable that freedom and unity of the country are really in peril, both literally and metaphorically. India, of course, is the world's largest multi-party democracy-larger than the oldest democracies on our planet. It is, of course, the biggest non-aligned country and has the proud privilege of being the leader of the Non-Aligned Movement at a time when the mankind is facing the threat of complete annihilation and the relevance of the NAM itself is being challenged by the exponents of the unipolar world. In this sense, what happens to India will go a long way in shaping the course of events in all other countries, particularly in Asia and the Pacific region. It all will not be chauvinistic to say that in making India strong, united and economically independent Rajiv Gandhi made the richest contribution

25. Brian Beedham. Indian Politics. *The Times of India*, 29 May 1991.

after Jawaharlal Nehru and Indira Gandhi. It is an irony of history that three Gandhis of India, Mahtama Gandhi, Indira and Rajiv, were killed at crucial stages in the history of post- independence India and that too in an atmosphere vitiated by communalism and fanaticism. This reveals that the monster of communalism and parochialism is pushing our country to the brink of a precipice.[26]

With Rajiv's passing away the last person of Nehru era has gone in posterity.

To make India safe for democracy and the world free from fear Rajiv Gandhi boldly went out to the only source-the people. From where can be derived the real strength for marching towards that tryst with destiny. And he broke the security barrier which he perceived, after experience of five years as Prime Minister, as a hindrance to rapport with those whose emotions and aspirations he was to articulate and express. His forbears and political ideals, Mahatma Gandhi, Nehru and Indira had done the same.

The Congress leadership's testy and somewhat exasperated response to efforts now under way, both within and outside the party's fold, to bring together present and former Congressmen is easily explained. Contrary to what it would have the world believe, the party is still in a dazed state. It will be several weeks, if not months, before it recovers its reflexes. Moreover, Sonia Gandhi's refusal to head the party has added to its woes. It is under these conditions that the party has to face the second and final phase of the elections. This is why the new president, P.V. Narasimha Rao, is moving with extreme caution merely to keep the Congress intact. Until the election results are out, the party can be expected to remain in one piece. But no one can say what will happen afterwards. Ginger groups have already sprung up here and there to ensure that they can negotiate from a position of strength onces serious attempts begin to form the next government. For all these reasons it is imperative for the Congress leadership at this juncture to refuse to open the door to all those who have started knocking on it. How long the leadership can keep the door shut naturally depends on the outcome of the poll. Should the Congress obtain a Working majority, pressure is bound to increase within its own ranks not to admit into the fold those who chose to part company with the party in its days of trial. But if a working majority eludes the party the door will be wide open for a massive influx of former Congressmen. Already several present and former Congressmen have prepared the ground for this eventuality. The Jan Morcha has declared its unilateral support to the Congress. While V.P. Singh has chosen not to comment

26. V.D. Chopra. National Tragedy. *Patriot*, 22 May, 1991.

on matters relating to the Congress, his Janata Dal colleague, Ramakrishna Hegde, has called on all Congress men, minus the coterie which surrounded Rajiv Gandhi, to come together, similarly, in defiance of his party's publicly stated stand, Mohan Dharia has gone so far as to speak of a merger between the Samajwadi Janata Party and the Congress. In much the same vein, Congress leaders such as Vasant Sathe, Dinesh Singh and K.C. Pant have gone public with their endorsement of the realignment theory. Fully conscious that any such realighment is bound to be at the expense of all those who thrived under Indira Gandhi and Rajiv Gandhi the Congress leadership has adopted a cautious approach to the issue. It has decided to admit individuals "strictly on merit" and by the same token to refuse wholesale mergers. Given the uncertain circumstances that prevail at the moment, and the ones that are likely to prevail in the near future, this was the only stand the party could conceivably adopt.[27]

Will there be a realignment of political forces? The question has acquired a fresh urgency in the wake of tragic assassination of Rajiv Gandhi. Both politicians and political pundits see in the Indian situation today new signs of polarisation which did not materialise in the past four decades or so, mainly because of the all embracing umbrella of the Congress and the dominant personality of a few individuals who guided the party's and the nation's destiny.

Since the Congress fortunes have mainly revolved around one personality or the other, Indian politics never acquired a natural momentum of its own. Vital components like ideology and programming never could strike roots. All this has changed now. For the first time, the 106-year old Congress has ceased to be dominated by one single personality, though it has a number of qualified leaders who stand on their own merit. This situation throws up tempting possibilities for readjustment and realignemnts. The highly volatile BJP phenomenon seems to have given an impetus to the old-time socialists, leftists and various shades of ex-Congressmen to explore the possibility of new combinations. Interestingly, each group sees for itself a new oppor tunity to share in power in the post-election scene.[28]

Indian politics, however, is a highly complex affairs. For, what is visible on the surface may not be a reality. And what is reality may not be visible. Delhi-based pundits often miss this point in their anxiety to rationalise both events and non-events. But that is a different story.

27. *The Times of India*, 1 June 1991.
28. Hari Jaisingh. The Polarisation Process. *The Business and Political Observer*, 1 June, 1991.

2

THE SILVER LINING

The entry for August 20, 1944 in Jawaharlal Nehru's Prison Diary read: "Indu had baby boy this morning 8 a.m. Both doing well. So I become a grandfather." With the untimely demise of Kamla Jawaharlal had also been a caring mother to his beloved Indu. His words of encouragement to an expecting Indira reveal a rare sensitivity. This act of creation is the fulfilment in some ways of a women's being .....I am glad you are going to have a baby...I have a feeling that it might actually do you good, even physically to have a baby..."

The birth of her first child was indeed an important development in the total blossoming of Indira's personality. Though very fond of children, Indira had often fretted at the possibility of not being able to have any, owing to a weak constitution and she had even considered adoption. The easy delivery of Rajiv greatly helped to reinforce India's confidence.

In his Ahmednagar jail cell, Jawaharlal reflected philosophically on the birth of his first grandson....."The birth of a new member of the family always makes one feel reminiscent... It is an unending panorama of human life with its sweetness and bitterness, its ups and downs." A non-believer in religious rituals himself, Nehru in good humour appreciated his sister Krishna's prayer offerings to Hanuman and Ganesh on the baby's birth. But at the same time he was very insistent on having the baby's time of birth recorded in the traditional way through a Janmapatra.[1]

In the confines of his prison cell, Jawaharlal spent considerable time planning a name for his grandon. For suggestions he turned to his fellow prison inmates. Acharya Narendra Dev, with his expertise in Sanskrit and the Maulana with his wide knowledge of Persian. Voting against the name "Rahul" by which the baby had initially been called, Jawaharlal explained to Indira that Rahul literally meant fetters or bandhan, which is how Buddha had viewed the birth of his son. The name that Jawaharlal personally favoured was Priyadarshi Birjees, the latter being an old Persian name for Jupiter the planet, suggested by Maulana Azad, Nehru, however, feared that it might become corrupted and Sanskritised into Brajesh. Ultimately the name Rajiv Ratna was accepted-Rajiv being a synonym of Kamla (lotus) and Ratna for Jawahar (jewel). The possessive grandfather confessed that he would be rather pleased if the family name Nehru was added. But he realised

1. Reba Som. Grandfather's First Impression. *The Hindustan of India* 26 May 1991.

that the full name. Rajiv Ratna Birjees Nehru Gandhi, would be too long and pompous" and so he finally surrendered to Indira and Feroze on the matter of the name. It was not until Rajiv was almost a year old that Jawaharlal was able to see his grandson. Nor was he in any great hurry as he felt rather uncomfortable with tiny babies, "they seem so soft and delicate", Jawaharlal wrote to Indira, "Rajiv's (that's how he spelt it) pictures are good. He looks quite human. He is attractive and has got a good humour look. In some of them he resembles you, in one there is a marked resemblance to Feroze."[2]

From prison, Jawaharlal followed with care the growth and development of his grandson in his first year. In his mind's eye he followed Indira and Rajiv as they journeyed in October 1944 from Bombay to Allahabad's Anand Bhawan which would now, he reflected, have a baby making it its home for the first time. For his little grandson's first summer Jawaharlal prescribed the sylvan settings of the pine-clad Kashmir hills. As Indira shared with her father the thrills of seeing Rajiv cut his first tooth and attempt to make a conversation, she also confided her concern at his delay in sitting up or beginning to walk. Jawaharlal's assurances to his daughter reveal his astute perceptions of life itself. To him "a slower and more solid growth, both physical and mental yielded better results."[3]

Jawaharlal Nehru gave Rajiv Gandhi the name of Rajivratna, a combination of lotus for his material grandmother's name Kamla and gem for the first three syllables of the first Prime Minister's name Jawaharlal. Nehru had a strong liking for naming the children.

Rajiv and Sanjay received no special favours by virtue of being the prime minister's grandsons, or 'the nation's grandchildren", as the press had dubbed them. At any time, the school had a number of sons of Indian nobility, which reinforces its image as an academy for the elite....Like most boys there, Rajiv enjoyed his time at Doon, after the initial homesickness. He spent his spare time in the wood and metal workshops making things, or at the photographic club. His grandfather had given him a Russian- made camera. The school encouraged outdoor activities, especially mountaineering, but Rajiv does not seem to have starred in this respect, or at the school sports of cricket and hockey. He is remembered at Doon School as a quiet, unassuming boy of average intellect, who nonetheless entered into the spirit of the place. He did not stand out as a scholar, and was considered to be 'very average' academically. His favourite subjects were geography and maths, in which in his final year he was in the upper half of the class

2. *Ibid.*
3. *Ibid.*

according to his teacher. He is remembered for his shyness, his wish to be ordinary and not be marked out as the prime minister's grandson. He recalls: 'I was embarrassed at being the prime minister's grandson.' When Nehru came to call at the school, said Rajiv, 'I stayed some where at the back; they couldn't find me.' Were it not for his membership of India's ruling family, he probably would not have been much remembered at school.[4]

As well as the constant foreign visitors, there were also other early foreign influences on Rajiv's upbringing. For a time, he had a Danish governess, a strict disciplinarian and ardent believer in cold showers and exercise. Later he was sent to exclusive kindergarten run by a German lady, Elizabeth Gauba, who had married an Indian. At that tender stage, Rajiv showed a special talent for drawing aeroplanes, and also enjoyed taking the lead in play-acting. When Nehru and Indira went to London for the Coronation in 1953, Rajiv and Sanjay were put into school in Switzerland for a short time. After early schooling in Delhi, Indira and Feroze had sent their children to boarding school at Dehra Dun, several hours' drive north of the capital in the Himalayan foothills. They went first to Welham Boys' Preparatory School, presided over by a formidable English disciplinarian, Miss Oliphant. Dehra Dun has many claims to fame, but is probably best known as the home of Doon School, one of a number of English-style public schools in India and where Rajiv and Sanjay went after Welham.[5]

Even while at School Rajiv fell behind most of his classmates. Doon believes in giving its boys a big hand in the running of the school but Rajiv never showed any remarkable leadership qualities nor was he a distinguished scholar. Most of his teachers remember him as being very quiet and shy "But he conformed beautifully to the school rules and never gave us any trouble.," recalls Vohra.

Rajiv's respect for his teacher and school rules, both as a student and as a parent (Rahul Gandhi also studied in Doon for two years), is something that all his teachers remark on even today. Vohra remembers how Rajiv never flaunted his Nehru connections to weave around school rules. He made sure that he never came back late even when his grandfather, Prime Minister Jawaharlal Nehru, came to visit him.

Nehru often visited his grandson but to avoid publicity, would wait in the Circuit House and send his ADC to pick up and drop Rajiv. Once when Nehru had taken Rajiv to nearly Chakrata, they were delayed

4. Nicholas Nugent. *Rajiv Gandhi*. London, BBC, 1990. See also *The Sunday Observer*, 26 May 1991.
5. *Ibid.*

because of the traffic and young Rajiv was so worried that he would be late for dinner that he forced his grandfather to drop him at school directly. Nehru came and left hurriedly, noticed only by the gateman.[6]

When Rajiv was sixteen, his father suffered the second of two heart attacks, and died. Rajiv recalls that it happened shortly after an attempt at recociliation between his parents. The family had taken a long and enjoyable holiday in Kashmir; 'some of the old strains had disappeared', he told simi Garewal in the video, India's Rajiv. Feroz was a few days short of his forty-eighth birthday when he died. Indira had confided to an American friend that she was deeply unhappy in her domestic life, saying she and Feroz 'quarrelled over every conceivable subject'. She told of her sorrow at having missed 'the most wonderful thing in life, having a complete and perfect relationship with another human being.' Rajiv remembers the good times and, being away at boarding school from the age of nine, may not have been conscious of the extent to which strains were growing in his parents' relationship. In any case, he had an extra father figure in Nehru, to whom he was devoted - more so than was his brother, Sanjay Nehru enjoyed spoiling both his grandchildren. Rajiv inherited from his father a love of working with his hands. Feroze had a talent for making toys and used to get his sons to help him in the small workshops they had at both the homes in Delhi. It was largely due to Feroze's influence, teaching them to take things apart and put them together again, that both Rajiv and Sanjay went on from school to study engineering. Rajiv says his father taught him the 'dignity of labour, not hesitating to work with your hands, being straight and truthful, not hestitating to speak out'. Rajiv also inherited from his father a taste for Western classical music since, according to his mother, 'the Nehrus were very unmusical people'.[7]

It was not so long ago that Rajiv Gandhi and Sonia used to go to Khan Market New Delhi holding hands for buying grocery, fruits and vegetables. They used to pick up crates of cold drinks and lots of fruits, Rajiv would then take out his wallet and make the payment while Sonia looked around. Indira Gandhi was the Prime Minister then and Sanjay was alive. Rajiv was an Indian Airlines pilot with not a worry in the world. With her partner now gone, Sonia clenched her hands into tight fists when the first sandalwood sticks were being palced on the body of Rajiv Gandhi. Immediately Priyanka was by her mother's side. she placed her arm on Sonia, the Pallav of her saree forming a protective shield on her shoulders. But Sonia did not relax. Priyanka then took

6. Savitri Choudhury. A School Mourns its Brightest Star. The Times of India, 26 May 1991.
7. Nicholas Nugent. *Op.Cit.*

Sonia's arms, draped them around her and gently forced open her clenched fists. Every stick that Sonia placed was around the feet of Rajiv Gandhi's body. Just before Rahul lit the pyre, Sonia removed a stick from the outer layer and placed a lone sandalwood stick inside-as close to the body as she could reach- in a personal and final tribute to her companion of 23 years.[8]

He was a small eater but the food had to be good. Before he become Prime Minister, one of Rajiv's regular haunts was the Bukhara at Maurya Sheraton, New Delhi. And even after, food was regularly brought from the restaurant to Race Course Road, New Delhi. He had a weakness for Mughalai food and kababs (made of goat meat) were his favourite. At an informal tea meeting with journalists last month (the menu included kababs), he recounted how during the 1989 campaign, he was in a muslim mohalla (area) in Kanpur at 1.30 a.m. He was famished and what made him more ravenous was the overpowering aroma of Kababs in the air. But in the hurly-burly of the campaign, he had to give it a miss. His other favourite dish was good, wholesome daliya (porridge). His security personnel never ceased to be amazed at the small quantitites of food Rajiv ate. "During trips out he rarely indulged himself with proper meals and preferred instead to snack," said one officer. Another restaurant he frequented was the Orient Express at the Taj. But he was most particular about water, carrying his own supplies. "In that matter, he was like a typical westerner," the officer said. Also very unlike an Indian prime minister, he was fond of the outdoors. One of Rajiv's favourite pastimes was angling. He keenly followed other sports too and would many a time surpirse his colleagues at meetings by asking for the latest cricket or tennis scores. When in town he spent a couple of hours everyday with Rahul playing badminton. His fixation for detail was something that he is said to have inherited from Indira Gandhi. When he called guests home for a meal, he liked everything to be in its proper place: From the forks and knives to the guests he was very particular about who should sit where. A journalist who was invited to one of these occasions recounted how one napkin had not been kept in its ring. "When he saw that, he threw a fit," the journalist said. Even when he moved into his residence at 10 Janpath last year, Rajiv supervised all arrangements personally. He replaced the electrical sockets (in the process giving the public works department staff innumerable headaches), decided where the VCR and television should be positioned and helped Sonia arrange the rugs, pictures and potted plants. "If the television antenna was angled wrongly, he would go about the business of setting it straight," said a security

8. *The Hindustan Times*, 27 May 1991.

officer. And if the car was giving him a minor problem, he had be first to dive under the bonnet before deciding that a mechanic was better equipped. He would even change a flat tyre himself," a security officer said.[9]

In a lighter vein, Dr. Subramaniam Swamy said "Rajiv Gandhi had a fantastic sense of humour and had a tremendous weakness for chocolates-a typical Parsi habit".

Strangely, it was my initial association with Rajiv that led to a deep and lasting one with Indira Gandhi. After the partition in August 1947, I was teaching at the Kindegarten Elizabeth Cobah School on Hailey Road (now called the Shiv Niketan School, New Delhi). In the later part of 1951, Rajiv, who was just seven and a half, came to study there. I remember him as a lovely loking but shy and introverted child, who greately enjoyed painting and drawing. He was a very sensitive boy-he would wince each time someone shouted at him but break into a beautiful smile if someone was gentle. But then I left the school in the middle of 1953. It was a little later, when Indira Gandhi was looking for someone to help her, that my name was suggested.

In the years that followed, the boys were mostly out of the house-first in Welhams and then in Doon School, Dehradun. However, during the holidays when they did come home, they were very happy to be by themselves. Rajiv, unlike Sanjay, was particularly reticent and withdrawn. The only time that he really opened up was when his father would visit the house. I remember they would play Mechano together for hourse, Rajiv's face lighting up on these occasions. As a child, Rajiv was also very considerate and gentle. I recall an instance in 1955 when Nehru and Indira Gandhi went on an official visit to Russia and East Europe. We, the kids and I, went along in a special Air Force plane to see them off in Bombay. On the way back, Rajiv was very sick and threw up. But not one of us got to know about it till we had landed. That was just like him, no fuss, no nothing. Even when he got married, he was a very thoughtful person, a family man whose world was his children, wife and home. Politics changed all this for him but even so he remained committed to his family and their home was a very special place for them, completely separate from the political world. Their house was a very meticulous one, neat and perfect, not chaotic at all.

After I opted for retirement, when Indira Gandhi died and he became Prime Minister, I visited Rajiv only on rare ocassions. My contact with them remained mostly through birthday cards and gifts that we continued to exchange. In fact, I last met Rajiv on Sonia's

9. *The Sunday Obseerver*, 26 May 1991.

birthday on December 9, 1990. We had a pot-luck lunch- just Rajiv, Sonia, Priyanka and me-and it was just like the old times. We sat at the table and chatted for hours. We laughed and Priyanka was thrilled to hear all those old stories about her father. The last memories that I have of Rajiv are happy ones and I am grateful for that. I remember him eating and talking and laughing on that day.

It is reassuring to see that Indira Gandhi's trait of poise and dignity in sorrow has been inherited not just by her sons but her grandchildren as well.[10]

Rajiv Gandhi was deeply attached to his family. He was concerned about Priyanka and Rahul having to grow up in a security cocoon. Priyanka adjusted herself very well, particularly after she joined Jesus and Mary College, Delhi University. Rajiv was delighted that Rahul could go to Harvard and told me more than once how well Rahul was doing there.[11]

Though there were many undergraduates from India in Cambridge at that time, some of whom-like writer Gita Mehta and her publisher husband Sony Mehta-have found fame in their own fields, Rajiv was not a great socialite and had eyes only for a quiet language student from Turin, Sonia Maino. He first set eyes on her in a Greek restaurant and, according to Rajiv, 'organised through a friend for them to meet'. It seems to have been love virtually at first sight as far as he was concerned: 'The first time I saw her, I knew she was the girl for me. Then we fell in love. Sonia was his first and only girlfriend. He introduced her to his mother as she passed through London on a trip....[12]

Rajiv Gandhi was a good pilot, intelligent and quick to learn," recalled Captain Nat Pereira, a former Indian Airlines director and pilot.

Capt. Pereira was the director of the Hyderabad-based IA Central Training Establishment in the seventies when Rajiv Gandhi was a student undergoing training for the Boeing 737.

Reporters on a visit to this prestigious air university years ago were shown the class room where he learnt his theory.

"If I entered the classroom, Rajiv Gandhi used to stand up and wish me. I never fussed over him and was objective while evaluating his performance," Capt. Pereira said.

Being the son of Indira Gandhi, who was then Prime Minister, there were quite a few trainners to go out of their way to be in his good books.

10. Usha Bhagat. A Shy, Lovely Looking Introvert. *The Times of India*, 26 May 1991.
11. P. Chidambaram. He Lived Too Dangerously. *The Times of India*, 26 May 1991.
12. Nicholas Nugent. *Op.Cit.*

For instance it was not uncommon to see some persons even offering to carry Rajiv Gandhi's bag.

But, all this did not affect Rajiv Gandhi who went about attending to his work without getting flattered, according to Capt. Pereira.

A similar opinion was expressed by another friend and colleague of Rajiv Gandhi, Capt. Prince Dandona, at present an Indian Airlines A-320 commander. Said Capt. Dandona: "People did favours for him, but he never got carried away."

Capt. Pereira said that on one particular occasion, Rajiv Gandhi expressed a desire to fly with him (Capt. Pereira). "I took him on the Delhi-Nagpur sector and pointed out some minor deficiencies in his performance and I found his grasping power very good," he said.

According to Capt. Pereira, Rajiv Gandhi always kept himself abreast of aviation knowledge. For example, whenever an accident or incident took place he always referred to a particular book which had made a study of the subject.

"As Rajiv Gandhi had a copy, I called him to my office and requested him to lend it to us. He said that he was flying to Delhi the next day and he would get a copy and send it to us which he did promptly," Capt. Pereira said.

"An incident which Capt. Pereira vividly recalls was the one involving a close friend and adviser of Rajiv Gandhi, Sathish Sharma.

"I once took Satish Sharma for the Boeing command training, but he did not come upto the mark. Satish Sharma immediately complained to Rajiv Gandhi about me. But Mr. Gandhi did not back him, but stood by my decision on his performance," said Capt. Pereira.

"I remember Rajiv Gandhi coming to the Delhi Flying Club on a scooter. Both of us used to fly the Pushpak," said Capt. Prince Dandona.

Capt. Dandona who was senior to Rajiv Gandhi found the latter's approach to flying extremely professional. "He followed the fly- by-the book principle and was a very disciplined person," recalled Capt. Dandona.

"He was a very good mixer, was very informal and never for once made anyone feel that after all he was the son fo the Prime Minister," he said.

Capt. Dandona who was with him at the Central Training Establishment in Hyderabad remembered that he used to call Rajiv Gandhi sergeant. "Whenever the lecturer asked question. I used to nudge Rajiv Gandhi and say, 'sergeant answer, answer.

We used to have lot of fun."

Rajiv Gandhi was also very particular about his weight and appearance, Capt. Dandona added.

Sharing the view of other Indian Airlines officials Capt. Dondona said, Rajiv Gandhi was an ideal person to deal with. He never used his position to seek out-of-turn promotions." He neither drank nor smoked," Capt. Dandona said.

Capt. Dandona said Rajiv Gandhi had a clean flying record. He never graduated to be a commnader because he moved to politics. Prior to being a first officer on the Boeign-737, he flew the Avro.

In the classroom, Rajiv Gandhi was very meticulous about keeping notes.

B.G. Menon of the Air Works India, a private aircraft maintenance frim, said he knew Rajiv Gandhi as a friend. "I have flown as a passenger in the same aircraft where he was first officer. When he knew that I was in the plane, he used to send for me and spent sometime in the cockpit," he said. Menon found Rajiv Gandhi's flying ability above average.

About 10 years ago, the Bombay branch of the Aeronautical Society of India organised a seminar on flight safety held at the Air India Auditorium at Nariman Point.

Delivering the inaugural address.

Rajiv Gandhi came down heavily on the directorate- general of civil aviation. The speech is still quoted in aviation circles.

Rajiv Gandhi was in Paris in June 1985 for the Paris air show. At this international Air and space exhibition, he was shown a mock- up of the cockpit of the A-320.

Though Rajiv Gandhi spent only a few minutes in the mock-up, he was stated to have asked "very intelligent" questions on this high-technology aircraft which impressed senior executives of Airbus Industries.

But then came 1984, and Doon School's nondescript pupil suddenly became the Star Alumnus. As they did for Rajiv Gandhi, things changed for the school. It suddenly became the object of intense media curiousity as (very often cynical) journalists hounded out every detail of the new Prime Minister's past. The media's obsession with Doon was compounded by the fact that Rajiv appeared to be surrounding himself with his old school cronies. The adage 'Doon Goons' earlier coined for Sanjay Gandhi and his infamous buddies was now applied to the new coterie. Kandhari remarks that more was made of the Doon coterie than what really existed. "Rajiv's style went against the usual darbari politics. The old guard were not willing to allow themselves to be superseded and hence the Doon slander," he feels. Soon parents from all over the country came to Doon chasing a dream for their sons. "We began to get far too much publicity and parents began to look upon Doon as a finishing school," comments Das, whose grandfather Sishir Ranjan Das started the school. When Das took over as principal three years ago, he claims he tried to play down the Doon-Rajiv Connection. Rajiv's biggest contribution to his Doon School, other than the unwelcome publicity, was more for the entire Doon Valley. During one of his numerous visits to Dehradun to see his Children, the unhindered limestone quarrying in the valley was brought to his notice by former principal Gulab Ramchandani. These quarries were causing unprecedented landslides, pollution and silting in the valley. Rajiv influenced his mother, then the Prime Minister to make an aerial survey of the valley, Indira Gandhi was horrified by what she saw and instituted the Doon Valley Board, headed by two citizens. Avdhesh Kaushal and Ramchandani. Later, Kaushal moved the Supreme Court and succeeded in getting 55 of the 58 mines closed. "We have to be thankful to Rajiv for the initial impetus he gave our movement," says Ramchandani.[13]

The boy who was not even able to become a monitor at school became Prime Minister. And while history will judge his exact contribution, and debates will rage over whether he was justifiably or unfairly criticised, one thing remains certain; his alma mater.

Rajiv Gandhi's remakarble victory at the hustings in 1984-that gave the Congress a record majority in the Lok Sabha that even his grandfather, the architect of modern India, Jawaharlal Nehru, had never secured-was the direct consequence of the wave of sympathy for his party in the wake of the brutal gunning down of his mother. However, the people voted in favour of the Congress in a massive way also because of Rajiv's untarnished image that contrasted sharply with the run-of-the-mill politicians. Thereafter Rajiv himself showed an inclination to live upto the expectations he had roused, and the accords referred to were the outcome of painstaking endeavours on his part. However, the brute majority of the Congress and the environment of sycophancy that surrounded the seat of power resulted in the onset of stangnation and drift that could not be checked by the young and ebullient Prime Minister's penchant for demonstrative acts whose positive features one could hardly overlook without being oblivious of their negative effects in the absence of the essential spadework. Thus the Indo-Sri Lanka agreement of 1987 floundered on the rocks of the stark reality with the Indian Peace keeping Force being compelled to wage war on an indigenous populace in alien territory, gaining practically nothing in return. The Pubjab accord remained unimplemented

13. Savitri Choudhury. *Op.Cit.*

and the lack of perspective in tackling the problem of dealing with secessionist terrorism only aggravated the situation there as every action in Punjab was marked by senseless drift and the restoration of the political process remained a far cry.[14]

In a way his real political career began on October 31. 1984, when Indira Gandhi was shot dead by two assassins, who were her bodyguards; and the tragic end of his political life came when he too was assassinated on May 21, 1991. Nevertheless, it will be utterly dangerous and myopic to solely regard Indira Gandhi's death as the result of an attack by a sikh fanatic, who had wormed himself into the inner security ring of the late Prime Minister's residence. Similarly, it will be naive to believe that the bomb which was operated through remote control was the handwork of some other fanatic. The real assassins were somebody else; the men who killed these two leaders of India were merely acting as tools. Any analysis of the secret forces which had planned and directed Rajiv Gandhi's murder is indeed a difficult task. The difficulty is both conceptual and functional, relating to search and selection of information and then of piecing together the entire material. Let us leave this question at that.[15]

When Rajiv Gandhi was Prime Minister, I was minister in his government. He gave me a lot of work to do and later added more. He personally asked me to intervene in the debates on Fairfax, the President's powers, the Thakkar commission report and finally, on Borfors. The period from 1987 to 1989 was one of great stress. In retrospect, he felt that Bofors had been handled badly in the early stages. When I was brought into the debate in early 1989, I looked into the matter afresh and gave him a confidential note. He accepted my analysis. I told him I would have to tell Parliament that A.B. Bofors had indeed paid huge amounts of money although it had not been established yet that any Indian or Indian entity had received any part of the money. This was a major departure from the earlier stand taken by the government, yet Rajiv did not hesitate to endorse my view. I discussed the Bofors case with him several times in formal meetings, in small groups and at a one-to-on level. I asked him if he knew anything about the Bofors payments and his answer was simple and straightforward: he had nothing to do with these payments and he knew nothing about them. As the Bofors drama unfolded, there were revelations from time to time but, so far as Rajiv was concerned, they made no difference. Not once did I find even a shadow of concern cross his face; not once did he avoid a straight reply. I was convinced-and remain convinced-

14. Sumit Chakravarthy. Balance Sheet of Rajiv Gandhi. *Patriot*, 25 May 1991.
15. V.D. Chopra. Rajiv Gandhi. *Patriot*, 23 May 1991

that neither Rajiv nor any member of his family had anything to do with the Bofors payments. It would be an insult to his memory if the Bofors investigation against Rajiv is allowed to continue. The government must put an end to these investigations now and close the matter.

Each crisis brought out the strength of his character. Rajiv knew who the real authors of the Defamation Bill, particularly the controversial Clause 13, were. He refused to pass the buck and accepted responsibility for the whole Bill.[16]

One would not be objective if one were to lose one's proportion in assessing Rajiv's reign as the Prime Minister. A novice in politics he did commit serious mistakes which were accentauted by his reliance on a set of political juveniles who acted as his advisers even though they were unable to comprehend their own failures and weaknesses. Thus he alternately pandered to both Hindu communalism and Muslim fundamentalism, something that bordered on opportunism. The Bofors controversy and the way he handled it reinforced suspicions of a highly shady transaction (even though to no allegation was proved before his assassination) thus rullyfying his clean image. His arrogant and haughtly out-bursts, though infrequent, betryaed certain authoritarian proclivities turning friends into foes. And yet, for all his shortcomings, Rajiv was a highly polished, decent human being who exuded a disarming charm-not charisma-that impressed one and all-supprters and adversaries. He was a man not cut out for politics on which he, however, left a lasting impression. Drawn into political arena by the conspiracy of circumstances, his success, failures and eventual assassination can all be attributed to the conspiracy of circumstances.

He might not have moulded history but was inexorably moved by the course of history which dictated his life and fate. The loss of India on his demise cannot be measured instantly. He will always be remembered as the Prince Charming of Indian Politics.[17]

It is true one of Rajiv Gandhi's first achievements as Prime Minister was the passing of the anti-defection Act. But the much- touted party elections were postponed over and over again. Before long the "brokers of power and influence" were back in business. Congress chief ministers were changed at will and the Union council of minisiters reshuffled nearly thirty times. Vested interests ruled the roost. Far from waging a war against casteism and communalism he appeared at critical times to compromise with them. His flip-flop on the shah Bano case, his decision to allow the shilanyas to be performed in Ayodhya in November 1989 just before the election, his ambivalent stance on the

16. P. Chidambaram. He Lived Too Dangerously. *The Times Of India,*
17. Sumit Chakravorthy. Balance Sheet of Rajiv Gandhi. *Patriot*, 25 May 1991.

Mandal commission report-all these were indicative of the fact that while he could not change the system he was quite helplessly yielding to it. Still Rajiv Gandhi's instincts all along were sound. He realised early that India could never hope to enter the next century with a measure of confidence unless it massively, inducted science and technology, accepted modern methods of management, opened up the economy to competition. The technological missions he set up to speed up development in such areas as water, edible oils and telecommunications were a daring innovation. His space programmes, like the nuclear energy ones, may not have met with resounding success. All the same he encouraged and was seen to encourage, endeavour on the scientific front. Similarly, he may not have gone beyond certain peripheral innovations to liberalise the economy. Still during his premiership, economic growth averaged over five per cent, tax revenues attained record levels, exports increased dramatically (as imports did too), employment was up. Above all, despite widespread and serve droughts, India did not witness any starvation deaths. Indeed absolute poverty declined perceptibly.[18]

18. The Times of India, 25 May 1991.

3
THE TRAGIC INNOCENT

Death shadowed Rajiv Gandhi ever since he took over as Prime Minister following Indira Gandhi's assassination in 1984. Even so, his violent end has shocked us. The question that should disturb us is: what has happened to this land of Gautam Buddha and Mahatma Gandhi? What went wrong? Who is responsible for the moral bankruptcy of the country? It is imperative that we search within us for some answers.[1] Ever since Rajiv Gandhi stepped into his mother's shoes after her assassination in 1984, he lived under a shadow of death. But nobody expected the end to be so soon and so gory. Most people still find it hard to believe that he is no more. In his election campaign this time, he got closer to the people and endeared himself to the masses. Alas! this cost him his life.

The weather on the May summer afternoon when he was cremated was unkind. Yet milling crowds escorted the gun carriage carrying his covered body and later thronged the Indira Gandhi memorial side of Shakti Sthal at Rajghat, New Delhi. The foreign dignitarties that assembled to pay homage to Rajiv Gandhi must have been unprepared for the sweltering heat. Most of them were dressed in formal attires or their national customes. Some of the VIPs from the western world wore hats or arried parasols. The women VIPs from the neighbouring countries of Pakistan and Bangladesh covered their heads with the ends of their sarees or "dupattas" and sat through the three-and-a half hour cruel afternoon sun patiently.

There was virtual scramble for bottled water in every enclosure. Even the priest who performed the last rites of Rajiv Gandhi succum-mbed to the heat when the family members and the VIPs had left. But the common people who have braved the sun waiting for the body from 1 p.m. stayed on till late evening watching the flames devouring the mortal remains of their departed leader.

Barely a few yards away, Indira Gandhi watched the soul of her first-born unite with the eternal one.[2]

The history of assassination of outstanding leaders of the Third World countries is revealing in itself. The Minister of information of Mozambique, Jose Luis Cabazo, announced in 1989 that his country had uncovered as espionage network of the CIA which had been detailed to destablise the Mozambique government. Behind the plot to murder Congolese leader Partice Lumumba was the United States

1. Arun Sadhu. The Politics of violence. *The Times* of India, 26 May, 1991
2. *The Hindustan Times*, 27 May, 1991.

Ambassador in the then Congo, Clare Hayes Timberlake. A special committee set up by the US Senate to investigate CIA activities threw light on some aspects of the brutal murder of Lumumba. The New York Times reported on November 23, 1975, that in the summer of 1960 the Deputy Director of the CIA for Planning, Richard Bissel, had asked Bronson Tweedy, the head of the CIA's African section, to study the possibility of liquidating Lumumba and to draw up a detailed plan for such an operation. The senate Committee also discovered that the then CIA Director, Allen Dulles, personally approved Lumumba's murder and considered this to be quite proper. The CIA operations in Chand, Ethiopia, Angola, Sudan, Chile and Nicaragua have been widely published in the American press.

In our region, six outstanding leaders have fallen victim to assessing hired by the imperialist agencies. Gandhiji was the first in the line. Pakistan's first Prime Minister Liaquat Ali Khan was the second; solomon Bhandaranaike of Sri Lanka was the third; Bangladesh President Mujibur Rehman was the fourth while Pakistan's Prime Minister Bhutto was the victim of legal murder. Indira Gandhi was assassinated in 1984. And now Rajiv Gandhi has been assassinated. The objective behind all these assassination was to destablise these countries. It is in this backdrop that cold-blood murder of Rajiv Gandhi needs to be seen.

This assassination has deepened the Political crisis in the country a crisis which had begun to unfold itself during the last two years. What is most intriguing is that it is in the midst of this crisis that certain influential circles have begun to advocate that a national government should be set up at the Centre. It is not a new concept. This concept has been put forward at every crucial point in the history of parliamentary system in our country. There is no doubt that in a vast country of India's size, the two-party system cannot and will not develop. India will always have a multiple-party system. Let us not make any bones about it. But the crucial question which political forces should join hands together, both in states and at the Centre to stimulate the process of nation-state building on the basis of secularism and democracy.[3] Among the strangest stories circulating about what happened outside 10, Janpath that fateful night of May 23, 1991 concerns former defence minister and estranged Rajiv friend Arun Singh. He was nearly lynched outside the gate by a frenzied, lumpen mob that abused him and threatened to break his legs.

Arun Singh was saved by the security guards and quietly left the scene. But his estranged wife Nina, once among Sonia's closest friends,.

3. V.D. Chopra. National crisis and whither Congress. *Patriot,* 27 May, 1991.

was determinued to get inside and offer her condolences. In the mmelee, she spotted Satish Sharma's car going in and with another friend of the Gandhi's hopped into the back seat. When Sharma turned around and saw who was there, he shouted for her to get out of his car at once. Nina Singh did not budge. So he leant back, opened the back door and screamed: "I need to get in and you need to get out".

Nina Singh was not available for comment but too many people saw it happen. Are such incidents an afftertaste of what has happened or a foretaste of things to come?[4]

All eyes were wet when young Priyanka bent to touch her father's feet before Rajiv Gandhi's body was taken out of Teen Murti House New Delhi, on May 24, 1991. Priyanka's gesture brought tears to Sonia Gandhi's eyes who stood by watching quietly.

Priyanka said a silent prayer at her father's feet for two minutes and moved to her monther's side suddenly, the mother and daughter leaneed on each other and even in that crowd they shared a private moment of grief.

The doors of the room where Rajiv Gandhi's body was laid for homage was closed to public. By now the family rituals were done and the body had been placed on a bier. A rose and jasmine garland was placed at the feet of the body. A screen had been held at the door for private ceremonies to be done, and to allow the family to have some moments alone with their dear one.

The body was draped in the national flag. It was fully covered. Everybody was shocked to see six feet tall Rajiv reduced to a diminutive size--such was the devastation caused to him by the fatal bomb blast in Sriperumbudur.

Sonia Gandhi and Priyanka stepped aside as friends, relatives and Rahul bent to pick the pall about 1 p.m. Rajiv had begun his last journey from the same spot that his grandfather Jawaharlal Nehru had 27 years ago, about the same time of the month.

Rahul held the front right flank of the bier, while Amitabh Bachchan, Suman Dubey, Satish Sharma, R.K. Dhawan, Gautam Kaul and some of Rajiv Gandhi's in-laws lent a holder to the man who had come to become a pivot of Indian Politics in the last seven years.

An unprecedented number of photographers and media persons recorded the event. As soon as the body was laid on the a gun- carriage of the artillery, several Congress workers and supporters surged raising hysterical slogans of "Rajiv Gandhi amar rahe". Many climbed on the gun-carriage and held on firmly to the edges till they had to be pulled

4. Sunil Sethi. Foretaste of Things to come? *The Times of India* 26 May 1991

back by Army men on duty. The sight of the body of Mr. Gandhi brought tears to the eyes of those present

Sonia Gandhi, Rahul and Priyanka were whisked away to the head of the cavalcade of chief mourners after the cars of the three service chiefs. A battery of photographers descended upon the family of Rajiv Gandhi who looked grim. Rahul looked in a state of shock, Priyanka stoic and Sonia Gandhi was trying stoic and hard to hold back tears. But as soon as the sombre procession moved, Sonia broke down. With trembling hands she removed her dark glasses and wiped her eyes.

A helicopter hovered in the sky dropping rose petals whose cool fragrance brought momentary respite from the sweltering heat. The funeral procession was led by an Army pilot jeep followed by a column each of the Army, Navy and the Air Force, the firing party and drummers. A flower bedecked Army truck pulled the flower bedecked gun-carriage. This gun-carriage was the same that was used to carry the bodies of Jawaharlal Nehru and Indira Gandhi.

The three service chiefs ied the chief mourners including Sonia Gandhi and her children and the rest of their relatives and friends. Black Cat commandoes walked along the VIP cars.

As the procession came out of Teen Murti frenzied cries of "Rajiv tera ye balidan, Yaad rakhega Hindustan" rent the air. Thousands of people were kept at baỳ, several left holding garlands and flowers they had brought as their tribute to the departed leader. The drummers beat a mourning beat. It was a different atmosphere all along Rajpath. Chaos and bustle of the political rallies which the lush green lawns on both sides of the road usually witness, was overtaken by a somber atmosphere. People lining on both sides of the road, eagerly waited for the procession to reach, to pay their last homage to the departed leader.

All eyes were gluded towards Vijay Chowk, spotting the gun- carriage on which the mortal remains of Mr. Rajiv Gandhi were placed. Once the procession turned towards Rajpath from Vijay Chowk, the people lining right up to India Gate stood in straight with flowers and garlands in their hands. A group of Naga girls stood in deep silence near India Gate with flowers in their hands. "We have come all the way to pay homage to Mr. Rajiv Gandhi ", was how one of them explained their presence in the scorching sun.

The flags of various political parties which usually adorn the lamp posts during ones were replaced by black ones. With a gentle flutter, they did adieu to the former Prime Minister who had made his presence felt on this very road on a number of occassions. So did the people present there, vividly remembering how Mr. Rajiv Gandhi, the Prime Minister, used to acknowledge the greetings of the people with that charismatic smile on his face while driving down the Rajpath to attend the Republic Day parades.

A large number of women and children were present on this stretch of the route. Braving hot weather, some of them waited for over two hours. The slogans Rajiv Gandhi Amar Rahen and Maa bete ka balidaan yaad karega Hindustan rent the air as the procession inched towards India Gate.

The entire area around Rajpath was virtually sealed by the securitymen. All connecting roads had been sealed. Utmost care was taken by the police to prevent main road.

Flags flew at half mast at India Gate as the cortege come inching its way from Vijay Chowk. Black flags had been put up on the lamp posts as a mark of mourning. Many people who came to witness the funeral procession also wore black bands. All the way from India Gate throughout Kasturba Gandhi Marg and ahead, a large number of people waited on both sides of the barricaded roads for a few hours. Police personnel stood alongside the road.

Jeeps of the military police and army vehicles led the funeral procession, headed by General Officer Commanding of Delhi area, Major General S.C. Kashyap.

The flower bedecked gun carriage on which was placed Mr. Gandhi's body draped in Tricolors was flanked by two vehicles packed with commandos.

Both Sonia Gandhi and Priyanka could be seen in a car immediately following the cortege. A large number of people could be seen running alongside offering their condolences to her. Many VIPs followed in the cavalcade of cars.

Delhi Pradesh Congress Committee president Prem Singh walked along with processionists. He said he would cover the distance on foot, "Rajiv Gandhi was my leader. I am his ordinary solider". A helicopter flew on top showering petals from time to time. A number of kiosks had been set up for water while people had towels, umbrella, handkerchief to save themselves from the scorching heat.

In the market centre shutters were down. The otherwise busy area was deserted, except along the fundral route. Heat and blowing dust added to the gloom. With heavy police arrangements and under the watchful gaze of mounted police, the procession drove along the Barakhamba Road, hundreds of people pressed forward towards the railings along the pavements to get a glimpse of the marigold garlanded portrait of the slain leader and the flower bedecked carriage.

The elaborate security arrangements made for the protection of VIPs in Rajiv Gandhi's funeral procession broke down on the as hysterical crowds swarmed onto the road and mobbed the cars carrying Sonia Gandhi and Amitabh Bachchan holding up the entire motorcade following the guncarriage with the body upon it.

Soon after starting from Teen Murti Bhawan, when the procession reached Duplex road, the police allowed the people standing on the pavements to join it leading to utter chaos. As soon as the people discovered the car with Sonia Gandhi and her daughter Priyanka in it, they surround it on all sides shounting slogans.

The heavily armed Black cat commandos walking alongside Sonia Gandhi's car with their automatic weapons held ready were brushed aside by the excited masses as they tried in vain to hold them back. Alarmed by the surging crowd, Sonia Gandhi had to close the dark glassed windows of her car for some time.

Soon after, the slogan shouting crowd discovered that Amitabh Bachchan and Rahul Gandhi were in the car behind her. Hyserical youths and lumpen elements swarmed over Bachchan's car trying to get a glimpse of him. The car came to a standstill as helpless policement and Congress-I workers tried to keep them away. Meanwhile the sirens of the other VIP cars and army vehicles held up behind wailed in vain again and again.

The cars moved haltingly at a slow pace as the Black Cat Commandos, the plainclothes securitymen, police constables and Congress workers struggled to hold back the frenzied crowds and make way for the motorcade which had got left much behind the guncarriage with Mr. Rajiv Gandhi's body on it.

Finally, the mobs were warded off as a car packed with securitymen flanked Bachchan's car on the right side while an Army truck carrying pressmencovered it on the left. On reaching Rajpath, Congress workers formed a human chain by holding hands to keep the crowds from getting into the way of the motorcade.

Meanwhile police constables had to literally form a wall around Amitabh Bachchan's car to keep back eagar fans and a couple of mounted policemen discouraged people from coming near it by aiming lathi blows at them.

The funeral procession was joined by thousands of peoples on reaching Rajpath, thus impeding its progress as it would its was slowly. To make matters worse, Sonia Gandhi's car broke down in the middle of Rajpath-she get down along with Priyanka and walked a short distance to get into an Air Force staff car as there was a sudden rush of onlookers to have a glimpse of them.

"Rajiv Gandhi" slogans rent the air at many places during the three-and-a-half hour procession. But at times, slogans were shouted for Sonia Gandhi, too, "Desh ko bachaenge Sonia ko laenge" (We will save the nation, we will bring Sonia) and "Soniaji sangharsh karo, hum tumhare saath hain" (Sonia start the struggle, we are with you) were some. At many a place, enthusiastic youth shouted this next to Sonia's car. And with folded hands she urged them not to.

The crowd ran behind the gun carriage bearing the former Prime Minister, Rajiv Gandhi's body. And along with the crowds ran Rahul Gandhi. He got off a blue Ambassador car near Modern School on Barakhamba Road New Delhi. At times he increased his pace and at times, he slowed down. A commando ran beside him. The crowds saw him run but didn't push or jostle him. A few tried to get close and he nodded his head. A short distance later he simply walked behined the carriage, down Sikandra Road onto Zafar Marg and finally opposite Shanker's Doll's Museum got into the car again.

Rahul also ended up walking for a good part of the time before that; he had get out where the procession slowed because of crowds.

History has been witness to two poignant moments at Shakti Sthal New Delhi where the mortal remains of a mother and son, both Prime Ministers in their time, were cremated with full state honours in a space of less than a decade.

A little less than seven years ago, grieving Rajiv Gandhi had lit the funeral pyre of his mother Indira Gandhi who fell to assassin's bullets in 1984.

On May 24, 1991, 17-years old Rahul Gandhi, son of Rajiv Gandhi lit his father's funeral pyre at a site nearby, on the banks of river Yamuna.

As the flames from the pyre leapt up, Rahul was seen comforting his mother, Sonia Gandhi, who was overcome by emotion.

The scene quickly reminded one of the piognant, emotionally surcharged moment seven years ago when Rajiv conforted Rahul, Sonia and Priyanka after lighting his mother's pyre.

Twenty kg ghee and 50 kg of "Havan Samagri" were consumed in performing the last rites of Rajiv Gandhi. One quintal of sandalwood was also used along with nine quintal of wood, ghee and havan samagri.

After sprinking the "Gangajal" on the body, Rahul and Priyanka placed the wood pieces one by one on the pyre, Sonia joined them by placing a few, while Amitabh Bachchan and Gandhi's maternal uncle Gautam Kaul lent a helping hand. Most of the time Priyanka was seen putting her hand around her mother who stood in mute silence.

As the body was consigned to the flames on the banks of the sacred river Yamuna, at a site close to the samadhis of Jawaharlal Nehru and Indira Gandhi, the eyes of millions of Indians on the spot or on television sets were rivetted on bespectacled Rahul, who kept a composed exterior.

Pandit Ganpat Ram Acharya, one of the chief priests supervising Rajiv Gandhi's final rites today, had done the same job at the cremation of Indira Gandhi in 1984.

The entire ritual was carried out according to Arya Samaj rites.

The volley of shots was the last salute. The vedic mantras kept their rhythmic intonation as son Rahul walked around the body of Rajiv Gandhi. It was 5.24 p.m. - time to light the funeral pyre.

The buglers sounded the last post as family members stood around the bier frozen to immobility under the grip of sorrow.

The flames licked the sky with unusual haste. Streaks of light fell on frames of Prince Charles leaning over to speak to PLO Chief Yasser Arafat while US Vice-President Don Quayle sat stoically behind Pakistan Prime Minister Nawaz Sharif.

Kept away by steel barricades and armed policemen the sounds of slain leader's admirers still reached the flames breaking the chants: "Rajiv Gandhi Amar Rahe (Rajiv is immortal). Jab Tak Suraj Chand Rahega ... Rajiv Tera Naam Rehega....." (Rajiv's name will survive as long as there are sun and Moon).

The final journey had started from Teen Murti New Delhi. He had lain in state for two days, while captains, kings and commoners filed past to pay their last tributes.

Rajiv Gandhi had played there in the sprawling gardens. Hidden behind Bougainvillaea bushes. Gambolled through childhood with pandas and tiger cubs. He had sprung to adolescene in this very house and in the womb of power as grandson of first Prime Minister Jawaharlal Nehru. Now he lay dead.

It is death which more than else proved his image as the "last prince of the age of innocence". The throging crowds who braved the midsummer sun were bo stereotypes drawn by the fierce loyalty and hatred which his brother Sanjay had enjoyed. Nor was it the worshipping crowed who were the chariot pullers of his mother Indira Gandhi's triumphal image of Shakti.

The 11 km funeral procession was marked for the national flag bedecked coffin carried on the shoulders of the three services Chiefs, even as the crowds surged forward. The children, Priyanka and Rahul, comforting mother Sonia, bearing her loss stoicaly. Even in her grief many others would not leave her alone. Those who swore by her also sat in the nearest available car for the roads were dusty, crowded and blisteringly hot........

In spite of the massive security arrangements it was the people who walked with the cortege braving the afternoon sun. At the Duplex Road round about as well as Vijay Chowk hundreds materialised from nowhere and successfully broke police cordons to be a part of the last journey. The VIPs kept looking out of their cars and put on grim faces at the first sign of Cameras.

It is only at Shakti Sthal that even the most prominent of hangers on were kept away from the bier. It was just the family: Sonia, Priyanka, Rahul, friend Amitabh Bachchan and cousin Gautam Kaul, the only person who had suffered rather than benefited from family connections. Sonia turned around to call up two gentlemen-every Congressman round or aspirant to the centre of power forgot "grief" and wanted to know the identity of these persons since they had never been seen in the corridors of power. They turned to be Rajiv's relatives-one a brother-in-law of the late Feroze Gandhi and the other the son-in-law of Feroze Gandhi's sister.

The hordes of VIPs, self-proclaimed and otherwise, were allowed up to the bier only after the family had come down to be consoled by President Venkataraman and his wife, Prime Minister Chandra Shekhar, former Prime Minister V.P. Singh et al.

It was a disappointment for the last minute climbers on to the bier for the TV cameras had shifted their focus and vanished with a swiftness which was unbelievable.[5]

Amidst silent tears and mournful chanting of Hindu 'mantras' the mortal remains of Rajiv Gandhi were collected in urns at the Shakti Sthal, on May 26, 1991. The distraught son, Rahul, collected his father's ashes from the rostrum where he was cremated earlier.

The ashes, which were collected in 30 copper urns, were taken to Teen Murti Bhawan and kept there till May 27 for the public to pay homage to their departed leader.

Security men has a tough time to keep the ashes from flying off when a dust storm hit Delhi folowed by heavy shower. Police and Congress volunteers, who has rushed to the spot, managed to cover the ashes with tin sheets and whatever was handy.

It was a heart rending scene when Rahul, Accompanied by Amitabh Bachchan, reached the Shakti Sthal to collect the ashes. Though stiff in his movements, Rahul went about collecting the ashes in a calm

5. Chand Joshi. The Requiem her Inoncence. *The Hindustan Times*, 25 Marg 1991.

manner. Ganpat Ram Acharya, who also performed the last rites of Indira Gandhi conducted the religious proceedings. A patient Rahul went through the rituals, which lased about an hour. Amitabh Bachchan was all the while standing next to Rahul, along with a small group of family members.

Senior Congress leader P.V. Narasimha Rao, former Lok Sabha Speaker Balram Jakhar, former Chief Minister of Kerala K. Karunakaran, former Union Minister H.K.L. Bhagat, Rajiv Gandhi's friend and aide Suman Dubey and V.N. Gadgil were also present at the Shakti Sthal. The former Prime Minister's aides R.K. Dhawan, M.L. Fotedar and Captain Satish Sharma were also present.

Two small trucks, decked with flowers, carried the urns to Teen Murti House, of the 30 copper vessels carying the ashes, Rahul carried two in the car he was travelling with Bachchan.

The security arrangement of the area was foolproof.

The urn containing the ashes of Rajiv Gandhi were taken from Teen Murti House, with full military honours to the New Delhi railway station on May 27 morning from where the sum were carried in a special train to Allahabad to be immersed at the Sangam.

Elaborate arrangements were made for the procession taking the urn to the station. The 'asthi-kalash' (urn containing the ashes) left Teen Murti at 9 a.m. in a special gun carriage. Three platoons, one each from the Army the Navy and the Air Force, presented the arms, a traditional military ritual, at Teen Murti. The procession was coompanied by the three platoons.

At the railway station, the three platoons again presented their arms. While a platoon travelling in the train, a total of six jawans were guarding the compartment where the urn were kept. Major General D.K. Sen of the Army Headquarters, also traveled in the train, being in charge of the entire liason.

The special train stopped at Gahaziabad, Khurja, Aligarh, Hathras, Tundla, Ferozabad, Shikohabad, Kanpur, Unnao, Lucknow, Rai Bareilly, Amethi, Pratapgarh and Prayag before reaching Allahabad. It reached the final desitnation at 6.30 a.m. on May 28, 1991.

From the Allahabad railway station, the ashes were taken to Anand Bhavan. The procession for the immersion of the ashes at the Sangam started at 11 a.m. and the ashes were immersed at 1 p.m.

Similarly, the urns containing the ashes were taken to the States and these were immersed in rivers at Various places.

Senior Congress leaders were accompanying the ashes to Allahabad while State leaders accompanied the ashes to their respective States.

People loved Rajiv Gandhi because there was a spiritual quality in this man which set him apart from other politicians. He was cut out to be a saint but, perforce, chose the wrong vocation. A great tragedy, indeed.[6]

6. Mrigank Mocher. Rajiv Gandhi, *the statesman*, 26 May 1991.

4
ADIEU SON OF INDIA

The Congress Party on May 21, 1991 expressed shock at the assassination of its President Rajiv Gandhi.

An AICC spokesman told newsmen in New Delhi at the party headquarters that "this is a deeprooted conspiracy of anti- national forces".

He said "We are stunned and shocked to hear this ghastly news," and described it as one of the greatest tragedies of Modern Indian History.

The former Union Minister, Mrs. Maragatham Chandrasekhar who was injured in the bomb blast broke down uncontrollably on being informed on May, 27 of Rajiv Gandhi's death, six days after his assassination.

Seventy-three-year-old Chandrasekhar was seriously injured in the bomb blast and was admitted to the Apollo Hospital in Madras "in a state of neurogenic shock". She was a few metres behind Rajiv Gandhi at the time of the explosion and fell unconscious.

A few of the steel pellets which flew from the plastic explosive had entered her left leg and she suffered a severe infection with fluid collection in her chest cavity which caused breathing problem.

The condition of Chandrasekhar who is under treatment in the intensive care unit, is improving steadily and she has resumed her normal diet, hospital sources siad.

President R. Venkataraman, condemned as a barbaric act of the "heinous" assassination of former Prime Minister Rajiv Gandhi, and said words cannot adequately express his grief.

Expressing his deep anguish at the death of Rajiv Gandhi, Venkataraman said in a condolence message that a brave and a dedicated son of India has been felled by an act of coward.

"This savage act should lead us all to resolve to fight the cult of violence in our public life", he said.

Venkataraman appealed for maintaining utmost calm and use the moment of grief to pray for peace in our motherland.

The President also appealed to all fellow countrymen not to allow passions to overtake them but strive to maintain peace and order in this hour of trial.

Bharatiya Janata Party leader L.K. Advani has said the news of Rajiv Gandhi's assasination "is shocking beyond words. No words are too strong to condemn the dastardly act".

He conveyed his condolence to Rajiv Gandhi's wife Sonia Gandhi, her family and his partymen from Ahmedabad.

The Bharatiya Janata Party strongly condemned the assassination of Rajiv Gandhi and asked the Prime Minister to order a high- level inquiry into the incident.

Party Secretary V.K. Malhotra said the Government must immediately find out who were behind the "tragic murder" of Rajiv Gandhi.

V.K. Malhotra said the killing of the former Prime Minister was "very bad" for the country.

He appealed to the people all over the country to remain calm at this "crucial juncture".

Party Vice-President K.L. Sharma described the killing was "most sad and tragic".

It had given an "unbelievable shock" to the nationa, he said. Sharma suspected a "deep-rooted conspiracy" behind the "cowardly act".

Shahi Imam of Jama Masjid Syed Abdullah Bukhari and his son the Naib Imam Ahmed Bukhari said they were deeply shocked to hear about Rajiv Gandhi's killing.

Our political beliefs aside, on humanitarian gounds his killing is very tragic and highly unfortunate, they said, With the death of Rajiv Gandhi it seems that almost the last of the Nehru family's scions have died.

It is a great misfortune for the country that terrorism and communalism have become so widespread and uncontrollable, they said. Strongly condening the killing Ahmed Bukhari said it was highly upsetting that this had happened.

Arun Nehru, former Union Minister and a cousin of Rajiv Gandhi, is cut short his visit to the United states and returned New Delhi immediately.

Nehru was deeply shocked and saddened as soon as he heared the news of Rajiv Gandhi's assassination in Tamil Nadu.

Vice-President, Dr. Shankar Dayal Sharma, expressed profound stock and grief over the killing of Rajiv Gandhi.

Senior Congress leader K.C. Pant, expressing his profound sorrow, said a great career has been cut short.

He said in Rajiv Gandhi's death the nation and the Congress Party had lost a great leader.

The Community Party of India (CPI) condemned the brutal assassination of Rajiv Gandhi.

Party's senior secretary Farooqui said that the CPI was extremely shocked at the murder of the national leader and concerned over the growing violence in elections and politics. All political parties had the responsibility to end violence in politics.

Rashtriya Swayamsevak Chief Balasaheb Deoras has described the assassination of the Congress-I president as "very unfortunate and shocking. Condemning the act, he said this is contrary to our culture.

Government will do everything in its power to indentify the forces behind the dastardly killing of the Congress President Rajiv Gandhi, Union Commerce Minister Subramanian Swamy said here today.

Describing the assassination as a ghastly act by anti-national forces, Dr. Swamy said the nation has lost a young leader and Rajiv Gandhi's death was an irreparable loss to the country.

"At the hour of crisis the nation must unite to foil the nefarious designs of whoever is responsible for the crime", Dr. Swamy observed.

Speaking on behalf of the Samajwadi Janata Party (SJP) Dr. Swamy expressed shock at the news and appealed to the people to maintain calm and peace.

The BJP tonight expressed grave shock and distress at the assassination of former Prime Minister Rajiv Gandhi.

BJP vice-president K.R. Malkani, said, "I am absolutely shocked and pained. I hope there is inquiry into the whole matter and the guilty are brought to book".

He said the whole air of lawlessness started with the assissination of Mrs. Indira Gandhi and the riots that followed. More recently, the coming to power of "lawlessmen like Mulaym Singh and Laloo Prasad" had further contributed to the general lawlessness in the country.

"The first primary and paramount task of the new Government after the current election will be to maintain absolute law and order and justice", he said.

"I do not believe it," said A.B. Vajpayee, senior BJP leader, when he was told of the death of Mr. Rajiv Gandhi.

Vajpayee, who came here in Lucknow this evening on his campaign tour, expressed his "deep shock" when he was awaken from his sleep late in the night to get his reaction. "It is the most disastrous and heinous crime." he said, Vajpayee conveyed his heartfelt sympathies to Sonia Gandhi and members of her family.

Expressing shock at the incident, Deputy Prime Minister Devi Lal described the incident as "unfortunate" and said the country should be saved from the violence.

Union Minister of State for Home Subodh Kant Sahay tonight admitted that former Prime Minister Rajiv Gandhi's death in a bomb explosion at Sriperumpudur in Tamil Nadu was due to lacuna in secuirty measures.

Reacting to Rajiv Gandhi's assissination Sahay said that the incident was the handiwork of "anarchists". He, however, said the group responsible for the explosion was yet to be identified.

Describing Rajiv Gandhi's death as a "national loss", Sahay said, "this is the blackest spot in my career as Home Minister".

Telugu Desam leader P. Upendra expressed shock at the assassination of Rajiv Gandhi.

Upendra condemning the "dastardly act" said the nation has lost a great leader. He said this type of act was "unheard of in a democracy".

Bihar Chief Minister Laloo Prash Yadav today expressed deep anguish and shock over the killing of Rajiv Gandhi.

He said that it was a "black day" in democratic history of our country.

Maharashtra Chief Minister Sharad Pawar described Rajiv Gandhi's assassination as "shocking beyond words".

The killing of Rajiv Gandhi had inflicted a cruel blow to India and the new generation of the country.

It showed the level of violence that had engulfed the country, he added.

The BJP spokesman J.P. Mathur said, "it is sad and soul horrifying to learn about the ghastly killing of Rajiv Gandhi".

He expressed the hope that the Government machinery and police will spare no effort to find out the culprits.

Former Goa Chief Minister Pratapsingh Rane described the assassination of Rajiv Gandhi as "a cowardly act by a mad man. Such acts have no place in a democracy", Rane said.

Maharashtra Gomantak Party leaders Ramakant Khalap and Prof. Gopalrao Mayekar have also condemned the death of Mr. Gandhi and said that it has shocked the nation.

Former External Affairs Minister Vidya Charan Shukla said the assassination of Rajiv Gandhi was a "cowardly attack on the democracy".

In Bhubaneswar, former Orissa Chief Minister J.B. Patnaik expressed his utter stock at the assassination of Rajiv Gandhi.

"Those who think that the country will disintegrate with the loss of Rajiv Gandhi are badly mistaken. We lost Mahatma Gandhi Indira Gandhi, but with each death, the country came out much stronger", said former Chief Excutive Councillor Jag Parvesh Chandra.

The pain is more because Rajiv Gandhi died at such a young age, he said.

Others who spoke at the meeting included former Lt. Governor Romesh Bhandari, Veena Verma, general secretary of the Mahila wing of "Congress, Minorities Commission member B.S. Ramoowalia, AICC member Padam Singh Sharma and All-India National Unity Conference general secretary Harbhajan Singh.

Bhandari said that disruptive forces who saw the Congress coming back to power assassinated Rajiv Gandhi to destabilise the country and create vacuum and chaos. It was the communal hatred which resulted in Rajiv's death.

Stating that we have to preserve the secular character of the country at any cost, he said tht the Congress alone can provide a stable and strong Government to keep the country united.

Veena Verma said that Rajiv Gandhi was a nice man no doubt, but it is a pity that he was surrounded by the wrong people. He said they were responsible for the 1984 riots and were taking Rajiv Gandhi "for a ride". Rajiv Gandhi was not against any community particularly the Sikhs. The best tribute to him is that the country should fight against communalism, he added.

Harbhajan Singh said that Rajiv Gandhi's death was a big challenge to the country. His assassination is part of international conspiracy to destabilise India, If the country wants its secular character, it must fight against communalism, fundamentalism and those who want to divide the country in the name of religion, caste and creed.

He also appealed to religious leaders to fight against communalism and those who are taking shelter under the name of religion. Religion is a personal affair of everyone and religion and politics should not be mixed, he said. Criminalisation of politics should not be tolerated.

T.N. Kaul, retired Foreign Secretary and Ambassador called upon all centrist parties in general and the Congress party in particular to close their ranks so as to meet the imminent threats arising to the unity, integrity and independence of the country in the wake of the assassination of Rajiv Gandhi.

In a statement issued in New Delhi he also called upon all like- mided leaders and parties to get together and work out a common programme to counter the existing political, economic, cultural religious, caste and liguistic divisions which threatened to disrupt the country.

Kaul feels that the assassination of Rajiv Gandhi is a blow to India's parliamentary democracy.

Indian trade and industry are deeply anguished at the assassination of Rajiv Gandhi.

While condemning the "dastardly act," they treat the former prime Minister's death as loss to Indian Industry, in particular.

It appears the era of liberalisation and industrial growth ushered in by the last Congress regime is still fresh in their memory, and they have been looking forward to another innings of liberalisation.

Dhuv M. Sawhney, President, Confederation of Engineering Industry (CEI): Indian Industry is deeply shocked at the tragic incident.

India has lost a young, dynamic and brave leader who had the vision of an emerging India and its Industry in the 21st century.

Indian industry had, during his regime, witnessed a major policy shift characterised by delicencing, decontrol and liberalisation.

It was Rajiv Gandhi who had initiated the process of globalisation of Indian industry.

Furthermore, he had constantly encouraged technology development and modernisation, and at the same time, supported the development of small and medium size units.

CEI had the privilege of interacting with Rajiv Gandhi even before he became the prime Minister.

We found in him a leader who was aware of the economic and other challenges facing India.

Rajiv Gandhi had always welcomed dialogue with CEI on as how to tackle national issues jointly.

A. Mazumdar, President, Assocham: The country has lost a dynamic and dedicated leader of great promise. Rajiv Gandhi was a leader of International stature.

The business community has lost a man who was modern in his outlook, and had a deep understanding of the problems facing Indian business.

H.P. Nanda, Chairman, Escorts: Well, I think, this is the worst thing that could happen to the country, it is almost a disaster.

People in business and industry were expecting someone like Rajiv Gandhi would lead the Congress Party to victory and salvage this sinking ship which is leaking on the economic, the law and order and the price front.

During the last four years, I had come to know him intimately. As you know, he was a class fellow of my son Rajan. In 1988, he inaugurated the Escorts Heart Institute.

When I was being operated upon for a heart problem, he visited me. When Mohammad Yunus, who is like a father to Rajiv and his family, was at the hospital recently, Rajiv and Sonia visited him many times and we discussed the situation in the country, its politics, the economy and aid from the world Bank and the Aid India Consortium.

I felt from my conversation, that the Congress in power under his leadership could resolve some of the problems. In his death we have lost a good leader.

A substitute will be thrown up, no doubt, but it will take a long time which we cannot afford.

L.M. Thapar, Chairman, Thapar group says, "We will always remember Rajiv Gandhi for the liberalisation and reforms he had introduced in the economy. Indian democracy has definitely suffered an irreparable loss. He was also a friend, philosopher and guide of the industry."

J.N. Sapru, Chairman, ITC, says, "I am kind of stunned at Rajiv's assassination. It is tragic, a grierious loss for the country and his family. We have lost a very fine man. I don't know what more to say................It is really shocking."

Bansi Dhar, Chairman, DCM Shriram Industries said, Rajiv Gandhi was a towering personality, both nationally and internationally, in keeping with the selfless tradition of an illustrious family, which for generations had dedicated so much to the nation, he has sacrified his life for the progress and stability of the nation.

Rajiv Gandhi's enlightened outlook has ushered in a new direction to the Country's progress and development. He had the vision to move the nation towards an open society, which is now being accepted by many other nations.

Ramesh Chauhan, Chairman, Parle Group said, we all were shocked beyond words. A lot depends on what happens during the next 2-3 days, and how the party adjusts to the loss of this very dominating and powerful personality.

S.S. Kanwar, President of PHDCCI stated that he was progressive in his outlook and truly secular and democratic. Anti nationalist forces are working for the disintegration of the country. I appeal to all that we must face this challenge unitedly and show maturity and ability to face this worst ever crisis.

Dr. B.K. Modi, President, Modi Xerox, who was in the UK attending a conference said that he was absolutely shocked. He would not believe what was happened. It was really tragic.

Rama Kant Manjal, Managing Director, Hero Honda Motors says, that It is a very tragic and sad incident. One doesn't know what turn politics in the country will take, what will happen to the Congress(I) and how the mood of the people will change the election results. The business community has lost a firm supporter and a person who stood for liberalisation of the economy and political stability.

Vivek Bharat Ram, Managing Director, DCM-Toyota says: "What can I say........It is an unfortunate, sad, traumatic experience. We have reached a situation of barbaric nature".

"We are seeing the backlash of all that Rajiv Gandhi stood for........secularism, unity of the country, the basic values. He has paid the price. It is a sad day for the country.

Rahul Bajaj Says it is a shock beyond belief. He stood for modernisation, freedom and competition. He will be greatly missed by the business community".

Dr. M.S. Patwardhan, Managing Director, NOCH, said the news was stunning, The consequences would be grave.

Nani Palkhivala stated that it is the death of Indian democracy in India would not survive if this kind of violence continues. The decision to continue with the polls in June was correct.

M.V. Arunachalam, Chairman, Murugappa group was of the opinion that in over 40 years, he had never felt so sad. We always prided in our tolerance and love for peace. All this is shattered now. The loss of such a mature person is one top of all the economic and political crisis faced by the country.

V.L. Dutt, Chairman and Managing Director, KCP said that it would be difficult to fore case anything now. Whiehever party comes to power will ace a very tough time. Had Rajiv Gandhi come to power, it would have been easier. He had internation stature, and this would have helped bring in funds and facilities from aborad. It is my hope now that we would get a statesman who will have the same capability. Rajiv Gandhi would also have continued his liberalisation policy despite opposition from some quarters. What we need is liberalisation to get out of the morass we are in.

R. Srinivasan, Manging Director, Wadia India said that now the formation of a stable government at the Centre would be very difficult.

C. Rajagopaln, Managing Director, Amco Batterial says, "The first task of political leaders is to check the growing cult of violence and the deterforating law and order situation".

Arun Thiagarajan, Managing Direct, Asea Brown Boveri says, the Congress has been synonymous with Mr. Rajiv Gandhi. If the old congressmen come back to the party, the Congress may gain in the ensuing election, otherwise, it may not be considered valuable, and the a BJP may gain as a result.

A.S. Lakshmanan, Chairman and Managing Director, Senapathy Whiteley say: Now much depends on who takes over as the new Congress President. A major realignment of political forces is likely, out of political forces is likely out of which two major parties will emerge, a rightist political party and the Congress.

Sanjiv Goenka, President, Indian Chamber of Commerce, Says: It is nothing less than a national calamity, and we pray to God to give us strength at a time India needs it most.

Ajit Dey, President, Calcutta stock exchange says: Uncertainty will prevail in the stock market for some time till a clear political picture emerges after the elections. Much will depend on the selection of the new Congress Leader.

Amitabah Bachchan said he was in a state of shock over the death of his close friends, Rajiv Gandhi.

In London to attend hearings in a defamation suit brought by his brother Amitabh Bachchan, the movie idol said, "I am in a state of shock. There is nothing I can say, I am just going to try to get back to India as soon as possible".

The Indian community in London went into a sate of mourning as news of the assassination spread. Many familities went to offer prayers at temples in Southall, Ealing and Wembley.

Industrialist Swraj Paul expressed extreme shock and said: "I can only hope that this will be lesson and that the country can revert to principles of non-violence".

Mahant Sewa Dass Singh, president of Akali Dal (Pherunan) in a letter to the President alleged that anti-India forces were diverting the attention from the real killers of Rajiv Gandhi, to the LTTE. These forces would soon assassinate more political leaders and that he too was on their hitlist, he said.

The Akali leader said that on January 3rd, 1991, he had informed Prime Minister, Chandra Shekhar, about the conspiracy to assassinate Rajiv Gandhi. He had told Chandra Shekhar in detail about the forces behind this conspiracy which were operation from outside the country and that some political leaders had links with the enemies of the contry.

The Mahant further said: "I will disclose the names of those who were responsibile for the killing of Rajiv Gandhi later on. These very forces are bent upon killing more political leaders of India and one day I will also be eliminated by them. I have definite reports that very shortly a few more prominent political persons will be assassinated. Mahant Sewa Dass Singh said.

"The anti-India forces are diverting the attention from the killers by blaming the Tamils or the LTTE. The LTTE has repeatedly denied that they have had a hand in the killing of Rajiv Gandhi. So I request to you goodself to ask the Government to direct the energies towards the real killers."

He also drew the President's attention to the reported statements of Simaranjit Singh Mann, Akali leader, that he would restrict the movement of the ashes of Rajiv Gandhi in Punjab. He said Punjab was not the ancestral property of Mann and requested the President to take action against "such elements who are siding with the enemies of India.

Maneka Gandhi, the sister "in" law of Rajiv Gandhi, was the first to visit the All India Institute of Medical Sciences (AIIMS).

A visibly shaken Maneka Gandhi, window of Rajiv Gandhi's younger brother Sanjay, accompanied by her son Varun, it was a "grivous personal tragedy" for her apart from it being a national calamity.

The Minister of State for Environment and Forests said in a chocked voice that she learnt about the incident at Piliphit (UP) from where she is seeking reelection to Parliament.

She immediately rushed to the Capital by road covering about 400 km. distance in about seven hours.

Naresh Mohan, President, The Indian Newspaper Society (INS) has expressed shock on the heinous and cowardly act of assassination of Rajiv Gandhi.

Condemning the brutal act, he said in a statement that in the death of Rajiv Gandhi, the country has lost a great national leader, under whose stewardship, the country has achieved tremendous growth leading to economic and social development.

Rajiv Gandhi lived for the unity and integrity of the country. He worded for the communcal harmony and lost his life fighting for the same. He has been an outstanding leader not only of India but the world over. His contribution and dedication would ever be remember Naresh Mohan added. N.P. I Chief of the Rashtriya Swayamsewak Sangh Balas-aheb Deoras strongly condeemed the "prutal and dastardly" assassination of Rajiv Gandhi saying such violence had no place in the value system of Indian culture.

RSS general secretary H.V. Seshadri in a statement from Mangalore condemmed the murder and called for immediate steps to nab the culprits.

In a statement from the RSS headquarters in Nagpur Deoras said the nation had accepted the path of democracy, which cannot co-exist with violence. "The killing of Rajiv of Rajiv Gandhi is the murder of not only an eminent national leader but also of the values of Indian culture and democracy and deserves to be condemned by the entire nation", he added.

The RSS Chief conveyed his condolences to the bereaved family and urged the people to maintain their balance and not give in to the machinations of anti-national and disruptive forces.

Four Sikh organisations "unequivocally" condemned the assassination of former Prime Minister Rajiv Gandhi dubbing is as "a senseless act.

In a joint statement, the organisations" representatives said "the Sikhs while sharing the country's grief, seek to caution the countryment against any attempt by vested and hostile interests ascribing or imputting blame for the tragedy on the Tamil and the Sikh communities".

Condolence message on the assassination of Rajiv Gandhi kept pouring in on May 28, 1991. The Shia Political Front condemned the act and expressed the hope that efforts would be made to counter the challenges posed by political violence in the country.

In a press statement, in New Delhi, the Front maintained that the cult of violence and political reprisals would lead the country to no where and would only weaken its democratic structure.

The Hindustani Ekta Manch, in a Press statement, mourned the tragic and untimely demise of Rajiv Gandhi. The Manch called upon the people to make a concerted bid to fight the violent forces in the country.

While condemning the dastardly act, Satya Adhar, a voluntary organization, described the slain Congress leader as a "progressive, broad-minded and charming person". The statement further said his concern for the worman and youth and the downtrodden "speaks volumes about his commitment to strengthen the social fabric of the country".

Various political parties, trade unions, religous and social organisations have expressed deep shock and anguish at the assassination of Rajiv Gandhi and have appealed to the people to maintain peace.

General Secretary of the Samajwadi Janata Party, Satya Prakash Malaviya said that a deep-rooted conspiracy has robbed the humanity of Rajiv Gandhi. Appealing to the people to maintain peace and harmony, Malaviya said that the best tribute to the departed leader will be to struggle against the communal, separatist and divisive forces and maintain the secular character of the nation.

Condemning the brutal killing, the Delhi Pradesh Congress Committee President, Prem Singh, appealed to the people to maintain peace and harmony at all costs. The greatest tribute to the departed leader would be to keep his philosophy and indeology alive, he said.

The New Delhi District Congress Committee while condoling the demise of Rajiv Gandhi condemned the assassination as a dastardly act. It called upon the people to act with the greatest restraint and not succumb to provocation and overbearing sorrow.

The Bharatiya Janata Party Delhi Pradesh in an emergent meeting of the State Executive Committee on May 22, 1991, Condoled the ghastly killing of Rajiv Gandhi. The resolution adopted in the meeting said that the demise of Rajiv Gandhi, one of the prominent leaders of the country, is an irreparable loss to the democratic traditions.

The resolution further said that there is no room for such violent act in democracy and there is no word to condemn such a heinous and barbaric act.

The RSS headquarters in a statement, strongly condemned the dastardly and of anti-social elements. It appealed to the public to remain calm in this hour of crisis with firm determination. The statement also expressed deep sympathy with the family of Rajiv Gandhi and others who have lost their lives in the bomb blast.

The Vishva Hindu Parishad Central Governing Council passed a resolution condemning the dastardly act. Expressing its deep sorrow at the untimely and tragic death of Rajiv Gandhi, the Parishad appealed to the citizens to cooperate and help check the growing tendency towards violence.

The Sant Nirankari Mandal held a condolence meeting on Wednesday. In a telegram to Sonia Gandhi, the Mandal Condemned the brutal murder of the nation's beloved leader Rajiv Gandhi.

The Quami Mushawrat Committee, expressing profound shock and grief over the tragic incident, condemned the assassination of Rajiv Gandhi as a dastardly act of political terrorism.

The National Front on May 23, 1991 complained to the Election Commission against what it called "missue" of the electronic media to carry out election propaganda for the Congress in the name of paying tribute to Rajiv Gandhi.

Talking to reporters in New Delhi after a meeting of the delegation of the National Front and Left parties with the Chief Election Commissioner, Telugu Desam Leader P. Upendra said they had brought to T.N. Seshan's notice the fact that Doordarshan was being used for eliciting and creating public opinion in favour of the Congress under the garb of tributes to the slain Congress president.

Upendra and Janata Dal spokesman Jaipal Reddy alleged that while eliciting tributes from the common people questions were being put to them about the performance of the Rajiv Gandhi Government during its five years in Office, eliciting a uniform response.

The national executive of the BJP recorded its deep sense off sorrow over the death of Rajiv Gandhi, saying it deprived the country a promising young life it its prime.

A tow-day national executive on its opening day, adopted four point resolutions, which wholly rejected the politics of murder describing it an "outrage upon country's culture, values and democratic polity".

It called upon all elements in the political life in the country to ensure that the violence do not get any encouragement directly or indirectly.

The death in a bomb explosion of Rajiv Gandhi came as a rude shock to the sporting fraternity of India.

They felt that with his traigic death an umbrella of care, concern and commitment to their cause had been sudeently removed from above their heads.

Rajiv Gandhi had the same interest in sports that his mother Indira Gandhi and grandfather Jawaharlal Nehru had.

It was with Nehru's blessings that the Asian Games Movement was launched and first Asian Games held in Delhi in 1951-Who can ever forget his immortal message on the occassion. "Play the game in the spirit of the game".

The Games returned to their place of birth 31 years later mainly due to the efforts of Indira Gandhi.

And it was then that Rajiv Gandhi showed his organisational ability by working round-the-clock to help make the 1982 Asian Games a thundering success.

Veteran cricketer Amarnath described the news of Rajiv Gandhi's assassination as "too cruel for words".

According to him, Rajiv Gandhi was a great friend of sports and sports persons. "Nothing can illustrate the fact better than the instance of his taking osme time off his busy schedule to call on me when I was recovering in a hospital for a foot surgery.

His kind nature and concern for others made him a sportsman first and a politician later, Amarnath added. Raja Bhalendra Singh, a former president of Indian Olympic Association, said in his capacity as a senior International Olympic Committee (IOC) member in India, "We totally condemn the dastardly act."

He said, "We cannot easily forget his personal contribution to the promotion, development and improvement of sports, not only in India but in Asia as well."

Aswhani Kumar, another IOC member in India, said India and Olympic world had lost a stalwart who "stood by free sport in India through thick and thin".

Vidya Charan Shukla, former IOA president, described the killing of Rajiv Gandhi as a barbaric act.

"Indian sports and sportspersons have lost a great champion of their cause," he added in a message from Raipur.

Expressing grief of the Olympic Council of Asia, its secretary general C.L. Mehta, said friendship through sports, trust and confidence in each other, were the mottos for which Mr. Gandhi lived and died a martyr.

Ace shooter and IOC Secretary-general Randhir Singh expressed grief on behalf of the entire sports fraternity.

Vijay Kumar Malhotra, President of the Archery Association of India, said Mr. Gandhi's interest in sports was evident from the fact that layout for sports was increased from Rs. 12 crore in the Sixty-Five Year Plan to Rs. 200 crore in the seventh.

Leading sportsperson and sports administrators were shocked to hear the news of Rajiv Gandhi's assassination.

Jagmohan Dalmia, secretary of the Board of Control for Cricket in India, said that Rajiv Gandhi was a great supporter of cricket and it was only because of his personal interest that the World Cup in 1987 and the Nehru Cup in 1989 was held in the country successfully.

Former Davis Cup and national coach, Akhtar Ali said, "We have lost a young, dynamic leader".,

B.K. Saha, President of Basketaball Federation of India, and one the Vive-presidents of the Indian Olympic Association said that the incident was the most tragic thing to happen to the country at this juncture.

Indian Olympic Association President B.Sivanthi Adityan expressed deep grief and sorrow over the assassination of Rajiv Gandhi.

Adityan said Rajiv Gandhi was a sportsman and a good shooter and India has lost a great sportslover and administrator.

The brutal murder of Rajiv Gandhi has shocked the Indian nation and plunged in into grief. I have no hesitation in condemning this dastardly deed which terminated the life of one who gave his all for the true progress of the nation. In the death of Rajiv Gandhi India has lost one of its noblest sons, a descendant of a family whose name is inseparably linked with our struggle for independence. Every Indian should abnor this abominable act which will always remain an indelible blot on the character of a nation known throughout the world for upholding the principle of non-violence.

The Catholic Community joins the nation in its mourning and will after up prayers for this great person, for all those who were killed with him, for their bereaved family and for peace and harmony in the country. (Archbishop Alan De Lastic, New Delhi)

Priyadarshni Academy's National Integration Award carrying cash of Rs. one lakh will henceforth be known as "Rajiv Gandhi Memorial Award for National Intergration".

Upon soaring expectations on a sunlist summit.
Came searing lava and the earthquake.
The flower of hope wilted in the ashes.
In the season of spring, a void and a Heartache.
Dazed in the maze of public sorrow.
Lost in pensive private grief.
We saw avarice in the eyes of cruel Fate.
In our sylavan home the trespass of the lurking theif.
Planet Earth he loved and was loved in turn,
In the arms of Mother Earth we saw him return,
Similing visage, his astral body without sear or burn,
His ashes in cosmic communion in the orb and the urn.

(L.M. singhvi)

5
THE GREAT VISIONARY

Rajiv Gandhi's death has come as a rude shock to business leaders in the capital. Many of them enjoyed close proximity to the Congress leader and thus experienced a deep sense of personal loss.

Industrialists were candid enough to admit that they saw Rajiv Gandhi as the only man with "capacity and vision" to pull the economy out of the present state of turmoil. "It was Gandhi's leadership which initiated the process of globalisation of Indian industry", says Dhruv Sawhney, president of the Confederation of Engineering Industry (CEI)

Though all of them agree that economic liberalisation will roll on in its own steam ("the IMF will dictate out policies in case the politicians don't give in", says L.M. Thapar), there is consensus that the process would have been faster under Rajiv's tenure. "His death will be a setback to long-term economic thinking", says Dr. Bharat Ram.

Dr. Bharat Ram enjoyed a close relationship with Rajiv (his son, Vivek, was the Doon School classmate of the ex-Prime Minister) and claims to have appointed him a pilot when he was chairman of Indian Airlines and to have given some hard advise before he made his debut into politics. "Make your own decisions, don't be a rubber stamp to you mother", Vivek Bharat Ram, a family friend of the Gandhis was in too, "distressed and shock" to say anything, "It is like losing a member of the family; Indians should be ashamed."

Disgust on his death was expressed by everyone. "Violence in politics has become a cult and every day the toll mounts, but when you knock off leaders, like the Gandhi's, it is time to think which way the country is heading", says Thaper. "He had been in the humdrum of politics for seven to eight years, he had matured and stood the best chance now of giving the country a good innings", he added. In a message from London, Hari Shankar Singhania, head of the JK group and vice-president of the International Chamber of Commerce (IIC) said that a dastardly act has cut short a promising career. The Federation of Indian Chambers of Commerce and Industry said, "it is tragic that on the eve of a new era, after a period of uncertainty and turmoil, the country should be deprived of his leadership".

Escorts chairman, H.P. Nanda, claims that the Congress president's deaih is the biggest disaster for the country, "the country is almost sinking". Commenting on Swraj Paul's bid to takeover Escorts.

Nanda recalled the firm stand taken by Rajiv Gandhi. "He made it clear in Parliament that NRIS have been invited to set up new industries and not to destablise well-run companies. It was under his directions that Paul was forced to sell his shares".

Everyone expects that good sense will finally prevail. "The economy has been in a quandry for the last two years and I hope that things will improve and the country does not slip further into violence and choas". K.N. Modi who enjoyed a close relationship with Rajiv Gandhi said "he was open to criticism". "His constant refrain us was to shed the close-door outlook and compete internationally but not by asking incentives, "Mr. Modi adds.

K.K. Birla in a written statement expressed condolence that the country can face the tragic event with boldness, "we can meet the challenge with courage and composure." Dr. Bharat Ram and Thapar agreed that there is no choice but for everyone, including all the political parties, to hold together in the larger interest of the nation.

Translating the loss in terms of stocks and shares, Harish Bhasin, president of the Delhi stock exchange, said that the downturn will be absorbed before the markets open. He is in touch with the major stock exchanges to decide on the cooling period to be provided before trading is allowed. In all probability the markets will open after the funeral. But if the sympathy wave results in a congress victory, shares will move up rapidly, Bhasin added.

The Indian public sector representatives also expressed profound grief at the assassination. Rajiv admirer, V. Krishnamurthy, the former chairman of the Steel Authority of India Ltd. (SAIL) was at Janapath on Wednesday morning to pay homage to the Congress chairman, said that the death is a blow to modernity.

More Political and social organisations have condemned the brutal killing of Rajiv Gandhi. They have appealed to all the right thinking persons to help in the restoration of peace in the country.

The Delhi petrol dealers association has expressed shock on the ghastly killing of Rajiv Gandhi. In a statement, the president of the association, Ashok Badhwar said his death has created a vacuum which is hard to fill. He appealed to the people to maintain peace and communal harmony which would be a true tribute to the departed leader who sacrificed his life fighting the menace of communalism.

Purshottam Goyal, former chairman, Metropolitan Council, paying glowing tributes to Mr. Gandhi described him as the symbol of peace who carried forward the peace efforts initiated by Jawaharlal Nehru and Indira Gandhi. He described him as one of the top ranking leaders of the world who kindled an urge for modernisation among the youth.

Swadesh Bhushan Jain, General Secretary, Jain Samaj Delhi, has expressed grief and shock on the assassination of Rajiv Gandhi, condemning the killing of Mr. Gandhi, he has stated that it is an act of violence to destabilise the country of peace loving people. In the death of Rajiv Gandhi, the country has lost a nationalist a preacher of peace and non-violence.

The trustees, management, teachers and employees of Feroz Gandhi College, Rae Bareli paid glowing tributes to Rajiv Gandhi at an emergency meeting held today. The manging secretary of the college, Onkar Nath Bhargava said his death was a personal loss to the member of the college family.

Delhi factory owners' federation president Lt. Col. R.S. Khurana said the death of Mr. Gandhi has sent shock-waves among the business community. He said the former Prime Minister was impatient with the slow response to change in economic direction. He had a strong vision for strengthening the economy through increasing productivity, reducing cost and bringing Indian goods nearer to international quality.

Several politico-economic and socio-religious bodies condemned the ghastly act of violence resulting in the tragic death of Rajiv Gandhi.

In their condolence message, the All India Freedom Fighters' Organisation, headed by Prof. N.G. Ranga, expressed great sorrow on the sudden demise of Rajiv Gandhi who during his Prime Ministership inspired the whole nation with a new vision to usher in an era of prosperity, progress, unity and social justice and new technologies capable of leading the nation towards the 21st centuary.

The freedom fighers' Organisation said that India has lost a brave son who had pledged to bring complete solidarity, stability and make India a strong nation. In a meeting, the organistion appealed to coutrymen, especially half a million freedom fighers to extend their helping hand to maintain complete peace and face this tragedy boldly with courage and confidence.

Freedom Fighters Relief Committee also expressed its deep shock at the assassination of Rajiv Gandhi.

In a Condolence meeting held on Friday, the pilots of Indian Airlines paid homage to their former colleague "Captain" Rajiv Gandhi. The Indian Commercial Pilot's Association on behalf of the pilots expressed their heart felt sympathy to his wife Sonia Gandhi and children Rahul and Priyanka. In a message, they said Rajiv would always be remembered by them as a special collegue, friend, mentor and guide.

In a condolence meeting under the presidentship of Ram Dhan, the Jan Morcha called this brutal act a grim warning of the grave consequences of politics of hatred, bitterness and confrontation. Arun Nehru, Arif Mohd Khan, Satyapal Malik and Dinesh Trivedi also attended the meeting.

The DPCC executive committee described the assassination as a well-planned conspiracy to destabilise the country at a time when the country needed stability the most.

International trade union federation and national trade unions, in a message, said that violence solved no problems-be it political, economic or social. This is a barbarious and despicable act and a coward attack on democracy, they added. Delhi Exporters Association, Federation of All India Foodgrain Dealers' Associations and the Central Consumers' Council also expressed grief on Rajiv Gandhi's death.

Other organisations which sent their condolence messages, were Authors Guild of India, Indian Federation of Small and Medium Newspapers, All India Scheduled Castes and Tribes Federation. Nehru Bal samiti, Indian Mountaineering Foundation, for Amity and National Solidariy, Cheshire Homes, All India Catholic Union, Rotary Club and Delhi (Midtown), Rajendra Bhawan Trust, Rajiv Brigade and All India Contonment Board Hospital Employees Association.

Serveral academics and organisations have paid rich tributes to late Rajiv Gandhi.

Condemning the barbarous act, they said that it is the handiwork of those forces, who want to destroy the country by raising spectres of communalism and casteism. Y.S. Mathur, president, former secretary, DUTA, have said the "like his mother, Indiraji, Rajiv Gandhi has laid down his life for the principles enunciated by Mahatma Gandhi and Jawaharlal Nehru. This supreme sacrifice will inspire the entire nation and the world community to espouse the cause of freedom, equality and world peace-the ideals he most devoutely cherished.

His was the vision of a secular, stable and democratic India, which stood him in good stand at the most crucial juncture in the history of India, like a colosus to keep the communal, casteist and fissiparious forces at bay".

All India National Unity Conference, under the leadership of Harbhajan Singh described Rajiv Gandhi as the champion of secularism and an embodiment humanism.

Syed Jafar Mahmud, in a statement here said that "Rajiv Gandhi was a great man, who fought for economic development, progress and was committed to true democratic and secular values. In his death, India and the world at large has lost a great leader".

P.S. Kaushal, general secretary of Vivekanand Foundation Delhi said "Words fall short for tributes to Rajiv Gandhi, who had laid his life for the cause of Motherland".

Paying his glowing tributes to Rajiv Gandhi, Ramesh Chennithala, president Indian Youth Congress said, "that the premature demise of this great visionary he was the embodiment of all the hopes and inspiration of Indian Youth. He appealed the Youth Congress Workers to come out on the street for election campaign and ensure victory to fulfil Rajivji's ideals and message for all times to come".

Others who paid tributes to Rajiv Gandhi's memory included office-bearers and members of Rajendra Bhawan Trust, Delhi Exporters Association, All India Islamic Congress.

"The untimely death of Rajiv Gandhi has resulted in the extinguishing of a resplendent career in Third World leadership India's pre-eminence in the cause of world peace so arduously espoused by Rajiv Gandhi cannot be depleted by such brutally planned acts of violence".

These views were expressed by the Vice-Chancellor of Delhi University Prof. Upendra Baxi while paying tributes to Rajiv Gandhi.

He said it should be made clear to all political parties in the country that the people do not subscribe to the cult of violence. Each one of the national leaders must assure the people that they would discourage violence within their own parties as a way of doing politics.

Professor Baxi said India will miss Rajiv Gandhi for a long time to come. His youthful dynamism, "his steadfast vision of a just world order and above all his desire to get us all moving to build a new India through practices of democratic pluralism constitute in legacy," he added.

Paying glowing tributes to Rajiv Gandhi at another condolence meeting eminent scientist Prof. M.G.K. Menon said Rajiv Gandhi wanted to deal with total problem and not part of it Citing an instance, he said in solving the water problem, Rajiv Gandhi was not only satisfied by only targeting the source but would delve with the intricacies of reaching the supply at the thereshold.

Describing him as a "young man in a hurry". Dr. Menon said time factor was very important for the Congress president. He was always impatient and yearned to see the completion of various projects before time he praised Rajiv Gandhi for laying stress on human resource development. But unfortunately his ideas in this regard could not be effectively implemented he added.

He further said, Rajiv Gandhi stood for an India which truly meant to be secular. That is why he had special reverence for all the faiths.

Addressing the meeting, former Union Minister Dr. Karan Singh said during Rajiv Gandhi's prime Ministership, there was generational changed in the political leadership of the country. The nation would realise in the next few years the terrible loss suffered by it due to his death.

Recollecting his tenure as Civil Aviation Minister in Indira Gandhi's Ministry when Rajiv was a pilot in the Indian Airlines, he said in his seven years in office, Rajiv neither sought nor was given any favour by the Ministry. He took his progessional duties seriously.

The University of Delhi's academic council met on May, 30, 1991 to condole the death of Rajiv Gandhi.

The council resolution lauded Rajiv Gandhi for "resolutely and courageously facing many difficult challenges" while endeavouring "to lead the country ahead on the path of democracy, secularism, scientific and technological progress". Also for "being the first Prime Minister who fully understood the need for an adequate legal structure to cambat growing atrocities against scheduled castes and tribes, he showed rare determination in enacting (legislation) and avidly sought the collaboration of state Governments in its implementation".

Several academics and other leaders paid rich tributes to late Rajiv Gandhi.

Condemning the dastardly attack on Rajiv Gandhi, the Jamia Teachers Association in a resolution described him as "an upholder of secularism and democracy in India. The way a great pillar to the Indian political edifice has been brought to an end is big shame.

The Jawaharlal Nehru University community has expressed its deep anguish, shock and grief over the tragic death of the former Prime Minister, Rajiv Gandhi, A meeting of the faculty, students and staff was held to mourn the death of Gandhi.

The Jawaharlal Nehru University Vice-Chancellor, Proft. M.S. Agwani who was in chair read the resolution in a choked voice.

The students and Vice-Chancellor, Jamia Millia Islamia University, Dr. S.Z. Qasim also held a condolence meeting here last evening Condeming this barbaric and cowardly act he said "the political assassination of Rajiv Gandhi is in reality an attack on all the noble principles".

More than a week after the brutal assassination of Rajiv Gandhi, message of condolence continue to pour in.

The Jawaharlal Nehru University Teachers' Association, New Delhi has deeply mourned the death of Rajiv Gandhi saying, "the dastardly act of violence has snatched away a young dynamic leader and caused irreparable loss to the country". The association has said that the heinous act, undertaken in the midst of a general election, was a deliberate and clear attempt to undermine democracy.

The Sindhu Samaj, alongwith other Sindhi Panchayats, has also expressed deep shock and grief at the barbaric assassination of the former Prime Minister.

In a resolution, the Samaj said that in the death of Rajiv Gandhi, the nation has lost a "great nationalist leader and apostle of world peace".

The Manufacturers Welfare Association, G.T. Karnal Road, Delhi had termed the assassination as "cowardly, barbaric and inhuman". In a statement, the association said: "Rajiv Gandhi's death has left a gap that cannot be covered".

A condolence meeting was also held at the South Campus of Delhi University, New Delhi. The Director, staff members and other officials came together to express shock and greif at the tragic demise of the former Prime Minister.

In a resolution, they recalled the contribution made by Rajiv Gandhi to nation building and said the void left by his death would be hard to fill.

A voluntary organisation, S Atya Aadhar, has also condemned the brutal assassination of Rajiv Gandhi. Terming the act as "cowardly and dastardly", the organisation has said that the loss of a "truly democratic and fair minded leader is indeed irreparable and sad".

The acting president of the Aligarh Muslim University students' Union S.N. Hyder Ali Khan, expressed deep shock over Rajiv Gandhi's assassination. "Through this gruesome act of violence an important leader has been taken away from the Indian people who believed in a non-violence and democratic values. This act of brutalism will go down as a black spot in the history of democratic values of our country. The students of AMU strongly condemned this act and express their deep sorrow to the bereaved family and the people of India", he said.

Tripura Chief Minister Sudhir Ranjan Majumdar, PCC president Radhika Ranjan Gupta and others said that the news of barbaric killing of Rajiv Gandhi had caused sorrow and gloom in Tripura, indeed, all over the country. They hoped that the country would bear the loss with fortitude and pursue the path shown by the departed leader.

Sanjay Dalmia and Shamsuz-Zaman, president and general secretary, respectively of the Organisation of Understand and Fraternity said "the most ghastly, brutal and cowardly assassination of Rajiv Gandhi has plunged the entire nation into the deep sea of uncertainty. No words could ever be found to condemn this brazen act of the assassins, but this is indicative of the most unfortunate aspect of our national life that is, growth of the cult of violence, which should not go unchecked.

Rajiv Gandhi stood for a cause and sacrificed his life in protecting the values so vital for the material and spiritual development of the nation. At this most tragic turn of Indian history the nation should rise as one man to protect and preserve whatever values are still with us and expose the nefarious designs of the divisive forces and make the firms committment that the nation cannot be cowed down by terrorism or any act of organised violence.

The blood of Rajiv Gandhi will not go waste, rather each drop of his blood would shine as the stars of glory and show us the way of building a new, powerful, prosperous and united India", they said in a statement.

The Chief spokesman of the world wide institution of Brahma Kumaris has described the assassination of Rajiv Gandhi as yet another sign of utter degeneration of values.

He said that Raj Yogini Dadi Prakashmani, the chief of Brahma Kumris, had appealed to all to unite in this hour of national tragedy giving up all differences and to make sincere efforts to defeat the negative forces of violence and hatred. At her call, all the 2000 centres of Brahma Kumaris spread over five continents. will hold special meditation for peace of the departed soul and will express deep sympathy for the bereaved family.

The Press Club of India condoled the death of Rajiv Gandhi. The managing committee of the club in a resolution conveyed "the heart felt sympathies" of its members and to the wife of the late leader, Sonia Gandhi and children Rahul and Priyanka Gandhi.

A number of eminent persons paid homage to Rajiv Gandhi at a function organised by the Delhi Social Welfare Advisory Board attended by a large number of voluntary organisation in New Delhi.

Former Union Minister Margaret Alva said that women of India must stand up and fight the growing cult of violence and hatred and "let sanity prevail", Whether in Parliment or outside Rajiv Gandhi, she said, provided "the voice of sanity".

To the call of "Garv se bolo hum Hindu hain" (Proud to be Hindu) she said, Rajiv Gandhi had wanted it to be "Garv se bolo hum Hindustani hain" (Proud to be an Indian). He did not want any aggressive campaign during the elections but wanted to apply the "healing touch", she added.

Romesh Bhandari said that Rajiv Gandhi was murdered by those people who did not want him to succeed in fulfilling his dreams and who were against his principles. Rajiv Gandhi wanted to defeat the forces of communalism.

Former Governor Kumud Ben Joshi urged women to fulfil the work left unfinished by Rajiv Gandhi of defeating those forces who in the name of religion were creating a atmosphere of hatred. It was necessary to create an atmosphere of love and peace all round.

The All India Small and Medium Newspapers Federation president said that the blood of martyrs like Rajiv Gandhi would go towards strengthening the foundations of the country and even if one had to sacrifice "hundred Rajivs, India would remain strong and united".

He alleged that the killing was part of international conspiracy. Rajiv Gandhi was the "messiah of the minorities and have nots". If Ram was of Advani, Ram was also of Rajiv Gandhi. To keep the country together the challenge before us is to separate politics from religion," he added.

Arun Asaf Ali said that they had almost forced Rajiv to join politics after the death of Sanjay Gandhi as a helping hand to Indira Gandhi. If we had not done so "perhaps he would have survivied."

The All-India Crime Prevention Society in a resolution extended its condolences to the bereaved family. The members expressed a resolve to work for implementing the ideals of the departed leader.

The Delhi Executive Association paid tributes to Rajiv Gandhi. The gathering recalled the immense contribution of him to boost exports and provide a special impetus for its growth.

S.P. Agarwal, President of the association, said Rajiv Gandhi was particularly interested in boosting exports and gave considerable time to the exporters to explain their view point.

Montek Singh Ahluwalia, a close associate and friend of Rajiv Gandhi, said he had the privilege of working in the Prime Minister's office for a couple of years and his sense of loss was therefore doubled. Ahluwalia said Rajiv Gandhi had deep concern for exporters and believed in modernisation.

Trade Fair Authority of India Chairman Moosa Raza drew a parallel with the assassination of American President John F. Kennedy and said, "Rajiv was young, charismatic and held out a hope for the country which we have lost".

The Indo-Arab Society has resolved to rededicate itself to positive action towards building more strong and abiding relationship in fulfilment of wishes of the late Rajiv Gandhi.

The Society as a condolence meeting held in Bombay recently under the chairpersonship of Najma Heptulla, Deputy chairperson of the Rajya Sabha, recalled Rajiv Gandhi's commitment for the Arab cause and his efforts towards the solution of the Palestinian question.

The staff and officers of Indian Airlines met in New Delhi to mourn the passing away of Rajiv Gandhi.

A resolution adopted during the meeting noted that before joining politics, he was one of the finest pilots that Indian Airlines had. The resolution observed, "while in Indian Airlines, he was always unassuming and maintained excellent relations with all sections of employees.

During the condolence meeting, a letter for Sonia Gandhi was also adopted as part of the resolution. The letter prays that the bereaved family gather strength to bear this tragic and irreparable loss.

Meanwhile, a stream of messages condoling the bereaved family condemned the killing of Rajiv Gandhi as a "dastardly and cowardly act", and expressed sympathies for the bereaved family. Also expressing regret at Rajiv Gandhi's passing away is Andrew H. Neilly, president of the International Publishers Association.

Amongst others who have condoled the death of Raniv Gandhi includes the Jain Samaj Delhi. In a statement issued today, it said Rajiv Gandhi's killing was an "act of violence meant to destabilise the country".

Man Mohan Singh, Chairman of University Grants Commission (UGC) has expressed "the deepest sorrow at the sad and most untimely death of Rajiv Gandhi". In a statement, he notes that the 'barbaric and cowardly act deserves universal condemnation".

States Manmohan Singh, "As Prime Minister of India Rajiv Gandhi worked to build a modern, technologically advanced, choesive and humane polity and society in India. His life and work will continue to inspire our people to wage a relentless war against poverty, ignorance, disease and against communal and caste hatred and violence".

Describing Rajiv Gandhi's death as a "great national tragedy", Singh extends his condolences to Sonia Gandhi and her children whose "loss is irreparable". He notes, "but they may derive some comfort from the knowledge that the whole country shares their grief and sorrow.

A stunining blow, said the New Delhi Municipal Committee on the death of this "great statesman and great human being".

"The name Gandhi has become synonymous with sacrifice for the nation, "said the Vishwa Ahimsa Sangh's Acharya Sushil Kumar. "India must unite to remove violence and terrorism. We have lost a man of love, honesty and harmony".

The Congress committee's labour cell has appealed to Sonia Gandhi to accept the post of party Chief, while the National Confederation of Central Government Employees and Workers says the government owes an explanation on the security arrangements. The assassination was due to vested interests which had created communal, caste, regional and language barriers over the past two years.

Convert Janpath and surrounding bungalows to Rajiv Gandhi memorial and change the name of Sriperumbudur to Rajiv Gandhi Nagar, demands the Indian National Young Lawyers' Congress.

The Messiah of the backward communities had been made it target, said the Babu Jagjivan Ram Smriti Samiti while the Gandhi Smriti and Darshan Samiti have appealed to all to strive for peace and harmony. The Friends of Soviet Union, which feels orphaned, said Rajiv Gandhi had continued the tradition of three generations of his family of promoting Indo-Soviet friendship as an important axis of foreign policy.

The People's Union for Democratic Rights says all political parties should consciously undertake the responsibility to maintain democratic norms and resist the temptation to engineer sectarian violence and generate communcal tension. The Ananda Marga Prachark Sangh has appcalcd to all come together to resist the growing violence.

A host of residents associations held condolence meetings. Among them are the DP Block residents Association of Maurya Enclave, the Sarita Vihar Pocket B Residents Welfare Association, the House Owners Welfare Association and the Rampura (MIG) residents welfare Association.

A stream of condemnation has come in from various other organisation too: the Delhi State Bharat Scouts and Guides, the Indian Council of World Affairs, the Bharat Sevak Samaj, the Mahila Dakshata Samiti, The Delhi Janvadi Mahila Federation, the All India Freedom Fighers' Organisation, the Ex-Andaman Political Prisoners' Faternity Circle, the All India Federation of the Deaft, the Society for the Rehabilitation of Physically Handicapped and Mentally Backward, International Youth for Humanity, National Forum of Advocates, Harijan Sevak Sangh, the Bar Association (Income Tax), the All India Tanzeem Aimma Masjid, the Centre for the Promotion of a Non-voilent and Nuclear- Weapons-Free World, the DCM Chemical Employees Lokhit Congress Union, The Prajapita Brahma Kumaris Ishwariya Vishwa Vidayalaya, the Rashid Market Welfare Association of and sshri r Niketan School.

Uma Bharati, BJP leader, has accused the Congress of trying to make political capital out of the tragic assassination of Rajiv Gandhi in the current elections to the Lok Sabha.

Describing the assassination of Rajiv as a "danger to democracy" Bharati told in an election meeting on May 28, 1991 sought to project Sonia Gandhi as the next Congress president even while her husband's body was lying in state at Teen Murti Bhawan.

She said Sonia Gandhi had acted sensibly by turning down the offer.

Bharati devoted a major part of her 80-minutes speech to the proposed Ram Janambhoomi temple at Ayodhya and said construction of the temple was a must. But whether it would be done by installing a BJP Government or by supreme sacrifices was left to the people to decide.

Referring to the National Front, Bharati alleged that V.P. Singh had done more harm to the country during his short tenure than during the entire congress regime.

No one was opposed to reservations for the backward communities, but the manner in which it was sought to be implemented was highly objectionable, she said.

Top Pakistani leaders expressed deep shock and grief over the tragic death of Rajiv Gandhi and termed it as a result of a cowardly act of terrorism.

President Ghulam Ishaq Khan in a condolence message said "India has lost a distinguished leader with a long record of service to the nation. Pakistani condemns in the strongest terms all acts of terrorism wherever they may take place," he said.

Expressing profound shock over the assassination, Prime Minister Nawaz Sharif said, "We are saddened by the passing away, under such tragic circumstances, of an important and distinguished political leader of our region".

Opposition leader and former Premier Benazir Bhutto said she was deeply grieved to hear about the dastardly act. She strongly condemned the terrorist action that took the life of Mr. Gandhi.

Chairman of the Senate Wasim Sajjad and a large number of Pakistani leaders have also condoled the death of the former Indian Premier.

United States Vice-President Dan Quale said that Gandhi was a leader of a new generation of leadership that was emerging around the world.

Japanese Prime Minister Toshiki Kaifu called Rajiv Gandhi a "greatman" who sicerely worked for India-Japan relations. Prime Minister Kaifu talking to Japanese journalists also condemned terrorist bombing that killed Rajiv Gandhi. The Indian Embassy in Japan opened a condolence book.

Swedish Ambassdor to the United Nations Jan Eliasson expressed 'shok and outrage' over the assassination.

The news of the assassination of Rajiv Gandhi was received by Canadians with horror.

Canada's external Affiaris Minister Barbara McDougallt told a sombre House of Commons that the Government of Canada was "deeply shocked" by the "senseless" violence.

Dr. Harpal Singh Buttar, a Sikh community leader, said the death was "a tragedy".

Nicaraguan President Violeta Chamorro sent a condolence note to Sonia Gandhi saying the killing brought back memories of her own husband's murder.

"In this moment of pain, I join you and your people, bringing memories of the bitter experience I lied through with the irreparable loss of my husband", Mrs. Chamorro wrote to Sonia Gandhi. The Nicaraguan Foreign Ministry released the note to the media.

Former President Daniel Ortega also condemned the Gandhi killing and recalled Rajiv Gandhi's support of Nicaragua's former leftist Sandinista Government.

Norwegian Prime minister Gro Harlem Brundtland said the attack has directed against India's democracy. Brundtland learned of the assassination during an official dinner with Czechoslovakia's President Vaclav Havel, in the Norwegian capital on a State visit.

Swedish Prime Minister Ingvar Carlsson said, "For me, Rajiv Gandhi was a close friend and important partner on international issues". He said he was shocked and saddened at Rajiv Gandhi's death.

Caribbean leaders joined the chorus of voices worldwide expressing shock and sadness over the assassination of Rajiv Gandhi.

Trinidad's Prime Minister Ray Robinson called the assassination an attack on democracy.

Condemning the assassination, Barbabo's Prime Minister Erskine Sandiford said he met the late Prime Minister four years a ago the Vancouver summit.

Frank Abdullah, Deputy Secretary General of the Caribbean Community (CARICOM), said Rajiv Gandhi "meant a lot to us here in the Caribbean and we deplsre the circumstances in which he met his death".

Brazilian President Fernando Collor said he was deeply saddened by the news of Rajiv Gandhi's death.

"I am certain that despite this tragedy, social harmony and conciliation shall prevail in the world's largest democracy", Collor said in a message to President Venkataraman.

Belgian Prime Minister Wilfried Martens appealed to the Indian people not to let the murder of Rajiv Gandhi stop their efforts to live in harmony.

Mexican President Carlos Salinas expressed dismay at the assassination.

In a separate letter to Sonia Gandhi, Salinas said Rajiv Gandhi's death meant the loss of "a great man of India, a promoter of peace and cooperation and a great friend of Mexico.

Malaysian Foreign Minister Datuk Abdullah Badawi said in Tokyo that the bomb that killed Rajiv Gandhi "was an attack on an established democracy that India is".

The Dalai Lama has condoled the killing of the former Prime Minister. In a telegraphic message to Sonia Gandhi, the Dalai Lama said "India had lost a great leader and the tibetans a great friend".

In a separate statement, he also appealed to the people of India to maintain peace and clmm.

The assassination of Rajiv Gandhi constitues a great loss for the poor people in the Third World countries, said former Nicaraguan President Daniel Ortega. He told reporters: "We express our disgust and repugnance, because there has been an assassination of a leader of the poorr people in the Third World".

Ortega said Rajiv Gandhi had been "a friend and a brother for the Nicaraguan people".

China's Prime Minister Li Peng paid tribute to Rajiv Gandhi in a condolence telegram sent to Indian Prime Minister Chandra Shekhar. Li expressed his "deep sadness" at the murder of the former Indian Premier, calling him an "extraordinary statesman" and a "friend" of the Chinese people. Rajiv Gandhi had made "positive contributions" to Sino-Indian relations, added Li.

Canadian Prime Minister Brian Multoney, arriving in Hong Kong for a four-day visit said Rajiv Gandhi was a colleague and friend who would be deeply missed.

"He was a wonderful collegue and friend, and we will miss him very deeply" he told reporters. Mulroney said he had sent a message of condolence to Rajiv Gandhi's widow and family.

The Natal Indian Congress and the Mahatma Gandhi Phoenix Settlement have issued a joint statement on behalf of the people of Indian descent in South Africa mourning the assassination of Rajiv Gandhi.

Egypt said it hoped the assassination of Rajiv Gandhi would not dent India's democracy.

"We regret this tragic incident and consider it a big loss", Deputy Prime Minister for Foreign Affairs Boutros Ghali said in Cairo.

President George Bush in Washington reacting to news of Rajiv Gandhi's death in a bomb explosion said "this is a real tragedy".

Bush, who said he had a "real friendship" with Rajiv Gandhi, said it was "just appalling" when people resorted to violence to settle political differences.

New French Prime Minister Edith Cresson said in Paris "after Indira Gandhi, her son......an assassination is always horrible."

British Premier John Major expressed his shock and sadness at the murder of Rajiv Gandhi, saying the former Indian Prime Minister, - "a very brave man" - would be missed "a very great deal".

In a separate message, British Foreign Secretary Douglas Hurd Called Rajiv Gandhi's killing an "awful tragedy" and said it was his devotion to India which had brought him into political life.

John Major, who had never met Rariv Gandhi but exchanged letters with him, said "all will be shocked and saddened about the very tragic news of Rajiv Gandhi's murder."

Soviet and Indian community in Moscow reacted with disbelief and shock to the news of Rajiv Gandhi's death.

Official reaction from President Mikhail Gorbachev with whom Rajiv Gandhi had built up a good rapport during their meeting every year since both came to office.

Rajiv Gandhi had an elaborate plan of publishing a commemorative volume has been finalised here.

This historical publication of international significance will be presented to Sonia Gandhi on the Republic Day 26th January, 1992.

The board of advisers formed for this publication consists of Naryan Dutt Tewari, Dr. Farooq Abdullah, S.S. Ray, R.K. Karanjia, Dr. A.P Kidwai, Amitabh Bachchan, Miss Jai Lalita, Dr. Ammar Rizvi, Padmashri Sunil Dutt, Jitendra Prasad, Mahabir Prasad, M.C. Bhandare, Padmashri Ali Jawad Zaidi and D.N. Sinha.

The editorial board of the publication consists of Girish Mathur, Ramesh Sinha, Shardendu, Sheo Shanker Misra and Mathura Prasad Sinha.

It may be recalled that a book titled "Rajiv Gandhi", the first book in the country in Hindi on the then Prime Minister written and published by Mathura Prasad Sinha was released in December 1987 by Narayan Dutt Tiwari in New Delhi.

6
IN SEARCH OF GLOBAL PEACE

Foreign diplomats in New Delhi describe the turnout of overseas dignitaries at Rajiv Gandhi's funeral as unprecedented since the World War Second.

The diplomats feel that the high level representation of various Governments at the funeral of persons who was out of office was due to the fact that Rajiv Gandhi struck instant relationship with a large number of people he met during his several visits abroad in the five years, when he was in office.

This indicated the stature Rajiv Gandhi had acquired as a world leader and the special rapport he had built up with a wide range of leaders.

A large number of foreign dignitaries kept pouring into Teen Murti House at New Delhi, on May 24, 1991 to pay homage to the slain former Prime Minister Rajiv Gandhi.

Among the foreign dignitaries were Prince Charles of Britain, the US Vice President, Dan Quayle, the former and the present Prime Ministers of Pakistan Benazir Bhutto and Nawaz Sharif, respectively, the Vice-president of the USSR, G.I. Yanayev, the former British premier, Edward Heath, the Mauritian premier, Anerood Jugnauth, the former Prime Minister of Japan Takeshita, The PLO Chief, Yasser Arafat, the Sri Lankan premier D.M. Wigetunge, the Nepalese Prime Minister-designate G.P. Koirala and his predecessor, K.P. Bhattarai, the German foreign minister, Hans Dietrich Genscer, the Afghanistan president Najibullah and the Bangladesh opposition leader, Sheikh Hasina.

There were delegations from Kenya, Zambia, Iran, Portugal, Denmark, Ireland, Tailand, Switzerland, New Zealand, Hungary and Vietnam, to mention of few.

The arrangements were orderly today despite the heavy security because of the presence of the foreign delegations. While the Indian Public field past under the portico in the front the side entrance to the building was reserved for the foreign dignitaries and the back entrance for the Indian VIPs, which included many politicians and film stars. Periodically, in the front portico, chants of Rajiv Gandhi amar rahe (Rajiv is immortal) and Soniaji sangharsh karo, hum tumhare saath hain (Sonia we are with you) could be heard. Finally at 11 a.m., as scheduled, the entry was stopped and barring the US vice-president, who came late, no one else was allowed inside.

Earlier in the morning, among the first to arrive were the vice- president of the Soviet Union, the Mauritian premier, the Kenyan and the Zamibian delegations.

The widow of the slain leader Sonia Gandhi, arrived around 9.30 a.m. with the film star and close family friend, Amitabh Bachchan. Dressed in a white sari, she was composed and walked past the waiting press photographers almost unobtrusively.

But the quiet was to be broken a little later when Benazir Bhutto, leading an opposition delegation, arrived shortly before 10 a.m. with her entourage and was mobbed by press photoprapherS on her way in and out of the building. Dressed in a yellow salwar kameez, with a white Dupatta draped over her head, she was easily the most sought after world leader by the press.

Other leaders of some neighboring countries also came in solemn processions. All of them were carrying beautifully, decorated floral wreaths. For those not recognisable by face by the securitymen, the country's name was on the wreath. The Bangladesh opposition leader was, in fact, not allowed in through the VIP gate. Later realising their mistake, the securitymen ran after her small delegation and requested them to return. She was sobbing after she emerged from the room.

When the Sri Lankan premier, arrived, a little later, an uncomfortable hush fell, where the journalists were standing. With the LTTE hand suspected in the ascassination of Rajiv Gandhi, the uneasy silence was broken only after he along with his small entourage, went inside the room.

With so many leaders arriving together, the small packing lot facing the Teen Murti library complex, was crammed. Everyone tried their best to make things smooth for the heads of states and other foreign dignitaries to avoid making them wait. But with so many cars already parked and many more continuously arriving some amount of confusion was unavoidable. Japanese leader Takeshita, for instance, waited almost 10 minutes in his car before he could go in where the body was lying.

One of the most touching sights was of Priyanka Gandhi and Varun Gandhi sone of Maneka Gandhi, leaving the Teen Murti house, escorted by Amitabh Bachchan. A little while earlier, Varun accompained only by two securitymen, had entered the building unnoticed by most as some foreign dignitary was leading his entourage. Priyanks, while leaving was heard telling one of the aides, she was going home for some time.

The two biggest delegations of nearly 30 persons each, were led by the Afghanistan president and the German foreign minister. Solemnity and sorrow writ large on their faces, the impeccably dressed German delegation was one of the most impressive.

Two other leaders who were mobbed by the press almost as much as Benazir Bhutto were, Nawaz Sharif and Yasser Arafat. On accompaied by a large delegation, stopped several times en route so that photographers could have their fill. Arafat, on the other hand, was recognisable only because of his uniform. Gone was the effusive and demonstrative Arab, a well-known face in India. He came and left quietly, hardly any change in his grim expression.

Among the last to arrive was Prince Charles, who came in his gleaming Rolls Royce, and looked quite overcome with all the media attention. In fact, the photographers were literally shooed away by those accompanying him as the British monarch appeared to be rooted in one place. Even when he got into his car the photographers continued to click away.

Another dignitary whose arrival was anxiously awaired through the morning, especially by the foreign press, was that of Ms. Hazel Hawke, wife of the Australian premier, Bob Hawke. She was accompanied by the foreign minister Garreth Evans and both of them were pushed by the media. She finally obliged, in what appeared to be an impromptu press conference under a tree, and spoke to some foreign journalists.

The honour for laying the biggest wreath went to the Italian delegation. With two long bomboo sticks attached to it, the nearly 7 feet-high wreath, was the most eye-catching one.

Soviet President Mikhail Gobachev and his wife Raisa in a message to President Venkataraman said "we are filled with indignation over the appalling heinous crime".

In separate message to Sonia Gandhi, wife of Rajiv Gandhi, the Soviet Leader and his wife told her "he was our great personal friend. We valued highly his wonderful human qualities".

The Gorbachevs told Sonia Gandhi that they were with her in the "inconsolable grief".

"It is a monstrous crime against an eminent statesman who has done so much for his country and to make the world a better and more just place". Soviet leader's message said.

"Please accept dear Sonia our sincere sympathy, friendship and support in this difficult hour".

The Soviet leader in his message to Indian President said "we are deeply shocked by the news of the terrible crime. Rajiv Gandhi, whom the Soviet people know well and respected highly, was a major modern statesman and political figure and continued the great national cause of Jawaharlal Nehru and Indira Gandhi and made an unflading contribution to Indo-Soviet Friendship.

"On behalf of people and the Government of the Soviet Union, I convey to you Mr. President and all the people of India deepest condolences at this heavy loss".

The Soviet Women's Committee has mourned the death of Rajiv Gandhi.

In a message from Moscow to Aruna Asaf Ali, it said the "news about the villainous murder of Rajiv Gandhi deeply shocked us. The Soviet people sincerely loved and highly respected him as an ardent patriot of India and a worthy follower of the cause of Jawaharlal Nehru and Indira Gandhi. He was widely known in the world as an outstanding statesman and a political figure putting in to life the priciples of democracy and civil reconciliation. His memory will stay in our hearts for ever".

In another message to Asaf Ali from Moscow, Ada Flora said "It is difficult to find words that could express our pain and grief in connection with the tragic death of highly respected and loved by us Rajiv Gandhi. Mankind lost one of its brilliant sons. We sent our most sincere condolence".

The Madras explosion virtually rocked Moscow. The tragic news spread even belfry the media confirmed it turning incredibility to grief. Rajiv Gandhi was loved by the people Soviet Union in much the same manner as his mother and his grand-father before him. India could talk of dynasties versus democracy, could find faults with its leaders, could vote them down and they set examples of accepting defeats with dignity, what mother, what son.

But the USSR gave the family its unquestioned love and respect. Every Indian who visited here can testify that these feelings had nothing to do with politics or diplomacy; It was the love of the masses who saw India in Jawaharlal Nehru, Indira Gandhi and Rajiv Gandhi. And they are right.

The political philosophy of Rajiv Gandhi unity, stability as a precondition of nation's emergence as a leading member of the 21 century's world community found a ready response here.

In the eyes of the country, Rajiv Gandhi was very much the chip of the old block but at the same time he was what India always presented as the law of life tradition and new thinking. It might sound too exaggerated, but these were exactly the feelings Rajiv Gandhi evoked in the hearts of the Soviets, both old and young alike.

Moscow is decidely becoming more concerned about the future of India in the aftermath of the gruesome murder of Rajiv Gandhi.

Officials and experts in Moscow consider the event not just a personal or human tragedy, which of course it is, but also a "very unfortunate development" for the political future of India, having reprercussions on India's relation with other countries.

The concern is primarily on three counts. First Moscow thinks that as the murder has taken place amidst unprecedented electoral violence, the Indian democracy itself, perhaps for the first time since independence, has been put on trial.

Second, it is pointed out, it has to be seen whether the Indian National Congress, "still the Chief Guarantor of democracy at the national level despite all its weaknesses", itself remains united in the near future.

Third, it has to be seen whether the right-wing forces led by the Bharatiya Janata Party, which follows, in Soviet views, an aggressive internal and external policy, is effectively confined by bringing about all Congressmen together with communists joining in.

Eric Komarov, who was specialised in studying the Indian elections, reflected the above concerns saying that he hoped the present Congress leadership should see to it that the Congress continues to remain an important component of developing a multi- party system in India, a major necessity for democracy. He stressed, "fragmentation of the Congress should not be allowed", while pointing out that he did not favour a return to the old Congress structures or one party rule.

Komarov said: "Other parties are there and they should develop, but the continuation of the congress is essential for India's unity. The Congress is the only party with all-India mass following".

His concern was partially based on the drama that took place in New Delhi when the Congress Working Committee put up Mrs. Sonia Gandhi's name but she declined the offer. Dr, Komarov said he failed to see why the united leadership was unable to make an immediate and more effective choice to preserve the party.

He thought a normal succession could not take placed because the party is overcentralised and the Indian political system has not yet evolved into a viable multiparty democracy.

He said: "See what happened when Charan Singh died. There was a leadership cirsis. So it is not just congress. Only the communists and the BJP appear to have worked out viable party structures.

The India Centre, a Moscow based Soviet think-tank, is now beginning to predict a quicker transition from a one party rule to new forms of political power. Dr. Andrel Volodin, head of the political section of the India Centre, told this correspondent that a "coalition appears inevitable, there may be a government of national unity".

This was also suggested by senior Indologist of the Centre, Prof. G.G. Kotovsky, who said: "The assassination of Rajiv Gandhi is a manifestation of the growing activities of the anti-democratic and right-reactionary forces", and it is these who will gain out of it, irrespective of the fact as who organised the killing.

Soviet TV commentator Alexander Serikov said the Rajiv Gandhi killing was a grim reminder to the Soviety people that separatism will inevitably lead to such terrorist acts.

Indeed, not only the Kremlin but also the Russian white house, as Yelsin's seat of power is called, did react, for the first time, on a major Indian event.

The Russian Congress of People's Deputies, now in session, stood for a minute in silence in the memory of Rajiv Gandhi on May 22, 1991, with Russian parliament foreign relations committee chief Lukin calling him a "great democrat".

Later, Lukin and Nikolai Travkin, chairman of the new Democratic Party of Russia, came to the Indian embassy to sign the condolence book on behalf of the Russian White house. They also held a meeting in Rajiv Gandhi's honour, first of its kind by the Russian leadership.

The Kremlin and the ruling communisty party also paid its condolences: President Gorbachev sent two message one to the president and the other to Sonia Gandhi. He also sent a third message to the Indian embassy in Moscow having failed to come there to sign the condolence book as he was bogged down in talks with the visiting Italian premier.

The Soviet people fell that in Mr. Rajiv Gandhi's assassination India has lost a "Young and talented leader who did a great deal for national consolidation and ensuring a leading role for India in regional and world politics".

In an interview to Novosti, Soviet experts recalled Rajiv Gandhi's contribution to promote Indo-Soviet friendship and cooperation. A notable achievement was the Delhi declaration signed by Rajiv Gandhi and the Soviet leader Mikhail Gorbachev, to realise the goal of a nuclear-weapon free and non-violent world, they said.

The soviet Indologist Andri Volodin said Rajiv Gandhi realised that India's development was impossible without fast scientific and technological progress. Rajiv Gandhi was an "outstanding politician with a braod outlook".

Another Soviet expert Tatyana Shaumyan regretted the assassination of the statesman for political reasons.

Leaders of the African National Congress (ANC) and various Indian religious and cultural groups paid tribute to Rajiv Gandhi at a memorial service held in the Johannesburg Indian township of Lenasia on May 26, 1991.

The memorial service, held at the Mahatma Gandhi Hall, was organised by the NC Lenasia branch, the Transveal Hindu Seva Samaj, the South African Tamil Federation, Central Islamic Trust, Transvall Indian Congress and the Sanathan Ved Dharma Sabha.

Besides Muslim and Hindu speakers, the memorial service was addressed by Senior ANC leader, Walter Sisulu, and Mosey Moola, former chief representative of the ANC in New Delhi.

Recalling the struggles of India, Mahatam Gandhi and the Nehru family, Sisulu said Rajiv Gandhi, in his short political life, won recognition as a world statesman and as leader of the Commonwealth and the Non-Aligned Movement.

"Among the oppressed people of South Africa Rajiv Gandhi won recognition as our friend and ally. He was in the forefront of the Commonwealth to impose sanctions, and to support the frontline states in resisting apartheid aggression", Sisulu said.

The Government, political leaders and people of Bangladesh are terribly shocked at the assassination of former Prime Minister and Congress president Rajiv Gandhi. The people, opening morning newspapers with a banner headline on Rajiv Gandhi's assassination, were horribly stunned.

Prime Minister Begum Khaleda Zia expressing deep shock at his tragic end said Rajiv Gandhi was a brave leader and an uncompromising advocate of democratic values: "We in Bangladesh are indebted to him for his sincere efforts to strengthen Bangladesh-India relations".

Begum Zia said his outstanding contribution to his nation and in the cause of regional and international peace would long be remembered.

Begum Zia's message addressed to Prime Minister Chandra Shekhar said at this hour the people of Bengladesh join you in mourning his death. Begum Zia also sent a condolence message to Sonia Gandhi, expressing her deep shock at the tragedy.

Acting President Justice Shahabuddin Ahmed condemning the dastardly assassination of Rajiv Gandhi said in his death India has lost a great India. Shahabuddin said as president of the Indian National Congress Rajiv Gandhi maintained its high ideals and principles of democracy and secularism despite many odds.

Cuban President Fidel Castro in a message to President Venkataraman said with great sorrow and indignation I received the news of the perfidious assassination of Rajiv Gandhi. I had the opportunity of evaluating his tenacity and fortitude in the hard struggle for the just causes of his people and the third world. In such painful occasion. I wish to convey to you may condolences and those of the Cuban people.

In another message to Sonia Gandhi, Dr. Castro said "I am profoundly shocked to address your in this moment of pain that is filling you for the irreparable loss of you husband Rajiv Gandhi.

Please accept the condolence and solidarity message that I wish to convey to you, your children and other family members for the physical disappearance of a person that for me was a very close friend, a cordial host, a comrade in the struggle for the development of our peoples and, above all. a man deeply intelligent, brave and human".

The Central Committee of the Communist Party of China (CPC) while condoling the demise of Rajiv Gandhi, described him as a friend of the party and a friend of the Chinese people.

In a message to the All India Congress Committee, the CPC Central Committee asked that condolences be conveyed to Sonia Gandhi, according to a spokeswoman of the CPC International Liasion Department.

The CPC Central Committee recalled that Rajiv Gandhi attached great importance to the development of Sino-Indian relations and ties between the CPC and Congress.

"The Chinese Community Party and the Chinese people will always remember him", the spokeswoman quoted the Central Committee as saying in the message.

The Chinese party and Government have over the past year and a half, made warm references to Rajiv Gandhi, crediting him with ushering in a new era in bilateral ties with his historic visit to Beijing in December, 1988.

In March 1991, the CPC had sent a high level delegation led by political bureau member Li Ximing, the highest ranking party leader to visit India since late Premier Zhou Enlai.

Li, who is also Beijing party secretary, had visited India at Rajiv Gandhi's invitation.

The common wealth movement, in which Rajiv Gandhi played the role of a bridgemaker in crucial conferences, mourned his death of Minister.

Leading the movement in paying tributes to Rajiv Gandhi was its Secretary general Emeka Anyaoku who called him a "great devotee and strong advocate of Commonwealth principles".

He said Rajiv Gandhi represented hopes for the younger people of the Commonwealth.

"His commitment to human equality and democracy made him an outstanding leader even in his short period as Prime Minister. It is a irony that he should die when he was illustrating the democratic process in action", Anyaoku said from the London head-quarters of the movement.

Another moving tribute came from former secretary general Sir Sonny Ramphal, who said Rajiv Gandhi had brought to Coomonwealth. Ramphal, who was secretary general from 1975 to 1990, said "he was therefore a very significant figure in the coalition of Commonwealth solidarity against apartheid and against Margaret Thatcher in those Commonwealth confrontations which he had. But he alwasy had the respect and friendship of those who were engaged with. Even those we were on the other side of the argument", Mr. Ramphal added.

He expressed optimism about India's future, saying the country had "tremendous reserves" to draw from.

He said Rajiv Gandhi's assassination will serve as a reminader of the threats of "violence, extremism and fundamentalist" that surround those who engaged in Political activity.

British Foreign Secretary, Douglas Hurd, has said that the assassination of Rajiv Gandhi, was for him the loss of a friend.

In an interview to the BBC, Hurd said he had all though recent years remembered a conversation with Rajiv Gandhi in Delhi in which he set out "simply and plainly his anxieties about India, what through could not be done." Hurd described India as a beacon of democracy, "a beacon which has often been besieged by storms- and there is clearly going to be a storm now-but the storms pass and there are still free elections, a free parliament, a free court, free media, so the beacon goes on shining."

Nothing that Rajiv Gadhi's death had come in the middle of an election campaign, Hurd said it would be wise "to announce a pause now for people to reflect but I hope the result of that reflection will be steadiness and a determination that the unity of India and the freedom of India should be preserved".

Hurd said development in India mattered to mankind and not just to this country to "This is a huge subcontinent which has become a nation, two nations, now three natins but India is the largest of them and the survival of those free institutions in that huge melting pot of India is really a test of man as a political being," he said. Hurd believed that India would always manage to rise above events.

The British Foreign Secretary also felt that Rajiv Gandhi's death was a loss for the Commonwealth. "He used the Common wealth and believed in the Commonwealth, but he was playing the traditional part of an Indian leader in the Commonwealth," Hurd said.

French Prime Minister Edith Cresons today deplored the death of India's former Prime Minister Rajiv Gandhi."After Indira Gandhi, her son......an assassination is always terrifying. Events in India are disquieting. All this comes at time when India is badly in need of stability".

Daniel Bernard, the spokesman of the French Foreign Office, said he hoped the assassination of former Prime Minister would not unleash a wave of violence, "Mr. Gandhi's death has caused both sorrow and consternation in France", he said.

Indiara Gandhi was admired by the French and her son Rajiv Gandhi too had established cordial relations with French leaders. In 1985, during the year of India in France, Mr. Gandhi had been given an extremely warm reception by both the French public as well as by the press.

During the 200th anniversary celebrations of the French Revolution, Mr. Gandhi who was still Prime Minister of India met President Mitterrand for long talks, Rajiv Gandhi argued the case for greater support and aid to developing nations. Mitterrand incorporated several of Rajiv Gandhi's proposals in a report he made to the industrialised nations summit which met concurrently in Pairs, Subsequent scandals however tranished his image here.

Liberation, the Paris daily concluded: "Rajiv Gandhi was almost pushed into office following the assassination of his mother. He never quite managed to step into her shoes. India's tragedy today is that there is no political personality who can take up where the Gandhi's left off".

Ghana is flying flags at Halt-mast in tribute to Rajiv Gandhi and head of State Flt. Lt. Jerry Rawlings has sent a message of condolence to the Government and people of India.

The flags are to fly at half-mast for three days. In his message Rawlings expressed Ghana's deep sorrow and profound grief at the brutal and cowardly killing of Rajiv Gandhi.

Rawlings described Rajiv Gandhi as a towering figure in the Non- Aligned Movement, a strong defender of the ideals of the Commonwealth and an ardent champion of the Third world.

"His untimely death is therefore as much a loss to Ghana and the Third World in general as it is to his native India". Rawlings said in his message.

Japanese Prime Minister Toshi Ki Kaifu deplored the assassination saying: "Rajiv Gandhi was a great man who had made efforts to improve ties between Japan and India. Terrorism should never be allowed".

"While expressing our condolences, we also pray from the bottom of our hearts for the repose of his soul".

Gloom gripped Nepal as the stunning news of the killing reached the Himalayan Kingdom.

Political leaders irrespective of party affiliations, intellectuals down to the man in the street strongly condemned this attack on one, who, they said was destined to lead the largest democracy in the world after the current elections.

The victory rally of the Nepali Congress today has been cancelled as a mark of respect to the memory of Rajiv Gandhi.

A real scramble for Indian newspapers carrying news and comments about Rajiv Gandhi's tragic killing was witnessed this afternoon at Sandesh Griha and other shops. The long queue had disrupted the regular flow of traffic in the New Road Market area. Outside the shop, lot of people were seen offering higher prices for the papers.

Among those who had lined up to purchase newspapers were many foreign and Indian tourists, besides officials belonging to many embassies located in Kathmandu.

This correspondent was flooded with hundreds of queries made over telephone throughout the day where the killers of Rajiv Gandhi have been apprehended.

The anticipation of most of the political parties and the people in Nepal was that Rajiv Gandhi whould form the government after the elections and it would be in the interest of this country. His perception about Nepal-India relationship was too very well known here. The optimism in the Nepali Congress in particular, which has received only a razor thin majority, was that with Rajiv Gandhi as India's new Prime Minister, the new Government in Nepal would be able to tide over most of the economic and other immediate problems.

An alert was sounded throughout Nepal, specially in the Indo- Nepal border areas, as the news of the assassination of for Rajiv Gandhi reached in Kathmandu.

Yog Prasad Upadhayaya, Minister for Home Affairs and Communications, who met the Premier Krishan Prasad Bhattarai at his resident said that the Government had alerted the security forces here against any after-effect.

"We are very keenly watching of the situation across the border. We will take necessary steps to see that peace is maintained in the country and there is no infiltration of undesirable elements from across the boarders", Upadhyaya said.

The assassination of Rajiv Gandhi constitutes a great loss for the poor people in third world countries, said former Nicaraguan President Daniel Ortega. He told reporters, "we express our disgust and repuguance, because there has been an assassination of a leader of the poor people in the third world".

"Criminals have eclipsed the life of a fighter for pleace and justice".

Ortega said Rajiv Gandhi had been "a friend and a brother for the Nicaraguan people".

Top Pakistani leaders expressed deep shock and grief over the tragic death of Rajiv Gandhi and termed it as a result of a cowardly act of terrorism.

President Ghulam Ishaq Khan in a condolence message said, "India has lost a distinguished leader with a long record of service to the nation".

"Pakistan condemns in the strongest terms all acts of terrorism wherever they may take place."

Expressing profound shock over the assassination, Pak Premier Nawaz Sharif said, "we are saddened by the passing away, under such tragic circumstances, of an important and distinguished political leader of our region".

Opposition leader and former Premier Benazir Bhutto said she was deeply grieved to hear about the dastardly act. She strongly condemned the terrorist action that took the life of Rajiv Gandhi.

The Chairman of the Senate, Wasim Sajjad and a large number of Pakistani leaders have also condoled the death of the former Indian Premier.

A Pakistan foreign office spokesman said Pakistan condemend all acts of terrorism and mourns the loss of the distinguished Indian leader.

Pakistani Urdu dailies today prominently flashed the news of the assassination.

A Sri Lankan sailor, who attempted an assault of Rajiv Gandhi, with his rifle four years ago has said he sent a message of condolence after Rajiv Gandhi's assassination.

The local Divaina newspaper quoted sailor Vijita Rohana on May 29 as saying he sent a telegram to Gandhi's wife Sonia expressing his condolences. Rohana, a memeber of naval honour guard, swung his rifle by the barrel as Rajiv Gandhi passed in front of him during a visit to the island on July 30, 1987. Rajiv Gandhi was hit on the back of the head and left shoulder.

The assault took place minutes before Rajiv Gandhi was due to leave Sri Lanka after signing a controversial pack with the then President of the Island nation, Mr. Junius Jayewardene.

"I had no personal grudge against Rajiv. My action reflected the resentment of the people against the agreement," Rohana told the newspaper.

Rohana, dismissed from the navy and sent to jail was released from prison a year ago.

Indians in Singapore condoled the death of Rajiv Gandhi. Meeting held at the lawns of the Indian high commission here adopted a resolution and paid tributes to Mr. Gandhi whose "untimely death is a grievous loss to India".

The resolution said, "we in Singapore are deeply shocked at the tragic assassinating of Mr. Gandhi, who was a great leader of India."

The former prime Minister of Singapore, Lee Kuan Yew also visited the high commission to sign the condolence book.

Describing the killing of Rajiv Gandhi as "brutal and barbaric" the Lanka President, Ranasinghe Premadasa said all Sri Lankans join him in condemning the "horrible and cowardly" act.

"This tragedy is one more reminder of the need for non-violence in public life", Premadas said, conveying his heartfelt sympathy to the bereaved family and the people of India.

Meanwhile, the Sri Lankan navy sent a maximum alert across the Palk Strait in view of the possible involvement of the Sri Lankan Tamil militants of the LTTE in yesterday's bomb explosion that killed Rajiv Gandhi and several others, official sources here said requesting anonimity.

The goodwill for the Nehru family was amply reflected in the profuse and touching tributes paid to Rajiv Gandhi in Britain. The extent of it was both surprising and unexpected.

That the tribute was led by Prime Minister John Major was in itself significant. Labour leader Neil Kinnock, the leader of the Liberal Democrats, Paddy Ashdown, and Dr. David Owen, former foreign secretary and Social Democratic leader, paid their homage to Rajiv Gandhi described as the last of the Nehru dynasty.

The British Queen, now touring the United States expressed her grief at the tragedy as did Margaret Thatcher, former Prime Minister, who is on a visit to South Africa.

Major described Mr. Gandhi as a "very brave man and a man of very rare qualities". He said that Mr. Gandhi had very many friends in the Commonwealth and in the Britain "who will miss him a great deal".

Kinnock said that Rajiv Gandhi's assassination was "devastating". The former Indian Prime Minister had a real vision for a modern democratic country and tried everythig he could to bring that to life and embodied "very best of modern India".

Paddy Ashdown said the assassination was a tragedy for India and bitter blow for democracy in the country.

The Secretary General of Commonwealth, Chief Emeka Anayaoku, said Mr. Gandhi's assassination was a huge loss to Commonwealth and India. He was an outstanding advocate of reconciliation in the Commonwealth. His commitment to human equality and democracy made him asouts tanding leader even in his short period as Prime Minister. His assassination was ghastly and despicable act. "It is an irony that the should die when he was illustraing the democratic process in action", he said.

Former Secretary General of Commonwealth Sir Sridath Ramphal, said Rajiv Gandhi Gandhi had brought compassion to Commonwealth and acted as a bridge builder inside the organisation. He said his role against apartheid was vital and enormous.

High Commissioner for India Dr. L.M. Singhvi called for world sympathy and support in the country's battle against forces of disintegration and terrorism. India needed fortitude to face the "terrible calamity". He said India lived in shame, shock and anguish following the assassination.

The President of the Indian Overseas Congress-I said that India faced a bleak future without Rajiv Gandhi.

British Premier John Major said everyone would be "shocked and saddened by the very tragic assassination of the former Indian Prime Minister Rajiv Gandhi".

Rajiv Gandhi was a very brave man, a man of very rare quality, Major said in a condolence message.

The opposition labour leader Neil Kinnock said Rajiv Gandhi's dead was "devastating".

Kinnock said "He had real vision for a modern democratic India and tried everything he could to bring it to life."

The liberal democrat leader Paddy Ashdown said, "It was a tragedy for India and a bitter blow for democracy".

A motion was placed in the House of Comon on May 22, 1991 condemning "the cowardly act of violence that killed Rajiv Gandhi." More than 45 MPs from all parties signed the motion on the first day.

The motion was palced in Parliament by Keith Vaz, Indian-born MP, Robert Hughes, David Alton, Ken Hargreaves and Sir Cyril Smith.

The motion says: "This House unreservedly condemns those who prepetrated the wicked, callous and cowardly act of violence which killed Rajiv Gandhi, the leader of the Congress party and former Prime Minister of India,considers that the Indian people have lost a figure of great importance in the life of their nation, and that the community of nations, including Britain, have lost a valued friend, reaffirms its faith in Indian democracy and believed that these acts of terrorism will not be permitted to undermine or subvert the world's largest democracy".

High Commissioner L.M. Singhvi said he had been besieged by calls of sympathy. Class came in till 4 a.m. on May 23, 1991 morning, Singhvi said. Among those who called were Prince Charles,

John Major, Labour leader Neil Kinnock, the Lord Chancellor and Foreign Secretary Douglas Hurd.

Singhvi said he also went to the airport to meet Rajiv Gandhi's son, Rahul Gandhi, who was on his way back to New Delhi. Singhvi said Rahul looked calm and composed at the airport as, he said, Rajiv Gandhi looked when he lost his mother Indira Gandhi.

Mr. Singhvi said Rahul returned to India with Mr. Amitabh Bachchan.

Addressing newsmen L.M. Singhvi said: "India will not be washed away by those who have adopted the creed of violence. They do not represent India, but only the aberrations of India".

The Labour national executive meeting adopted a motion to express "deep sorrow at the horrific death of Rajiv Gandhi and other people in Tamil Nadu". Rajiv Gandhi, the motion said, was a "progressive leader who sought to serve his people with courage and wisdom and to encourage cooperation and understanding across the world". The conference emphasised "its abiding faith in the capacity of India to solve its problems by peaceful means".

Sources of meetings were held, meanwhile, among the Indian community in London, Manchester, Birmingham and Leicester. Southhall, the scene of celebrations after the assassination of Indira Gandhi, was quiet.

Shops in Indian-habited areas of West London downed shutters as the Indian community in Britain mourned the death of Rajiv Gandhi.

People from all religions have offered prayer meetings since Rajiv Gandhi's assassination on May 22, 1991 in marked contrast to the reaction to Indira Gandhi's killing in 1984.

Most *gurdwaras* and mosques in Britain in addition to Hindu temples, have held prayer meeting to condole Rajiv Gandhi's death, the president of the largest Indian organisation in Britain said.

"There is a vast differece in the reaction this time. The vast majority of the people have not been happy with the murder because they have come around to the view that political problems cannot be solved by violence", Piara Lal Khabra, president of the Indian Workers Association said.

Secretary General Javier Perez De Cuellar has expressed deep shock at the assassination of Rajiv Gandhi, saying the entire world is appalled by the dreadful etc.

De Cuellar sent a signed cable to Sonia Gandhi conveying his 'most sincere condolences'.

"Rajiv Gandhi was a remarkable leader whose impact was felt not only in his own country but around the world. Called upon to take high national office following the tragic and untimely demise of his late mother, he rose to many challenges with imagination and determination".

De Cuellar said it is all the more tragic that his assassination comes of at the time when India once again giving evidence of its long standing devotion to the democratic process. A stern trial of character and will may now face India, her leaders and her people.

"I know they will have the goodwill of the entire international community in facing this challenge," he said.

"Sadly it falls to me on behalf of the United Nations and on my own personal behalf and that of my wife to extend to you and to the memebres of your family my most sincere condolences at this moment of irreparable loss to you," the message said.

Warm tributes were paid to the former Prime Minister, Rajiv Gandhi's commitment to the Non-Aligned Movement, world peace and disarmament and also his leadership qualities at a plenary session of NAM held at the UN headquarters on May 23, 1991.

In a rare gesture, NAM called a special session to pay homage to its former chairman.

The Indian ambassador, C.R. Gharekhan, thanked the movement for standing by India at their time of sorrow.

He said Rajiv Gandhi, as leader of the Non-Aligned Movement, had devoted considerable time to thinking about the direction it was taking and was instinctively an intervationalist.

Earlier, members of the UN Security Council paid homage to Rajiv Gandhi, describing his death as a rude shock to India and world peace.

The UN Secretary General Javier Perez de Cuellar was the first to sign the condolence book at the Indian mission.

He was followed by ambassadors and diplomats from various mission expressing sorrow and shock over the assassination.

New York mayor, David Dinkins and many diplomats and intellectuals were among those who paid tributes to Rajiv Gandhi.

Dinkins visited India's consulate general in New York and signed the condolence book.

A number of American scholars and professors also visited the consulate general and signed the book. Several Indian Community groups held a condolence meeting last evening at the consulate at which speakers paid homage to Rajiv Gandhi.

Iraqi President, Saddam Hussain, has said the death of Rajiv Gandhi was a great loss for humanity and the developing countries.

In a message to Sonia Gandhi, the Iraqi president described Rajiv Gandhi as "a great political personality" and lauded his role in the international arena.

Vietnamese leaders have paid glowing tributs to Rajiv Gandhi for his outstanding contributions to India's national construction, socio-economic development and in the defence of national unity and integrity.

In separate messages to the President, R.Venkataraman and the Prime Minister, Chandra Shekhar, they said that Rajiv Gandhi was an eminent activist of the Non-Aligned Movement and had worked tirelessly for global peace, independence and social progress.

Assassination of Rajiv Gandhi shocked the Indian Community in the United States and many broke down as the ethnic and other television network tried to interview them to seek their reaction.

Major televisions network cut into their regular programmes to announce the death of the Congress President in a bomb blast and ethnic TV network was broadcasting non stop news on the assassination and subsequent developments suspending all its programme.

In the United Nations, several diplomats expressed their sorrow and condemned increasing political violence in the world of which Rajiv Gandhi, they said, was a victim. The assassination and political future of India was the subject matter of discussions throughout the afternoon.

Indian Ambassador to United National C.R. Gharekhan fought back his tears as gave his reaction on a television network.

The Indian National Congress of America held a condolence meeting late in the evening at New York where homage was paid to the Gandhi and his acievements recalled.

In the news reports, it was being emphasised that for the first time now, Indian political structure would be without a dominating memebre of the Gandhi family but most reports said Indian democracy would survive the tragedy.

During interviews, members of the Indian community condemned the assassination and some said even though they had not agreed with several of his views, killing had no place in a civilised and democratic society.

Apparently with riots after Indira Gandhi's assassination in mind, a Sikh gentleman, did not want to be identifies, said the whole community should not be held responsible for the act of one individual.

In a touching gesture of sympathy, friendship and support President George Bush called at the Embassy of India in Washington on May 24, 1991 to convey his condolences on the untimely demise of Rajiv Gandhi.

The President's visit was the high point of an unprecendented display of concerned interest in the United States to the news of Rajiv Gandhi's assassination. From the media to Congress to the administration, expressions of friendship for the slain leader, anxiety about India's future and confidence about the strength of its democratic underpinnings have been unexpectedly profuse.

"He was my friend", said Bush as he was greeted by Ambassador Abid Hussain. "He was a really good friend. In our business we make friends, but this one was for real".

The President then signed the condolence book. He wrote: "With respect for a great leader (leader underlined), with love from Barbara and me. For a great friend-my respect to India's people.

President Bush said that the assasination of Rajiv Gandhi was a real tragedy and said: "I do not know what the world is coming to"

Bush said that he and his wife had a real personal friendship with Rajiv Gandhi and so his death was a personal loss. "When you look at his contribution to international order and think of his decency", said Bush, "Rajiv Gandhi's assassination is a real tragedy".

"And when people will resort in a democratic country or anywhere to violence of this nature, it is just appalling," he said.

Said Bush: "It is a sad thing that this young man should have lost his life in this way. It is a tragedy."

Members of US Congress and Indian Community leaders paid tributes to Rajiv Gandhi, at a memorial at the Washington Cathedral.

Speaker after speaker recalled Rajiv Gandhi's commitment to build up India as a united, secular and modern state.

They specially lauded his efforts to bring India and America closer.

Congress woman Helen Delich Bentley called Rajiv "a prince of man" and a "universal personality who belonged to us all".

She deplored the "senseless act of violence which caused Rajiv Gandhi's death and said democracies would never allow an appeal from the ballot to the bullet to succeed.

Congresswoman Constance Morella said former President Ronald Reagan used to say that to him Rajiv Gandhi was like a son.

She recalled that Gandhi had lowered taxes, reduced economic regulations and "moved closer to the west".

Former high State Department official Alan Keyes said India had set an example of democracy to countries which generation after generation had been parliaments give way to tyrants and military dictators.

The United States has pledged whole-hearted support to India to track down Rajiv Gandhi's assassins. The US Federal Bureau of Investigation and the Central Intelligence Agency have received instructions from the "top" to "do everything possible within their worldwide netwcok to uncover the plot behind Rajiv's assassination".

These instructions to the top US intelligence gathering and counter terrorism agencies come just hours after US Vice- President Dan Quayle promised Sonia Gandhi in New Delhi that "the US will stand by India in its hour of trial".

The Federal Bureau of Investigation is mainly responsible for law enforcement within the US, but as part of that beat and with changing times the agency's brief has enlarged and now reaches out of to all nations of the world either directly or through a complicated web of intelligence arrangements with other agencies.

The FBI, it should be noted, is the most sophisticated agency when it comes to counter-terrorism anywhere in the world. In South Asia, the FBI has a significan presence and it is reliably gathered that in tandem with the Israeli intelligence, the FBI is familar with the doings of the LTTE in northern Sri Lanka.

To unravel the political motives, if any, behind the killing of Rajiv Gandhi, the Central Intelligence Agency (CIA) has also gotten into the act. The CIA is trying to determine what could be the political motive and the origin of the motive. Both the CIA and the FBI will be inputing their knowledge into the Indian CBI and RAW. A similar arrangement was palced in action at the time of the "Kaniskha" Air-India bomb blast over the Atlantic Ocean, but this time the effort is far more.

Interpol, the international police organisation, has also sent out its highest priority alert to all its worldwide posts. The alert includes satellite pictures of the suspected woman assassin. Law enforcement that the hunt being launched for Rajiv's assassins is unprecedented and sources feel confident that given a bit of luck the case would be cracked open.

The *Independent* (London) wrote: "The murder Rajiv Gandhi marks the death of a dynasty and, almost certainly, of the political movement that the family had come to dominate. Congress(I) was the Gandhi family in a way in which the Democratic Party never belonged to the Kennedys.

The bomb blast also seems destined to bring to a head the political, religious and social crises that in recent years has called into question the survival of Mr. Gandhi's country as a democratic and seculars state..........His death is all too likely to be the signal for further atrocities.

When a world leader (Rajiv Gandhi was without doubt one even out of office) dies, it is customary, even ritualistic, for other world leaders to pay tributes to him or her. However, most often that is done out of ceremonial politeness rather than from any felt sense of personal loss. But anyone who read between the lines the tributes heaped on Rajiv Gandhi could not have helped noticing the fact that they were tinged with a sense of personal bereavement. For instance, Pakistan President, Ghulam Ishaq Khan, could just have said (considering the strain from which Indo- Pakistani relations have never really been free) that he was shocked at the assassination of Rajiv Gandhi, and stopped at that. Even if he wanted to be more generous, he could have gone to the Indian High Commission and written the same thing in the condolence book. But, according to newspaper reports, he was "visibly moved" when he went to our High Commission to condole with Rajiv Gandhi's family-nay with the people of India-over the death... And what he said and wrote could not just have been for purposes of protocol which did not demand effusiveness. The Prime Minister of Sweden, Ingvar Carlsson, has said: "For me Rajiv Gandhi was both a close friend and a collaborating partner in emaningful international issues. This (the murder) is yet another example of how good and progressive ambitions have been shattered by brutal violence".

Benazir Bhutto has viewed the tragedy in a broader perspective. "In this time of great flux," according to her, "it is essential to rise above narrow considerations. And it is in this context that one misses Rajiv Gandhi most because he was above such considerations and could also lift others above such narrow feelings." According to a report in *The Hindu,* the whole Arab world has been convulsed by Rajiv

Gandhi's assassination because he had maintained live contact ("through correspondence when he could not meet them") with all state of Arab society. Can there be a greater tribute to his stature than the fact that it did not diminish in spite of his adopting a pro-Saddan stand during the recent crisis when almost the whole of the Arab world seemed arrayed against Iraq? The average Indian may well ask in Hamletian terms: "What's Hecuba to him, or he to Hecuba, that he should weep for her?" To go by the reaction not only of world leaders but also of the world, the answer is: A great deal, Countries judge a leader not by what he has, or has not done for them. At a time when the concept of a global village is fast gaining currency, the entire world is bound to admire a leader, in power or out of it, alive or dead, who wishes to envelope entire humanity in a sort of Whitmanesque embrace, and will hope that, like the phoenix, he will emerge from the ashes to which his mortal remains were reduced.

7
LOVE AND AFFECTION

Rajiv Gandhi was a symbol of people's dream of India as a great nation on the world map. With his passing away the whole nation, time and history of coming era is bowed to salute the great son of India.

The tragic exit of Rajiv Gandhi from the national scene marks a break in the long chain of continuity in Indian politics. When he succeeded Mrs. Indira Gandhi in 1984, after she was gunned down by her own security guards, he instantly came to symbolise as a crucial link in the change-over in the polity, especially of the age-old Congress culture, while he bridged the generation gap at one go. The vital link has now broken. This throws open all the complexities of the turbulent Indian politics. This is surely not a happy setting as we have tended to ignore inconvenient questions under the umbrella of the 105-year old Congress which has been intimately linked with the Nehru-Gandhi family. The Congress culture under Rajiv Gandhi might have acquired a degree of sophistication, thanks to the impact of the computer and young enthusiasts' flirtation with politics. But in its basic characteristics and working, the party has remained an amorphous bunch of thought and trends. All the same, the patchwork quilt of the Indian National Congress has acquired a certain fusion which is its real strength in Indian society. Rajiv Gandhi was not Indira Gandhi, and he did deviate for a while from her policy thrusts and style of functioning. However, soon he realised the importance of taking the old guards along with his new aides. Indeed, there have of late been definite signs of Congress rejuvenation. Indira Gandhi had her own charisma. So was the case with Rajiv Gandhi. Their personalities were good enough to attract the masses. This helped to make the Congress going as a mass based organisation, from Kashmir to Kanyakumari. How the party is going to adjust itself to the new situation and evolve new responses to keep its platform intact will be watched with keen interest. The mass-based appeal of its leaders like Jawaharlal Nehru, Indira Gandhi, and Rajiv Gandhi virtually made the Congress synonymous with stability of India. The question which has now begun to be asked is whether the new crop of leaders will be able to generate enough confidence among the people to keep the Congress and the nation going. The implications are obvious especially in view of the fact that the party does not seem to have an outstanding mass leader at present whose appeal cutsacross divisions of religion, caste, and region. This does not mean that a Lal Bahadur Shastri cannot emerge from within the rank.[1]

1. Hari Jai Singh. Post-Rajiv India. *The Business and Political Observer,* 23 May, 1991.

The party has a number of shrewd and sharp leaders, who probably could not grow enough in the past or preferred not to assert themselves in the face of powerful personalities of the established leaders. A lot will depend on how the present set of leaders respond to the new challenges facing the party and the country. More than the party, it is the problems and challenges before the nation which are simply daunting. Democracy is definitely flourishing, but what is the quality of this democracy? The growing criminalisation of politics and the accompanying politicisation of the underworld have not only made our democratic structure vulnerable but have seemingly eroded the confidence of the people in the ifficacy of the parliamentary system. Worse, criminals have realised how indispensable they are and have begun to infiltrate the political mainstream by contesting and even winning election themselves. Inevitably, the input of ideology has shrunk perceptively. Secularism with its inherent tolerance is today intellectually devalued. The growth and acceptance of fundamentalism too must be traced to the decline of liberal ideas, sentiments and politics. There is a general debasement of the political system. Politicians and the political process have lost moral authority. Divisiveness is now finding new outlets. The new infrastructure of politics consists not of grassroot individuals sensitive to the local ethos but of musclemen and mafia. The frenzy with which money is extorted, black money which need never be accounted for, and the attempt to sway the electorate with sops have made the vote not only the end but the means for speedy appropriation of the country's resources by a small political elite.[2]

There is so much sorrow and tragedy in the manner of Rajiv Gandhi's death that it is hard to write about him just yet except in eulogistic tones that obituaries naturally assume for those who die young. In my case an objective assessment is particularly difficult because I knew Rajiv as a friend before I knew him as a politician. But, if I do not try and assess his contribution to Indian politics objectively and unemotionally I feel that I would be doing him a disservice and would, in fact, be no better than the cupbearers and sycophants who in the end destroyed him. I first met Rajiv during the Emergency (1975-77).

In fact, it could not have been more than a week after his mother had locked up the entire Opposition and declared this necessary for putting 'democracy on the rails'. Among the guests at this particular dinner was Biju Patanik's son, Naveen, whose father was among those jailed. The other guests were mainly socialites, young scions of industry and commerce and glizy creatures from the worlds of advertising and

2. *Ibid.*

art. They hovered around the Gandhis, kowtowing, flattering and utterly abject in their devotion. The only person who seemed to notice Naveen Patnaik was Sonia Gnandhi who said uncomfortably that it should not be nice for him to have his father in jail, or words to that effect.

This was the only remark that could be described as political that evening. There followed a succession of similar parties throughout the Emergency to which I was invited but always urged by everyone else in the circle not to say anything political. This resulted in my not speaking to Rajiv at all because with Emergency excesses raging outside it seemed ridiculous to be talking to Indira Gandhi's son about, for instance, whether he liked flying Avros or jets. Finally, when the Janata Government came to power I could restrain myself no longer. Catching Rajiv sitting by himself at yet another party I asked him how much he knew about the 'excess! He looked me straight in the eye and said, "Very little. But whatever I did find out I told Mummy."[3]

As he said this a look of such relief dawned on his face that I realised that far from not wanting to talk about politics he had actually been longing for someone to mention what had become the unmentionable. We talked at length that evening about what he had felt about the emergency, what he had known and what he thought about his brother's politics. He never attacked either his mother or brother but always tried to explain why they had done certin thing. There was so much candour and sincerity in what he said that it was hard not to be completely and utterly charmed by him, as were most other people who met him at a personal level. Many meetings and political conversations were to follow that first encounter and I discovered that although Rajiv's understanding of political things was limited he had the sort of overdeveloped sense of decency and honour that was exactly what national politics needed. Without realising how prophetic my words were going to turnout to be I often said to him that he was the right brother to be in politics. It was, in fact, thanks to a lot of persuasion from me that he gave his first interview (I think) to Sunday magazine and that is how MJ. Akbar first met him. I remember him being really nervous about the interview and insisting that he would give it only on the condition that I sat through and signalled to him if he was about to say anything wrong. He needn't have worried. Akbar was completely in his thrall by the end of the interview and it was carried on the cover. Then Sanjay died and he was sucked, much against Sonia's wishes, into the political vacuum his brother left. His immediate reaction was to try and collect around him people with the same sense of values and these

3. Tavleen Singh. Remembering Rajiv Gandhi. *Indian Express*, 26 May 1991

tended to be school friends like Arun Singh. In the inner circle around him at that time there were few people against whom aspersions of any king could be cast. On the fringe, however, lurked always the likes of Satish Sharma and other loser types from the Doon School, Uttar Pradesh.

It was Rajiv's misfortune that when he became Prime Minister it was the latter who hemmed him in. This was particularly true after differences cropped up between him and Arun Singh. Then this little caboodle of the worst of his friends became the inner circle, the only ones with the magic key of access to the Prime Minister's house. They flaunted their access a parties, stomped into government affairs as if they had his permission to do so and used his name in a thousand ways all guarnteed only to bring discredit and trouble. Rajiv, himself, compounded the problem by using as his spokesmen crass, abrasive persons of the Mani Shankar Aiyar variety who made it easy to forget Rajiv's own charm and who were also unable throughout to project any of the good things his government did. And, good things there were. There was, for instance, the first serious attempt to liberalise India's shackled, stagnant economy. There were attempts to make people aware of how fast the rest of the world was moving and how we would get completely left behind unless we realised what was happening in the world of computers and new technology. There were, initially, serious attempts to restructure the Congress Party so that the power of corrupt, party bosses and influence- peddlers could be reduced. But, because of the inability of his spokesmen to project anything except their own boorishness, most of these achievements remained in the background as did some of the excellent work done by people like Sam Pitroda. Rajiv's own increasing inaccessibility-God only knows under whose stupid advice, made him unpopular with the Press. So everyone was literally waiting to pounce when Bofors happened. This again, was handled with such monumental ineptitude that Rajiv came across as guilty even bofore the evidence began to be compiled. Forgetten immediately were his political successes, his charm, his decency and all that remained was the image of an effete, isolated prince surrounded by a corrupt and foolish collection of courtiers. It is not the worth of image you win elections with. He lost. Would he have won this time the 1991 elections? I very much doubt it. And again I blame the people around him and their senseless, self-defeating sycophancy. So, all prevasive was this atmosphere in the circle around him that he was never encouraged to think about mistakes he may have made as Prime Minister. My last meeting with him was along with a group of foreign correspondents, and someone asked him what mistakes he thought had made and the only one he could come up with was that "somewhere along we had lost our communication with the people". Tragically, it was his sincere attempt to rectify this, by drastically reducing security measures, that killed him.[4]

It is difficult to believe that Rajiv is no more. Mine has been a long--and fond--association with him. We have shared many moments of happiness and many hours of trial. I have known him since 1958, it has been 33 years. I have known him since I was a student, and I have worked with him in politics. Rajiv had a wonderful sense of humour, a deep sense of consideration and was a very, very humane person. He attached great importance to human bonds and was apt to recall shared moments with nostalgia. All this made you cherish your association with him. His kindness and sense of consideration was apparent from the first day that I met him. I remember in 1958-or was it 1959? I was coming to Delhi from school. The occasion was the first international trade fair for which the Pragati Maidan grounds had been laid out. As I was a boy then, someone was to come to the airport to pick me up. But the person wasn't there. Rajiv was to go to Teen Murti House where he was living with his grandfather, Jawaharlal Nehru. He perhaps realised that I was a little panicky, so he didn't go. He spent one and a half hours with me, until my escort was located. I remember him insisting that he remain with me unitl the escort was found. The last time I met him was at Chhindwara, where I was campaigning for my election. He had learnt that the going was tough for me. On May 8, he cancelled four meetings in four districts and came to Chhindwara. Instead of the scheduled 35 minutes, he spent two-and-a-half hours there. Finally, when he left, he undertook a night take-off from an airstrip that had no night facilities. Trucks and jeeps were lined up along the runway, with their headlinghts on. Rajiv did not mind any of this, because he felt that he was helping a friend. His last words to me were "See you in Delhi. Obviously, you cannot lose". What were the differences between Rajiv and Sanjay? well, I was fortunate to be Sanjay's friend and equally fortunate to have been close to Rajiv. Frankly, in the last year or year-and-a- half, there were hardly any differences between the two. But basically, Sanjay was far more frank brusque in his behaviour, where Rajiv was more introverted in his reactions. It is difficult to think of the Congress after Rajiv. But one thing is certain. The party has not sunk, so it does not have to have to be salvaged. There are inherent strengths and the party will chug along. It will adopt and implement the policies and programmes of Indira Gandhi and Rajiv Gandhi. That is the best tribute we can pay to our great leaders.[5]

4. *Ibid.*
5. Kamal Nath. A Very Humane Person. *The Sunday Observer*, 26, May, 1991.

We were at school together. And later at Cambridge. But I hardly knew him at either place. He was three years junior to me and in a school where you spend a total of five years, a three-year difference in age constitutes an almost unbridgeable generation gap. As, indeed, I never got around to thanking him for rounding up his Indian friends at Cambridge to go and vote for "that Indian" who was standing for President at the Union. Dalip Mehta, now Chief of Protocol at the Ministry of External Affairs and one of those who was so coralled by Rajiv, told me about this nearly 20 years after it happened I was amazed. For, although Rajiv and I were in neighbouring colleges--he at the upmarket Trinity College and I at the humbler Trinity Hall--our paths rarely crossed. The only occasion I remember running into him was as I was going into the Union Chamber, listed, for the first time in my life, as the opeining speaker in the order papers for the day, and hence both in a somewhat nervous flutter as well as dressed to the gills in my black *bundgala* and whilte trousers (the trousers, alas, a size too short, so the edges rode above the shoe-line towards the ankel!) Rajiv was standing at the entrance and, as I passed by called out after me with an enormous smile: "Where do you think you are headed to, yaar? The floods?" Miraculously, I nevertheless got the speech off my chest. It was only after he became Prime Minister and I joined PMO that I all got to know Rajiv. It was an official relationship. I never called him anything but "Sir". I was never invited into his home. The only time he came to mine was to convey his condolences when my mother dead. Almost all our conversations were related to the work at hand. But because I travelled with him everywhere he went, all over India and to something like 50 countries abroad, I got to see him from very close up, more closely and more often, perhaps, than anyone else bar his Personal Secretary, 'Vincent George', in many different settings, in many different modes. The other interaction was at the intellectual level. Over the years, I became his ameneuensis, translating his thoughts into words, crafting the phrases and expressions which conveyed with an accuracy that matched his exacting standards precise points he wished to convey. Drafts would usually go into five or six versions, sometimes even upto 15. There was one long letter to President Gorbachev I prepared for him. He fed it around with him punching in addition, scoring out passages, working on every word till we would found just the right one he wanted. The lap-top computer went with us from helicopter to helicopter, up into the azure skies with Air Force one, carted from one grimy circuit house to another. From start to finish, it took almost three months for him to be satisfied with the outcome. That was the kind of pernickety precision he demanded. of others. and of himself.[6]

And it was through excercises like these that I discovered the Rajiv I knew. Six years-now wiped out in one blinding split- second of devastation. Perhaps it is the fact that he is now irrevocably gone and I shall never see him again that makes me recall, again and again, the Rajiv I knew in the aftermath of the assassination attempt on him at Rajghat on Gandhi Jayanti 1986. As an expert in ballistics (one of his many pastimes) knew exactly what had happened when the firing occured. He whispered into President Giani Zail Singh's cars that they must faster walk an send their families back before proceedings to Shantivana. With death having called but yards away, Rajiv kept him cool, gave precise instructions for the safety of others, refused to allow theleast race of panic or even concern to be reflected from the leadership to the people, and ensured normalcy by completing the entire programme laid on for the morning. A few hours later, we were airborne for Nagpur. He called me into his cabin and we were alone together almost all the way. We worked on the speech he was to deliver at Sewagram. He opened up to me about non- violence, of how true non-violence is when you don't ever desire revenge let alone seek revenge or inflict revenge on one who has raised his hand against you, for how the highest act of bravery is to remain non-voilent in the face of violence, of how it is by atoning for your own mistake that you can best make the "enemy" recognise the error of his ways. That long morning it was revelation for me to discover the extent to which Rajiv had observed the Gandhian ethic. Somebody had just tried to kill him-and would, but for a break, have succeeded. There was no animus in his heart or his voice against the man. Only a firm conviction, more firm than ever before, that violence leads to no solutions. He also spoke to me of the security arrangements. He said that none of this elborate aparatus was really going to protect him. The only protection was "up there", he said, pointing to the sky. When the time came he added, the time would come. Till then, there was somebody up there protecting him. The same evening he sat on a lighted stage looking down on an enormous crowd assembled in the main Nagpur Maidan for the cultural show inagurating the South-East Zonal Cultural Centre. He was a sitting target. The least I felt I could do was to stand behind him. The function lasted nearly two hours. He didn't once flinch. He did not once betray any nervousness. But his eyes must have searched the darkness for the killers hiding there. And in his heart and in his head, he knew that there were hundreds of crazened men and women plotting and

6. Mani Shankar Aiyar. The Rajiv I Knew *National Herald*, 28 May 1991

consipiring to finish him. He remained unfazed, unafraid, upright.[7]

Just before Rajiv was assassinated, he gave an interview to New York Times, who he said: "I have been on the road 23-and-a-half hours a day almost every day since the first of May. At the end, I am swollen and bleeding or have a cut arm. Here and in Kerala there is thick cheek-pinching. And sometimes in Muslim neighbourhoods they kiss me-you know one, two, three times, that special hug.

The country weeps. The world mourns. I feel a terrible emptiness within and there is no drowning this sorrow. At the moment our consolations are few, and torments many. When the tears have dried, the anger subsided, the horror diminished, the scar will remain. The shame will remain. So will the heartache. I ask myself, shell-shocked and benumbed, is this the land of the Buddha and Gandhi. India in my own lifetime has been an example to the world to be emulated. Are we today becoming a warning? Rajiv Gandhi was at the peak of his vigour. He died standing on his feet in the midst of the people he loved. He had a natural way of entrancing people, of offering affection, consolation. He had that rare and genuine gift to lift his followers up and provide them inspiration and hope. What scored on my mind was his composure, but even more appealing and refreshing was his youthful passion and engaging warmth of spirit. His assassination is a political watershed, no, it is a bloodstained blot on our democracy. History has been derailed and I do not know who will put it back on the rails. Political power now lies on the street for grabs by political tinsel. Already sinister forces, domestic and foreign are at work to destroy the Congress Party and the Nehru legacy. These must be crushed if this nation is to be saved. I cannot think of a more dismal national scenario. When Indira Gandhi was gunned down, the spring went out of my life. Now it seems, for us the clock has come to a grinding stop. When she departed we had Rajiv Gandhi to take up and carry forward her great work. Today alas! There is a vacant place across the horizon. He is irreplaceable. Why do I say that? Because with him are gone, decency and goodness in public life. With him have gone uprightness and tolerance. Gone is the hope for modernisation, for a technological an scientific revolution, gone the burning dedication to secularism, for Hindustaniyat (Indianness) and Insaniyat (mankind), Obscurantists, religious fanatics, narrow- minded bigots are on the prowl and they must not be allowed the upper hand. In his death he will continue to fight them as he did in life. We shall overcome. Fate holds all the cards. Against fate there is no armour. The Nehrus are a star crossed family. They attract the lightening. Only Motilal Nehru and Jawaharlal Nehru

7. *Ibid.*

died peaceful deaths. Sacrifice, supreme sacrifice comes to them naturally, that is why this country responds to them as to no one else. There is no parallel for this in history. It is unique.[8]

My first meeting with Rajiv Gandhi was in 1981 when as the President of the Kerala Students Union I invited him to add him to address a rally. He had just entered politics and what struck me most was his openness and simplicity. He was candid and forthright, yet gentle. We worked very closely during 1982-84 when I was president of the NSUI. We interacted for hours on end. What impressed me most was that he remained calm and unaffected even in moments interesting incidents I remember is that of the National Convention of the NSUI in 1984 in Nagpur. When we went to tender our resignations following certain adverse publicity, he told us with a twinkle in his eyes, "No, a man learns from every mistake he makes". In 1985, after I took over a general secretary of the Youth Congress and was selected to lead a delegation to China, he invited us for a cup of tea. He told us that China was an ancient nation with a unique socio-political system. He told us to see what we could learn and assimilate from them. That was Rajiv, always ready to learn from new experiences. In 1987, when I was 28, he made me a cabinet minister in Kerala. I was perhaps the youngest ever in India. He told me to take on the responsibility as it was essential that young people have administrative experience. One thing I will not forget is when he look time off his very heavy schedule in 1986 while the Muslim Personal Bill was being discussed in Parliament to attend my wedding reception. For him personal relationships came above everything else.[9]

It was the day after my swearing-in as parliamentary secretary, that I went to the Prime Minister for guidance. He said take decisions, the right decisions, and come to me only if you cannot decide. Mind you, he said, you will not make mistakes, but if you do, your neck will be out. It is with this confidence that he allowed us to work and take decisions without wavering. On the 10th May, 1991, he was in Mangalore to campaign. We received him at Talapady on the Kerala-Karnataka border. He got into our car and settled down in the front seat. But his head was about to hit the fan on the left side of the door. I held my hand and cautioned Rajiv, saying "Sir, mind your head." He paused and replied, "Yes, I will have to mind my head." These words sent shivers through me. I knew he was anticipating the worst of dangers. When we proceeded to Mangalore he wanted the security to be removed. He wanted to be with the people without any barriers; Chief Minister

8. K. Natwar Singh. Beloved Leader. *The Hindustan Times*, 26 May 1991.
9. Ramesh Chennithala. Personal Ties. *The Times of India*, 26 May 1991.

Bangarappa protested but Rajiv would not budge. I got the feeling that he was determined to be with the people come what may.[10]

Whatever few visitors met him were impressed by his calm polite behaviour and bewitched by him smile! The smile with which he climbed the steps of the rostrum at Sriperumbudur, on the night of May 21, 1991, ten years later. His mission in 1981 was to help his mother for the party, the mission that took him to his tragic end, was to help the party she had left behind to regain power. This 10 years span, on the one hand, marks the rise of a 36 years-old young man who gave the country an aura of youth, hope and confidence, during the crucial period when the older generation was being overtaken by him. Whether power came to him because of his emotional appeal or Indira Gandhi's legacy, the fact remains it was Rajiv, then inexperienced in the air of politics who traversed the meandering route to power to become Prime Minister and yet remain popular and charming. Those were the days, when an appearance of his would bring to a halt all activities, domestic or public, for they would all go to see him. His entry and adulatory acceptance of that was a high watermark in India's democratic polity where despite the violent end of a Prime Minister the transition of power remained smooth and peaceful. His macabre end, the most devastating act, marks on the other hand, a watershed in the country's politics. Why was a 46 year- old life full of vibrance and zeal cut short? He had shown, during these last 18 months, that it was not only the razzle- dazzle of power that has enable him to remain at the head of a monolith of a complex party like the Congress. He had also the resilience to withstand the loss of power--with a smile. He had not bowed under pressure, nor left the country's shore. The initial outburst of exuberance, the love for special imported cars, the excursions to exotic lands gave way to political maturity in handling both eagles and doves the Congress is surfeit with.[11]

The superthermal power stations was one of his first concepts, the bringing in of younger bureaucrats to key ministries was another bold attempt to give a push to a heaving bureaucracy in 1982. There was of course the British and Americans remark that it showed that India could be as modern and contemporary as any other developed country. In the summer of 1985, as one watched Ted Koppel throw questions at him at prime time in Rajiv Gandhi did every Indian proud. The smile bewitched the women on the streets and in Washington. A member of the Indian Prime Minister's party was showed preference and cooperation with such warmth and generosity that one wondered where one

10. Oscar Fernandes. I Must Mind My Head. *The Times of India*, 26 May 1991.
11. Vijay Dutt. The Smile is Gone. *The Hindustan Times*, 26 May 1991.

was really in the US. "He reminds us of our own president Kennedy." The smile had gone the trick. It is an irony that Rajiv was destined for a fate similar to that of Kennedy. These past months had made Rajiv realise that India lived beyond New Delhi. He had transited smoothly from the urban, upper-middle class public-school product and was transforming himself into a man of the masses. If the background of Doon School, Utter Pradesh was initially a handicap the early year at Teen Murti, New Delhi came in handy now.[12]

Anyone who knows the Rajiv Gandhi and family will tell you that the most striking thing about it is the obvious love and caring that pervades almost all its actions. The parents and the two kids spent as much time as they could doing things together- playing badminton, visiting their farmhouse, chatting. Whenever Rajiv said goodbye to guests at the door, he would hold on to Sonia as if she were all that mattered to him. This element of "touch" was true of the couple when they were newly-weds, and was true as recently as the day they cast their votes in New Delhi- Doordarshan footage shows Rajiv guiding Sonia's hand to the ballot box, besides a smiling Rajesh Khanna. These four Gandhis have always been tightly knit. Being for years, the only apolitical people in an especially political dynasty, the company of the pilot, his Italian-born wife and their son and daughter was often a refuge for Indira. And once the threat of assassination brought a security blanket around them, the family came even closer than before. Never did one of them behave as if they were scions of a ruthlessly calculating ruling elite. "They are like any other middle-class Indian," says a Gandhi intimate. They had the usual share of family problems and issues. I like all mothers, Sonia would open up the hems of the kids' school uniforms so that they could be used for a few months longer. Granny Indira would have none of that, insisting that new sets of uniforms be brought. But Sonia would make sure that her kids were not different from other children.[13] Rajiv was a doting yet firm father. One government officer who remembers the Gandhis visits abroad says that Rajiv Gandhi and Sonia would try to make sure that the kids were exposed to as much of the country's culture as possible, taking time to explain the various sights to them. Outside the Capital's Junior Modern School at Humayun Road, New Delhi, many parents arrive every morning to drop off their kids. In the late 70s, among the adults could be found one person dressed in casuals and mixing with fellor parents. The man, Rajiv Gandhi, who would drive up with his children in a Matador van, whenever he was in town. Misconceptions about Rajiv's children abou

12. *Ibid.*
13. Sreenath Sreenivasan. The Family Next-door. *The Sunday Observer*, 26 May 1991.

-nd. The general impresion is that they are snooty brats who speak only English. "Do Rahul and Priyanka have any friends," is a frequent query. Not only do the fluent Hindi-speaking 21-year- old Rahul and his younger sister have friends, but they also have social circle to equal that of any fellow college-goer. Their school and College friends visit the Gandhi home regularly. Youngsters who have been with Rahul and Priyanka recall how Rajiv was always friendly with them, joining table tennis and badminton games. Rajiv's influence on the behaviour of his son and daughter is obvious. Priyanka, a second year Psychology student at Jesus and Mary College, Delhi University who loves to eat *golgappas,* is an emotionally strong person. With her mother in a state of collapse and Rahul away in America, it was Priyanka who took charge of family matters after her father's death. Unlike the usual image of the spoiled VVIP son who barges into discos and picks fights, Rahul is a thorough gentleman. He is respectful towards the myriad aides and servants at home and addresses them only as "aap" (you) and "bhaiya" (brother). An avid sportsman who is an excellent shot, he has inherited Rajiv's love of fast cars. Part of Rahul's undergraduate course in Government at Harvard University deals with "International Terrorism" - an area of study in which he has shown special interest. Not only does he has no security detail in the United States, but many of his collegemates are not even aware who his father is. Earlier this year, the students of a Delhi University group invited the former Prime Minister for dinner and a discussion to its college. To everyone's surprise the invitation was readily accepted. While some less prominent personalities had earlier refused to address the group, here was a man accustomed to speaking before tens of thousands, willing to address an informal gathering of 100. Unfortunately, the programme-the dates chosen were initially February 26, and later, March 11-had to be deferred as just before the second, the fall of Chandra Shekhar's Government. Rajiv was extermely apologetic for the inconvenience and promised a rescheduling of the programme as soon as the political situation settled. The students were looking forward to meeting Rajiv when the new academic session began in July, 1991.[14]

And then there are tales of Rajiv's graciousness. When he hosted dinners for heads of government at Hyderabad House (which he modernised with cordless microphones and the like) New Delhi, he would always arrive a few minutes early, to make sure all the arrangements were alright Carpets would be straightened, and flowers rearranged under his direction. This eye for detail was something he acquired from his mother.At official dinners, he could be seen talking

14. *Ibid.*

to even the junior-most officers and their wives. He would always encourage everyone to mix around: "Don't make these ladies only groups," he would say.

At the airport during his 1985 state visit to Japan, the Prime Minister's plane had to return to the runway due to a technical snag. Everyone was expecting Rajiv to be furious; instead he was his smiling self. One of the members of his entourage nervously suggested that it was divine intervention that had ensured his safe landing. "This has nothing to do with divinity-it is just bad maintenance on the part on Air India," he remarked, instantly lightening a tense atmosphere. Sonia was a politician's wife who was not interested in politics, and didn't like being in the public eye. Her attention was focussed more on her children and her home. Nothing brought out her devotion to the family as clearly as her simply, yet tastefully, decorated house, filled with eight dogs and warmth. On the plane that brought Rajiv's body to the Capital, the coffins of Rajiv and his Personal Security Officer Pradeep Gupta, were lying near one another. While Rajiv's coffin had many flowers laid across the top, Gupta's was bare and neglected. When Sonia noticed this, she silently picked up a few of the flowers from her husband's coffin and placed it on top of Gupta's.[15]

I did not know Rajiv but I had a few opportunities to observe how sycophants-and regretably it includes some of the so-called journalistic elite (read courtiers) -ensured that the young man never really got down to sorting out the nitty-gritty of workaday problems facing the country. He was the leader and he like it to be said. More ominously, he liked to hear it. Came the fall, loss of office. And slowly, perceptibly a different Rajiv was taking shape. Only he was being more authoritarian in party matters, but overall there were signs of maturity for all to see. For one thing he became accessible, even to the non-conforming Press. He started doing his own sums and it was not such a bad idea for a man who until then had let others do the ground work, not all of them above board. This was the time when I came to understand Rajiv even without really knowing him. But even as he was evolving as a national leader in his own right he created quite a few enemies for himself and not all of them inherited from his mother's or brother's era. There were people who would have liked to see him removed from the scene. Well, he is no longer there. And that reminds me of one of the rare occasions I had to meet him. It was a dinner hosted by one of his chhota (small) colleagues in his Cabinet. The courteous host's attempt to introduce me to him was cut short by a familiar Rajiv one-liner preceded by a smile: "Of course, I know him and he is an angry man" I

15. *Ibid.*

am still angry with the intolerance, the violence that has eaten up the vitals of India that is Bharat.[16]

Words cannot describe the shock everyone felt at the news of the killing of Rajiv Gandhi in such tragic circumstances. That his death has created an extraordinary emotional upheaval among millions of people is a testimony to the powerful standing that Rajiv established among masses in such a short period. Rajiv, a leader in the Jawaharlal mould ritually bypassed security men and mingled with crowds. All along the election campaign trial he displayed a sort of craze for mixing with people. In an interivew he was asked why the Congress lost in 1989? His reply was "Somewhere, we lost communication with the people" and now while communicating with the people he was lost. In him we have lost yet another dynamic leader, a man of the masses. It is time to revive the Gandhian spirit, avoid ill-feelings, preserve unity and save the country drifting from the ideal of securalism.[17]

I really got to know Rajiv Gandhi in 1964 when my father stayed at Panditji's house after he came out of prison. We'd met before in Kashmir, but this was the first time I had a chance to know the man. There after we had little contact till my return in 1975 when my father took over. When I became Chief Minister, we met often, and developed a kind of rapport. I trusted him and he trusted me. Rajiv was someone you could talk to. I knew his mother, his grandfather. I knew Lal Bahadur Shastri, Morarji Desai and Chandra Shekhar. But Rajiv was more receptive. With him it was never a unidirectional talk. He would tell you his difficulties and how they could be removed for some ultimate aim, not his chair but for the nation. You could be frank with him, put your cards on the table. He liked people who called a space. And when I would butt in he would say, "Farooq, first listen to me, let me place the facts before you and then, let's talk." He had a patience I have rarely seen. He was totally modern in his thinking. He never cared what religion you belonged to, what language you spoke, the region you came from or your sub-caste. He was like Jawaharlal. His religion was India which was something I appreciated. I am a Muslim but I hate the fundamentalists. Like all his family, Kashmir had a special attraction for him. In 1988, when he came in through all that snow and was asked not to go any further than Banihal, the road being dangerous, he still insisted on going. He drove, and drove himself. He said he must go and see for himself the condition of the people in winter. He saw there was no electricity, no water, there was nothing. We were left to God. And in the villages his heart bled. He left Sarla Grewal there and ensured

16. M.L. Kotru. A Promise Unfulfilled. *Indian Express*, 26 May 1991.
17. Rajiv Gandhi. *The Hindu*, 25 May 1991.

everything was cleared in 12 hours. He made everybody work through the night.[18]

It was amazing how he mingled with the common people. I remember how once he stopped by at a *dhaba*. Over tea, he chatted with the people there, ignoring the securitymen. He asked them about their difficulties, what they thought he should do. And hugely enjoyed himself. You can imagine the reaction. Here was the Prime Minister of India casually chatting with the common people. He always had a smile on his face. Even in moments of crisis I have never seen Rajiv looking troubled or in turmoil. I will never forget how Rajiv helped me to remain outside the Chandra Shekhar government, although I had earlier agreed to join it. But in my heart of hearts I felt it wasn't right to come to Delhi when Kashmir needed me. I told Rajiv I would be grateful if he would speak to Chanera Shekhar first. On Mrs Gandhi's birth anniversary he caught hold of Chandra Shekhar at 1 Safdarjung Road saying, "Here's Farooq. He's told you he will join you and me that he does't want to because of Kashmir's pressing needs." They sought to convince each other, but eventually Chandra Shekhar agreed. The 1989 agreement between the National Conference and th Congress was an experiment Rajiv and I entered without eyes open. We saw a dnagerous divide approaching-religious and regional. We decided to come toghether not for party considerations but out of concern for the nation. Our trust was not betrayed. But we could not attain the speed with which we had to move. I don't blame Rajiv. There were several other people responsible for that experiment not taking off.[19]

Withj the death of Rajiv Gandhi the national pulse has stopped. Flowers have shrunk, petals dropped. Smiles have been replaced by screams, the illclad poor Indian is under stupor. He has perhaps lost the hopes of Panchayati Raj. The dusty Indian soil lies trampled under the asaults of traitors. In Rajiv Gandhi was the soul of nation. He was the fragrance and pride of India. He was a brilliant engineer who tackled the national problem ably. As we remember him droplets of tear go down the cheeks. Rajiv Gandhi was unparallel. His deep wishdom and nationalist zeal would always serve as valid reminders. The stars have dimmed and the moon has suffered an eclipse. While the great some has departed we should not forget his ideals. We should not forget his dreams to mame a stronger India. The country passes through a hard period. We must get over the crisis wisely. We must also preserve the peace and public order. The best condolence possible to Rajiv Gandhi would be to act unitedly against the forces of anti natio-

18. Farooq Abdullah. He was a Person. *The Sunday Observer*, 26 May 1991.
19. *Ibid.*

nalism. We all must shake off our false vanity and parochial setiments to build a bigger India.[20]

In the words of Simi Grewal, "He was such a courteous, warm and responsive human being. He had no pretensions what soever. It was the people around him who had the hang-ups."

Rajiv Gandhi loves masses, a champion of democracy and a person of rare courage and conviction.

Rajiv Gandhi was a gentleman, very much like his granfather, Jawaharlal Nehru. He was an extraordinary combination of two of the finest people I have known-Nehru, and his father, Feroze Gandhi. The first time I met him was during the Emergency when I was hitting the family hard-not Rajiv Gandhi, but Sanjay, V.C. shukla and others. I was invited to lunch by a dear friend of mine, Inder Chopra, who was in the foreign service, Romi Chopra's father. Then Rajiv and Sonia turned up. And I was surprised at his wit and humour, his grace and his smile. He was always smiling. This was a great trait of his. Even during the Bofors days, I always found him smiling. So, there I was, bashing his family. But I found that he was totally detached from the Emergency. In fact, I had feeling that he was agreeing with all that I said. That was the beginning of a genuine friendship. Two or three months ago, after he heard that I was ill, he sent this very expensive, American medicine for meningitis to Bombay through Murli Deoras. We could not use them, because I had a different kind of meningitis. Then he came himself to see me at the Breach Candy hospital in Bombay. After his visit, everything changed for me. Suddenly I became some kind of a prime ministerial patient. None of us can forget that visit; he was so charming, so gracious, a gentleman to his finger-tips. I remember the campassion, the feeling. He was a friend, a gentleman, politician, statesman and a man of tremendous compassion. That was the last time I met him.[21]

He took so much interest when I started The Daily. It was a great success but I had to sell it because I could not afford to run it. He took such interest because it was something new. He loved things young and new. This was tabloid journalism and he wanted to know all about it. He read it avidly, and when I could not afford it any more, he did not let it die-he helped me. I found no change in him even when he was out of power. I fact, for me, he was always the Prime MInister. Very often, while talking to his secretary, George, I would say "Can I speak to the Prime Minister?" and there would be laughter. It was not something artificial, this was no maska-polish. It was just something natural. He

20. Rajiv K. Dikshit. Pride of India. *National Herald,* 25 May 1991.
21. R.K. Karanjia. A Gentleman to His Fingertips. *The Sunday Observer,* 26 May 1991.

was the Prime Minster, that is all. The ideal Prime Minister India has had. The most important thing was that he realised he had made mistakes. And if he had come back, I know Rajiv would have changed the system; completely revolutionalised it.[22]

Rajiv Gandhis sacrifice will have been in vain if Congressmen do not engage themselves seriously in restoring the national consensus, the disruption of which caused his death in the first place. In his death he has intervened on a scale reserved for epics in the caste and communal strife that was the stuff of the elections being contested. It devolves on his partymen to further arrest the nosedive and recover the mideleground that once belonged to the Congress. This will be a suitable tribute to Rajiv Gandhi. How whould Congressmen address themselves to this task? The year 1967 was the first assult on the Congress monolith. That year began the authoritarian phase in Congress rule when Indira Gandhi split the party and centralised authority. Part of the subsequent history consisted in ex- Congressmen regrouping with Lohia socialists on the one had and the Jana Sangh on the other, with the CPI-M often finding itself in this company because of its compulsions in Kerala and West Bengal to attack Congress citadel. Over a period of time, the anti-Congress stance of this opposition transformed itself into exasperation with the stranglehold of the Nehru-Gandhi dynasty on both the Congress and the Delhi gaddi (seat). We were a feudal as well as a Hindu society. We were confortable with dynastics and we defied our leaders, placet them on a pedestal from which they could not be dislodged. It was the ingenuity of the anti Congress mind that brought to the centre stage a retiring Jayaprakash Narayan to counter Indira Gandhi's charisma. JP had renounced power and renunciation was the stuff for deification. It was in the crucible of the Bihar movement that the Janata Party was forged. Pressure was applied on Indira Gandhi. She blundered on with the Emergency, pacing the way for the Janata victory in 1977. Since the welding was imperfect, the Janta Party broke up and Indira Gandhi regained power from 1980 untill her assassination in 1984. Two important trends emerged, which Congressmen would do well to bear in mind: One, Indira Gandhi's national coalition consisted of sprinkling of brahmins at the apex with harijans, backwards, minorities and other castes forming the bulk of this coalition.[23]

Rajiv Gandhi had the stature to carry with him men like Ghulam Nabi Azad, Shiv Shankar and Pranab Mukherjee who had no political base whatsoever. The new leader must have a political base. He must

22. *Ibid.*
23. Saeed Naqvi. The Task Before Congressmen. *The Independent.* 24 May 1991.

represent social groups that have come under the sway of Mandal. Once the contentious edge is taken off Mandal as a means of political mobilisation, the consolidation behind the *mandir* will not seem quite as menancing and confrontationalist. In pursuit of a mature, effect leadership, the party may have to open its doors to those who had strayed away earlier. This is the way to build on Rajiv Gandhi's tragic death.[24]

"Don't mention that I no longer wear a bullet-proof vest. But yes, I have shed it, "Rajiv Gandhi, once the country's most heavily-guarded politician, candidly said. In any case, it seemed obvious as the hordes of ecstatic men and women squeezed close to him, clutching at him and practically pulling his white Kurta off his shoulder while he smilingly elbowed his way through the masses crowd to reach the dais in Bhilwara in early May, 1991. By the time he reached Madras, after a gruelling month- long schedule, the security forces had resigned themselves and helplessly watched him plung enthusiastically into the crowd. In Jaipur, a couple of weeks before, the police had resorted to a light lathi charge as hundreds of people mobbed him. But he had stopped them. At Ajmer as scores of excited young men clambered on to his jeep inching its way through a packed crowd to the Dargah, Rajiv clamed a hysterical police force "No don't stop them," he said as they pressed forward in hundreds to garland him, to apply a *tilak* on his forehead and place on his head the traditional *Rajasthani Safa.* And he in a gesture reminiscent of his mother Indira Gandhi, graciously threw back the garlands at the women and children.[25]

Whether it was in Aligarh, Varanasi or Bhilwara, at a public meeting Rajiv would call out: "Let the women come near," waving aside the security forces. Apparently, Election Commissioner T.N. Seshan, who had earlier been responsible for Rajiv Gandhi's security when he was Prime Minister, had repeatedly warned him. But for Rajiv the choice was stark. In the 1989 elections, the electorate had rejected the aloof and arrogant Rajiv Gandhi. Surrounded by the security forces, Rajiv remained cut off from the people he had earlier disarmed by his open and accessible style of compaigning in 1984.[26]

But in the April-May-run up to the 1991 polls the accessible Rajiv was back, capaigning as he had in 1984 before he became Prime Minister, putting his faith in the dictum that political leader is safest among his own people. His personalised style was interlaced this time with some of the tried and tested flourishes of Indira Gandhi's camp-

24. *Ibid.*
25. Rita Manchanda, The Last Campaign. *The Sunday Observer*, 26 May 1991.

aigning style. There was the torch which she shone on her face as she sat in the front seat of an Ambassador diriving through the night. And of course her characteristic gesture of flinging back the garlands at women and children, the jai hind raised at the end of the meeting. Like her, on the trail Rajiv never tired of stopping, of getting out of the car to greet the clusters of people gathered all along the way. A couple of kilometres drive into the city could easily take over two hours. He would plunge headlong into an *enthusistic crowd,* make an unscheduled stop at a roadside *dhaba* to amiably chat with a student, a local shopekeeper or a farmer, to share their problems, to, for a moment, make them feel that they mattered to this patient, ever-smiling man who rivalled the good looks and charisma of a film star. And there was also the distinct Rajiv touch. Whether it was a car or a plane Rajiv Gandhi quite habitually would take the wheel. To sriperumbudur too he drove himself while he informally chatted with two journalists. It was Rajiv Gandhi who had popularised the practice of the relay interview in the car adopted subsequently by all other major leaders. Gone was his aloofness, and in Amethi, Rajiv Gandhi could be seen casually sharing a fistful of *chana* (gram) with a photographer, the only food any of them had all that day. Gone too was his peremptory arrogance and impatience with local Congress leaders. At Bhilwara, a local Congress leader mentioned to Rajiv Gandhi that he had organised an impromptu meeting with some Congressmen 25 kms away. The old Rajiv would have had no time for such a meeting. Besides, he was running several hours late. But Rajiv found the time [27]

Rajiv was the unrivalled star campaigner of the 1991 elections, but whether his personal popularity, his film star-royalty appeal would be translated into votes for the Congress candidates, was an open question. What kept him going-with barely three or four hours of sleep campaigning for 20 hours a day in the heat and dust? Rajiv laughed and drew into the conversation fellow Congressmen sitting with us in the Contessa car. "Ask him, he has been doing this for over 20 years," he said. "It is the people's enthusiasm, their love, their response that gives you the energy to keep going", said Rajiv.[28]

Rajiv Gandhi's weakness as a result of lack of experience and natural feel for politics had become obvious during his period of apprenticeship to his mother. He had surrounded himself with his equally inexperienced frinds and cronies who were strangers to Congressmen and the party's tradition and culture, shown scant respect for old party veterans and displayed a strong preference for computer culture. His

27. *Ibid.*
28. *Ibid.*

installation in the office of Prime Minister did not persuade him to try and overcome these weakness. Instead they got reinforced. The best in Rajiv Gandhi surfaced on the occasion of the tragedy of his mother's assassination. He bore the pain in his heart with a stoicism and quiet dignity which was particularly impressive precisely because it is so rare in India. Rajiv Gandhi did not act unflappable. He was unflappable. He was not out to prove that there was a young man the country could trust as it faced an uncertain future on account of the growing Pakistan-backed terrorist-seccessionist threat in Punjab and the impasse in Assam. He is made that way. He was being the natural self. Millions of fellow-Indians, who, thanks to the vastly expanded Doordarshan newtwork saw him perform his mother's last rite with certain dignity, were overwhelmed by his demostration of quiet courage and cast him in the saviour's role. This obviated the need for Rajiv Gandhi to engage in self-introspection, realise his inadequacies for the awesome responsibilities that a cruel fate had heaped on him, look for experience, such as was still available in the Congress, and respect it. The foundation for the troubles which burst on him in 1987 had been well and truly laid in 1984-85. When the explosion occured in 1987 in the shape of V.P. Singh's deliberate and well- planned challenge to him and was followed by a detrrioration in Rajiv Gandhi's relations with the then President of the republic, Zail Singh, who finally claimed the right to dismiss him, Rajiv Gandhi did not lose his nerve. I met him a number of times in the evening after head had a most gruelling day in Parliament and every time I always found him relaxed, friendly and communicative. His handling of problmes was, as is widely recognised, messy and less than competent. But if he was not a natural warrior, he was no deserter eithre. Those who believed he would quit politics and even leave India in the wake of defeat in 1989 did not know the man. The 1984 mandate was frightening development. Implicit in it was a level of popular desperation and expectation no one could possibly have coped with and fulfilled. It should have frightened Rajiv Gandhi. I doubt if it did. On the contrary it exhilarated him as it could exhilarate only a movie in the dangerous world of popular passions and power.[29]

29. Girilal Jain. Neither a Fighter Nor a Deserter. *The Sunday Mail* 26 May 1991.

8
GREAT EXPECTATIONS

It is ironic, that Rajiv Gandhi should have fallen a victim to violence which he had tried to put an end to by signing four accords during his Prime Ministreship (1984-89).

The first of the accords, the high points of his regime, was on Punjab which he signed with Akali leader Sant Harchand Singh Longowal on July 24, 1985 in a bid to end over a decade of terrorism in the State.

Assembly elections were subsequently held in Punjab on July 24, 1985. The Akalis won the elections and formed a Government. The accord and the elections resulted in a sudden steep fall in terrorist activities. Peace, however, remained elusive as the full implementation of the accord got bogged down by one controversy or the other.

Terrorism returned gradually to the State with renewed vigour making it difficult for the State Government to function. As a result the state was again placed under President's rule on May 1, 1987.

Rajiv Gandhi ended the six-year-old Assam Students' agitation on the foreign nationals issue by signing an accord with the All Assam Student's Union (AASU) on August 15, 1985.

This was also followed by Assembly elections in the State on December 16 the same year. An Asom Ganga Parishad (AGP) Government was formed on December 22, 1985.

Like Punjab, the north-eastern state also ran into rough weather over the implementation of the accord with the state Government accusing the Prime Minister of draging his feet on the Centre's obligations under the accord. The AGP later became a constituent of National Front.

The situation had come a full circle in the state when the Chandra Shekhar Government dismissed the AGP Government headed by P.K. Mahanta and placed the state under President's rule, charging that the state Administration had failed to check the militancy of the United Liberation Front of Assam.

Mizoram come next on the accords. Rajiv Gandhi signed the Mizoram accord with Mizo Ntional Front supremo Laldenga on June 30, 1986, putting an end to the thirty-year-old insurgency in the then Union Territory.

On August 21, 1986 Laldenga, who had been leading the insurgency, formed a coalition Government with the Congress, pending elections.

In the elections, held on February 16, 1987, the MNF was returned to power. Laldenga assumed office as Chief Minister as the head of the MNF Ministry and Mizoram became a full-fledged State.

The Laldenga Government however did not last long and the MNF was defeated in the elections held on January 21, 1989 in which the Congress won a majority.

The last in the series of agreements reached by Rajiv Gandhi was the Indo-Sri Lanka accord, aimed at ending the ethnic conflict in the island nation.

He signed the accord on July 20, 1987 with the then Sri Lankan President J.R. Jayawardene. This was followed by another on July 28, 1989 which promised to ease the tension in the two countries' relations and raised hopes of an end to the Sri Lankan Tamils problem there.

The agreement had also envisaged phased withdrawal of the Indian Peace Keeping Force (IPKF) from Sri Lanka beginning from Jyly 29. But it did not come about due to various reasons.

The actual withdrawal of the IPKF began on October 16, 1989 as per another agreement reached earlier on September 18.

Despite these accords violence remained unabated in Sri Lanka with the Liberation Tigers in Tamil eelam persisting with its demand for an independent Tamil in the island nation.

The LTTE issue also led to the dismissal of the Dravida Munnetra Kazagam Government headed by M. Karunanidhi in Tamilandu. The Chandra Shekhar Governmetn at the Centre placed the State under President's rule charging the Karunanidhi regime with aiding the subversive activities of the LTTE.

The Government of India, on May 21, 1991 declared a 7-day state mourning as a mark of respect to former Prime Minister Rajiv Gandhi.

All Central and State Government offices, school and colleges remained close on May 22.

A combination of idealism lack of political-maturity and eageneress for quick-fix results explains why so many of his warmly applauded initiatives-notably the accord on Punjab and Assam and the power-sharing agreement with the National Conference in Kashmir-turned sour. As against this he was able to find a peaceful solution to the Gorkha and Mizo agitations. It is that same combination which accounts for the misadventure in Sri Lanka. On the foreign policy front as a whole, Rajiv Gandhi's performance was, however, most creditible and, on occasions, even brilliant. The six-nation, five-continent initiative, the Delhi declaration, the initiatives regarding South Africa, the positions on North-South issues-all testify to his stubborn belief that

India should speak witth a distinctive voice in the concert of nations. This mixed legacy reveals much that can stand the country in good stead as it emerges from the trauma of Rajiv Gandhi's assassination. India years for order, stability, security and growth. These will be difficult to come unless our leadership is endowed with a dynamic and caring vision of the state and society, a clarity of prupose, an experienced understanding of how our system operates and how it can be changed, with decisiveness, flexibility, drive and energy. Rajiv Gandhi possessed some of these qualities in good measure. Some others he did not possess. But his qualities as well as this drawbacks, his achievements and his failure, his promises and his inability to delivery on them, all taken together, constitute a precious storehouse of insigh's and pointers to how India can survive and florish in the future.[1]

The large-scale violence in Andhra Pradesh that followed the assassination of Rajiv Gandhi puts the question mark on the claim of Chief Minister J. Janardhan Reddy that the Government took prompt and effective steps to prevent the sampage by vandals. The decision of the State Government to institute a judicial inquiry into the incidents of the demands of Telgu Desam leader N.T. Rama Rao (NTR) but it can also be seen as an effort to shift responsibility of a serious failure. Some people turned a tragedy into an occasion for attacking political rivals with impunity. These should be arrainged for their offences. The decision of TDP leader NTR to go on an indefinite fast is clearly an over- reaction. He has reason to be aggrieved. But intemperate words and violent deeds have become parts of our contemporary political culture, and all parties are guilty of them. Rajiv Gandhi's assassination has generated what is said to be a sympathy wave, and NTR fears that the Congress would benefit. NTR's fast would thus be seen as a step determined by electioneering. Rama Rao should call off the fast since the Government has conceded his demand for inquiry. His anguish, however, is understandable as his own property as well as the property of his party have been damaged and looted by the unruly and allegedly Congress mobs. Of course the State Government bears the responsibility for failing to stop violence that played havoc with the lives of many. Now, even belatedly, it must see that the law takes its own course and the guilty are punished and government efforts are sincerely made in that behalf. It is inexplicable why the State Government has not acted against those whose participation in the acts of violence has been corroborated by the policemen present on the spot. Not a single arrest has been made, despite clear evidence that violence was directed

1. *The Times Of India*, 25 May 1991.

against selected targets. The Government has not even spelt out the time in which the enquiry committee should give its finding. All this indicates non- seriousness in the government attitude. The TDP and its allies have reason to fear that tide of sympathy might give the Congress the bulk of the remaining 25 Lok Sabha seats for which the polls are due on June 15. The Congress leaders have been meticulously keeping the assassination as the main talking points. The passage of the urn containing the ashes of Rajiv Gandhi throughout the state before immersing the remains into the Godavari river is partly political demonstration. Special arrangements have been made for the movement of the procession bearing the urn through those districts which are of vital importance because of the boycott call given by the PWG (People's War Group) activists. Though such moves probably are to be considered natural in India's current political style, these offend the basic values-the sanctity attached to grief and respecting Rajiv Gandhi's death as a national tragedy, above partisan quarrels of the moment. The TDP and allies have worked out a plan to foil the attempt. Their trump card is the counter campaign to export the misdeeds of the ruling party.[2]

There were grief and sympathy in Assam over the tragic death of Rajiv Gandhi.

There were sizable crowds at the local party headquarters in Guwahati almost throughout the day. At Silchar, party supproters and people took out a procession this afternoon, according to reports reaching the State Capital.

State Congress chief Hiteswar Saikia, who was campaigning in Nagaon, left for Delhi. "It is a great loss for us", he said.

Assam Gana Parshad leader and former Chief Minister Prafulla Mahanata said that the death represented a threat to democracy. The Centre, he felt, must be more careful not to allow such incidents to recur. Tamil Nadu was after all under Central rule.

Janata Dal chief Golap Borbora also codemned the killing and said it was a sad demise for the former Prime Minister. Pankaj Bora of the Congress(S) said that the incident was most unfortunate. United People's Congress of Assam leader Phani Sarma felt that democracy itself had ended in India. Bharatiya Janata Party leader H. Bhattacharya said that the killing must be condemend with all the vehemence one could muster.

The administration alerted the police to prevent any outbreak of violence. The day remained incident free, with educational institutions remaining closed.

2. *Patriot*, 1 June 1991.

Leaders of various political parties expressed shock at the brutal assassination of Rajiv Gandhi. Strongly condemening the incident, prominent leaders of all parties urged that those responsible be caught and punished.

Bhartiya Janata Party (BJP) national secretary Madan Lal Khurana, stating that he was shocked, said political assassinations have no place in democracy. He appealed to the people to maintain peace at this time of national crisis and regretted that some Congress workers were shipping up anti BJP feelings over the issue. Khurana said he had asked Lt. Governor Markandey Singh to take steps to prevent violence in Delhi.

BJP Delhi unit president Prof. O.P. Kohli said it was a dastardly and cowardly act to be condemned by all. Extending deep sympathy and condolence for Rajiv Gandhi's family on behalf of this party, Prof. Kohli said people should exercise restrain and ensure tht there is peace.

Congress's South Delhi candidate for the Lok Sabha poll Romesh Bhandari called it a pre-planned brutal assassination and a part of a diabolical plan to subvert the democratic process in the country. The Congress(I) Workers should maintain peace and harmoney in their respective areas by forming mohalla peace committees, he added.

All-India Mahila Congress-I joint secretary Kiran Choudhury expressed shock and sorrow at Mr. Gandhi's killing. It has been a great loss to the nation and the party, more so to the cause of uplifting women. It will be difficult to fill the varcum he has left behind, she added.

Rajya Sabha member from Haryana Surinder Singh describign Rajiv Gandhi as a great leader said with his death the nation has suffered an irreparable loss.

Former President Zail Singh said the sad demise of Mr. Gandhi was a great shock. He appealed to the people to make all effort to maintain tranquaility and expressed hope that the democratic process will be completed undisturbed.

Describing, Rajiv Gandhi's killing as "outrageous", Indian Union Muslim League General Secretary G.M. Banatwalla said his passing away has caused irreparable loss to the country.

Condemning the murder Vishwa Hindu Parishad General secretary Ashok Singhal said terrorism and democracy could not go along together. He asked the people to maintain harmony and restraint.

Indian Council of World Affairs president Harcharan Singh Joshi said Rajiv Gandhi had remained vice-president of the ICWA from 1982 to 1986. Congress workers took out a peace march in Kamla Nagar area in tribute to Rajiv Gandhi.

The Delhi Pradesh Janata Dal condemned the killing and said people should ensure that peace is maintained.

President Shiromani Akali Dal (Master Tara Singh) Jathedar Rachhpal Singh said Rajiv Gandhi's death has left a void cannot be filled.

Convenor Quami Mushawarat Committee Jawed Habeed expressed shock over Rajiv Gandhi's killing.

Habeeb said when the nation was going through the traumatic experience of unprecedented communal strife people should not give in to blind rage all instead maintain restrain and peace.

Vice-President All-India Hindu Mahasabha Indrasen Sharma termed in inhuman and extended condolence to the grieved family members. The Sant Nirankari Mandal sent a telegram to Sonia Gandhi condemning the brutal murder and extending condolences.

The BJP Delhi unit in an emergency working committee meeting held today condoled the sudden and dastradly demise of Rajiv Gandhi expressing deep anguish over the dastardly act. The passing away of Rajiv Gandhi is an irreparable loss to the nation. Condemning his assassination the BJP meet appealed to the people to remain calm and not fall prey to any excitement.

Delhi Pradesh Congress Committee President Prem Singh appealed to the people to maintain peace and harmony at all costs so that the dream of India's "great son", Rajiv Gandhi to keep the country united remained with all and any kind of aggressive passion, hatredness and violence could be avoided.

He said the death of our beloved Indian leader was the greatest tragedy happened in the history of independent India. Rajiv Gandhi was a symbol of peoples dream of India as a great nation on the world map. With his death the whole nation, time and history of coming era was bowed to salute the great son of India.

The Khidmatgar Committee expressed deep anguish and shock at the killing of Rajiv. Condemning the brutal and heinous crime. Committee president Mohammad Taqi said the sad news had made him deaf and dumb.

The central committee of the Communist Party of India. (Marxisit Leninist) condemned the bomb blast which killed Rajiv Gandhi and said the killing of political parties' leaders was not the way of political struggle.

The Samajwadi Janata Party called the assassination of Rajiv Gandhi a deep rooted conspiracy which had robbed one of the bravest and brightest sons of the soil. A greatful nation can never forget the manifold services rendered Rajiv Gandhi for the people. The best tribute for him will be to struggle against the communal, separatist forces and help maintain the secular character of the country.

Vice-Chairman of Kisan Congress, Romesh Sharma, has urged the President to suspend the elections all over the country in view of the caretaker government's inability to manage law and order situation. The convenor of the Teachers cell of AICC, Dr. S.S. Rathi, has stated that Mr. Gandhi was the prime target of the conspirators trying to divide the country. "Unfortuantely certain political forces are providid-ing strength to these international conspirators."

Several social organisations including the Citizens for Democracy, PUCL, Radical Hamanist Association, YWCA of India, and Sam-poorn Kranti Manch have expressed deep shock over the assassination of Mr. Gandhi. In a joint press release, they have apealed to the people to maintain communal harmony and peace and to fight against all efforts to incite passions against any section of people.

The people of Haryana were shocked and grieved to hear the news about the assassination of Rajiv.

It was only a few days ago that he freely mingled with the people of the State. During his election campaign he addressed several public meetings throughout the State. And it was at these meetings that he tried to establish mass contacts.

There was no security cordon around him and the people had given him a rousing welcome everywhere he went.

Meanwhile, curfew has been imposed in Ambala and Sirsa districts as a precautionary measure. While the curfew in Sirsa is for 12 hours from this morning, the furfew in Ambala is for an indefinite period.

The Haryana roadways buses did not ply and elaborate police arrangements were made to prevent any untoward incident. The repolling in 12 booths of Haryana have been postponed. It was schedeled for May 22.

Leaders of different political parties held an all-party meeting at Ambala and Rohatak and condemned the assassination.

Leaders of different political parties including Bansi Lal of Haryana Vikas Party expressed shock and condemned the dastardly act.

In a statement, Bansi Lal condemned the assassination and ap-pealed to the people to maintain peace.

The Haryana Pradesh Congress Committee (HPCC) mourned the assassination of Rajiv and strongly condemed the barbaric act which has brought the country to the worst point of its history.

Birender Singh, the president of the HPCC in a Press statement has expressed great shock and anguish over the cowardly act and said the assassination of Rajiv at a time when the country was anxiously looking towards him for stability, after a spell of chaotic political unertainty it witnessed during the last one and a half year's Janata Dal and Janata Dal-S regimes, has inflicted a great blow to the democratic polity of India.

Rajiv Gandhi, symbol of India's unity and national integrity led the country at the most critical and difficult moments after Indira Gandhi's assassination and provided a stable and clean Government from 1984 to 1989. The country made all round strides during his stewardship. His assassination at the hands of anti- national elements, out to destabilise the country, has come as a national calamity and the great void caused would be difficult to fill, the Haryana PCC chief asserted and said that in the death of Rajiv Gandhi, the country has lost a great leader, a benefactor of the poor and the downtrodden and a chamption of world peace.

Former HPCC President Shamsher Singh, expressed deep anguish and shock on the barbarous assassintion of Rajiv Gandhi at the hands of enemies of the nation and democracy.

He said that this is the greatest ever tragedy faced by the nation and added that countrymen and the Congressmen particularly should rise to the occasion to face the challenge.

An emergent meeting of the Haryana Pradesh Congress-I Committee (HPCC-I) was held on May 23, 1991 to condole the assassination of Rajiv Gandhi.

The meeting noted with concern that at a time when stability and governance of the nation was formost on the national agenda, the forces of destabilisation, internal as well as external, struck the deadliest blow by killing Rajiv Gandhi.

"Mr. Gandhi had become the symbol of stability, communal harmony, unity and integrity of the country. The forces of destabilisation struck at a time when the Congress-I was at the threshold of forming a stable Government. The assassination of Rajiv Gandhi has once again vindicated the stand of the party that it alone can fight the divisive forces", the party said.

The meeting paid homage to the departed leader for the services rendered by him to the country and its people.

On May 24, 1991 when Rahul was lighting the pyre. I remembered my father, the way he must have felt when Jawaharlal Nehru was cremated. Nehru also wanted that India should get on with modernisation and make progress shunning all the weaknesses away. I was thinking, "Oh my God, how much Rajiv had learnt in these 15 months of opposition! And how much of it he was going to put in action!" How cruel sometimes God can be. He removed Jawaharlal Nehru at that time. And today, when the country is in far greater danger than it was in 1964.....Here was a man who had learnt from his mistakes. He had learnt to listen and then to think himself, which is a big achievement. And there are very few people who accept that they have made mistakes. The biggest thing about him which I felt whenever I met him is that he was never down in the dumps. The enthusiasm he generated gave you such encouragement that you came back with greater strength after meeting him. And he was a person who could listen, whom one could tell one's inner feelings. Now when he is no longer with us, one remembers so many things. Once he told me how the kashmir tangle was near its solution and the Siachin issue had been absolutely cleared between India and Pakistan and maps and charts had been drawn, when suddenly Zia went away and it was switched off. Recently he went to Iran and won another friend for India.[3]

On December 8, 1986, he was to come to Kashmir for a function of the agricultural university. It had snowed very heavily. From Leh, he flew to Srinagar but could not land there. So, the flight had to be diverted to Udhampur. From there, he drove. The security personnel told him he could not go further.

But he said he had to reach. So the large stones were continuously blasted to clear the roads and he kept driving and somehow reached Srinagar. Because there was heavy snow. Srinagar was without water and electricity. And then he said to me. "Farooq, today for the first time I am realising what the people of this state must be going through, the kind of misery they have to suffer." The next day, we took him to show a bridge at Pampore. Where we stopped stood a small dhaba. Its owner, and old man, came up to Rajiv and said, "Will you have a cup of tea at my dhaba? And Rajiv said, "I will have tea at your dhaba on the condition, that you give me the Kashmiri bread too." Look at the humaneness of the fellow. Here was the Prime Minister of India having tea at a dhaba. Later we started for Gulmarg but could not reach there because of bad road conditions. So we stayed at Tangmarg. Here one could see the family man. Here were Rajiv, Rahul and Priyanka throwing snowballs at one another.[4]

3. Farooq Abdullah. A Man who Learnt His Lesson. *The Times Of India*, 26 May 1991.
4. *Ibid.*

About 200 Pakistan-trained militants held a condolence meeting in a jail near Jammu to mourn the death of Rajiv Gandhi.

They observed a two-minute silence in memory of the later leader.

A resolution adopted at the meeting recalled Rajiv Gandhi's attachement with Kashmir, as one who wanted to see the Kashmir Valley prosperous and said in his death the state had suffered a great loss.

As many as 15 Kashmiri youths spoke on the occasion and paid tributes to Rajiv Gandhi.

Destiny had it say in the case of Congress president Rajiv Gandhi.

Soon after addressing an election meeting Rajiv Gandhi drove straight to the airport to fly to Madras by a special chartered plane.

As he reached the airport, the crew members informed him that the flight might not take off as the engine had developed some snag. Visibly upset, Rajiv Gandhi decided to stay in the circuit house overnight.

Even before Rajiv Gandhi reached the circuit house, along with others, came a message that the snag had been set right and the flight was ready to take off. Then, Rajiv Gandhi rushed back to the airport and boarded the flight.

Kerala Pradesh Congress Committee president A.K. Antony described the assassination of Rajiv Gandhi as a great loss to the nation and said that if he had come back to power this time he could have done many good things for the country.

Chief Minister E.K. Nayanar has expressed his deep anguish at the brutal assassination which he described as "most unfortunate".

The former Kerala Chief Minister said, Rajiv Gandhi was a fearless and thorough gentleman politician. He said that in the Congress election manifesto, Rajiv Gandhi had promised so many good things for the benefit of the people.

Antony recounted his days as the party's general secretary when he had the privilege of working with Mr. Gandhi and added that the latter was very kind to his co-workers.

The KPCC-I president said that after the 1989 Lok Sabha poll debacle, Rajiv Gandhi tried to avoid security cordons around him because he wanted to mingle with the common people. Untimely death was the price he had to pay for his eagerness to mingle with the people, he added.

Later, Antony left for Delhi to attend the Congress Working Committee meeting to decide about the funeral proceedings and a new leader. Opposition leader in the State Assembly K. Karunakaran has already left for Delhi.

Madhya Pradesh Chief Minister Sunderlal Patwa opposed the Election Commission's decision deferring the Lok Sabha poll to June 12 and 15 following the assassination of Rajiv Gandhi.

Keeping in view the duration of national mourning, he felt that there was no need to postpone the elections for such a long time.

He told newsmen here that he had talked to his central party leadership which assured him to take up the matter with the Election Commission.

He parried the question whether the incident would affect the election result, saying "wait and see."

He, however, said he had full faith in the conscience of the people who, he felt, would take a proper perspective of the issue. He observed that it was not an electoral issue in any way.

"Describing the assassination as a "violent blow" to democracy, Patwas called for a united effort by all political parties to check recurrence such heinous crimes.

Almost all the towns and cities observed a bandh in Madhya Pradesh to mourn the death of Rajiv Gandhi.

Section 144 of C-PC has been promulgated in about ten towns as precautionary, measures. The towns include Indore, Ujjain, Bhind, Jabalpur, Bilaspur, Sagar and Morena.

In several places BJP workers were made the target by the agitated Congressmen. In Piparia an attempt was made to set ablaze the house of the BJP, Legislative Member Murli Dhar Maheshwari.

In Bilaspur, Sagar and Ujjain some buses were damaged by the supporters of Rajiv Gandhi. In Indore a minor lathi charge was made to disperse the unruly crowd in the Rajwada area. Chief Minister Sunder Lal Patwa on his return from his election tour straightway drove to the BJP office to take stock of the situation arising of the assassination of Rajiv Gandhi. He issued a Press statement condemning the brutal murder of Rajiv.

The president of the Madhya Pradesh Congress Committee Arjun Singh who had reached Bhopal after his hectic election tour left for Delhi to attend the meeting of the Congress working Committee. He described the assassintion of Rajiv Gandhi as: 'cowardice and henious'.

The Congressmen in the State wearing black stips took out a silent procession in many parts of the state. Several state congress leaders have expressed their giref over the demise of Rajiv Gandhi.

Mizo National Front president Zoramthanga expressed his sorrow and anguish over the brutal assassination of Rajiv "the architect of many peace accords".

In a condolence meeting held at the MNF party office at Aizawi, Mizoram Soramthanga said Rajiv Gandhi brought peace to the trouble-torn State by singing the Mizo accord with the underground MNF in 1986.

The situtation in this noisy town took a violent turn soon after the news about Rajiv Gandhi's killing in a bomb blast was heard. Congress sympathisers went berserk and ransacked the offices of the CPI in the town and indulged in heavy stoning of vehicles entering the town.

Tension in Aska, Kerala was much greater. The whole town observed a bandh as the Congress workers protested against the killing of their party president.

Chief Minister Biju Patnaik lashed out against the murderers of Rajiv Gandhi and said that he would like the investigating agencies to "take every possible step to locate the culprits, bring them to book and hand them."

Addressing a Press conference, the Chief Minister said he was terribly upset at the murder of Rajiv Gandhi and described it was a deliberate act of conspiracey to kill. "My heart goest out to Sonia Gandhi and the children who I hope will be able to bear this great loss", he said.

Janata Dal leader and Orissa chief minister Biju Patnaik is a worried man today. He has every reason to be one. The cruel assassination of Rajiv Gandhi at a time when Patnaik was creating a favourable wave for his party in the state has come upset the Janata Dal's calculations there. The poll outcome may be a repeat of 1984 when the Congress bagged 20 of 21 Lok Sabha seats in the state thanks to the sympathy wave which swept the country in the wake of Indira Gandhi's assassination. The Dal leader, however, discounts such a possibility in Orissa on the ground that the situation is not like which prevailed in 1984. Even the induction of Sonia Gandhi as the Congress chief would have done little to improve the party's chances, Patnaik points out. Patnaik's strong objection to the polling date in the state being deferred from May 26 to June 15, 1991 clearly indicates his assessment of the present situation. The septuagenarian chief minister fears a downslide in the tempo his party had been building up till date. In the 1989 Lok Sabha poll, Patnaik led the Janata Dal-CPI-CPM combine to a resounding victory. With a 19 per cent swing away from the Congress-I as against the national average of eight to nine per cent, the three-party alliance romped home with a record 18 seats (JD-16, CPI one and CPM one). Much water has flown down the Mahanadi since minister's chair. The collapse of the non- Congress government for the second time, the split in the Janata Dal and the mandir issue overtaking Mandal has put

Patnaik into discomfiture. But Patnaik's popularity amongst the Oriyas has remained more or less intact due to his conscious attempts to project his rebellious image to regain the lost pride and glory of Kalinga. Beat up corrupt public servants; I am a naxalite; No Mandal in Orissa; Free from the fiscal clutches of New Delhi; Dishonest Marwari traders go back. These and several other controversial statements of Patnaik have kept the media and the public guessing the real intentions of the last surviving politicians of the Nehru era.[5]

For long Orissa remained neglected largely due to the appathy of the centre. The stagnation in the agricultural and industrial sectors in the state worsened during the decade-long Congress-I regime headed by J.B. Patnaik despite a massive mandate to the party in both the 1980 and 1984 Lok Sabha elections and subsequent assembly polls. Corruption in high places and the non- performance of the J.B. Patnaik regime was the rallying point for the Dal leader who had raised high hopes among the voters that his first task would be to put the Congress-I leaders on trial for their corrupt practices. The vigilance raids on the residences of the Congress-I leaders including J.B. Patnaik and some top bureaucrats soon after the Dal leader assumed charge of the state created a flutter in political circles. Patnaik's anti- corruption crusade was further reinforced when he justified naxalites beating up corrupt officials and looting feudal lords. Even patnaik called upon the people to beat up corrupt public servants after taking the permission of the Chief minister. The Chief minister's office was flooded with hundreds of telegrams seeking his permission to beat up erring officals.

Having succeeded in creating a fear psychosis among the officials indulging a in corruption, Patnaik's latest attack on unscrupulous traders who, according to him, are mostly Marwaris was aimed at stripping them of their economic dominance in the state. And at the same time the Dal leader successfully checkmated the right wing Hindu revivalist Bharatiya Janata Party, preventing the latter from wooing non-Marwari traders and urbanites.[6]

A total bandh was observed in Punjab as the news of Rajiv Gandhi's killing last night sent a wave of shock and anguish in the region.

A number of Congress leaders of the State including the PCC president Beant Singh and R.L. Bhatia described the killing as a heinous and barbaric crime and cowardly act. The Leftists condemning the murder in the strongest terms put it as a loss of big leader. The Akali Dals and other Panthic parties however matained a stoic silence. President of the Punjab Janata Dal, Teja Singh Tiwana, while con

5. Nageswar Patnaik. Upsetting the Equations. *The Independent*, 25 May 1991.
6. *Ibid.*

demning the killing of Rajiv said - "we may have political differences with anyone but violence of any kind has no place in any democratic set up."

A number of Congress leaders led peace rallies at Amirtsar, Ludhiana and Patiala. They appealed to the people to maintain calm and exercise restraint in this hour of grief.

Some tension was reported in Jalandhar but authorities said the situation was under control. Menawhile, police and security forces were put on alert in the entire state.

News of Rajiv's death was revceived with shock and disbelief in Amritsar where people were out in streets early to discuss the situation arising out of the tragedy. In Guru Nanak Dev University among his severest critics Mr. Gandhi's killing was viewed as repayment for his wrong policies.

A senior SGPC functionary while commenting that if the country was falling apart politically it was due to the gross mishandling of the situation by the Gandhi family. He however hastened to add that the SGPC did not approve of violence of any kind. He said he was sorry for the killing of a man of Rajiv Gandhi's stature. Meanwhile, the Government is believed to have ordered an extra vigil on the Indo-Pak border while issuing a red alert. Very little traffic was observed on the national highway.

Controversy has dogged the proposal of elections in Punjab ever since the decision was announced by the Centre. Opinion was sharply divided on whether the State's situation would ensure conditions required for holding a reasonably free and fair election. Most major national political parties' leaders met President R. Venkataramn to dissuade him from ordering elections in Punjab. The threat that even if elections were held, most political parties might boycott the polls appeared imminent. But by pressing ahead with the decision on elections in Punjab, Prime Minister Chandra Shekhar reactivated various political elements in that State, long silenced by terror. Indeed, the revival of the elective process witnessed an unexpected rush for filing of nominations as various political parties and militant organisations resiled from their earlier stand of boycotting the polls. The Congress decided to boycott the elections. When the Election Commission sensibly agreed to delink Punjab's election from the polls in the rest of the country to ensure the presence of adequate para-military forces in the State, fears began to be expressed over the unduly long period of campaign and the risks that it involved. These apprehensions stood vindicated when polling in one Lok Sabha and six Assembly constituencies had to be countermanded following the killings of the candidates.

And at a time when violence threatened to endanger the very creadibility of the polls, doubts were also expressed whether a new government installed at the Centre might not indefinitely postpone the polls: It is, therefore, a matter of no surprise that the assassination of Rajiv Gandhi has only added to the imponderables about the Punjab elections. The postponement of polls in the rest of the country added a new problem for Punjab, since it entailed a delay in the arrival of additional companies of para- military forces in the state. It was a in view of this that Punjab Governor O.P. Malhotra had urgently requested a postponement of the polls in Punjab to June 29 or 30, expecially since the killings of candidates were continuing. More than a dozen candidates have been killed in the past four weeks. The problem of providing security cover to candidates has been accentuated by the refusal of a number of candidates to accept the offical security offered. In a welcome development, the Punjab Government has decided to extend its security cover to all candidates simply on "moral requests", instead of responding only to written ones as decided earlier. The Centre, too, has done well by responding promptly to Gen. Malhotra's plea and deciding to despatch 12,000 para-military personnel immediately, to be followed by another 16,000 so that the State's programme for beefing up security before polls need not be deferred. Some concern has been expressed over reports that the Centre has allowed arms licences for prohibited weapons to certain bodies which have been publicly demanding a separate Sikh homeland, apparently for their self-defence. It is said that the State Government was not consulted. If true, arbitrary actions such as this must be rescinded. The decision by Union Minister of State for Home subodh Kant to contest the Ludhiana Lok Sabha seat has fuelled allegations that the Centre has entered into a deal with some militants. Facts of the case are unknown. However, the Centre, in its anxiety to hold elections in Punjab, must do nothing that goes against the country's long term interests.[7]

Army was called out to assist the civil administration in maintaining law and order in the State capital Where situation was tense following the news of assassination of former Prime Minister and Congress President, Rajiv Gandhi.

It staged a flag march in those localities where authorities were apprehending trouble. Army was also asked to stand by in other parts of the State to meet any eventuality.

The incidents of looting, arson and clashes between Congress-I and workers of other political parties have been reported from Kota, Ajmer

7. *Patriot*, 1 June 1991.

Udaiput, Bhilwara, Chittorgarh and Bikaner.

In Ajmer, about 30 persons including nine policemen were injured when police resorted to lathi-charge to disperse a violent mob indulging in looting arson and stonethrowing.

Congress workers at Udaipur, Chittor, Bhilwara and where polling for Lok Sabha elections was to be held tomorrow, pulled down the banners and cut outs of non-Congress-I candidates. In Udaipur they damaged some vehicles.

In Kota the Congress workers came out on the roads around midnight and raised anti-BJP slogans, they indulged in stone throwing also.

A total bandh, called by the Congress-I was observed in almost all major towns in the State.

The Rajasthan State Transport and private transporters withdrew their vehicles in view of tension in various parts of the State.

The State Government today declared a holiday to mourn the death of Rajiv Gandhi. A close vigil is being kept on the interantional border with Pakistan.

According to a Government spokesman the bandh was by and large peaceful barring stray incidents of stone throwing at some places. Police and para-military forces are patrolling the areas where tension was reported.

An urn containing the ashes of Rajiv Gandhi were brought in Jaipur on May 27, 1991 for immersion in five lakes of Rajasthan.

The urn was palced at the Albert Museum in Ramniwas Bagh before immersion to enable people to pay their homage, according to the Pradesh Congress office.

The urn, was carried by RPCC chief Paras Ram Maderna and former Rajasthan Chief Minister Harideo Joshi, for immersion in Galtaji lake in Jaipur, Pushkar in Ajmer, Martkundia in Chittorgarh, Baneswara, and Kolauat in Bikaner.

Five persons, two of them officials, were reportedly killed in police firings and related incidents a the mute anger of a shocked state threatened to engulf the streets and take on the contours of a war of revenge.

Paramilitary forces patrol the main arteries of the state capital and the national highways to meet any threat of an outbreak of large-scale violence.

The news of Rajiv Gandhi's death percolated through Madras only after stunned citizens opened their morning newspapers. By the time the state of shock could transform itself to that of anger battalions of the armed police had taken position in sensitive zones-specially in the twilight areas where rival official factions, castes and communities were evently balanced.

There was ao real dawn in the State-only an extension of the shadowy right of violence and gloom. Even before the first rays of the sun could be seen the battered of body of whisked away in an ambulance and a convoy without sirens or anything which might distrub the calm of the sleeping city.

The first confirmation of the news of Rajiv's death available with the early morning editions of the Tamil papers saw clustered groups of the young out on the streets enveloped by a sense of impotent anger.

The first objects to invite the wrath of the small groups of marauding young men were the huge cut-outs and posteres of the DMK and its former Chief Minister M. Karunanidhi whose Government was dismissed for failure to tackle the militant activities of the LTTE which is being held responsible for the assassination.

In Madras city even as strong police contingents tried to move into position rampaging nob of over enthusiastic AIADMK cadre attacked establishments and institutions associated with the DMK.

The DMK general secretary K. Anbazhagan's residence was attacked by a mob who burnt his car and were beaten back as they attempted to ransack the house.

That anti-social elements were also trying to take advantage of the situation was apparent from the attempts of a notely group waiving AIADMK flags to break open and loot shops in the Pulianthoppu area. They dispersed only after police fired teargas shells.

In the state capital's middle class dominated T. Nagar area the Janata Dal office was burnt by a crowd which seemed to have come with the single minded purpose, and many of them could be seen speeding away on their two wheelers to join the attack on the offices of the DMK's party paper Murasoli which was set on fire. Extensive damage was done before the police intervened.

Attempts to set fire to petrol pumps were reported from North Madras while in the industrial area of Ambattur groups indulged in heavy brickbatting.

Troops staged a flag-march and police opened fire in Jalpaiguri today following arson and violence which left one person killed and 10 injured.

The crowds were stillon the last notes of the chours when the sound of demonic cymbal rent the air blowing Rajiv Gandhi to pieces.

Ironically, Rajiv died with the last strains of the song which had been sung: Its words:

Rajiv's life is our life,
if not for Indira Gandhi's son
there is no life for anyone.

The children were still clapping to the rendition by composer Shankar-Ganesh and joined him in the chorus.

While the identity of the assassin of Rajiv Gandhi and the involvement in it of any organisation remain a matter of speculalation at this stage, political leaders in Tamil Nadu opposed to the DMK have lost no time in pinning the blame for the ghastly tragedy on it, either directly or by implication. The PCC-I Chief, Vazhapadi K. Ramamurthy is in the forefront of the campaign to exploit the assassination by directing popular wrath against the DMK with his own inferences about the complicity of the party because of its proximity to the LTTE. That the CBI team entrusted with the responsibility of unearthing all evidence is yet to start the job in earnest has not prevented Mr. Ramamurthy from accusing the DMK in a Press conference of having hatched a deep-rooted conspiracy for "the annihilation of political rivals through hirelings." All this only lends credence to the charge of DMK leader M. Karunanidhi that the objective behind the orchestrated denunication of his party is to derive electoral advantage by whipping up popular sentiments against it. Indeed, the spate of organised attacks on DMK leaders and the property of the party as well as its National Front allies cannot be dismissed as a spontaneous reaction to the tragedy. Among the seven people killed in Tamil Nadu are two DMK workers in Thiruvarambur, allegedly by an AIADMK mob, while the party candidate at Andhiyoor suffered extensive burns when she was locked up in a house, which was later set afire. The police stood as passive spectators when Congress-I and AIADMK workers indulged in arson at the offices of the DMK organ Murasoli and the CPI-M journal Theekathir. These motivated and well-planned attacks clearly seem to be part of a plan to ensure that the DPF wins the election virtually uncontested by terrorising DMK supporters to stay away from the polling booths. Ramamurthy's charge that the DMK has ushered in the bomb culture has elicted the rejoinder from Mr. Karunanidhi that the training camps for militants were functioning from 1983. While calling for the immediate deportation of all Sri Lankan Tamils from the state, AIADMK leader Ms. Jayalalitha chose to appeal to her flock to remain calm and refrain from violence only after much of the damage has been done. Since the high-level inquiry instituted by the Centre is yet to start its work, Tamil Nadu politicians would do well to resist the temptation of making political capital through a witchhunt of their rivals. Instead, all assistance should be given to the authorities and the commission being set up to find out the culprits responsible for the assassination and the conspiracy behind it. Public acrimony can harm the conduct of the investigations whose successful outcome is important for the country.[8]

Prominent political parties in Tamil Nadu on May 23, 1991 demanded a judicial enquiry into the violent incidents that took place in the state following the assassination of former prime minister Rajiv Gandhi.

At an all-party meeting convened in the secretariat by the government this evening, the parties felt that the enquiry should help in assessing the damage to property and payment of compensation to the victims.

The three-hour meeting attended by the DMK, AIADMK, Congress, PMK, CPI (M), CPI and other parties observed a two minute silence to pay homage to Rajiv Gandhi. It condemned the assassination and appealed to the people to maintain calm.

The meeting decided that strong action ought to be taken against anti-social elements who indulged in violence and complaints be immediately looked into.

They sought the cooperation of all converned for the proper maintenance of essential services and appealed to the people not to believe baseless rumours.

The meeting, convened at the direction of Tamil Nadu governor Bhishma Narain Singh, was also attended by top officials.

Meanwhile, the DMK demanded the resignation of Bhishma Narain Singh and his two advisers and own moral responsibility for the "unprecedented deterioration" in law and order in the state, following the assassination of Rajiv Gandhi.

In a statement here, DMK deputy general secretary K. Manoharan alleged that the police were silent spectators to the large-scale looting, arson and violent attacks on DMK partymen and their election and newspaper offices.

Alleging that a serious security lapse was responsible for Mr. Gandhi's death, he said even the elementary details of VVIP security were not attended to. "It is a matter of shame for the Tamil Nadu police that some police officials fled the scene immediately after the blast," he said.

The law and order machinery was crippled in the state and, as the state was under President's rule, the governor and his advisers should resign, he said.

8. *The Hindustan Times*, 25 May 1991.

Meanwhile, rumours of some DMK leaders being arrested here today kept the telephone lines of news agencies and newspaper offices busy.

Denying the report, senior police officals warned that such rumours should not be believed," the police said.

The anxious callers also enquired about the general law and order situation in the city and whether any police station had been set on fire.

In the aftermath of the assassination of Rajiv Gandhi, the stray incidents of murder, arson and looting that have rocked the country from Tripura to Tamilnadu are a sad commentary on the state of the law and order situation. Given the grim reality that many parts of the country suffered from lawlessness, despite a nation-wide red alert, immediately following the tragedy, it is evident that either the government machinery is inherently flawed or violence has acquired cultural legitimacy in our country, or both. If even the once-peaceful state like Tamilnadu is rocked by an outbreak of violence, we have no option but to admit that the spread of lawlessness is near complete. The continuing violence in the different areas of Tamilnadu reflects the inadequate response of the police and administration. The lives of many innocent persons, who have been victims of the mindless fury of the mob, could have been saved. Why the state machinery awakens always after the deed is done is inexplicable. The myth that President's rule can ensure better maintenance of the law and order situation than is done by an elected government is not upheld by the paralysis of the

Tamilnadu administration headed by Governor Bhishma Narayan singh. The handpicked Governor of Tamilnadu, Bhishma Narayan Singh, has much to answer for. Aside from the strange behaviour displayed by policemen on duty of Rajiv Gandhi's meeting at Sriperumbudur on May 21, after the fatal explosive detonated. Tamilnadu's police force appears to have failed to contain the repercussions which were easily predictable. Leaders of all parties should refrain from making irresponsible and provocative statements. While the CBI team has been investigating the identity of the assassin or assassins of Rajiv Gandhi, nothing is gained by politicians engaged in electioneering blaming each other for this dastardly crime. Such utterances may be prompted by electioneering or indignation. But these can only vitiate the already tense atmosphere. The assassination was not a simple crime. It probably has many remifications. Let the specialised agencies complete the investigation. A judicial inquiry under the Commission of Inquiry Act has also been ordered. That is why it is not possible to appreciate the efforts being made by TNCC president Vazhapadi K. Ramamurthy and AIADMK chief Jayalalitha, since the death of Rajiv

Gandhi, to charge their electoral adversary, the DMK, with responsibility for this crime. How the LTTE has come to secure a menacing presence in Tamilnadu, if truthfully restated, would compromise many, including the AIADMK. Let the investigating agencies unfold the conspiracy behind the crime and what part the LTTE played in it. To do otherwise might draw a red herring across the trail and prejudge the findings. The attacks on leaders of the DMK and the National Front and the damage of the properties of the party allegedly by AIADMK and Congress activists cannot be justified and Congress and AIADMK leaders must restrain their followers. What is to be done about Sri Lankan Tamils in India is a separate matter, and no instant solution can be found. What ought immediately to be done would require political and administrative will of the highest order. Tamil refugees and their camps should be searched for weapons and explosives and these should be immediately seized. Tamilnadu should not be misused by terrorists as their base of operations. AIADMK and Congress leaders should comprehend the concealed danger that lies in this tense situation and must refrain from misusing the tragedy to arouse passion against rival groups. The country is passing through a difficult time. At this juncture the leaders are expected to agree on the immdeiate requirement-that public order, and safety to all innocent people must be guarnteed. Political violence. Has caused immeasurable damage and internecine bloodshed. These must not be countenanced by any major party or persons who are in a position to influence public opinion.[9]

People in his home state expressed shock and indignation over the assassination of Rajiv Gandhi.

Shops, business establishments and entertainment centres remained closed making it a spontaneous homage to the departed leader.

Candidates of all parties stopped campaigning on their own and groups of people collected on road crossings, forgetting their political differences to discuss the news which they received only in the morning with disbelief and dismay.

The UP Government ordered a seven-day mourning in the State and issued a red alert to keep extra vigil in all the districts. All government offices and educational institutions remained closed today. Flaps flew at half-mast on all government buildings in the State capital and district heaedquarters. The chief secretary directed the district magistrades tp Leepa Watch an the situtation to keep a watch on the situation.

Leading the mourners, Governor B. Satyanarayana Reddy strongly

9. *Patriot*, 29 May 1991.

condemned the killing and said "Mr. Gandhi's whole life was dedicated to national development and welfare of the society. His death has caused an irreparable loss to the nation."

He appealed to the citizens to face this loss gravely and maintain the unity and integrity of the nation.

Chief Minister Mulayam Singh Yadav in a statement condemned the brutal assassination and said the country had lost a young and dynamic leader.

Gloom descended on the Pradesh Congress Committee office at Mall Avenue with party leaders making a beeline to it. They held a meeting and took stock of the gravity of what had happened. A sobbing PCC chief Mahabir Prasad in his condolence message said the country had lost a great leader.

While BJP leader Atal Behari Vijpayee described the assassination as a 'cowardly act', Pradesh BJP leader Kalyan Singh termed it as 'an unfourtnate happening'.

Many other political parties issued statements to condemn the killing. Many student and youth organisations also recorded their heartfelt feelings.

The Lucknow Municipal Corporation held a condolence meeting presided over by Mayor Dr. Dauji Gupta.

There are several reasons which account for Rajiv's charisma and appeal among the Amethites. "When he came here to contest elections in 1984, it was as if a messiah had arrived," said Wakar Ahmed. "The way he mingled with the people was not the way most Congressmen would do. He always stopped to greet them on his way with a smile." Pradhan of Bhoi village, Lal Bahadur Singh, said that whenever Amethi residents visited Rajiv in Delhi, his security staff was instructed to allow them into his house without much ado. "People from other states, including senior party functionaries, often had to wait for days for an audience with Rajivji. But we were special." Bahadur Singh also pointed out that Rajiv did not particularly care for sychophants. "During one of my trips some three years ago to Delhi, my first reaction was to greet him warmly. But Rajivji cut me short and said 'Now stop giving me badhais and tell me what benefits you hope to get by coming all the way to Delhi." Giriraj Singh, a former MP from Sultanpur and presently president of the district Congress unit, recalled that Rajiv made every minor functionary of the district party unit feel important by giving him a platform to atriculate his views and involving him in important decisions concerning the district affairs. Bahadur Singh remembers an occasion in 1988 when Rajiv had come to a village near Amethi to address a public gathering. "Since I was neither an MP nor the district unit president I sat right behind. But Rajivji spotted me and from the dais shouted across and insisted I sit right next to him."[10]

Equally emotionally and nostalgically recalled are Rajiv's sterling contributions towards the development of Amethi. "He transformed usar (Barren) land into an oasis of prosperity", said Giriraj Singh.

Industries, roads, railway lines, schools and colleges, hospitals- schemes which are dreamt of in most Indian villages have become realities in Amethi. Giving the example of his own village, Bhoi, Bhadur Singh said 15 years ago people ran to see a passing automobile as it was a rare sight. "Today my village is connected by road and rail." Singh also said that in the pre- development era, a government posting in Amethi was regarded as a "penalty." "The situation has reservsed today. People hanker after posting in our district and then no one wants to leave." All this, they feel, is due to Rajiv's deep felt commitment for his con- sitituency. "Other MPs forget their constitutencies once they are elected.

"Prime minister Rajiv Gandhi visited Amethi seven or eight times a syear," said Bahadur Singh. Congress functionaries also spoke of Rajiv's "workacholism" at the peak of electioneering. "He would be on the move from 8 am to 2 am, snatching only four or five hours of sleep. He would eat a packed lunch yet continue working cheerfully. Most of us used to fall ill after moving with him for a couple of days," said Giriraj Singh.

Singh's residence in Gaurigang was thronged by thousands of people on Wednesday, all wanting to confirm if the dreades news was true. "They sat and wailed. At sundown I told them to go home and pray for Rajivji and not do anything drastic or violent. I told them that would be the most befitting tribute to their leader's memory. And they listned and kept up their word".

Only Singh's five-year-old grandson, Mukesh, could not control his anger. "He pulled a photo of Rajivji from the wall and said, "Dadaji only a chor or badmash (a thief or bad character) could have killed him."[11]

Chief minister, Jyoti Basu, praised Rajiv Gandhi for his attempts to build a consensus on issues of national importance and suggested that similar efforts must go on so that solutions to these issues can be found.

"No party can save the nation on its own. If we cannot sit together, the nation cannot be saved," he said at a condolence meeting to mourn the assassination of Rajiv Gandhi. Basu did not rule out the involve -

10. *The Independent*, 24 May 1991.
11. *Ibid.*

ment of a foreign hand in the killing, and criticised the PCC president, S.S. Ray, for trying to tarnish the image of the Left parties by suggesting that they were responsible for the assassination.

Basu fondly remembered Rajiv Gandhi's promise to help the Uttar Pradesh chief minister, Mulayam Singh Yadav, on the mandir-masjid issue. "He was sitting next to me at a national integration council meeting when Mulayam asked for help. Rajiv immediately agreed," he said.

Declaring the he had never made personal attacks on Rajiv Gandhi, the chief minister said that he had welcomed Rajiv Gandhi's last-minute initiative to stop the Gulf war. "I wished him well when he went to Moscow and Teheran to solve the crisis. He did the right thing. He may have got two extra votes for his efforts. But even if he did, it was our duty to wish him well," Basu said.

But, Basu strongly condemned S.S. Ray for pandering to the "forces of destruction" in the state and regretted that no state Congress leader had criticised the Congressmen responsible for such incidents. He said that Congressmen went on a rampage in Jalpaiguri and the military had to be called out but Congress chose to remain silent.

Referring to Ray, Basu said that the PCC (I) Chief was "giving specific instructions to anti-socials to create trouble." He said that Ray has "stopped very low" and is trying to "divide India and foster its enemies." He said that the Left Front and Janata Dal workers have shown signs of patience in face of this assualt though the administration was initially taken by surprise. He added that the remarks by Mr. Ray has forced the Left Front and the Janata Dal to organise a separate condolence meeting and not attend the one called by the Congress (I).

The Chief minister added that the Congressmen had earlier restored to violence after the assassination of Indira Gandhi and had stopped rioting only after Rajiv Gandhi asked them to stop.

The Left Front chairman, Sailen Dasgupta, condemned the assassination, suggesting the involvement of a foreign hand and also criticised the state Congress(I) for indulging in shameful acts in the hour of sorrow. He added that such acts merely tarnished the image of the Congress (I).

Ashok Ghosh of the Forward Bloc, Nikhil Das of the RSP, Samar Guha of the Janata Dal and Nandagopal Bhattacharya of the CPI also spoke.

9
PROBE PANEL

The Centre has despatched a special investigation team headed by the Central Bureau of Investigation (CBI) to Madras to probe the assassination of Rajiv Gandhi.

Union Minister of State for Home Subodh Kant said that the team comprised experts from the Intelligence Bureau, National Security Guards ad the Research and Analysis Wing (RAW). The team has already taken up its work.

Forensic experts from these organisation had already begun investigations to establish the modus operandi and the type of explosives used in the blast that killed Rajiv Gandhi. The team has been asked to submit its report as early as possible, the Minister said.

Subodh Kant presided over the high-level meetings which was attended by the Union Home secretary, R.K. Bhargava, the Intelligence Bureau Chief M.K. Narayanana, the Special secretaries G.S. Mander and A.A. Ali, the head of paramilitary organisations and other senior officials.

He said, "the governemtn under no circumstances will allow the law and order situation to deteriorate to the extent it did in the aftermath of the assassination of Indira Gandhi in 1984".

Reports of incidents of burning of cut-outs of DMK and TDP leaders had come in from Tamil Nadu and Andhra Pradesh but there had been no incident of organised violence anywhere in the country.

In the northern parts of the country, the people were observing a self-declared bandh and in most of the areas, traffic was off the roads, the Minister said.

He said, "the people are in a state of deep shock and no one has gone in for violent protest."

All the State Governments have been asked to step up vigil and maintain a round-the-clock watch on the situation, he said adding that the State authorities had been alerted before the Doordarshan and Radio broadcast the news of Rajiv Gandhi's killing at 11.16 p.m. last night.

Talking about the situation in diffeernt States, Subodh Kant said a bandh call given by the Left Front and the Congress in West Bengal hand kept people and Government and private vehicles off the streets.

In several States, suburban train services were also withdrawn to prevent the agitated people from making them targets of public violence, he said.

The Home Ministery has set up a special control room to monitor the law and order situation round-the-clock in the country, he said.

Union Law and Justice Minister Subramaniam Swamy said the Government had also taken adequate precautionar steps for maintaining law and order in all parts of the country in the wake of the assassination. The Government had by and large suceeded in keeping the situation under control, he added.

On the assassination fo Rajiv Gandhi he said while it was for the investitating agencies to find out the forces behind the attack, it was clear that the assailant was capable of operating a sophisticated remote control device. It appeared to be a well- organised conspiracy, he added.

The Government on May 27, 1991 announced the appointment of Justice J.S. Verma of the Supreme Court to inquire into the assassination of Rajiv Gandhi. The probe will confine itself to find out if the assassination could have been averted and if there were any security lapses.

The one-man commission of inquiry will submit its report within three months. There was a 45 minute meeting between prime minister Chandra Shekhar and president R. Venkataraman before the announcement of the judge was made. The cabinet had decided on an inquiry by a sitting judge of the supreme court a day after the assassination.

The government had written to Chief justice of India, Mr. Ranganath Mishra to nominate a setting judge. Union minister of state for home Subodh Kant Sahay made it clear that the judicial probe will be confined only to the security aspects and not to the investigation of the assassination which is being done by a special Investigation Team of the CBI.

Many judges felt that the appointment of a sitting member would hamper regualr work in the supreme court where there is a huge backlog of cases awaiting disposal.

An official spokesman said the terms of reference for the commission is:

a) whether the assassination could have been averted?

b) whether there were lapses or dereliction of duty in regard to the assassination on the part of any individual responsible for Gandhi's security?

c) Deficiencies, if any in the security system or arrangements prescribed and operated in practice which might have contributed to the assassination. The spokesman said the commission may recommend to the government remedies and measures that need to be taken for the future. The commisson will decide on the place where to hold sittings as well for its office to function. Fifty eight-year old Justice Verma joined the Supreme Court in June 1989 after having served as the Chief justice of the Rajasthan High Court.

J.S. Verma, a sitting judge of the Supreme Court who has been appointed head of the one-man commission to inquire into the assassination of Rajiv Gandhi, has the onerous task of unravelling the mysteries of the sinister deed. The commission is expected to go into the entire gamut of issues concerning the assassination. It has been asked to submit its report as early as possible but not later than three months. Inquiry commissions have in the past tended to take their own time to submit their reports. The inquiry will lose much of its relevance and utility if it not finished in time. It is, therefore incumbent upon the Central Government to ensure that all infrastructural facilities are provided to the commission to complete its assignment at the earliest. Needless to say, few incidents have in recent years shaken the nation as the killing of Rajiv Gandhi. The need to indentify the brains that masterminded the heinous act cannot be overemphasised. It is apparent that considerable planning and dexterity has gone into the dastradly operaion at Sriperumbudur which nearly pushed the nation down the precipice. Obviously, it could not have been the handiwork of a woman alone. The investigating team which will work in concert with the commission has the responsibility of bringing to book all those involved in the conspiracy. For all one knows, the attempt might not have been merely to bump off a promising leader. It might have had the larger objective of destabilising the system in vogue in the country. If it is so, there is every reason for the perpetrators of the carnage to strike again. It is in this context that the commission's finding will help the Government in coping with such threats from within or without. That it took one whole week for the Government to find a judge to head the commission of inquiry should be seen against the backdrop of the supreme Court Judges' reluctance to take up such assignments. In the light of the unnecessary criticism that Justice M.P. Tahkkar, who inquired into the assassination of Mrs. Indira Gandhi, had to incur and the shabby treatment meted out to Justice D.P. Madon, who was appointed to inquire into the Meham incidents, their reluctance is, of course, understandable.[1] If, ultimately, the judges relented and the apex court could spare a sitting judge, it is a measure of the importance they attach to the inquiry. Thus, the judiciary has shown a great sense of responsibility in complying with the Government's request.[1]

The terms of reference of the Justice J.S. Verma Commission appointed to inquire into the Rajiv Gandhi's assassination are wisely limited to the issue of whether there were any security lapses at Sriperumbudur. It shows that the government has learned a lesson from the mistakes of the past when judicial commissions of inquiry were given broad and ill-defined powers. This resulted in a judicial body ending up playing a quasi-investigative role for which it was clearly ill-suited. This was best exemplified by the incongruities which surfaced when the Tahkkar Commission was asked to look into the larger conspiracy surrounding Indira Gandhi's assassination. While Justice M.P. Thakkar's attempt to identify the killers led to his infamous" needle of suspicion" remark against Mrs. Gandhi's close associate, R.K. Dahawan, the Special Investigation Team (SIT) that was conducting a parallel inquiry, drew contradictory conclusions. This lent an unsavoury political undertone to the investigation, quite apart from damaging the credibility of the parties involved. The fact that government chose to reject the Thakkar Commission findings even while with holding certain "sensitive" portion from the public only led to further allegations of impropriety. It is hardly surprising that last year beleagured Supreme Court judges passed a unanimous resolution refusing to accept such assignments in the future. The Chandra Shekhar government has, therefore, taken the right step by separating the Verma Commission's duties from those of the SIT. The task of actually indentifying the killers is a detective's job, for which the SIT possesses the requisite skills. Already the SIT has shown a sense of purpose by pressing ahead with its investigation. The Verma Commission on the other hand is, however, ideally equipped to suggest broad policy guidelines for ensuring greater security to high-risk individuals, besides, of course, looking into any acts of commission by the law-enforcement agencies in Tamil Nandu. In the circumstances, demands made by the Congress, the BJP and the CPI that the Verma panel's powers be extended to enable it to unravel the larger conspiracy are clearly out of place. While one shares the BJP's concern to have the perpetrators of this dastradly act identified as soon as possible, emotional outbursts should not be allowed to obscure hard realities. Piecing together the clues, in what appears for the moment to have been a carefully engineered conspiracy will take some time and effort.[2] In the interim, parties would be better advised to refrain from scoring political points

1. *The Hindustan Times*, 29 May 1991.
2. *The Times Of India*, 31 May 1991.

that might needlessly handicap or prejudice this critically important investigation.

Controversy has reared its head over the terms of reference of the Commission set up to inquire into Rajiv Gandhi's assassintion. It was with some difficulty that the higher judiciary could overcome its reluctance to involve itself with Commissions of Inquiry following the unhappy experienced of the Thakkar, Thakkar-Natarajan and Kuldip Singh Commissions. Public scrutiny of the works of these three commission led to the most serve criticism and even to questions about the impartiality of the judges concerned. Justice J.S. Verma has shown great public spirit in undertaking a difficult task. His acceptance of the job as the "court's duty" recognises implicitly the fact that the quality of a commission's work alone is the best protection against "scurrilous" attcks. While the official notification on the formation of the Commission and its tasks is still awaited, press reports about the likely terms of the reference suggest that these will be concerned with the security system and possible lapses and dereliction of duty. The narrow campass of the inquiry is not improved by Dr. Subramaniam Swamy's glib assurance that the judge will be free to go into any matter he desires. The Congress, BJP and CPI have already questioned the focus of the inquiry. The BJP specifically calls for an investigation into the "whole mystifying conspiracy" and its international ramifications; the CPI asks for all aspects of the assassination to be examined, including its "political ramifications". On the face of it, it might seem sensible to separate the work of the special investigation team, headed by D.R. Kartikeyan and the Verma Commission and so avoid the kind of contradictions and consequent loss of credibility that occurred in the parallel and overlapping investigatins of the Thakkar Commission and Anandram special investigation team in the Indira Gandhi assassination case. Many assassinations have political dimensions. The search for the Sriperambudur killer or killers leads logically to a search for the accomplices, motives and then perhaps conspirators. An investigation into a "political conspiracy", if any, seems unvoidable since it cannot be precluded at this stage. The Government must examine when and how this aspect can be gone into.[3]

A developing country without all the resources and traditions that make the practising of Westminister-style democracy easier, India has been persevering to promote the system in the belief that it is a sound system for a nation of our diversity. The myriad views and cultures enrich this nation but they also sustain its growth. Intolerance and the use of arbitrary violence cannot be permitted to snuff out hopes of

3. Indian Express, 1 June 1991.

building the total culture of India. The commission's task is not going to be easy, but it is to be hoped that all agencies will help it to complete the vital national task. As important as their cooperation in the probe is the need to complete the inquiry quickly. Often, the purpose of such an exercise is lost in the long time it consumes for its work.[4]

Prime Minister Chandra Shekhar on June 4, 1991 agreed to the Opposition demand in the Rajya Sabha for widening the scope of Justice Verma Inquiry Commission probing the assassination of Rajiv Gandhi.

Shekhar, who intervened in the short-duration discussion on the security lapses, told the House that Congress President P.V. Narasimha Rao had written to him about it and the Government had sent him some proposals for amendment to the 'satisfaction' of the Congress party, of the terms of reference of the Commission. The Government, he said, was now awaiting the Congress response to the proposed amendments.

Shekhar, however, made it clear that the amendments to the terms of reference of the Commission would have to be discussed with Justice J.S. Verma. He said once that Commission was appointed, its terms of reference could not be altered without the knowledge of the probing.

The Prime Minister assured the members that some legal luminaries too would be consulted before affecting any such amendments.

Though Shekhar made it clear that he would not cross the limits, he tried to meet most of the points made by the opposition members by the time of his intervention.

Shekhar stoutly denied that there had been any security lapse in protecting the former Prime Minister. He termed the method of assassination used as 'unique' as a 'human bomb' was employed for the first time in the world.

The Prime Minister said at the elections meeting site in Sriperumbudur, metal detectors had been used. Frisking done and garlands which were to be presented to Rajiv Gandhi were screened. Chandra Shekhar said he had no information regarding absence of ambulance and reported fleeing of policemen after that incident and said the Government would look into these.

Chandra Shekhar said the Government had received from time to time inforamtion regarding threats to Rajiv Gandhi adding, "We had been alerting States on this as well as passing them to Rajiv Gandhi himself."

4. *The Hindustan Times*, 23 May 1991.

He said earlier there were other risk areas." But two to three months and back we got infrormation that Tamilnadu might be another risk area we had accordingly alerted the state Government", the Prime Minister said.

Chandra Shekhar said nearly 1400 security men had been deployed for the security of Rajiv Gandhi from the Madras airport to the site of the election meeting which included an experienced Inspector General of Police, two DIG's, SSP's and other senior officials and the State Governor was in touch with the AICC for making these arrangements.

Serious security lapses that are coming to light regarding the arrangements for Rajiv Gandhi's election meeting have made the Verma Commission of Inquiry very important and crucial. The nation is shocked to find that even elementary security arrangements such as the provision of an ambulance and a SPG cover were absent for some mysterious reasons. Basically three factors stand out as of now about the security arrangements. First the lack of the SPG cover, secondly, the absence of the mandatory medical ambulnce and thirdly, the absence of frisking of the people who rushed to Rajiv Gandhi on the fateful day in that remote village in Tamil Nadu.

One can give any number of reasons now as to why these lapses of an extremely serious nature had occurred. There are many other questions that are being raised at different levels. The government has done well in accepting the demand of the Congress to widen the terms of rererence of the inquiry but it is not known if the charge that certain foreign elements were behind the assassination of Rajiv Gandhi would be covered by the expanded terms of reference. Whatever be the claims of the government about what it had done to protect Rajiv Gandhi, there is a strong feeling among the people that he fell a victim to the machinations of internal and external forces which were keen on weakening this country and in breaking it up. This sentiment was clear in the debate in the Rajya Sabha on this issue, though some were more vocal than others and some were even more explicit.

The Congress member, NKP Salve, told the House that the terms of reference of the inquiry should be expanded to include the alleged role of foreign elements in the conspiracy to assassinate Rajiv Gandhi. The Union Law Minister Prof. Subramaniam Swamy, was not so categorical but he was certain that the forces of destabiliation forged a nexus with the forces of fundamentalism to eliminate Rajiv Gandhi, who was the only hope for the country to forge ahead. That the assassination was an attempt to check India's march to modernity was widely accepted. But at a different political plane was the charge of S.S. Ahluwalia, who made some extermely serious allegations and asked Prime Minister

Chandra Shekhar, why an ambulance was not provided at the site of the public meeting to be held at Sriperumbudur. Ahluwalia recalled an altercation he had with Chandra Shekhar in the Central Hall some time ago when the latter had said: "There would be nothing left of the Congress to recover politically. Ahluwalia was shocked at what had happened. This government owes a lot of explanation to the country about the glaring security lapses near Madras. One hopes that the Verma Commission will unravel the truth."[5]

5. National Herald, 6 June 1991.

10
MR. CLEAN - THE GENTLEMAN

Rajiv Gandhi was born to politics, if not rule. His great grandfather, Motilal Nehru, a lawyer, was president of the Indian National Congress in 1919. The year of the Amritsar massacre. His grandfather, Jawaharlal Nehru, was independent India's first Prime Minister (1947-1964). His mother, Indira Gandhi, reigned for all but three of the 18 years from 1966 until her assassiantion in 1984. Rajiv's father, Feroze Gandhi, was a journalist and Member of Parliament.

Yet politics was not Rajiv Gandhi's chosen career. His amibtious younger brother, Sanjay, was sponsored by their mother as heir to the Nehru dynasty. At Doon School and at Cambridge, Rajiv was unassertive and unsung. He failed to be made a prefect. At Cambridge, where he read engineeing at Trinity, he failed his final examination and went home without a degree. "Flunked it," he told an interviewer after becoming Prime Minister. "I didn't do well enough."

At Cambridge, Rajiv met his would be wife, Sonia an Italian girl who had gone there to learn English. Unlike Sanjay's spirited wife, Maneka, Sonia proved a prefect submissive daughter-in-law for Indira Gandhi. "My upbringing is such," Sonia said in a rare but revealing interview, "that I feel my husband is superior to me and his mother even more superior."[1]

Rajiv trained as a pilot with Indian Airlines, flying Avros before graduating to the Boeing 737. His airline career was ended in 1980, when Sanjay was killed piloting a private plane. He entered politics reluctantly saying: "The way I look at it is that Mummy has to be helped somehow."

The magazine, India Today, found him the quintessence nice guy. If fate had not intervened–in 1980 and in 1984–the magazine suggested, "he would have gone through his life flying his planes, taking photographs of his children, spending relaxed evening with his close circle of friends, staying out of controversy's way." But Rajiv Gandhi's political genes asserted themselves. He was a novice, but not a stranger to the world he entered when he fought and won his brother's Amethi constituency (to the chagrin of sister-in-law Maneka, who wanted it for herself). He was appointed a general secretary of the Indira Congress. Although Rajiv never held Cabinet office under his mother, he quickly became the second most powerful figure in politics. His first year as Prime Minister, 1985, was one of promises seemingly fulfilled. The

1. Eric Silver. Gentleman. *The Hindustan Times.*

atmosphere of Indian politics was transformed. Rajiv accepted as his mother had never done, that regional indentification was not synonymous with treason. This conciliatory approach produced agreements to end revolts in Punjab, Assam and Mizoram. Under Rajiv's direction a start was made in liberalising the economy. The new government declared war on corruption and began to put Congress's own murky house in order. Rajiv's dream of bearing India into the modern world on the back of a supercomputer (what, one sceptic termed "cow shit to bulshit in one generation") suddenly seemed attainable. Internationally, Rajiv steered a profitable course between the super powers, but found relations with his troublesome neighbours, Pakistan and Sri Lanka, less tractable. India was heralded as a leader of the non-aligned, a campaigner for peace and racial equality, but it was not yet a power in its own right. Rajiv Gandhi, as one Indian commentator once put it, was "an officer and a gentleman thrown among whellers and dealders. "Now, at a moment of India's maximum instability, his death (as the age of 46) feels like that of a general clubbed to death by his own sepoys, as in the Mutiny.

Rajiv, symbol of nation's unity and national integrity led the country at the most critical and difficult moments after Indira Gandhi's murder in 1984 and provided a stable and clean administration from 1984-1989. India made all round strides during his premiership.

Rajiv Gandhi had the life of a hero and earned the death of a martyr. He was an example of an ordinary man developing into a super man by dint of circumstances.

He combined a dynamic personality with vigour. He lived for the cause of his party and died a martyr's death. His barbaric, inhumane and cowardly assassination is a blow to democracy. As a leader represents a mass of people and their thinking, it will be correct to say that killing of a leader is directly proportional to the murder of democracy.

It is wrong to think that a political party can be weakened or snuffed out by such dastardly acts of violence. The cold-blooded felling of Rajiv Gandhi will only strengthen the party he so ably represented.

The investigation into Rajiv's murder should not become another routine affair that drags on for years without much headway. International help should be sought if necessary to nab the group that masterminded the dastardly killing and the facts brough out in the open.

We hang our heads down in shame. We shed tears of sorrow for what has come over our ill-starred country. Our hearts go out to Sonia and Rahul and Priyanka. Their ioss is strange that three Gandhi's lives should have had such tragic ends. Though the Mahatama was no relation of the other two, he was their Bapu as he was ours. If he could be murdered by one of his own childeren, if should not have surprised anyone that Indira Gandhi would meet her and at the hands of men to whom she entrusted her life and who were physically closest to her. And the third Gandhi, Rajiv, should have fallen to a bomb planted by people for whose security he had committed his country's armed forces. It is significan that in the cases of all the three Gandhi's their assassins had no personal enmity against their victims; they kelled them for what they stood for. I had the good fortune of meeting Rajiv Gandhi many times. He was a contemporary of my daughter at Cambridge. A couple of times I was a passenger in the plane piloted by him and recipient of cups of tea he sent me. His manners were impeccable and his charm irresistible. I had several meetings with him when he became Prime Minister. When he signed the Punjab accord with Sant Longowal I went up to him in Parliament to congratulate him for the courage he had shown by taking the Punjab bull by the horns: I told him that for what he had done for the nation he deserved the Bharat Ratna. When he reneged from the accord, I denounced him in Parliment and in these coloumns. I told him that though he was a perfect gentleman, he as was a poor politician. He took both praise and criticism with a smile. The last time I met him was in my own home when he dropped in to join my son's 50th birthday party. What adds poignancy to the tragedy is that he should have gone at a time when it seemed that the Prime Ministership of the country was once again within his grasp. He was a gentleman- politician who did not realise that the two don't go together.[2]

As the leders of India's freedom movement died, one after another, the history of the country's post-independence four decades got inextricably linked with the fate of the Nahru-Gandhi family. With the assassination of Rajiv Gandhi therefore a definite phase in Indian history has been drawn to a close. An involuntary and reluctant entrant into politics, Rajiv Gandhi was drawn to fill the void left by the treacherous killing of Indira Gandhi by her own security gurards in October 1984. The mantle he inherited was burdensome, made so more so by the viciousness and divisiveness that was injected into Indian society by the circumstances in which Indira Gandhi took and held power. This viciousness was increased manifold by the manner in which Indira Gandhi was persuaded to deal with Punjab secessionists who had captured Harmandir Saheb of Armitsar. Doubts were expressed in many quarters about the sagacity of perpetrating a dynastic succession; but when Rajiv Gandhi took office there really was no alternative to him and the country wholeheartedly approved of him. That the

2. Khushwant Singh. The Third Gandhi. *The Hindustan Times*, 25 May 1991.

political fortune of the country and that of the Nehru-Gandhi family had got intertwined in the popular mind was convincingly affirmed when the people gave Rajiv Gandhi the most massive electoral mandate. The young Prime Minister silenced the skeptics further by the fresh approach that he promised to introduce in Indian politics. This departure from the old order was heralded at the Bombay session of the AICC in 1986 when he spoke of liberating the Congress party from the clutches of office-seekers and power-brokers and, instead, builing it up at the grass-roots level. A debutant in politics, during the first two years of his Prime Ministership, Rajiv Gandhi epitomised a desire for a change for the better in politics, economics and public life. He refused to be influenced by past prejudices or recoil from taking bold initiatives.[3]

The Assam, Punjab and Mizo accords that he negotiated established his credentials as a genuine peaceseeker. In the field of economics, a liberaliser by instinct, Rajiv Gandhi sought to de bureaucratise the heavily regulated economic system that he had inherited from his mother. His encouragement of computerisation, consumer products, electronics and the automative sector produced an era of record growth in manufacturing and living standards. That generated by far the most rapid rate of growth during the period of the seventh Plan. And if his policies were instrumental in creating Indian yuppies, they undeniably also led to a decline in the number of the absolutely penurious.

As a child I recollect being presented to Jawaharlal Nehru by my grandfather and that must have been the first time I met Rajiv. He was a young man, and I foundly remember him playing with me, a little boy he had taken under his wing. To me he always was a person to look up to. The world realises worth of a man only when he is no more. Today everyone accepts that Rajiv was one of the most sincere men of his generation. I got to know him when I was very young and as I used to tag around after him, he would take the pains to explain every question of mine. This quality remained with him. There was never a time when one could not ask him a question and expect a frank answer. One incident I remember occurred when I was about 8-year old and had dropped in to Teen Murti House with my grandfather. While playing with Rajiv and Sanjay, we splashed ink all over the floor and were extremely apprehensive about Indiraji's reaction. Ultimately Rajiv took the blame and punishment, though I was responsible for the offence. This quality of his was later often exploited by people.

During the last nine years when I worked with him I found him to be

3. *Patriot*, 25 May 199'

very systematic, organised and disciplined person. He was always clear about his point of view but being essentially a democratic person, would allow others to over rule him and this sometimes proved harmful. However, his commitment to principle and policy was steadfast.[4]

I think I can now call him Rajiv. In the beginning, he was Prime Minister. After the defeat in 1989, we fumbled with PM and ex-PM before we settled on CP (Congress President).

I first met him in September 1984 when, as general secretary, he came to Madurai to address a rally. In the seven years since, he became the most important person in my life. I was last with him during the night of April 24-25, 1991. At 5 am. on April 25, he took my right hand, patted me on the shoulder, wishes me good luck and asked me to rush to the airport lest I miss my flight to Madras. I was leaving to file my nomination. If he had lived, he would have been in my constituency (Sivaganga) at noon on May 22, 1991. Knowing the demands that were made on him and the need to campaign in marginal constituencies, I has asked those in charge of his tour why sivaganga had been included in his itinerary. I was told that he had himself indicated the constituencies in Tamil Nadu where he sould campign and Sivaganga was on his list. I was deeply touched. I was looking forward to welcoming him in my constituency. Rajiv was one of the most decent human being I have known. In small groups and at a one-to-one level, he impressed everyone with his charm and hospitality. Whether it was editors of newspapers or leaders of the opposition or scientists or businessmen or voluntary groups, none left his room without being impressed by his sincerity and willingness to listen and learn. He spoke his mind freely, some times too readily and frankly, pre-empting a different point of view, but he was open to reason and was willing to change his mind. He was full of vigour and life. He was fresh as a flower whether it was 9 in the morning or two hours after midnight. He was prone to colds but had enormous reserves of energy. He constantly used eye drops and throat lozenges. In fact, he took too many of these lozenges when he was on tour.[5]

Personally, I owe a great debt of gratitude to Rajiv. In spite of efforts by some people to carry tales and poison his mind for certain things that I have been saying in the national and party interest, he never misunderstood me. Not only that, he respected my views and agreed with them to a large extent. In April 1991 I had admitted myself to the Escorts Hospital, New Delhi for a heart check-up. I was there for only a day but somehow Rajivji learnt about it. I was having my bath when

4. P.R. Kumaramanglam. My Boyhood Hero. *The Times Of India,* 26 May 1991.
5. P. Chidambram. He Lived too Dangerously. *The Times Of India,* 26 May 1991.

Rajiv reached the hospitzal. My wife was totally taken back. When she told me from outside, I just peeped out and said, "Rajiv I am sorry but I cannot come out immediately. I am having a bath". And he laughed saying "Sathe, you please take your time, will wait." And he remained in the hospital room with us for about half-an-hour. He told me that unless I was very sure about my health, he would not like me to take any risk by contesting an election. Also, as there was speculation if I would shift from Wardha to some other constituency, he asked me if I wanted to go somewhere else. I told him I did not want to shift but I would leave the final decision to him. He ensured that I got the ticket from Wardha. However, some party people started compaigning against me. When Rajiv Gandhi learnt about it, he decided to come to my constituency even though it was not included in his tour schedule. He cancelled a meeting and reached Wardha at 1.30 a.m. He addressed the meeting and told the crowd: "sathe is a man with an open heart. Whatever he thinks is right, he says it. Sometimes he must have rebuked you. He even rebukes me. But we badly need people like him." And with these words, not only did he steal the hearts of the audience, he gave a slap to those partymen who were opposing me.

As others were asking him to leave immediately for Nagpur. I told Rajiv that even though it was so late. I had kept food ready for him at the circuit house. He was pleasantly surprised and said nobody even thought that he also needed food. Then he told me how wherever he went, he was pinched by people and there were scratches all over his hands ana arms because people everywhere wanted to touch him. Sometimes they would come and hug him and kiss him. And he said, look, this is my real food, it is the people's affection that sustains me, that keeps me going.[6]

In all the six years I knew him, he walked in the shadow of death. And never once did he allow the fear of death to stand in the way of taking the decisions he felt were the right ones to take. He was the bravest man I knew. Left to myself. I would call his memorial resting place Dhairya Sthal. He had enormous compassion too. One of my main tasks was to provide succour (from the Prime Minister's Relief Fund and Government sources) to the thousands of unfortunates who came to him for help. Polio- stricken children, Handicapped young men and women, brighteyed and alert, but crippled by a distorted limb, a blighted leg, a twisted arm hanging helplessly in the air. Yount women, abandoned by their husbands. Old men and women abandoned by their familites. There was real pain in his eyes as he would throw an arm around an abandoned shoulder or clasp their hands in

6. Vasant Sathe. His Food was Affection. *The Times Of India*, 26 May 1991.

his. And that pain would lift into true joy when he espied the kids.

He really loved children. They would mob him as we went from village to village. He loved to laugh. His zest for life was also a zest for fun. Throw him a punch line and he would explode into a hearty guffaw. He'd be tickled pink by my alliterations. A clever turn of phrase-and the corners of his mouth would turn to a smile. It was a smile that travelled from his eyes to the dimple of his cheek and right across his broad white teeth. He would mercilessly rib me about my excessive weight, the pot belly I carry like a pregnancy on my waist. The last time I was to see Rajiv was at the Nawab of Arcot's Eid-Milan dinner in Madaras on the 18th April. I had flown into the city separately earlier in the day and met the Crown Prince at lunch. Some one had mentioned this to Rajiv. As we sat down to dinner, Rajiv leaned across the table groaning under mounds of beryani, a dozen varieties of chicken and an armada of mutton, and called out to me, "So, you've been at this since lunch time have you?" I smiled back. Abdus Samad of the Indian Union Muslim league (now, ironically, one of my chief opponents in my constituency of Mayiladuthurai) begged me through dinner to get Rajiv to say something about the IUML at the Marina Beach meeting scheduled immediately after dinner. It was only when Rajiv was seated on the dais that I got the opportunity to pass the message to him. "Samad wants you to mention his League. In any way at all. But please mention it," I whispered to him. "How?" he asked me "I don't know," I shot back, "but, fortunately, I'm not the boss!" He gave me that bewitching smile of his. They were the last words I ever spoke to him. He was due in my constituency at 9.20 on the morings of May 22, 1991. On the last day of Rajiv's life, I took the morning off from canvassing votes to jot down the points I thought he should touch on in his speech in Mayiladuthuri next day. I phoned my notes through to Pillai at Rajiv's 10 Janpath office. Pillai told me that the Boss was at that moment on his way to Vishakhapatnam, from where he would be flying directly to Madras. He said that the Tamil Nadu Congress Committee Presiden Vazhapadi Ramamurthy holding over the Fax message to Rajiv at Meenambakam airport. I see Rajiv glancing at it, then tucking the message into his shirt pocket. I see it travelling with him as delirous crowds wave him on through vilivakam and Poonamalee to his tryst with destiny at Sriperumburdur. I see the woman with the garland bending down to touch his feet as Nathuram Godse did to Mahatma Gandhi. And I hear the deafening explosion that carries Rajiv and my speech away to eternity.[7]

Today it is called upon to provide a stable government even while

7. Mani Shankar Aiyar. The Rajiv I Knew. *National Herald*, 28 May 1991.

countering the lethal forces of communalism and casteism which threaten to rip Indian society apart. It will also have to shoulder the gigantic challenge of freeing the economy from the clutches of the state even while catering to the needs of the country's vast population of the needy and the deprived. The suggestions and whispers of a possible realignment of forces after the elections give reason to hope that once again India will keep the demons of divisiveness at bay. Be that as it may, the country owes a huge debt of gratitude to Sonia Gandhi. Her dignified conduct ever since the brutal death of her husband has immensely enhanced her reputation in the eyes of the Indian people. Her principled refusal to play a political role could well appear in retrospect to be a landmark in the history of free India. In one fell swoop the has enabled the Congress to re- organise itself along radically different lines, to overhaul its 'culture', to pave the way for all forces opposed to authoritarianism and atomism to make common cause. None of all this, however, will deter the harbingers of catastrophe. The venomous attacks on the Nehru-Gandhi family in sections of the Western press must be seen for what they are: an onslaught against a strong and united India. For example, The Sunday Times, (London) in its editorial on Rajiv Gandhi's assassination, regrets the fact that from the very beginning independent India was not split into a hundred Hong Kongs. But these cassandras at home and abroad did not want India into existence: neither can they will it into oblivion.[8]

Rajiv Gandhi bloomed before his time, faded before the spring, and died prematurely. His carrer is a sad comment upon the state of the Congress. When his mother died, the Congress turned to him for the same reasons, that it first turned to his wife, Sonia Gandhi, upon his own death. That is, it turned to him for three reasons, which do the party no credit. First, the way the Congress had been run by Indira Gandhi, had reduced all potential leaders to pygimes. Therefore, lack of proven talent in Rajiv Gandhi was no great dis-qualification she had not allowed any rival Congressman to prove his talent either. Second, it turned to him in sychophantic or slavish homage to Indira Gandhi, in particular, and the Nehru family, in general. Third, it turned to him because he would be good for gathering votes. What sort of a prime minister he would make and whether experience had equipped him for the job, did not count very much in the eyes of the Congress caucus that chose him. That he turned out to be a good prime minister for a year or two is entirely because he broke out of the ways of the caucus, even rejected the examples his mother had set, and chose to be guided by

8. Dileep Padgaonkar. No Deluge After Rajiv. *The Times Of India,* 29 May 1991.

his own instincts and values. Thanks to a good upbringing, an inherited culture and his own good sense, his instincts and values were good. They served him well. They explain all the excellent initiatives he took upto about the middle of 1986. But they were not substance enough to enable him to meet the great needs of his demanding office. They could not go on producing good policies and actions. His office required a good team of capable and honest colleagues, which would help him overcome his own lack of experience. That means he needed a party which had a good working culture. But the Congress had none. Therefore, Rajiv Gandhi's lack of experience began to weigh him down more and more, and for all the apparent dash and vigour he showed, he fell into the terms of a coterie. His mothe knew how to create and exploit and destroy coteries. But he did not. His coteries used him. The remainiging years of his Prime Ministership, therefore, became increasingly undistinguished.[9]

I remember the days when Panditji (Nehru) moved to the Teen Murti House, New Delhi there were simple quarters then, not much of what's there now. The children, Rajiv and Sanjay, would come home for holidays from Doon School. Bunty (Amitabh Bachchan) and Ajitabh would come over to play along with our children. So would Mohammad Yunus's son. After completing their studies, Rajiv joined Indian Airlines and Sanjay set up an automobile repair shop at Punjabi Bagh, Delhi Rajiv and Sonia got married at the house on Safdarjung Road, New Delhi. We always used to call Sonia "Bahurani". Within a short while, whe could speak fluent Hindi. She loved cooking baingan ka bharta (baking vegetables). After Sanjay's wedding, the children had separate quarters in the Safdarjung house. Rajiv was a good father. Whenever he was off duty, he would play with the children, as did his mother, or take them out for long drives. On their birthdays, he would shoot their pictures. Dinner was the only time when the entire family sat together. Rajiv was very fond of ice-cream-he would make it on the machine himself. Most of the days, he woke up late. His mother would leave early and ask me to pass on messages. Sanjay was the snappy one, on the dot with appointments, planning the day. Rajiv used to have only Campa Cola, and no water, tea or coffee. Earlier, it was only Coca Cola. Sanjay, on the contrary, had only water to drink. After Sanjay's death, Rajiv stood by Indira. Whatever they did as the ruling family, they were very helpful to people in need. I used to know all the people close to them - R.K. Dhawan, M.L. Fotedar, M.N. Sharma, Indiraji's PA, Naqvi Sahib.... It was only later, after Indiraji's assassination that even my own friends were afraid of being seen with me or Dhawanji.[10] Words fail to

9. Pran Chopra. Rajiv Grew in Substance. *The Sunday Observer,* 26 May 1991

10. Nathu Ram. Rajiv Gandhi. *The Sunday Observer,* 26 May 1991.

convey one's sense of horror, anguish and revulsion at the news of the brutal assassination of Rajiv Gandhi by a bomb blast near Madras on May 21, 1991. This was an act of cowardice on the part of whosever was responsible for it. But the manner in which it was carried out strengthens suspicions about a calculated conspiracy behind it, bringing out its striking similarity with the circumstances that led to the death of Rajiv's mother, Indira Gandhi. Rajiv Gandhi's killing has come in the wake of an unprecedented outbreak of violence that marred the first day of polling for the countrywise elections to the Lok Sabha, taking a toll of 50 lives. This barbaric killing cut short the life of one of India's very promising young personality who bestrode the country's political scene for the last six and a half years, first as the head of government and then as the leader of the largest single party in Parliament. Whatever the nature of one's political differences with him-and there were not a few occassions when his actions evoked sharp criticism and srong opposition from a large spectrum of political opinion-there is no gainsaying that Rajiv Gandhi's activities left a deep and indelible impress on events both at home and abroad. Without him on the scene, politics in this country will not be the same again. Rajiv's tragic demise removes from the national political arena the most prominent figure of the present generation-the generation that was born just before independence but was brought up in free India. Rajiv Gandhi was an ardent advocate of India's emergence as a modern and perosperous scientific industrial and technological power by the turn of the century. Soon after assuming reins of power following the death of his mother, he began to articulate this vision of the new India he envisaged. No doubt it was a vision that suffered from many a shortcoming but the fact that he chose to propagate such an idea was projected as an example of this refreshingly new approach to problems beyond the confines of petty politicking and intrigues normally associated with politicians.[11]

Rajiv Gandhi had been a decent individual outside the realm of politics which had no attraction for him in his student days. When circumstances conspired to draw him into to vortex of politics after the death of his younger brother, Sanjay Gandhi, in an air crash in mid-1980, he initially gave sufficient testimony of his determination to bring in a whiff of fresh air in the suffocatiing political atmospher heightened by palace intrigues that marked the reign of his mother. This refreshingly new approach he retained in the first years in office as the Prime Minister when he sought to restore the consensual approach to national problems and opted for serious negotiations to tackle the seemingly

11. Sumit Chakravarthy. Balance Sheet of Rajiv Gandhi. *Patriot*, 25 May 1991.

intractable issues facing the country whether in Punjab or north-east. These yielded the Punjab, Assam and Mizo accords-all in his first year in office in 1985-that brightened the prospects of moving the nation forward. Side by side, Rajiv promised to revive the process of democratic functioning of the Congress by taking active steps for holding organisational elections, strove to banish the unhealthy practice of defections in public life by piloting the anti-defection law, and launched a blistering attack on power-brokers in the party and the country at large. All this had the salutary effect of bolstering his Mr. Clean image based on morality in politics.

All those who value the values advocated by Rajiv Gandhi must put their heads together to continue the fight for a stable, secular, self-sustaining, democratically developing and non-aligned India willing to work for the cause of world peace and yet not prepared for surrendering to the dictat of others.

11
THE LOVE OF POWER

The cult of violence unbashedly promoted by elements who have no faith in the democratic process, nor the country's interest at heart, has claimed another crusader for peace and non-violence in Rajiv Gandhi who, like his mother seven years ago, met with a violent death but refused to distance himself from the people. The nation's most popular leader passed away in the prime of youth at a time when it appeared he was on the comeback trail after having been in the opposition in Lok Sabha for a year and a half. His passing leaves not only the Congress party leaderless at a most critical juncture in the nation's history but the country without charismatic personality who had matured after seeing adversity and was loved and respected by friends and foes alike. As destiny would have it, moments before his brutal death at Sriperumpudur, Rajiv Gandhi paid homage to his assassinated mother Indira Gandhi by garlanding her statue and bowing to it with foleded hands reverentially. He then mingled with a crowd as he has been doing day after day during the past one month of hective campaign. Throughout the campaign, Mr. Gandhi had been preaching non-violence and communal harmony and warning the country of the dangers of falling a prey to communal slogans or responding to religious appeals. He maintained that in a composite society such as India, people of all faiths had to live in peace and harmony and no provocation was strong enough to discard Gandhi's path of nonviolence and secularism. Leaders of political parties and Congressmen who thronged the departed leader's residence at No.10 Janpath felt that the best homage to Rajiv Gandhi was to carry forward his unfinished task and to see that there is no communal flare up and anti-social and disruptive elements are not permitted to seize the opportunity to spread disaffection and chaos as they had done in the wake of Indira Gandhi's assassination. The Security is on maximum alert. It is difficult to visualise how the Congress will recover from the shock because its entire working revolved round the personality of Mr. Rajiv Gandhi, as is the case with other parties too. The party is left with no charismatic leader and shall have to rise to the occasion and through a process of consensus elect a new leader. The country is in the midst of the tenth general election and only the first phase, marked unfortunately by violence, is over. The two other phases take pace on May 23 and 26. After Congress's defeat in the 1989 election Rajiv Gandhi has been trying to work out where he went wrong and to correct himself and evolve a cohesive vision of India. In a frank, though at times sharp exchange with this correspondent a few months ago, he admitted that his political immaturity and reposing unqualified trust in people, who later stabbed him in the back, and cost him dearly. Added to this his failure of communication had created an unwanted distance between him and partymen. For want of proper management of things he had become vulnerable. He had joined politics with a technical bend of mind "while flying an aircraft you press the button and the response is immediate. But I learnt to my cost that in politics it is not so. You keep pressing but there hardly ever is a response and if there is one, it is very much delayed." In the past few months Rajiv Gandhi gave the impression of having politically matured and he had become less vulnerable. But in an age where chivalry is not to be expected, Rajiv was an eyesore to all his opponents and regarded him as an unbeatable rival.[1]

The death of Rajiv Gandhi is not the death of an individual. He was an episode in the political history of India. and his visit to Tamil Nadu was nothing but death's camouflage at play or, at least, a case of fate transitorily meeting its obligations. The intellect reels at the barbarity of his death, no malter at whose hands it was, for he had in his character many traditional virtues. Such as the dignity, honour, encourage and the fine selflessness of his illustrious grandfather. In temperament, too, he like Jawaharlal, was equable and generous. He consistently provide to be competent 'as in the signing of the Punjab, Assam and Mizorum accords). He was not set, except in his love of the country and the people. Even before becoming Prime Minister he seemed to be master of an expertise which was fast vanishing he was immensely intelligent but also immensely percipient. New facts made a tremendous impression on his capacious but sensitive mind, but he never made a fetish of novelity. Of course, it was left to Mr. Rajiv Gandhi to create the consciousness that new facts were emerging in all quarters and that they required a new interpretation, that most of our problems needed a fresh analysis and that the most venerated principles had to be restated. The world was undergoing ethnical combinations in which no elements were left unchanged. The constituents of society were being altered, both in proportion and quality. The old economic were going out of date since they were deduction from a state of things which had ceased to be. Current beliefs in every department of life were imperceptibly changing, as proved by the supreme Court judgement in the Shah Bano case. However, it was to the credit of Mr. Rajiv Gandhi that he combined an awareness of what was new with devotion to what was old. Therefore, the legislation he introduced to render nugatory the verdict was less a capitulation to fundamentalism than a concession to

1. M.K. Dhar. Crusader for Peace. *The Hindustan Times*, 22 May 1991.

the religious sentiments of a religious minority which had over the years developed, rightly or wrongly, a siege mentality. Another instance was the plan for the purification of the Ganga which was important to him as the preparation of the country for the 1st century. He had, so to say, the 18th century sense of living in a world which was not made yesterday and emphatically would not be remade tomorrow, and he saw the long descent of the most novel problems. Like Burke, he would not destory (merely because some plasterwork was shaky) what many generations had built. As the same time, he was wholly in tune with the present age and aware of every nuane of the modern world. He would not admit there was any merit in a thing merely because it was new. He would examine it first, and seemed to possess an instinct which told him where along the line of contemporary speculation that point was to be found from which the next advance might best be made. Rajiv Gandhi's attack on power brokers at the Congress centenary celebration in Bombay was a case in point. That, in the event, new power brokers replaced the old and proved his undoing was his misfortune rather than his fault. All the same, he had always had his instinct in a remarkable degree and his channel of thought, once a backwater, became under the guidance of his mother the fashionable stream. He came to see deeper into human problems and nature.[2]

Though born into India's most politically active family, Rajiv Gandhi remained aloof from politics till destiny dragged him into it. Like a meteor, he streaked across the Indian sky. Nehru and Indira Gandhi held office for a long time. The former had the additional advantage of a cooperative Opposition. Rajiv Gandhi had a short stint as Prime Minister but his achievements were no less greater than those of his predecessors. In spite of the most hostile Opposition, Rajiv Gandhi ensured a special position for India in the international community. His personal popularity was evident from the presence of so many dignitaries from various countries at his funeral, though he did not hold any official position. Run-of-the-mill politicians ridiculed his background as a piolet. But it was the thorough training a pilot has to undergo that taught him to take decisions without dithering.[3] Rajiv Gandhi's assassination is a profound tragedy of many dimensions. It is a tragedy for the world which is short on men of vision who would ceaselessly work for assuaging passions and tensions in order to bring humanity closer together and rid it of the scourage of fear and conflict. It is a deep tragedy for India for Rajiv was the symbol of unity, stability, sanity and goodwill in India. The crisis of the country has been infinitely

2. Mohammad Vazeeruddin. India's History. *The Tribune*, 29 May 1991.
3. Arabindra Bose. Coming to Terms with Grief. *The Statesman*, 29 May 1991.

deepened with his heinous act. It is a personal tragedy for the family which has already suffered so much in just one decade. The political trends unleashed in the last two years wherein lie the roots of this tragedy must be closely analysed, but before we do that mentioned of a personal side to this tragedy may be permissible. Rajiv Gandhi was a warm human being and a thorough gentleman. He had an endearing sense of humour and an infectious laughter. He never failed to appreciate a joke and could laugh at himself too, which he did with a chuckle. There are not many in politics especially in India who display any sense of humour and do not take offence at the sightest allusion to the ludicrous side of human affairs.

The dastardly act falls in line with the atmosphere of intolerance and hate sedulously fostered in India in the last one year in the name of religion or caste. The people were being fed on a daily diet or either caste fanaticism or religious fanaticism. The incitment to caste fanaticism was masquerading under the label of equity and social justice and minority communalism was openly wooed as a vote bank. But the biggest culprits were the stormtroopers of the BJP. They oozed poison in the name of the God of love and sacrifice. Never has there been such blatant abuse of religion in the service of political power in post-independent India.[4]

He was called alot of names in his all too brief lifetime: Mr. Clean, which rapidly descended to Mr. Corrupt ("Har qalli mein short hai, Rajiv Gandhi chor hai," (in every street there is a shouting that Rajiv is a thief) a charmer, a liar, stupid, naive, cunning, manipulative, perhaps he was all these things, or a combination of them. But I think of him essentially as a reluctant politician, brought kicking to centrestage against his will, after the premature death of his brother, Sanjay Gandhi-who really was an arch manipulative politician-by a mother who had become obsessed with the notion that the Nehru family was destined to rule India for ever Rajiv wanted no part of such a scheme of things, which is why he chose to marry a foreigner and went into the most apolitical of professions-flying aeroplanes. But fate willed otherwise. When Sanjay was killed, Rajiv surely dreaded the prospect of politics the two brothers did not see eye to eye on the Emergency-and it must have taken a great deal of persuasion on his mother's part to get him "to help Mummy," as he innocently put it to an interviewer. He had hardly gone up to his ankles in the political water before his mother's foolhardy "Operation Bluestar" claimed her as its major victim. Suddenly, the unprepared Rajiv found himself to be the focus of the "Sympathy wave" and before he knew what was happening, he

4. V.P. Dutt The Assassination and After. *National Herald*, 29 May 1991.

was in the driver's seat. Considering his utter lack of preparation for the role he did marvellously in the first couple of years of his premiership. Even his detractors-and I became one later on-have to admit this. The economy was liberalised, the share market boomed and India really seemed to be marching into the 21st century. Rajiv Gandhi, Vishwanath Pratap Singh and Arun Nehru formed a marvellous and most effective trio. Salacious characters like Dhirendra Brahmachari were shown the doors and a number of hot-shot aides like Arun Singh and Montek Singh Ahluwalia brought into the Prime Minister's Office (PMO).[5]

So unique a combination of qualities, rather than the office of AICC general secretary he had held before becoming Prime Minister, made him a major force. He ended up, in the words of renowned British writer, as "a very great servant of the state and a greater human being." Of course, Rajiv Gandhi had his quota of faults. But who has not? Did not Homer nod? For instance, to many there was something chilly in his all ofness from the passion of the marketplance, not quite human. Could he suffer and rejoice like an ordinary creature? That was the question many asked. Assuredly he could and did, retaining till the end the light- heartedness of a boy. As the expression goes, he maximised life, getting and giving of the best. He wanted a new India to be brought out of the magma of the old. But it was the Indian people's freedom from melodrama, their national gift of meiosis and their steady nerves which seemed to convince him that a new society could be built, a society in which there would be less social and economic injustice and less exploitation of many by man. Mr. Rajiv Gandhi had an independent mind and the courage of his convinctions. Otherwise the anti-defection bill would not have been among the first measure he introduced on becoming Prime Minister in his own right with a massive mandate. He stood by whatever he considered just and right, irrespective of the consequences. The greatest proof of it was provided by the Punjab, Assam and Mizo accord, particularly the former, considering that his election plank was basically anti-Sikh. It was this courage, this fair-mindedness, which made him popular among all sections of people. He was far too cultured a leader to tolerate barbarity. He would not otherwise have ordered an enquiry into the 1984 atrocities on Sikhs. Little wonder, therefore, that the masses looked upon him as young Moses who was to lead them to a new, secular, egalitarian way of life. He had the idealist's ardour and his sensitivity to suffereing was not mere rhetoric but a profound emotion. To recall the words that Alexander Pope used about Harley, in the wake of Indira Gandhi's

5. Rahul Singh. The Reluctant Politician. *The Independent*, 27 May 1991.

assassination Mr. Rajiv Gandhi proved to be a "steady man with a great firmness of soul,." Even a dictator like Zia-ul- Haq said as much, though not in so many words. There were many strong colours in the nature of Rajiv Gandhi but he diffused a gentle, compelling radiance.[6]

The most charming man of Indian politics and the shining star of the Nehru family has been snatched away by the most cruel death. This is a blot on the Indian democracy. This family sacrificed almost everything for India and for maintaining democratic traditions of India. In the politics of India-a reenactment of the Mahabharata-another great hero has fallen. At that time it was Veer Abhimanyu and this time it was the Veer Abhimanyu Rajiv. In this great battle everyone contributed to the brutal end of this hero. We deserve to hang our head in shame. Rajiv will be remembered by the people just as Abhimanyu.[7]

History has been the rise and fall of many states. Each conducted itself on the principle of first, struggle for survival and, then, expansion through domination. Many eventually fell by the same instrumentalities through which they had emerged, survived and expand. Mahatma Gandhi's India represented a new point of departure in history. Without recourse to violnce, the Mahatma had brought into being a free country. This was the first time ever that history had seen nonviolence used successfully as a political instrument. That same India, under Jawaharlal Nehru's stewardship, advocated a revolution in the mindset that had hitherto guided international relations. Where, since the dawn of history and before, the quest for dominance had been regarded as normal and natural. Nehru's India advocate and end to dominance in any form and the opening of an epochal new era of peaceful coexistence. Panditji's Non-alignment challenged every conventional asumption of international relations and every conventional goal of diplomacy. Instead of confronting the rival blocs with an alternative vision of an international order of equality in place of dominance, cooperation in place of strife, coexistence in place of deferrence, nonviolence in place of violence. Within the country, the domination of the vested interest was frontally challenged by the application of the revolutionary principles in which Gandhiji and Panditji founded our modern nationhood.

Democracy took political power from the grip of feudal chieftains and placed it in the hands of the people. Secularism undermind the domination sought by sectarian zealotry. And socialism uprooted the comfortable domination of the economy by large landowners and a handful of Capitalists. No wonder then that during these 42 years of

6. Mohammad Vazeeruddin. India's History. *The Tribune*, 29 May 1991.
7. Daman Prakash. Great Tragedy. *National Herald*, 1 June 1991.

independence. India has seen many challenges, that would have fragmented nations of lesser intrinsic strength or lesser will. We believe that far from imitating models developed elsewhere, it is the mission of India to build, in the light of the precept given us by Gandhiji and Panditiji, a society and a nation which would serve as an example to the world on how to deal with the post-nuclear world and the new technology that now lies in human hands. Nuclear technology has given humankind the power to destroy itself and our planet Each in the briefest wink of history. 'Technology has also opened unparalleled opprotunities for a fulfilling and bountiful life for all the citizens of planet Earth. How is one to avoid the former fate and ensure the latter? The answer lies in the human mind. Gandhiji and Panditji advocated an entirely new globel reality. India, by its example, can show the world the path to not only global survival but also to the most glorious era ever in all human history. This noble goal we can realise only by remaining true to the principles of Gandhiji and the vision of Jawaharlal Nehru. We are uniquely placed to undertake this role because we, in India are the inheritors of a great historical experience in organizing a multi-lingual, multi-ethnic, multi- religious, multi-caste, multi-regional society. The village of the new technology has to learn from our experience the basic lesson of how hamanity is to live together not in segregated states but as one human family.[8]

Those who are at the top do not allow other to come near their position due to insecurity, but the parties' member are also to be blamed for allowing the leader at the to do what they want. The Indian political psyche seems to believe in one leader worship. Political activists look up to only that one leader, there by denying another a chance to make any serious attempt to reach that level. This in turn leave them with no other alternative but to two the line of the supreme leader because their own political survival starts depending on him/her. While blaming the Nehrus for perpetrating dynastic rule in a democratic country, we should also consider the fact that none of the second rank leaders in the Congress ever tried to increase their area of influence beyond their respective states or regions. The current second rung leader such as P.V. Narsimha Rao, N.D. Tiwar, Pranab Mukherjee and Sharad Pawar, who have been in higher level politics for more than 15 years, have failed to assume a national image. Although most of them were in union governments either with Indira Gandhi or Rajiv Gandhi for years, they have, in effect, remained state level politicians. This is a sad commentary on the political system in India.[9]

8. Rajiv Gandhi. *Nehru Centenary Memorial Lecture.* New Delhi, 13 November 1989.
9. Bharat Kumar. A Dynastic democracy. *The Independent,* 26 May 1991.

The leadership style of Indira Gandhi was characterised by intolerence of party bosses, impatience with factions, greater reliance on populist slogans and mass mobilisation techniques than on the instrument of the party and finally a preparedness to reach out to the Indian people overarching the party, to seek from them a kind of plebiscitary endorsement for her politics and her leadership. To her the party was no more than a tool at best and an inconvenience at worst. This brought handsome electoral returns and Indira Gandhi emerged as the single most valuable resource of the party. Everything else because secondary only to be manipulated to strengthen the asset. Thirteen years of hegemonic leadership inevitably produced organisational decay as vital organs of the party lay in diuse. With no elections in the party, filling up of party posts through appointment of "loyalists" and the disruption of the normal authority structure, the Congress party became more and more moribund and lost contact with its supporters and sympathisers. Rajiv Gandhi inherited from his mother such a Tammany Hall type of Congress organisation when the mantle of leadership fell on him under tragic circumstances. As soon as the initial euphoria and sympathy subsided, problems resurfaced and a seriously debilitated party was unable to help him face upto them. In fact, the party itself had become an encumbrance. To set the matters right Rajiv wanted to "restore a democratic functioning within the party" and declared that party elections would be held in the following months. But nothing happened.[10] Again, at the Congress centenary celebrations in December 1985 he threatened to deal firmly with the power-brokers and wheeler dealers and to expose "all the paper tiger". Again nothing happened.

Certain words or definitions used for instant communication purposes, tend to get unfounded durability. A section of the media and intelligensia, for intance, picked up with facile ease the conceptual formulation of "dynastic rule" and began to critically fix it to the Nehru-Gandhi tenure. This is a big semantic hoax, and needs to be debunked. When Gandhi proclaimed Jawaharlal Nehru as his heir in the thirties, despite the presence of many other Congress Stalwarts like the venerable Sardal Pate, C. Rajagopallahari and Maulana Azad he hardly did so to perpetuate the dynasty of Motilal Nehru. Motilal himself was a top leader of the party on his own right, along with stalwarts like C.R. Das and others. But the Mahatma designated Jawaharlal as his heir because he perceived that next to himself the Indian masses were more atuned to the handsome, sensitive Jawaharlal than to any other leaders. Putting it differently, Mahatma Gandhi saw as day-light the fact that Nehru was more atuned to the Indian masses

10. Ram Joshi. Congress: Hegemony to Consensus. *The Times Of India*, 20 May 1991.

everywhere in this vast country than any other leader, other leaders largely held sway over their own regions of provinces, not beyond them. The Indian masses as a whole responded to Nehru much more enthusiastically than to any of his comrades in the freedom struggle. Jawaharlal commanded the language and the pitch, the style and the personal charsima, that tended to deeply move the Indian masses. Gandhiji, as the supreme leader of the national struggle, never belittled or ignored the dedication or the limited influence of other Congress leaders, but he, at the same time, reckoned Nehru's intellectual superiority and stature, and the tremendous capacity to move the masses. He therefore declared Jawaharlal as his heir not to perpetuate Motilal's dynasty in the Congress but to successfully conduct the freedom struggle of an unarmed people against the mightest Imperial power at that point of time. He had to keep the country prepared to the eventuality of his accidental absence from the scene during the Indian struggle for liberation. Also, there had to be someone to lead the cause, even if freedom was won during his lifetime, as it indeed came about. The Mahatma also wanted to ensure that Jawaharlal should head the first Independent India's government. Since then till his death, Jawaharlal Nehru remained the unchallenged leader not only of the Congress but of the entire nation. All other leaders, whether in his own party or in the opposition, remained totally overshadowed by him, both intellectually and in terms of love, trust and respect he evoked from the Indian people, irrespective of their religion, language, caste or creed.[11]

One recall when once in the early sixties, Jawaharlal expressed his desire to quit the Prime Ministership to devote his whole time and every to revitalise the party. Not only were Congrssmen driven to the verge of despair, and people in their thousands began prayers to dissuade him from taking contempated step. Even the top leaders of the Communist Party went in a delegation to persuade him not to do so, in fact the Central Committee of the Party adopted a resolution urging Nehru to continue to lead the country! Gandhiji did not plant the Nehru dynaty on the people of this country. On the contracy, the people themselves repeatedly gave the mandate to Jawaharlal Nehru Neither did he impose his daughter Indira by way of birth-as dynastic rule operte in the octual cannotation of the word-or through intrigue on the nation. After Jawaharlal passed away in 1964. Indira Gandhi did not even make a feeble attempt to become the Prime Minister. The contest in the Congress Parliamentary Board and the Working Committee was between Lal Bahadur Shastri and Morarji Desai. The later was

11. Ashis Barman. It was Not Dynastic Rule. *Patriot*, 1 June 1991.

defeated and Lal Bahadur became the Prime Minister. After Shastri's death abroad in 1966, there was a contest in the CPP between Morarji Desai and Indira Gandhi in the united Congress and Mrs Gandhi was backed by a large majority of the Congressmen as the party's choice for Prime Ministership Desai was defeated democratically, and had abided by the results. Thus Indira Gandhi was never placed in the Prime Minister's chair by the alleged dynastic logic-a fashionable charge of the carping critics. Not only Indira Gandhi's Prime Ministership came about through democratic norms exercised by her party. Within the confines of the parliamentary processes, but her continuation in the seat of power-along with her ouster in 1977-came by way of democratic verdicts of the people. The Indian people have never relented from excercising their judgement regarding the merit or otherwise of their elected leaders. Thus, they had refused to blindly follow even Indira Gandhi. In the wake of the disastrous devaluation of the rupee by Indira Gandhi in 1966, the people of Indira punished her party by defeating it in nine States for the first time. It is another matter that the leaders of the anti- Congress parties, including men like Charan Singh and the socialists, miserably failed and ended up totally descredited. The Congress headed by Indira Gandhi drew proper lessons from the misteken steps of devaluation, and later adopted radical policies to bounce back to power in the opposition rules states. But electoral triumphs of 1971-72, following the split in her party in 1969, hardly paved the socalled dynastic Nehru-Gandhi rule. In the wake of Emergency excesses and strong-arm tactics, the angry people of this country threw out Indira Gandhi personally, along with her party's dominion. The people reposed high hopes on the Janata Party and leaders like Jayaprakash Narayan, Morarji Desai, Charan Singh, Chandra Shekhar and so on. But, bothe the Janata Party and the leaders connected with it, including the two non- Congress Prime Ministers, namely Desai and Charan Singh, belied their hope.

People, angry with these discredited leaders and the hotchpotch party they had fathered just to gain personal power, ousted them in 1980 and brought back the Congress led by Indira Gandhi to the governmental seat. This triumph was the democratic asertion of the people in favour of Indira Gandhi and her party, as much as was the Janata Party victory in 1977. There was nothing dynastic in this return of Indira Gandhi and her party.[12]

One key to the understanding of Rajiv Gandhi before he became Prime Minister was his low profile and reticence, though many who knew him well even in those days averred that he was an extermely

12. *Ibid.*

engaging conversationalist whose talk was not a brilliant monologue or a string of epigrams but as exercise which quickened and elevated the whole discussion and brought out the best of other people. He would take the hesitant remark of a shy man (he himself was one) and discover in it unexpected possibilities, would probe and expand it until its author felt that he had really made some contribution to human wisdom'. His guests would then leave walking on air feelig no special obligation to him (that was his technique) but convinced that they were bigger men than they had thought! In conversation he had a delicate courtesy which was without a suspicion of patronage. Hence he had admirers of every type and in all parties, the only grumblers possibly being the small fry who believed that a leader should chain his soul to the party he headed.

Another charge often levelled against Rajiv Gandhi was that he had a genius for picking on wrong persons for his friendship. Some of them were surely unworthy of it, but Rajiv Gandhi knew from his mother's experience, if from nothing else, that the personalities of "friends" would shift and change as they were lighted up by a change in circumstance. Very few were independent of their envorinment. Rajiv Gandhi was prepared for the lighting changing, but looked for those who had the light within themselves, as in an opal or a star-sapphire. There was nothing slacklipped in his geniality. He could be a stern critic of incompetence (remember what happened when a fire broke out in the Asiad village as the country was preparing to host Asian Games?) and make devastating comments. One such comment on Anjaiah may he led to the birth of the Telugu Desam Party, but what matters is that he was willing to take the risk. Besides, he had strict moral standards. In the graver matters of conduct, people were surprised to find that this urbane young man of the world had a stiff knuckle of puritanism, the stiffer because it was so completely intelligent. He proved equal to every situation; none was intractable. He had repeatedly shown as Prime Minister that he was endowed with strong critical mind and a fastidious taste but that he also had reverence for the plain man and his modes of thought. His arguments were directed against specious generalities. He believed in and revered human reason but not the contorted visionary reason of the metaphysician. It was common sense, the ordinary consciousness, a wise appreciation of the working rules of human society, the free-play of the intellect that could understand the intractable subject matter it worked with which he prized.[13]

Don't forget that after 1984, Rajiv Gandhi had power, real power, power neither Jawaharlal nor Indira ever had, a power of over two-thirds majority in parliament, the power to amend even the constitution

13. Mohammad Vazeeruddin. *Op. Cit.*

at will. More than that, he had the whole country behind him. He floundered, not because he was not a savvy politician but because he really didn't believe in anything deeply enough to get it done. In all the interviews you read, he talks of how the system defeated him. But that's not new: a system, any system, builds up a network of vested interests which will resist the slightest change in that system. Rajiv Gandhi had the mandate and the power not just to change, but to destroy the system if he had wanted to. But first, he had to know that he wanted to. In the absence of that, all we got was a bit of tinkering here and a bit of tinkering there. He begam tinker with the economy and liberalise it; the moment someone sounded a danger signal, he applied the brakes. He began to tinker with Doordashan and liberalise it; the moment affected politicians made a noise, he dropped Janvani and Bhaskar Gosh and the like. He began to reform our education system but never carried that through; our electoral system, but let it continue; in fact to get our society ready for the 21st century but opted instead for reactionary measures like the Muslim women's bill. Of course he was wrongly advised, but it's the leader who chooses his advisors. If only he had the convictions, the right advisors would have come his way. If only he had trusted his instincts! Just go back to what he initiated and you find a liberal, open mind at work. And his own instincts were right because Rajiv Gandhi was basically a very decent human being. That's what you saw when you met him. That's what we saw on television and that's what we see in the pictures. A warm, decent, human being who charmed everyone he met. Left to himself by his mother, he would have grown to a ripe old age, flying his beloved planes, achieving his lifelong aim of flying jets, and being a good family man.[14]

But having not been left to himself by Indira, and being forced to lead a country against his will, who knows what he might have done if the bomb hadn't happened.

None of us can choose the manner of our going but for Rajiv Gandhi, the gods chose the most inappropriate way. They-the gods or the ghouls-chose to blow away his face, and it was Rajiv's face which until the last retained a quite disconcerting innnocence. It was disconcerting because no man who is 48, has any right to look so lamb-like, so seemingly untarnished by the wickedness of this world. He has certainly no ritht to such purity if he is in politics and is its focal point. But there it was in all the photographs. You saw it especially in pictures which caught him laughing: the mouth is open wide, the eyes crinkled up, the whole aspect one of total abandonment. We seem to have intruded upon a particularly unguarded moment. Yet the moment is very public,

14. Anil Dharker. If Only. *The Independent*, 26 May 1991.

and the moment is also very frequent. Cast a look at other photographs of him: Rajiv with world leaders. There he is clasping Margaret Thatcher's hand or standing at attention by the side of Bnazir Bhutto or laughing at some sally of Mikhail Goebachev's. You see in the pictures not only that he is much younger than they-he is younger than even Benazir,though not in years-but that in meeting them, he is meeing them with an openness which speaks of total trust. Surely that's not right? Surely a leader should be guarded, suspicious, knowing? Surely a leader shouldn't exude so much warmth that you feel he means it? Warmth and charm: Whether you met him briefly or over a longer peiod, whether it was at a crowded press conference or at a quiet get-together, you came away feeling that you had met a man who had these two qualities in abundance. He could be, you felt, a good friend. That's what I felt too in the one extended meeting I had with him. This was in Delhi when he was Prime Minister and he decided to call in 'experts' in various fields to have breakfast meetings with him. Breakfast-a real five-course one-lasted a full two hours. We had enought time to speak; in fact the impression each one of us got was that we could have stayed till lunch hadn't it been for our own sense of guilt that affairs of state were waiting, Rajiv Gandhi seemed so much to enjoy the relaxed conversation. He might, of course, have been playing the good host, but it seemed to all of us at this meeting-and to others at other times-that good food, good conversation and light- hearted banter were things he enjoyed most. Nothing wrong with that, you might say. A lot of us do too. Agreed, but then a lot of us aren't Prime Ministers.[15]

Here is an extract from a letter Bapu wrote when he had heard about the death of my mother: "...Why grieve, over the inevitable? And death is the common measure of all that lives. Imagine the torture that birth would be if there was no death! Loss, therefore, is a conventional word. Then true friendship is tested finally by the death of the loved one....Let Him take what He has given. Let us then praise His great name..."All that Bapu wrote in that letter applies to to Rajiv Gandhi now. When innocent people were being killed daily in more than one state of India and his heart was bowed with all the griefs of the nation, Rajiv Gandhi as Prime Minister still found time to write personal letters to very ordinary citizens like me. Such was the man Rajiv Gandhi, full of the milk of human kindness. Let us muster courage and rededicate ourselves to the sacred mission for which Mahatma Gandhi, Indira Gandhi and Rajiv Gandhi lived and died-their ceaseless fight against communalism, obscurantism, revivalism and religious fundamentalism of

15. *Ibid.*

all types.[16]

I was never one of Rajiv's close friends. He came to Cambridge University to study for his Mechanical Sciences Tripos (he never completed the course) in 1962, the year that I left the University. His buddies at Cambridge were Arun Singh, Suman Dubey, Sanjeev Mukherjee (son of India's first air chief), Michael Albuquerque (husband of Doordarshan newsreader Usha Allbuquerque) and Deep Kaul (son of T.N. Kaul). To their credit, Rajiv's pals never tried to use their closeness to him to their advantage. One who tried, Deep Kaul, was banished from the coterie. Mani Sahnkar Aiyar and Rajiv overlapped one year at Cambridge but their close association only stated after Rajiv become Prime Minister. M.J. Akbar, too, only got to know Rajiv well after 1985. Though I had met him briefly on a few occasions earlier, the first time that I saw Rajiv for a prolonged period was when I accompanied him as part of the press party on his first major trip abroad as Prime Minister in June 1985. For almost a fortnight, I watched him at close quarters at press conference, receptions, sight-seeing tours, addresses to various groups and gatherings. I remember vividly the first time we spoke on that trip. It was on the first day itself and we had arrived at Cairo from New Delhi. I had worn a very brightly coloured sports shirt for the plane journey, thinking that I would have sufficient time on arrival at Cairo to change into something sober at the hotel. But right from our touchdown at Cairo airport in the morning, we were rushed straight to the Egyptian president's palace and thereafter it was one hectic meeting and reception after another. In the evening, still in my outrageously multi-hued shirt, when we were all being taken around the famed Citadel, I finally got a chance to speak to Rajiv and, since we had not met for quite some time, also to introduce myself. "How could I have failed to recognise you in that shirt of yours," he said poking me in the ribs with a smile, "I've been noticing you even since we got down at Cairo airport!" We both had a hearty laugh. That was Rajiv, fun-loving, informal, he put you straight at ease. In that sense at least, Rajiv was so different from both his mother and his brother. Neither of them had a sense of humour and you couldn't really relax with either of them. Rajiv was hugely likeable and made you feel comfortable with him, even if you were a stranger. There was nothing imperious or daunting about him, as there was with his mother. As I said, I observed Rajiv closely on that foreign trip. At the beginning he was quite unsure of himself, fumbling at press conferences and getting his facts wrong. In Algeria, at a press conference he was even uncharacteristically rude to an American reporter. But he was a fast learner. As

16. Omar Luther King. Vicious Killing. *The Hindustan Times*, 28 May 1991.

the journey progressed, he grew in confidence and in stature and by the time we had reached the USA, he had almost become a seasoned pro, like his host President Reagan. The two men hit it off instantly. The contrast with Indira Gandhi's earlier disastrous trip to the USA could not have been greater. But the high point of the Rajiv Gandhi trip was the lunch meeting at the Washington Press Club. For some reason the Club asked me to represent the entire Indian press corps by sitting at the high table, along with Rajiv and Sonia Gandhi, and a few selected members of the foreign press. Even the likes of Buta Singh, Narasimha Rao and Romesh Bhandari were relegated to lesser tables. At one corner of the dining room were seated some Khalistanis, who had insisted on attending the lunch and the Washington Press Club, in true liberal tradition, had allowed them to do so. After the President of the Press Club had introduced Rajiv Gandhi in the typical irreverent and humours fashion common among American journalists on such occasions, Rajiv gave an imprompt speech which was a model for the occasion: short, informal, to the point and witty. I could sense that the normally hard-bitten Washington press corps, which has a reputation of making mince-meat of visiting dignitaries, had been completely won over by Rajiv. At the question and answer session that followed, he was equally good, fielding tough questions deftly and, when needed, with humour. When asked about the Punjab problem, he looked hard at the table where the Khalistanis were sitting and replied that he would like to "remind the gentlemen sitting over there" that the capital of the early 19th century Ranjit Singh's empire-which the Sikh extremists want to restore as "Khalistan"-was actually Lahore. While the audience laughed the Khalistanis looked distinctly embarrassed. I returned from that trip feeling proud of our new leader. True, he was no great intellectual, but he was a learner and he seemed pragmatic. The reluctant politician had in a very short time become somebody who had begun to enjoy politics. I saw him again on a few occasions, when he wanted to talk about the Punjab problem. There, too, he made a marvellous start. But then something-I really don't know exactly what-went seriously wrong. Perhaps he became cocky, perhaps power went to his head, perhaps his security needs cut him off from the people, perhaps the Bofors scandal paralysed him. But he somehow lost that marvelous instinct that he had in the first couple of years of power. Retribution came with the challenge from the expelled V.P{. Singh and the 1989 election. On October 1990, I was in Delhi and it happened to be my 50th birthday. My Cambridge friend, Taj Hotels Vice-president Camelia Panjabi, also happened to be there. "Let's have a party and let's also call Rajiv Gandhi," she said. I hadn't interacted with him for a long time and I had also been writing critically of him during his last couple of years in power. But I called him anyhow and he came, saying that he would just stay for a few minutes but stayed for over two hours. At the party, the youngest guest was two-year-old Alisha. She pointed to Rajiv and said, "Who he?" Everybody, including Rajiv, had a good laugh. "At least it shows that I don't appear so much on Doordarshan," he joked. It was the Rajiv of old. And it looked like he was going to be given a second chance to run the country. He blew his first chance, but I think this time round he would have done a better job.[17]

The nation is deeply shocked at a dastardly murder that has not only cut off a promising career in its prime, but which deeply offends every civilized instinct of the Indian people. In this hour of renewed bloodshed thought turns automatically to that cruel killing in 1984 when Indira Gandhi was so tragically sacrificed. In a sense India has not really recovered from that grim event, and the related happenings that came before and after. Rajiv Gandhi has walked in the shadow of death even since. Opinion will differ as to when he was actually inducted into political office and why; but there can be no two views on the courage that he displayed in taking up his mother's somber responsibilities in the certain knowledge that he was risking his life. But no one can over have imagined that death would strike now, so suddenly, and in Tamil Nadu of all places. This election campaign has been brutal in many respects; it has gone beyond normal political skirmishing to question certain fundamentals about the Indian Republic and its most cherished beliefs. In the process, it may be said to have discarded many of the niceties that give a certain gentlemanly gloss to contests under the Westminster system of governance, and unleashed stark and basic passions and powerful medieval urges. Yet, the south has, by and large, remained untouched by these developments which have been reflected mainly in the violence, bloodshed and electoral abuses reported from Bihar and Uttar Pradesh.[18] The loss is great at a human level for Rajiv Gandhi was a living father and a devoted husband, more endearingly attached to his family than many men in public life. But the national loss is incalclaubel, for the blow is not just to a person but to a process and a concept. In the opinion of many Rajiv Gandhi would have been in a position to from a government once the 10th Lok Sabha had been elected and to restore some stability to a badly bruised polity. It is sad enough that he should be cut off on the eye of this expected vindication. What is to be regretted in-finitely more is the impact that his untimely death, and the manner of it, is bound to have on the political system and, indeed, on India's future. One suspected that as he matured as Pri

17. Rahul Singh. The Reluctant Politician. The Independetn. 27 May 1991
18. *The Statesman*, 22 May 1991.

me Minister he let the world see his latent aversion to too roseate dreams about humanity and also its profund consciousness of homely worth and homely wisdom. His enthusiasm was for what was practicable, for the business of carrying on courageously the work of the world. He had many of the attributes of a popular leader though he was unrhetorical and fastidious and seemed to hate all that was showy and glossy, and his mental processes were often too subtle for popular comprehension. He had profond respect for the fortitude of human nature, the courage with which Indians stumble up the steep ascent of life. It was, therefore, the business of this leader not so much to put quality into his following as to elicit it since the quality was already there. Evidence of that was to be found in his repeated and categorical statement that every member of his team was on probation.[19]

Above all, Rajiv Gandhi had enormous trust in his countryment and believed that there was no odd they could not overcome if given the correct lead. And it was a trust they never betrayed.

19. Mohammed Vazeeruddin. Op.Cit.

12
HIS PUBLIC LIFE

History may be pitilessly objective in evaluatiing the Rajiv Gandhi years as an era which witnessed the most rapid deterioration in the quality of politics and public life in India. Instead of giving the Congress a bright, young fresh look. His later years in office saw new ugly facets added to what has come to be known as the Congress culture. His own basic honesty and decency failed to assert themselves in making the crucial decisions affecting both his government and the congress and yet Rajiv Gandhi and the Congress along held the potential to stem the rot. After all, Rajiv Gandhi, even more than his mother, was the Congress. He was both its maker and unmaker. His sudden exit from the scene puts a frightening question mark over the future of the Congress and the country. The trouble with the party is that it has no acceptable national leader. The congress as it exists today, would disqualify itself as the party of national consensus. Perhaps it is time for leaders of such Congress splinters as the Janata Dal, the Janata Dal(S) and the Jan Morcha to come together to revive the Indian National Congress of old. This is Indian's hour of tragedy (in a greater sense than it was on January 30, 1948, or October 31, 1984,[1] The period and extent of trauma is likely to be more than the previous two assassinations because the void left by Rajiv Gandhi is very, large.

The first half of 1987 found Rajiv beset with almost every imaginable difficulty. The year had started with the very real risk of war with Pakistan and continued with a series of rows and scandals which reflected adversely on Rajiv's leadership, culminating in the resignation from the government, and subsequent expulsion from the party, of Rajiv's most trusted and respected colleague, V.P. Singh. Operation Brass Tacks and the near war with Pakistan contributed in their own way to Rajiv's difficulties. They had provided the pretext in January for transferring V.P. Singh from the Ministry of Finance, which he had headed for two years, to Defence, The ostensibel reason was that the Defence Ministry needed a full time head at a moment when the country felt itself threatened by Pakistan. Rajiv's repeated denials that V.P. Singh had been moved at the insistence of aggrieved industrialists were not entirely convincing and became less so in the light of later developments. V.P. Singh had earned the reputation as a powerful and effective Finance Minister who had succeeded in controlling inflation as well as raising tax revenue by more efficient collection and by

1. *The Tribune*, 23 May 1991.

tightening controls on evasion.[2]

There was a ridiculous innocence about Rajiv Gandhi. His grandfather, Jawaharlal Nehru, had some of this innocence, but otherwise it did not run in the family. By her last days his mother, Indira Gandhi was a devious and suspicious melancholic. His younger brother Sanjay, had mambition-great heaps of it-but no observable quality which could endear him to strangers. Sanjay, should have filled his mother's shoes. He was the keeper of the dubious political flame. But then in 1980 his aeroplane fell out of the sky over Delhi, and Rajiv became heir apparent. I first met him around time. I liked him. Most foreigners and foreign correspondents did. Among Indians, this liking was often viewed harshly and with suspicion. We liked him, we were told, because he was amirro-image of ourselves. He spoke English better than Hindi, he had married an Italian, he read English novels (usually bad ones; Robert Ludlum was a favourite), he loved computers and computer games. In short, he neither knew nor understood the great chimera: "the real India". All this was true enough and yet his original intentions were admirable in their innocent way. I remember that first meeting: June 1981, on the root of a *rajah's* palace in Amethi, Uttar Pradesh. He had been persuaded (mother doing the armtwisht-ing: who else could she trust?) to stand for his dead brother's parliamentary seat. A joke went round one of the opposition parties. "Congress candidate is BSc Cambridge Fail. Our man is MA Jabbalpur Pass.." That was near the mark. I didn't expect brightness from Rajiv. He was famous as a steady kind of airline pilot whom Indian Airlines had not seen fit to promote to jets-a nice guy. Dr. Jekyll to hsi brother's Mr. Hyde. But at that time the brightness, orlack of it din't seem to matter. He sat on the roof and said all the things that anyone who has ever been dissatisfied with India (which is everybody who has ever been to India, as well as most people who live there) has always wanted to hear; and been as innocent, as Rajiv in wanting to hear it.[3]

Let's face it, the country didn't work. The politicians were feudal and corrupt. People were losing confidence in the system. A whole class of people-the managerial, executive class of which he was a member-had been alienated from politics. They needed to be brought in, to clean up the stables, to make the trains run on time. He was earnest and I think he meant what he said, I wrote it piece and dubbed him "Mr. Clean". After he won the seat, I saw him spurn a triumph as gift of luzurious sweets from Delhi's best hotel. A small act, but the determination to start well-an end to corruption, new voters begin herel-was

2. Micholas Nugent. Scandal. *The Statesman*, 1 June 1991.
3. Ian Jack A Tragic Innocent. *The Independent*, 24 May 1991.

touching. And then, in 1984, his mother was murdered. Thousands of "Sikhs died, especially in Delhi, as Hindu mobs exacted their idea of revenge. Many need not have died. The army could have been called out much earlier than it was Sikh suburbs could have been protected. But Rajiv did nothing for too long. "When a great tree falls, the earth shakes," he said of the butchery. That was not such an innocent statment. It seemed to excuse the butchers. Still, for year there was a marvellous honeymoon. He won the ensuing election with the largest majority in the 40-years history of Indian democracy. India, especially elite, urban India, fell in love with him. He may have been one of us, but he was also one of them. Caste didn't matter to him, his father a Parsi. He played Stevie Wonder records. He arranged political accords (always short- lived) with the Sikhs in the Punjab and the Assamese in Assam. When I went to see him in the Prime Minister's office, he was in many ways as innocent and boyish as ever. Free enterprise was the message how. Away with trade restrictions, government licences: "taking India into the twenty-first century" was the pharase and the plan, whatever that meant. I asked him if he believed in God. "No", said Rajiv. I gave him full marks for the lack of humbug, and out of 10 for political nous. In an outer office one of his aides, one of the new marketing men (ex-Cherry Blossom shoe polish, Calcutta) was already confinding that they had got it wrong, that they could not cope with the feudalism and the corruption and would therefore have to be more feudal and more corrupt. That happened. The gloss wore off. Rajiv Gandhi became as cynical and manipulative as his mother, and perhaps as anyone must be who governs India. He should have got out when he lost the last election. Many people expected him to, and also to quit India for an exile's life in Italy or Britain, safe under armed guard. He stayed because he had grown to love power. A terrible mistake. Innocence again.[4]

I was stunned at the barbaric assassination of Rajiv Gandhi. It is a pity that when we are ushering in the 21st century and the world is progressing at a very fast pact, our country is going through one trauma after another. Beginning as a novice in politics in 1984 Rajiv Gandhi became one of the most well-known leaders in the world. His eversmiling face will forever be remembered by every Indian. The Nehru family has done a lot for India and those who criticise dynastic rule must realise that it is just one family in India which has had a make the supreme sacrifice-not once, but twice-in a span of seven years.[5] The

4. *Ibid.*
5. Chandana Chakraborty: A Brutal Assassination. *The Telegraph*, 27 May 1991.

assassination of Rajiv Gandhi, is the biggest shock this country has had since Indepedence. It is difficult to believe that he is no more. Finally, after a long time there had emerged a silver lining on the dark clouds on the nation's horizon. It was widely expected that the people if India would once again repose confidence in Rajiv Gandhi and his ability to provide a strong, stable and vibrant democracy. How different he was from everyone: His sincere and thorough bred gentlemanly manner and demeanour was far above the petty and sectarian attitudes of most of our other leaders. The violnce and chaos that we have witnessed in the process of the current election is truly insane. That these barbaric acts would one day engulf Rajiv-a man so full of love and affection always smiling, is difficult to believe. One will always miss his over-powering personality. Now that this earth shattering event has taken place, we are grief stricken and realize our folly. I hope we awaken to the danger posed by the spreading cult of the gun. It is time for the healing process to begin, and all of us fight earnestly to obliterate violence from the mainstream of Indian society.[6]

Only when would we be able to learn from our mistakes and start a new chapter towards building a strong, stable and caring India which Rajiv Gandhi so fervently believe in: What he could not achieve in his life time, his sacrifice should be able to inspire us to achieve. With the tragic assassination of Rajiv Gandhi, the country is once again at the sort of cross-roads where it stood when Indira Gandhi was assassinated in 1984. Indeed, if anything, the choices today are more difficult and the path ahead strewn with greater dangers. There is violence all around, a greater sense of a vacuum, and all manner of atavistic passions are riding high. A big question-mark also hangs over the future of democratic process in India, because increasing numbers of disaffected groups are taking to methods that are wholly inconsistent with the norms of civil society. Thus a great responsibility devolves on all Indian citizens to ensure that they keep their passions in check and do nothing which will exacerbate the already taut nerves in the country. The President of India has done well to scotch moves to declare an internal Emergency and to postpone elections by up to six months. These moves would only have undermined faith in the system. Far better to go with the elections as soon as possible, and to consider options like a national government (which R, Venkataraman himself had been in favour of last year) only after the poll results are known. The immediate moves to for a national government and to declare an Emergency have more to do with personal political ambitions and calculations than any real concern for the future of the country in a

6. Rajiv Mehta. Supreme Sacrifice. *The Independent*, 25 May 1991.

moment of dire crisis. It seems that our politicians have learnt nothing. The decision of the Election Commission to postpone the elections until June 12 and 15 has to be viewed in this overall context. Even though questions may be raised over whether it was necessary to postpone them by so many days, it must be conceded that until the tension in the air settles down, it would have been unwise to go on with the voting as scheduled. It is almost certain that there would have been even greater violence than witnessed on the first day of polling, when 50 people reportedly lost their lives. The government has also been done well to announce a commission of inquiry and the formation of a special investigation team, to go into the assassination. Preliminary reports seem to suggest LTTE involvement. The assassination of Rajiv Gandhi has plunged India into its deepest crisis to date. When Jawaharlal Nehru died, there was the mighty Congress party to which the people looked. When Indira Gandhi died, the party had all but disintegrated, but Rajiv was there-having been studiously groomed for a succession over four years. Today, the choice seems to be between a bunch of non-leaders and a grieving wife with no expreince or penchant for politics. At the level of political discourse, the present situation could well presage an uncoordinated lurch away from the centrist Politics of the Congress. For those who inherit the party or more accurately, the motley collection of none-to- upright individuals who pass for one, the focus of endeavour must be to prevent this. For, in its 105 years, the Congress had come to mean all things to all men, there by gaining an unparalleled national presence. It was in this that its strength lay. If, in the absence of the stren hand to guide it, it gives in to the ever-present dangers which inviegle Indian politicians, the curtain would truly have been rung down on a play that had once promised to go on forever. And yet, there is one bequest that Nehru, Indira and Rajiv have left behind which must be preserved and built upon by the nation. This is the fundamentally modern and forward looking view of India and the world. Today, when the nation is in the grip of all manner to atavistic passions, nothing can be more important then the single-minded pursuit of the modernist ideal which the Nehru-Gandhi family personified. It is all too easy, when the grief abates and the wound heals, to lose the central passion of a leaders life. Just as for Gandhiji it was satyagraha, for the Nehru-Gandhi family it was the vision of India as a modern nation-state. Meanwhile, the task befor the central government headed by Chandra Shekhar as also the various state governments is to ensure that the spreading violence is contained. Failure to do so will further weaken the faith of the people in the law and order machinery.[7]

7. *The Economics Times*, 23 May 1991.

This is something that the nation can ill afford. It is also incumbent upon the union government to pay some what more attention than it has been doing in the last few weeks to running the government. Though this intention may be understandable in the light of the elections, the economy is too close to collapse to be able to afford such a luxury. Such decisions as have to be taken must be taken forthwith so that the slide towards bankruptcy is halted. About a fortnight ago, Rajiv Gandhi allowed himself to think aloud in the midst of a punchy election speech about the dire consequences of another hung parliament. Soon thereafter, the BJP's leading ideologue, K.R. Malkani took many people by surprise by suggesting that in a hung parliament, the BJP might seek Congress support to run the government. Malkani's suggestion drew for the gushes of protests from leaders of the Congress-I as well as BJP though I found it difficult to believe that a seasoned RSS leader like Malkani would have indulged in that kind of political kiteflying without consulation with at least some of the top brass of the RSS-BJP combine. Congress leaders from Rajiv Gandhi down ruled out all possibilities of a political combination between the two parties after the election. In the election, however, some token linkages between the two have stirred considerable public interest. A National Front leader and former cabinet minister is being opposed both by the Congress and BJP, while in at least one election meeting in the South local leaders of the two parties were seen sharing the same platform. But, of course, two slender swallows do not a summer make. The assumption behind Malkani's statement was that the BJP would emerge as the single largest group in the Lok Sabha. Since it would need some substantial support from other parties the best party to solicit support was the Congress because it has been the long-time design of RSS to weave the two parties gogether into a "truly nationalist party". However, Malkani's basic assumption many have an overdose of wishful enthusiasm. While many poll observers forecast a substantial swell in the BJP presence in the next Lok Sabha compared to the 85 members it had in the previous House, I have not known of any one so far who has predicted that BJP would emerge as the single largest party. Personally I find it difficult to believe that BJP will get more than 100 seats in the tenth Lok Sabha. A hung parliament, as noted, will necessitate a coalition. A very senior Congress leader who is close to Rajiv Gandhi disclosed confidentialy a couple of weeks ago that his party would interpret a second hung parliament as an electoral mandate for a coalition government. But the million dollar question is: who is to coalesce with whom?[8]

8. Bhabani Sen Gupta. Birds of a Feather Flock Together. *The Independent*, 24 May 1991

In November 1989, the National Front had two electoral allies; the Left Front and BJP. Neither was ready to join a government formed by the NF, but both committed themselves to support it from outside. Thus was the coalition of November 1989 formed, an entirely indigenous product of Indian political improvisation, It, however, did not last. The present election is a multipolar contest. Only the National Front and the Left Front are tied up in an alliance. The Left parties are even ready to join a coalition government with the NF if their own performance measures up to the expectation of its leaders and followers. Which means that there will be a stable coalition of the NF and LF if together they can command a majority in the Lok Sabha. But right up to poll eve, most election observers do not believe that the two allies can make it to power; indeed, some of the better known, but not necessarily wiser, pollsters predict the alliance trailing both the Congress-I and BJP. Once again, for whatever it is worth, let me put down my own expectation: the Janata Dal will spring many surpirses on the election observers when the final results are known even if it were unable to stake its claim to form the next government with the support of its LF allies. Assuming that the Congress once again comes up as the single largest party in the Lok Sabha but short of 50 MPs to form a government, to which parties and groups will it then turn? The Congress has its own allies-the AIADMK and the Chimanbhai Patel 's party in Gujarat. There will be several other small groups- Chandra Shekhar's SJP, Kanshi Ram's BSP, Muslim League, and even a small group headed by Bansi Lal. The Congress' first preference, of course, will be to clobber up a coalition of these small groups and control the main levers of power. The well-known political plumber, Subramanian Swamy will immediately get busy to graft a constellation around the Congress solar system. The problems will be the price to be paid for each group depending on its number and political weight. Chandra Shekhar if he is returned from Ballia-will of course not join the coalition as anything except prime minister, a position the Congress will be reluctant to yield. But he may claim for one or more of his henchmen protfolios that the Congress may find it difficult to part with without sharpening the contradictions within it. Will Kanshi Ram demand to be deputy prime minister if he could muster a gaggle of 10 to 15 MPs? Coalition building in a hung parliament is compelling. But in the peculiar head and bustle of the present election, with all parties gunning at one another ouside theNF-LF alliance, it may prove to be extremely difficult to beat a coalition to shape. And much harder still to ensure that it endures.[9]

9. *Ibid.*

"I Goofed", Rajiv said. The answer was disarming, and the battery of questions with which one had gone armed became suddenly irrlevant. The time was early 1986. After an unprecedented year- long honeymoon with the Indian Public, Rajiv Gandhi has just made his first mistake: a sharp like in the prices of a variety of petroleum products, V.P. Singh as Finance Minister was still giving out sheets of paper justifying the decision. But the public anger had been so palpable that the government, beat a hasty retreat and rolled prices back half-way down. Rajiv Gandhi agreed to an off-the-record meeting, to explain what had happened. And in his office, the young prime minister was candour personified. He hadn't realised how strong the public response would be he said. What was the extent of political damage he had suffered? The condour continued: "A lot," There was no dissembling, none of the fudging of issues that became familiar during the Bofors years. One fact stood out about Rajiv through half a dozen meetings since 1985; face to face, it was impossible not to like him. The handshake was firm, the eye contact direct, the answers to the point, the style relaxed, and the smile easy- even when the political temperature began to climb. You could disagree with what he said, or notice that the candour had begun to wane, but the personal charm was always devastarting. At the first meeting, a couple of short weeks after he had swept the 1984 elections, he seemed an ordinary person sitting in an imposing office inherited from his mother, talking the ordinary man's language. "Why do we need all these boxes and things to complicate our tax laws? Why can't it be made simple, have reasonable tax rates without qualifications and exemptions that only give employment to tax consultants?" Or again: "Why can't we have proper roads, instead these potholed things over which I have been travelling throughout the election period?" And then: "People's expectations are scary." The last meeting was barely a month before Sriperumbudur, with a group of Delhi-based editors. Naryan Datt Tiwari was waiting in the ante-room outside, escorted by R.K. Dhawan and M.L. Fotedar: the too over his double candidature had just happened, and parleys were obviously proposed. Once the editors had settled down. Rajiv buzzed for Vincent George, asked him to usher Tiwari in. As the veteran politician entered, Rajiv told the editors: "I thought we could also have the advice and wisdom of a senior Congressman like Tiwariji, "But it was said with a wink that Tiwari could not see, and gave the game away. The UP politician sat glumly through the 90-minute session, without saying a word. Other images come to mind: in the Great Hall of the People in Beijing, walking up to meet Deg Diaoping. Rajiv was clearly nervous as he walked up the corridor to a closed door. He swallowed, licked dry lips. The door opened at just the right moment and Deng walked out, a short, old man with a strong, clear voice. The handshake seemed to go on forever, and there was a clear political message in the warmth of Deng's opening, almost fatherly words. Rajiv's smile expanded. He must have realised that the visit would now be a success.[10]

Later, there was a dinner at his Janpath residence when he was out of power. Half a dozen guests, mainly politicians and journalists. The politicians a were cloying sycophantic: everything was so wonderful when you were in charge, now things are going to the dogs, they told him at every opportunity no matter what the context. Sensible political discussion became imposible. It must have been difficult to stay sane and balanced when surrounded only by partymen. But the minute the conversation veered round to non-political issues, the contemporary mind came through: sensible, balanced, alert. The Prasar Bharti Bill was being discussed in Parliament, and Rajiv was clear that this was not enough: technology would make it impossible for Doordarshan to retain its monopoly, because direct satellite transmission was round the corner. So private channels would have to be allowed. The conversation ranged from education to international relations and the economy and Rajiv was a stimulating discussant. It wasn't always like that, of course, Back in 1981, Rajiv had just been sworn-in after his first victory at Amethi. The big issue that session in the Lok Sabha was the Antullay cement Scandal, and R. Venkataraman as Finance Minister was valiantly defending the Oppositions' bouncers. Rajiv was a backbencher, but hopped from one seat to the next, prodding the Sanjay goons to heckle and raise cain, giggling at their antics. A note was then scribbled and sent to the Treasury benches. A cabinet minister got it, and promptly jumped up like a jack-in-the-box to mouth some inanity-obviously taking the clue from Rajiv's note. He din't have difficulty speaking for himself later. In fact, the problem was that, as an interviewer, you found that his answer had finished almost before the question had been asked. His mind obviously responded very quickly, and the early response was usually a one liner. He soon learnt to follow that up with a more elaborate response. Then the one-liners disappeared altogether, as the answers became more measured, less transparently honest. On a two-day helicopter run with him through rural Maharashtra, you could see the politician at work. As the chopper descended to land Rajiv would look through the porthole to assess the crows. A quick brushing down of the hair, and as soon as the door opened, he would jump down, waving enthusiastically. "Inspector Zende", Mani Shankar Aiyar called him when he donned this avatar. And Rajiv was very much the public works inspector. The escorting

10. *The Economic Times:* 27 May 1991.

minister or offical would suggest going to one drought-relief project in the area, Rajiv would say let's go somewhere else. Suspicious of the prepared visits, the schooled responses to anticipated questions, he snapped at officials who tries to answer a question he had addressed to an illiterate villager: Let her speak". Standing up in a moving jeep that was running cross-country, and undeterred by the mid-day sun in May, Rajiv would choose the direction of travel, trying to somehow penetrate rural reality, find out how government programmes were really working. At the night halt at Sholapur, Mani discouraged any talk of an interview. "These tours are not meant to be interview opportunities". Rajiv walked up, asked how the visit was going journalistically. Was an interview possible? "Yes, Why not? Let's do it tomorrow. Mani will tell you when". He must have been bored sometimes. A dinner-reception in Bombay: all the government and party bigwigs assembled. The sofas are arranged along the walls of the largish room, the women on one side, the men on the other, and no one is talking. Rajiv, the Doon School chum who could shake a leg on a dance floor, must have wondered at the awful boredom that was the hallmark of the evening. But he din't show it, and tried gamely to keep up a polite chatter. Another dinner: this time a formal one in Hyderabad House, for the visiting North Korean Prime Minister. No one of the Indians present know Korean, none of the Koreans seem to know English. Conversation across nationalities is clearly impossible. As Rajiv listens to the translation of the visitor's dinner speech, the eyes-droop, trying desperately to stay open. Obviously not enough sleep the night before. At the end of the evening, he walks down, gets into the driver's seat of the silver-grey Mercedes. Suresh Kalmadi whispers something into his ear, then runs round the back and gets into the front seat alongside. The car whizzes off, there is no sign of sleepiness at the wheel.[11]

Oscar Wilde said that style is always more important than substance. Not that Rajiv had no substance. But he certainly had style. At Prime Minister Rajiv Gandhi was always ready with a quick repartee that not only lessed the tension during the Parliament debates but also helped him get out of Opposition attempts to corner him. His quick will not only helped lighten the atmosphere in the House but enabled him to come unscathed while crossing swords with several veterans MPs known for their barbs. On several occassions he matched his wits against Opposition stalwarts. Once Rajiv Gandhi was making remark in Lok Sabha about the strength of his party in Lok Sabha and said in 1990, "the party would even take over the Opposition benches", countering him. Prof. Madhu Dandavate pointed towards heaven and

11. *Ibid.*

said "it is because after some years we will go to that Upper House." Rajiv Gandhi was quick to retort, "We are not in any rush to send him to that Upper House. But we are glade that he acknowledges that the Congress will be replacing the Opposition leaders even on those benches." When the then Finance Minister VP Singh prolonged his 1986-87 budget speech for nearly two and half hours, an apparently exhausted Prof. Dandavate intervened to ask "is there no ceiling on speech." CPI-M veteran Somnath Chatterjee wanted to know in the middle of the speech how many pages were still left. "If you accept all the proposals I will stop right now", V.P. Singh hit back. "In sheer exhaustion members may accept your proposals" replied the irrepressible Prof. Dandavate. But Rajiv Gandhi had the final word. "Obviously the reliefs that we are giving are exhausting the Opposition members", he quipped. The former Prime Minister Mr. Rajiv Gandhi's last words were don't worry. Relax"- uttered to woman constable who had tried to prevent the woman assassin from getting clost to him. Miss. Anusuya, a constable of Kancheepuram in Tamil Nadu Who is undergoing treatment in a hospital in Madras for injuries sustained in the blast. That Rajiv Gandhi pushed her aside when she tried to block the way of the woman later identified as the assassin. "I prevented her from reaching Rajiv Gandhi but he pushed me aside. I was pushed back a few feet. Meanwhile, the assassin garlanded Rajiv Gandhi, touched his feet, and then came the explosion, all in a flash," she said. Only a vew seconds before the assassin garlanded the VIP, Rajiv Gandhi, as if to seek Miss Anusuya's foregiveness for pushing her, had patted her on the shoulder and said, "Don't worry Relax. The constable said Rajiv Gandhi never said anything there after. Rajiv Gandhi dead? Says who? As long as there is even one living breathing soul in this fated country of ours who shares Rajiv's dream of an India without hatred, without power games, without discrimi ation, he will forever remain alive.[12] Mere men die. Martyrs don't.

12. Nazareen Challawala. Rajiv The Independent, 28 May 1991.

13
THE GANDHI - NEHRU LEGACY

The violent death of Rajiv Gandhi has sent shock waves through the entire nation, shaking even those not particularly well deposed towards the former Prime Minister or his Congress party. The shock is as much at the cruelly unexpected end of Rajiv Gandhi, as at the passing of an institution, which for better or worse, had barring few interludes, steered the nation through its traumatic independence up to the present day. But with the death of Rajiv Gandhi, the shadow of the Nehrus fades away entirely, and a hesitant nation must, for the first time since its independence, find its own bearings. It is some of this hesitancy perhaps that manifested itself in the wild outpourings of a very public grief by myriad individuals throughout the nation, at the death of a man who few of them could have known, still less hoped to benefit from, on his projected return to power. It was also in part this hesitancy to square up to a completely new situation by Rajiv Gandhi's recently orphaned Congress flock, that showed itself in their badly timed attempt to shelter behind the bereaved, and herself no less shaken Sonia Gandhi, the unwilling and improbably inheritor of the Nehru mantle. And yet, the legacy of the Nehru's is strong enough to make even this plausible. For post-indepencence India, whether one concedes it or not, the Nehrus, were much more than its first political dynasty. They could even be called free India's home spun version of royalty. And it was not coincidence either that the assassin of Rajiv Gandhi should have struck when she did, for indeed he courted death, in defying the restrictive safety norms of his security or mingle with his 'commoner' public. But in this he was only being true to a tradition that pre-dated even his illustrious grandfather-to the long freedom struggle, in which a small highly literate elite, had to rely upon a more numerous, but unlettered and politically naive constituency for its stock of foot soldiers in order to sustain its turbulent political struggle. A largely rural constituency, which if it could not understand the alien concepts of universal suffrage and civil rights, was game for replacing its rapacious foreign overlords, with hopefully more being local ones.[1]

The critics of the Congress often talked of the party having become the private property of the Nehru dynasty, but few had expected that the senior leaders, on their own, would come forward to confirm the critics" charge. The scandal was some how averted the next day with Sonia declining to wear the crown which the party bosses had obsequiously offered her on the very morrow of their leader's passing away.

1. Baljit Singh. A Break with the Past. *The Business and Political Observer*, 4 June 1991.

One is intrigued why in the midst of all round grief the party leadership chose to stage this demonstration of sycophancy. What could have been the possible consideration that led them to make Sonia their Great Helsman? It was obvious that they calculated that after Rajiv's assassination there would be an effusion of "sympathy votes" for the party in the elections if his widow was presented as his successor. But this could have been achieved and possibly will be managed-even without making her the president of the party. The hi-fi radio and television coverage, not to speak of the Press and the video, of the funeral of the departed leader, is bound to have its impact on the voter, and the Congress election managers are certainly aware of it. And if the grief-stricken Sonia makes a tour of the remaining constituencies, would it not fetch the sympathy vote? If that were so, why then this instant reflex of the Congress bosses to instal hear as party president? If one goes into the history of the party's functioning particularly in the last 25 years, one gets an idea of how it has become conditioned to the doctrine of dynastic rule. It is sometimes said that Nehru groomed Indira as his successor, this is strongly disputed by his admirers and adulators. Perhaps, the truth lies somewhere in between. Certainly, Indira Gandhi was groomed for politics, and that was inevitable in a family where almost all adult members were sucked up in the freedom struggle. After independence, she became the official hostess at the Prime Minister's residence. It is possible that Nehru lent a helping hand to her coming up in the Congress hierarchy, and it is equally possible that others, to be in the good books of the leader, pushed her up.[2] When she became Congress President, the initiative came from those who wanted to use her in their bid to displace the eysore Communist Ministry in Kerala, which Nehru was reluctant to dismiss outright. There is good reason to believe that Indira's pressure had a decisive effect on the Nehru's decision to dismiss the Namboodiripad Ministry in Kerala in 1959.

As for his successor as Priem Minister, Nehru left it to the newly formed syndicate, the consortium of top organisational bosses of the party. It is to be realised that Nehru wanted to uphold the party organisation, as he, like the other members of Congress old guard, looked upon the Congress organisation as the instrument that helped them win independence. So, when he knew that his days were numbered, he not only let the syndicate be formed, but almost asked it to manage the succession after him. That was why Lal Bhadur Shastri was inducted into the Cabiner when Nehru had the paralysis stroke at Bhubaneswar. And on Nehru's death Kamraj, as chief of the syndicate, managed Shastri's election as president and kept Morarji was not the

2. Nikhil Chakravarty Interregunum, *Sunday Mail*, 26 May 1991.

syndicate's choice. Again in January 1966, when Shastri died, the syndicate campaigned for Indira and again Kamraj managed to keep Morarji out and chose Indira as Prime Minister. The syndicate's calculation was the she, being young, could be persuaded to carry out its begest and so would provide the facade for its own rule. Once elected Prime Minister, Indira collected her so-called kitchen cabinet, as she did not relish the idea of being the syndicate's puppet. After the 1967 electoral setback for the Congress. Indira got rid of the syndicate and got another brand new set of aides to replace the kitchen cabinet. The congress split came as the climax of the *kurukshetra* between Indira and the syndicate, Which lost heavily at the subsequent 1971 generl elections which she swept with her populist measures, and the next year she won the Assembly elections with the magic slogan of Garibi Hatao. It was from this point that a new chapter of Congress functioning began, with Indira as the supreme vote- catcher. No elections were held within the new Congress and she became dizzy with election successes. Then came the backlash of the JP-led Nava Nirman upsurge articulating popular discntent at growing corruption and misgovernment. So, panic gave way to complacence, and the slide down to emergency with the classic sycophantic call of Indira-is-India. The emergency undermined the fabric of government and destroyed the party functioning. This was the period which saw the supreme leader not only groomng her second son but virtually installing him as the successor. Came the debacle of the 1977 general election and she fought back her adversaries; it was in this phase that Sanjay went through his baptism and in the 1980 election earned his ligitimacy. When Sanjay died in an air crash., Indira had the unique opportunity of grooming one of her many experience Congress leaders to be her vice-chief and potential successor. But she did not choose the democratic course; when opted for the dynastic rule and without the least hesitation summoned Rajiv from the world of non- political pursuits to be announced her prince-of-wales. It is important to bear in mind that there has never been an inner party election since Indira split the party in 1969. Even when she was cornered within the party after the fiasco of the Emergency, she walked out of it to form a new Congress party specifically named after her, for the first time in the annals of Indian politics. The leadership principle is thus an inherent concomitant of dynastic rule.[3] It is no wonder that the little men who now man the big signboard of the Congress have nothing else to fall back upon to elect their leaders but just the code of dynastic succession.

There is no point in just blaming Indira and Rajiv Gandhi for conv-

3. *Ibid.*

erting the proud party of independence into a servile appendage of the Nehru-Gandhi family. The truth is that voters have shown time and again, that they prefer the family to the party organisation. So the entrenchment of dynastic politics must be ascribed in fair measure to voters. On becoming Prime Minister in 1947, Jawaharlal Nehru lost little time in cutting other party stalwarts to size. In his treatment of Acharya Kripalani, Purshottamdas Tandon and even Rajendra Prased (in the case of the Hindu Code Bill), he demonstrated that his will reigned supreme. Of course, he presented this as the will of the government, not of the family. But to him goes the distinction fo first blurring the difference between the two. When he die, the Congress still had many stalwarts of the independence struggle around, and so it was the party that asserted itself, not the family. Lal Bahadur shastri became Prime Minister. And when he died in 1966, it was the party organisation that selected Indira Gandhi. The family mattered for getting votes, but was not in any fundamental sense equated with the party. Indira Gandhi changed that by splitting the party in 1969. The party bosses were confident that the people would vote for the party organisation and not the family in the subsequent general election. They proved wrong, and the family triumphed. The event was misinterpreted by most people (including myself) at the time. The party bosses had over time come to be equated by voters with the landed, richer sections of society, while Indira Gandhi promised to fight for the poor and oppressed. So many naive observers interpreted her triumph as one of the left over the right. They were soon proved wrong. In 1977, the Congress was thrashed in the general election, and Indira Gandhi herself was beaten in her constituency. Clearly it was a vote against her, not against the party organisation. So the organisation once again asserted itself, and tried to cut her down to size. For the second time Indira Gandhi split the party, and the issue was once again decided by voters in the 1978 state elections and 1980 general election. They voted overwhelmingly for the family against the organisation. This time nobody could portray the battle as one of the Left versus the Right. There was nothing socialist about the Emergency, or about Indira Gandhi's post-1977 slogans. Indeed, voters had by then become quite cynical about politicians promising instant socialism. But Indira Gandhi's tattered reputation proved superior to the even more tattered reputation of theirs. Some argued at that stage that voters had a special rapport with Indira Gandhi personally, and not with the family as such. This theory was soon exploded when she died and a servile party immediately chose Rajiv Gandhi as its leader (in contravention of its normal procedures). The choice was massively endorsed by voters.[4]

Only people with middle-class sensibilites would have been horrified the way they were when the Congress Working Committee decided to elect Sonia Gandhi president of the Party. They understand neither the psyche of the Indian masses nor the realities which have kept the Congress the only mass-based national party. It is not for the first time that the Congress has been accused of perpetuating the rule of one family in the party. The only new element this time was that the Congressmen wanted to entrust their leadership to a person who happens to be of foreign origin, who acquired citizenship of this country very recently. Ture, dynastic succession goes against the basic tenets of democracy and it should have no place in any modern democratic institution. But what should one do if the institution in question has moulded itself entirely around now family? That may be considered a handicap for a political party in a modern democratic setup, but that, in fact, is what gave sustenance to the Congress party for 25 years. Soon after Independence Congressmen placed their fate in the safe hands of Pandit jawaharlal Nehru and then forgot how to run a party democratically. In the later years generation after generation of Nehrus were available to see them through one election after another and whenever a crisis developed, they knew the family was around to solve it. They could rest assured that the leader will pull the party out of the crisis. In the circumstances, if Congressmen had elected a leader from within, that would have been diametrically opposite to what they were trained to do all these years. It was natural for Congressmen to look to the family as the only force that can keep the party united-and also see them through in the most difficult election that the party was facing, before the cruel assassintion of Rajiv Gandhi. One should also keep this in mind that this 105 years-old institution has seen no organisational elections in that last quarter of a century, that it has no organised membership roll; and that all its office-bearers are appointed from above without any democratic pretensions.

The dependence on Sonia Gandhi, therefore, is quite understandable. She may be of foreign origin, but she is the only person now left in the family who can actively participate in any kind of democratic movement because both the children have not attained the age to stand for elections. Sonia Gandhi's election as party president would have been very reassuring for the party and reassurance is what it needs now. It is not necessary that the Congress president must lead the governme-

4. Swaminathan S. Anklesaria Aiyar, Why Voters Like Dynasties, *The Times Of India*, 30 May 1991.

nt : it was not so about a quarter century ago. When the party president and the prime minister used to be two different personalities. The practice of combining both the posts began only with Mrs. Indira Gandhi. If one wants Congress to become the Congress of pre- independence days, it will be expecting too much from a party which has really forgotten how to react democratically. They should be given some time to think and act rationally.[5]

Rajiv Gandhi had the stature to carry with him men like Ghulam Nabi Azad, Shiv Shankar and Pranab Mukherjee who had no political base whatsoever. The new leader must have a political base and must represent social groups that have come under the sway of Mandal. Once the conditintious edge is taken off Mandal as a means of political mobilization, the consolidation behind the Mandir will not seem quite as menacing and confrontationist. In pursuit of a mature, effective leadership, the party may have to open its doors to those who had strayed away earlier. This may be the way to build of Rajiv Gandhi's tragic death. On how to learn from tragedy, we must turn to Ghalib: *Gham nahin hota hai azadon ka besh-az-yak nafas. Barg se karte hain roshan sham-e-matakhana harm.* (The man of vision does not mourn a tragedy for long: when lightning strikes his house of mourning, he must have the presence of mind to conver it into illumination".[6]

The atmosphere on the eighth floor of the Indian Institute of Medical Science was grim that October 1984, afternoon. Dr. K.P. Mathur-Indira Gandhi's personal physician, had just tearfully announced that it was all over. Who was to succeed Indira Gandhi? That was the question on everyone's mind. In his memoirs, My years with Indira Gandhi, records the behind-the-scenes drama that culminated in Rajiv Gandhi becoming the Prime Minister. Rajiv and Sonia Gandhi's responses to the crisis, described in the following lines:

I moved to the foyer of the eighth floor, where the Congress Chief Ministers stood along with some of their ministerial and party colleagues from their states. I talked to Narayan Dutt Tiwari, Chief Minister of Uttar Pradesh., S.C. Mathur, Chief Minister of Rajasthan, Bhajan Lal, Chief Minister of Haryana, and J.B. Patnaik, Chief Minister of Orissa, individually and each one of them said that Rajiv should straight away be sworn-in as Prime Minister. They, too, strongly opposed the idea of any interim arrangement. I conveyed their views to those present near the operation theratre and they agreed that a final decision on this issue should be taken after the arrival of Rajiv, who

5. S.P. Singh. Congress: Relax Actions, *The Economic Times*, 27 May 1991.
6. Saeed Naqri: Time for Congress for Overt Symbolism. *Patriot*, 23 May 1991.

was to land in Delhi from Calcutta. Rajiv arrived on the eighth floor of the Institute at 3.15 p.m. accompanied in Pranab Mukherjee and Arun Nehru. Anguish was writ large on his face, but he displayed remarkable courage in controlling his emotions. After greeting those of us who were on the verandah, he quickly went into the room adjacent to the operation theatre where Sonia was standing in one corner.[7] A very serious situation now started brewing in the verandah while Rajiv as inside the room with Sonia. Arun Nehru who had already talked to G. Parthasarathi, Balram Jakhar and the other senior ministers present took me aside and said that the decision was that Rajiv should straightaway be sworn-in as Prime Minister by the Vice-President without waiting for the arrival of the President. He said that he had talked to most of the senior leaders present at the Institute and everyone had agreed with this suggestion. He also said that Rajiv too, would accept this, though he did not specifically say that he had discussed it with Rajiv and obtained his consent. He said that Zail Singh was already in a hostile mood and he might refuse to swear-in Rajiv without his being formally elected leader by the Congress Parliamentary Party and insist on swearing-in the seniormost cabiner minister following old precedents. He said that no such risk should be taken. Any interim arrangement which Zail Singh would make would be of his choice and it was quite clear that his choice would be Pranab Mukherjee. An interim tenure of Pranab Mukherjee as Prime Minister could cause complications and this should be prevented under any circumstance. On the other hand, if Rajiv was sworn-in by the Vice-President before the President landed in Delhi, the President would accept the fait accompli even if he did not like it. I reached quite strongly against this suggestion. I felt that it would be quite unwise to proceed with this proposal as the President would rightly take it as a clear challenge to his authority and, worse an indication of a lack of faith in him and, therefore, as an insult. If driven to this position, the President might not accept the validity of the swearing in by the Vice-President and this would mean very serious legal and constitutional complications. Much to my surprise, I found that Arun Nehru's proposal had the enthusiastic support of most people present. They were of the view that once Rajiv was sworn-in as Prime Minister the Presidnet was unlikely to raise any question about the valid was clasping Sonia by both hands in a corner of that room and talking to her very animatedly. Sonia was holding him tightly and with tears rolling down her cheeks was ardently pleading with him not to agree to be Prime

7. P.C. Alexander. My Years With *Indira Gandhi*, New Delhi, 1990 see also. *The Sunday Observer*, 26 May 1991.

Minister. Rajiv was kissing her forehead and trying to convince her that he had to accept the office as it was his duty to do so in that hour of grave crisis. Rajiv saw me standing immediately behind him and knew that I was impatient to talk to him. Time was ticking away and a hundred things had to be attended to after getting Rajiv's decision, and I decided to make an effort to tear him away from Sonia. I whispered to him that I had to talk to him immediately and that the matter was so urgent that I could not wait any longer. He then turned around and came away from Sonia with a gesture indicating to her that he was assuming that she had agreed.[8]

By this time a few women close to the family had entered the room and, finding it difficult to talk to me without being overheard by others. Rajiv took me into the small bathroom attached to it. I mentioned Arun Nehru's proposal to Rajiv very quickly and also the fact that it had been supported by the senior leaders present and my own strong recommendation that it would be advisable to wait till the President arrived and be sworn-in by him. Rajiv immediately agreed with me without the slightest hesitation. He said that the right and proper course was to wait for the President's arrival and to have the swearing-in with his approval, and by him. Rajiv then took Arun Nehru inside the bathroom and himself told him about his preference. What could have developed into a major crisis was thus finally averted by Rajiv's prompt decision. It was about 4.10 p.m. by then and I came out and told those present of Rajiv's decision. There upon, we all got busy with the various tasks we had to attend to before the President's arrival. I have given here an account of this very intimate meeting between Rajiv and Sonia at that dark hour of a great personal tradgedy for them after a good deal of hesitation. Normally, I would have avoided any reference to such a strictly personal talk between them, but I was disturbed by certain malicious reports that Sonia had been very keen that Rajiv should become the Prime Minister and had, in fact, pressed him to step into the vacant position. Though such allegations deserve no serious notice. I feel that I owe it to history to place on record what I saw and heard as a witness. I thought a good deal about the propriety of my recoding this part of that tragic day's events and came to the conclusion that I would be failing in my duty if I did not do so. The scene of Sonia with tears rolling down her cheeks, pleading with Rajiv with great emotional fervour not to accept this crown of thorns is one of the poignant memories of that day ethched deeply in my mind.[9] In fact the Congress countinued to throw up leaders and its organisational structure-the All

8. *Ibid.*
9. *Ibid.*

India Congress Committee, the Working Committee and the parliamentary board-remainded alive and active throughout his long tenure as Prime Minister. If his colleagues sought and accepted his advice on most occassion, it was only because Nehru was a democrate and worked for and through consensus. After the assassination of Indira Gandhi again, the party took only hours to decide upon its new leader. That it chose Rajiv Gandhi did give the impression that it had fallen short of talent, though infact, the party was undergoing a generational change at the time and the new generation leaders and yet to take over from the old guard. The family factor may have played a key role in the choice, but there was no doubt that Indira Gandhi had been grooming him to head a new generation party leadership.

In spite of the fact that an orderly growth of the new generation leadership had been snapped suddenly by the brutal assassination, Rajiv Gandhi was clear about the task before him when he declared a war on "power brokers" at the Congress centenary celebrations in 1985. The war, unfortunately, was declared a bit too soon, long before the young leader had been able to put in place the new generation leaders and at time when the nation, after having voted so overwhelmingly for the Congress in the interest of national unity, would not have looked kindly at any split in the party. Instead of Rajiv Gandhi calling the shots, thus, it was the entrenched old guard, aided by "family friends" and New Delhi based "Left intellectuals", who dubbed his government as "the babalog (elderly men's) government", that struck, making it imperative for Rajiv Gandhi to hold his hand and rehabilitate the "veteran leaders loyal to the family". A split, however, was imminent and was caused by V.P. Singh, who adopted the familiar Indira Gandhi style populist politics, but does not have her finesse. Nevertheless, the split made Rajiv Gandhi even more dependent upon the veterans.[10] Whatever be the means utilised politics-desirable or undesirable, legal or illegal, moral or immoral-they leave their imprints on the polity. Here polity is seen as distinct and different from politics. The Indian polity is no exception. Both before and after Independence, the Indian polity has been influenced by one-party dominance that of the Congress. Rajni Kothari charactrised it as a weak opposition from without and basic opposition from within, whether effective or not. In fact, the crystallisation of an opposition in the form of various political parties both on the right and the left of the Congress occurred as offshoots of the Congress.

In the sense, one-party dominance has made the Indian polity basically centrist in nature. And depending on which force was in

10. Devendra Chintan. Politics of Consensus. *The Business and Political Observe,*: 29 May 1991.

power in the Congress, the pendulum of the Indian polity swung either to the right of centre or to the left, but only marginally. The reasons for this were two-fold. These offshoots of the Congress, whether to the right or to the left, choose to remain on the frings of the centre and the parties on the extreme right and the left were either short lived, like the Swatantra Party or split up like the Communists. In fact, on the right of the centre in the Indian polity there is no alternative for the right-oriented Indian electorate other than Bharatiya Janata Party. If the BJP is not acceptable to the right-oriented voters because of its communal over-tones, they are forced to choose from the centrist parties. Since there is no party which can be called marginally right of the centre, the choice is actually reduced to choosing between those parties which are marginally to the left of the centre (Janta Dal and the Samajwadi Janata Party) and the Congress. The Congress of course, being the centrist party always offered a mixed-bag to the electorate. It has in its hands all cards even if they are not of the highest value. Hence, dislodging the Congress from power always required mistakes on the part of the Congress such as the declaration of emergency and the Bofors scandal. What about Indian electorate which forms but the base of the Indian polity?[11] The Indian electorate has shown more maturity than the political parties of different hues. Whenever the Congress made mistakes, the electorate has given the other parties a chance to rule, and whenever the country faced a crisis, whether from outside or from within, it has voted for stability. But like most political parties, the Indian electorate has also exhibited its prefernce to how-ever around the centre, either to the right or to the left but mostly to the left. Regional parties which came into power as alternatives to the Congress proved to be no exception (Telugu Desam, DMK and AIADMK)[12] Sonia Gandhi may or may not have given the final word. She might yield to pressure from the late Rajiv Gandhi's backroom boys to accept the presidentship of the party. But the frantic effort of the Congress Working Committee to make her president has exposed the fragility of the 106-years old organisation. At the time of writing this protagonists of the "draft Sonia" line still hope that she will accept the challenge after performing the last rites. In fact, the CWC's unanimous decision to settle for a rank outsider only reveal desperation to avert an acute leadership crisis. The irony of the crisis is that as things stand today, Sonia Gandhi along can avert the current challenges facing the party. Amidst an array of veterans, she alone stands as a unifying force. Party leaders do not hide the fears that if the

11. G. Pandey. Voting in a Crisis. *The Independent*, 27 May 1991.
12. *Ibid.*

sticks firmly to her decision, the Congress will face a serious leadership crisis. Even before Rajiv Gandhi's body arrived in the capital, it was obvious that the top Congress leaders were sharply divided on selecting a new leader. It was thought that P.V.Narasimha Rao would have the widest acceptance. This was owing to his senior position and because Rajiv Gandhi himself authorised him to look after party affairs when Rajiv was on election tour. But by May 22, 1991 forenoon, it became evident that some of the influential leaders were against this. In informal consultations, some of them insisted that the leadership issue need not be decided before the last rites to the departed leader were performed. Among others, Sitaram Kesari and M.L. Fotedar were the advocates of such a line. They were soon joined by others. By then word reached 10 Janpath that Vice-President Shankar Dayal Sharma, a former Congress president just before the Emergency, also planned to have his say in the matter of choosing the new leader. But there were not many in the Rajiv establishment to buy his views. This too had, enhanced the process of seeking the easiest way out by electing Sonia Gandhi. Such a deep leadership crisis was not unexpected in a party like the Congress. First, unlike the late Indira Gandhi, Rajiv Gandhi had not groomed anyone as his successor. Neither had he made any efforts to develop a second line fo leadership. Indira Gandhi, on the other hand, had carefully trained Rajiv soon after the death of Sanjay. Rajiv first became party general secretary. Then he acquired greater responsibility and experience in handling the large number of Congress(I) men whom he had later described as 'power brokers'. Second, the very organisational structure of the Congress precludes any king of leadership role to any other than the party president who should also be the prime minister. Careful endeavours are made to curb the emergence of any other leader at the national level. At the state level, if any chief minister tries to establish himself by building up a base of his own, he is given the marching orders. This has been the cardinal principle of enforcing unity in the organisation. No doubt, the method has worked in ensuring loyalty, unity and discipline which have been the pride of the Congress Organisation. However, it has also proved disastrous in times of crisis, such as now in the midst of a decisive poll battle.[13] So far, the late Rajiv Gandhi was the sole campaigner for the Congress. The campaign was solely built on his charisma. But now even if a new leader is chosen immdeiately, he or she will find it impossible to attain the kind of acceptance that will compensate for the absence of Rajiv Gandhi.

13. P. Raman. Congress At The Crossroads. *The Economic Times*, 26 May 1991

A Congress devoid of the trapping of dynasty would be scarcely different from the Janata Dal. Rather than Continue to be divided, centrist politicians may decide that it is better to unite and thus comfront the revivalist feelings sought to be raised by the BJP. There is clearly a fundamental difference between Congressmen-of whatever he-and the followers of L.K. Advani. The former are emphatic on the need to remove the insecurity that is inherent in being a minority but, if necessary, creating a small tilt in their favour in the instruments of governance. The latter are clear that "majority" opinion-as in Pakistan-must prevail and that if the minorities do not adjust to this, they should be given short shrift. It is the opinion of most that such an attitude would create intolerable social strains should it become the accepted policy of government, strains as deep as those that have been created by the "Mandal Messiah" V.P. Singh. The tactics followed by V.P. Singh show the limits of reconciliation between individuals with a supposed common Congress heritage. Let there be no mistake about this. It was not by accident that Sanjay Gandhi placed such total reliance on V.P. Singh. Despite a greater facility with words than the former, the Janata Dal leader has in effect made his party a clone of the Congress as it was. There is in it only one leader, who announces decisions after a process of consultation seemingly centred around his own intuition. There are the cheerboys, the V.P. Singh's case Ram Vilas Paswan and Sharad Yadav, and there is ruthless marginalising of dissenters even those such as Arif Mohammed Khan who were istrumental in projecting Mr. Clean Mark 2 in 1987-88. A BJP on right, a Congress in the centre and the radical parties on the left with a sprinkling of fringe parties all around. This seems to be the direction towards which India seems to be heading should be focus in the 1990s move away from personalities to policies, from confrontation to consensus, from micro-views to macro, the traumas that the nation has endured this past decade may yet have served a purpose.[14]

Indeed, in his own persona, Nehru symbolised various identities giving him a general Indian identity, which subsumed the particularities. He as a Kashmiri Brahmin. Yet settled in Uttar Pradesh; a person who belonged to the entire people without belonging to any one region. This remained the hallmark of the family, significantly imparting it with all-round acceptability in a country as diverse as India. And it was such a person as Nehru who laid the foundation, albeit unwittingly, of the Nehru- Gandhi dynasty. That Nehru did so unwittingly was because he did not anoint his daughter, Indira Gandhi, his successor. In fact, he had opted for his deputy Lal Bhadur Shatri. It is

14. M.D. Nalapat. Congress At a Watershed. *The Times of India*, 1 June 1991.

difficult to tell what shape Indian and Congress politics might have taken had Shastri had a longer innings, but his sudden demise brought the party to a crisis. And party leaders, governed by their survival instinct, opted for the then lowest common denominator-Indira Gandhi. She was a person acceptable to all factions, and one whom every coterie thought would be easy to manipulate to serve its end. It is the same instinct and perhaps the same motivation which today has made the party leaders opt for Sonia. It is another matter that the best laid plant at times go awry. Indira Gandhi proved more than a match for any one faction, let alone anyone Congress leader. She had, moreover, plans of her own, based on the realisation that her heritage gave her a head start over, the others. In the face of opposition from the Syndicate, she split the arty in 1969. Though it did not seem so at that time, the dynastic character of the succession process was direct consequence of the transformation of the Congress after the 1969 split. It was then that the Congress (R) emerged the victorious heir to the old Indian National Congress which had dominated the country's politics for a greater part of the 20th century. After having defeated leading Congressmen in a struggle for national power, Indira Gandhi created a new Congress organisation which was personalised and centralised, where there would be no danger of independent provincial leaders threatening her position. The dependence of the party on the family consequently grew.[15] It was in the aftermath of the Emergency, that the first genuine opposition was mounted to the family when a bulk of the leaders opposed the entry of her son, Sanjay, into a critical decision, making position within the party. There was a debate whether the Congress could get an identity outside the family. Reaching, Indira Gandhi split the party again in 1978. This time it was not on an ideological issue as was her tussle in 1969 with the Syndicate, but purely on the question of succession. Though never stated in as many words, the message was clear. If the party leaders wanted her, they would have to accept her son. After the 1980 polls, which Indira Gandhi won decisively, it became apparent that Congressmen were willing to accept her terms. For, above all, they wanted power. So began the "home-coming", and so ended all apprehensions within the party over the succession issue. The Party's dependence on the family was complete. When Sanjay died, it was the party who wanted the elder son, Rajiv, to enter politics. The some what introverted Rajiv did not like the idea. His wife, Sonia, is believed to have opposed the move strongly. Yet, it was the Congressmen who besieged the mother and the son. To say that all this

15. Arindana Sen Gupta. Indian National Congress: End of An Era. *The Sunday Observer,* 26 May 1991.

begging and gorvelling was orchestrated by an ambitious mother is again a simplification of the situation and a failure to understand the Congress psyche. After a decisive resolution to the succession issue in the Seventies, partymen knew that their political future was enmeshed with the future of the family. It was again the same survival instinct. In the process, some basic facets of democracy were perhaps subverted. Congressman, central or state leders as well as party workers, were no longer so dependent for their future on their own performance. Irrespective of their record, party MPs would get elected so long as the supreme leader could generate a wave for the party. So, service to the people was supplanted with the test of loyalty to the leader. After all, it was a question of being given a party ticket for the leader. After all, it was a question of being given a party ticket for the elections. In short, loylty also became an easy meal ticket.[16] How can a major party, which boasts many martyrs to the cause of national integration, be called "pernicious" because it maintains its true identity with the people's aspirations? The attempt to make Sonia Gandhi Congress president does smack of sheer opportunism for the coterie close to the Nehru-Gandhi family has a vested interest in perpetuating hereditary rule. But this does not necessarily fully the party's contribution to Indian democracy. Sometimes, it seems that Nehru would have been wise to accept the balkan plan as suggested by Mountbatten Bloody caste and communal conflicts might then have been averted. Violence during elections understandably raises doubts about the survival of democracy but "precipitate change" would not be prudent. The idea of a national government is preposterous though the presidential system may prove effective in the long run. The Congress party has been facing a sever challenge to its monopoly of power. On top of this Sonia Gandhi turned down the offer. The Congress has plunged into perhaps the gravest cirsis in its long history.[17] The greatest tragedy of the Congress has been its failure to acquire a distinct identity. The rot set in just before Independence, forcing Janata into the opposite camp to stake his claims to Pakistan. The nadir is reached when a group of apparently able- bodied adults looks for crutches and does not feel ashamed to take political advantage of a woman who is dazed with grief after he husband's assassination.

Yet the glory that was the Indian National Congress is not all lost. Men and women in remote villages still spin sliently on their charkhas without bothering about power brokers who seek to give a fresh lease of life to the Nehru-Gandhi dynasty's rule. It is time secular Indians,

16. *Ibid.*
17. Santanu Das. Identity Crisis in Congress. *The Statesman*, 2 June 1991.

who have traditionally identified themselves with the rich heritage of the Indian National Congress, came forward to fill the vacuum at the top.[18] From early morning of May 22, 1991 or rather from the midnight itself, one began to hear voice of enthusiastic, well-meaning but stupid sycophants within the ranks of the Congress demanding that Sonia Gandhi be elected President of the Party and successor to Rajiv Gandhi. The appeal was not only madness. It also bordered on inhumanity. The family has suffered enough. It should have been allowed to withdraw into the peace of private life so that Rajiv's young children could live their own life. This would not have precluded either of them from taking part in politics in future. But no, for utterly selfish reasons for Congress power politicians decided to use the Gandhi-Nehru name for short tearm advantage. However, it is Sonia Gandhi's determined no that has saved the Congress. It now appears to have recovered its balance. The unanimous election of P.V. Narasimha Rao as President is bound to restore faith in the democratic credentials of the Congress. It will reap its benefit in the next round. The Congress has thus silienced the Opposition by avoiding charges of dynastic succession. Anyway these charges have increasingly soundded hypocritical. There are of course high-minded men and women who on principle oppose dynastic rule. But can it be said that the Opposition practises what it preaches? Does not their moral indignation over the Congressmen's appeal to Sonia Gandhi smack of double standards? What merit and experience did Ajit Singh possess when he succeeded to the position held by Charan Singh in his party? Did not Bhairon Singh Shekhawat induct his son-in-low as party Secretary? Who does not know that V.P.Singh himself was a party to bargain over the leadership of the Janata Dal Parliamentary Party in December 1989 which included Omprakash Chautala's succession to the Haryana gaddi? The principle of family rule has deep roots in the age-old caste system based on birth and the all pervasive feudal mentality it has fostered. Did not Devi Lal put it crudely last year when he said: *What is wrong with family succession. Does not a blacksmith's son become a blacksmith, a cobbler's son a cobbler, and a bania shopkeeper's son a shopkeeper? Why then should not Chief Minister Devi Lal's son become a Chief Minister"? Devi Lal's crude mind changed Chief Ministership into a hereditary occupation. It is, therefore, gratifying that the Congress has opened a new page. The fate of the Congress is important because there is no other party or group of parties united in a coalition of principle which can provide an alternative majority.[19]

18. Biman Bose: Congress. *The Statesman*, 2 June 1991.
19. Madhu Limaye. Congress After Rajiv. *The Hindustan Times*, 4 June 1991.

14
THE CONGRESS CULTURE

With the sudden and brutal removal of Rajiv Gandhi from the political scene, the Congress party has been called upon to make yet another transition in a short span of less than seven years. In its long and chequered history, the Congress has successfully made several transitions and the present one too could have been made with relative case had the Congress been organisationally in a better shape. Actually it is in a terrible state of atrophy unable to respond quickly and appropriately to a challenge of such enormity. In the past it was different. The Congress had effectively managed dramatic and far-reaching changes in leadership, ideology, support structures as well as techniques of mass mobilisation both before independence and after. In fact, there are few political parties anywhere in the world which have demonstrated a similar capacity for endurance and self- transformation as the Congress has done over the years. It has been one of the most successful of nationalist movements anywhere to have smoothly made the transition from protest and agitation to governance and has provided India a stable, effective and democratic government virtually for the entire period since independence, a particularly turbulent time in modern Indian history. The Congress party's ability in so adapting itself to the new role has been due to its built-in pragmatism, its proven skills in internal conflict management and its consensual approach to national problems designed to accommodate through the party's mediating mechanism the competing demands of a highly diverse polity. Although the Congress retains some of these strengths, it does so in an attenuated form since these have suffered erosion due to progressive de-institutionalisation in the party after the emergence of the personalised style of leadership under Indira Gandhi. After the split of 1969 and especially after the victory in the parliamentary elections of 1971 on the populist slogan of *garibi hatao* (remove poverty) Indira Gandhi gained unprecedented ascendancy which gave her a degree of autonomy from the constraints of the party which even Nehru did not have in his heyday. He too had his charisma and a power-base independent of the party. But he tolerated and worked through established party organs and procedures, however frustrating this must have been at times.[1] He was tolerant of factions in the party and was more eager to reach a consensus than force a showdown. For the second time in seven years, the Congress party is attempting a dynastic succession in the wake of the assassination of the leader. In November 1984, the

1. Ram Joshi. Congress: Hegemony to Consensus. *The Times Of India,* 30 May 1991.

choice, and the rationale, was easy. Rajiv Gandhi had been nominated and was being actively groomed by Indira Gandhi as her political heir and successor. He had at least a few years of hard political experience and was nominally also a parliamentarian having being elected from Amethi in June 1981. Consequently, even though he had not wrested control of the party's levers of power-which was largely due to his more democratic temperament, unlike in the case of his brother Sanjay who had earlier steam-rollered into the cabal of decision--markers--there was a sense of consensus when Rajiv Gandhi succeeded his mother. This time around, there is no such air of consensus. Indeed, there are several party leaders who see themselves as contenders to head the destinies of the Third World's largest and oldest democratic party. Among them are P.V. Narasimha Rao, Narain Dutt Tiwari and Arjun Singh, to name only a few. But the possibility of such a democratic seccession has obviously not gone down well with the inner coterie of Rajiv Gandhi who, in the power vacuum, are still the key power brokers. Consider the clique which surrounded Rajiv Gandhi and formed his palace guard: Satish Sharma, R.K. Dahwan, Makhan Lal Fotedar, V. George, again to name only a few who controlled access to the office of the prime minister. None of them have any political base and Dhawan and Fotedar, at least, owe their positions to their services to the Gandhi family. Captain Sharma was totally a Rajiv Gandhi crony and as a place guard, he has made many powerful enemies with his abrasive ways. For the survival of this guard-and the conterie of dozens of hangers on who surrounded them--it is essential that power still be vested with the Gandhi's. And hence their hurried attempts to stanch any process of democratically electing a leader for the party by resorting the dynastic succession of the Nehru-Gandhi clan. Unfortunately for them, Sonia has seen through their strategy and declined the offer.But is Sonia's refusal the last word in the matter? One doesn't know, but it is certain that the coterie of Rajiv's cronies will be working overtime to make her change her mind after the funeral. Of course the specious line is that Sonia is undoubtedly the best person available to the party to cash in on the sympathy factor which Congressmen feel will go a long way in helping the part get a majority at the hustings.[2]

But considerations in drafting Sonia Gandhi apart, the Congress leadership is clearly caught in a cleft stick, with or without the services of Rajiv Gandhi's widow. To be sure, Sonia Gandhi's foreign origin and her Christain faith are bound to be exploited by political oppenents, especially the BJP. To the BJP, which is the party posing the strongest challenge to the Congress and which has chosen to make religious

2. Sailesh Kothary. Caught in a Cleft Stick. *The Independent,* 25 May 1991

propoganda the theme of its election campaign, the best thing which could come its way is if Sonia would take charge of the party. Then, her strong Catholic belief and the fact that she only chose to renounce her Italian nationality as late as 1983, two years after her husband was elected to Parliament, are bound to become central issues in campaign rhetoric. Even without Sonia Gandhi to lead the charge, the Congress is in no position of clear strength as the election campaign picks up in the next few days. With so many senior leaders and no clearly designated No.2, the politics of groupism and factionalism are bound to be unleashed as each leader will try to make his bid for the top spot. And in the power struggle which is bound to ensure, a consensus is hardly a possibility whichever candidate is finally elected. Given the party's unenviable track record of infighting, it is unlikely that the rank and file of the Congress will stand stolidly behind the new leader as the battle of the hustings begins again. Indeed it is more likely that disgruntled party bosses will work at cross purpose with the new leadership, if only to view the possibility of losing the elections as an opportunity to settle old scores. And a divided Congress is hardly the party which can hope to garner votes by harping on stability as its electoral theme.[3]

Before Indira Gandhi had changed the party's organisational pattern in early'70s, the Congress was like a massive river system. An array of eminent leaders, both at the Centre and in the states, constributed to its strength at every level, each one acting as a tributary of the river. Even if the main catchment area dried up, the river never got dry. That was how the Congress was bilt. Now, instead of contributing their mite, the leaders anxiously wait for the party chief's visit to their constituency as the only means of winning the election. This is the current dilemma of the Congress. It goes to the credit of Rajiv Gandhi that he had introduced some kind of democracy in the organisation. Congress sessions and AICC sessions were held rarely during his period, but he had reestablished the Congress Working Committee as a forum for vibrant discussions. However, Rajiv Gandhi could not shake off the iron grip on the chief ministers and state leaders. Even as late as two months back, Shardad Pawar was cut to size. The frequent change of chief minister and Union ministers, PCC president and AICC office-bearers were all part of this old device that invariably led to organisational castration of the otherwise able leaders. It is in this context that the CWC's frantic decision on Wedensday to elect Sonia Gandhi as its leader has to be seen. The Congress leaders are frank about the reasons. Rajiv Gandhi sacrificed his life for the country. Now his widow had the right to inherit his legacy because she alone could take advan-

3. *Ibid.*

tage of the people's spontaneous sympathy for the martyr, P.V. Narasimha Rao, the senior most leader and perhaps with the widest acceptance, could have been respected and mature leader. But only someone close to the departed leader could have received the type of sympathy that had given a two-third majority to Rajiv Gandhi in 1984. This was the main factor that prompted the Congress leaders to look to someone who had little experience in politics. Understandably, the Congress needed some kind of a wave to help it get a majority. From all accounts, stability, the party's main election plank, had not have impressed a wide section of people in the Hindi belt. The National Front has been able to wean away a considerable chunck of the weaker sections, including the Harijans and backward castes in Bihar and certain other packets. As a result, the Congress strategists have felt highly disturbed over the performance on the first day's polling.[4]

Therefore, it was imprative for the Congress to fully make use of the sympathy wave to counter the two other waves. This was what they did by opting for Sonia Gandhi as their leader. Second, the choice of Sonia Gandhi was the easiest way to avert a tussle for leadership. Many in the Rajiv establishment still feel that with experienced persons like Narasimha Rao, Pranab mukherjee or N.D. Tiwari at the helm, they would lose their current role as advisers. Sonia Gandhi, at least for a few year, would have to depend on them for survival. In other words, the existing Rajiv establishment could continue to keep their hold over th country's affairs as they did during the initial stages of Rajiv's rule, and to a lesser extent afterwards.

Third, the backroom boys at 10 Janpath and 24 Akbar Road, New Delhi were highly exercised over the concerted efforts by the influential supporters of Chandra Shekhar to take control of the Congress organistion in the name of realignment of political forces. As a first step, the Chandra Shekhar loyalists had suggested that the Congress working committee should give a call for strengthening of the Congress by inviting former Congressmen to come together.

Shardad Pawar and Chimanbhai Patel had contacted several Congress leaders with this suggestion. They tried to sell the idea that no single leader within the Congress(I) could fill the void left by the death of Rajiv Gandhi. A collective leadership was necessary to meet the challenges posed by the divisive elements like the BJP and Janata Dal. The backroom boys were quick to see through the game. A little before noon on Wednesday, some of them met Narsimha Rao and Arjun Singh caution them against falling into the trap of realignment of forces and

4. P. Raman. Congress At the Crossroad. *The Economic Times,* 26 May 1991.

national government at the Centre. Instead, the Congress should go ahead on its own. No one who did not enjoy the trust of the late leader should be allowed to take control of the Congress on any pretext. They also argued that if the Congress survived crisis after cirsis, it was due to its unique type of organisation. In a country like India only a party with monolithic leadership with powers vested in one leader could provide cohesive leadership. Sitaram Kesri, R.K. Dhawan, M.L. Fotedar and Pranab Mukherjii also put forth the view that under the circumstances, selection of Sonia Gandhi as Congress president would solve all such problems. It was then decided to put off the CWC meeting to 5 p.m. on Wednesday and discuss the issue at an informal meeting at 10 Janpath a little before it. At this meeting, almost all senior members, including Pranjb Mukherjee, Narasimha Rao, Arjun Singh and N.D. Tiwari as well as R.K. Dhawan and M.L. Fotedar, were present. By then, K. Karunakaran had also come round to the view that Sonia Gandhi would be the best choice. He had his own reasons for this. If Sonia Gandhi assumed the leadership, it would help the United Democratic Front led by him to win back the support of the solid block of Catholic cotes in Kerala. Sonia Gandhi's decision to spurn the offer has come as a bolt from the blue. Many in 10 Janpath, New Delhi still believe that Sonia-Gandhi has not yet given the final word. She only wants to remove the impression that she accepted power even before he husband's body was cremated. This may or may not be true. But in case she sticks to her stand, it is bound to push the party into a deep leadership cirsis from next week. Already, different forces are at work both inside and outside the party. Lobbying has been intensified. At the moment, it will be difficult to forsee who will emerge as leader. Whoever it might be, the Congress may not be the same again. If Sonia or any one related to Rajiv Gandhi fails the Congress it may become the centre of another realignment of centrist forces.[5]

In 1967 elections Congress was severely mauled at the Centre and in the states and SVD governments came to power in many northern states. This was the result of people's anger at the arrogance of Congress politicians in power. This followed by Congress split in 1969. In 1971 elections Congress of Indira Gandhi had a landslide victory because it gave adequatre share of power to the minorities, backward classes, weaker sections, women and harijans and gave them adequate representation to contest elections. The trounced opposition parties could not stomach the poll disaster and look the streets creating violence and anarchy. To contain this chaos, Indira Gandhi clamped emergency. All agitations collapsed and useful work including family

5. *Ibid.*

planning was achieved. But emergency facilitated bureaucratic and police excesses in North India. Voters, frightened at family planning excesses in North India blindly voted against Congress in frenzy and threw out the Congress in all states in the North. The theory trotted out by the press and non-Congress parties that the rout of the Congress was people's verdict against Congress and was a vote for freedom, democracy and liberty does not hold water because the south loves democracy, liberty and freedom no less than the north. The 1980 elections gave a landslide victory to Congress in the Centre and in all the states in North India, Congress lost power in the south because there was an anti-establishmenbt sentiment among the people on account of Congress mis-rule. The 1989 elections in Parliment can be explained only on an anti- establishment sentiment among voters and a Rajiv wave in south India and North-east among newly enfranchised youth. Congress lost very heavily in North India. But, the states in south India which had non-Congress governments gave a spectacular victory to Congress. To attribute the debacle of Congress in 1989 election to alleged hatred of Congress and the spectacular success of BJP to Hindutva is untenable. The Hindus of South India and North- east India are no less religious and no less attached to Hinduism than people in the north. Why did they not repudiate the Congress? Why did they boot-out BJP mercilessly? This can be explained only on the hypothesis of anti-establishment sentiment all over India and Rajiv wave in South India and the North-east. By clever seat adjustment BJP along with the other non-ruling parties became a great beneficiary of the anti-establishment sentiment in North India. The Ayodhya issue had no significant effect on Hindu vote, but BJP undeservedly appears larger than life.[6]

The much touted theory propounded by the press and our intellectuals that opposition unity in 1989 elections was the main cause for defeat of Congress is ingenuous. It presumes that there is an unalterable anti-Congress electroate in the country, that it was being split among opposition parties enabling Congress to win on a minority vote. The landslide victory of Congress in South India in the teeth of this opposition unity and rule of opposition unity and rule of opposition parties in 1989 elections destroys this theory. The masses and common people in India are amazingly secular. It is sheer stupidity to assume that they will be swayed by Hindutva to vote for BJP. It seems to me that the coming elections are most likely to prove the Waterloo of this obscurantist and obstreperous party which has brought Hinduism into contempt and has posed a serious threat to social harmony and the security and

6. K Ramachandra Rao. Congress Prospects Bright. *National Herald*, 22 May 1991

stability of the country. The Harijan pogroms, caste wars, anti-reservation riots and agitaions and the electoral compulsions of praising Dr. Ambedkar and competing promises to enforce Mandal reports are clear indications that the feudal order in the backward Hindi states is slowly but surely getting eroded. This will ring the death knell of higher caste hegemony and domination in the Hindi belt. This will be a death blow to BJP, RSS and VHP and is sure to usher in the golden age for India. Caste, religion or money no longer influence the vote of the masses. They have hold only on our intellectuals from privileged classes. The honorary US lobby in India exclusively consists of these intellectual attracted by the US largesses and US foundations. The leadership of the Communist parties in India is mostly from the higher castes. These leaders are hungering for a share in power in the Centre. In their obsession, they entered into opportunistic, unprincipled alliances. In the forthcoming elections, they are likely to lose out to Congress. Their ideological confusion over the present state of affairs in the USSR and East Europe is bound to affect their doctrinal and intellectual credibility. The Congress is likely to be the beficiary. So, the Congress has a fair chance of returning to power at the centre. The future of BJP appears very bleak depsite its tall claims. The elections may well call the bluff of BJP, for the harm it has caused to our society and to India, this party deserves little sympathy and no tears over its demise.[7]

When Indira Gandhi fell to her bodyguards' bullets the Congress Party's natural choice was her son, Rajiv Gandhi. For partymen, as well as for a majority of the countrymen, he represented what his mother stood for. The same ability to be appear to be above all factions, religions, castes and regions in the country. The succession was, therefore, smooth. The issue which had been decided by Indira Gandhi in the Seventies was not reopened. Ostensibly, Rajiv represented both continuity and change. For the world, he seemed to be the same recognisable face of India. But by the time Rajiv, the third generation, arrived, there was a growing political problem. The problem was that in the perception of people, the governing elite was unable to move the country, either in the direction of greater economic growth or towards greater equity in income. Regional and community tensions, which were simmering for the past one decade, were fast reaching a flash-point. Perhaps Rajiv recognised this and gave therefore the slogan of change. But all he could manage to do us usher in a superficial change, identifiable more in the yuppisation of the middle class, rather than in the radical accomodation of newly emergent interest groups. The basis power equilibrium remained the same, with major forces in the politi

7. *Ibid.*

cal system carefully poised to protect their own interest. The apparent effect was greater stability within Indian than in other developing countries as aspect which gave both the country and the Nehru- Gandhi family international recognition-but this was at the cost of necessary political accommodation. The highly personalised and centralised manner of functioning which Rajiv inherited from his mother, kept the lid on the cauldron, but the danger of it boilling over nevertheless remained. And it did following Rajiv's defeat in the 1989 election. Religious, regional and caste tensions came to the fore even as a National Front (NF) minority government tried to grapple with inherited problems. Ironically, the NF government's failure made the Congress, and its leader Rajiv Gandhi, once again an attractive proposition to the people. Rajiv was, indeed, on his comeback trail when an assassin aborted what looked like a triumphant return journey to power. And that has changed the country's political agenda.[8]

When Rajiv became Prime Minister on October 31, 1984 and successfully led the Congress to secure independent India's most massive electoral mandate, Rajiv Gandhi enjoyed one advantage which was denied to his mother. Indira Gandhi was part and parcel of the Congress party and the government at the Centre whereas Rajiv Gandhi, being a debutant in politics, could afford to announce a break with the past and yet command the loyalty (or obeisance?) of his partymen. The Congress badly needed such a break, having by then become a political organisation of office- seekers and power-brokers with no contact with grassroot-level workers, not to speak of the people at large. At the centenary celebrations of the Indian National Congress, he promised to bring back some of the democratic traditions given the go-by by the Indira regime. Untainted by the politics of the day, he started out as an idealist willing to wipe the state clean and start afresh in both Punjab and Assam. If the two accords he signed on these contentious issues came unstruck eventually, the fault was not entirely his. At any rate, the perceptible change in the atmosphere in post-accord Punjab and Assam was testimony enough to the virtues inhereint in the initiative. In everything he did in the first two years of his Prime Ministership, Rajiv Gandhi came out as a genuine peace-maker and a person keen to bring about change in the arena of national politics, the economy and public life at large.[9]

But idealism, even with the authoritarian hold on both government and party, is not adequate to make a successul politician. As he came

8. Arindam Sen Gupta. Indian National Congress: End of An Era. *The Sunday Observer*, 26 May 1991.
9. *The Tribune*, 23 May 1991.

to realise that politics is not so much the art of the possible as the science of reconciling contradictions in the policy and society, Rajiv Gandhi, instead of vigorously pursuing the ideals, preferred to widhraw himself into the shell of traditional Congress politics. Thus the power-brokers survived, the brokerage was substantial and the organisation with withered for want of grassroot contact and democratic elections. The Punjab accord could not be implemented while the Assam accord did not progress beyond the conversion fo the agitating All-Assam Students Union into a bumbling Assom Gana Parishad government. In economics, his government mindlessly plumped for liberalisation promoting elite interests and governmental profligacy. But it is undeniable that the Rajiv era saw the Indian Capital market grow into a vibrant economic accelerator. In foreign policy, too, Rajiv Gandhi successfully balanced India's relations betweeen the two super powers while simultaneously expanding channels of communication with China. There was glitter but not much substance. But as long as he was there, India seemed to count in the eyes of the nations of world.

The traumatic shock which the Congress has suffered on account of the assassination of Rajiv Gandhi is no less than what it had experienced at the time of Mrs Gandhi's death. But the impact of the two tragedies on the party has not been identical. In 1984, the Congress did not encounter any difficulty in choosing a leader round whom it could rally. Though a novice, Rajiv Gandhi was promptly accepted as an effective link with the past, capable of keeping the party intact and leading it to victory at the hustings. Now the question confronting the party is: Who could fill the bill as the successor? This is not the first time that the party finds itself caught in the throes of a succession drama in tragic circumstances. When the first Prime Minister Jawaharlal Nehru, died, the then Congress president, K. Kamaraj, took the initiative to settle the succession issue. His emphasis was on collective leadership and with the support of other senior leders, he assessed the preferences of the members of the parliamentary party. Lal Bhadur Shastri, who had an edge over Morarji Desai, was elected leader. After Shastri's sudden death in Tashketnt, the leadership question was again settled by the parliamentary party in a keenly contested election. Indira Gandhi, by defeating Morarji Desai, became Prime Minister. When she died, President Zail Singh, on the suggestion of a few Congressmen, invited Rajiv Gandhi to form a Government and the parliamentary party later formally elected him leader. There has thus been no hard and fast rule by which the Congress has been settling the leadership question from time to time. At times a group of leaders take the decision and the AICC unquestioningly accepts it. Or, the leader is properly elected. There is, however, a major difference between the present situation and the conditions that prevailed during the earlier changes in leadership. When Rajiv Gandhi was assassinated, he was the party president and not the prime minister. The party's immediate task, therefore, was to elect a president and not the Prime Minister. The leadership of the parliamentary party is a different issue which will be settled after the general election. No doubt, the election of the party president has a significant bearing on the election of the leader of the parliamentary party by virtue of the fact that the same person used to hold these two offices.

The Congress did give the impression that it was almost orphaned on account of Mr. Rajiv Gandhi's assassination. That might explain why the working committee in such an unseemly hurry chose Sonia Gandhi as party president. With hindsight one might say the working committee should not have acted in haste. Without getting the prior consent of Sonia Gandhi, it should not have chosen her as leder, particularly when she had not recovered from the shock of a personal tragedy. The party's inclination to look up to the Nehru family for leadership in times of crisis was once again demonstrated. At the same time the anti-Sonia campaign launched by certain sections outside the party left a bad taste in the mouth. They could have waited till her reaction to the working committee's offer was known before casting aspersions on her loyalty to the country because of her foreign origin. The Congress is at the crossroads. For the first time, the party seems to be getting out of the clutches of dynastic rule and the pangs of transition are being felt in the organisation. For almost 40 out of the 45 years of independence, some member or other of the Nehru family had been at the helm of affairs of the country and the average Congressman has been accustomed to the benevolent 'dictatorship' practised by the leadership. This arrangement, despite certain advantages, has reduced the party to an organisation of spineless sycophants. Coterie rule became the order of the day as decisions taken at the top were thrust upon the party. Even when the leadership went wrong, it was applauded, not corrected. Frequent changes of Chief Ministers and PCCI chiefs according to the whims of the high command would not have been possible had the party been functioning on democratic lines. A major lesson which the Congress should have learnt by now is that excessive dependence on a leader, however great, or a family, however illustrious, will deprive it of the inherent strength to stand on its own feet. The party certainly needs a change in its outlook, style of functioning and leadership structure.[10] The battle of the ballot is still to be faught in a substantial

10. P. Tharyan. After Rajiv - Congress at Crossroads. *The Hindustan Tinmes,* 1 June 1991.

measure. The Congress party, after choosing a new commander to fill the place of its beloved leader, so treacherously killed in the midst of the campaign, will be joining the battle against destabilising and communal forces. The country's imperilled democracy has to be safeguarded. The first round of polling held on May 20, 1991 had covered about 40 per cent of the electorate. The other 60 per cent has yet to exercise the franchise. Rajiv Gandhi's absence from the scene should not lead to a slackening of the will to fight or loss of a sense of direction by the Congress party. The remaining campaign period of more than a fortnight should be fully utilised to carry the message, which Rajiv Gandhi was effectively doing to the people. The choice of the new Congress President is important. The working Committee saw the urgency of the matter and at an emergency meeting unanimously elected Sonia Gandhi for the post. In the trauma of her husband's assassination, Sonia Gandhi declined to assume the responsibility. That was understandable, but all efforts must be made to persuade her to reverse her decision in the interest of the party and the country. Neither the Congress Working Committee nor the Congress Parliamentary Party has any doubt about the wisdom of the choice. The general feeling among members was that Sonia Gandhi was the person most fitted to lead the party and the country at a period of crisis like the present. The Nehru-Gandhi legacy has to be kept alive and the stability of the political system safeguarded. In some respects there is a parallel between Sonia Gandhi's choice at present and the election of Rajiv Gandhi in 1984 after the assassination of Indira Gandhi. Critics who cast doubts about the political experience and ability of Rajiv Gandhi proved wrong. The leadership he gave to the country was one of the finest. Sonia Gandhi equips her for the job although she chose not to strike a high profile in the political arena. She could be expected to carry on the Congress legacy and lead the party to victory at the hustings.[11] The Congress party's task, as Rajiv Gandhi started clearly at the start of the election campaign, is to "rescue the country from the divisive and manipulative politics of caste and religion" and to rekindle the people's hopes and aspirations. He articulated specially the aspirations of the post-independence generation, of which he was one. Rajiv Gandhi noted that people of this generation "want a new Indian India in which they can dare to hope for a better, more fulfilling life." He spoke of his dream of "the great Indian people marching confidently into the future."

The So-called loyalists who had been occupying curcial positions managed to frustrate Rajiv's efforts to introduce internal elections and

11. *National Herald*, 27 May 1991.

democrati functioning in the Congress. The inescapable result was that the party moved further away from the people, lost its ability to incorporate new social and economic groups, got thoroughly demoralised as soon as a concerted assault was mounted by a united opposition in 1989 and collapsed like a house of cards. It is a tribute to Rajiv's leadership qualities and not to the Congress party's resilience that in a short time of 18 months he marshalled his forces to return to the battle determined to win. It is a tragedy of horrendous proportions that he was not allowed to see the outcome. Has the Congress then outlived its usefulness? Is the Indian polity at such a stage of development that it can move on without the Congress? The answer to both the questions is negative, not yet at any rate'. At this point in time it is impossible to visualise any pattern of (polarisation that would obviate the need for some groups and segments of our society to seek in the Congress party effective articulation and aggregation of their collective interests. Besides, and more importantly, the Congress continues to represent, in a manner no other party does, basic elements of that consenus on the basis of which the building up of the Indian nation-state was contemplated and groundwork laid. The need to reifforce that ideological foundation has not decreased but increased and has acquired urgency in view of the threats from divisive forces and the spectre of the polity falling apart. Disintegration of the Congress at this juncture may have serious negative consequences for the polity through greater systemic instability making the goals of democracy, social justice and economic growth more difficult to attain.[12]

It has to be said, and said explicity: a heavy responsibility now lies with the Congress party. It is at the moment understandably in a dazed condition. A party which has, throughout the years, sunned overtures to democratise its organisation and depended wholly on a supreme leader, could not but be pushed to a traumatic state by the tragedy occurring at Sriperupudur, Madras, Precisely because of this state, it may be sorely tempted to exploit the tragedy for its maximum advantage in the left-over parliamentary polls now rescheduled for the second and trhird weeks of next month. Some elements within the party have indeed commence to dream a repetition of the 1984 ride to victory on the crest of the so-called 'sympathy wave'. They can however try to render the dream into reality only by playing up passion. Should they fall for the temptation, who knows, they might even succeed in their immediate goal. But such success will be the precursor of disasters of an indescribable magnitude. For passion will be answered by other passion, and India, in the course of a few weeks, will be a vast,

12. Ram Joshi. Congress. *The Times Of India,* 30 May 1991.

open-ended killing field. It is for the wobbly leadership of the Congress to consider whether this is the denauncement they prefer for Inda.

There is an analogous matter which has to be addressed particularly to Sonia Gandhi. Her intitial reluctance notwithstanding, tremendous pressure is likely to continue to be brought to bear upon her, during the next few days, by circles within the Congress to assume the mantle of her departed husband and therby save the party. It will be a horrendous mistake if she gives in to the pressure; she should not deviate from her first judgement. The Nehru-Gandhis have paid enough price of their obsessive desire to hold the reins of power and be in absolute control of the nations's destiny. The sad thing has to be said: the price they have paid is the inevitable outcome of personalised authoritarian politics. If the nation has to be saved, we have to move away from that genre of politics. In case Sonia Gandhi is trapped into taking over the Congress leadership, she would, after a brief interval, provoke intense wild emotions that are likely to vitiate the atmosphere nearly irretrievably. Because of her European extraction, she would also stir xenophobic instincts. Reaction of the nature might be throughly irrational, a few of them might even be deliberately engineered, but it is still crucial to accept the hard realities as they are.[13]

Rajiv Gandhi's brutal killing is an immense national tragedy, but it must not be compounded by other follies. The survival of the nation is more important than the survival of the party. Apart from all that, the family, there is no question, needs a respite from public focus at least for some while.

The manifestos of the front line parties presented a splendour of confusion and withheld basic issues relate primarily to national security, economic soverignty and foreign relations. Certain major questions are components of these issues. These are religious militarism, terrorist and secessionist campaigns in Punjab, Kashmir and Assam, the LTTE menance in parts of the south, industrial disabilities ad the benign neglect to which India has been consigned by the world at large. The present paralysis and future feats of India are the outcome of the failure to confront these issues and hammer out a coherent response to them. The election campaigns were spectacular in trivia, dim in perception of the issues and policies that must resolve them. Unemployment, BoP crisis, foreign exchange crunch, industrial inefficiencies, infrastructure breakdowns, rural-urban confrontation languages and ethnic frictions, poverty and destitution are not issues. They are humiliating problems. The nation will always be forced to try

13. Ashok Mitra. The Nation and the Party. *The Independent*, 28 May 1991.

and tackle them as best as it can. The sheer intensity of chaos and disorder will force the government regardless of its party affiliation to employ measures to reduce tension to manageable levels. The frenzy and hysteria of electioneering, that delectable spectacle of democracy, threw these up as life and death issues and buried the real ones without ceremony. Every party was promising what the other were. And bettering the deal at the next rally. One party that stood out in the courage of its conviction is the one that has promised a Ram temple. If that is a priority of the party and its constituents, so be it. No other priorities, real or imagined, were in evidence. If this is intellectual bankruptcy of the so called national parties, it would have been a tolerable disaster. It is callousness and insensitivity which is an insult to voters. Fortunately, the voter has neither the time not the inclination to realize this affront.[14]

K.C. Pant, defence minister in the Rajiv Gandhi cabinet, is in favour of establishing a collective leadership in the Congress, adherence to the one-man-one-post principle and a realignment of political forces that would involve the return of all former Congress members to the party fold. Pant said in New Delhi, on May 31, 1991 that given the seriousness of the problems facing the country, he should welcome all like-minded people getting together "if it facilitates steps to face these challenges", Given the huge budgetary deficit, the precarious balance of payments position and the pressure on prices, it would be necessary for the new government to take hard decisions. Further, the unity and integrity of the nation would have to be preserved at all costs and the growing violence contained, he said. Given these objectives and challenges. He thinks people who belong to the Congress culture will find it easier to get together and tackle these problems," he said. While a great deal would depend on the outcome of the polls, Pant said he had sympathy with the viewpoint that all "Congressmen" should come together. Asked if this meant that all former Congress members who are now in the Samajwadi Janata Party, Janata Dal and other parties are welcome, Pant said given the challenges facing the country, any realignment should be considered.

Referring to the election of P.V. Narasimha Rao as president of the Congress, Pant said in the given circumstances it was a good choice. Rao, he said, was a person with a great deal of experience and he "deserves the support of all Congressmen at this critical juncture." On his part, Rao would have to see that the Congress is strengthened at the grassroots level and at all other levels, taking into account the

14. Nirmal Goswami. What Elections Cannot Solve. *The Business and Political Observer*, 29 May 1991.

democratic traditions of the party and aspirations of party workers all over the country, he said. Pant, who had come out against the coterie around the Gandhi family just before the 1989 elections, said he was of the view that there was need for collective leadership in the Congress(I). In fact, the way the Congress used to function, it was designed to take into account various points of view and also to prevent abnormal over-centralisation, the former defence minister said,"I believe that is the democratic approach."

When pressed, Pant admitted there had been phases when there was more centralisation than required Unfortunately, wherever this happens, ther is a danger of rootless self-seekers clustering around the centre of power and wielding authority without responsibility, he said. Asked if he subscribed to the view that the posts of party president and leader of the parliamentary party should be held by different people. Pant said he hoped the party would adhere to the one-man-one-post principle. "Broadly speaking, this is a healthy principle," he said. Pant said the Congress was an old party which had been functioning for over a century. The freedom struggle attracted people drawn by the moral challenge. They had made sacrifices and had given something because the struggle itself fostered a set of values which revolved round this approach. Mahatma Gandhi had laid stress on moral aspects and that was a valuable legacy. In additon, there was a clear cut ideology which envolved over the year. Thus, Congress culture is understood by people as meaning a commitment to democracy, socialism and secularism and an approach to foreign policy which recent events have fully vindicated. People who belong to this culture will find it easier to get together and tackle problems, he said.

Rajiv Gandhi's death is a big loss for Indian democracy. The tragedy occured at a time when the country needed strong political leaders. His most important qualification was his undisputed leadership of the country's biggest and oldest political party. In the larger interest of the nation, it is necessary that the Congress leadership rise above petty party politics. It should adopt a longsighted policy to bring an end to the politics of bitterness and open the doors for old Congressmen to rejoin the party. This is necessary to ensure an absolute majority for the party. The party must project Chandra Shekhar as the future Prime Minister because he has proved his capability to lead the nation during his short tenure, Unfortunately, he is a leader without a party. The Congress is the most established party in the country and it will be in the best interests of the country that old and present Congressmen forget their personal differnces and come together. He will be an asset both for the party and the country.[15]

Even if Rajiv Gandhi had lived to form a government, he would not have been able to solve the problems created by the Congress culture of institutionalized corruption and appeasement of the minorities. Punjab, Jammu and Kashmir, Assam and Naxalite- dominated Andhra Pradesh were in turmoil long before the BJP called for nationalism based on majority culture. The leading democracies of the west are all essentially Christian states where minorities are not harassed but certainly denied high profile representation in national life. The violence which culminated in Rajiv Gandhi's ghastly murder can only be tackled by a party like the BJP with dedicated leaders and cadres. It will remove violence from politics and treat it as an act against society. Violence is also the result of over-population. The minorities share of the population has increased from eight per cent at the time of independence to 20 per cent leading to the utter failure of family planning. As a result, we now have 200 million unemployed young people. If only one per cent of them became desperate, we will have two million recruits for anti- national organizations-twice the strength of our army. All parties have become immoral and are unable to rule the country, and the BJP is the only hope because it tries to rally the majority in the name of Indian culture.[16]

The Congress's first reaction to feelers from former Congressmen wanting to return to the party was predictably negative. But Narasimha Rao's public statements in the few days since taking over as party chief add up to a more pragmatic line on this question. He neither rules out all possibility of reunions nor throws wide the party's doors to all comers. With power equations within the existing party, in the aftermath of Rajiv Gandhi's assassination, still in a state of flux, the Congress(I) is unprepared to deal with a variety of new entrants. Among them are Chandra Shekhar, with Mohan Dahria as intervener, the Jan Morcha which has exhibited a desire to merge with the Congress, and, as some reports will have it, sections of the Janata Dal which are not happy with their present alignment. All these possible candidates are making their bids from positions of weakness and the Congress can afford to wait and watch and pick and choose. Narasimha Rao has rightly ruled out throwing the doors wide open and has described the Dahria formula as ill-timed and unrealistic without ruling out a case by case approach. Rao's primary task is to present a united face to electorate. However, consideration of the larger question of the future

15. Subhash Agarwal. Congress and Rajiv. *The Business and Political Observer*, 31 May 1991.
16. M.V.R. Balasubramanium. Rajiv Gandhi. *The Statesman*, 26 May 1991.

shape of the Congress cannot be long postponed. A realignment of centrist forces after the election is desirable on two counts. One is the need for an effective, coherent alternative to the communal threat instead of the present fragmentation of secular, centrist forces. The imperative of electoral arithmetic is another reason. The President of India is not alone in stressing the need for an honest coalition in the event of a hung Parliament. The Congress may be able to count on the Left if the Congress emerges after the polls as the largest party without acquiring a majority. It would surely be more comfortable in alliance with like-minded groups at least in so far as economic policy goes.[17]

It is in this context that the return of former Congressmen must be seen. Only a stable, confident government can hope to tackle the hard economic and political decisions that lie ahead. If the Congress is to be in a position to do so it must also take steps now to stabilise itself, contain the factional struggles in the party and guard against the power games of the so-called coterie.

17. *Indian Express*, 4 June 1991.

15
RENEWAL OF CONGRESS PARTY

In his last television interview, hours before his assassination Rajiv Gandhi had said that the Congress required to change its thinking in view of the "new realities".

The party required the change because all its policies were developed at a time when India's capabilities were very limited, Rajiv Gandhi felt.

He emphasised that "now, it is not like that. It is very different and we are stronger. We are able to face the challenge with more self-confidence and I think we must make use of this self-confidence and new strength. The faster we move, more confident we would be".

The interview was given to Madam Daniella Kaneva of Bulgarian television on May 21 during his flight from New Delhi to Bhubaneshwar and Visakhapathnam. Rajiv Gandhi then flew to Tamil Nadu where he was assassinated.

Asked whether his understanding about the new realities in the country and his approach to other political parties were shared by the new generation of politicians in the party. Rajiv Gandhi had said, "yes, yes, very much so."

"We have found that in Karnataka. We have got a new generation (of politicians) there. In Andhra Pradesh, we have a new generation and in Maharashtra too," Rajiv Gandhi said.

Confident that his party would win a majority on its own. Rajiv Gandhi had listed three problems of great importance to him.

"Internally, there are two factors. One, during this period very sharp divisions have been brought about in our society-caste, religion and even regionalism. All this must end, "the former Prime Minister said. According to him, the second factor was economy. For 15 months "we have (almost) had no government and the economy is in a mess".

Thirdly, the global situtation had changed a lot. From bipolar, it had become a unipolar world, he said.

He said, "that we want is a true democratic system in which every country has a say. We must work towards that and that must be the goal of the non-aligned movement now."

To a question that India did not play an effective roll at the United Nations though it was a member of the Security Council, Rajiv Gandhi said, "we have to make use of our presence wherever we can."

Rajiv Gandhi favoured restructuring of the UN in the changed circumstances. "With the denete it is totally redund in its present form," the former prime minister said.

Asked to give his assessment of the BJP, the reasons for its catching up since the last elections, Rajiv Gandhi said, "most likely, the BJP will come this time as the second largest party.

Rajiv Gandhi felt that wherever the centrist forces other than the Congress disintegrated, they left a vacuum which the fundamentalist forces filled in.

He cited the examples of Kashmir and Maharashtra. The congress and the National Conference had a very close working arrangement. The two centrist parties got together and they left the field open "where we have the fundamentalist parties coming up." In Maharashtra, after the merger of the Congress and the Congress (S), the Shiv Sena came up, he observed.

Replying to another question, Rajiv Gandhi said he was very much for a national opposition because if there was a second national party, "we will have a national perspective."

If the BJP shaped on the religious lines, it could be dangerous. But if the party instead looked at political realities and economic problems, it would perhaps be a good step, Rajiv Gandhi stated.

Rajiv Gandhi's murder in the middle of the 1991 election campaign exposes the extent of the brutalisation of the world's largest democracy. The political responses to that ghastly act and its aftermath also prove once and for all that there are no simple solutions to the puzzles of Indian politics. The official period of mourning saw intense politicking of the ugliest kind. Sycophancy and treachery, factionalism as well as the compulsion to hang together to escape hanging separately, display of object partisanship and an intangible but nevertheless reall sense of the need to protect and promote national pan-Indian, interests all these went hand in hand as the orphaned Congress came to terms with its suddenly revealed limits. The left and the National Front demonstrated the extent to which their supposedly autonomous politics was predicated on the Congress and that indeed their point of reference too was the individual assassinated at Sriperumbudur. Indian democracy, itself appeared to need reaffirmation in a drastically changed context. Insidiously but inevitably the anti-democratic elements too crawled out of the woodwork. Rumours regarding cancellation of elections, imposition of Emergency, cobbling together a "national government" to bypass the democratic process which was considered inadequate to cope with exigency-all these fed the fires of incipient authoritatianism, political cupidity or plain despair of tired old men unable to comprehend either the changed nature or the inherent vitality of Indian democracy. At the same time Mr. L.K. Advani urged his BJP-RSS-VHP-Bajrang Dal sotrm troopers to exhibit their "killed instinct".[1]

The tragic assassination of Rajiv Gandhi has left the Congress turly ohphaned. Headless, the party is now groping confusedly to fill the void. That in itself is indicative of the extent to which the Congress, whose destiny the last 40 years or so has been shaped by the Nehru-Gandhi family has been over-dependent upon the mystique of one family. Ironically, if this illustrious family has sustained the party for over four decades through the leader-ship it provided, by doing so if also undermined its strength as a modern democratic party. Today the Congress appears as an organisation, that having ruled for a long, seems to have lost its moorings. The proud inheritor of a 100-years long legacy of the nationalist movement for freedom and development, the Congress in its present state is only a highly distorted shadow of its original. An essentially centrist movement embracing a broad coalition of national interests, the Congress had not only spearheaded the freedom movement but also thrown up a line of eminent leaders to guide India after independence. One of them, Lal Bahadur Shastri, succeeded Jawaharlal Nehru in 1964. After Shastri's untimely death, Indira Gandhi was elected the Prime Minister. However, when Indira Gandhi refused to be manipulated by a caucus of leaders, the feud led to a split in the party, in 1969. Therefore after not only did the party shrink but as Mrs Gandhi grappled to assert herself over the other leaders, the party all but ceased to exist. In fact the party soon became an appendage of the leader. Consequently, rootless persons, animated by ambition, propagated a pernicious personality cult that further eroded the party's lower level organization. The old Nehruvian preference for consensus in solving contentions problems became dysfunctional. Party affairs came to be managed increasingly through backroom manoeuvres; regional and local party chiefs as also Chief Ministers and Governors were manipulated like puppets on a string, and democratic sustenance of the party at grassroots level totally overlooked as internal elections were repeatedly bypassed. Emergency in 1975 was the logical outcome of this aberration and when in 1977 Indira Gandhi and the Congress were defeated, it inevitably led to another split in the party. The years that followed saw the Congress transform itself into a highly centralised body totally dependent upon the leader. It was therefore natural that when India Gandhi fell to the assassins" bullets, the mantle of the party fell upon her son Rajiv

1. Arvind N.das The Real is Irrational. *The Times Of India*, 31 May 1991.

Gandhi. The young heir, fortunately gave a worthy example of himself when he tried to liberate the party from the clutches of the power-brokers and promised to restore inner party democracy. Political expediency compelled Rajiv Gandhi to scuttle his ambitious reform of the party.[2] Now that he is no more, the Congress cannot survive unless it reorganies itself. The Congress must, first of all, restore inner-party democracy. Personalised loyality tests should be discarded in favour of faith in the Congress's true heritage the spirit be queathed by Mahatma Gandhi and Nehru. Only when Congressmen realize this would they do true justice to the memory of the Nehru-Gandhi family who sacrified so much for the country and the party.

After Rajiv's death the party needed to resolve quickly and satisfactorily the problem of succession. Its first attempt in that direction was clumsy and showed a complete lack of sensitivity towards Rajiv's widow. Once she refused there was no other way for Congressmen but to return to the consensual process of choosing one from among several contenders through open and free discussions. The party must now seriously start the process of restoring internal democracy through organisational elections, consultations at all levels, and rejuvenation of the organisation at the local, district and state levels. The Congress will have to sensitise its adaptive and incorporative mechanisms to rebuild linkages with the socially, economically and educationally disadvantaged groups among whom political awareness is rapidly rising. A polity of deepening social cleavages will always need a party like the Congress restored to its consensual dynamics to play a stabilising role.[3]

The Gorbacheve spoke of his "wonderful human qualities" in their message of condolence. Li Peng called him "an outstanding statesman". Yasser Arafat was far more eloquent when he said:"The knight has fallen amidst his people while exercising democracy and embracing the people whom he adopted." Messages poured in from Washington, London, Paris, Islamabad and virtually every world capital as soon as the news of Rajiv Gandhi's assassination reached.

What was it that made the world stop for a moment and ponder over the impact of a lethal bomb blast in an obscure Tamil Nadu village of Sriperumbudur? It would be a mistake to think that Rajiv's extensive tours of the world and contact with world leaders were solely responsible for this international attention. It was more than that. It was the surname that Rajiv Gandhi carried and the family to which he belonged. The Nehru Gandhi family has over the years, emerged the country's premier family, one which had transcended the boundaries

2. *Patriot*, 27 May 1991.
3. Ram Joshi Congress. *The Times Of India*, 30 May 1991.

of region, religion and caste to become a distillate of the spirit of India.[4]

In a sense, therefore, the world leaders' reaction to Rajiv's death was really a reaction to a momentous happening in India, which has placed the country's politics at the crossroads.

However, on thing is certain: An era has come to and end. An era which did not begin either with Rajiv, or with his mother Indira Gandhi, but many years before Independence, when Mahatma Gandhi appointed Jawaharlal Nehru his political heir. The India of the future will no longer be the same-neither will the Congress party, nor national polity. The eopoch of Congress hegemony on national politics and the Nehru Gandhi family's hold over the Congress seems to be over. The country is now poised to enter a phase in which political permutations and realignments will shape a different sort of Indian politics. The world is concerned, the nation anxious and the Congress party panic stricken. For, changes in the basic political rules of the world's largest democracy involves everyone at home and abroad. The issue is, of course, more immediate for the Congress because its future largely depends on how speedily it can adjust itself to the changed circumstances.[5]

How things shape up in the short run-that is, how the succession issue is resolved in the post Nehru Gandhi family era-also dependens on the Congress Party. To assess that, it is necessary to examine the party's initial reaction as well as its likely behaviour in the near future. The party's first reaction was predictable. In an effort to defer the consequences of uncertainty, 24 party leaders-18 congress working committee (CWC) members and eight special invitees-decided on May 22, 1991 night that Sonia should be the leader of the party. A person without any political experience, perhaps with little interest in politics, and grieving a personal loss, was the consensual choice. Why? There are two possible reasons for this. First, Sonia's entry, felt Congress leaders, would crystallise a "sympathy wave" for her in the elections, riding on which the party would be swept back to power. Second, she alone was the most acceptable choice in front of a faction-ridden party. If factionalism within the Congress party is seen to be as old as the party itself, the second reason boils down to the acceptability as well as the dominance of the Nehru Gandhi family. Indeed, no one dared to say "no" to Sonia at the CWC meeting, even if they opposed her candidature in private. Congressmen are known for their strong survival in stincts. And obviously their choice of Sonia was determined by that. As

4. Arindam Sen Gupta. Indian National Congress: End of An Era. *The Sunday Observer*, 26 May 1991.
5. *Ibid.*

in the past, it is this very instinct that has made partymen not only accept, but lionise the family's predecessor Jawaharlal Nehru, Indira Gandhi and now, Rajiv. So much so, that Congressmen have come to be known as a bunch of sycophants, grovelling before one family and propagating dynastic rule.

Seen in this perspective, Congressmen appear to have been equally responsible for building the Nehru Gandhi dynasty, as Nehru or Indira Gandhi might have been in nursing the ambition of seeking their progeny in power. But to see Congressmen merely as sycophants is to judge a domestic reality through western sensibilities. The fact that the people themselves have endorsed the dynastic rule-as successive elections have shown-suggests a far more complex phenomenon. Similarlym, it would not have been possible for the Congress to have remained until recently, a party of consensus and a wonderful melting pot, in which the interests of disparate groups got resolved, had it merely been an aggregation of sycophants,. Simplifications, therfore, do not explain the dominance of the Nehru-Gandhi family in the Congress.

To understand it, it is perhaps necessary to go back to the days of Jawaharlal Nehru. The first Indian Prime Minister's father, Motilal Nehru, was a top leader fo the nationalist movement and an associate of Mahatma Gandhi. Nehru, therefore, had impecable credentials when he joined politics. Inclined towards things Western, Nehru was the very antithesis of Gandhi. If Gandhi was a religious man, Nehru was an agnostic; if Gandhi carried with him the Hisduised tradition of India, Nehru represented a break from it; and if Gandhi could at times be superstitious, Nehru was scientific in his approach. The two deffered in their idiom, attire and their worldview.[6]

The Indian polity is bound to witness a major change as a result of this ghastly assassination. The assassination is a tragedy. But I still hope it will do some good to India in two ways: firstly, that it would lead to widespread revulsion against the cult of individual violence and secondly, it might contribute to the democratisation of the country's largest political party. It appears to me that in future the cumulative effect of this assassination might be to refocuss the concerns of political parties on issues and ideologies rather than emotions and slogans. Right now, barring the Left Parties, the other political parties are mainly dependent on emotions and slogans. I am also certain about a dramatic change in the format and functioning of the Congress Party. Of course, a lot dependens on the backbone that the residual leadership of the Congress shows. At present, it largely consists of a group of

6. *Ibid.*

sycophants and toadies. I am sorry to say there is little character left in the party. The challenge is theirs. Only if the character of the party is rebuilt will it have a future. Otherwise, it will get divided into hundreds of factions, and schisms. It is for Congressmen to think and act. Of course, rebuilding the character of the party at this stage might appear a tough proposition and even seem a distant dream. If for nothing but their very survival, the Congress leadership will have to ponder over ways to save the party. They have no other alternative However, I do feel that the assassination of Rajiv Gandhi will in no way jeopardise the future of the Left movement or parties in India. They have their own vista and they can use the existing situation to their advantage. I don't think that there is any organic relationship between the perspective of the Congress and that of the Left. The Left parties have very great vistas opening before them but whether they are successful in garnering a good crop out of these vistas depends on their ability to transmute class, religion and ethic issues and turn them into class struggles. For this, they will have to adopt themselves to the realities of the Socio- economic and political milieu. Whether they are able to do so depends upon their degree of success in combining and adhering to principles with flexibility in strategy and tactics.[7]

It will be relevant to recall here that in the late sixties when a similar crisis was unfolding itself, though perhaps of not the same magnitude a similar move was initiated by an influential section of the Congress. In fact, at that stage some of the Congress leaders including the then Congress president Nijalingappa, began to enlist the support of the Jana Sangh and the Swatantra Party but farsighted leader of the Congress Indira Gandhi foiled this game by rallying all democratic and Left forces in the country. Over the decades the charater of the Congress has been changing. The Congress has always been a mass movement. However, both during the freedom struggle and subsequently after independence, under the leadership of Jawaharlal Nehru, the Congress had adequate transmission mechanism-organisational instruments which enabled it to know the mood of the people and their problems. More importantly, it is through these transmission channels that peaople exerted pressure on the Congress leadership to evolve its policies which reflect the aspirations of the people. For certain historical reasons, these transmission lines got weakened and finally in the pyramid of the organisational structure of the party the gult between the top leader and the rank and file Congressmen considerably widened. It is a strange paradox that for nearly two decades the Congress has not held it s organisational elections and that too in

a

7. Ashok Mitra. Rajiv's Death. *The Sunday Observer*, 26 May 1991.

historical situation when in one country after another ruled by the communist parties, the movement for democratisation of the political system and of the parties has surfaced itself with full force. Equally important is the fact that although the Congress, and especially Jawaharlal Nehru, had been passionately attached to the democratic political party system, the party slowly though surely became a highly centralised organ of political power. In this process the instruments of party organisation were weakened and the party began to lean heavily on the popularity of its outstanding leaders. That being the position, when the most popular and outstanding leader of the party has been assassinated, the party is thrown into a serious crisis. Though it is for the Congress leaders to decide as to who should head the party at this crucial point in India's history, the future of the democratical system in India is directly related to the future of the Congress. Among the political formations in the country, the Congress is still not only the biggest political force but also continues to symbolise the democratic and secular traditions of the country. The crux of the problem is that the era of a highly centralised political system of a party like the Congress has come to an end. With it ends the sneaking hope that the camouflage of a centralised political system will help the Congress to revitalise and regenerate itself.[8] The Congress if it has to survive as a major political force in the country, has no other option but to democratise itself and build a collective leadership. There is no short cut to it. Democratisation of the Congress and building a collective leadership will certainly confront the party with new problems. The Congress leaders, the Congress Chief Ministers in particular, have their own ambitions. However, if the mature Congress leaders assert themselves they can rebuild the party and fill the gap created by the tragic death of Rajiv Gandhi. No single individual in the Congress can fill this gap today. The historic task facing the Congress is to redefine its policies, make them more precise and, above all see if the Congress leaders can come to honest political agreements with other democratic, secular and radical forces in the country. Without a vision of a broad democratic front which consistantly and vigorously works for the transformation of our society and deepening of a democratic political system, the Congress will not be able to act with cohesion and purpose. If the Congress leaders do not embark on this path they may find regional fractions as the reactionaries will be. This must be prevented and it can be. Only a forward looking Congress can become the focus once again of all radical-minded and secular forces in our ancient nation. The Challenges which the Congress is facing are enormous and the Congress alone can face these challenge unitedly, rising above petty amibitions and prejudices.[9]

The Congress party's capacity for self-inflicted wounds is enormous. Only a self-destructive propensity can explain why the party could not have done on May 22, 1991 what it did on May 29 in electing Narsimha Rao as prty president. This would have totally avoided all confusion of the "Sonia Gandhi" episode. In the event, it was her sensible refusal to accept the job-and the even wiser persistence in the refusal-that cleared the way for the only sane decision in the circumstances. Why is the Congress so perversely accident-prone? It is that habits of dependency are difficult to share off? Or could it be that senior leaders were caught off guard by the of the "coterie" and decided to fall in line with a commendeered CWC decision for fear of splitting the party over the leadership issue? Whatever the reason, after an unedifying inter-regnum of dither and cross purposes, the Congress is mercifully on its way to recovering its composure. There is no contradiction between party unity and healthy rivalty within the party. After all, the Congress has been and still is an umberella organisation for a wide range of regional, class and sectional interests. These can be brought to states of temporary equilibrium only through inner-party struggles. Conflict is best managed by going through party procedures of consultation and election rather than by submitting to the dictat of a single person advised by an out-of-touch and self-serving kitchen cabine. With Rao as party president and without the complications, proposed by some sections of the party, of five vice-presidents, it should be possible permanently to separate the functions of party chief and parliamentary leader. It is to be hoped that the lessons have been learned and the party is preparing for an orderly post election choice of its parliamentary leader during which individual record, experience, image and support base will come into play, of course, mischief may still be affort after the election of which the main line Congressmen should be way. If they are not vigilant and give collective leadership a fair chance, the "coterie" may once again try to hijack the party in the "interests of party unity". India is becoming an increasingly difficult country to govern. The British cabinet system which we have chosen to follow has an inbuilt bias towards a presidential prime minister. This tendency was carried to an extreme in the list two decades without making the business of governance any easier. The Congress party now has an opportunity it must not lost to go back to its pre-Indira Gandhi phase and to develop a collegiate form of leadership in which the Prime Minister is primus inter pares and not the sole receptacle of the

9. *Patriot,* 27 May 1991.

Congress party's hopes, wisdom and power.[10] For this to come about, it will be necessary to restore grassroots democracy in the party and turn it once again into a bottom-up party instead of the top-down organisation it has become. Only then can the party hope to provide a respensive government accountable to the people and capable of mediating the alarming array of societal conflicts in the country.

Then if India's political system was designed for kings, the Nehrus were natural for the role, and took as if born to it. Few medieval kings could have exuded a grandeur comparable with that of a Indira Gandhi holding morning darbar at her residence. Few commanded equal adulation. And if an initially hesitant Rajiv Gandhi was averse to mixing with the common public, he soon learnt of the advantages, indeed necessity of this for maintaining a sympathetic public profile, so essential to retaining what is referred to in the political lingua franca as his 'political base'. But the Nehrus' relationship with India was not entirely one sided. If they enjoyed a unique level of public trust and adulation, they did in their turn endeavour to justify it in keeping the several heterogeneous nation states clubbed together by colonial England, and handed to Jawaharlal Nehru and provide modern India with a modicum of government. Their record on both these scores was at best patchy. However, it is significant that a country in which caste and religious demarcations were clearly delineated, the Nehrus, high-caste Hindus themselves, were never indentified with their caste or the majority community to which they belonged, and managed to present themselves as Indians foremost. No small legacy this, considering the caste"religious associations of present from of leaders. If anything, both Indira and Rajiv, whose record campares rather poorly with Nehru's were, Golden temple and Delhi riots notwithstanding, frequently portrayed as prominority. Still, infairness it must be conceded that by the turn of the last decade, and 40 years down the road, the Nehru legacy had gotten more than alittle frayed at the edges, both because of the follies and foibles of Rajiv Gandhi and as a consequence of the fast deteriorating internal and international environment.[11]

For the Congress Party he has left behind not only its revived and reftrebished legacy but also the challenging task of convincing the nation that though he is gone his indomitable spirit lives. That task the party had successfully, accomplished after the dastardly assassination of Mahatma, it also rose to the occassion in the much more difficult circumstances after the shooting down of Indira Gandhi. The task is

10. *Indian Express* 30 May 1991.
11. Baljit Singh. A Break With The Past. *The Business And Political Observer,* 4 June 1991.

even more daunting today, though not at all hopeless, because the party has come to depend so much on Rajiv Gandhi. Hope arises from the fact that the party had been reinspired with the ideals with which it has been traditionally associated.

The most outstanding evidence of that is the open confussion of mistakes and deviations of the past. The corrective got credibility not only because people trustee the word of Rajiv Gandhi, but the trust, in fact, was based on the realisation that, unlike some other leders, he had not imposed his ideals on unwilling colleagues but that he spoke only after he had brought his party collegues round to his way of thinking. Credit is due to him not just for unwavering personal committment to the ideal of secularism but because he had recharged the Congress with that thought current. In accomplishing this he had to go, through a gruelling struggle with himself (to develop patience with his wayward colleagues), with the people (to attune their minds to the fast moving technological revolution in the world) and with his political rivals (who were out to reverse the course of Indian history towards the darkness of the dark Age) That he had succeeded in galvanising the first two to his way of thinking is apparent from the tremendously enthusiastic response he was getting from the common people. It was also reflected in the courage and determination with which he took up the fight against the forces of communalism. More than anybody else it is he who made the nation aware of the dangers inherent in the ideology of the BJP Shiva,Sena, VHP etc. Like his illustrious forebears secularism was not for him a hot-house plant imported from somewhere. He adopted it as the best in the religio-cultural traditions of the Indian people. Beliefs of people, he felt deserved full respect from those who undertook to lead them. Although he kept his own religious belief, whatever it was, as a strictly private affair (in this respect he was some what different from his mother and much more like Jawaharlal Nehru), he made it well known that he did not treat the beliefs of others, whether of the minority communities or the majority, with anything like cynical disdain which is arrogantly flaunted by arm chair intellectuals. It is the latter attitude which is responsible for whatever weakening it witnessed in popular adherence to the secular ideal. When critics talk of the failure of Nahruvian model they confuse it with the theoretical models of atheist materialists. Nehru's image is blurred largely because he has been monopolised by this set of self-proclaimed Nehruites who have hardly much in common either with his theoretical approach or with his practice.[12]

The unanimous election of P.V. Narasimha Rao as President of the

12. D.R. Goyal, Rajiv's Challenging Legacy. *National Herald*, 25 May 1991.

Congress is a recognition of the fact that he is the party's best bet. His rich political and administrative experience can stand him in good stead in his new assignment. Ror Fao, the immediate challenge is to lead the party to victory at the hustings for which he will have to convert the sympathy Rajiv Gandhi's violent death may have generated into votes. It is a measure of his realism that he has already added secularism to the party's stability slogan to make it more appealing and maeaningful in the changed situation. Nevertheless, it will not be easy for him to sell the stability idea when Rajiv Gandhi is not around and when a party posts have not been held for over two decades even as careerists and opportunists have been albowing out traditional Congressmen. Rao will be doing a service to the party if he is able to encourage wider participation to all sections of the party and being it closer to the people. The process of alienation of the party from the people can be reversed only be democratising the functioning of the party and making it an instrument of change. Needless to say, the nation still has great expectations from the party and Rao's task is to enable it to redeem itself. A crucial test of his leadership will be when soon after the elections the leader of the Congress Parlimentary party, who will also the Prime Minister if the party wins sufficient seats, is elected. It is the first time the party is contesting an election without projecting someone as the potential Prime Minister. Notwithstanding the unity party leaders displayed in his election the Congress-I is far from united. The electoral compulsions might have had a restraining influence on them but in easier climes and without the domineering presence of a leader of the stature of Indira Gandhi or Rajiv Gandhi, it would be difficult for them to keep their differences under wraps. Mr. Rao has the unenviable task of retaining their support without undermining the party's larger interests. Although the move to have four or five vice-presidents to "Assist" him was given up-and rightly so-he will have to reconcile himself to the reality that he is at best the first among equals.[13] Of course, he cannot be oblivious of his limitations in comparision to his immediate predecessor who had age, flamboyance and familiar heritage to his advantage. Rao will, therefore, have to adopt a consensual and hence a democratic approach to the running of the organisation. Rebuilding of the party is Rao's immediate task after the elections are over.[13]

By electing P.V. Narsimha Rao, a senior and non-controversial leader, as the party president the working committee has settled the leadership question for the time being. The formalities will be completed only when the AICC approves him as the regular president.

13. *The Hindustan Times,* 31 May 1991.

Besides, the party president need not be the leader of the parlimentary party. As party president, Narasimha Rao faces a difficult task. The fact that he does not fit himself into the Nehru-Indira-Rajiv line might cramp his style of leadership initially. But this need not turn out to be a handicap in carrying out his onerous responsibilities. Though age and health seem to be not favouring him, his administrative experience, political acument and erudition are likely to stand him in good stead. A traditional Congressman, he is unlikely to act erratically as some of the youngsters tend to do. In a dispassionate and sedate fashion, he can be expected to tackle the problems of the party. Narashimha Rao's immediate task is to lead the party to victory at the hustings. Though the sympathy wave generated in its favour in the wake of Rajiv Gandhi's assassination has improved the party's electoral prospects, it has to intensively its campaign in order to ensure victory. It has not only to stress the stability factor but also to convince the voters that it is capable of delivering the goods. The campaign thrust of the party is now the promise to "keep Rajiv's dream alive". The people expect a clarification of the dram from the leadership. In other words, what are the ideals and policies, for which the party stands? The answer is contained in the new slogan which Mr. Narsimha Rao has given to the party- "stability with secularism". He has pointed out that what India needs most is a strong and stable Government that can "protect the unity of the present and nourish the vision of the future". In new Congress-I, chief has rightly emphasised that there can be no stability without secularism. On the poll front the party has to fight mainly the BJP and the National Front and it would be honourable if the fight is along ideological lines. The Congress need not be shy of its traditional values and ideals although it is imperative that it should change with the times. Secularism has been a cardinal principle with the party and whenever it has attempted to dilute it, the party has suffered a setback. But secularism does not mean pampering any particular community. The Congress has a responsibility to defuse the communal tensions that have been building up in recent moths and the time is quite conducive to it. Even the BJP has been compelled by circumstances to stress less on Ram and more on stability which means that the party has realised the risk in overplaying the communal card at this Juncture. If the Congress-I makes secularism a key issue in the elections not only will it improve its electoral prospects but it will be rendering a signal service to the nation. Another major task of the new leadership is to preserve the unity of the party by keeping divisive forces at bay. The party is known for its factional squabbles and when the elections are over, these might become worse. A certain degree of firmness is required on the part of Narasimha Rao while dealing with the various faction leaders spread all over the country. In this respect, he may find himself in a less advantageous position than his predecessor. The best way to strengthen the party is to restore democracy within the organisation. The fact that organisational elections have not been held for more than two decades has been a slur on the party. Narasimha Rao's effort should be to hold these elections at the earliest. If inner-party democracy is ushered in, the Congress will find itself rejuvenated. The election of Narasimha Rao as the party president gives no inkling of the likely leader of the parliamentary party who will be the Prime Minister in case it wins a majority of the Lok Sabha seats. It would be in the fitness of things if the leadership of the party and that of the parliamentary party are separate. Congressmen need not feel upset if a contest for the parliamentary party leadership becomes inevitable. The search for a consensus leader has at times gone to absurd lengths. After all, election for leadership is the sign of a lively democracy. Mr. Narasimha Rao, party president, should make sure that the democratic process in the party goes on uninterrupted. Whatever the outcome of the general election, the Congress-I likely to play a pivotal role in national politics, although over the years it has lost its pristine glory. It is the only national party in the sense that it has a presence in every nook and corner of the country. By upholding its ideals, democratising its functioning and strengthening its organisational structure, it may be able to regain its vitality as well as clout among the people. Much depends upon how the new leadership acts and the response in gets from the rank and file. With the end of the Rajiv era, a new chapter has begun in the annals of the party and time along will show how it will unfold itself.[14]

The Gandhi family has contributed to neo-feudalism by eroding the independence of institutions and making so many of them subservient to party hacks. But almost every other party, when given the chance to govern, has done the same. Voters have experimented repeatedly with non-dynastic options, which unfortunately have failed repeatedly. Had the Gandhi family alone been guilty of misusing institutions and power, it would have lost out to others who respected, and efficiently ran institutions. In fact personalities ruled supreme over principles in party after party, faction after faction.

Voters are not incurably feudal at heart. When given a ruler who provides some semblance of impartial justice and governance, no matter that he has many flaws, they vote on non-feudal line (as in West Bengal). But in general they do not feel they have non- feudal options,

14. P. Tharyan. After Rajiv Congress at Crossroads. *The Hindustan Times*, 1st June 1991.

and therefore look to the Gandhi family as a solution to the neo-feudal reality they face. The situation is unlikely to change till there is an overhaul of the Constitution to curb drastically the power of politicians, guarantee the automomy of institutions, ensure the punishment of guilty politicians and civil servants, and provide for speedier justice in the courts. Till that happens, a young feudal seion like Priyanka Gandhi will continue to carry more credibility with voters than a score of Congress Party bosses.[15]

15. Swaminathan S. Anklesaria Aiyar. Why Voters Like Dynasties. The Times of India, 30 May, 1991.

16
THE CONGRESS PARTY AND THE CHALLENGE

The monster of bloody violence has been on the rempage for quite sometime now in different parts of India. On May 21 it struck at the national level. The bomb that killed Rajiv Gandhi was aimed not at an individual. Its target was the life of the leader of the leading political party engaged in the campaign for the most crucial general election since the country's independence. The balance of forces is poised so in our polity today that this assassination has the dangerous potential of disrupting the democratic process and plunging the country into a civil war. The climate has already been surcharged with tension and fratriciadal hatred generated by the political happenings of the last two years, now once again overheated during the current general election campaign. Incidentally that this assassination has taken place in a State that is under direct President's rule falsifies the Centre's claim of running an administration more alert than those at the State level. The shock at the brutal killing of Rajiv has not only stunned the entire nation, but perhaps has had a chastening impact on political leaders at large realising the gravity of the gathering environment of a civil war. However, the Congress party followers at many places seem to have gone berserk-partly spontaneous, partly calculated which brought back fears of a repetition of the ghastly anti-Sikh pogrom in the wake of Indira Gandhi's assassination in 1984. This time the alertness of security arrangement has so far prevented the situation going out of control. This is however an insecure respite because the tension persists with the polling for the Lok Sabha half-way through while the Chief Election Commissioner's blatantly pro- Congress partisanship, demonstrated repeatedly with unashamed zeal, has in a large measure, undermined the authority of the high office in the public eye so much so that a code of conduct for the Election Commission itself seems badly needed. Which has only added to the hazards of uncertainty prevailing all round.[1]

In this dark twilight, President Venkataraman's reported initiative for a dialogue with leaders of major political parties to explore the possibility of an all-party national government at the Centre is undoubtedly a statesmanlike endeavour. Narrow partisan approach by any party, great or small, high or low, will only divide the nation in an extraordinary crisis like the present. There have been massive cam

1. Nikhil Chakravorty, Congress Faces Big Challenge,. Patriot, 26 May 1991

paigns and agitations in recent months which have only helped to rent asunder the fabric of national which have only helped to rent asunder the fabric of national unity. No doubt communal tensions have been whipped up- not only by formations branded as communal but others too which sanctimoniously claim to be above communalism. Public postures and secret deals contradicting such postures have become commonplace for political leaders anxious to garner votes. At the same time, problems of forbidding dimension assail the nation today. Whoever is invested with the power to govern this country by virtu of the verdict of the ballot box, will be confronted with intractable issues-ranging from Kashmir and Punjab to economy and IMF loan and then on to the Mandir-Mosque dispute- none of which can be settled by any one party even if it commands a comfortable parliamentary majority. Nor can the crisis of today be solved by going in for an emergency as suggested in some quarters-rather such an emergency will aggravate the crisis beyond repair. Nor is the putting off of polling in the remaining Lok Sabha constituencies going to normalise the situation; rather this may very well accentuate the tension. In fact, none of the major issues awaiting decision of any new government can be tackled without the consensus of all. And such a consensus shall not come unless and until all the major parties are charged with the responsibility of governance. The idea of an all-party government therefore is not just a fire-brigade approach but implies a serious attempt at unifying the nation at this juncture. Normally, the initiative for a national consensusneed not have come from Rashtrapati Bhawan. It should have come from within the political spectrum, particularly from the leadership of the party claims to be the largest in Parliament. Not only did the Congress command and the largest number of members in the last Lok Sabha, though failing to get a majority, but it has throughout been claiming to be the only party with a nationn-wise spread, But the Congress today is in a state of irremediable atrophy. This is amply demonstrated by its bizarre move to make Sonia Gandhi the party president. What could be the possible consideration that has led senior leaders of the Congress to make Sonia their leader? It is obvious that they have calculated that after Rajiv's tragic assassination there would be an effusion of 'sympathy votes for the Congress in the rest of the polling if his widow in distress is displayed as his successor in the party. Further, it is no secret that there are provincial warlords within the party who would find it difficult to choose the leader from among themselves, and so as a means of keeping each other out, they have chosen Sonia for the post of the party president. It is worth noting that when Sonia declined the offer of party presidetship, two stalwarts, Arjun Singh and N.D. Tiwari have thrown their hats in the ring.

However, the calculation of the Congress bosses may go wrong and only betray their bankruptcy. A general election is a serious business, and large sections of the awakened electorate this time particularly may not be easily hoodwinked by such stunt decision. On the contrary, the selection of Sonia Gandhi may provide easy grist to the mill of the traducers of the Congress. It is not that there is to be any objection to her being a foreign-born Indian citizen. The stark fact of the matter is that she is nobody, in the political life of this country, and it is indeed grotseque to find her at the held of a leading political party.[2]

The tragedy intorudces very major concerns for the future because it confirms the worst impressions we have. Looking to the immediate future in the post-assassination period, one good thing is that despite the awful excess in Tamil Nadu, on the whole, people have behaved sensibly in that there has been no repeat of the anti-Sikh genocidal pogrom of 1984. Coming back to the present, every well informed school child expects some kind of sympathy effect to get translated into votes. The curious situation is that two-fifths of our Lok Sabha elections is over. Approximately three-fifths of the seats will be contested in the next two rounds. In the incompleted Lok Sabha, not taking into account Punjab, Assam and Jammu & Kashmir, elections to two- fifths of the total number of seats is over and will not be affected by the assassination. The balance three-fifths will be in political terms, in some way or the other.[3]

The Cogress Working Committee (CWC)'s offer to Sonia Gandhi to take over as party president shocked quite a few people. But the offer was an inevitable fallout of Rajiv Gandhi's death at a time when the process of the 10th Lok Sabha elections was half way through. Whether Sonia would have made a good party president or whether she should subsequently have been made Prime Minister if the Congress obtains an absolute majority in the elections, are different issues. The main issue offer highlights right now is this: the Congress leadership was left with no other alternative but to offer the coveted post to Sonia. The party leadership faced certain compulsions which led to the offer. But let us look at the background process which led to these constraints. It is the Congress supreme leadership itself which is responsible for the party's present plight. Right from the time of Jawaharlal Nehru, the Congress has not thought in terms of a second ranking leader from its cadre. When Nehru died on May 27, 1964, the same question as the one facing the party now arose: Who after Nehru? Then fortunately, the low profile Lal Bahadur Shastri lived upto expec

2. *Ibid.*
3. N. Ram. The Congress. *The Sunday Observer,* 26 May 1991

tations. But once again, after, Shasrti's sudden death on January 11, 1966, there was no leader with a strong national image. Indira Gandhi was brought in since the next Lok Sabha elections were round the corner and people still had memories of the Nehru era. Indira Gandhi came to power as Nehru's daughter. Her decisions to nationalise banks and abolish privy purses helped her landslide victory in the 1971 elections. She soon started emerging as the party's only top ranking leader, though till the Congress split in 1969, the party did have prominent leaders such as Morarji Desai, K.Kamraj and S. Nijalingappa. But after the formation of the Congress, Indira Gandhi saw to it that no other leader including veterans like Y.B. Chavan and Jagjivan Ram could grow. The eventual outcome of this one-leader policy was that she could smoothly induct her son Sanjay and, after death, Rajiv into politics. When Indira Gandhi died on October 31, 1984, the party had to elect Rajiv as the prime minister, though he had no experience in the government, primarily because there was no one to take over. Rajiv Gandhi continued the same policy and curbed the growth of all other leaders. This decades-long practice is what made it impossible for his party colleagues in the CWC to think of any one else but his wife Sonia, who has no experience of politics. The situation is not very different within other parties. In the Bharatiya Janata Party, besides L.K. Advani and Atal Behari Vajpayee, it is difficult to think of a third equally prominent leader. Similarly, the Janata Dal minus V.P. Singh is a leaderless party. And the only real leader in the so-called cadre-based CPI-M is Jyoti Basu. This trend indicates that something is fundamentally wrong not only in the structure of the Congress but in the very method of looking at leadership dynamics and developing second ranking leaders in all our political parties. The Indian population has always looked up to the Premie Minister for providing a strong leadership to the entire country. Other than members of the Gandhi family, in the last few decades, only V.P. Singh was able to reach the national leader standard, but his decline began soon due to his decision on the Mandal commission. Neither Morarji Desai, who took over with a big bang against the backdrop of the Emergency nor Charan Singh, who claimed to be the sole protector of farmers, could claim to have elicited a national response.[4]

Was the Congress ever a political party in the real sense of the word? Has there ever been a time when it was not dependent on the charisma of one perosn? Does anyone recall any sustained periods of time when the party was run on truly democratic lines rather than on the personal influence of that person? The passing of Rajiv Gandhi, and the pathetic

4. Bharat Kumar. A Dynastic Democracy. *The Independen,*. 26 May 1991.

attempt by the Congress Working Committee (CWC) to replace him as party president by Sonia Gandhi, under scores the importance of these questions. The record certainly indicates that Congressmen, starting with Nehru, Patel and the rest of them, have always tended to 'obey' a leader in the search of a consensus rather than do thing the way they are done in Western political parties, upon which the Congress is supposedly modelled. At first the leader whose wishes invariably prevailed was Gandhiji. Once he had wrested control of the party after the Nagpur Congress in 1920, he did pretty much as he pleases, and as the conduct of Motilal Nehru and others showed, the only place for dissidents was outside the party mainstream. This was true of Nehru as well, who gained total control of the party after he worsted Purushottamdas Tandon in the early 1950s. But by now those disagreeed had to leave the party altogether. But the saving grace in the case of both Gandhiji and Nehru was that both were products of British liberalism. Neither regarded the party as a personal fiefdom and would not have dreame of using it in quite the way tht Indira Gandhi later did. But what matters is this culture of *ji huzoor* (yes, sir) was there, and all it took to convert the Congress into a private army of non- too-subtle sycophants was a determined by assualt by a politician like Indira Gandhi, when a political free-for-all developed after Nehru had gone. 'India is Indira' etc. has always been inherent in the ethos of the Congress party. That it should manifest itself once again in the form of a unanimous endorsement of Sonia Gandhi, whose inadequacies for the post of party president need no reiteration, should not therefore cause my surprise.[5]

What is surprising, however, is that those who proposed he name, and those voted for it, should have persumed not only that she would accept, but also that the country would stand by their choice. The move, which happily backfired, (though if Mrs. Gandhi is 'persuaded' to change her mind, things would be back to square one) proved what a well-known journalist has maintained since December 1989, namely, that the once mighty Congress party has been reduced to a nameplate on 10, Janpath. But now that the nameplate has been blown off by the balst that felled Rajiv Gandhi, who, in spite of everything, was probably the country's best bet, where does the party go? Will it be able to arrive at its famous 'consensus' or will it simply wither away? Worse, will it fragment into parties which look like the Congress(S)? One for each state, that is and none for the country as a whole? These are early days to say definitely what will happen but one thing is certain: faced with a situation in which not only is there no supreme, there is not even a second rung leadership of the Kamaraj, Atulay Ghosh, S.K. Patil sort,

5. T.C.A. Srinivasan Raghavan. The Congress. *The Economic Times*, 27 May 1991.

or even a heir apparent like Rajiv Gandhi, the little man upon whom the responsibility has fallen, will either run bleating to Sonia Gandhi, or scrable away like so many ants out of a anthill.[6]

CPI-M general secretary E.M.S. Namboodripad, has asked the Congress to reexamine the attitude towards the Left parties in the post Rajiv political scenario. In an open letter to the Congress president, P.V. Narsimha Rao, has asked the Congress present electoral strategy, steeped in hostility to the CPI (M)- lead political alliance in west Bengal, Tripura and Kerala and the National Front, would do may good either to India or that party itself, and if that strategy should not be subjected to a reexamination there the coming poll. While congratulating Mr. Rao on his election as party president, he said he was not saying much as he was aware that Mr. Rao was taking on a "crown of thorns". Yet he wished Rao the courage to tackle problems he might face. The deep crisis into which the Congress and India had fallen after Rajiv Gandhi's assassination was the direct result of the Congress Organisational functioning devoid of inner-party democrary for the past 20 years, he charged. Nomboodripad said after Rajiv Gandhi assassination, a "caucus" within the party had tried to make use of Sonia Gandhi as a "pawn" to retain control of party affairs. But Rao's election was viewed as a "miscarriage of the conspiracy". Developments, along with statements by various Congress leaders on the need for restoration of inner- party democracy, signifed the opening of a new chapter in the history of the country and the Congress, he said and the most important task which merited Rao's immediate attention was bringing to justice those responsible for the killing of Rajiv Gandhi. He said the Congress working committee should "strongly condemn the violence indulged in by Congress workers in different parts of the country against political opponents" during the observance of mourning for Mr. Gandhi. The house of N.T. Rama Rao and former Union Minister Ram Vilas Paswan, had been among the targets of attacks, CPI(M) offices and workers in many states, including Kerala and Tripura, had come under attack, but the Congress leader had not condemned these incidents, he said.

There is much speculation on what the left parties will do in the event of a hung parliament, especially if the Congress emerges as a single largest party a few seats short of a simple majority. Will the CPI-M offer to support the Congress? Will they even go as far as to participate in the government? Will Jyoti Basu emerge as a consensus candidate and become the Prime Minister? This speculation has been fuelled by the reported reluctance of Rajiv Gandhi to criticise Basu at public

6. *Ibid.*

meetings in Calcutta and the West Bengal chief minister's titillatiing hints about all kinds of possible permutations after the elections. As we journalists love to say, Basu is playing his cards close to his chest and since he is not ready to reveal anything, we speculate. One fails to understand the coyness on the part of the CPI-M. Admittedly, during an election campaign the left parties cannot be publicly seen distancing themselves from their chief ally, the Janata Dal or hobonobbing with their arch enemy, the Congress. But if Basu and his colleagues are half as astute as they are said to be, they must have seen the writing on the wali-there is no way the Janta Dal can form the government and the Congress is most likely to emerge as the single largest party. Further, BJP needs to be contained and fought and even the CPI-M has bever doubted the Congress party's anti-BJP stand. Why not then come out into the open and proclaim that if the Congress needs support it will be provided?

The truth is that the CPI-M is a victim of its own muddled strategies of the fast few year and is now hard put to it to extricate itself from its dilemmas. Having made anti-Congressism as the cornerstone of its ideology and policy in the last two decades, more so after the Emergency, it now finds that it cannot justify to its rank and file or its odd bunch of political friends a pro-Congress tilt. The CPI-M has more in common with the Congress than with the socialists, regional parties like the TDP and, obviously, the BJP. But this has not stopped it from hobnobbing with all of them at one time or the other. All because of a bizarre antipathy towards the Congress. Basu and Gandhi share the same approach towards communalism, the unity and integrity of the country, foreign policy and now, even the economy. But Basu is obliged to take potshots at the Congress, and not merely at the state level. Basu did not agree totally with V.P. Singh on the .Mandal issue and should logically be rabidly against Lohiate socialist who are anti-communist, but he freely shares a platform with them. In such a situation, how can Basu come out in the open and announce his support to the Congress? He will be simply purged out of his party. The old guard led by E.M. S. Namboodiripad would never allow any hobnobbing with the Congress, though they had no qualms about cuddling up with the BJP on the same bed with Singh in the middle. The dichotomy, which CPI-M fellow travellers will tell you is canny political strategy, is one more symptom of how out of touch the CPI-M is with reality. It has failed to understand the significance of changes in eastern Europe and is content with pursuing an obsolete line because it feels secure. Today the CPI- M presents a sorry picture. It still commands a good cadre base and has sound thinkers in the ranks but none theless has been reduced to a regional party at best. It often sounds like a part of social democrats and has jettisoned even classical communist postures. It has failed to recognise the bigger dangers for the country and has got bogged down in petty, personality-based politics. These elections provide a chance to the party to redeem itself. Let Basu, who still enjoy clout within and outside the party take the first step. He should convince the party that its best interests and the good of the country lie in all secular and progressive forces coming together and battling obscurantist elements like the BJP who are hell bent on taking the fascist and regressive road. The CPI-M has a historical role to play; will it live up to expectations.[7]

The assassination of Rajiv Gandhi on Tuesday will throw up a new political situation, where anything can take place, observes the Communist Party of India(CPI). It expects new realignment of political forces, which will alter the course of politics in the country. The party is also confident that the Congress will survive the void created by Rajiv Gandhi's death. The party, however, reiterates its earlier stand of not forming a government with the Congress. Even though not altogether ruling out such a possibility. It may be recalled that the CPI-M politburo member Jyoti Basu had earlier made a statement, hinting at the possibility of forming a government with the Congress to combat the BJP threat. As expected by many political parties, especially the BJP, the Congress will not disintegrate, asserts the CPI. According to the CPI, the Congress leaders will have to keep the party together, as its falling apart would bring about a shift in power. The party also feels that the sympathy factor will play a crucial role in the forthcoming elections.

The Bharatiya Janata Party described the elections of Sonia Gandhi as the Congress president as the "utter bankruptcy of the Congress". Reacting on Sonia Gandhi's election as the Congress president, BJP all-India secretary J.P. Mathur said, it showed utter bankruptcy.

The elimination of Rajiv Gandhi from the scene has created a deep sense of void not only in India but throughout the world. The personal loss of Sonia, Rahul and Priyanka Gandhi is, of course, irreparable. But the feeling is shared by the whole nation, indeed by the whole world. The tearful crowds at the funeral of Rajiv Gandhi and the tributes from all parts of the globe, cutting across geographical and ideological boundaries, speak for the stature which he had attained.

Rajiv Gandhi had come to symbolise the hopes of all those who seek to convert the East- West detente into an atmosphere conducive to building a just and peaceful world. Especially the hopes of the developing countries whose most articulate and forceful spokesman he had

7. Sidharth Bhatia. The Left must Take The Right Road. *The Independent*, 22 May 1991.

come to be. No surprise that the non-aligned met in a special session at New York to condole his death. Nor should it surprise anyone that serious apprehensions are being expressed about the future of NAM after him. Fears are also expressed about the future of democracy in India. And they are not altogether unfounded. The alternatives to his party and leadership have only given jolts to democratic polity by whipping up communal and casteist prejudices. The language of reason and decency which is the precondition of democratic practice has also been associated with him more than with any other leader. Most of his opponents invariably yielded to the temptation of using base passions to achieve political ends. The Congress party bears the awesome responsibility of ensuring the continuation of that culture and tradition. Used to living under the comforting shade of the umbrella of a Jawaharlal, an Indira Gandhi and, then, a Rajiv Gandhi their first reaction was of bewildered orphanament. The immediate reaction was to press Sonia Gandhi to take the mantle of her late husband. Carping critics have tried to see it as "political bankrupty". The Bharatiya Janta Party. flouting all canons of noble culture and conduct, have hastened to dub the grief-sicken lady as a foreigner and an alien. It only shows to what depths of pattines and degradation they can descent in their cynical pursuit of power. They are now trying to sell the idea that Congress minus Rajiv Gandhi cannot be as good an instrument of stability as their own party. People will surely decide whether their party, red in tooth and claw with the blood of innocents and totally devoid of the milk of human kindness and decency can be accepted in the role of a socio-political stabiliser. The request of the Congress Working Committee to Sonia Gandhi, apart from the first panicked reaction to an event which was beyond their wildest imagination, has also to be seen as its determination to reassure the people of India and the world that the policies and practices hitherto assiciated with it will not be abandoned. It was also a legitimate expression of gratitude to the departed leader whose family had made the Congress and instrument of service to Indian people as well as to humanity at large. On a more mundane plane it was perhaps an attempt to avoid contest for leadership at a time when the party is in the midst of a gruelling electrol battle. To interpret such inner-party rivalry and contention as paucity of leadership as the BJP has done reflects a mentality which does not admit of plurality of leadership in a party, and adheres to the Fuehrer principle. It is quite natural, of course, for those who have been natured in the RSS which is based on the principle of *Ek-chalak-anuvartitva* (follow one leader). The Congress, indeed, has never been short of leaders. At every stage in its history there have been plenty of them representing all varieties of belief and opinion in this vast and varied nation. They have had differences and contentions, sometimes even bitter, but they have always succeeded in hammering out a path for the future which was acceptable to the largest number of people in the country.[8]

In discussions of the Congress Party over the last 15 years, the increasing role of the dynastic factor has been rightly stressed. However, in drawing the right lessons that can prove useful in rebuilding the party and saving it from disintegration, it is necessary to analyse this factor with some discrimination. For, the political culture that prevailed under the founder of the dynasty (Jawaharlal Nehru) and that which unfolded under his descendants were vastly different. True, even Nehru preferred to be the "undisputed leader", was intolerent of challenges to his authority, and was at times petty-minded in dealing with those he considered as his rivals (Patel, Tandon, Kripalini). But, all the same, he was able to share power with a wide range of people, drew a galaxy of talent in the process of governance and, while rataining immense personal power, contributed not a little to the building of institutions. Power was shared down the line too, producing the "federal consensus" based on a shared vision of building one nation, but from diverse centres. There was no attempt to foist the wishes of the Centre, nor was there any need to. Leaders with a strong regional base (Kairon, B.C.roy, Kamraj, G.B. Pant, C.B. Gupta) were given due regard. And when the balance of power shifted in a given state, e.g. when the organisational wing challenged the ministerial wing through the free play of democratic politics, this too was taken due note of. In Nehru's time too chief ministers were changed but more often than not this was brought about by changing power equations in the field, not something imposed from above just because someone with a strong following had emerged as has been the case under his discendants. The federal principle was also attempted to be carried further down-community development, panchyati raj, cooperative, voluntary bodies engaged in social reform-although Nehru was unable to stop the virus of bureaucratisation of all these initiatives which in turn led to growing centralisation. Third, under Nehru the party organisation continued to be the operative structure of electoral and party politics; those in change of party organisation carried a lot of clout. That this gave rise to "bossism", was, of course, true. But it was still the party leaders who was in command; even mafia-type elements were not absent but they were under his complete control. Today, the roles have reversed.[9]

It is the erosion and wnaton disregard of this institutional nereus of

8. *National Herald*, 28 May 1991.
9. Rajni Kothari. Consensus Again. *The Times of India*, 29 May 1991.

shared power, its federal spread and grassroots strength and a widespread party organisation (which together provided checks on centralisation and personal rule) that has, especially over the last 20 years, led to the decline of legitimacy of the Indian state and of the Congress organisation as its operative framework. Hence, the compulsion for dynastic successions, the usurpation of real power by cliques, and coteries in the name of the "leader", the trndency to treat the state as a private domain and the considerbaly increased reliance on money power and other means of dealing with adversaries, including assiduous use of the mass media for personal build-up and inspired propaganda. Any attempt to recapture the erstwhile consensus and re-build its institutional infrastructure must, of course, take account of the radically changed situation both in respect of the polity and in respect of the social terrain in which it is supposed to function. Widespread public discontent, growing polarisatin of social forces and a governing structure that is unable to deliver the good provide the new context of power. Meanwhile, new dangers have emerged; a highly militant form of communalism, the growth fo a new and turbulent culture of violence, and alienation of the youth and the middle classes which, if not channelled constructively, could well be mobilised by fascist elements. The skills needed to steer the democratic path in this changed reality will have to be quite different from those that were needed under the Nehruvian umbrella. And yet the passing of the "dynastic" fix to which so much of the system had got riveted does throw up the challenge of rebuilding the lost consensus and the corroded institutions. Both the Congress and the non-Congress parties committed to a democratic, just, pluralist and united India must face up to this challenge. Perhaps more the latter than the former. But for this they must leave behind old fixations like anti-Congressism and come out on a positive thrust of recapturing the essence of a democratic, federal and secular polity that draws upon the lessons of the past-both positive and negative-and at the same time deals with the new challenges that have emerged. What we need is a new framework of consensus. As was provided by the Congress system before it got corroded by the dynastic factor and the coteric rule that emerged under it.[10]

Rajiv Gandhi's strength was that he could depend on the obedience of the Congressmen, in whatever decision he took and whatever they felt about it. That is one aspect of the stability that the Congress could an does promise. The dynastic aspect also spotlights his weakness. He had not gone through the mill; he was a stranger to the party's members and culture; above all, he thought that technocratic solutions were

10. *Ibid.*

available for essentially sociopolitical issues and conflicts. An assumption is made that Rajiv Gandhi would have secured a working majority, if not a comfortable majority, at the hustings. This is speculation. But even if we accept such predictions at their face value for the sake of argument. I cannot see it as sufficient justification to form the so called national government. A particular party's ability or inability to get a majority is primarily its own concern. There is no reason why it will not be possible to form a genuine coalition government between, say the Congress, the Left and the Janata Dal.[11]

It is difficult to imagine a more tragic and shocking event than the brutal assassination of Rajiv Gandhi, just when he was in the process of leading his party back to a victory at the polls. I can testify to this personally, as I campaigned for the Congress myself in several States for fiteen days and could judge the trend of the electorate. For those of us who knew him over the years, and who saw him grow from an adored grandchild of Jawaharlal Nehru into a competent airline pilot, and from there watched the dramatic way he was catapulated into the Prime Ministership, his going is felt as a personal blow, as if we have lost a member of the family. The cult of violence and assassination has deprived the nation of a man who was just reaching full maturity, who had learnt many valuable lesson from his first term a Prime Minister as well as his spell in the Opposition, and who was now psychologically and politically ready to lead the country at least for the next decade upto the dawn of the twenty-first century. For the Congress Party, which as a result of historical circumstances had become almost totally dependent upon him for its national leadership, his sudden departure has been a traumatic event. Although technically the party is still called 'Congress-I' for all practical purpose it has become the inheritor of the mantle of the Indian Naitonal Congress. A well- meaning but insensitively times resolution electing Mrs. Sonia Gandhi as president party was passed without her prior consent, and , as it turned out, the move proved infructuous as Sonia Gandhi politely but firmly turned down the invitation. The party will no doubt carry on for the next few months with P.V. Narasimha Rao as president, but the whole event has brought to the fore the importance of broadbasing the party machinery. Unless people with substantial support among the masses are involved in the decision-making process, an important element in our democratic functioning will be distorted.[12]

Elections to the party from the grassroots upwards will obviously take some time, but even before that it should be possible to call a broadbased meeting consisting of all central and state party legislators,

11. Girlal Jain. Rajiv's Weakness. *The Sunday Observer*, 26 May 1991.
12. Karan Singh. After the Strom. *The Hindustan Times*, 3 June 1991.

organisational office-bearers and prominent Congressmen in order to confirm the new president and also to chart out the future course of political action. It would be desirable if this exercise is completed soon so that the political vacuum created by Rajiv Gandhi's untimely demise is not allowed to persist.

The Congress at last seems to be sorting out the leadership question it has been facing after the assissination of Rajiv Gandhi. This is evident from the reports that a consensus is emerging in the party that P.V. Narasimha Rao should take over as party president and continue in the post till such time it elects one. This is sensible considering that he is the seniormost among Congress leader and least controversial. The fact that he does not command the allegiance of a strong faction makes him more acceptable to a large section of the party which cannot afford to face a show of disunity, caught as the party is in the fight for returning to power at the Centre. Actually, Narasimha Rao should have been asked to take over as an Acting or Interim President last week itself soon after the assassination of Rajiv Gandhi, but this was not possible thanks to the ill-advised moves of the coterie which chose to resort to subterfuge and propose Mrs. Sonia Gandhi's name for the Presidentship and that too-as it came to known later-without seeking her consent. Wisely, she has declined the offer having perhaps seen through the game of the vested interests who thought she could continue controlling the party in her name. Many people had feared that after Rajiv Gandhi the Congress would split into various factions which might choose to walk on different tracks. It looks as if senior party leader have come to feel the need to remain together and steer the party through a difficult time, proving the sceptics wrong. Its performance at the polls is likely to improve if they remain united. And if there are problems of mutual adjustment, these can be tackled-perhaps successfully-after the elctions. One reason why the party is not in a disarray at the moment is the shared feeling that it can come to power on a sympathy wave. Unity is always important for a political party and more so now when over 300 Lok Sabha seats are yet to go to polls.[13]

The immediate task for the party is to win the Lok Sabha election. And after the election the party will have to bring about the much-needed reforms in its structure and the ways of functioning. One such task that can be brought about soon after the election is the seperation of the office of President of the party from that of the leader of the Congress Parliamentary Party. The AICC and the PCCs and the various other elective bodies will need to be activised so that the party can survive and be of use to the country. Organisational elections which

13. *The Hindustan Times*, 29 May 1991.

have been postponed in the past will also need to be held soon to encourage wider participation by the rank and file. The Congress has still the largest mass base in the country and given unity and purposeful effort, it can serve and play its due role despite the tragic loss it has suffered in the death of Rajiv Gandhi. Its leaders must meet the challenge.

The assumption of the Congress presidentship by P.V. Narsimha Rao marks the reemergence of the "traditional Congressman" within the top levels of the party, meaning individuals who have served in the organisation for decades and come painfully up through the ranks. The dynamic of the freedom struggle had dictated a set of parameters within which the party operated substantial autonomy to local units (including in the selection of their leaders0, attempts to build a consensus before taking decisions, preference for a platform appropriate to an umbrella party and rejection of socially exclusive or divisive slogans. Despite splitting the party in 1969, Indira Gandhi did not at first deviate substantially from this model. She allowed the local satraps, as well as senior collegues such as Y.B. Chavan and Jagjivan Ram, substantial freedom. Cabinet meeting were chacracterised by debate, as were party get togethers, competing views jostled for attention, as exemplified by the mergence of the Congress Forum for Socialist Action (radical) and the Nehru Forum (conservative) in the early 1970s. A Vasant Sathe could come before a CFSA really in 1973 and demand the nationalisation of all private industries without damage to his political career. A.K.V. Raghunatha Reddy could make criticisms of the functioning of the very government of which he was a minister of state and yet survive. But by late 1973 the climate began to change. It was around that time that Sanjay Gandhi emerged as the principal adviser to his mother, and began building up a cadre of individuals who were "personally" loyal. By the time the Emergency was declared two years later, three-fourths of the local party units had their composition altered. It was no longer fashionable, for even necessary, to cultivate a local base. In place of seeing the party's base as the aggregate of the bases of the local leaders, the theory was floated that the base depended sloley on the "supreme leader" and that all others had merely to join the badwagon. Some did but others who did not, found themselves excluded. In 1977 election, one reason for the Janata victory was the non-participation of the bulk of the former Congress rank-and-file in campaigning "Let the storm-troopers the poll, after all it is their party now" was the mood. The stormtroopers lost, and Mrs. Gandhi was once again faced with the need to have a party machine. She mended fences, gave back much lost importance to traditional functionaries and limited Sanjay to a low-profile role exvept during the final days of the Janata era when he and Kamal Nath manipulated the clash between Morarji Desai and Charan Singh. The 1980 Congress, again in power, was not what Sanjay wanted. But he set about changing that, promoting favourite such as A.R. Antulay and V.P. Singh to take charge of vital states. By 1984 the "revolution" interrupted by the 1977 defeat would have been completed. But in June 1980 Sanjay died, leaving Indira Gandhi at the crossroad. Should she return to a "traditional" party structure, or move further along the path to a personalised one? She chose the latter, making clear by end of 1980 that Rajiv Gandhi was her chosen successor. During 1981 and 1982, Rajiv surprisingly almost got transformed into a pre-1974 Congressman. He would give respect to state leaders, attempt to find consensus solutions, downplay the importance of personal loyalty. It was only after Arun Nehru became his principal adviser in early 1983 that this changed. With characteristic efficiency Arun Nehru began combing the ranks of the party and outside for individual who would be personally loyal. Fund-raising was intensified, links with business groups strengthened. Political manipulations such as the coup against N.T. Rama Rao in Andhra Pradesh were set in train. But a year and a half was too short to complete such an ambitious process. The 1984 elections, whcih can unexpectedly once more saw the drafting of a majority of candidates from the "traditional" stream though there were also a fair sprinkling of new Congressmen.[14]

The new Congressmen had no time for such frivolous pursuits as developing a mass base for himself. That was the functiong of the leader. He would focus on more substantive issues, such as getting more and better publicity and increasing the range of his influence and affluence. Had Arun Nahru continued in the innermost circle of Rajiv Gandhi beyond 1985, there is little doubt that he would have rid the Congress party of most of its traditional elements. However, these elements were once more saved, this time by the suspicious in Rajiv Gandhi's mind that the individual being groomed by his cousin were loyal not to him but to Arun Nehru. This was the only point of difference. The plan-to create a refurbished party in which the M.J. Akbars and the Mani Shankar Aiyar would dominate-was still active.

14. M.D. Nalpat. Congress At A Watershed. *The Times Of India,* 1 June 1991.

But its implementation got delayed due to the Bofors controversy, when Rajiv Gandhi had to seek the support of the traditional partymen in order to check V.P. Singh's rebellion against him. This supprt was willingly given. But in exchange all that the traditional party men got was continued survival. Power was firmly in the hands of a small group of individuals concentrated in the Prime Minister's house. Shortly before the last election this group was joined by the formidable R.K. Dhawan. Had Rajiv Gandhi not fallen victim to a bomb, and had the returned as Prime Minister, there is little doubt that power winthin the party would have been controlled by a very small group of individuals acting in his name. Even after his defeat in 1989, he did not lie low as his mother had done but removed "traditional" Congressmen such as Veerendra Patil and Channa Reddy from power and was on the verge of pushing out an individual with a very strong local power base, Sharad Pawar. The Congress cannot return to its old roots. Too much violence had been done to them these past decades for that. But it can return to more accepted ways of functioning, going back to the theory that hundreds of small bases are far stronger than one huge one. It can returnto a respect for the autonomy of state units and to an avoidance of decision-making based on the personal advice of a coterie rather than consultations with many. After long years of ecvlipse, the traditional Congressman has once more stepped onto the centrestage.[15]

P.V. Narasimha Rao, Congress president, told the Congress Parliamentary Party (CPP) in New Delhi, on June 3, 1991 that while Rajiv Gandhi's assassination had shocked the national and the Congress, all partymen should rise to face the challenge posed to the "system" in the country. Addressing the general body of the CPP comprising Rajya Sabha members as Lok Sabha members are yet to be elected, Narasimha Rao said that he had not in the wildest of his dream though such a situation would arise when the CPP whould have to meet in the absence of its leader, Rajiv Gandhi. In the history of natins there were occasions when great events took place. But the men who participated in those events were not equally great. "This is perhaps the phase that the Congress party is passing through now," he said. Stressing the need to fulfill the unfinished tasks of Rajiv Gandhi, Narasimha Rao said this task was all the more difficult because none had expected the present situation. "We will have to consider waht we small men and women will have to do to save the country, the party and the system in the absence of a strongmen like Rajiv Gandhi's he said.

15. Ibid.

17
HIS SOCIAL PHILOSOPHY

Rajiv Gandhi bequeathed India a rich social legacy. He gave India's 200 million middle-class a sense of indentity, self-respect, pride. He made them come out of their shells to stake a claim to India's politics and economy.

In power for barely five years (1984-89), Rajiv Gandhi has nevertheless bequeathed a rich social legacy upon India. Moreover, most of the social processes he has set in motion, not to mention the economic forces he unleashed, are irreversible. Like his grandfather and mother, he moulded India in his own image, which was very different from those of his forebearers. The last of the Nehrus has done India proud, left it a better place than the one he inherited.[1]

Cutting across party lines, the Rajya Sabha members on June, 3 1991 paid rich tributes to the former Prime Minister, Mr. Rajiv Gandhi, and condemned his "horrendous assassination" on May 21 last as a blow to democracy, secularism and national aims of grwoth with social justice. The nation must ponder over it and fully comprehend the manifications of this great tragedy, they said. In a length resolution, proposed by the chairman, Dr. Shankar Dayal Sharma, and passed unanimously by a visibly sad and sombre House, the Rajya Sabha recalled the role played by Rajiv Gandhi at home and abroad and assailed the "diabolical and premeditated conspiracy that had beunmbed and shocked decent people around the world". It described Rajiv Gandhi as a visionary who wanted to see India enter the 21st century as a modern and prosperous country. On the opening day of the two day special session of the Upper House convened primarily to seek approval of the imposition of the President's rule in Haryana, the proceedings were adjourned after paying homage to Rajiv Gandhi. All praised Rajiv Gandhi's personality and maintained that not only India but the entire would had suffered an irreparable loss. They called for a united effort to fight the violent and disruptive forces as a befitting tribute to the charismatic leader who had been removed from the scene at the Prime of his youth. Paying a personal tribute to Rajiv Gandhi, Dr. Sharma said "some elements do not wish us well by persuing the cult of violence. This poses a challenge to all of us who believe in the peaceful methods of ballot and debate to attain our goal of progress and development. This challenge had to be met with all our might". Noting that Rajiv Gandhi had "retained a youthful exuberance and courageously discharged his oner-

1. Chandan Mitra. The Legacy. *The Sunday Observer,* 26 June 1991.

ous responsibilites till the end although he was not initially inclined towards politics,' Dr. Sharma said the country had reposed high hopes in his "youthful and charismatic leadership." Dr. Sharma said Rajiv Gandhi was a visionary and an idealist who conducted himself with courage and fortitude. He had taken up several new programmes and was gearing up the rural and district administration. Rajiv Gandhi believed in taking up problems directly and this was the reason for the Punjab and Assam accords. He was also seeking to promote regional cooperation, and had signed the accord with Sri Lanka and also made a historic visit to China which proved to be a turning point in India's relations with that great nation, "Dr. Saharma said. The six-nation initiative and the Delhi declaration, apart from the Africa Fund and the contribution towards the freedom of Namibia, were some of Rajiv Gandhi's singular achievements, Dr. Sharma added. Dr. Sharma said the house shared the grief of the Sonia Gandhi and her children on the death of Rajiv Gandhi, whose "warm smiling face and youthful charm" would always be remembered. The Prime Minister said in the country of Mahatma Gandhi. the fact the terrorists had succeeded in removing a personality like Rajiv Gandhi did not portend well. The nation must be prepared to face the forces responsible for this act. Rajiv Gandhi took the reins of the nation at a challenging time. The way he tried to tackle the Punjab and Assam problems showed his intelligence and well-meaning intentions. Shekhar praised the tolerance shown by people in the aftermath of the assassination and said the killers could not wipe out the values for which Rajiv stood. In a short span of public life, Mr. Gandhi has left an indeliable imprint on the world. He had dreamt of a prosperous and modern India with smile on the faces of crores of people, Mr. Shekhar said. Speaking in flowing and flowery Hindi language Atal Behari Vajpayee showered priase over the slain Congress president Rajiv Gandhi never allowed political differences to come in the way of personal relations, he said, and related how Rajiv had arranged to send him to the USA for medical treatment "This may be a small favour, but it touched my heart," he added. Vajpayee warned that no party should try to use this gruesome murder for petty political gains. "This would be an insult to the spirit of Rajiv Gandhi". Describing the assassination as a "tragedy of unparalleled proportions, the leader of the House, Yashwant Sinha recalled Rajiv Gndhi's commitment to international economic order and world peace that had won him universal acclaim. Describing Rajiv Gandhi as an ardent believer in modernity, peace and progress, Mr. Sinha said violence could have no place in our society. The leader of the Congress party in the Rajya Sabha, Shiv Shankar said Rajiv Gandhi was removed at a time when the prime ministership was within his reach. "The congress party has lost the captain of its ship; but the ship must sail on". Shiv Shankar said many feel that Rajiv Gandhi did not get a fair deal from his opponents and had to face the court of the people on unsubstantiated charge. The leader of the opposition, Gurupadswamy (JD) said despite our differences in the past, "we looked upon Rajiv Gandhi as a person who could lead the country to the 21st century". He symbolised modernity against the tendencies of revivalism. His assassination indicated that the country was drifting from "barbarism to degeneration". He added that India was a sick country as it had brutalised its politics. Samar Mukherjee, a senior CPM leader, said this tragedy should not be viewed as an isolated incident. Rajiv Gandhi's assassination was fraught with international ramifications. The force responsible for this must be identified and death with as foreign imperialism was interested in utilising them for creating chaos in the country. P.Upendra (TDP) said assessments might differ about Rajiv Gandhi's performance as the Prime Minister, but his sincerity of purpose was unquestionable. After Jawaharlal Nehru, he was the only Prime Minister who managed to establish close contacts world leaders. N.E. Balaram (CPI) said the best tribute to Rajiv Gandhi would be to work for unity and integrity of India, Surendra Bhatcharya (RSP) said such incidents might occure unless we successfully combat violence, Nagen Saikia (AGP) said Rajiv Gandhi fought for the cause of humanity and world peace. G. Swaminathan (AIADMK) pointed out that Rajiv Gandhi not only proved a good Prime Minister but also a good leader of the opposition. J.S. Arora (Akali Dal) while condemning the assassination of Gandhi said the roots of democracy were still tender in India and needed to be nurtured carefully. Recalling his long association with the Gandhi family R.K. Dhawan (Congress) said he stood for values and was a man of words. He related how while seeking his (Dhawan's) resignation in the wake of the inquiry commission report pointing an accusing finger against him for the 1984 riots Rajiv Gandhi had promised that he would be taken back as soon as he was cleared for the charges. Rajiv Gandhi did exactly that, Dhawan said. He also narrated how Rajiv Gandhi prevented the use of offical machinery after the death of his younger brother, Sanjay Gandhi. Jayanthi Natarajan (Congress) who was present at the site of assassination, was almost on the verge of breaking down when she described how she owed everything even her life, to the departed leader. Rajiv Gandhi had saved her life by sending her away just before the blast. "For me, Rajiv Gandhi's death was a personal loss," she said. The resolution passed by the House to mourn the death of Rajiv Gandhi described him as a leader who dedicated himself to the sacred task of building a new India-an India strong, united, peaceful and progressive, and India evolving, in the genius of her time-honoured ethos of oneness and synthesis, towards modernity, an India making her contribution to the building of a better, more humane, world environment. While condemning the "horrendous assassination," the resolution said this was a time when India must ponder over a fully comprehend the ramifications of this tragedy. "The nation must beware of any further attempt to convulse and disrupt national life". It added: "This House condemns the diabolical and pre-meditated conspiracy threatening the very foundations of our civilization, culture and identity as a free, sovereign and independent nation...... It is vitally necessary that the national responds to that dreadful deed by the manifestation of resolute determination upholding our nationa values unitedly and fear-

lessly and by our rededication to the task of national reconstruction and the building of a letter future for the world as a whole". Nothing less would be an appropriate tribute to the memory of Rajiv Gandhi, the resolution stated. Rich tributes were paid to the memory of late Rajiv Gandhi, at a meeting organised by the Delhi unit of the National students Union of India in New Delhi on June 3, 1991. The meeting was attended by several prominent Congressmen and leaders of various organisations. Professor Upendra Baxi, Vice Chancellor, Delhi University, stated that Rajiv Gandhi was not just a leader of the third world, but a leader of the whole of humanity, Film Actor Rajesh Khanna who was also present on the occasion said that he was first impressed by Rajiv Gandhi's abilities "when he intered politics on the death of his mother, Indira Gandhi. Top scientists and technologists of the country in a separate meeting also paid their tributes to the departed leader stating that in is death "we have not just lost a person, but a direction for the future of science and technology in India." A statement adopted at a meeting of scientists, management experts, technologists and engineers said the tragic death of Rajiv Gandhi was a shattering blow to the scientific community. Recalling his contributions and commitment to science and technology to help in the eradication of mediocrity in all walks of life, they said he wanted scientific attitude to percolate to all the citizens. The Statement recalled Rajiv Gandhi's compassion, affection and "unprecedented partiality" towards the scientific community. The scientists and technologist said: In paying our tribute to this great personalit who adorned the Indian scene, the scientific community can pay its homage only be rededicating itself to the cause that he believed in, namely of bringing all round development in India through science and technology. The scientific community earnestly hopes that this ideal of Rajiv Gandhi will not be forgotten in the years to come". The meeting also adopted a resolution, moved by Prof. C.N.R. Rao expressing condolences to the members of Mr. Gandhi's family, All those present at the meeting, held at the India International Centre, stood in silence for a while paying homage to the departed leader. The Telecom Commission Chairman, Sam Pitroda said during his first meeting with Mr. Gandhi in 1981 he realised that he was the hope for a new generation. Dr. V.S. Arunachalam, scientific adviser to the Defence Minister recalled Rajiv Gandhi's deep interest in dfence research and the encouragement to scientists. Dr. P.K. Iyengar said Rajiv Gandhi believed that technology could be achieved only through science and the development of the society could be ensured only through technology. The mission approach for excellence was devised by Rajiv Gandhi, he said. V. Krishnamoorthy, former Chairman of the Steel Authority of India, said Rajiv Gandhi was the first Prime Minister who could understant all facets of science and technology. Dr. P.N. Tandon said Rajiv Gandhi was more modern than many scientists and was an information addict. Dr. A.P. Mitra, former Director General of the CSIR, recalled Rajiv Gandhi's encouragement to young scientists. Foreign dignitaries, Congress leaders and members of Parliament (MPs) also paid rich tributes to Rajiv Gandhi, hailing him as an apostle of peace, a world leader, a statesman and a champion of human rights". Participants at a condolence meeting, organised by the Indo Arab Society, condemned the growing cult of vidlence. Ali Muhsen Hamid Chief representative of the League of Arab National, said Rajiv Gandhi's support for the Palestinians was "great". Senior Congress leaders including Natwar Singh and several Arab diplomats attended the meeting.

With the death of Rajiv, and unless the leaderless Congress manages to pull off a miracle in closing ranks and projecting itself as a deserving inheritor of the Nehru mantle, the nation no longer enjoys the "Nehru alternative, and could be in for a period of uncertainty, as political forces realign themselve. The nation could also be in for a spell of BJP rule, with its own as yet uncertain prospects and inherent dangers, given north India's present close to flash point communal temperatures. However, the nation need not necessarily take a nose dive as is being widely speculated upon on the west. For, if the Nehruvian model, provided a modicum of stability and sustained growth, its latter years were witness to a marked straining of political decorum, with crass politicking, cronyism, ethnic and communal strife, and a surfeit of bureaucracy, all on the upswing, and strong but unusually timid Congress government loath to face head on. On the other hand, Rajiv Gandhi's initial fledgling attempt at economic liberalisation, were quickly sidetracked and misued by a throughly corrupt patronage system, and rather than benefits, brought the nation to the verge of economic disaster, outlining the limitations of even bold initiatives, in the absence of honest monitoring mechanisms. Again given his populist electoral rhetoric and the peoples high expectations from him, it is questionable, in the light of his past record that a relatively weak, congress government could have demonstrated the required discipline to resolve political problems, and keep the government deficits in check, so as to take the pressure of the economy. India's new crop of political leaders, though not extirely free of the patronage albatross, neither carry such a surfiet of social-idological baggage, not court such a level of expectations, and should they chose to exercise their initiative, could more easily achieve the dramatic breakthroughs that this country urgently requires, both in the economic as well as the political and social fields. This is as true of a post-Rajiv Congress, as it is of its opponents. Whether the party that comes to power in Delhi will eventually wear do this or not depends on its ability to break with the past, and take hold, not necessarily popular initiatives, even at the expense of its immediate political future. While such initiatives may or may not actually be forthcling, the death of Rajiv Gandhi and with it the Nehru clan, does brings with its dark clouds, a faint silver lining of hope. It now remains for India's new emperors to cash on it, and fast, for unlike the Nehru's they neither enjoy the luxury of universal acceptance, not a strong economy to tide them over, and if their politically harsh decisions attract the flask of the nation, perhaps their reward will be in history.[2] The resurgence of Hindu nationalism in India in recent years is also part of the worldwide revival of religion, especially in the Islamic states. Hindu nationalism, unlike the Nehruvian ideal, defines itself in opposition to Islam and, to that extent, negates a fundamental principle of mainstream Indian nationalism as understood so far. Interestingly, Hindu nationalism is a mirror image of Islamic nationalism and its ideologues are seeking to impose the same king of organisational structure on Hindu society that is the hallmark of Islamic social organisation. This is a perfectly valid and legitimate strand of nationalism. But what is valid need not necessarily be desirable. In its current from the definition of nationalism by the BJP-VHP-RSS is divisive and ruind contrary to the essence of Hindu civilisation itself. By definition, Hindu civilisation, or at least its dominant ideological tendency is inclusionist. It also hinges upon a nebulous, yet emotional, concept of nationhood because the physical boundaries of Hinduism are coterminous with India's borders which, culturally although not administratively, include Nepal. For example, the inclusionist civilisa

2. Baljit Singh. Break with the Past. *The Business and Political Observer* 4 June 1991.

tional ideal and its concurrently nationalist theme is represented evocatively in a poem by Rabindranath *Tagore-Hethai Raja, hetha Anarja hethai Drabid, Cheen/Shak, Hun dal, Pathan, Mogol, ek dehey holo leen* (here Aryans, non-aryans, Dravidas and Chinese/Shaks, Hunas, Pathans and Mughals have all merged into one body). This being the essence of the Hindu nationalist pride, it is difficult to conceive of an exclusionist ideal gaining acceptance. To begin with, the definition of Hindu itself would run tinto insurmountable problems. But from this to jump to the assertion that those who speak of Hindu nationalism are enemies of India is far-fetched and counter-productive. And that is what the Congress in recent decades has done, under the polluting impact of left ideologues. Once strident critics of Nehru, the Left intelligentsis subsequently became his hero worshippers. Nothing wrong, except that in worshipping Nehru they counterposed his qualities against the "evil genius" of Sardar Patel. This is what forms the ideological basis of the BJP's legitimacy today. Though its unwitting stridency, the Congress has allowed itself to be consumend, by Left nationalism. The answer to the challenge posed by the BJP is not to be found in the militant rejection of Hindu nationalism as an illegitimate strand of Indian nationalism. The BJP can be combated only through the projection of an all encompassing nationalist ideal that is neither majoritation, nor mioritarian. The Congress has to redefine Indian nationalism in political and power terms, steering clear of religious definitions. That would eventually condemn both the divisiveness of the BJP's appeal and the crass opportunism of V.P. Singh's alliance with the Shahi Imam. The Congress would have to redefine Indian nationalism in Bhakti or Sufi terms, which steer clear of orthodox religiosity withoug rejecting religion as a legitimate social variable.[3] "When I came here to campaign last time, you were asking for colour TVs". Now, you are complaining about the price of dal," Rajiv Gandhi admonishingly told some vilagers in Rajasthan in April, 1991. The point had gone home: During 18 months of non-Rajiv rule, Indian society and search for upward mobility had come crashing down, attention had focussed back to subsistence. Indeed, so integral was Rajiv Gandhi's identity with the upwardly-mobile aspirations of the burgeoning Indian middle- class that the Congress is said to have toyed with putting out a slogan like "Double your income in five years -Vote Congress." The idea was finally dropped, but the very fact that such a slogan was even conceived, reinforces the central thrust of Rajiv Gandhi's yuppieised view of political ideology. It would, however, be simplistic to characterise the Rajiv years as the age of the Indian yuppie. The yuppie occ-

3. Chandan Mitra. Indian Nationalism, *The Sunday Observer* 26 May 1991.

upied the top stratum of Rajiv's target group. His appeal reached out to the entire middle-class, both urban and rural. He gave them a sense of identity, self-respect, pride. He made them come out of their shells to stake a claim to India's politics and economy. It is an irreversible trend now. Its sheer size-approximately 200 million- makes it impossible for any party to ignore the middle-class as a political variable. The BJP's characteristically downmarket attempt to rope in the lower sections of yuppiedom through strickers like "Let's go for Ramrajya,Let's go for BJP" stands testimony to Rajiv Gandhi's success in galvanising the middle- class and moulding a political constituency out of them. The quality of middle-class life has experienced a quantum leap in the Rajiv Gandhi years. The pace of growth now, admittedly, is slower, but it is a matter of time before the middle-class, its political and lifestyle aspirations significantly whetted, reassets itself. Because many of these changes in the quality of life have been imperceptible, it is not easy to quantify them; now probably does the middle-class consciously recall that is present, vastly enhanced, lifestyle, is the most significant contribution of Rajiv Gandhi. But to looked for memorials to Rajiv Gandhi, one has only to step inside any middle class home, past the Maruti car of van parked outside, The colour TV, the VCR/VCP, the washing machine, ethnic pillow covers and branded clothes or shoes, are only a few examples of how life has changed since Rajiv. And in the almirahs there are bound to be share certificates. Rajiv Gandhi was also the presiding deity of the share market boom; it was under his tutelage that the share market reached out to the ordinary, middle-class house holds.[4]

Rajiv Gandhi had felt that there will be no threat to his life from women. During his visit to Rewa in the second week of May, 1991. Rajiv Gandhi had instructed the security officials to allow women in the security ring. "Women cannot be a threat to my life", Rajiv Gandhi had told women near the meeting platform. "The women should not be stopped" Rajiv Gandhi had reportedly told the officials. In Padamdhar Park, the venue of the public meeting, women heard Rajiv Gandhi speech by violating the security ring. Call it crass, call it brash, consumer society is here to stay. The washing machines won't go back into their packages the credit card will remain ubiquitous, branded apparel, including foreign labels like Benetoon, will be what the well-dressed middle-class will wear, supermarkets will mushroom. The Indian middle-class will steadily catch up with its western counterparts. Unlike the affluent sections of the middle-class in other Third World countries, the Indian middle-class will get all these trappings of upward

4. Chandan Mitra, The Legacy. *The Sunday Observer*, 26 May 1991.

mobility here manufactured indigenously-or, at least, assembled from CKD/SKD kits. In a sense this had to happen-Rajiv or no Rajiv. But, because he personified the yuppie lifestyle, combining comsumerism with class, it lent respectability to this cultural phenomenon. His Gucci shoes may have been the butt of many jokes, but he persisted with them unfazed. He din't mind being photographed, wearing Levi's geans, T-shirt and hat, a camera slung from his shoulder, and fishing-rob in hand when he went holidaying with his family to Mizoram in 1985. Indeed, he persisted even with his holidays, despite squeals of derision when he had Amitabh Bachchan and Sonia Gandhi's relatives accompany him on cruises to the Andamans and Lakshadweep. The message that went out was clear: The middle-class need not be apologetic about being itself, doing the things it liked doing. For those who could afford it, these were things to aspire to. With the implementation of the Fourth Pay Commission's recommendations, salary levels in government, public sector and related jobs shot up dramatically, making it possible for increasing sections of the middle-class to pursue their consumerist dreams. The slump that has since come in this pursuit is proof enough of the boom's link with Rajiv Gandhi.[5]

It takes a tragic assassination to set things in perspective even as it creates a dangerous trubulence in the political waters of the country. We have been living in Carolesque times in which strange Jabberwokian political formations have been hovering over the political horizon ever since the unthinkable happened. Leading the pack is a political mutant which has suddenly developed a "killer instinct". The party of god has temporarily abandoned the Almighty in favour of something more corporeal but equally intangible. The BJP now claims to be the only party capably of providing the country with stable government though it has never had the good fortune to govern the nation. The party was quite easily the fastest growing political supermarket in the country even before Rajiv Gandhi was brutally killed. Having already statiated the voter with its cafeteria approach to Ram, Roti and Insaf (Ram, Bread and Justice). It is now offering a special discount on stability and governance as well. The act that it has two potential prime ministers-one of whom served as the country's foreign minister and the other as information and broadcasting minister all of 28 months-and not much else, worries it not a whit. Neither does the fact that it has no leader of worth from outside the Hindi belt. Taxing the credulity of the common citizen, the party expects people to vote with their feet, abandoning the Congress which, even after the death of Rajiv Gandhi, can still bank upon a pan-Indian identity that is far

5. *Ibid.*

stronger than that of any other contender. Besides the Congress has considerably longer years of national administrative experience in its ranks than all the others put together.[6]

These past days, I have been thinking with grief, as have all of us, of the passing of a good politician and a better man. Not that I was close to Rajiv Gandhi or shared his views quite the contrary. I thought that some of his policies were short-sighted, his views were not coherent and that too often he spoke without adequate reflection, more interested in scoring a point than winning his adversary. Rajiv Gandhi's entry into politics was not just as the son of Indira Gandhi but as the Great White Hope, the Prince Charming who would defeat the demented demons violating our society, usher in a new era of honesty, equality and change. Primarily, to those of us born in the decade after independence, Rajiv represented change, for the better. Remember his scorching remarks to his avaricious partymen at the 1985 Congress centenary in Bombay, denouncing power-brokers and favour-seekers, decrying the lethargy in the party and the distance between leaders and the people. It struck an immediate chord in each one of us, especially people like myself whose family has a long tradition with the Congress. "He's speaking our language", was the deligthful feeling. We believed a bright young avata had truly arrived. Here was a man who could speak our language, who was in step with us, who understood the hopes and longings of a million years and hearts because he wasn't part of the Congress politics of manipulation and caucuses. He was one of us. Fresh from the ranks, an ordinary guy with a family and interests in music and photography. That he was better off than many other Indian's and was a privileged scion of the Nehru clan did not seen to matter. What mattered-unlike in the case of Sanjay who was, quite simply, an illiterate brigand who drewother thugs to him-was that he was an okay guy. One of us. Not flashy, not pushy, not Prime Ministerial controversial material. Of course, we had our disagreements. My first meeting with him was soon after he had won the Amethi by-election in 1981, he drove up to the home of a correspondent of The Times of London in jeans, a leather jacket, a cheerful simile. His vehicle, self-driven, was a Fiat. We got into a discussion about A.R. Antulay and the cement and FSI candals in Maharashtra. "He took the money by cheque," he said resisting my description of Antulay's action as abuse of office. After a sharp debate, he grudgingly acknowledged: "It may have been misuse of office." We had another sharp exchange on the Bhagalpur blindings. But within a week of that exchange, Antualay was out of the Maharashtra Chief Minister's gaddi (seat of power) osten

6. Anikendra Nath Sen. Post Rajiv Politics. *The Times Of India*, 4 June 1991.

sibly bowing to a court judgement. As much as anything else, Rajiv represented romance. In the true sense of the world. Not in a mushy, messy sense. Romance in politics-freshness and change in a pool of stagnation and stink.[7]

We are sailing perilosuly close to anarchy. Violence is in the air. The assassination of Rajiv Gandhi should tell us more sharply than anything else the folly of pitching one group of people ethnic, religious, class or caste against another. This is not an ordinary murder. It was surely contemplated with great deliberation and executed with murderous efficiency. What happened to Rajiv could happen anybody else. It will not undermine the state. Neither the assassination of Mahatma Gandhi in 1948 not the cold-blooded murder of Indira Gandhi in 1984 made any dent on the majesty and stability of the state. But what they did was to indicate the boiling lava on which it was built. And it is to that our attention should reverted. The concept of a federal state was accpted in good faith by the founding father of the Constitution after the position of seperatism that had polluted the country had been drained following Parition. One had hoped that once Pakistan was created, the rest of India would settle down to the task of building a strong, united nation. To a large extent the task has been accomplished. The nation has never been economically more prosperous; the forces of unity are stronger than the forces of disruption, but that does not mean that the later have disappeared altogether. They exist and we have been noticing them in Jammu and Kashmir, Punjab and Assam.

Two short-term measures are indicated. One is a tightening of gun laws and the licensing of arms; the other, the efficient and speedy implementation of land reforms. Simultaneously a faith in the judiciary has to be established but would understandably take much longer. Bothe the Congress and BJP have in their electoral promises, included speeding of justice and judicial reform. The Congress, for example, has promised legal aid to the poor expanded on a massive scale, speedy disposal of cases at all levels, establishment of speical courts and of additional benches with concomitant increase in the number of judges. Similarly, the BJP has promised measures to discourage interminable adjournment of cases, raising the retirement age of high court judges to 65 and provision of mobile courts for rural areas. What is important to note is that there is, among political parties, an awareness of the need for improving the law machinery. Helpful as these measures are, they are not enough to restore normalcy in the country. Far too many tensions have been aroused for them to be easily reduced, and too many

7. Sanjay Hazarika. For We Shall Never be Young Again. *The Hindustan Times*, 2 June 1991.

expectations have been raised for them to be easily met. The pitching of the rural against the urban, the backward against the forward castes has set in motion tensions that are not easily assuaged. Politicians now have a duty to put these propositions in cold storage. The immediate task is to restore sanity in the country. Mandal and Mandir can wait.[8]

Stemming possibly from his own relative ignorance of rural India, was Rajiv Gandhi's determination to bring traditional, rural culture alive to the city. The trend had begun during Indira Gandhi's time, but it did not have the kind of official sanction and patronage which Rajiv was to provide it. The Festivals of India had begun before Rajiv took chanrge, but he made them almost into instruments of policy, a component of his socio- cultural package. There was much to be criticised about these extravaganzas. But, they did serve a purpose. The cocooned middle class, which always believed that culture began and ended in the cities, was exposed to the splendour of folk culture both through the widely televised Festivals of India aborad and the Apna Utsavs at home. Of course, his accent on packaging rural culture, bred its own distortions and also give rise to a "culture-vulture" mafia which siphoned off enormous resources from the exchequer to line their pockets and build gigantic farm houses on Delhi's outskirts. Many of these shows were dominated by form rather than content and ended up as pure extravagazas. But Rajiv legitimised the packaging of culture and gave the official stamp of approval to the ethnicity boom. The annual Surajkund Mela, for instance, has come to stay; besides generating income for the village artisans, such shows have, undoubtedly helped in bridging the cultural gap that divides metropolitan India from its vast hinterland.[9]

Rajiv Gandhi's assassination has put into bold relief the fevers and anxieties that have made Indian society so sick of late. It has revived the blood-stained memories of the fateful course of its recent history. It began its so-called trust with destiny in the midst of frigthful riots which claimed half a million lives on either side of the new borders. How this carnage had wanted the minds of some people became all too clear when one fanatic killed the very man who has led the freedom movement. The country has found it beyond its moral means to outlive this bitter legacy. Far from being able to cleanse the body politic of the poison of hatred, it has, both wittingly and unwittingly, allowed it to spread. Political parties have all too often sought to take issues to the street so that both mob violence and police firing have by now become a daily routine. The frequent atrocities against Harijans in many parts

8. M.V. Kamath. Reaping the Whirlwing. *Current*, 1 June 1991.
9. Chandan Mitra. The Legacy. *The Sunday Observer*, 26 May 1991.

of the country, the murder of Indira Gandhi by one of her bodyguards, the rise of sessionist movements in Punjab, Assam and more recently in Kashmir, run by wellarmed terrorist outfits and aided and abetted in some cases by Pakistan, and unscrupulous politicking based on aggrandised communal, caste and ethnic identities all tell the same story of a country being torn apart. The use of a human bomb to kill Rajiv Gandhi has given a new twist to this story in sofar as it points to another source of infection in the body politics. That the suspected assassin was a member of an LTTE suicide squad is a mere conjecture which has yet to be proved. But whatever the result of the judicial inquiry, there is little room for doubt on two points. First, substantial presence of LTTE militants among the Tamil refugees can be taken for granted. Secondly, so fanatically committed a body of men cannot be expected to be neutral observers of the political scene in the host country. They are bound to make their presence felt more and more as months go by in ways which can pose a new threat to the integrity of the country. The sooner the parties get their minds rid of the delusion that the system will go on working somehow, that the way to unity lies through new area of communal, caste and ethnic conflict, that it will soon be time for business as usual, the better will be their chances of saving the country from the forces they themselves have so wilfully conjured up. A repetition of tried phrases flaunting of self-images that events have blown up can be of no avail. We pride ourselves on being a tolerant society. The fact is that if it was tolerant of doctrinal differences in religious matters in the past it was also extremely intolerant of anything designed to do away with the rigid caste divisons. Untouchability is nothing but a relic of a particular vicious form of intolerance which has not yet been completely done away with. As for the level of political intolerance it is visibly growing every day.[10]

Violence, is not a matter of law and order or tightening one's gun laws or of exhibiting anguish at every act of terrorism. It's a direct and unavoidable product of a system which exists as a ritual that is not understood, and consequently generates an increasing reservoir of dangerous frustration. Mahatma Gandhi rather than British Prime Minister John Major grasped this. The best men, he said, cannot be elected and parliament "is simply a costly toy" and "if India copies England she will be ruined". Is it possible to deny that there is too much for comfort in this predicition if we look at the national scene today? When the system is unable to contain the demands made on it there is a spillover into violence. But there is another sort of spillover euphemistically called a breakaway from 'normal politics'. Instances of

10. Sham Lal: Self-Image: *The Times of India*, 2 June 1991.

this were the JP movement in which officials were told to disobey orders they considered to be illegal or undersirable, and the Zail Singh bid to topple Rajiv Gandhi in 1987 by means that were constitutionally questionable. The conventional answer to all this is that we must learn to be more truly democratic. Yet if we have, on the one hand, a people and country which we call India and, on the other, a system called democracy and they do not fit, must the first adapt to the second or is it better sense to believe that the solution is the other way around?[11]

Where is India heading? As if last year's (1990) anathema of self-immolations by several youth on the Mandal issue and the butchery of hundreds of persons in Ayodhya were not enough. Rajiv Gandhi's brutal assassination and a loss of 200 lives in the first phase of elections in the world's largest democratic exercise has added fuel to the already burning Indian political inferno. The gory assassination of Rajiv Gandhi has left a trail of unanswered queries. The first and foremost question which reverberates in the mind of a common man is regarding the politics of violence. The burgeoning cult of violence in our politics and a nefarious nexus between the white attired politicians and black-listed history-sheeters of the under-world (many criminals have been given tickets in the 10th Lok Sabha elections) show the cracks and crevices which are now palpable in our democratic monolith. Then comes the question of security. What price security? The hightech blueprint of Rajiv Gandhi's assassination bears ample testimoney of the assassins cerebral prowess. Persons saddled with the security arrangements of VIPs and VVIPs should stop calculating and anticipating any attack on the traditional lines. They should broaden their operations. India, the country of truth and non-violence which had earlier preffered rather unanimously her peace and tranquillity to her citizens and even to her invaders, today presents an antithetic spectacle from its past. The cataclysmic upheavals in the country lead us to hang our head in utter shame. These disastrous events have eroded India's prestige aborad. The epicentre of all these ctastrophes is the common man. Today, he feels torn apart between caste and religion. He feels restless and insecure. The chronic problems of poverty, spiralling prices, unemployment, illiteracy have added agony to his misery. He is perplexed and directionless. And he desperately wants a stable government with a strong leadership which should have the guts and grit to waft the country to safer shores far away from the present vortex.[12]

11. N.J. Nanporia. A Functioning Anarchy. *The Times of India,* 2 June 1991.
12. Jaideep Barman. Politics of Violence. The Hindustan Times, 4 June 1991.

18
ENVIRONMENTAL PROTECTION

We have only one earth. It has generously supported life through million of years of evolution. Its remarkable powers of regeneration have kept it rich and bountiful even in face of human greed.[1] On the eve of the World Environment Day on June 5, 1991 the science and technology cell of the AICC-I on June 4 recalled the contribution of Rajiv Gandhi as India's Prime Minister to global environment security. Rajiv Gandhi had launched the "Global Environment Protection Fund". He had also upgraded the Department of Environment to the Ministery of Environment and Forests and introduced the Forest Act to stop deforestation in the country in the name of development, cell consultant Ashok Rai said. Indira Gandhi had been the first to underline the place of environment in global perspective. Her leadership of the global environment movement at Stockholm and Nairobi conferences followed by Rajiv Gandhi's initiatives put India in the front rank of environment-conscious countries. Rajiv Gandhi is also brought environment to the centrestage of development activity through launching his "Clean Ganga" programme the massive wasteland development programme and making environmental clearance compulsory for all projects. He was in favour of environmental and energy audits for all industrial units. Meanwhile a meeting of toplevel scientists is scheduled here for tomorrow to pay tributes to Rajiv Gandhi and emphasise his national vision in science and technology. Among the speakers are Dr. C.N.R. Rao, Planning Commission member, Prof. M.G.K. Menon former Science Advisor to the Prime Minister, former Presidents of the Indian National Science Academy and other top scientists. It is appropriate that the theme for this conference is "Technology for a Better World Environment". For thousands of years, India has developed more in the spiritual direction than in the material direction India traditionally has believed Man and Nature to be one and inseparable. This has given us an awareness of Nature, a feeling for Nature. With the technological revolution coming into India, there has been some tension between the two directions. We have developed our technology. We have developed our industries and we have found ourselves more and more separated from our traditional spiritual depth and strength. This has caused some problems in our social structure. Today, we once more look towards building both aspects

1. Rajiv Gandhi *Message on World Environment Day, New Delhi* May 25 1985

equally. Protecting the environment is very much part of this effort. India has special problems because of the sheer size of our population. The pressure that population puts on the environment is perhaps more in India than in any other country. Thisis compounded by the development process, and by poverty. Because of poverty people have to rely more on what is available to them and accessible to preserve Nature. But we are bringing about right from our school stage an awareness of protecting the environment, an awareness of the dangers of damaging our environment Ultimately it is the people's awareness that will help us protect the environment. No amount of legislation will bring about the type of projection that is required in a country like India. Such seminars help the process of awareness. And I hope that we shall have many more such seminars at all levels, not just in Delhi but in all parts of the country to build this awareness. In a developing country one has to balance, the costs and benefits of exploiting resources and protecting the environment, whether it is in terms of destruction of certain areas to put up industry or to put up mines or other development projects, whether it is in terms of pollution of rivers, of air or various areas. We must bear in mind that ultimately there is no short cut. If we do not pay a price today we will invariably pay a much heavier price tomorrow. We must build this into our awareness.[2]

We have enacted many laws which do not allow certain types of industries to come up in certain areas, and we are trying to give a policy direction so that protected areas will get industries that do not pollute and are clean. We have incorporated this consideration into the very process of clearance of projects. No project can even start unless it has full environmental clearance. We have also gone a step further and ensured that if a particular forest has to be cut to accommodate a project, an equivalent area is replaced at some other location preferably near the same area. Our forest cover in India is already much too low. Water pollution is one of our major problems. We have tackled our first major project-that of cleaning up the Ganga. This is a project which is close to the heart of every Indian and it will not only bring about a new spiritual feeling but, much more than that, it will also give clean water to thousands of villages and millions of people living in the Gangetic base. Some times the problem is fairly simple. It is just a question of better administrative control to get things going. Many of the towns along the Ganges do not have sewage protection plants. Some have. Oe, I know, was closed because electricity bills had not

2. Rajiv Gandhi Inaugural address to the Second World Congress on Engineering & Environment, New Delhi, 7 November 1985

been paid. Sometimes the problem is difficult specially with industrial pollution. Although the concentration levels are low, the toxic levels are high. This is where engineering design must come in. We have to build in adequate anti-pollution measures at the very first stage of setting up industry. We must adequately identify the particular toxins and remove them before we get the plant going. We have had a very bad experience in Bhopal with air pollution-with a chemical plant getting out of control. Again, it is not just a question of safety measures but a much deeper question of also taking adequate protection measures in case something goes wrong-really having a full fail-safe structure. We have seen that this does not take place in many chemical plants. Industry while chasing profit, does not pay adequate attention to the dangers of particular chemicals. We know that highly toxic chemicals are still carried in drums, in tankers across the country. We have stopped it in our country. But we know that this happens even in developed countries. Industry is not taking the responsibility of protecting the environment from its side effects. This responsibility must be squarely fixed on industry. It is by bringing about an awareness of the dangers of failure or slip that the people will accept the extra cost of protection. The extra cost, when it is spread out over all the consumers and over the full time span of a particular process, is very easy to bear, but when that cost comes at a particular time, as it did in Bhopal, it becomes a much harder problem, not only in terms of relief measures for the Governments that are involved but also in terms of compensation for the industry that is involved. And a little foresight in planning, proper safety measures will prevent such accidents and will prevent such high costs. The prioriteis on pollution must be an integral part of all new technologies that we are developing. The emphasis must be in shifting to low pollution industries and also to industries that use less natural resources and cause less damage to our environment. We have found in India that by protecting specific areas we are able to protect the environment. By protecting a particular animal like the tiger, we have protected not just the tiger but we have protected the whole environment in that area. Through such integrated projects, integrated in regard to protection and integrated in the matter of location and grading of industries, having proper laws to control the amaging effect of industries, we have started out on actually improving the environment in spite of the pressure of development and the pressure of the population. This is only a first step. This awareness must be brought about to a much greater degree in our country. We are doing this. It is equally important to bring about this awareness in other countries more specially in the developing countries where there is a feeling that environment protection costs a tremendous amount. But the costs that we have to pay by changes of climate, by natural clamities caused by environmental damage, the costs that we have to pay if we do not protect our environment today will be much greater tomorrow. This awareness right across the globe is what we must work for today.[3] Nehru loved children. He also loved mountained and forests. While we are on our way to development, we tent to move away from nature. It would not be so. We are trying to go back to nature. We are trying to bring children closer to nature. We have to ensure that in our bid to progress, we do not do any such thing as to pollute the environment. As Ziaur Rahmanji said, environment changes when we construct a road or bound or lay a railway line. We have to pay attention to this and smaller things as well. Generally speaking, we pay attention to big animals, like trigers and elephants, but we ignore birds, insects etc. But all these keep the cycle going. If there is any break, will face difficulties. Economic development becomes meaningless if there is no water to drink, no air to breathe and no oxygen to inhale. All development will stop if the environment changes so enormously as to cause floods or brought. Panditji and Indiraji, both emphasised on preserving our environment; not only to preserve but also to improve it if it has been damaged in any way. We are also trying to do this. In our lifetime we will not be able to achieve much. But you have to carry forward this task. Let me hope you will tell your friends whatever you see and learn here. This exhibition will go to schools also Let me hope you will preserve and improve the environment of India when you grow up. Recently, heavy losses were caused due to environmental pollution in a factory in Bhopal. We have to keep all this in view. We have to develop forests again wherever they are being cut, changing the land into desert. We have to save the animals from being killed. Experience tells us that not much progress can be made when we try to preserve simply the forests, but forests can be preserved whenever we try to save the tiger or some other big animal. With that, it is also possible to preserve the environment. We have to implement such programmes as would improve the environment. If this happens, the future generations will be living a beautiful India.[4]

The Launching of various schemes, tree planting, processions, exhibitions and seminars marked the observance of World Environment Day throughout India, on June 5, 1991. The Zoological Survey of India (ZSI) announced an ambitious plan to develop 94 more national parks and 131 sanctuaries to preserve the country' genetic heritage. In New

3. *Ibid.*
4. Rajiv GAndhi's speech while Inauguarating An Exhibition on Environment, New Delhi, 14 November 1985

Delhi, the ministry of environment and forests organised several functions, including a mass tree planting programme near the Paryavaran Bhavan. Meanwhile, United Nations secterary-general Javier Perez de Cuellar called upon the government and people of the world to act urgently and responsibily in the crucial endeavour of preserving and protecting the natural environment. In his message De Cuellar said economic development and alleviation of poverty would improve the prospects for sound management of the environment as the poor in developing countries were often forced for the sake of survival, to take actions detrimental to their long-term welfare. Assistance to them now can help them protect and develop their own resources in a sustainable way in the future, he said in the message. Pointing out that the global warming problem had been created by wasteful production and consumption, the secretary general said the solution cannot be the imposition of limits on the capacity of the poor people to satisfy their needs and aspirations. If the requirements of the planet's ecology impose constraints on global material growth, then equity demands a redistribution of opportunities and of resources to those in need, he said. The environment is a global resource that must be managed effectively. Sister-in-law Meneka Gandhi may be hogging the limelight in her characteristic brusque and brazen fashion, but it-was Rajiv Gandhi who really placed the environment on the nation's agenda. His programme, moreover, was much more meaningful-not confined to gimmicks like barning smoking on domestic flights which is Meneka Gandhi's only tangible "achievement". In this first speech after the famous 1984 victory, Rajiv Gandhi unveiled the Ganga Action Plan which instantly touched a chord even with the environment-unconscious rural multitudes. Despite criticism regarding wastage of funds the fact is that north India's lifeline and that eternal symbol of Indian civilisation, the Ganga, has regained a considerable degree of its pristine glory. He also unveiled a programme for regenerating vast wastelands and constituted the National wasteland Development Board. Many such schemes failed to take off or were aborted midway. Some were rijacked by fly-by-night non- government organisations (NGOs) who fleeced the government, draping their greed in a ever altruism. Rajiv's problem here, too, was that he could't see through-people and was taken in by the articulating abilities of shabbily clad professional environmentalists who made a killing at the expense of the taxpayer, exploiting Rajiv's sincerity of purpose. Yet, Rajiv put India on the world environment map. The trend had begun, like many other trends, during his mother's lifetime, but it was Rajiv who gave this a thrust and profile. Whatever may be his achievement, he has certainly instilled a consciousness regarding the environment, especially among children. Hopefully, this consciousness will translate into realistic schemes by the time the next generation takes over the reins and India will be spared the environmental catastrophe towards which it is, at present, hurtling almost unstoppably.[5]

There are few regions of comparable size on the globe where environmental coherence and interrelatedness is os pronounced as in South Asia. From the equatorial seashores of Sri Lanka, through the tropical deltas, plants, deserts and plateaus of India, Pakistan and Bangladesh to the sub-temperate mountain ranges of Bhutan and Nepal, there are continuities, cycles and confluences in climatic, hydrological, biotic and cultural terms. Yet within this overall monsoonal ambience bounded by the Himalayas and the Indian Ocean, there is unparalleled diversity and a number of eco-niches. livelihood and cultures with specific manifestations down to the village, community and micro-watershed level. And all this contains within it several millennial layers of resource use, adaptation, tehnologies, production, modes of exchange and management and governance. Until the middle of this century, the ecological basis of human sustenance in South Asia had not suffered serious dislocation despite over-exploitation of pastures and forest and damming of rivers by the clolonial state. The main assault on natural resources began with the launching on rapid industrialisation and urbanisation on the Western pattern. The current crisis situation of massive deforestation, lead degradation, brought proneness, desertification, toxicity and industrial air-water pollution is the direct consequence of this development enterprise. It is now obvious that this is no sustainable even in the short run and if persisted will lead to irreversible collapse. Hence the search for sustainable and conservationist alternatives to curb the damage and to encourage recovery and regeneration. Unfortunately, the environmental concern is still a weak and marginal expression of adversely affected communities, academics, journalists, activists and voluntary organisation. Its parameters and ramifications are as yet poorly understood by decision-makers and the general public. The policy framework, institutional set-up and political will are still indequate "Environmental issues lack political expression in South Asia while the forces responsible for and benefitting from ecological damage are usually well organised and articulate. Even the voluntary sector which has raised the alarm and initiated local resistance and corrective effort has remained fragmented, lacked an overview and failed to develop a mass base. The internal situation in the South Asian region within each country and between the countries is marked by instability in political

5. Chandan Mitra. The Legacy. *The Sunday Observer,* 26 May 1991

and economic terms. There has been a resurgence of old conflicts on religious, casteist, ethnicity and regional basis with new assertions for economic and political power. In most cases the legitimacy of centralised power by dominant regional or social elites is being questioned. Of course, all this is in the context of mainstream development either demanding a greater share of the national cake or an opportunity to take command of their own development and resources in a conventional manner. Only rarely is there local realisation that the people's own resource base is endangered by development and they have to assert themselves to protect it. Even though these grass-roots movements have been highlighted by voluntary organisations and independent academics and journalists, they do not matter much in national or regional political discourse".[6]

In Rajiv Gandhi the world has lost a leader who made "outstanding" contributions to the fields of environment science and technology at both national and international levels, according to former Environment Minsister Digvijay Singh. It was under Rajiv Gandhi's initiative that the National Wasteland Development Board and the Ganga Action Plan were set up in 1985. Three years later he steered the promulgation of the Environment Protection Act and formulated the New Forest Policy. He also gave directions to procure up the initiative to recommend a special global fund for subsidising environmental projects created from a percentage of world trade turnover. The "revolution recommendation" was "very well received by the world community". The former Prime Minister had held the portfolios of the departments of science and technology, atomic energy, space, electronics and ocean development, besides environment and forests, and had held frequent parliamentary consultative meetings to discuss these issues. Rajiv Gandhi elevated the Department of Environment, set up by Indira Gandhi and former to a full-fledged ministry. He also constituted a special All India Congress Committee cell on science and technology to inculcate a sense of commitment in these fields at the party level. In Today's world, leaders are figments of people's perceptions. And given the growing sense of negation and cynicism that modern India experiences, today's leaders can repidly become tomorrow's lepers with one flick of the public mood, Like a pendulum gone crazy, Rajiv Gandhi, more than any other leader we know, suffered this fate. Our perspective of Rajiv Gandhi is, of course, biased. For us, it was somewhat of a personal journey. We come to know him when he was prime minister because of our interest in environment. And he always came across as a person deeply interested, willing to

6. Kishore Saint. South Asia-Ecological Imperative. *Indian Express* 1 June 1991.

listen, including criticism of his government, and prepared to act. Rajiv Gandhi had begun to take an interest in environment even before the 1984 elections were over. While campaiging was going on, he had set up four groups to discuss four key issues on which he wanted his new government to take immediate action once he got elected. One of those groups was an environment and wastelands. In his very first address to the nation as Prime minister, Rajiv Gandhi won the hearts of many environmentalists by stating that his government would take up a massive programme for afforestation and start a series of projects to clean up the Ganga. He himself retained the environment portfolio and backed the ministry to the hilt. Our first occasion to see him closely came at a meeting of all secretaries to the government in early 1986. The meeting was specially concened to discuss the subject of environment together with a few environmentalists. Environment being an inter- ministerial issue, he wanted all ministeries to understant its importance. The meeting soon became a litany of protests. From Raja Ramanna, then secretary, department of atomic energy, to all secretaries dealing with power, coal, mines, steel and whatever not, whose projects and had been held up on environmental grounds, every one began to criticise the Forest Conservation Act. Rajiv was the only person who spoke up for the Act and it was then we realised where the interest in environment within the entire government was coming from. It endeared Rajiv to us but it also made us realise how limited was the entire government's commitment to the subject.[7]

Almost as if to confirm our thoughts, we received a few days later an extraordinary invitation to address a special meeting of the council of ministers on a report on the state of Inida's environment that we had edited. The letter left us stunned. We had never known Rajiv personality. We were not even aware that he knows our work well. We later learnt that T.N. Seshan, then secretary, department of environment, had given him a copy of the report and Rajiv had come back a few days later with a note saying that he wanted the editors of the report to speak to all his ministers. Even Seshan was surprised by the reaction. Our entire 416 page report was extremely critical of the government. The Prime Minister office explained to us that there was considerable resistance within the government to environmental issues, especially when this led to delays in clearance of projects. This meeting was, therefore, the young prime minister's effort to get his colleagues to see the importance of environmental concerns to development. For us, of course, it was a daynting task. We wanted to be openly critical of how the government was governing the country' natural resources but we

7. Anil Agrawal and Sunita Narain. Green Politics. *The Economic Times,* 26 May 1991.

were not sure how well this would go down with the very people who ran the government. Would we not be considered young upstarts? But the meeting went off well. Rajiv/s reactions pur us at rest. Every time we pointed out how government policies were leading to environmental destruction, he would smile. One minister even remarked that in some of our slides, he had seen signs of pralay.[8]

A suggestion was then made that the same presentation be made to Parliament. Rajiv suggested instead that the presentation be made to each of the parliamentary consultative committees attached to the various Union ministries. These being smaller groups, they could discuss the presentation in greater detail. This of course, was a tall order for us. Addressing as many as 27 committees one after another was not something we greatly relished. It would tie us down for months. We decided to address only those which were particularly important from the point of view of environment. Rajiv Gandhi again presided over the first such presentation we made, in his capacity as minister of planning. As soon as he sat down, he leaned over to ask whether we would be making all the presentations. But when we said that we would be doing only about 20 or so, he immediately looked disappointed. He explained that it was vital for us to get MPs interested in the subject, "So try and do as many as you can," he suggested. And during the meeting, he kept prodding us to be more provocative. The meeting which was to last an hour went on for hours while his staff kept postponing his other appointments. Seeing his keen interest we decided to gothrough all the 27 presentations, And soon we realised what Rajiv was trying to tell us. Interest in the subject was extremely limited. If the minister had some interest, discussions after our presentation would last for some time, otherwise the meeting would end immediately. Rajiv Gandhi, as defence minister, presided over our parliamentary party on floods and drought and how environmental degradation is affecting them. Can you give us a presentation relating only to this aspect with lots of visuals, charts, stellite pictures, etc.? The logic I have sold them is that with environmental degradation even low rainfall becomes a (flash) flood and the waterwashes into the sea (taking the top soil) and then is not available as goundwater, thus, a vicious circle." It was clear from the note that we had not been able to educate legislators to the extent that he had wanted us to. He explained that we spend an enormous amount of money on drought relief and rural employment, and if some of that money could be effectively used to improve the environment, then that expenditure would be well spent and the next drought easier to deal with. So we made another hard

8. *Ibid.*

attempt to prepare a lecture. We went around collecting information from all over the country. The ministry of environment had previous little. The ministry of water resources argued that deforstation does not have much impact on floods and the ministry of agriculture had no information that the problem of droughts was internsifying because of environmental destruction. Nobody in Rajiv's government believed his thesis. We battled hard to get the data we wanted and were finally ready for the budget session in 1987. Rajiv fixed the date. Bhajan lal sent out the invitations. The meeting began in the Central Hall with ove 200 MPs and senior ministers present. But as soon as prople lernt that Rajiv could not come, everyone trickled out, except about half a dozen. By then, of course, the Bofors gun was booming. Rajiv had no time left for legislators' education. Pressures were increasing from UP and Gujarat legislators on Narmada and Tehri dams. While he gave in to some projects, he held out on others. Even though he was himself beginning to express doubts about the Forest Conservation Act, he invited Seshan to meeting of state legislators in the UP hills to defend the Act. Despite the increasing distance from the ministry of environment he asked Sam Pitroda to develop a special technology mission for wastelands development. He also asked the planning commission to develop agricultural plans specifically suited to different agroclimatic zones.[9]

In global geopolitical terms South Asia remains captive in Cold War parameters even when major realignments are under way-in super power relations and new arrangements are being forged for economic development on the basis of regional proximity for instance, in Europe and in East and South East Asia. There is no recognition of the enormous cultural and natural advantages South Asia holds as a region for cooperation for ecologically sound and sustainable development. A new perspective for working together in this direction can also be a means for dealing with many of the internal conflicts and inter-country problems, ecological viability, economic prosperity, internal and international security, social justice and political stability and democracy in South Asia cannot be assured without a positive and strong disposition for peace and cooperation in the region. This has to be devoid of dominance and exploitation on inter or intra-counrty basis. It has to provide for the realisation of the full economic and cultural flowering in a highly decentralised manner and on an ecoregional basis. In sum, a new South Asian political ethic is called for in the present crisis situation. One of the powerful and unique endowments of South Asia is its ethos of normative human living in harmony with the laws of nature. This has become manifest again and again in the revelations

9. *Ibid.*

teachings, and life examples of countless prophets, divine incarnations devotees and has been encoded in the institutions of religion and in folk traditions. This living sense and matrix of practice can be a rich source of knowledge and principles for an ecologically sound future.[10]

Prof. Priya Ranjan Trivedi, of the Indian Institute of Ecology and Environment of June 5, 1991 stressed the need for a comprehensive global action programme to prevent environment degradation that threatened the very survival of manking. Delivering the first Rajiv Gandhi memorial lecture on the theme of "climate change-need for global partnership" on the occassion of the World Environment Day he said "unless we take some urgent steps to protect our environment we will be heading towards catastrophes that might annihilate the entire mankind. The trends of environmental degradation continue unabated forests are shrinking, deserts expanding and soil eroding. Thel depetion of stratospheric ozone layer that protects us from ultra violet raditioen appars to have escalated, he said. Against this back-drop he said global warming was now causing widespred concern all over the world. Prof. Trivedi noted that the mankind should desist from pushing the climate, inadvertently to trigger an abrupt change in living conditions, upsetting the man life style. In this context he said the problem of controlling the processes that could trigger global climatic change was international in scope. "It is one of the most challenging ecological problems face, because its solution is closely interwoven with world-wide economic growth, energy consumption, population growth and food production," he said. Highlighting the need for an urgent action plan to prevent harmful climatic change. Prof. Trivedi said "although climate change is a young science, this is no excuse for delay." He explained "societies invest in many programme such as defence to protect against an uncertain but potentially disastrous threat. Similarly, investing in strategies to slow global warming is a sort of insurance policy against catastrophes that have far greater odds of occuring than most events for whiich we buy insurance."

10. Kishore Saint. South Asia-The Ecological Imperative. *Indian Express,* 1 June 1991.

19
HIS MIND AND IDEOLOGY

When asked politicians have a bad image, so would be encourage children to aim at politics, Rajiv replied:

"Of course. Well, firstly I don't think politicians have a bad image-certain politicians have a bad image, yes. And it is true of certain people anywhere-you see businessmen, you see industrialists. In any field there is always a group which is the black sheep. But politics is the most important thing in a country. Because ultimately the functioning of everything comes back to politics. It is a pity that people have started taking less interest in politics. There was tremendous interest gnerated during the freedom struggle prior to our independence and a lot of people came into politics. And that it what gave the freedom struggle its thrust and its strenght. And after we won independence, everybody though: Now we are independent, now it doesn't need all the atention, and fewer people started coming in. And that is very dangerous and harmful. Some you must take interest, good people must come in and realise the importance of politics.[1]

Rajiv was born to politics, if not to rule. Yet politics was not his chosen career. His political genes asserted themselves. He was a novice, but not a stranger to the world he entered. He was appointed General secretary of the Congress in 1981, soon after his election, winning Amethi seat. His first year as Prime Minister in 1985 was one of promises seemingly fulfilled. Under Rajiv's directions a start was made in liberalising the economy.

Deep-seated transformation of inegalitarian economic and social structures cannot be undertaken without deepseated political transformation. We want to create at the grassroots a responsive leadership which, because it is directly and intimately responsible to the people, cannot hide behind the tired cliches and well-worn formulate of the para but has to find new solutions levant to the new challenges. We intend to endow these bodies with maximum democracy and maximum devolution. What is really important is that consensus on social change and change itself must be secured by argument, persuassion and other nonviolent and democratic means, not by violence, deceit or other unethical methods. For the first and the last rule of our politicial life must be that right ends can be secured by right means alone. As Panditji, under the tutelage of Gandhiji, repeatedly stressed, only the

1. Rajiv Gandhi. *Children at His House. New Delhi* 8 July 1985.

right means can lead to the right ends. In a broadcat made during a visit to the United States a few months after the martyrdom of Mahatma Gandhi, Panditji said:

> "I have become more and more convinced that so long as we do not recognize the supremacy of the moral law in our national and international relations, we shall have no enduring peace. So long as we do not adhere to right means, the end will not be right and fresh evil will flow from it. That was the essence of Gandhiji's message."[2]

We have also learned from Panditji and the other founders to our democracy that Constitutional and legal provisions have to be reinforced by certain norms of political and administrative action.

The democratic process results in a party being elected to power. But once it has formed the government, the government must be run as a government for all the people and not only as a government for those who have voted for that party. Where leadership is narrow, insensitive and rigid, the available instrumentalities of promoting harmony and peace are of little use. That is why it is essential for the political leadership to be personally and deeply involved in not only setting broad goals but also in the detailed work required to attain these goals. Jawaharlal Nehru showed how enlightened leadership could lead to the resolution of seemingly intractable problems. Panditji's vision of India encompassed our millennial past and looked out to a millennial future. It was not conditioned by immediate problems and immediate concerns. Rather, it drew its inspiration from the essential continuities of India's civilization. It charted its perspectives from the need to restore Indian to its position in the vanguard of all that is of the best in human civilization. Panditji's solutions to problems of everyday politics and everyday administration based themselves on the fundamental moral values of our tradition-truth, nonviolence, tolerance, compassion, one humanity and one world. He was the very personification of synthesis, of the composite culture of India, of its unity in diversity. When he looked to the future, he did not limit his vision of India's destiny or India's role in the world to statistical measures of rates of economic growth and other such material indices. He visualized resurgent India as giving the moral leadership to the world, of leading the world in thought and philosophy, in culture and the arts, in science and technology, in equality and justice, in human dignity and human rights,

2. Rajiv Gandhi. *On Nehru and India.* New Delhi, 13 November 1989.

in morality in public life and probity in personal conduct. It is that vision of India which I share. It is that vision of India which the country shares.[3]

Indira Gandhi's decision that Rajiv should step into sanjay's shoes and become her principal adviser and putative successor caused no surprise nor much comment, though the intelligentsia did demur that India was being apparent determination to keep power within her bloodline. Interestingly Rajiv himself was rather hesitant in responding to his mother's call. As an airline pilot he had been content to live quickly quietly with his Italian wife, Sonia, and their two children. He had studiously stayed out of the limelight while his younger brother had hogged it. He was reluctant to take the plunge into politics even though he realized that he could not deny his mother the help she needed and was asking for. Sanjay's young, ambitious and fiery widow, Maneka Gandhi considered herself to be the rightful heir to his mantle and was prepared to fight for what she believed to be her right. In her view, Rajiv was not only a usurper but also unfit for the role expected of him.[4]

No words can describe the horror of it all. Rajiv Gandhi, by all accounts on his way to befoming the Prime Minister of India again, assassinated in the most horrifying way. First, Sanjay Gandhi, killed in a plane crash, then Indira, shot by her own bodygruards, and now this. The Gandhi family, once at the dizzying heights of power and in control of the country's fortunes, must now seem destined to a most tragic fate. Our tragedy is that in the manner of death of the three Nehru-Gandhi prime ministers-Nehru of old age and his daughter and grandson through assassinations - is the downward grap of India. From the euphoria of independence, the chance it gave to our people to join in a common endeavour, to the violence which is now a by- word of our national life. Where earlier there was idealism, there is now the utmost cynicism, with violence being used as an acceptable part of everyday life, especially of political life.

The 10th Lok Sabha election has already seen more of it used than any earlier ones. This election has also been more hate being used than ever before, with each and every political party laying claim to this most dangerous of weapons, pitting one community against another, one caste against another, one class against another. With so much hatred and violence in the air, it all had to explode at some point.

Tragically is has done so and taken away the man we had begun to think of as Prime Minister again. In a sense Rajiv Gandhi had not stopped being PM even in the eighteen months he was out of power:

3. *Ibid.*
4. Inder Malhotra. Dynasty. *The Statesman,* 1 June 1991.

his supproters refused to accept that he would be anything but PM.

In the last few weeks, he had began to believe it more and more himself, as his initial reluctance to face the electorate changed when he was faced with the enthusiastic popular response he recveived at public meetings. His growing sense of confidence could be seen in his party's manifesto which suggested that he would chart a new path for the country, away from the hamstrung ideologies of the past. More than anything else, Rajiv Gandhi's manifesto-and his election campaign-promised stabiity, a state missing from our country and something which we had all begun to yearn deeply for. With Rajiv Gandhi's brutal killing, is there any hope of it at all? In the interest of our country, let us pray that it is. In the interest of all of us, let us pray that Rajiv Gandhi's supporters, aggreived and angered as they all must be, will think of the country first and not indulge in the kind of blood-letting which followed Indira Gandhi's murder. The perpetrators of the cirme must be caught and dealt with according to the harshest penalities of the law, but no one else, certainly not the innocent who died in such numbers in 1984.[5] We must, instead, get together in the aftermath of this tragedy and put the pieces of this nation together. Unusual situations demand unusual solutions. India's constitutional experts can explore the possibility of Prime Minister, Chandra Shekhar, and his council of ministers advising the President to call of the elections. Further, if the life of the existing parliament can then be extended to its full term of five years, the President can ask the leaders of all political parties to come together and form a national government. To continue with the electoral process now would be senseless since the leader of the largest political party has been killed, and the largest political party is now leaderless. Continuing with the elections could also lead to even greater violence.

Rajiv's reluctant entry into politics is well known. It was obviously not an accident that he wasn't interested; things seemed to have been planned that way. If they had been planned that way. If they had been born in post-independence India, Jawaharlal Nehru and Indira Gandhi would probably not have been in full-time politics. It's rare for people with their background to get into its hurly-burly. Panditji's entry was natural during those times however and since Indira grew up in this atmosphere, her entry into the political world was inevitable.

But it was obviously decided that Indira's children wouldn't go into politics. Otherwise why would both Rajiv Cambridge and Sanjay as a Rolls Royce apprentice? Why would both sons pursue their own careers, Sanjay making cars, Rajiv flying planes? We do not know at

5. *The Independent*, 22 may 1991.

what time Indira Gandhi changed her mind. Possibly it was soon after Panditji's death: while he was alive, politics must have seemed a nobel challing calling; a chance to really serve your country rather than just a chance to really serve yourself. Indira's initiation into the murkier aspects of politics began soon after Lal Bahadur Shastri's death when the back-room politicians began to use her as a front for their own machinations. It was then that she began to look for people she could trust. The process which started then culminated in the induction of first Sanjay, then Rajiv into politics. Sanjay at least liked it. In many ways he was the epitome of a particular kind of politician. Rajiv hated it, and his loathing of it and of the normal run of politicians is illustrated by two famous incidents.

The first occurred at Hyderabad airport when Indira Gandhi was still alive. Welcomed in the usual fawning manner by sycophantic politicians, Rajiv reacted angrily (and rudely) to the Andhra Pradesh Chief Minister, T. Anjiah. The second was Rajiv's famous "power - brokers" speech, delivered as President of the Congress party at its centenary celebrations in Bombay. Both these incidents sprang from a contempt for all politicians. Rajiv may not even have realised this; he may have thought that he was reacting to unnecessary sycophancy and the evil of power-brokers. The point is that both these things are not only necessary but vital to the run-of-the-mill politician, and in reacting against them with contempt, he was echoing the feeling of every non-political Indian-and especially the middle calss. No wonder Rajiv became everyone's favourite. His surrounding himself with people he knew that came to be known as his coterie-was really Rajiv's attempt to distance himself from the hated politician. It was, you could say, his way of retaining his innocence. Being open and trusting, he needed to cocoon himself even more than most. The people he surrounded himself with: childhood chums like a Amitabh Bachchan or Gautam Kaul, or people he could talk to like fellow pilot Satish Sharma or Indian foreign service mandarin Mani Shankar Aiyar knew even less about politics than he did. That, to say the least, created a problem which until his death he had not resolved. Given his circumstances-the fact that the mantle of prime minister fell on him rather than having to be earned-his alienation from the scheming politician might actually have been an advantage. Can't you just see how we all, sharing the same feelings, could have exulted in a leader who turned his back on the venal side of politics? Can't you see how we would have said, "Yes, my god, this man is really above these things" and given him our trust, and our votes? We would, provided Rajiv Gandhi had a conviction of his own. Perhaps that's being unfair. Perhaps he did. Perhaps he really did want to build the less unequal society he often talked about: a fairer, cleaner, more just India, for all its citizens, not just the favoured few. That too finds an echo in most of us, even those of us who wallow in our society's inequalities everyday. But however well-meaning that conviction, it's an unfocussed one because it is generalised and satisfied with itseld because it is so well-meaning. For Rajiv Gandhi to have used his advantages of birth and inheritance, it wasn't just enough that he shared with most of us our prejudices and a vague dream. It was necessary for that dream to be a burning conviction, that would brook no opposition, which would sear through bureaucratic impediments or the obstacles put up by vested interests.[6]

History takes its own time to settle on a generally accepted assessment about the greatness or otherwise of a personality. Some are filtered out in due course to be labelled 'great', while the rest are relegated to limbo. In the case of Rajiv Gandhi, it is unlikely that in the middle of national elections, in an atmosphere charged with political controversies, and so soon after his removal from the national scheme, an objective evaluation of the man will emerge. One will have to wait for the verdict of history. Within a short span of eight years of public life-about a year as party secretary, five years as Prime Minister and a year-and-a-half as the leader of the Opposition- Rajiv Gandhi was ripe for world attention. The convergence of a bevy of world leaders to pay homage to him when he was a mere Opposition leader was a revealing phenomenon. They did not come to New Delhi because he died a dramatic death, nor because he was the son of Indira Gandhi, nor, indeed, because he was a former Prime Minister. In these days of violence and transitoriness, there are many famous people who die a violent death, or are the progency of distinguished parents, or have held high office; but they will not be honoured as Rajiv Gandhi was. One may think that all this glorification reflects the fact that India is still a great country. This is probably true, but does not explain the whole phenomenon. There is the story of a citizen of the old Greek city-state of seriphus who taunted the famous Themistocles, a citizen of the city-state of Athens, by saying that the latter's fame was due not to himself but to the greatness of Athens. The mistocles retorted: "Yes, I shouldn't be famous if I were a seriphan: but nor would you, if you were an Athenian." In Rajiv Gandhi's case too, it was the importance of his country combined with his own qualities that made him the focus of world attention.

His brief but intense public life falls into four phase. The initial phase was one of aloofness from politics and all that it implied. Oncepreva-

6. Anil Dharker. If only. *The Irdependent* 26 May, 1991.

iled upon to join politics, the second phase showed him as General secretary of the Congress. He plunged quickly into party affairs and familiarised himself with politics and politicians. Some ugly things happened in this period, but, in all probability, he was not responsible for these: some lesser politicians obviously were. One unsavoury even was the pulling of the rug from under the feet of the Andhra Pradesh Chief Minister, N.T. Rama Rao, in misguided effort to install a Congress Government in the State. Then, there was the crude attempt by the party to bargain with Dr. Farooq Abdullah to infiltrate into the Jammu and Kashmir Government, to set up a puppet regime there and to breathe down the neck of Kashmir is and prevent a popular government from functioning. This, indeed, was the beginning of the present mess in the state after more than a decade of adjustment and goodwill. And finally, there was Operation Bluestar, which not only cost Mrs. Indira Gandhi her life but led to the shameful anti-Sikh riots, involving the loss of several thousand innocent lives. While it may not be right to put the blame for these awareful events on Rajiv Gandhi, it is a moot question whether in the very first week of his Prime Ministership, he could not have quelled the anti-sikh riots in Delhi any faster than he did. The fact that nothing was done to bring the culprits to book remained a sore point not only with the sikh community but everyone interested in secularism, justice and fair play. It was a blot on the Government led by Rajiv Gandhi and kept a large number of Sikhs alienated from him. This failure may well have been the cause, among other things, of the escalation in terrorist violence in Punjab.

It was largely because of the sympathy vote following his mother's assassination that Rajiv Gandhi came to power with more than a three-fourths majority in the Lok Sabha. In this phase, his initial policy pronouncements were refreshing and added up to a desirable structural change. Most of these had an economic focus but he plunged with equal enthusiasm into the political issues of the day. He sought to cope with the separatist movement in Punjab and the sons-of-the-soil agitation in Assam. He demonstrated a capacity to negotiate effectively solutions to many a problem. The settlement of the Assam problem, an extremely thorny issue, was, on the whole, creditable, although the element of justice and equity in that settlement remained in some doubt. But, Rajiv Gandhi succeeded in the case of Assam largely because he did not let his party take control of the state Government. He conceded the right of the other parties to govern the state and thus prevented a secessionist movement from taking strong root. Equally important was his accord with Longowal in Punjab and it was a pity that a fairly decent settlement with a popular leader came to naught with Longowal's assassination. The whole question was then thrown open and terrorism and insurgency spread, capitalisig on the fact that the culprits in the Delhi riots had not been brought to book.[7]

By 1983 the politician in him had already begun to look for an identity. The biggest problem with him was that he had no political belief or conviction of his own, and so he was seen merely as his image-markers wanted him to be seen. In the early '80s, the PR-men around Rajiv had given him an image of an outsider, but there was mounting pressure on him to take over the controlling levers of the party, to become a partyman and to stand by collegues even if his image got sullied in the process. The inevitable reorientation of Rajiv began with the debate in the Lok Sabha on the Antualay affair when, to the dismay of many who had seen a new ray of hope in Rajiv's induction to politics, he began a laboured and convoluted support of the controversial Maharashtra Chief Minister. Antulay's act was "not corruption in the strict sense of the term", Rajiv said at that time, in what sounded like a faint but accurate echo of his mother's much- remembered litany-"corruption is a global phenomenon". Though still pent-up in the Motilal Nehru Marg bungalow, Rajiv was approaching the centrestage of politics through exactly the same route as his younger brother had taken. It was the extra- constitutional route. By then Mrs. Gandhi had perhaps realised that her over the hold over the Congress party was dependent on the extent to which she could distribute state patronage, by means fair or foul, among her supporters. And she could do so only through the agency of an extra-constitutional authority- Sanjay at first; Rajiv later. In that sense, the relation between Mrs. Gandhi and Rajiv was perfectly symbiotic in the early years. Though the "Rajiv brigade" had by then begun silent forays into lucrativ areas like defence, petrochemicals and fertilizers, the trademark Khadi cap to of the Congress did not fit him yet. Partymen had little access to him through a door which was stoutly barricaded by an army of old friends and ambitious relatives. The barrier finally was dissolving in 1983 when Rajiv began to cobble together a team of his own an weed out quite a few old-timers. It was in this phase that he took a series of tough actions, dismissing Chief Ministers with the gusto fo the Red Queen in Lewis Carroll's Alice in Wonderland, even yelling at some of them in public places, like the airport. Besides, soldiers of fortune in his camp, like Arun Nehru, had already consolidated their position in the party and the government and were poised to trigger a chain of ill-conceived actions. Their aftershocks were to haunt Rajiv, and Mrs. Gandhi, as long as they lived. The dismissal of N.T. Rama Rao's ministry in Andhra Pradesh

7. A.M. Khusro. Rajiv Gandhi. *Indian Express,* 5 June 1991.

was one such action. So was the dismissal of the Farooq Abdullah led government in Srinagar and its replacement by Gul Shah's puppet regime. The move in Hyderabad resulted in the emergence of Telugu Desam as a permanent rival of the Congress; the Kashmir operation finally brought out of the bottle the genie of militancy. In Puniab too, Mrs. Gandhi made the fatal mistake of Operation Bluestar, an incredible overkill masterminded from a shadowy background by Rajiv's advisers. However erroneous these decisions were, these indeed were the benchmarks as Rajiv advanced to secure full control of the party. Without riding roughshod over Chief Ministers, he perhaps could not have established his own pecking order in the minds of partymen. Without pampering backstreet bulles like Nehru, he could not have raised a private army of hatchetmen who could do dirty jobs and yet make the buck stop there. In 1985, after Rajiv had obtained full control of the party and had become the Prime Minister, he put a new coat of paint on his image-hawking himself as Mr. Clean by abusing "power brokers" in his party at the Bombay seession of the AICC, and seeking to be projected as a moderniser-an Indian variant of Emperor Meijiby talking vaguely about the 21st century (the only concrete action was reduction of import duty on consumer electronic components from 310 per cent to 90 per cent).[8]

The selling of the Mr. Clean image was disaster. Arun Shourie had begun calling him "Mr. Whitewash" from the very beginning, an aphorism which seemed prophetic as the Bofors drama began unfolding itself from the summer of '87. In the process, those who were potently unclean were either shunned by Rajiv or wer shuning him themselves. So he was left with no solid constituency for himself, with neither Alibaba nor the forty thieves being on his side. Meanwhile, with every passing budget, the 21st century, instead of looming colser, appeared to recede more and more in distance. While only the consumer and service sectors boomed, agriculture and basic industry were neglected and the import bill had become so high that only hefty IMF loans could bale out the economy. Surprisingly, being bereft of any tangible political thinking, and thus having no clear idea of the direction in which he would like the national to be led, Rajiv could not put together a team of aids worth the name. In 1987, he was about to lose power in the wake of his conflict with Giani Zail Singh, the then President. He survived by the breadth of a hair, and tht too after paying a heavy price. Between 1987 and 1988, he made a series of ignominious compromises with the same people whom he had himself thrown our chair after assuming premiership. Notable among these are the return

8. Sumit Mitra. Rajiv's Politics. *The Sunday Mail,* 26 May 1991.

of Praban Mukherjee and R.K. Dhavan into his favour. As a result of such flip-flop, Nehru, V.P. Singh, Arif Mohammed Khan and many of his cronies turned against him. But he was unfazed. He thought he would win back his mother s supporters at the expense of his new constituency, a plan which never went off well. Till his last, his favourites had no roots in the party whereas those who had roots in the party were never really his favourites.[9] Realisation should have dawned on him at the electoral debacle in 1989, but he was really left with very few options. He could neither regain the nation's confidence nor the trust of his friends.

This is a catastrophe of massive proportions. It's such a blow to those sane and sober elements fighting the forces of divisive politics. Only the futuere will tell us the impact of Rajiv's untimely passing away. He was a very warm person, sincere and honest in his utterances. Unlike other politicians, he didn't tailor his views to meet his political requirements. He was a very warm person, sincere and honest in his utterances. Unlike other politicians, he didn't tailor his views to meet his political requirements. He always spoke to you straight from the heart. I was struck by his sincerity. Politics had not touched his basic self. If hadn't turned him into the hardboiled type of politician, It was this which made me express my frank opinions to him without worrying about being misunderstood. As railway minster, I was lucky in that he had confidence in my team. So we got his full backing on policy decisions. He was quick to grasp the core of a problem, no matter how complicated, and then decided fast among the options available. If he hadn't gone, then under him we would have seen some hard, unpopular decisions in the next couple of years. He could have pulled the country out of the bottomless pit into which we seem to have fallen. I see tough times ahead now. Whoever becomes the new Congress leader will take time to fully gain the confidence of the people.

One aspect of his personality was that he was always in good humour. I remember, on the 13th of this month, he had come to Madhya Pradesh to address election meetings. We were traveling in a helicopter when he turned to a senior politician and said, "Is it Ok if just Madhav and I address the next meeting?" The man said he just wanted to speak for two minutes. Rajviji said, "If only you would speak for two minutes I'd ask you to speak everywhere, but you do anything byt that." He had a twinkle in his eyes when he said that. It always amazed me how cool Rajiv was. In 1986, in the plane back from Maxico, he called me to his cabin for dinner. We hear a faint whistling noise all through the meal. Finally, the flight steward came and said there were problems, that one

9. *Ibid.*

of the engines was't working. Coolly, Rajiv replied that he knew all along. I have seen him similarly cool during the severest of severe crises. I think he was unfairly maligned for having a coterie. It happens all over the world. How can you expect a top leader not to have his close circle of advisers? It's just that the advisers shouldn't become too big for their boots and start flaunting their closeness to the seat of power.[10] We have lost the man who could have taken us into the 21st century.

Rajiv Gandhi's assassination is not the killing of an individual, it is an assault on whatever India has stood for since it achieved independence in 1947. It is a success for the continued offensive against India's democratic, secular, self reliant, non- aligned and progressive policies. The enemies hope by this dastardly act to destabilise and Lebanonize India. This heinous crime has been committed at a critical moment when India was almost in a state of siege, battling with formidable political, social and economic problems. Rajiv Gandhi represented a certain ideology and principles. These were rooted in the glorious traditions of our national movement as espoused by Mahatma Gandhi, Jawaharlal Nehru and later, by Indira Gandhi. It was on these principles that rested the foundations of a democratic, secular and united India. From the very inception of independent India, these principles have been under attack from powerful vested interest both from within and outside India. The history of independent India is the history of bitter struggle between the forces which wanted the country to deviate from the path chosen by the founding fathers. One can remember the bitter debates which raged around the issues of secularism, democratic processes, federalism, official language, Hindu Code Bill. There have always been two trends around these issues. It is to the credit of Jawaharlal Nehru, Indira Gandhi and Rajiv Gandhi that they resisted all pressures and stuck to the basic ideology of India.

The struggle has not been an easy one. India had become independent after the communal bloodbath and bitterness of partition. The prepartition conflict between the ideology fo the Indian National Congress and the two-nation theory of the Muslim League had left a bitter legacy. And yet the fact that independent India decided in favour of secularism is a tribute to the moral strength of the Congress led by Jawaharlal Nehru. Another major achievement of the Congress was the abolition of zamindari, which later led to the implementation of land reforms in most of the Indian states. The far reaching socio-economic impact of the abolition of Zamin dari has tra nformed India's

10. Madhavrao Sciendia. Politics Had Not Touched His Basic self. *The Times Of India*, 26 May 1991.

rural scene. In the sphere of social reform, the Hindu code Bill is a milestone. It provoked the sensibilities of even some of the top leaders of the country and yet, the Congress implemented a social change equal in magnitude to the abolition of sati or the widow remarriage of the 19th century. Abotition of untouchability and reservation for the SC/ST in jobs has significantly reduced the disparities generated by the caste divisions.[11]

The evolution and strengthening of the democratic institutions has been a major contribution of the Indian National Congress. This achievement has to be seen in the light of the failure of the ruling elites in our neighbouring countries. India alone among the south Asian countries has maintained and developed its democratic processes, and this, in spite of mounting attacks from within precisely on these structures. It is the commiment of the Congress to democratic process that India has held nine general elections which have been unparalleled in their size and magnitude. The Congress has held elections many times even when it was obvious that it would lose power.[12]

Internally, he began to take a fresh look at the economic policies on the basis of India's own experience and that of the socialist countries This was partly reflected in the election manifesto of the Congress There are sufficient indications that he was keen to build bridges with the Indian Left on the basis of a minium programme. In fact, it is said that some preliminary discussions on this question took place between him and some of the important Leftist leaders. It is in the interests of Indian left not to admit it openly, but this is a fact. In fact, in the last phase of the election campaign some of the Left leaders began to talk about a realistic policy depending on the what they called the correlation of political forces. Perhaps, there was a school of thought among the Indian communists that the possibility of the Congress-Left relations on the lines of 1969- 71 cannot be ruled out

This shows that Rajiv Gandhi, through his own practical experience, had come to the conclusion that to build a modern India, all the secular and Left-of-the centre forces should unite. The dynastic 'thesis' which has become a weapon in the political struggle, does not bear scrutiny. That both in 1989 and in the present elections, he was asking for popular supprt on the basis of the policies and his own popularity clearly proves this point. That is why the right-wing forces along with character- assassination of Rajiv Gandhi, inflamed the passions and thus clouded the reasoning faculty of a section of the Indian population through communalism and 'Mandalisation' of politics. This vitiated the

11. Kalim Bahadur. The Forces Behind the Assassination. *Patriot,* 23 May 1991.
12. *Ibid.*

atmosphere. The agencies which were operating behind the scene must have sat back, relaxed, after kindling the fire of harted and revenge and said, after Mark Antony:

"*Now let it work, Mischief,*
though art afoot,
Take thou what course thou
will.

And it has taken that course, of assassination of Rajiv.[13]

His politics of reconciliation, flawed as it may have been, is the only way forward for India. Reconciliation. Not repeat not Consensus. That is the bungling mistake that Congress, Janata Dal and other political parties have made time and again. Reconciliation means you are prepared to change and shift position while sticking to your basic views without harming the interests of the other. Consensus means self-abasement and surrender of an independent will. This is not meant to be an epitaph for Rajiv. I am not qualified to write it. It is not meant to shower fulsome praise on him. I had too many differences with his views to do that. But it is, I believe were an honest, from-the heart attempt to reflect on what I believe the qualities that stirred, charmed and enthused a generation. Here was an airlines pilot-granted that he had the advantage of being the prime minister's son and the grandson of another-who showed that you don't have to be an obsequious khadi-dhoti wallah to make it to the top. One of Rajiv's great strengths was his youth. He had so much to live for, so much to do, despite all our caviling and carping. There was a lump in many throats, certainly in mine as I groped for thoughts and words while watching his son, daughter and widow standing so compellingly alone and with such dignity as the flames devoured a man beloved by a generation. All that we are left with are memories. And the sure knowledge that even if one day, we can dream again, yet we will never be young again. To paraphrase Jawaharlal Nehru: 'the romance has gone out of our lives and there is mediocrity all around."[14]

Rajiv Gandhi's tragic end changes the political landscape of the country in more senses than one. It will have an impact on the last round of polling, now postponed till next month, and it will mark a new beginning for the Congress, for the first time without a member of the Nehru-Gandhi family for more than half a century. The Congress decision to elevate Sonia Gandhi to the party presidency is little more than a holding operation till the elections are over. These

13. V.D. Chopra. Rajiv Gandhi. *Patriot,* 23 May 1991.
14. Sanjay Hazarika. For we Shall Never Be Young Again. *The Hindustan Times,* 2 June 1991.

consequences, taken together, will serve two purposes: it will blunt the edge of the Bharatiya Janata Party's assertive Hindutva offensive and will see in accretion of strength to the Congress party. Thus, ironically, the end of the Nehru era this election represented in some ways is likely to be postponed some what by the manner in which Rajiv was brutally assassinated even while compaigning in electoins. Elections to around 300 constituencies are still to be held, and a hung parliament that was destined to emerge out of this electoral exercise on the basis of sober political arithmetic may not materialise, after all. Unless the Congress makes a hash of things, the sympathy factor will now work in favour of the party and could bring it an absolute majority. The tragic interruption in the electoral process does not negate the BJP's agressive championing of recasting Indian polity in a different mould. But it does act as a brake on its blizkrieg technique of hijacking the electorate to its tent. There will now be a pause and time to reflect on the verities put forward by the BJP, and they will work again the party because its appeal to the mass of the electorate is based on emotion and the rousing of elemental passions.

It is human nature to try to return to the old verities at a time of great emotional and psychological crisis, and the snuffing out of Rajiv's life is one such crisis. The tendency of many of those disillusioned with the Congress-and their numbers are not insignificant-will be to seek solace in the immediate future in the party of the independence movement. There are consequences too for the Congress party. Realignment is a word that can hardly be used in the strict sense in Indian politics, which has become opportunistic and self-serving in the extreme. But provided the leadership collectively acts wisely to surmount the crisis facing the Congress and the country, there could be a bonus for it through the return of many of the politicians who had left it. This would seem hardly to apply to men like Vishwanath Pratap Singh or Ram Vilas Paswan, but the attraction of the Congress pole can only grow with the party entering a newphase.[15]

The danger is that if individual leaders in the Congress do not moderate their ambitions and pressures, the party could veer towards another split which could prove ruinous to it. If the strongest potential candidate, Sharad Pawar, were to throw his hat in the ring at this stage, it could divide the party. A section of the party might well look longingly to a Congress under the leadership of Chandra Shekhar, who has won his spurs in the short period he has occupied the prime minister's chair, but such a dispensation in the immediate context would, more likely than not, force a split on the party. Congressmen cannot but be aware

15. S. Nihal Singh. Where Do we Go from Here? *The Independent,* 25 May 1991.

of th fact that their strong suit of stability would be hopelessly eroded if they quarrel among themselves on who should don the Nehru Gandhi mantle.[16]

If politics were the last resort of a scoundrel, as many in India would seriously believe, then Rajiv Gandhi would not even have had a toehold in it. This less adventurous elder son of Indira Gandhi was parachuted onto the political arena-in his own words- to "help-mummy". In fact, it was he who needed a lot of mummy's help, for he had neither the savvy of his brother, Sanjay, who had died in an air crash in June 1980, nor the cold, ruthless individuality of his mother. He spoke just as easily as any other '80s-model yuppy down the lane, but he did not have a fraction of the oratorial brilliance of his father, Feroz. A mere "Gandhi", he contested the polls in 1980 and won from Amethi, the constituency vacated by the death of Sanjay. The public at that time took him for a reluctant apprentice who had been forced by circumstances to join politics. Both he and his mother did their best to heighten his image of being a recluse of sorts in politics, an ET in the big, bad world of men in Khadi caps and safari suits. His initiation into bit-time politics began with the organisation of the 1982 Asian Games, when nearly 200 IAS, IFS and IPS officers kowtowed to him as the top leader of the organising committee. He had neither the experience not the expertise to manage large events, but the '82 Asiad was a platform for Mrs. Gandhi to tell the country who the next boss was. By then, Rajiv had begun functioning from a spick-and-span bungalow on Motilal Nehru Marg which was fitted out like any business office in the City of London, and had surrounded himself with a gaggle of boxwallah-turned-countries. By 1983, Rajiv was already calling most of the shots, a fact known quite far down the line of the party, as well as bureaucratic, hierarchy. But very few people would talk about it then.[17]

As a politician, Rajiv rose only as far as circumstances could take hi, but his talent were too limited even to allow him a long stay at such high altitude. Even his enemies admit that he was a nice friend, a gentleman at heart and a picture of generosity at any negotiation table. But he was hamstrung by two shortcomings: mediocrity, and an inability to stick to any particular constituency of peergroups and supporters. In Indian politics, the late Lal Bahadur Shastri, and many other idea-less perfect vacuum had risen to powerful positions only because of their permanent "gang loyalty".[18] Rajiv did not have an iota of such calcualtive herd instinct, a factor which shaped him as a good human being but quite a disaster as a politician.

16. *Ibid.*
17. Sumit Mitra. Rajiv's Politics. *The Sunday Mail,* 26 May 1991.

It has gone, the smile that endeared him to the country, the smile with which he came into politics, to help his mother and be a bridge between her and the party, broken suddenly with the death of brother Sanjay. It was in the winter of 1980-81 that he had finally succumbed to the pressures of his mother and begun to emerge out of a strictly private life, a shy affable family man into the backrooms of political power. It was a quiet entry, with no fanfare or jubilee glare. He had got a modest room in the Akbar Road, New Delhi single-storied building with a small room on the side occupied by Makhan Lal Fotedar, while across a glazed hall, in the rear was a slightly bigger room which was given to Vijay Dhar who was specially brought in from Srinagar to help friend Rajiv. There were no frills, no usual signs of power brokers. On two much used tables, there were two old type writers, one for V. George, then a rather lanky man and the other for Kumar, a short wiry typist. The former was for Rajiv and the latter for Dahr. The atmosphere was uncharacteristically quiet and business- like with party-members and other visitors generally waiting for Fotedar in the front verandh. Rajiv Gandhi spent unobtrusively long hourse discussing plans for self-sufficiency in power and in preparing blue prints for perking up the administrative system. The hours were long, extending beyond midnight. The ground rules for Dhar and such like was to keep in the background, faceless, anonymous beign who were expected to slog and sweat for 16-18 hours and were expected to keep their endeavours strictly forbidden. Rajiv nurtured the culture himself by keeping in the background, a reluctant debutante, who had after reluctance agreed to help out a mother, who was then struggling determinedly to emerge from her personal tragedy and keep the Government and the party from going into shambles. Wife Sonia was opposed to his being pushed into politics, but ultimately conceded to the needs of Indira Gandhi.[19]

I can hardly remembre when I first met Rajiv, it was so long ago, yet sometimes in the last two days it has seemed as if out first meeting was only yesterday. There was nothing very memorable about that first meeting. I had gone to Madam's (Indira Gandhi's) house and Rajiv was sitting in the drawing room with a friend. Madam introduced us, he said 'Hello' and after a few minutes took his friend to another room. This must have been sometime in the late 70s, perhaps 1979. Rajiv was then in the Indian Airlines. After that I saw Rajiv, Sonia and their children off and on, during some of the occasions when I went to meet Madam. I cannot say I spoke at any great length to any of them in those

18. Sumit Mitra. Rajiv's Politics. *The Sunday Mail,* 26 May 1991.
19. Vijay Dutt. The Smile Is Gone. *The Hindustan Times,* 26 May 1991.

days, it was mostly limited to polite greetings, after which they would go to their part of the house, leaving us politicians to talk to Madam. The time I really saw the whole family together was after Sanjay's death. We all rushed to Madam's house as soon as we could. I found Rajiv to be a tower of strength on the occasion. It was he who was consoling Madam, holding her most of the time, right though the entire ordeal uptil the funeral and beyond. In a few months I started to meet Rajiv more and more often as he became increasingly involved in politics, specially after he won the by-election from Amethi in 1981 and became a Member of Parliament. He began to appeal at the AICC and CWC meetings, which we, too, attended. In those years, he did not speak much at these meetings, but listened to every- thing carefully. Unlike many who said he was a reluctant entrant into politics, I always found Rajiv taking keen interest in political affairs.[20]

Normally, I get up at about six and I do a couple of hours of work. Then about 9 o'clock I start office work-either I go to office or meet the general public here on the turf for about an hour. Then from 10 to about 12.00 I meet various people who are, you know, intelligence, director RAW, all the sort of government inputs; people working in my office, people like general secretaries and joint secretaries of Congress, and that leaves me about an hour and a half till 2 o'clock to meet other people who are to meet me. Afternoons normally I keep for meetings-as today we have a Cabinet meeting after this-or for longer discussions. The morning meetings are really short, not going into depth but just getting information, and the afternoon is for discussions, either small groups or large groups, and really policy thinking- sometimes it goes until 10 at night but usually it is till about 8.30 or so. And then I have my home work just like you. I get lots of boxes, you must have seen yes Minister. We get many more boxes than they.[21]

Politics is about power, and Congressmen are about the hunger for it. One way or another, they will seek it. It is that process which could well deal the Congress its death blow as different groups of Congressmen go their different ways because there is nothing to hold them together any longer. To be sure, what emerges may still be called Congress-this or Congress-that (brand-names are important, after all) but whether it is the same party which dominated India from 1947 is far from certain. For one thing, the supreme leader syndrome is likely to vanish because today there is no one who can even remotely lay claim to being one. Also, the overall Nehruvian consensus having broken down, the nature of politics has changed. Fundamental to this change is the likely reemergence of a 1950s type relationship between the

20. Pranab Mukherjee. New Ideas. *The Sunday Observer,* 26 May 1991.
21. Rajiv Gandhi. *Children At His House.* New Delhi. 8 July 1985.

Centre and the states, in which the country is run on power relationships which are far more equal than has been the case since 1971. With more states going the way of Maharashtra, where Sharad Pawar has an independent political base, it is very unlikely that someone can lay claim to being the disputed boss. Much will depend on what happens, at one level, in Uttar Pradesh and at another, in the Hindi states. Uttar Pradesh sends 85 members to Parliament and anyone who can manage to capture around 60 fo those seats could become a primus inter pares amongst Congress politicians. Extending the same logic, anyone who can capture over 60 per cent of the 227 seats in the Hindi- speaking states, will become even more powerful. But what of the four southern states then? They send 127 MPs to the Lok Sabha. Will they accept a Hindi-belt politician with the same eagerness that they accepted the Nehru-Gandhi family? Unlikely in the extreme. This could create a North-South divide in the party, which will have major implicatins for the power relationships not only within the party but also between the Centre and the States. But all this is in the long run. Immediately, the party has to find a way of surviving the current election. One school of thought believes that the assassination of Rajiv Gandhi will fetch it the sympathy vote in a repetition of the 1984 election. Another believes that there is no one left to sympathise with, in the political sense, at any rate. So Sonia Gandhi or not, the party cannot get the sympathy vote, because that would mean voting not for someone from the Nehru-Gandhi family, but for local upstarts, whom other local upstarts will not support. For example, if a Janardan Reddy in Andhra Pradesh or a Bangarappa in Karnataka can help the Congress win a large number of seats in the absesne absence of Rajiv, would he not become very powerful? Why would Chenna Reddy help him or the Veerendra Patil group help Bagarappa? Precisely similar situations can be foreseen in all other states as well. So it is safe to predict that those who do not already have a mass base, like Sharad Pawar, will not be allowed to develop one. Moral: lots of infighting, which was always there. But this time there is a difference: there is no referee. This is likely to be the central feature of Congress politics for some years to come, and in that sense it will be exactly like the other centrist alternatives like the Janta Party in 1977, and the Janata Dal in 1989 have been.

The north-south divide, if it develops, could have an important bearing on the nature of the politics of the regional parties as well. It is well to remember that a number of them developed largely as a response to the Indira Gandhi style of politics.[22] The removal of a

22. T.C.A. Srinivasan Raghavan. The Congress. *The Economic Times*, 27 May 1991.

monolithic organisation depending on an individual could open the way for a coming together of large number of political interests which are at present represented by small regional parties.

It is quite possible that the southern Congressmen may make a separate peace with the regional parties. The alternative for them might well be the prospect of political oblivion, to avoid which, like ture Congressmen, they may go to any lengths. This would follow the classic pattern of first forming new parties, and then merging them with whomsever offers the best chance of acquiring power. It is also important to bear in mind the presence in Uttar Pradesh and Bihar of the Janta Dal. This is a party which has sought to cultivate traditional constituencies of the Congress and has done so with a measure of success. If that sort of politics succeeds, as it looks like doing because of demographic reasons, northern Congressmen may well have to make their own peace. What that would do to the Congress now is also an open question because it would entail, at its most fundamental level, a complete realignment of caste power equations in Uttar Pradesh and Bihar. Nor would it do to overlook the drawing power of the BJP. So far, the Congressmen have professed faith in secularism because the Nehru-Gandhi family insisted on it for both personal and political reasons. That imperative not being there any longer. At some Congressmen might make a beeline for Hindutva. It is probably fair to say that the Nehru-Gandhi family hands over to the nation as its political legacy an empty shell. Coteries with no independent power base will try to manipulate it, and may even succeed for a time. But in the long run, only the naive or the optimistic will expect the Congress to be the political force that it was. Therein lies the real failures of the Nehru-Gandhi family.[23] They killed the goose that laid the golden egg for them. The barrenness will be felt by their followers who have no one to turn to now.

A true assessment of the contribution of Rajiv Gandhi to India will have to wait for some time till peace prevails. This is largely so because he played a key role in determining the course of events in each and every sphere of the nation's activity. Even to provide a general overview of his contribution to each of these vital sectors is not an easy job nor can it be done in a hurry. Rajiv Gandhi worked with rare passion and devotion formulating a future for this country that was appropriate to its standing and status in the comity of nations. He was aware precisely what the country needed and when. He also knew how to accomplish transformation of a poverty-ridden country into a modern nation. It was true politics was something he never relished but he was conscious

23. *Ibid.*

of the fact that political activity was the only vehicle on which the nations travel to great heights and glory. Thus he become a politicians-a word he ironically preferred to avoid-only as a matter of necessity and only as an instrument to achieve what he wanted for his country. In his very first election speeches in December 1984 after the death of his mother, he expatiated in great detail his vision of India. He spoke to the rural masses a language they had never heard before. He was the first and only political leader who dared to mention computers and modern technology in his elections speeches and sought to explain to the illiterate masses how the new frontiers of technology could transform their lives and this ancient land. Unlike others he never directed his ire against superstition and age-old practices. He never despised those, who for whatever reason stuck to these antiquated practices. In fact Rajiv Gandhi never saw any dichotomy between modernity and tradition. Indeed he would visualise them as two sides of the same coin. If one gave the shape, the other gave the spirit. Given this intellectual convicition it was easy for him to see how tradition and technology could work together producting a fascinating mosaic of the beautiful Indian cultural canvas. Even as he took over as the Prime Minister he said "we have to conserve and cherish our heritage-political, cultural and philosophic. We have to establish a right relations with our natural resources strengthen our new self-reliance."[24] Rajiv Gandhi was acutely aware of the problems in acquiring new technologies, especially those of the state of the art level needed for making India one of the advanced nations. But unlike other political leaders who generally preferred political methods to acquire technologies, he chose a new and an innovative and most correct method-to seek the technologies on the strength of our own capabilities.

This meant India striving to qualify for getting and absorbing new technologies hitherto never tried in the country. It was a bold experiment and he had executed it with determination and finesse and, what is more, producing remarkable results. In just five years after he took over as the Prime Minister, India became one of the very few countries in the world to possess and practice technologies that were extremely rare. He brought the telecom revolution making India the only developing country to manufacture rural telephone exchanges that could work in all weathers. Be it in optical fibre, microchip or laser technology Rajiv Gandhi had succeeded in bringing India into the company of a galaxy of selected advanced nations. In establishing the C-DoT, he had paved the ground for a continuous flow of technological

24. K.V.S. Rama Sarma. Rajiv Gandhi. *National Herald*, 23 May 1991.

support to the Indian industry. Even as he talked tirelessely about new technologies and the wonders that computers could do for the country's agriculture, industry and education, he never lost sight of the importance of the man in developmental activity. The basic theme of his speeches was national interest, self-reliance and new technologies to make the man deliver better results. Ted Koppal of the ABC News of the US had told Rajiv Gandhi in an interview that Charles de Gaulle had said that "men have friends nations have interests" and asked Rajiv Gandhi why was it so important that he and President Reagan got along as individuals Rajiv Gandhi replied that national interests always involved human beings. He told Koppal "National interest is important and we cannot deviate from national interest. But we do deal with human beings and I certainly would like to feel that I am dealing with a human being and that is why I appreciate personal contacts and getting to know people." The innovative thinking that marked his approach to technology was also visible in other areas like economy and foreign relations. In the economic sphere he believed in gradual introduction of automation and was opposed to hasty easing out of labour-intensive techniques. His tenure as the Prime Minister has witnessed the liberalisation of several policies which had become irrelevant over a period of time. He believed in steady opening of the Indian market to foreign competition. But he was against unfair competition. So while he would encourage the sheltered Indian industry to face competition he would ensure that this would not lead to collapse of the Indian economy. An association with a foreign industry would benefit the Indian industry in many ways he would say.[25]

Rajiv Gandhi's death deprives India of a leader with a modern mind and a great vision. His assassination comes at a crucial moment of the nation's life. In a fragmented and directionless state of the nation's polity, he was hoping to restore stability. He was working hard to bring the Congress Party back to the centre stage. The Janta Dal led by V.P. Singh and its splinter group under Chandra Shekhar, which managed to keep the Congress out of power after the 1989 elections, were no doubt offsprings of the Congress ideology. The stem of the original plant which brought freedom and government the nation for over four decades, however, contiuned to be the party headed by Rajiv Gandhi. He was inheritor of the mantle of Jawaharlal Nehru, Lal Bahadur Shastri and Indira Gandhi.

Rajiv Gandhi was struck down as he was engaged in bringing home this fact to the people over the length and breadth of the country. He was sure they would be convinced and vote his party back to power.

25. *Ibid.*

The Congress was looking to him to provide a successful leadership that would enable it to recapture its old glory.

With Rajiv Gandhi at the helm, the country would have proceeded in the same direction in which he took it during the term of Prime Ministership to which he succeeded on the death of his mother, Mrs. Indira Gandhi in October 1984. His vision was of a progressive, modern India, untainted by the scourge of age-old proverty and illeteracy, retaining her cultural traditions and value and holding her head high in the comity of nations. He had created around him a loyal dedicated and talented team of officials and experts capable of translating his ideas into reality, although some of their sophisticated methods were found jarring by old-timers in the political and official establishment.[26]

In the last interview of his life, Rajiv Gandhi was able to speak philosophically about India and where its political turmoil was leading it-in between impromptu whistle-stops. But he agreed that the growth of strong new parties was an indication of a political coming-of-age in India, where one party could no longer have a monopoly. "But I feel these are the wrong kinds of parties," he said, a reference to the BJP. "A tremendous frustration is building up in the people, which is causing these swings from one party to another," he said. "They are frustrated that the system is not delivering, not meeting their aspirations." He added that he thought the problem went back into the late 1960s, after the death of his grandfather, Jawaharlal Nehru. He said the Congress party had tried "to bring those aspirations down to a kind of realistic level. But we have to do so much more," he said. "we have to make the system much more efficient."[27]

Rajiv Gandhi mused about some of the plans he had for the next administration he hoped to form after 1991 Lok Sabha elections. Commenting on popular ciriticism of the government-controlled television services in India, he talked about opening up broadcasting to private corporations, but under "some-sort" of government oversight. "We will not allow it to end up as regional chauvinisms," he said.

As Congress President, Rajiv Gandhi did not seriously pursue democratisation in the party structure, but in matters of foreign policy, his global initiatives and dealings with world leaders doubtless commanded attention and respect, although no dramatic results were obtained. There were, of course, some new openings with Pakistan and an improved relationship with Benazir Bhutto. But, these came to naught with the exit of Rajiv Gandhi and Benazir from power. In the final phase, Rajiv Gandhi has to be reckoned as an effective leader of

26. T.V. Venkitachalam. India Without Rajiv. *National Herald,* 26 May 1991.
27. Barbara Crosette. We Hope to Do Much More. *The Times of India,* 26 May 1991.

the Opposition, although India's parliamentary system itself has, over the years, lost its dignity, poise and high performance. In opposition to V.P. Singh's Caste-based reservations. Rajiv Gandhi took up a position in favour of reservations based on economic criteria. Although the Congress Government had taken a some what ambivalent stand on the Mandir issue, eventually the party as well as its leader opposed the demolition of the mosque and propsed the construction of the temple nearby, unless the contending parties failed to agree, in which case the decision of the courts was to prevail. The impact of Rajiv Gandhi's thinking and his refreshing approach to economic policy is discernible in the 1991 election manifesto of his party, which is innovative in many aspects and is designed to improve the performance of the economy and leave its depressing past behind. He had the capacity to acknowledge his mistakes, learn from them and apply correctives, and towards the end of his short career, he was a much wiser man. All in all.[28] Rajiv Gandhi turns out to be a remarkable politician in terms of a highly enlightened thought process and a capacity for effective negotiations and policy decisions, but leaves something to be desired in implementing decisions and persuading party functionaries to do what he wanted.

28. A.M. Khusro. Rajiv Gandhi-An Assessment. Indian Express, 5 June 1991.

20
COMMUNALISM AND NATIONAL CRISIS

Rajiv Gandhi was assassinated on the verge of his triumphal return to power; not on the crest of any sympathy wave but largely due to the revulsion of the people at the doings of the anti Congress parties, backstabbing each other and egging on violence in the name of religion or caste. This turn-around of the popular mood surfaced first in Bhopal, even before official electoral campaign started, when the people of the city gave a huge welcome to Rajiv Gandhi. This was followed by Jaipur. Both the State capitals are BJP citadels, thus there was the indication that the latter's supremacy in Madhya Pradesh and Rajasthan was waning fast. The Congress was rapidly acquiring the image of a challenger breathing down the neck in all the BJP- ruled States. The next major indicator of the ascending curve of popularity of Rajiv Gandhi, and in collective association of the masses of his party, was when he received the tumultuous welcome all along the route in his ride to Kanpur from Jhansi. These mass welcome established the fact that the Bofors hysteria, which pitchforked to popularity V.P. Singh and allowed the RSS-BJP combine to laungh its vicious character assassination of Rajiv, had got its deserved burial. What was more, the people began to divine the opportunism inherent in the synthetic all-in opposition unity against the Congress and the lust for personal power of its conglomerate leadership, regardless of national consequences. The JD-BJP leadership was slowly being stripped in the eyes of the people, despite the Mandal and Mandir Ploys. The communal frenzy created by the BJP and its bandwagons, its organisational clout and immense funding capacity whatever their mysterious sources-made RSS-BJP-VHP campaign visibility almost stunning. In contrast, the JD's presence even in Uttar Pradesh and Bihar looked tattered. For that matter, even the Congress campaign took a back seat. Yet, out of the four opinion polls conducted in early May, two showed the Congress heading for an absolute majority, while the other two earmarked its position as the "largest single party", if the elections took place at that point of time. But, every day, the Congress headed by Rajiv Gandhi, was improving its position further. In contrast, the BJP- Shiv Sena alliance is Maharashtra reached a critical stage after SS supreme Bal Tackeray publicly hailed Nathuram Godse for killing Mahatma Gandhi. As if this was not shocking enough his fascist protege Chhagan Bhujbal, much less devious than the BJP leadership, exploded an atom bomb by demanding that Mahatma Gandhi's statues should be destroyed and in their place Godse's statues should be Godse's be constructed'. Such vicious electoral propagnda helped to create an atmosphere of blind hate conductive to the assassination of Rajiv Gandhi, who stood for national unity and independence on the rocks of secularism, but the BJP was getting rapidly discredited in States like Madhya Pradesh, Rajasthan and Himachal where it ruled. The aftermath of the Rajiv's assassination would seriously impair the BJP's electoral prospects, despite the rhetorics of its leadership, in the entire country. It would be now difficult, if not impossible, for the BJP even to retain its 86 seats of ninth Lok Sabha. The Janata Dal too would suffer in its bastions like Bihar and Uttar Pradesh: The glaring evidence was the panicky attempts by Laloo Prasad Yadav to rope in Jyoti Basu for a joint electoral campaign with Janata Dal stalwarts in States like Bihar and Uttar Pradesh.[1]

Rajiv Gandhi's assassination has come as a cruel shock to a nation which is already in tatters. However, his death will not go in vain. The shock it has generated throughout the country is unbievable. People of all religions are numbed with grief and feel genuinely concerned about the path of violence the country is taking. His assassination has made the people realise that neither Ram no caste nor religious frenzy can save the country at this critical moment.[2] A true Hindu spirit which cuts across lines of nationality and religion is the need of the hour. That will be the best tribute that a bereaved nation can offer its fallen leader who died because he stood for secular values and peace. If the country heats back the forces of communalism and casteism, Rajiv Gandhi's sacrifice will not be futile.

Does Mahatma Gandhi rank among political thinkers? The answer to this must be an ambiguous "no" for his original contribution to political thought, or even to the definition of Indian nationalism, was nominal. He was a creator of symbols and an interpreter of ideas, rather than an ideologue. But through symbolism, he did broadly define the ideological contours of Indian nationalism, self-reliance and Hindu-Muslim unity being its cornerstones. In imparting substance to the framework of Indian nationalism, Nehru moulded it with his own ideas. In the process, he carefully excluded the alternative current reprsesented by the right-wing in the Congress party. Nehru's vision broadly incorporated the Left ideal, although Leftists including Congress socialists such a Acharya Sangh (RSS) and the Hindu Mahasabha. In addition to such leaders, there were others who wanted the Hindu nationalist viewpoint to be accommodated within the broad spectrum of Congress thought. The two most prominent of these

1. Ashis Burman. Time For Secular and Left Cooperation. *Patriot* 6 June 1991.
2. S. Menon. Rajiv Gandhi. *The Telegraph*, 27 May 1991.

leaders were Sardar Vallabhai Patel and Dr. Shyama Prasad Mookerjee. Patel's premature death probably enabled the Nehruvian vision to gain hegemony, marginalising the challenge posed in later years by Purushottam Das Tandon. The other Hindu nationalist in the Congress Dr. Rajendra Prasad, had cleverly been "kicked upstairs" by Nehru. He fretted and furmed against that breathtakingly modernist piece of social legislation-the Hindu Code Bill-but could do nothing about it. Dr. Mookerjee, on the other hand, tried to work with Nehru from outside the Congress for many years, but eventually quit in disgust over the "appeasement" of Sheikh Abdullah. As founder of the Jana Sangh, he sought to lay the foundation of a populist, non-orthodox, Hindu nationalist alternative to the Nehruvian vision. Post- Nehru, the ideological spectrum of Indian nationalism moved further left-wards. This was somewhat paradoxical considering Indira Gandhi could hardly be described as an ideologically committed Leftist. But political expediency compelled her to join hands with sections of the Left, and the induction of Pro-CPI academics in her think helped the process of Leftisation of the Nationalist ideal. Consequently, accommodation of the Hindu nationalist current into the mainstream of Indian nationalism seemed unnecessary. The appeal of that tendency had also declined sharply, especially after the mid-1960s, symbolised by the Jana Sangh's marginalisation in Indian politics.[3]

The assassination of Rajiv Gandhi is persistently being condemned by various organisations. All-India Muslim Youth and students Forum has described his killing as unfortunate which has cut short a promising career. In a statement, convenor Anis Ahmed said Rajiv Gandhi was a true friend of minorities. He was a dynamic and upright person, he added. He also criticised the attack on the house of Ram Vilas Paswan here and demanded an inquiry into the matter. The killing of Rajiv Gandhi's a blot on the democratic set-up of the country, said Rizwan Ahmad Siddiquie, President, National Unity Forum. He said those at the helm of country's affairs should hang their head in shame as they have repeatedly failed to protect human lives.

Obituaries of Nehruism have been written for almost a quarter of a centruy now. But in its own way, the Nehru legacy somehow managed to survive. It was robbed of its element of consesuality by Indira Gandhi, the overt liberalism with the capital "L" that marked his worldview also declined steadily. Yet, the India we still know is essentially Nehru's India. It is his definition of nationalism, with minor modifications, that continues to dominate our understanding. With the assassination of Rajiv Gandhi, the Nehruvian era draws to a close

3. Chandan Mitra. Indian Nationalism. *The Sunday Observer* 26 May 1991.

even physically. In any case, it had become increasingly difficult to sustain the Nehruvian definition of Indian nationalism as its sole definition. But Indira Gandhi and her son had somehow managed to retain the essence of his ideological legacy, probably because neither was in ideologue and could hardly have been expected to redefine nationalism in their own vision. What constitues the Nehruvian vision of India nationalism? Defined in its original form, its components were secularism, egalitarianism and liberalism-all being held together through a democratic political system. It becomes immediately obvious that the Nehruvian concept is inclusionist and not exclusionist, that is, it does not seek to define Indian nationalism in contradiction to others. Secondly, all its components are derived from western political thought. Of course, it is essential to point out here that most modern political thought is Western. Since the advent of colonialism, hardly any original ideas have been generated either at the level of political theory practice outside the west. The only non-western definition of nationalism to assert itself successfully in recent times relates to Islamic fundamentalism. Borrowing heavily from both western notions of egalitarianism and marrying them with pre-capitalist millenarian ideals, the Iranian ideologue, Dr. Ali Shariati, formulated a theory of Islamic nationalism which provided both the ideological thrust and practical blueprint to the Khomeini revolution. This is significant, because in the domestic context, the Nehruvian vision today is being challenged not by a Left revolutionary ideal, but by a concept of nationalism that hingers on religion. The point is that non-western, particularly oriental political philosophies derive their sustenance from religious thought and not secular political theories.[4]

India undoubtedly is passing through and unprecedented an political crisis. The cirsis surfaced in an acute form after the 1989 general election to the Lok Sabha when a minority government headed by V.P. Singh was installed at the Centre with the support of two conflicting political forces, the Bharatiya Janata Party, on the one hand, and the Left parties, the CPI-M and the CPI in particular, on the other. The V.P. Singh government collapsed when the more important of the two pillars supporting it, i.e. that of the BJP, was pulled out. The communalisation and "Mandalisation" of the polity of the country, which took place during the recent years, further deepned the crisis. It was in the midst of this crisis that another minority government, this time headed by Chandra Shekhar and supported from outside by the Congress, came into power. This government also did not last long because of the inherent contradictions between the Janata Dal (Socialist) and

4. Chandan Mitra. Indian Nationalism, *The Sunday Observer,* 26 May 1991.

the Congress. This was followed by the dissolution of the Lok Sabha and mid-term poll. Rajiv Gandhi's assassination through a well-conceived and neatly planned conspiracy took place in the middle of the election campaign. This cold-blooded murder of the former Prime Minister, decisively unmasks how grim is the situation and how India's unity and integrity are facing unparalleled threats.[5] This murder does not merely expose the extent of the brutalisation of the world's largest democracy. There is more to it than meets the eyes.

The education system and the mass-media, the two principal weapons of influencing mass opinion, have utterly failed in transforming the superstitious and religious, scientific and progressive values, these two instruments, in the control of the state and the dominant social groups, have been employed in quite the opposite direction. As a result, religious nations have, in fact, been strengthened over time, instead of being displaced. In India today, atheism is anathema, totally tabooed. To be an atheist is considered to be a sign of gross deviance. In our search for secularism, we have completely ignored, in fact, ruled out, the atheist option. A glance at the census records reveals that almost all Indians chose to identify themselves with one religious community or the other hardly any being "non-communal" in the sense of not identifying themselves with a particular religious community. The role of religion in guiding one's actions in the wider social domain, including the political sphere, can be displaced if an atheistic consciousness takes the place presently occupied by religion. The Atheist Movement, however, has miserbly failed in India. Even the Indian Marxists have failed to offer a radical sociological critique of religion. It was, however, Karl Marx who had suggested that a critique of a particular society must begin with a critique of its religion, which, in effect, reflects the social, economic and political relations of that particular society. Our arm-chair academics, in particular, most of our sociologists, have done little to present before the masses the social, mundane, this-wordly roots of all religious phenomena. They have shirked away their responsibility of exposing how, in the ultimate sense, all religions are forces created for and employed in the maintenance of social domination by vested social interest groups. If this were explained, in suitable idiom to the masses, there can be no doubt that they would hestiate to be swayed by communal appeals by sectarian organizations. This, of course, is not to argue that mere ideological counter-propagnda can win the battle for secualrism. It is true that the roots of the communal problem lie deep in the wider economic and social processes. Yet, it is undeniable that the ideological battle is

5. V.D. Chopra. Multi-Dimensional Character of National Crisis, *Patriot*, 3 June 1991.

possibly the most crucial and decisive one.[6]

Soon after assuming office the ruling party leadership as well as its supporters, the BJP and the Left Front, realised that each problem they touched became more complicated than ever before Corruption combined with inefficiency was the hallmark of administration Files gathered dust on ministerial tables because each minister had to work overtime just to remain of the chair he got. Militant activities in Kashmir and Punjab assumed unprecedented magnitude. To that was added the overflow of Tamil terrorism from Sri Lanka to Tamil Nadu the graduation of Assamiya chauvinism of SGP into separatist militancy of ULFA. By the time the curtain was rung down on the frace of JD Government there were clear signs that various terrorist groups had started working in concert with one another. Prime Minister V.P. Singh would not have been unaware of these developments unless ambition had turned him sand blind. About the economy and the nation's standing in international field the less said the better. Whatever growth was seen in the earlier phase was only because of the momentum of the previous period. It was a matter of disgrace for a country which had all along treated its national endeavour as a part of the international for peace and progress. It was also a cause of anxiety for the whole of international community as is evident from the reactions to the ghastly murder of Rajiv Gandhi. I am mindful of this rapid downhill drift the rulers of that time resorted to gimmickry which threatened to tear as under the very fabric on nationhood built over a century of hard and gruelling struggle. The BJP launched what with his characteristic braggedacio. Advani called "the biggest mass movement" on the Ayodya dispute. It was no love of Ram or Hindutva, it was the political manoeurve of the BJP in reponse to the Mandal manocuvre of V.P. Singh. Interestingly enough the motivation of V.P. Singh also was neither social affirmation nor equity (such Conceptualisation is only an after-though to give a repectable vaneer to a cynical political trick): he had made the announcement just to upstage Devi Lal who was threatening him with rural urban polarisation. It was a veritable game of musical chairs being played by political trickers V.P. Singh had outflanked Chandra Shekhar with the help of Devi Lal. The latter was feeling cheated because his beneficiary was not showing the necessary gratitude in return. Thus the nation was being shattered into pieces by whipping up volatile sentiments on the basis of retualism, Casteism and communalism while this was happening in the heartland, the peripheral areas were coming under the shadow of separatist-chauvinism. Under the pretext of reordering centre state relations the national centre was

6. Yoginder Sikand. Search for a Secular Society. *Patriot,* 4 June 1991.

being reduced to what the National Front Chairman. N.T. Rama Rao, had once termed as "a conceptual myth".[7]

Who benefited? V.P. Singh claims that he sacrified power to uphold the principle of secularism and to protect the right of Muslim over the Ayodhya shrine. He believes people would forget what he had done before the BJP pulled the carpet from under his feet. He had secured the support of the BJP with the promise that his government would not do anything violative of their manifesto. And that included abotiton of Articles 370, promulgation fo Common Civil Code, conversion of the Minorities Commission into a Human Rights Commission. Sure enought he kept quiet on all the questions while giving different assurances to the VHP-BJP, on the one hand, and the various Babri Zealots, on the other. The upshot of his politics was that by the time he was forced to lay down office the country was filled with communal hatred and violence of the most ferocious type. Only a perversely stupefied community would believe that such a leader was their benefactor. The Muslims did not believe him as is evident from the totally negative response to the appeal of the Shahi Imam. What about the Backward Classes? Only the self-styled Leftists, currently acting as drummer boys of V.P. Singh treated Janata Dal's Mandal policy as harbinger of a revolution, of sicial transformation, in faour of poor. So far as the really humbled and the humaliated of the land are concerned they saw it as a new whip in the hands of their well-known traditional, tormentors. The oppression against the landless, whether Harijans or Backwards, touched the lowest depths with the affluent among the Backwards getting hold of only state power but also the gun power. The combined effect of the BJP-JD strategies is that in the current elections an unprecedentedly large number of consituencies had to be declared by the Election Commission as prone to violence. The electoral process had to be protected not only from the alienated and foreign aided militant groups but also from the self-proclaimed guardians of citizens' security and democratic values. What did the Hindus gain? Not even the hope of constructing a temple in Ayodhya. Just to keep the hope alive the BJP has put up candidates in 478 constituencies so that people may get an illusion that they can come to power and redeem the promise. Anybody with even a modding acquaintance with the realities of politics would tell you that the party cannot even put up symbolic fight in more than two hundred of them, what to speak of winning a majority in Lok Sabha. And for developing this illusory hope into frenzied support they led hunderds of Hindu young men into the jaws of death. To be sure the interests of the Hindus are not confined

7. D.R. Goyal. Stability Wins out. *National Herald*, 1 June 1991.

to revanchist possession of a mosque and converting it into a temple. They being the majority their interests are best served in an atmosphere of peace and tranquility so that trade and industry, science and technology and various other aspects of national life make satisfactory progress. If towns have to live under the dark pall of fear and life remains paralysed by strife they stand to lose more than any other community. These realities of life dominated the minds of people when elections to the Lok Sabha were announced. The need to end strife and stabilise the nation was upper most and true to its traditional character the Congress grasped it. As leader and spokesman of the party late Rajiv Gandhi articulated it most effectively when he declared that the whole country, the entire people, were his constituency. And people were responding to the slogan of stability with renewed confidence. The cruel death of Rajiv Gandhi at the hands of a barbarous assassin has added a sharp edge and poignancy to the call for stability. In a flash the people have come to realise that the politics of confrontation among various communities and sections of people can lead to destruction of the democratic system, nay of civilised existence. The only hope lies in the politics of reconciliation and consensus of various interests which the Congress alone has been pursuing. The assertion of the BJP that it is a disciplined and stable party and therefore best suited to provide stability sounds like a bad joke. A party which changes policies from election to election, and which has to important more than half of the candidates for election, can make such claim only because it will not reach the point where it will be tested. Even in the midst of this election they have been shifting. First it was Ram, then Roti and Insaaf were added, and now Ram is sought to be replaced by stability. The parties of the National Front and the Left Front seem to have realised the wisdom of the Congress Party as well as of Rajiv Gandhi. The tradiness in due and full- throated acknowledgement is only a compulsion of the electoral exigency. Stability has triumphed. The only regret is that its chief spokesman fallen victim to the conspiracies of destabilisers.[8]

On several subjects, Rajiv Gandhi returned to his fears of more separatism in India. Which has disrupted life in three states- Assam, Punjab and Jammu and Kashmir. At Madras airport earlier in the evening (May 21, 1991) he explained they would elect an administration that would pass a resolution of autonomy or independence. He talked about education, one of his favourite subjects. He said he wanted to free the highly plained why he was against allowing Punjab to hold state elections, saying that there was every like-politicised universities from

8. *Ibid.*

too much control and let them find their own level. "Some will be good, and some will be bad," he said. "Now they are all awful." He argued that family planning was "very much a non-starter" in India, "We need education for the woman, the girl child. We need a good jobs for everybody. We need child and maternal healthcare. And we need overall economic growth. The government must act so that the result is family planning, which would follow these things". Above all Gandhi said, he was determined" to kill all controversies over religion". He said he has not worked that Hindu fundamentalists and the BJP would go to the holy city of Ayodhya and tear down the Babri Masjid, the 16th century mosque, to build a temple to the Hindu god-king Rama. He said he thinks Hindus were jolted out of their crusade by the violence they caused last year when zealots tried to storm the mosque. "The BJP does not have the guts to do that again," he said.[9]

The election of P.V. Narasimha Rao as the president of the Congress has removed the uncertainty about the leadership of the largest party in the country. The leaders of contending factions within the Congress have therefore opted for a cease-fire at least for the time being, as they are astute enough to realise that any inner-party squabbles or open tussles for the capture of posts and positions within the party organisation just now, might bring disaster for them all in the remaining poll contests. The experience on May 20 has had a chastening effect on the Congress leadership as the party is reported to have fared below expectations in that round. With the leadership issue solved at least patched up until after the general election results come out-the Congress is definitely better placed now to improve upon its performance in the first round. This will be, to a very large measure, due to the so-called sympathy vote that the party expects to harvest on the assassination of its leader under the most shocking circumstances. The fact that Rajiv Gandhi sacrificed his life while campaigning for the party will undoubtedly betch more support for it from the electorate while the morale of the party ranks is expected to be uplifted by the supreme sacrifice of their leader. It is in this context that the Congress leadership would not certain openly any talk of any alliance or understanding or merger with any other parth just at this moment. Because that would deflect in no small measure from the halo of having been committed to the behest of the martured leader. That is why Mohan Dharia's importunate appeal to let the Congress take over Chandra Shekhar's SJP has been summarily rejected by the Congress working Committee. Such bargainings are for tomorrow, not just now. The intensive phase of the election battle in the foming fortnight is thus

9. Barbana Crosette. We Hope to Do More. *The Times of India*, 26 May 1991.

expected to have a cleansing impact for the Congress party. At the same time, one should have no illusion about the power of mischief of the venal coterie so long operating from the top, particularly now that it is bound to be desperate on having been suddenly deprived of the protection of the leader. The sympathy vote will thus no doubt be an important factor in the remaining part of the election battle that no Opposition party can afford to ignore. At the same time, one has to take into account the fact that the wider public might adversely react towards the Congress in areas where it let loose ruffians to recklessly attack opposition party premises and property of their members particularly in the South along with a number of indicent in the North as well. Althouth this comes nowhere in its magnitude to the anti-Sikh pogrom by marked-out Congress ruffians in the wake of Indira's assassination in 1984, the Congress authorities will have to beware of such lapses on the part of section of their party. The political environment today does not permit at all any unleashing of violence whether communal or caste or between intra-party adversaries. On gets the feeling that the public temper today is much more worried about the outbreak of insenstate violence than at any time before.[10]

Another precious offering has been laid at the alter of modernity and secularism. Mahatma Gandhi, Indira Gandhi and, now, Rajiv Gandhi have been felled not because either of them provoked any personal enmity but because their ideas and practices were perceived as hindrance to the relisation of their dreams. As Bal Thakery, the Shiv Seha supremo and a closeally of the Bharatiya Janata Party (BJP), has pointed out that Mahatma Gandhi's killer was inspired to perform the heinous act by the ideology which considered the thought and practice of the Mahatma the cause of India's vivisection in 1947. Godes, says the S.S. Chief, prevented another partition by pumping the lethal bullets into she body of the Mahatma. With their iron-in-the-well mentality these people fail to that what brought about partition is the very approach which they advocate if India, after Independence, has remained steady and not broken up like many other new nations, it is because of the way of life set out by those people. The long line of leaders from A.D. Hume and W.C. Bannerjee to Rajiv Gandhi have been engaged in a saga of pulling India out of the darkness of medievalism, thickened by the stagnating impact of colonialism and building a new grand edifice of a superstition free, enlightened and modern India. There have been setbacks in the course of this struggle but after every setback the main formation, the Indian National Congress, emerged with enhanced determination and increased vigour to

10. Nikhil Chakravarthy. Sympathy Vote. *Patriot,* 2 June 1991.

pursue the path towards the tryst with destiny. Its resilient, non-dogmatic approach enable it to adjust, modify and evolve policies needed to meet every new situation, every fresh challenge. That is how it is today the oldest democratic party in the world. Rajiv Gandhi was the proud inheritor of that legacy. The situation in which he had to assume the nationas leadership was however far from easy. Not only objective but also subjective. The country was shaken by divisive forces which had developed lethal teeth. The Congress Party had received serve jolts in the preceding decades. What onece was a predominatly secular organisation with only a small, insignificant fringe of doubters had got rather overburdened with a large section of what Rajiv Gandhi described in his Congress Centenary speech at Bombay, as "power-brokers and influence peddlers". Unabarhed talk of playing the power game by concentrating on the majority community had been in the air. It goes to the credit of the departed leader that he pulled the party out of that morass so that in 1991 it was able to produce a manifesto which was more an echo of the warriors for secularism like Gandhi, Azad and Nehru than the expression of the political tribe which treats people as voting blocs to be manipulated and managed.[11]

They are indeed effective. The Bharatiya Janata Party's effort to blur, even obscure, its communal image and appear as a right-if- centre alternative have undoubtedly won it support among the middle classes. With Rajiv Gandhi's assassination seen widely as an attack on the Indian nation, the BJP's militant ultranationalism could make it even more attractive. If only it could usurp the Rajiv levacy and project itself as natural successor to his twin planks of stability and a strong India. This is precisely what the party is trying to do, though with a difference. It is not only seeking to capture these planks minus their policy framework, but attacking it as the chief villain. That is what its attack on Nehruvism is all about. The BJP's ciriticism of Nehru's politicies is not that they have not worked, but that these were based on alien ideology. But, what, party, does that mean? True that the concepts of socialism and communism were developed by thinkers outside India; but so has been the entire corpus of modern knowledge, including the concepts of liberalism and market economy, on which are BJP's economic package is based. So indeed are the concepts of ethnic nationalism and nation state that come so handy to the BJP for justifying its objectives. Not that BJP leaders do not know about ideas and ideologies being universal, only the talk of alien ideas helps away the voter. If ancient Indian wisdom were all the BJP were to draw upon, it would be left with only anamoral **rajniti** that would shock even a

11. D.R. Goyal. Rajiv's challenging Legacy. *National Herald*, 25 May 1991.

Machiavelli. The BJP may sell its wares under Sanskrit names, but that does not make them "made in India". The question, therefore, is not where its policies were manifactured, but whether they can ensure a stable government and a strong nation. The BJP may employ the Kautilyan subterfuge of picking up all the populist promises made by all the parties, and going one better on these, but they cannot do the impossible. Here is an example: if the Congress has promised to "hold the price line of essential commodities", the BJP has done one better by promising to 'hold the price line" of all, even while "reducing non-plan expenditure", ensuring "remu nerative prices to the farm labour" and "removing all restrictions on the movement of farm produce throughout the country". Sorry for the BJP, but not even Brahma can do this. All that these promises mean, in effect, is that the party wants to push up food prices and throw the farmer again to the mercy of the wholesale traders, commission agents or arhits, its main constituency. The party's professions abound in such contradictions which only shows that not much thinking has gone into its economic package, that is notheing more than a collection of all populist promises and a good does of "alien" liberal capitalism.[12]

The gory incidents of communal carnage during the recent months highlight the need for spirit of tolerance, catholicity of outlook, respect for each other's faith and willingness to abide by rules of self-discipline. This has to be both at individual as well as group level. If individuals selfishness, disergardful of feelings and rights of others, is bad, much worse is the group selfishness, disregardful of feelings and rights of other groups. As it is, we present a picture of a nation where in the people are at war with each other. We must bear in mind that unlike what has been done in some of the countries in our neighbour hood, our founding fathers opted for the establishment of a secular polity. This was in keeping with what great sons of India-Vivekananda, Aurobindo, Gandhi, Tagore, Radhakrishnan and Neru-had stood for. The spirit of India has been one of assimilation of the various elements that came into our country. When she failed to abide by that spirit, she herself declined. When Mahatma Gandhi asked us to open our doors to all the winds, but not get swept off our feet, he was essentially articulating and stressing tradition of India. India, as pointed out by Dr. Radhakrishnan, strove throughout her history for the freedom of spirit and the union of hearts. She did not destroy differences, but discovered their underlying affinities. The essence of Hinduism, which has been fount-head of our cultural and religious heritage, has been

12. Devendra Chintan. Stable Rama Rajya. *The Business and Political Observer,* 5 June 1991.

the spirit of tolerance, catholicity of outlook and freedom of thought. Heresy hunting is something wholly alien to it. If growing incidence of violence thereatens the unity of India and the cause of secularism, it equally poses a danger to out democratic polity. Democracy in its nascent stage or in the countries where in it has not taken firm roots cannot withstand for long the stresses and strains of turmoil and disorder. Such conditions also prove to be a propitious soil where in sprout the dangerous seeds of military rule. Human history reveals that in such an atmosphere there comes the man with the sword on the horse back-be it a Hitler, a Mussolini or their prototype. He is initially hailed as Messiah and a saviour to resotre law and order and provide security of life and property, but once he gets entrenched, history tells us, he acquires the traits of a despot and dictator, intolerant of criticism and unwilling to put up with opposition and dissent. Such a regime would mark the demise of democracy and the values associated with it.[13]

History also teaches us that it may not difficult to dethrone democracy, but once democracy is banished, it is most difficult to revive it and bring it back to the people. One of major tasks or challenge would be establishing mastery over communalism because it is not longer academic, it is no longer sporadic. The old methods, obviously, will not work in bringing the communal situation under control, the rule of a government must be to defend and cherish the secular principles, come what may. We must put an end to this nonsense because we now know that the nation is yet to realise the truth of this proposition that without secularism, without communal harmony, there can be no national unity, no democracy, no civil society, no rule of law, no pursuit of justice, no serious economic development.[14]

Whether the country will be able to recover its balance in the midst of the prevailing communal, caste and ethnic conflicts and the new government to be formed later this month being the situation under control, are questions to which only time can provide definite answers. All that can be said just now is that the margin of safety for the nation as well as the room for manoeuvre for the parties are shrinking with each passing day. That in this situation a veteran leader of the Left should assure the public that there is no cirsis shows how hopelessly out of touch the parties are with the grim realities on the ground. Do not the presence of so many governments at the Centre in sixteen months, the unprecedented delay in the presentation of the national budget and enforcement of a new fiscal discipline, the big resources crunch and the decline in the country's credit rating, the rising tempo

13. H.R. Khanna. Politics of Violence. *The Hindustan Times*, 27 May 1991
14. N. Ram. The Congress. *The Sunday Observer*, 26 May 1991.

or violence in public life and the spectre of political instability that haunts the nation, all add up to distressing evidence of a looming crisis. Or have the food stores in the cities to go empty, the economy has to register negative rate of growth, and communal and ethnic conflicts have to grow fare more virulent.[15]

Rajiv Gandhi has laid down his life for upholding unity, integrity and stability of the country, which is being threatened by communal forces. It is high time for secular and socialistic forces to unite to fight against communal forces. In the national interst, it is incumbent upon secular and socialistic minded political leaders of various political parties to unite to defeat the communal forces at the polls. All weak candidates should withdraw themselves from the contest in favour of strong candidates who can defeat the candidates backed by communal forces. By adopting one-to-one contest the secular and socialistic forces will win to uphold the unity, integrity and stability of the country. This is the only way to curb communalism through the ballot and this will be the best tribute to the memorty of Rajiv Gandhi.[16]

15. Sham Lal. Self Image. *The Times of India,* 2 June 1991.
16. Fani Akbarabadi. Era Comes to and End. *The Hindustan Times,* 6 June 1991.

21
SECULARISM AND FUNDAMENTALISM

Rajiv Gandhi is dead. The bomb which killed him was directed not only against him but also against the entire Indian nation-its secular edifice and democratic system. We are too close to this tragedy to objectively assess its impact on the course of political development in our country in the foreseeable future. That Rajiv Gandhi was killed in the mist of the mid-term poll to the Lok Sabha conceals more than what if reveals. India has so far managed to sustain a secular democratic system of government on a scale which has no parallel in the world. This achievement in itself is remarkable in more then than one sense, because despite various limitations a democratic system has not only been established in the whole of India, it has also withstood some profound shocks-the partition of India in 1947, mass migration of population after partition.[1] Pakistani invasion of India in 1947, Sino-Indian conflict in 1962, Indo-Pak war of 1965, Indo-Pak conflict of 1971 and the assassination of Indira Gandhi in 1984. India's secular and democratic political system survived all these challenges.

It is often argued that political mobilization on the basis of religion can be checked byemphasizing that religion is merely a private affair, an individual relation between the believer and the divine, having no wider social and political ramifications. But this, however, is to completely ignore the primarily social nature of religion. As socialists have been at pains to stress, the worship of God is, in fact, the worship of the community itself. Social norms, values and customs are given religious sanction and legitimacy, to make them all the more difficult for potential deviants to transgress or violate. Since the political sphere si, by far, the pre-eminent element in a given society, the social rules, in the guise of religious laws, also extend to the political domain. Thus, all religions lay down rules for governance and, therefore, are intimately connected with politics. For instance, in Hinduism, the Manu Dharma shastra lays down the duties of the king and the citizens belonging to the different castes. The king must rule in accordance with the Varna Ashrama Dharma. The two most widely accpted Hindu religious books, the Ramayana and the Mahabharata are both epics dealing initimately with politics. Likewise, in Islam, the Khalifah or the Caliph is both the religions as well as the temporal head, and he must rule in accordance with the Islamic Shari at. All religious, besides establishing a bond between God and the believer, also envisage their ownparticula-

1. V.D. Chopra. National Criss and Whither Congress. *Patriot,* 27 May 1991.

r versions of an ideal society, including an ideal polity. In this sense, politics is an essential component of the religious paradigm. This being the case, politics may only be separated from religion if religion itself is displaced on the ideological sphere by a non-religious, atheistic consciousness. An atheistic consciousness, of course, if far from the irreligiousness that is often associated with it. On the institutional plane, the and social psychological role played by religion would have to be fulfilled by other intermediary social institutions, such as occupational associations and the like.[2]

A secular India alone is an India that can survive. India and secularism must remain synonymous to assure the glory of our civilisation and the future of our country. In every village of India, in every basti, and in every mohalla, there are people of different faiths, of different languages, of different cultures who live together as neighbours. Secualrism is a condition of our existence. It is the essence of our tradition, Secularism and our nationhood are inseparable. We are a multi-cultural society, but we are not a multinational society. We are one people, we are one nation, we are one country and we have one common citizenship. Most civilizations posit nationhood and diversity as antithetical. The single greatest contribution of India to world civilisation is to demonstrate that there is nothing antithetical between diversity and nationhood. Through 5000 years of living experience, we have demonstrated to the world that our unity in diversity is a vibrant reality. Today's world is in desperate need of learning from India's experience. Peace and survival in the modern age depend on non-violence, on tolerance, on compassion and understanding, on peaceful co-existence between diverse philosophies and diverse ways of life. Through technological development the world is becoming smaller and is growing into a global village. The world is equally in need of unity and diversity. India's secularism is a global need because global secularism is inseparable from human survival; it is inseparable from global interdependence; it is inseparable from global cooperation.[3]

We shall never let another partition of India happen again. We shall never again let the forces of communalism triumph over secularism. Through forty years of Independence we have shown that we are one nation. We have faced external aggression as a united nation. We have stood firm as one nation against the internal forces of fundamentalism and fanaticism. It is illustrated most dramatically by what has happened in Punjab. The protagonists of secession found common cause with

2. Yoginder Sikhand. Search For a Secular Society. *Patriot,* 4 June 1991.
3. *Rajiv Gandhi in Parliament.* Ed. by M.C. Shah, Delhi, 1990. See also National Herald, 2 June 1991.

religious fanatics. Together, they roped in terrorists, murders, hired assassins, gun-runners smugglers and common cirminals mising politics with religion, mixing religion with criminality. Gurdwaras were turned into criminal dens till operation Black Thunder, proving that terrorism was not for religion, not for religious purposes, but for ulterior motives. The people were disgusted at the defilement of the shrines and the misuse of religion. They were disgusted with the intimidation of the *Granthis* and the oppression of the *sevadars*. The people has triumphed. The forces of communalism have not accepted defeat. They are always on the prowl, always looking for an opportunity to make mischief, always trying to insinuate themselves into the political life of the country working from behind the scene or using others as a front. If the secular forces stand together, communalism can be contained, the danger arises when political parties, for opportunistic reasons, lend the weight of their support to narrow causes. There are political parties represented even in this House that have become tools wittingly or unwittingly of fundamentalism and fanaticism masquerading as religion. Some political parties live on stoking the fears of religious minorities. Others live on stoking the religious passions of the majority communities. And then there are those who convert petty arguments and minor disputes into communal conflagrations. There are those that create disputes where none exist. There are those that incite passions only to pose as protectors of the faith. The Congress is pledged to have nothing to do under any circumstances with such forces.[4]

The challenge to secularism as is not from one quarter, but from fanatics of all faiths strring trouble in various ways. There are those who ignore our composite culture and project to followers, a distorted and motivated picture of India's history, creating grievances where there are none, making political capital out of distressed religious sentiments. It is for the state governments to be alive to, such attempts to set up an intelligence system for advance information about trouble makers and trouble spots. It is for state governments to take preventive action and quick, corrective measures. No state government, Congress or non- Congress, can claim an unblemished record. All state governments, Congress and non-Congress, have attempted to tackle the problem. No state government has ever been refused a full assistance of the Centre in preventing or tackling the problems in a particular situation. This is a national issue and it is an issue that demands a national response. The elements of a response, formulated through a general consensus and the consent of the country, is what is needed.

4. *Ibid.*

The secular injunctions of the Constitution must be carried out in good faith and with deep dedication. Religion must not be mixed with politics. No one doing so can run for elections today after our recent amendments. But still there are some political parties who amend their constitution and bring them into conformity with the nation's Constitution. The minorities needing educational and economic help must be assisted to avial of equality of opportunity as guaranteed by the law. Genuine grievances must be tackled quickly. Imaginary grievances must be quickly exposed. The macinery of law and order must be insulated from all religious prejudices from all communal overtones. Jawaharlal Nehru staunched the bloodletting of partition, reassured the minorities, reformed the obsolete and oppressive mores of the majority community. He gave Indians of all faith the confidence that the state is above all prejudice, above all discrimination, above all narrowness.[5]

What has happened in India in the early nineties is that a concerted move is a foot to wean away the majority community, i.e. Hindus, from the main secular edifice. This is how the Gandhi-Nehru frame of nationastate building is being destroyed. In this connection, it has to be admitted that successive governments, of whatever ideological complexion, have more or less helped in this process of reversal. Even the Congress when in office, has not been consistent in its loyalty to Nehru's concept of secularism. In its keenness to secure votes, it has been willing to compromise on secularism. This has sometimes brought short term advantage, but in the long term scenario it has strengthened communalism. The situation has been further compounded by rise of Muslim fundamentalism in the developing countries in general and in our own region, in particular. It appears that in the last phase of his life Rajiv Gandhi through his pragmatism and experience had begun to realise that there was no short-cut to realise that there was no short-cut to building a modern nation-state except on the philosophy of Jawaharlal Nehru. One hopes that under the leadership of the newly elected Congress pressident P.V. Narsimha Rao, this process will be carried forward. In the totality of the situation we find that the medieval outlook is coming into sharp conflict with the modern and secular attitudes. The process to counter the growing offensive of medieval philosophy is not going to be easy. Historically speaking the jews were denounced in Nazi Germany as a threat to the economic prosperity of the German nation and its unity. In India today, Muslims are being made the scapegoat of both political and economic crises of the country. On cannot expect our working people, particularly the pease-

5. *Ibid.*

antry, the agricultural workers, the Harijans and the backward classes, to support with any enthusiasm the modernisation of the economy without weeding out from their minds their deeply-rooted feudal outlook. One cannot accept veneration for a reactionary feudal socio-economic outlook and yet hope to work for its liquidation. This is the challenge which the Indian nation faces today and this challenge can only bet met by all the secular and democratic forces unitedly. Seen in this context, the Indian Left, strategically placed as it is has a historical role to play.[6] The era of fighting the 'two enemies' simultaneously has come to and end. India has already entered a period in which the monster of rising fascism has to be fought unitedly. One hopes that new Congress president P.V. Narasimha Rao, in keeping with his past, will rise to the occasion.

Mahatma Gandhi's blatantly anti-modern compromise with the Muslim clergy on the Khilafat issue may have been motivated by the noblest of objectives, but was definitely not a secular decision. From this to Jinnah's disillusionment with the "hypocritical Hindu" was not a long journey. What the Muslims needed were modern education and economic opportunities, what the clergy and Gandhiji were giving them was khilafat and obscurantism. The partition of the country, the flight of large number of educated. Muslims to Pakistan and the widespread pro-Pakistan and the widespread pro-Pakistan sentiment among large sections of Muslims after that resulted in their alienation from the mainstream for quite some time. It is this feeling that made them easy votes for those who could promise them just protection. The Congress, particularly under Indira Gandhi, fully exploited this communal card as did many other parties, including the Left. So did all of them, including the BJP is in all of its incarnations, exploit the caste factor. The BJP therefore, is perfectly justified in branding them all as pseudo-secularists. Only, that does not strengthen its claims to secularism or lend credence to its promises of a stable government and a strong nation.

Nor does it entitle the BJP to question the secular credentials of the Congress under Rajiv Gandhi. Whatever his other mistakes, Rajiv Gandhi cannot be accused of having deliberately acted in a communal manner, to appearse or punish any community. He was a thoroughly religious politician, though he did fall a prey often to the communal propensities of his followers or was carried away by a desire to please everybody. All experience shows that communal politics has invariably weakened the Indian nation. The threats it is facing in Kashmir, Punjab

6. V.D. Chopra. Multi-Dimensional Character of National Crisis. *Patriot,* 3 June 1991.

and the northeast have been caused in no mean measure by the communal tendencies of even its secular leaders.[7]

If India has to develop as a strong nation-as it has to-it shall have to practise secular politics and ensure full rights and opportunities to all irrespective of caste or creed.

Secularism is our answer to those who seek religious domination, to those who demand a position of privilege for the dominant religious community as the quid pro quo for letting the minorities even exist. As there are those who contest this view even now, let me recall Panditji's definition of secularism:

> "It means freedom of religion and conscience, including freedom those who may have no religion. It means free play for all religions, subject only to their not interfering with each other or with the basic conceptions of our state. It means that the minority communities, from the religious point of view should accept this position. It means, even more, that the majority community, from this point of view, should fully realize it. For, by virtue of numbers as well as in other ways, it is the dominant community and it is its responsibility not to use its position in any way which might prejudice our secular ideal."[8]

Panditji conceived of socialism as the third great pillar of our contemporary nationhood, as our answer to attempts at economic domination. When Indiraji saw that the struggle to serve the people was being thwarted by legal legerdemain, she brought socialism into the Constitution. We are one nation and not a union of nations precisely because our nation has room for all manner of diversity. By preserving and promoting all our cultures, we have evolved a composite culture. By transcending ethnic identities without dissolving them, we have created a higher loyalty to the nation, preventing ethnic, linguistic, religious or regional differences from consolidating themselves into divisive political boundaries. Another pathbreaking innovation which Panditji and his colleagues brought into our Constitution, under the guidance of Mahatma Gandhi, was its enshrinrment of affirmative

7. Devendra Chintan. A Stable Rama Rajya. *The Business and Politivcal Observer*, 5 June 1991.
8. Rajiv Gandhi. *On Nehru and Indira.* New Delhi, 13 November 1989.

action in favour of traditionally disadvantaged sections of society. We pioneered the concept that it was not only necessary to end discrimination against the disadvantaged, it was equally essential to empower the disadvantaged through special access to the legislatures, educational insitutions and government jobs, to translate the assurance of equality given in the Constitution into a political, social and economic reality. This constitutional innovation was in sharp contrast to the practice of the older established democracies.[9]

His secular, modern outlook was beyond question. He never wanted power for power itself, but rather to use it as an instrument to serve the people. The two arenas in which I had the privilege of working under his guidance are trade unions and Parliament. I found him to be precise, clear and extremely principled. There was a time when I was leading an agitation of central government employees demanding an amendment to Article 311 of the Constitution. He spent hours discussing the matter and finally gave a satisfactiory decision.

The most interesting aneccdote was when the Fourth Pay Commission Report was published and he found it would sot cost the government a substantial amount. He called me and asked how I had managed to pull the wool over the eyes of finance minister V.P. Singh. He was amazed when I told him I had shifted the demand from DA to basic, which was a red herring VP settled the matter, not realising the real issue lay in the DA formula. Rajiv, however, did not consider with drawing from the government's commitment but only asked the workers to be more productive and efficient. It was this approach which changed the very atmosphere of industrial, relations and boosted the economy during 1985-1990.

Another interesting aneccdote deals with subramaniam Swamy threatening the speaker and his subsequent affidavit in Parliament. Rajiv was extremely upset and said that in no way should the prestige of Parliament be sacrificed and that Swamy should apologise. Similarly, when the V.P. Singh government fell, many of us requested him to stake a claim.[10]

But he refused, saying he had given his word to the people of India that he would not become the Prime Minister, unless he had their mandate. He did the same even in March 1991 when Chandra Shekhar decided to resign. During the last two years his constant worry which he expressed to all of us was the atmosphere being whipped up by V.P. Singh and L.K. Advani. He was very worried about the country being pushed back to medieval times. He used to inform us that our main

9. Ibid.
10. P.R. Kumaramnglam. My Boyhood Hero. *The Times of India*, 26 May 1991.

opponent was BJP whose main objective was to convert India into a communal country. The last few years one saw him literally chase the security away to meet the people whom he loved. When V.P. Singh's government withdrew the SPG and when all of us made a hue and cry, Rajiv told us that the government knew best. It is this combination of an atmosphere of hatred and the withdrawal of security that took him away from us at this crucial moment.[11]

A major contribution of Rajiv Gandhi is that he has cleaned the Gandhi-Nehru framework from the dross that had accumulated over it. Today the dividing line is clear. Nobody misunderstands secularism as negation of, or indifference to religion and tradition. It is clearly seen as an approach which rouse the base, predatory and combative strains in them all. The philosophical approach was underpinned by insistence on technological leap forward, reflected in the slogan of march towards the 21st century. A nation equipped with the latest productive technology. Rajiv believed, would be a nation well insulated to the siren voices of the bullock-cart age. It was indeed ironical that these who criticised his respect for people's beliefs in the name of secularism were the foremost in ridiculing his ideas on technological advance. No surpirse, therefore, that the votaries of anti-Gandhi and anti-Nehru ideologies sensed a serious threat to their future in a Rajiv-led Congress. That is why the forces which hoped to thrive on caste and community antagonism launched the hitherto unprecedented onslaught on the ideological political edifice inherited by the Congress. As everyone knows it has been a no-holds-barred affair. The basic principles of the Constitution, the jurisdiction of the highest law courts, the sanctity of the President of India, the authority of the Election commission-all the symbols and components of secular polity have been challenged and held up to ridicule. All varieties of the challenges to that legacy have been whipped up to ferocious frenzy. Communalism of the darkest hue, throwing away even the fig-leaf of semantic dissimulation, is audaciously calling itself true secularim and denigrating the time-tested ideals as pseudo-secualrism. Significantly enough the foremost protagonist of this ideology declares willingness to join hands with the crudest forms of casteism and regionalism. What other interference can be drawn from the declaration of the BJP that while it would not join in a coalition with the Congress or the parties of ex-Congressmen it would be willing to share power with NTR's Telugu Desham, Karunanidhi's DMK and the fire- eaters of AGP? Thus the current election scene has assumed extraordinary significance as a contest between the forces of integration, represented mainly by the Congress, and the forces of disruption

11. *Ibid.*

whose nucleus is the BJP. It is a referendum on the question whether Indian genius and ethos are reflected in the tradition of Tilak, Gandhi, Azad and Nehru who based themselves on the best civilisational values of this soil or in the throught thought of Hedgewar, Godse, Advani and Thackeray whose ideological framework stands on the superficial Western perceptions of Indian civilisation. It is no coincidence that Bal Tahckerary unashamedly justified the assassination of Gandhiji and the BJP accuses Bal Gangadhar Tilak of minorityism. Notably, all, except the Congress, have maintained a thunderous silence over these perverse outrages.[12]

The same kind of reactions have been evinced on the decision of the Congress Party to make Sonia Gandhi the party president. Rather than appreciating the spirit of the breaved family to carry on the battle in the course of which Rajiv Gandhi laid down his life they have reacted with vulgarity to call her a foreigner. In other words one who is not born in this country, or has not adopted the religion which the BJP calls Hinduism, cannot be treated as an equal citizen even though practice and the Constitution entitle him or her to it. By the same token Nellie Sengupta, Annie Besant, Sister Nivedita and Mira Behn would have to be excluded from the category of Indian patriots.

It is not known so far who hurled the bomb at Rajiv Gandhi. But the person is not important. More important than the instrument of the ghastly deed is the mentality that impelled the hand that used the bomb. Rajiv Gandhi, in his death, has posed a test for the people of India. Do they prefer the legacy which Tilak and Gandhi and Nehru bequeathed or the views of the imperialist sociologists which the BJP and its associates are advocating as nationalism?[13]

On mixing religion with politics BJP leader L.K. Advani said in an interview with News Week, published on June 3, 1991 it was not the first time that this charge was levelled against the party." I am not apologetic about it anymore. What we believe in we say firmly."

"We tell our critics your secularism is bogus. It is not concerned with the welfare of the Muslims, only with their votes. Has the lot of the Muslims improved in the last four decades? He asked.

Advani said Hindu society by its very nature could not become fundamentalist because it was not a monolithic structure.

There is no one form of worship. How can it become fundamentalist?"

On the BJP's attitude towards Muslims and other minorities, L.K.

12. D.R. Goyal. Rajiv's Challenging Legacy. *National Herald*, 25 May 1991.
13. *Ibid.*

Advani said, "my party is unequivocally committed to the secular constitution of this country. We would not allow any change in this Constitution that takes it towards theorcracy.

"When we talk of a Hundu Rashtra, we speak about it in the same sense as one would say that Britain is a Charistian country or France is a Christan Country.

"That does not mean a non-Christian in France is a second class citizen, or that Britian is a theocracy.

"We guarantee equality, justice, freedom of worship to all. These are the three ingredients of secularism as I understand it. According to other political parties, whose attitudes I have described as pseudo-secular, secularism means disowning the essential personality of this country."

Asked about communal clashes in placed places he visted during his rath yatra, L.K. Advani said, "every newspaper, every political party, every government keeps telling the Muslims that his chariot tour means riots for you...... I don't blame them.

There has been a subtle move to denigrate national leaders, including the father of the nation Mahatma Gandhi. Just to serve narrow selfish ends. In other words, there has been an attempt to recast Indian nationalism in narrow terms. All this has been possible because, as you observe, the masses have been made to drink the heady wine of bigotry and hatred.[14]

Rajiv Gandhi, despite his weaknesses and shortcomings, stood as bulwark against obscurantist and regressive trends and laid down his life like his mother. It is the turn of the political leaders to give up their divisive politics and rise to the occasion. There is no doubt that the Indian people who have weathered similar blows before will do so again and vote for democracy and secularism a true tribute to Rajiv Gandhi.

In India the elected monarchs wield the power of the purse on the basis of black money levies and hence monarchism previals in this nominal Republic. Republicanism, secularism egalatarianism, rule of law, independent thinking and respect for judicial and legislative norms and procedures are all interlinked values. Monarchical loyalty to leaders, religious, linguistic and caste chauvinisms, flouting of judicial and legislative standards, street violence, adulation of fuehrers, self-advancement through sycophancy and deterioration in governance also go together. This is not the fault of individual leaders alone. They were all helpless victims of a vicious system.[15]

14. D.N. Goswami. Trying Times. *The Times of India,* 1 June 1991.
15. K. Subrahmanyam. Monarchism in India. *The Business and Political Observer,* 3 June 1991.

In the face of aggressive political mobilization and counter-mobilization on religious lines, the secular fabric of the Indian polity has now come under tremendous strain. Posing an immense threat to the very unity and integrity of the Indian state. In a bid to prevent the country from hurtling headlong into the bottomless pit of perpetual religious strife of the Lebanese sort, feeble voices are now being heard arguing for a strict separation of religion from politics and the polity as a whole. The question, however, to be asked before offering this staple suggestion, is whether merely separating religion from politics and the state would suffice to preserve and promote secularism. This solution has been put forward and nauseum from the Nehruvian era onwards, with little or no positive consequence. Mere verbal protestations and moralistic pontifications of this sort, from lofty pedestals and isolated ivory-towers, seem to have had no magical effect in controlling the fast escalating communal frenzy that has now engulfed the country. It appears that the mere separation of the state from religion or even the equal consideration by the state of all religions (the Indian version of secularism) is hardly sufficient to promote secularism and contain communal conflict. For, even if the state were to distance itself completely from religion or from a particular religion, the virus of communal hatred would still have enough fertile ground to flourish in civil society at large. Communalism would still thrive in the non-political social domain. For instance, even though the RSS and the Jamaat-e-Islami Hindi are professedly non-political, they gain their strength and legitimacy from their unbridled propagandistic activities in civil society. If secularism were accepted merely as the separation of politics from religion, then, clearly, there would be no check on the activities of the professedly non-political communal organizations in the social sphere. This suggests, therefore, that true secularization of society itself is secularized, there can be no doubt of the fact that politics will be forced to follow suit. If Indian society is sufficiently secularized, there would be little scope for communal parties to appeal to the baser instincts of religion and caste in a bid to derive political mileage. Unfortunately, however, very little has been done towards secularizing Indian society as a whole. Instead, what we find today is that large sections of society have very dramatically turned to religion as a means for establishing their identity. This, however, is a religiosity of an entirely new character-a synthetic religiosity, primarily political and ethnic in nature, deprived of any great spiritual content.[16]

An era has ended. With the tragic passing away of Rajiv Gandhi, the dream of a peaceful India has been shattered. It is still difficult to

16. Yoginder Sikand. Search for a Secular Society. *Patriot*, 4 June 1991.

believe that he is no more with us. His assassination cannot be condemned by mere words alone. The people of India must stand united at this moment of national grief and work towards the achievement of a truly secular Inda. This is what he dreamt of; this is what he stood for; this is what he died for.[17]

The assassination of Rajiv Gandhi is the biggest tragedy of the decade. A leader whose only fault lay in the fact that he believed in secularism and democracy has been snatched away from us in such a cruel manner that it is still difficult to believe he is no more. Rajiv Gandhi may have made mistakes when he was Prime Minister, but events in the last one-and-a-half-years did indicate that it was only he who could provide the much needed political stability in the country. His disappearnace from the political field, especially at a moment when he was in all probability going to be the next Prime Minister of the country, has shattered the masses. Though he is no more with us, his dreams will continue to guide the country for all time to come.[18]

Secularism, can only be established and promoted through a complete transformation of the ideological as well as social, economic and political domains. Without this, it appears that our feeble appeals to combat the communal menace would fall on deaf ears.[19]

P.V. Narsimha Rao's statement to The Times of India that the Congress will adhere steadfastly to the "Nehru line and the BJP's swift riposte to it should serve to draw the ideological battle lines more sharply in the remaining rounds of the 1991 elections. Jettisoning his party's past inhibitions, Mr. Rao, much to the discomfiture fo the JD-NF-Left combine, has gone so far as to argue that there is no viable alternative to the Nehru line "outside the pale of fascism". Not to be outdone, the BJP president, Dr. Murli Manohar Joshi, has lambasted the 'Nehruvian model' and held it responsible for every conceivable ill plaguing the nations. However, to be truly significant, this bitter exchange cannot be conducted at the level of invectives alone. On vital economic and foreign policy issues, for example, the Nehruvian positions clearly need a hard look in view both of the dramatic changes the world has witnessed in the past three years and of the country's own uneven performance over the past four decades. The Congress itself has implicitly amditted as such much in its election manifeso. The need to free productive forces in the country from stultifying bureaucratic control and gross political interfence has never been more

17. Surinderjit Singh. A Brutal Assassination. *The Telegraph,* 27 May 1991.
18. Ajay Kumar. Rajiv Gandhi. *The Telegraph,* 27 May 1991.
19. Yoginder Sikand. Search For a Secular Society. *Patriot,* 4 June 1991.

pronounced. Likewise, the emergence of a new world order following the collapse of the Berlin wall and the Gulf war calls for a through review of what remains of the non-aligned movement as well as of our bilateral relations with countries which matter vitally to our security and economic concerns. Again, while the Congress is on a sounder footing when it evokes the Nehruvian concept of secularism, it still has to do some explaining for the compromises it has stuck from time to time with fundamentalist Muslim and Hindu forces. All the same, Rao's latest formulation on this issue-"to exist in India is to co-exist" reveals a strong commitment to a secular order which alone can guarantee India's survival as a caring, democratic and modern republic. The BJP, too, cannot rest content merely with the argument that the "Nehru line" is "pseudo" because it is based on "imported concepts". Nor will it suffice to repeat parrot like that it derives inspiration from the country's "glorious cultural roots" and specifically from the teachings of Swami Vivekananda, Swami Daynanda, Sri Aurobindo, Lokmanya Tilak, Shyama Prasad Mookherjee, Deen Dayal Upadhyaya et al. For these figures in the BJP's pantheon took markedly different positions on a host of issues pertaining to Indian nationalism. For instance, Sri Aurobindo wanted Indian nationalism to be "largely Hindu in its spirit and traditions..........but wide enough to include the Muslim and his culture and traditions and absorbs them into itself." Veer Savarkar warned that the "Hindus cannot take this country as jointly owned by those who came running from their countries and sought protection here or those descendants of ex-Hindus, who for the greed of power and money or of fear, renounced their glorious faith and became converts, or those who are descendants of those barbarous invaders who spoiled our very sacred land, demolished our sacred temples......the country cannot belong to them". M.S. Golwalkar, the long-time head of the RSS, went a step further: "The non-Hindu peoples in Hindustan must either adopt the Hindu culture and language, must learn to respect and hold in reverence Hindu religion, must entertain no idea but the glorification of the Hindu race and culture.......or may stay in the country wholly subordinated to the Hindu nation, claiming nothing, deserving no privileges far less any preferential treatment-not even citizens' rights." Indeed, when Dr. Murli Monohar Joshi alleges that the Nehru line is based on "imported concepts" he does no more than echo Golwalkar's warning that Hindus should shake themselves "free from the mental shakles of foreignisms, foreign ways and fashions of modern life."

This then is the dividing line. On the one hand are ranged those who believe that co-existence is the essence of Indian existence; that the foremost duty of the Indian state is to protect those who are weak in number, wealth or status; that modernisation need not be at the expense of time-tested tradition. On the other hand are those who, despite their recent adherence to insaaf (justice) roti (bread) and stability, oppose these republican virtues under one guise or another: by debunking "pseudo-secualrism" and "minorityism", frowning on modernity, suspecting cosmopolitanism, hailing a culture and a polity which carry the ominous hallmarks of a theocracy.[20] No one can minimise the appeal of this mix of religious exclusivism and social conservatism, not the least because it is kept alive by the fundamentalists among the minorities.

Unity, patience, endurance among the leaders and all concerned are needed to face the situation after such an unexpected sudden death of a bold humanitarian leader like Rajiv Gandhi. Contributions of Rajiv in world politics and world peace movements were great. In spite of all difficulties and disturbances his devotion to secualrism shall made him ever dear to all those believing in it and in fraternal global perspectives.[21]

20. *The Times of India*, 5 June 1991.
21. Bhuban Mohan Dasgupta. Era Comes to an End. *The Hindustan Times*, 6 June 1991.

22

NATIONAL INTEGRATION - TOWARDS OPEN SOCIETY

Rajiv Gandhi, the child of the nation, has been killed. I can scarcely believe it. A part of my heart is bleeding, weeping silently but tears refused to flow down. Something has frozen inside and refuses to melt in the fire of anger and anguish. A flower, a youth, has been blown out of existence, leaving the nation and the world at large wondering if mindless terrorists will kill men, women and children and dance over their dead bodies in Punjab, Kashmir, Assam, and now in the south of this land of ours. Dedicated to vedic values, non-violence, peace and harmony as preached by Mahatma Gandhi, the father of free India, the urgly face behind the mask is revealing a ghoulish grin. One wonders if India born in the vedic ages is going to survive as a world power for serene, noble ends. Will the feelings and compassion be dead leaving India a brittle land of skeletons or will it survive by overcoming the cruelty sulking in bitterness in the heart of men? Rajiv was young and filled with dreams for his country. He said once that he wanted to make history, not only read it. Will the generations that inevitably follow one after another produce pure men and women? Will the era of Gandhi and Nehru be fogotten or will the future of mankind make itself sublime? Rajiv is dead but may his life be a legacy to be cherished by the sons and daughters of India. Young men and women must decide.[1]

Rajiv Gandhi's departure leaves a big gap in the Indian political equilibrium and suddenly unleashes new forces in the national polity. In the flashfloods that have followed on one is sure of even the safety and survival of the values and norms. Perhaps, turbulence is inbuilt in the system. So any break with the past is bound to be equally violent. However, the future thrust depends on whether our rulers care to learn lessons not only from history but also from recent events. India is a great nation. The mess has been created by politicians and it is for the people to make them behave not like lumpen elements but as honourable citizens of an ancient civilisation. Perhaps, it will take a couple of elections before the message goes home and India is rescued from the clutches of vested interests. In his own way Rajiv Gandhi had began to address himself to one onerous task ahead but his sudden violent death has left that job unfinished. His abrupt departure has left the nation at the crossroads of history. Whether the country and people once again move in the right direction or not will depend on the quality of leaders we elect. In a period of rapid transitions, we have no choice

1. Arun Asaf Ali. Legacy to be Cherished. *Patriot*, 23 May 1991.

but to seek political coherence in majorities or coalitions. The hope lies in the common sense of ordinary Indian citizens. It is here we feel reassured of better wisdom in the post-Rajiv India. However, the ultimate steps that translate public pressures for change into systemic reality are the ones those in power alone can take. It is said that the history of politics in India is a story of tragedy that began in hope.[2] The challenge today is far more grim since we are called upon to overcome the tragedy and work to build a stronger and united India.

Nations, like men, often have no choice but to live dangerously. Their destinies, however, are made not by the dangers they run into, but by the way they conduct themselves in facing these. The manner in which India has recovered its poise after the traumatic assassination of Rajiv Gandhi, certainly speak eloquently of its maturity. The angre to Indira Gandhi's assassination in 1984 was more in the nature of a tribal response. A tribe is bound together by the bond of blood and any attack on one of its members is viewed as an act of enmity against the entire tribe to avenge which is a duty of all of them. Notwithstanding other factors, the legacy of tribal culture payed a major role in both her assassination and the riots that followed. If India has behaved more like a modern nation after Rajiv Gandhi's assassination, much of the credit for that belongs to the assassinated leader who played no mean role in imparting a modern outlook to the nation during his only term as Prime Minister. It is the prependerance of the middle classes, that grew exceptionally apace during the 80s, as also the lessons the nation learnt in 1984, that are responsible for its maturer conduct now. One whishes the departed leader had done the same to his party. For, the way it has conducted its affairs since the tragedy struck is hardly worthy of a party that displayed such remarkable resilience when the nation lost Mahatma Gandhi Jawaharlal Nehru, Lal Bhadur Shastri and Indira Gandhi, three of them was gunned down in 1948 and the Cassandras expected the Congress to split between Jawaharlal Nehru and Sardar Patel, the two prominent successors took hardly any time to close their ranks and rally the party and the nation behind the new leader. Similarly, when Nehru left the scene, the party confounded those who had been talking of "After Nehru, what?", rather than "who", by choosing a diminutive Lal Bahadur Shastri as leader and uniting behind him to provide a collective leadership. Shastri's death at Tashkent in tragic circumstances too found the party alert and prompt in electing Indira Gandhi as leader. It is quite another matter that she chose to defy the syndicate later and caused a split in the party.[3] The

2. Hari Jaisingh. Post-Rajiv India. *The Business and Political Observer*, 23 May 1991.
3. Devendra Chintan. Politics of Consensus. *The Business and Political Observer*, 29 May 1991.

mere fact that Nehru was succeeded by a Syndicate gives the lie to those who accused him of being a banyan tree under which notheing else could grow.

The brutal assassination of Rajiv Gandhi has sent shock waves across the country. The people of India have to bear this tragic death of the youthful leader who sacrificed his life for the unity of the country. The cult of violence has to be rejected at all costs and at all places. Mahatma Gandhi taught us that Indian way to resolve conflict is not to struggle over values and claims to scarce resources and power in which the opponent is either neutralised or injured or eliminated but that our aim should be to develop harmonious relationships between different castes, religions and other groups and to replace hatred with love and affection. The poll violence should steer the whole nation to examine the value system the country intends to follow. In competitive politics, the political partieis are engaged in a race for political supremacy. What is the principal purpose of the race? To gain political power either to build or to destroy the nation for personal or party gain. Much intelligence and energy are going into this effort. Yet it seems more important than ever than an even greater effort is made to achieve positive and mutually helpful human relations. This cannot be done by merely political forces. Most of the present breed of leaders have taken to politics as their main source of income and livelihood. In the Gandhian era leaders gave up their lucrative professions and took to politics not as means of livelihood, but to join the struggle for independence. They did not expect anything in return.[4] Their values must be revived to build the nation and maintain its unity.

Rajiv Gandhi was murdered because he not only symbolised the unity of India but he also stood like a granite wall between forces of subversion and the unity of the country. The secular and democratic edifice built by Jawaharlal Nehru, consolidated brick by brick, by Indira Gandhi through well-throught out political and socio-economic policies, could not be weakened and destroyed without physically liquidating Rajiv Gandhi. If Jawaharlal Nehru and Indira Gandhi laid the basis for the transformation of socio-economic structure of the country, Rajiv Gandhi was creating a new India, which was on the threshold of becoming a great global power. Again, if Jawaharlal Nehru conceived the concept of non-alignment and become one of the founding fathers of the movement, Indira Gandhi, both as the Prime Minister of the country and later as the leader of the Congress, began to elevate and revitalise the non-aligned movement in the historical situation in which the world had begun to be dominated by one superpower, though

4. K.D. Gangrade. Resolving Conflict the Gandhian Way. *The Hindustan Times*, 5 June 1001.

perhaps temporarily. It was in this historical situation that Rajiv Gandhi was killed. The most agonising and disturbing development which took place after the assassination of Rajiv Gandhi, and that too even before his mortal remains were consumed by the fire, was the so-called "palace intrigues" that began to unfold themselves. And so the gossip mills also began to work overtime. Rumours were floated regarding cancellation of elections and imposition of emergency. Influential political circles started talking about the formation of a national government. Though these rumours were killed by denials, both by the President House and Prime Minister Chandra Shekhar, they did an immense damage to the country. These rumours sapped the self-confidence of the Indian nation and created an atmosphere of instability. If the country had witnessed violence and arson, following the assassination of Rajiv Gandhi, the process of destabilisation of the country would have entered a dangerous phase.[5] That this did not happen confirms how robust are the democratic and secular instincts of the Indian people. The Indian people once again rose to the occasion and foiled the game of "balkanisation" of the country through anarchy, chaos and disorder.

Rajiv Gandhi's assassination, a dastardly act, needs severe condemnation. Rajiv, the young, dynamic politicians had carved a strong position for himself in the Congress.

As Prime Minister of India, (1984-1989) in the first half of his tenure he administered the nation excelleently. But his downfall was evident when he sacked V.P. Singh. By that time, the Bofors scandal was also hovering over his government. Though people and sympathy for him, he could not recover the lost ground.

The Nehru-Gandhis have paid enough price for their obsessive desire to hold the seign of power and be in absolute control of the nation's destiny. Rajiv Gandhi's murder is an immense national tragedy, but it must not be comprounded by other follies. The survival of the Nation is more important than the survival of the party.

The chief characterstic and strength of our civilization have been its unity in diversity. As a civilization we have never attempted to impose uniformity, we have never attempted to dilute diverity. We have been open to the best of influences from outside even when such influence came in the wake of military conquest. We have refused to let the spread of human genius be limited by artificial barriers. The continuihg theme of our civilization has been synthesis, that is, the fusing of numerous cultures into a x composite culture, where individual

5. V.D. Chopra. Multi-Dimensional Character of National Crisis. *Partiot,* 3 June 1991.

identities are retained while common traits are shared. It has bred in our thought processes a sense of tolerance, a ready acceptance of that which is different, a celebration of the diversity of humankind. Panditji ascribed the continuity of our civilization to its "tender humanity, a varied and tolerant culture, and a deep understanding of life and its mysterious ways."

These values and traditions, which constitute the running thread of our civilization, are the explanation for its cultural continuity. More than any other single factor, it is the Indian tradition which has enabled us to face contemporary challenges. We have had the immense advantage of the idea of India- *Bharatavarsha,* as our ancients called this land-having predated modern concepts of political unity and having survived all manner of vicissitude, military political and economic. Going at least as far back as the Rig Veda some five thousand years ago, Indians have recognized the contours of their idea of India, an idea which is always above the shifting frontiers of political entities. The natural frontiers of the idea of India were given us by nature itself. Ranged along the northern rim was the immense massif to the world's highest mountains. Surrounding the Indian peninsula were the vast oceans. Twelve hundred years ago, Adi Sankra, the unifier of the Hindu religion and the exponent of some ot its greatest metaphysical insights, established four places of pilgrimage in the borth, south, east and west of India. These, in a spiritual sense, have constituted the frontier pillars of the idea of India. Pilgrimages to these dhams deeply ingrained the idea of India into our national psyche. The other great religions of India-Islam, Christianity, Sikhism, Jainism, Buddhism, Zoroastrianism, and others-also established placed of pilgrimage around the country. They too transcended shifting political boundaries to enter the national psyche and contribute to the evolution of the idea of India. In building a modern, united, contemporary India, we have benefited enormously from this edea of India. The idea of India has not only risen above passing political divisions, it has also risen above the racial, linguistic, cultural and religious diversity of the country. Every ethnic group, howsoever defined, depply believes-and with confidence asserts-that it is part of the entity called India. Equally, each ethnic group, ranging from overwhelming religious majorities like the Hindus to numerically small minorities like the Zoroastrians, finds it natural to coexist with the other ethnic groups. From time to time through our history there have been attempts to build on narrower identities. But such attempts have not endured. In the long run, the larger idea of India has marginalised those who, in political terms, have attempted to build themselves on narrow identities. Above all, the continuity of our civilization has been hased on an implicit recognition of the entire gamut of values comprised in the single word "non-violence." The roots of the Indian concept of nonviolence lie in the philosophy of the Budha, further developed by our civilization over the last 2500 years.[6]

The BJP has been protesting that it is wrongly dubbed as communal although it does not stand for a theocratic state and is the mosque-temple controversy, it says, is intended only to strengthen the national sentiment, because Rama is but a national symbol. Let's not question the BJP for a while about the felicity with which it can express itself in three rupas at a time; how the same RSS cadres can talk of the Hindu dharma as VHP volunteers and the Indian nation as BJP activists. Nor let's debate about what they mean by Hinduism-a universal religion as the VHP projects it, or as the multi-ethnic culture of India as the BJP sometimes interprets it. These, and many other questions about India's political, ethnic and economic maps may be vital to its survival as a nation-state, but are better avoide in the present charged atmosphere. But let's ask the BJP just a few simple, straight questions. Do all the citizens of India constitute this nation-state, or no? And if they do, do all of them, including many Hindus, consider Rama a national symbol? And even if Rama is a national symbol, is he the only one of the kind? What about Krishna, or Buddha, Mahatma Gandhi and countless other avatars, "330 million" gods, chakravartins? How many symbols does it take to make a nation, after all? And, is temple too a national synmbol? Or, but a place of worship, a religious symbol? What about mosques and churches? And what of those who accept the National Flag, the National Anthem, the Constitution as national symbols, but fall short of accepting Rama as one? Do they cease to be Indians for that reason even if they accept Rama as a mythical VVVIP? The answers should be obvious. How come, then, that the BJP hopes to convince anybody that its support to the Ramajanmabhoomi agitation is not communal, its attempt to use it for votes is not tantamount to the exploitation of the communal sentiment and its projection of religious symbols as national ones is not theocratic politics? Its hopes lie in the mismanagement of the country's politics, and economy for long by professedly secular leaders who did not hesitate to play any communal, casteist or sectarian card to stay in power. If others can do that and pass off as secular, why cannot the BJP do one's better by poohpoohing their pseudo-secularism, communalising the term itself and claiming that it is the only genuinely secular party? The logic is not without basis. It is true that secularism in India has come under severe pressures and strains all along. Their history can be traced to the trend of Hindu

6. Rajiv Gandhi. *On Nehru and India.* New Delhi. 13 November 1989.

insularity dating back to Goswami Tulsidas and Guru Nanak, as a retreat from the excesses of the alien bigoted Muslim mullahs who had a vested interest in distancing their rulers from the natives and stopping the process of cultural synthesis between tasawwuf and bhakti. Other factors include the British view of the Muslims as their main enemies in India, the losses the Muslim feudals suffered during the permanent settlement, the way the Hindus embraced English education which was spurned by the Muslims, the use of religious symbols by the leaders of both during the 19th century, the change in the British communal preferences around the turn of the century., the British attempts to reduce the Hindu prepondereance in the service to accommodate their new favourites and perpetuate the communal divide.[7]

The 1989 electoral verdict and the failure of the non-Congress parties to stick together for even a year robbed the young leader again of his chance to democratise and revamp the party. Come elections and he had to once again fall back upon the familiar state party bosses. And then came the catastrophe, denying him any chance to give India a stable and modernist government and rejuvenate his party around a new consensus. One can, therefore, appreciate the Congress dilemma in electing its chief. A young leadership is just not there; the veterans are out of tune with the spirit of the ranks. They have been "loyal soldiers" for far too long to don the mantle of generalship. What one cannot appreciate, however, is the indecent haste with which the Bharatiya Janata Party has sought to hijack the Congress's stability card. While it would be unfair to prejudge or preempt the investigation by blaming this or that terrorist group, individual or froeign power for the crime, nobody can disagree that the atmosphere of hatred created in the country during the recent past, particularly last year, is immensely conducive to violence. It either incites politics of murder or sanctifies it. The role of the BJP and the Janata Dal in spreading this divisive politics of hatred needs no elaboration. While the Janata Dal has responded discreetly and gracefully to the new situation, the BJP has rushed indecently to fish in troubled waters. In doing so, it has failed to realise that if at all any party could gain from the tragedy, it is the one that has been struck by it. The Congress will put its house in order sooner or later, though it should do that sooner, rather than later, in its own interest. For the rest, there has been no big change in the electoral prospects of any party. The pollsters have all along been predicting a hung Parliament, with the Congress emerging as the largest party in the Lok Sabha. That situation has changed only marginally, though the

7. Devendra Chintan. A Stable Rama Rajya. *The Business and Political Observer*, 5 June 1991.

margin may prove decisive in giving the Congress an absolute majority. The confusion about the Congress's prospects will last only until it elects a leader. The moment it does that, it will become a force to reckon with, because even after Rajiv Gandhi, it has a large number of leaders, none of whom is in any way inferior to any the BJP or the JD can field. Neither Mr. V.P. Singh nor Atal Bihari Vajpayee or L.K. Advani has yet attained a stature greater than that of a .P.V. Narasimha Rao, a Arjun Singh, a Sharad Pawar or a N.D. Tiwari. Chandrashekhar may have added a few inches to his height during his "four months", but his party is too minuscule to exploit the advantage.[8]

On the way to the rally near Madras, Rajiv Gandhi had been riding in the front seat, window open. A special flourescent light mounted on the dashboard of the Indian-made Ambassador car played on his face, so that the people could see him. They threw in flowers, their faces frenzied with happiness. The biggest smiles in India live in the gentle south. He threw the garlands back at others, along with scarves and shawls presented to him at stops along the way. At one point, he stopped to greet a shy woman being jostled by the crowd. He placed a scarf around her neck and spoke to her. She covered her face with her hands and than clutched the cloth and held it close to her. In the national election campaign, in 1989 Rajiv Gandhi had been criticised for being too aloof, too insulated from the people he hoped to lead. This time around, determined to carry his message directly to the people, he went on punishing road journeys, stopping at hamlets to shake hands and ask for votes as if he were a town council candidate. "What else can I do?" he told us as we pulled away from Ponamallee, a town along the route. He had been asked dozens of times a day whether he was afraid. His security was almost nonexistent tonight. A hundred times one of those hands that reached into the car to grab his arm or stroke his hand could have stabbed or shot him. He looked at the sleeve of his kurta. "I have been on the road 23 hours a day," he said. "At the end I am swollen and bleeding or have a cut arm. Here and in Kerala there is this cheek-pinching. And sometimes in Muslim neighborhoods they kiss me-you know: one, two three times, that special hug." I asked if he had any special regime, any vitamin supplements or diet designed to sustain his energy, particularly in the heat of an Indian summer, where temperatures reach 110 degrees. He laughed. "Most of the time I get nothing to eat at all," he said. In the car, there were a few bottles of water and a thermos of tea or coffee. Gandhi made on concession to comfort. When he died, he was wearing expensive run

8. Devendra Chintan. Politics of Consenus. *The Business and Political Observer,* 29 May 1991.

-ning shoes, easier on the feet for long days at the hustings.[9]

Rajiv was responsible for making me chuck up things in America, where I was a writer, public affairs analyst and consultant, and followed career as a journalist since 1981, and I must say that he was given a bad deal by the opiion-makers in this country. They carried on a virtual slander campaign, about his "remoteness," his "inaccessibility," his "security ring". And what happens when he lifts it-he's killed. I want people like Arun Shourie, N. Ram, Rajni Kothari and your own Harish Khare-who sat in their goddam chairs and wrote hypothetically about things and created a hate atmosphere-to answer to Sonia now. Today, when I read in the same press all these accounts of the greatness of Rajiv and his last hour, I feel nauseated. I met four-five days ago, at Agra. He showed up at 3 am. He looked to tired..... he seemed to be carrying on his shoulders. There was no respite for him even at that late hour. He had to meet us, the local Congressmen and the press. He even found time to feel the bump of a cop who had been hurt at one of his meetings. I felt sorry for him, he cut a tragic figure. But he was like a man possessed, you know. Or else, why would he do all this? He could have led a cushioned life; just the royalties from books that his grandfather and mother wrote would have been enough to give him a comfortable life. But you can't have a heritage like his and spurn public life. He was just a very ordinary-next-door- neighbour-type guy, a trait he never lost whether in power or out of it. In the company of the Reagans and the Thatchers of this world, though, he had a regal presence. And he didn't become cynical even when the slander campaign against him finally destroyed him. The defeat in 1989 didn't turn him into an ideological extremist. I remember asking him once about his vision of India. He said we have to remove the sense of slothfulness in the Indian people-the trait which makes the villagers wait for the government to come and cover a ditch, and which makes the shopkeeper clean up the area only in front of his shop. About economy, he used to say it was just a matter of common sense. Don't give me arcane jargon, he used to say. He would point out that it cost more to collect tax in the New Delhi area than the tax revenue collected. Why can't we, he would ask distribute water free if the government was losing out anyway. But he hadn't reckoned with the bureaucracy, which sabotaged him at every step, through leaks. When Indira Gandhi had so many bullets pumped into her, Rajiv had said, "Did she deserve that?" No one deserved to die the way he went eithre.[10]

9. Barbara Crosette. We Have To Do Much More. *The Times Of India*, 26 May 1991.
10. Rajeev Desai. Shourie and Ram-Please Answer to Sonia. *The Times of India*, 26 May 1991.

Notwithstanding the forcefull assertion by the leaders of the Congress and the Janata Dal to form the new Government on their own strength, attempts are being made for a reconciliation of all centrist forces committed to certain values. It is obvious that in the midst of an election campaign no political party can afford to make pronouncement, which mar its prospects at the hustings. Even then, there is no dearth of leaders in the Congress and the Janata Dal who have openly pleaded for such a reconciliation. Senior Congress leader Vasant Sathe has called for unity of all Congressmen under the Congress flag. He has pleaded for 'home coming' of all those Congressmen who had gone out for one reason or other. Obviously, Vasant Sathe, while making this appeal, was keeping in mind the assertion by Janata Dal leader V.P. Singh that he still treats the Congress as his home and he has not left it. On the contrary, he was driven out from his house. V.P. Singh is not that vocal in asserting his ties with the Congress, but his another colleague, senior Janata Dal leader from Karnataka; Ramakrishna Hegde, has openly pleaded for unity of the Congress and the Janata Dal in the post- assassination situation.[11]

While talking to reporters in Bangalore on May 27, 1991 Hegde said that if the National Front falls short of majority after the elections, it would seek support from Congressmen minus the "coterie". (It may be recalled that the non-elected close associates of Rajiv Gandhi like R.K. Dhawan, Mr. Satish Sharma, Suman Dubey and M.L. Fotedar and supposed to be the "coterie" or as some Congressmen would like to call it "cabal". This group is not only hated by former Congressmen, now in various opposition parties, but even by many Congressmen who are still in the party). Hegde ruled out merger of the Congress and Janata Dal. But his trusted lieutenant, Karnataka State Janata Dal President J.H. Patel, did not rule out the possibility of a realignment of political forces after the poll. At a proper press conference on May 27 at Bangalore, Patel asserted that the danger to the country is today more from the BJP than the Congress. The BJP coming to power after the elections will be disastrous for the country". While ruling out the possibility of an alliance or understanding between the Congress and the parties belonging to the National Front till the two remaining rounds of polling are over Patel said: "However I see a major political realignment after the elections with all the secular, democratic and socialist forces coming together including the Congress." In Congress itself, two district trends are visible. Those who prefer a collective leadership in the post-Rajiv era are clearly inclined for a reconciliation of all present and former Congressman. This group, which has the backing of new Con-

11. Shameen Faizee Centrist Forces. *Patriot*, 31 May 1991.

gress president P.V. Narasimha Rao is more inclined towards a reunion with Congressmen in the Janata Dal and a broader alliance with the like minded parties including the Left. It is believed that P.V. Narsimha Rao, before his elevation to the post of party president, exhorted Congressmen to follow the politics of consensus. He is reported to have advised his partymen, not only to unite within the organisation, but also with the like minded forces outside the party. Political circles in the Capital are agog with the reports that bridges are being built between the top leaders of the Congress and the Janata Dal for a possible realignment of political forces in the post-election period. A meeting betwween Narasimha Rao and V.P. Singh is also being mentioned which, according to reliable sources, took place on the initiative of the Janata Dal leader. The other group in the Congress headed by Maharashtra Chief Minister Sharad Pawar is more inclined towards the SJP and particularly caretaker Prime Minister Chandra Shekhar. Actually, before the election of Narasimha Rao as party Chief, Pawar actively campaigned for making two announcement from the CWC. He wanted an interim president for the party and projection, of a name for the Prime Ministership. It is believed that in his bid for Chandra Shekhar, Pawar roped in his counterparts in Karanataka and Andhra Pradesh, S. Bangarappa and Janardhan Reddy. Kerala party chief and former Chief Minister K. Karunakaran was projected as possible candidate for the party presidency. After the consensus on Narasimha Rao, the Chief Minister of Karanataka and Andhra Pradesh deserted Pawar. But he has still not lost the hope. He continues to canvass for Chandra Shekhar. Another interesting personality in favour of drafting Chandra Shekhar as possible Prime Minister, if the Congress wins the majority, is film star Amitabh Bachchan, who is also a family friend of Rajiv Gandhi. May be Amitabh Bachchan wants to repay the debt to Chandra Shekhar who favoured him in February, 1991 by withdrawing all investigations by the CBI against his brother Ajitabh Bachchan. Interestingly, bothe these groups in the Congress are against the so called "cabal" of Dhawan, Sharma, Fotedar and Sitaram Kesri and the "shouting brigade" of Ratnaker Pande, S.S. Ahluwalia and Viswajit Singh. Incidentally, almost all in the "cabal" and "shouting brigade" are members of the Rajya Sabha and have never faced the electorate.[12]

The unanimous election of Sonia Gandhi as Congress president by the party's Working Committee clinches the issue. The Congress leadership, such as it is, has acted in the belief that the "sympathy wave" resulting from Indira Gandhi's assassination played a major role in winning a landslide victory for it is the 1984 poll. It is to be seen whether

12. *Ibid.*

this calculation is justified. But be that as it may, the Congress has once again gone in for a dynastic succession in a repeat of 1984. Fortunately, the popular response to the tragedy, unlike in 1984, has generally been reasonably calm. This is consistent with the nation's long-term needs. This suggests that the decision to postpone polling by almost three weeks has been a case of over- reaction. A three-day postponement could have sufficed. But that decision is at least understandable. The same cannot be said at all for the move to form a so-called national government. A national government is a euphemism for an attempt to freeze politics. That would be undesirable at any time in a democracy. It would be particularly dangerous in the given situation when a struggle is on to redefine the very organising principles for Indian society and polity. The Hindutva and Mandal platforms have raised fundamental issues and these must be settled one way or another through the electoral process. Partisanship is the very stuff democratic politics is made of. It cannot be made an excuse for scuttling politics. In this moment of national grief, however, let us put all this aside, and look at the man many of us have known, some intimately as friends and some others not so intimately and not as friends but still from close enough quarters. I may be forgiven if I believe that I belong to the second category. Ever since I came to know him in 1985 when he was well ensconced in the office of Prime Minister, I have often asked myself, and others have asked me, as to what I think of him. The answer his has invariably been the same. "A good man fallen among thieves". That is how I felt about him when he was around and that is how I feel about him after his most tragic death. To say this is not to denigrate politics and politicians. I for one have no desire to engage in this kind of moralistic posturing. On the contrary, I regard politics as an essential part of human existence and practitioners of this highly dangerous and precarious profession as representatives of the larger ethos. Thus if the sandard of our public life is not particularly high, it is because the standard of our private life is also not particularly inspiring. The point I wish to make about Rajiv Gandhi is that he was not meant for politics and politics was not meant for him. Again this is no reflection on Rajiv Gandhi either, politics calls for what one-time British Prime Minister Harold MaCmillan called the killer instinct. Good men often lack this instinct. Rajiv Gandhi certainly did. He could not even be frank becaue he could not bring himself to face any kind of unpleasantness is a face-to-face-encounter.[13]

As is well known, more than a cruel turn in history in the shape of Sanjay Gandhi's death in 1980 pushed Rajiv Gandhi into a role he was

13. Girilal Jain. Neither A Fighter Nor A Deserter. *The Sunday Mail,* 26 May 1991.

obviously not prepared for either in terms of training or temperament. Indira Gandhi was keen that he stepped into the deceased younger brother's place as her possible successor and the she prevalied. The irony of it all is not so much that a "reluctant" Rajiv was pitchforked into the deadly business of politics against his own and Sonia Gandhi's better judgement-I do not believe he was all that reluctant-as that Indira Gandhi too acted partly against her own judgement. She was aware he was too much of a gentleman for the harsh-realities of politics. Or, at least, it seemed to me then. I raised the subject at one of my meetings with her. At the very mention of it, she went into a long monologue on the leadership qualities of Sanjay Gandhi. She did not talk of Sanjay's ruthlessness, determination and passion for power. But it was implicit in what she said. On her statement, Rajiv Gandhi was a study in contrast. I was, of course, not the only person whom Indira Gandhi spoke to in this manner. I know it for a fact that she spole to any number of individuals in this refrain. Many of them concluded that she was putting on an act, as she often did in other matters. Perhaps she was. After all, she was more than proud of being Nehru's daughter, she was a dynast; she was convinced that the Nehrus and, as a corollary, the Gandhis, alone could rule the country and as such determined to do all that she could to ensure that her only surviving son succeeded her. But if she was keen on him, she was also sceptical about him primarily, in my view, on account of his gentlemanly ways. As I saw things, so much had come to hinge, fortunately or unfortunately, on Indira Gandhi that it was vital in the nation's interest that someone should be ready to move into her place if something should happen to her suddenly. And that someone could only be Rajiv Gandhi since by then other Congress leaders had been fully emasculated, or, to put it differently proved to be men of straw. Those who came back into the 'fold' after his death could not possibly stake a claim to succeed her.[14]

To begin with, his role could only be of a flag-bearer for the transition period, the rest depending on his performance and finally on the verdict of the electroate. But that too was not to be. History again took a cruel turn. This time Indira Gandhi herself was moved down and in circumstances which ensured not only that Rajiv Gandhi stepped in as Prime Minister for the transition period, but also that he was given an overwhelming mandate for a full five-year term. Thus, as the Mahatma's assassination helped Nehru sell his approach and consolidate his power, Indira Gandhi's ensured Rajiv Gandhi's succession to her not only as Congress president but also as Prime Minister.[15]

14. *Ibid.*
15. *Ibid.*

A redefinition of political categories appears to have begun-surprisinghly, even before two-thirds of the electorate has voted. The admission by Janata Dal president S.R. Bomai, that a political realignment may well take place after the election, taken together with CPI(M) leader Harkishan Singh Surjeet's assessment of post-poll prospects, is more than a straw in the wind. The SJP's moves for a post-poll deal with the Congress are well known. Significantly, the Jan Morchas leader Arif Mohammad Khan, has now offered to step down in favour of the Congress candidate in Bahraich, in a bid to pool resources to defeat the BJP. Of course, in case the Congress wins a comfortable majority, it need not depend on the Janata Dal and Left parties to form a stable government. But surely, Bommai and Surjeet, not to mention Arif Mohmmad Khan, are looking beyond pure electoral configurations. Their concept of realignment is ideological, not necessarily electoral. What we are witnessing, therefore, are hesitant beginnings of a new redefinition of Indian politics in BJP versus he non-BJP terms. Blind anti-Congressism, which has marked non-Congress politics since Acharya Narendra Dev broke away from the parent party in 1948, is truly over. Instead, political parties are slowly seeking to define themselves vis-a- vis the BJP. The attempt by the forces of Hindutva to recast nationalism in a religious mould, has evidently alarmed the others. Besides, following Rajiv Gandhi's assassination, the Congress may not succeed in exercising the same degree of hegemony over the centrist ground of Indian politics. In the final analysis, political parties are gearing up for a sharp polarisation between the centrist and non-centrist forces.[16] The broadly liberal, secular parameters of Indian nationalism as defined by Jawaharlal Nehru are under challenge. Therefore, those forces which largely accept the Nehruvian definition for centrism, are seeking to rally to preserve this legacy. Of course, there are significant differences of perception among them. It is debatable, for example, whether V.P. Singh's crass pursuit of casteist politics can be accommodated within the matrix of centrism. In any case, the coming together of centrist forces will not be quick or, amount to political unity. But, political polarisation for and against the BJP appears certain. Such a polarisation can be meaningful only if it does not develop into blind, dogmatic anti-BJPism. For, while polarisation of political forces into two distinct categories may be welcome, ecouragement to bigotry of one type against another cannot. Political opposition must be based on argument on principles and not on dogma.

Speculation about the realignment of political forces that may result

16. *The Business and Political Observer,* 29 May 1991.

from an indecisive electoral verdict had of course, started even before Rajiv Gandhi's assassination. What the tragedy has done is to trigger overt moves for such a realignment. The gambit has, predictably, come in the form of proposals for former Congressemn's return to or rehabilitation in the parent party. From inside the Congress, the idea has been canvassed publicly by Vasant Sathe and more discreetly by Sharad Pawar, while its wider appeal has been illustrated by the former Jan Morcha's "unilateral" electoral support for the party and Ramakrishna Hegde's loud political rethinking. Special anxiety for such a reunion has been evinced, for obvious reasons, by luminaries of the Samajwadi Janata Party, if not directly by its ex-Young Turk leader. Subramaniam Swamy's talk of a post-election alliance between the SJP and the Congress I has been followed by Mohan Dharia's spured suggestion for seat adjustments here and now, while Devi Lal's felicitatory message to P.V. Narasimha Rao was markedby more than formal warmth. The Left, too, has been early to hit the realignment trail. After CPI-M leader H.S. Surjeet's significant pronouncements on the subject party general secretary E.M.S. Namboodiripad's "open letter" to the new Congress president hardly shows unwillingness for friendly relations with the Marxists' pet aversion of the past if their preserves of power were allowed to remain intact. The BJP has also been throwing hints that it does not rule out participation in a coalition, though every one of its possible partners in such a set-up sweats implacable hostility to it. As the fate of Dharia's overture shows, a realignment process has little chance of becoming more than a proposition before the completion of the elections. It is too abrupt a departure for the parties concerned to make form their positions, amounting to a repudiation of their own campaign rhetoric, half way through the exercise; and the choice before each of them is unclear in view of the uncertainty about the electoral outcome.[17] The realignment, however, is a distinct possibility, if not an inevitable prospect, in the event of the people's mandate producing a hung Parliament. Its ultimate shape will be decided by the arithmetic of the post-poll situation. While numbers will further or frustrate the reunion and reconciliation moves, the run-up to the elections, particularly their second and third phases, has made two things clear. The capacity of the SJP to influence the process, in the first place, is severly constricted. More importantly, from the voters' point of view, no professed principle or political plank would appear likely to inhibit major political camps in their quest for Sharad Pawar, if the mandate permits no higher hope. We have to be a more open society. We must allow an open and continuing discussion on

17. *The Hindustan Times*, 1 June 1991.

issues that afflict Indian people. Such openness is an assurance that problems will be sorted out in a confrontation-free atmosphere and remedies will be found taking into account the sensitivities of all segments of Indian society. In fact, we ought to texture our twenty-first century India very differently-in simple, uncomplicated and natural way, allowing legitimate political interests to have a free play keeping in view that no political arrangement can sustain itself on negativism. It can only flourish with a definite sense of direction, ideological coherence and action plan. The polarisation manthan can work if political leaders free themselves from the sterility of concepts that have emptied themselves of all meaning. Unfortunately, every political consideration today is reduced to that of electoral interest. In the absence of a principled approach, the present attempt at realignment, looks like a long painful exercise. The realities of Indian politics are too harsh for the Mohan Dharia and the Chandra Shekhars to click at one go. Paralleling these developments is a change in the political sensibilities of the people. So, the real process of realignment can only begin after the poll results. For, the electoral fortunes of different parties will actually set the pace for who aligns with whom, and at what price and for what purpose. The Indian political churning has indeed reached a very interesting stage.[18] With the death of Rajiv Gandhi era that began with Mahatma Gandhiji unifying India, Jawaharlal Nehru laying the foundations of its progress. Indira Gandhi strengthening its roots and structure and Rajiv Gandhi paving the way for it to enter the 21st century has come to an end. India is today at crossroades but the lights that Jawaharlal Nehru had lit are shining bright and should lead us into the future, protecting these lights is the task of every Indian.[19]

Rajiv Gandhi as leader of the Congress was the only person who could hold the country together. With his assassination, separatists have removed the plank on which the stability of the country rested. The country is in deep peril and lies totally exposed to external destabilising forces. He was killed at a time when he seemed to be emerging as the next Prime Minister,[20] The assassination should not be viewed in isolation as it seems to be a part of a bigger game of imperialist forces. Rajiv Gandhi will remain in the hearts of Indians forever.

18. Hari Jai Singh. The polarisation Process. The Business and Political observer, 1 June 1991.
19. K.V.S. Rama Sarma. Jawaharlal Nehru. National Hearld, 27 May 1991.
20. Dhrubajyoti Gupta. Rajiv Gandhi The Telegraph, 27 May 1991.

23
HIS ECONOMIC LEGACY

Any objective assessment of Rajiv Gandhi's performance as Prime Minister or as the leader of the Congress party cannot miss his contribution to the country's economy, and particularly to the evolution of liberal economic policies for faster growth. Whether it was for his youthful, modern outlook or the freshness of his approach to developmental problems, Rajiv Gandhi chartered a new path beckoning the nation to the 21st century a path full of promise and hope. Towards this end, he sought to transform the highly bureaucratised and regulated economic system he inherited from his mother. Indeed, he blazed a new trail by liberalising the industrial licensig policies and by giving a thrust to what are known as the 'sunrise industries.' In the budget he presented himself in 1987, he also gave clear notice to public enterprises to improve their performance in a competitive environment. Unfortunately, later in his tenure his energies were spent more in facing the concerned onslaughts of the opposition over the Bofors issue. This hampered his advance towards further liberalisation of economic policies, especially in regard to foreign private investment. Yet, the success of his policies was reflected in the overall performance of the economy during the eighth Plan period (1985-89), with the GDP exceeding the targetted five per cent growth rate and industrial growth averaging eigh per cent per annum.[1]

Rajiv Gandhi's liberal stance on economic issues is seen in a more crystallised form in the recent Congress manifesto which promises further debureaucratisation, more free flow of foreign investment and a phased withdrawal of state presence in areas where the private or joint sectors have established proven capabilities. His return to power would have triggered new growth impulses in the besieged economy.

The political turmoil the country has been going through ever since the National Front government came to power in December 1989, has taken a heavy toll of the economy. Despite a series of budgetary abd extra-budgetary taxation measures over the past few years, the government revenues are in a bad shape. The trade gap has widened. The Bop situation has worsened after the Gulf crisis. This is reflected in the wideranging import curbs. With mountaing inflation and decelaration in industrial growth, the economy is fast slipping into a quagmire of stagnation. At one stage, it looked as though the country would tide over the BoP crisis before long with the help of an IMF loan. This hope

1. *The Business and Political Observer,* 23 May 1991.

has received a jolt with the assassination of Rajiv Gandhi and the consequent postponement of the remaining poll process. This development will not only further delay the presentation of the Central budget, which is supposed to spell out the fiscal and other policy changes in terms of the IMF requirements, but make the very process of adjustment more difficult. In any case, the prolonged political uncertainly does not inspire confidence among multilateral agencies and donor countries about the country's ability to put its house in order. The task of the new government after the polls will, therefore be more onerous. It will have to take some imaginative steps to augment budgetary as well as foreign exchange resources, besides taking effective steps to put the economy back on the rails. Any further does of direct or indirect taxes will prove counter-productive. The only way out is privatisation of public enterprises to mobilise resources needed for strategic investments, particularly in the infrastructural sector. But it will be necessary to go beyond disinvestment of 20 per cent of government equity in selected public undertakings, in favour of mutual funds and other public financial institutions, as proposed in the interim budget. Similarly, in order to meet the BoP crunch, in addition to approaching the IMF and other donors for long-term concessional loans, a major thrust will have to be given to export and investments by NRIs and other foreign investors.[2]

While political development over the past one-and-a-half years, including the present elections, and the impending post-poll political adjustments are part of the democratic process, the challenges on the economic front have become too serious to brook any complacency. In fact, the success fo democracy lies in our ability to solve the economic problems which touch the very lives of the people. The country has already paid a heavy price for the delay in tackling them. Time is running out.

India was headed for the second type of crisis well before Rajiv Gandhi came to power. The rate of growth of the government's non-developmental expenditure had been far in excess of the growth of its revenues ever since the early 60s. It was hence only a matter of time before the government's finances deteriorated to the point where it had to borrow larger and larger amounts for the banking system and going for more and more deficit financing, just to meet its annual (revehue) expenditures. This point was reached in 1981-82. Since a persistent budget deficit is also one of the reasons for the persistent trade deficit, India would have fallen into a debt trap at most three or four years later than it actually did, even if Rajiv had not tried to step up the pace of

2. *Ibid.* May 24 1991.

development. The most significant feature of the step up in growth that took place after Rajiv Gandhi became the Prime Minister was that it was achieved not by increasing the ratio of investment to the gross national product, but by enacting important policy reforms that raised the productivity of the industrial sector. Mr Gandhi was the first Indian Prime Minister to recognise that the economic policies of Nehru and Indira Gandhi had outlived their purpose and become millstones around the country's neck. Protection against foreign competition, which was originally intended to give, infant Indian industries room to grow and one day challenge their rivals in the industrialised world, had instead encouraged the use of obsolete technology to the point where almost nothing India manufactured apart from textiles and garments could find a buyer outside the country. In the same way, policies like industrial licensing, which were originally intended to ensure the efficient use of scarce resources resulted in excessively capital intensive projects on the one hand, and caused enormous delays in investment. These created a regime of permament shortages that shielded producers from domestic competition and made it unnecessary for them to use their plants and their capital resources more efficiently.[3]

Lastly, laws meant to prevent monopolies created them instead, by shielding existing producers from competition from new entrants into the industry. The experience of other countries has shown that the moment of truth comes for such autarchic economies when they find that they are unable to earn enought from exports to pay for imports. They have then to choose between imposing serve curbs on imports and bringing down the growth rate, borrowing heavily abroad to finance imports and thus postponing the day of reckoning for a few years, and making the necessary root-and- branch reform of economic policies that would, after a transition period, enable the country to emerge with an outward looking, export-oriented economy that is able to pay for its growing exports. The third option also requires a large does of foreign borrowing to meet the rise in imports that takes place during the transition period but this phases itself as exports rise. Rajiv Gandhi's government adopted the third of these options, but because the reforms it made were not thorough-going enough he unintentionally ended with the second opetion. The fiscal and foreign debt crisis that hit the country in 1990, was a direct result. The sweeping reforms that his government introduced in 1985 and 1986 have been too well catalogued to need repetition. Some of those were a drastic reduction in the rigours of industrial licensing, a host of measures to encourage

3. Prem Shankar Jha. Rajiv's Economic Legacy. *The Business and Political Observer*, 25 May 1991.

the growth of new industries; a sharp reduction in the scope of the monopolies and restricitive trade practices act; reforms of direct taxation, a major liberalisation of the import of capital goods and of components for sophisticated manufactures under a phased manufature programme; and a succession of carefully worked out reforms of the Indian capital market that were designed to make people to put more of their savings in the capital markets and less in the banks. The result was that private investment jumped in 1985-86 by 40 per cent and continued to soar thereafter, that the share markets went on an 10 months long boom; that GNP grew at 5.5 per cent annum and the rate of industrial growth went up a full 1-5 percent from around seven per cent a year between 1980-81 and 1984-85 and 8.5 per cent between 1984-85 and 1989-90; and that exports rose more rapidly than at any time. But the reforms failed in two respects: they did not generate enough additional revenues cover the government's rising expenditures, and party as a result of this, they failed to raise exports by enough to cover the ising import bill. The immediate cause of the fiscal crisis that Rajiv Gandhi left behind in 1989 was the failure of the Public sector to generate the expected resources. Faced with the slow growth of revenues, he resorted to borrowing to make good the deficit and implement the seventh plan fully. But behind this lay the incompleteness of his reforms. For instance, the reform of industrial licensing left out the MRTP and FERA companies to whom all licensign procedures concinued to be applied as before. This meant that the very companies that could most quickly deploy resources in a new area of production and thereby prevent existing companies from making abronmal profits because of shortage were kept out for long period as before, so that the shortages never diappeared.[4]

Socialists of all brands agree that socialism is a means for social reconstruction. Nehru and for that matter Rajiv Gandhi starts from the same basis. Nehru evolved his own ideas about socialism and gave it a practical shape. Writing to his daughter Indira in 1933, Nehru said, "Socialism, I have told you, is of many kinds. There is general agreement, however, that it aims at the control by the state of the means of production that is, land and mines and factories and thelike, and the means of distribution, like railways. etc, and also banks and similar institutions. The idea is that individuals should not be allowed to exploit any of these, methods or institutions or the labout of others to their own personal advantage", (Glimpses of World History, Vol. II, 851-52). Truth must triumph, said Gandhi. That mankind must survive and cooperate was the clarion call of Nehru and Rajiv Gandhi to the whole

4. *Ibid.*

world. His greatest contribution was the conviction that "India will pull itself up by work and sacrifice. If it consents to do so, but never, never under theknout". Nehru the socialist, wanted to establish a society where the suffering people are fully covered by various social security measures. Nehru, the economist, desired to fulfil this dream only as a by-product of development, not as its prequisite.[5] A down-to-earth social reformer, no cause was dearer to his heart than wipingl out the tears from the face of every citizen of India. Today, the Nehru philosophy serves as an inspiration and illuminates the right path more brightly.

Rajiv's grand-father, Jawaharlal Nehru visualised an incresingly greater role for the public sector in the economy. That philosophy is now under attack and that light he had lit is now facing the threat of being extinguished Nehru was aware that to preserve the Gandhian contribution, it was necessary which could not be achieved by merely introducing adult franchise. Adult franchise in a country like India dominated by illiteracy was a double-edged weapon. And as Marx said universal suffrage may give the right to govern but does not give the right to govern but does not give the power to govern. Nehru obtained for the Congress--which to him was an embodiment of India-the right to govern. He sought to accomplish the more difficult task of power to govern by striving for a participative democracy. On the one hand the ushering in of the public sector had promised and begun yielding results to the masses and on the other Nehru set out to decentralise the decision-making process so as to give the masses the right to rule themselves. For after all a nation of India's dimensions and complexity could not be ruled but by its own people. The various measures Nehru had brought forward to take democracy in a true sense to the grassroot level were part of his desire to generate in each and every Indian an abiding interest in the political system of the country. Accomplishing this in a nation of diverse religious faiths was a massive problem, unless the people of all faiths work in union and with a common commitment Nehru always had a secular outlook and this helped him in evolving the secular policy of India, though he was religious in an undogmatic sense. That he had succeeded in his mission is amply proved by the contributions each community has made to India's overall development. There were of course, defects in Nehru's policies but they were certainly much less compared to any other statesman. If Mahatma Gandhi had prepared the nation and handed it over to Nehru, Nehru had placed the nation firmly on the road to progress and glory and bequethed it to Indira Gandhi During her entire tenure as the Prime Minister, she

5. N.C. Joshi. Nehru's Vision, *Patriot*, 27 May 1991.

worked with total devotion to further strengthen the roots of India's democracy, secularism and socialism. The great leaps the public sector had made India so strong and self-reliant that even the World Bank had to pay tributes to India's economic management of those years. Indira Gandhi had promoted secularism in every sphere of life. It is not a mere accident that during her tenure as the Prime Minister three miniority leaders - Dr. Zakir Hussain Fakhuddin Ali Ahmed and Zail Singh-were chosen by the Congress as its Presidential candidates and they occupied the exalted place of the Presidentship of India. The biggest test to India's political system came during her lifetime when her party was defeated in 1977 elections and she played the role of an opposition leader. He triumphant return to power in 1980 was an eloquent testimoney to India's democratic convictions and commitment. Those three torches which proclaim the basic policies of this country passed into the hands of Rajiv Gandhi in December 1984 and he, like his mother, live for his convictions and laid down his life.[6]

There is no doubt that Indira Gandhi's brutal assassination paved the way to Rajiv Gandhi's leadership of the party and the government so soon, and amidst such thundering triumph. But then all political parties in every democratic country tend to select its leader according to the perceived popular support behind the individual, in order to ensure the party's success at the hustings. So it was inevitable under the circumstances for the Congress to select Rajiv at that point of time.

But, then, the people of the country rejected the Congress, headed by Rajiv Gandhi in 1989, largely on the basis of unfounded charges of personal corruption levelled against him by his former collegues who ganged-up with even the most retrograde BJP. Rajiv Gandhi and his party accepted this democratic verdict instead of trying to exercise any dynastic rule, which never get over-turned by democratic poll mandate. The national history, thus, amply bears out that the slogan of "Nehru-Gandhi dynastic rule" is bunkum, whether Sonia Gandhi is ultimately persuaded to head the party or not. It is preffered by either lazy minds or rival politicians with narrow, propaganda purposes. Democracy and dynastic rule are alien to each other, and no amount of sophistry on the score can alter this fundamental contradiction, even if partisan minds fail to reckon this basic incompatibility due to their blinkers.[7]

The whole of Eighties saw a sustained industrial growth of eight per cent, thanks largely to these and other liberalisation policies. But these very policies also led to large-scale imports of components and raw

6. K.V.S. Rama Sarma. Jawaharlal Nehru. *National Herald*, 27 May 1991.
7. Ashis Barman. It was not Dynastic Rule. *Patriot* 1 June 1991.

materials to sustain. The country went in for large borrowings and several analysis now describe the industrial growth of the Eighties as debt-financed and hold it largely responsible for the balance of payments crisis the economy is facing now. But the other view is that if Rajiv Gandhi had continued to remain in office even after 1989, he would have taken adequate measures to halt the downslide. In the area of fiscal policy, Gandhi introduced a longterm fiscal policy that envisaged a stable direct taxes regime. However, these reforms could not be implemented as political controversies overtook Gandhi's interest in economic affairs. The other casualty was the proposed capital market reforms and changes in the public sector. One of the promises Gandhi made time and again was to free the public sector from the cluthches of bureaucracy and allow it to function as autonomous companies. But during his five-year tenure, he could not even bring out the promised white paper on public sector, which was expected to set out a new path for public sector undertakings. Whatever Gandhi's failings, officials agree that the former prime minister brought in a whiff of fresh air to the government. His personal charm, a questioning mind, willingness to experiment with change were qualities that far surpassed his failings. And when the history of Indian economic progress is written, the five years when he was at the helm of affarirs should stand out as a watershed.[8]

Like most Indians, I am in a state of shock. Yet I can't refuse the request from 'The Economic Times, to say something about Rajiv Gandhi. It is not possible to be objective or to maintain bureaucratic detachment. In the days to come, a lot will be written about him by persons more qualified than I. They will write much more competently about his leadership qualities, personal charm, courtesy and calm in the face of adversity. The image which is most vivid in my mind is that of 1987 when as the prime minister, Rajiv Gandhi as the prime minister assumend temporarily the charge of finance minister. The budget was to be formulated. The officials of the ministry spent nearly 100 hours, spread over all times of the day and night, discussing various budget proposals and the economic strategy to tackle the problems of the day. It was at once apparent that his interest in matters economic was deep and abiding. Otherwise, he could not have spent so many hours, despite his other responsibilities, in free and totally frank discussions on various proposals. While he shot down many a favourite bureaucratic idea, we one our part can also claim to have succeeded in changing his views on many ideas that he tossed around. This was a measure of his eclecticism. A ver y interesting debate took place on the question of

8. A.K. Bhattacharya. The Rajiv Years. *The Economic Times*, 27 May 1991.

restricting the budget deficit. As usual, demands were many and resources were few. The previous year's budget deficit was high and it was felt that the next year's deficit should be much lower. I think the figure that was finally decided was something around Rs. 5,200 crore. The issue on which there was a difference of opinion was whether the Prime Minister should also give a firm advance commitment not to exceed this figure. One view was that such a commitment at the level of the prime minister will ensure discipline. The other view was that it will make the budget inflexible. There was also a risk that if the commitment was not kept, the Prime Minister's credibility could suffer. After listening to both sides, Rajiv Gandhi decided that if the budget deficit had to be reduced, a firm commitment should not only be give but it also much be adhered to. In a well-known paragraph, he gave his categorical views on the need to keep the deficit down and announced his personal commitment to keep the actual deficit within the projected level. This was a risky announcement and could have been avoided without anybody complaining. But he took the risk and the commitment was actually kept.[9]

There is also the image of 1985, the Prime Minister just having taken office and full of new ideas about tax reforms in India's fiscal system. A new bold budget was presented. Several innovations were made. Later in the year, for the first time in India's fiscal history, a long-term fiscal policy was introduced. Then there is the image of 1988, when the balance of payments problem was beoming actue. A decision was taken at the level of the prime minister to give a strong boost to exports. A cabinet committee was formed under the Prime Minister's chairmanship. Meetings were held almost daily. A number of dicisions were taken and exports started showing a sharp increase. Onver these years, there were several discussions about the management of the banking system. There were controversies about specific individuals, union activities and the performance of individual banks. The Prime Minister listened, went into the pros and cons of each argument and then took a decision. At one time, there was a controversy in Parliament about some large loan transaction. Both the Finance Minister and the Prime Minister were angry, asked for full facts and decided to set up a committee to go into all aspects objectively. Contrary to the tradition of secrecy, the report of the committee was made public. Suitable action was taken after consideration of the advice of the governor of the Reserve Bank of India. The first instinct of the political authority was to dismiss the entire top management of several banks. But on being

9. Dr. Bimal Jalan. He was Impatient with Slow Change. *The Economic Times,* 23 May 1991.

informed that this may have international and domestic reprecussions, the decision was reviewed, after some persuasion that confidence in India's banking system would not be allowed to suffer. Many more images, comes to my mind. On a brief visit to Delhi from Washington, I called on him the very day that he gave up office as Prime Minister. He was calm and confiden enquiring about life in Washington and talked at length about the unfinished talks. There was a reception in honour of Nelson Mandela, where he enquired about the impact of the Gulf crisis and how India should tackle it. He gave his own political perception-how the cirsis was likely to be played out, and wished us good luck. At the President's reception on January 26, 1991, he once again reverted to the impact of the Gulf crisis and wanted to know more about the economic implications and where we would go from here. There was a domestic controversy and he wanted to make sure that what he said formally took into account India's bilateral economic interest. How do I sum up his vision of India and its economy? There is the sheer Nehruvian vision of a strong, independent and self-reliant India. There is also the vision of a technocrat, wishing India to be much more competitive, internationally oriented and technologically avanced. There is impatience with the slow peace of change, the difficulties of making the economy move faster within the social and political constraints. Above all, there is a strong vision of India playing an important role in international affairs as a Third World country. And a clear perception that this required India's economy to become more dynamic and selfsustaining. There were, of course, faults. And mistakes were also made. But I am unable to talk about them today.[10]

At his first major press conference after he had become Prime Minister, Rajiv Gandhi was asked how he would like to describe his government, since Indira Gandhi had earlier promised 'a government that works'. The son's response was quick: 'a govenment that works faster'. Certainly, the economy moved faster during the Rajiv years. Growth accelerated to 5.6 per cent during the seventh Five-Year Plan (1985-90), faster than during any previous quinquennium. Industrial growth averaged over 8 per cent. The numbers below the poverty line dropped rapidly from 38 per cent to 28 per cent, according to the official statistics. There was also a noticeable uplifting of the over-all economic mood. There was the boom in the consuption of consumer goods, the rapid burgeoning of the middle class, the exponential growth of the capital markets. There was tremendous growth in the number of new industrial projects (as reflected in industrial licences, letters of intent and registrations with the DGTD), a spurt in foreign collabora

10. *Ibid.*

tions as Indian industry went on a modernisation spree, and a long-delayed boom in exports, which more than doubled in the four years between 1985-86 and 1989-90. It is this over-all climate of optimism and accelerated growth by which the Rajiv Gandhi years will be remembered. But there was the downside as well; growing budget deficits, stagnant sayings, and the mounting foreign debt, which by the time he demited office in 1989, totalled a staggering Rs. 100,000 crore-and made India the world's fourth largest debtor-nation. Clearly, growth came at a price, and it would seem that the country was in some senses living on borrowed prosperity. Impatient with the pace of change, and unwilling to accept the limitations within which the economy had to function. Rajiv frequently lost an inherited Nehruvian temper. He called the planning commission a 'bunch of Jokers', had a raging argument with the same body over its attempts to limit the growth of civil aviation and dressed down senior officials at a review meeting on the technology missions. New initiatives flowed by the dozen. There were the technology missions, a new education policy, new employment policies, laws proposed to drastically upgrade the role and powers of panchayats and manicipal bodies, an attempt (in some cases shortlived) to restructure government ministries; education became human resource development, housing became urban development, an ommibus transport ministry and an omnibus industry ministry which included company affairs and the department of public enterprises, an internal security minister.[11]

The underlying theme was modernism, typified by the talk in the first couple of years of getting ready for the 21st century. This some times boiled down to trivia; brown paper government files with traditional red tape gave way in the Primi Minister's office to plastic files with elastic bands that snapped a file shut and gave greater confidentiality, Computers were ordered to be placed in most government offices (but it took a while before senior officials began using them, and many of them never did.) But even before he assumed office, there was the concern with telecommunications, and the active induction of an unknown non- resident like Sam Pitroda to try a wholly new approach to telecom technology development, through the creation of the Centre for Development of Telematics. Earlier, in the 1980-81 period, whortly after he entered politics he played a role in shaping the government's response to the second oil shock of 1979, by emphasising the need for repid increase of demostic oil production; which trebled in the sixth plan (1980-85). The approach was often target oriented, the mission approach, not holistic or systemic. So many villages to be given drinking

11. *The Economic Times*, 23 May 1991.

water, so many to have drought programmes. The government's speedy response to the drough of 1987-88 (overplayed, but serious nevertheless) was such as to ensure speedy disbursal of funds to the state governments, and for the Prime Minister himself to tour the villages asking questions as to how the programmes were working, and whether people were benefiting. Each tour ended with a detailed meeting of central and concerned state officials, where on the spot decisions were taken on the problems that had been spotted during the day's tour. There was a purposefulness here that few Prime Ministers have shown, a willingness to get into the nilty-gritty of government programmes. The approach of fiscal policy was equally forthright. Asked in the first few weeks of his period in office as to what he throught budget policy should be, he said that taxation policies should be simplified tax rates mode reasonable and collection effective. The 1985 Budget had his stamp all over it. So did the unsuccessful move to impose fiscal discipline through a long-term fiscal policy. Economics liberalisation came into its own during the Rajiv years. In retrospect, it would appear that all too little has been achieved, that the Indian economy remains among the most controlled in the world. But a serious attempt was neverthelass made to achieve modernisation, world scale production, and internatinal competitiveness. The approach was often adhoc, with no clear step-by-step programme outlined for achieving the ultimate objective. Nevertheless the initiatives flowed fast and furious; minimum capacities instead of maximum ones, broadhanding of licences, a white paper on the public sector (which never saw the light of day despite several drafts) an export thrust through the formation of a cabinet committee on exports which at times met daily. When he came accross a voluntary environmental group that had done path-breading studies on the degree of degradation that had taken place, he took the unprecedented step of asking the group to make a formal presentation to the full cabinet, and then followed it up by arranging for similar presentations to all MPs and then separetely to the various consultative committees of parliamentarians attached to the different ministries. But his very first initiative after assuming office-the creation of a National Wasteland Development Board to achieve five million acres of afforestation on wastelands annually-came to nought, with the targets missed by a mile and the board itself caught in unseemly squabbles that made it a divided house. Devoid of the Congressman's traditinonal suspiciousness of the private sector, he inducted several leading industrialists into government and public sector functioning-Ratan Tata and Rahul Bajaj were made and Indian Airlines, respectively, in yet another experiment that failed. And when Soviet President Mikhail Gorbachov came visiting, the man chosen to give a detailed late night presentation to the

Soviet leader was not nay of the government's leading scientist-bureaucrats but the then chairman of Hindustan Lever, Dr. A.S. Ganguly. There was a refreshing willingness to deaprt from conventional methods in many of these initiatives. The results were not always what he intended. But Rajiv's years in office will be remembered for the serious attempt that was made to give a new direction to the Indian economy. The results were mixed, but the country was the richer for it.[12]

Bankers in Bombay reacted with shock and indignation at the assassination of Rajiv Gandhi.

Chairman and managing director of the Industrial credit and Investment Corporation of India (ICICI) Narayan Vaghul said that India's credit worthiness abroad would not be adversely affected if after the elections a stable party emerges and forms a government. It would not be correct to judge things at present since we are in the middle of an electoral battle and the country should be able to come out of the crisis. Mr. Vaghul expressed his shock at the assassination of Rajiv Gandhi which he described as tragic.

Executive director of the State Bank of India S.M. Parande describing the assassination as "terrible" said that it would change the course of our history. Mr. Parande foresaw a change in the direction that the country would take now. It is an organisation's strength and momentum that sees it through the troubled times, he added.

Also optimistic was general manager of the Canara Bank Mutual Fund B.R. Acharya. He too refused to see the possibility of a hung Parliament. He was hopeful of stable government at the centre and said that with stability one could tide over the economic crisis.

Chairman of the State Bank of India M.N. Gopria expressed shock at what he called "dastardly attack" on Mr. Gandhi. He hoped that the people would show restraint and the country would come out of this crisis.

Executive director of the Bombay stock Exchange (BSE) M.R. Mayya too expressed condolences for the departed leader. Mr. Mayya hoped the country has the forbearance and fortitude to see through these sad days.

Seeing it as a good opportunity for the Political parties to coalesce partner of the Mecklai Financial and Commercial Services (MFCS) Jamal Mecklai felt that it is the best time for all the parties and leaders to become friends once again and concentrate on lifting the country out of this impasse.

12. *Ibid.*

Welcoming the idea of national government being mooted in some circles, he said that from the political standpoint this seems to be the best time for political joint ventures. A national government consisting of membners of all parties which matter will do the country a lot of good, he added. He described the situation today as one where 'fingers are crossed but the hearts have to be filled up with smiles'. He emphasised his optimism saying that we can only go in one direction from here-up.

The Standing Conference of Public Enterprises (SCOPE) Chairman Moosa Raza condemned the barbaric act and termed it as a great loss to the country.

Raza described him as a friend and staunch supporter of the public sector.

One of the speeches that Mr Gandhi delivered at the inauguration of the International Congress of Public enterprises '87' organised by SCOPE reads: "The public sector has been made the tool of our development process. It is the cutting edge of our development and whenever you are in the forefront your always have more problems".

Raza said that now that Rajiv Gandhi belongs to history. we the people of India owe it to ourselves to carry forward the ideals of peace, harmony, secularism, modernism and democracy he lived for and died for.

In his message of condolence to Sonia Gandhi chairperson of Modi Enterprises K.N. Modi stated that the entire nation was grieved on the tragic assassination. He said, "In this hour of grief, there is a need that all of us should keep calm and peace, avoid violence and remain united to face the many challenges before the country with courage and determination and build a modern and prosperous Indiaby following the progressive and dynamic policies of Rajiv Gandhi, who was a champion of the cause of the masses and strived hard to make India competitive and liberalising economic policies. "The biggest homage to him will be complete his half done task by eradicating poverty and unemployment and solving many difficult problems facing the country".

The president of the Federation of Associations of small Industries of India, A.N. Srinivasa Rao, has expressed deep shock at the dastardly assassination. He recalled the liberalisation measures initiated by Rajiv Gandhi and the introduction of long-term fiscal policy as well as the restructuring of exercise duties by means of MODVAT, which enabled the small scale sector to have an edge in competing with the large sector. He exhorted the small units to translate the vision of Rajiv Gandhi of a strong India into reality.

We have to see that the time involved in evaluation and in licensing is reduced. We quibble over small amounts of differences may be by a few crores of rupees one supplier might be cheaper and another supplier might be more expensive; but in evaluating that, we take three years; and then there is no meaning in one supplier being cheaper than the other because we are paying almost one-third more than what we would be paying in the first place. Not only that by the time we take a decision we get outdated technology, because we have been arguing about it for so long.[13]

I am not an economist and, at the same time, I must say that on most such occassion economists disagree with each other as much as they agree with each other. When we talk about something like the Seventh Plan, the questions that are really in front of us are the political choices on the economic plans that have been given to us by the economists. The exercise has to be as political as it is purely economic because ultimately what we are working for is the development of the poorest people in the country.[14]

If we look at the performance of our economy in the past six years, since the Congress government came back, the economy has done extermely well in a situation where the economies of major countries were in difficulties, and the economies of developing countries were seeing inflation rates of 300 per cent 400 per cent and even close to 1000 per cent. Under those conditions, we have had a growth rate of approximately 5 per cent and an inflation rate well under control. Sir, we do not take credit for that. Indiraji looked after the country during those days. But what we are looking towards now is the future. The future is not going to be a joyride or a cakewlk. This is going to require trementous hard work. If we are not willing to do that, if we are not willing to give that much for our country, then we do not deserve a free, independent country. The basic framework was 93 per cent of our own resources for development, not to go running with a bowl to other countries. We had an easy way out. Other countries have taken the easy way out. But the result is visible. We will not allow India to go that way. We will not look at short-term solutions that may compromise the sovereignty of our country.[15]

To remove poverty, we have to look at technology. If we think for a minute what we mean by removing poverty, ultimately it comes down to improving the level of technology that is available to ourpeople. I am talking of just the level, not make the villager run a super computer,

13. *Rajiv Gandhi on Economy*. New Delhi. New Delhi, Lok Sabha 13 April 1983.
14. *Ibid.* 16 December 1985.
15. *Ibid.* 5 March 1986.

but improving his plough, improving the seeds, improving the fertiliser-that is all technology. So when we talk of development, when we talk of progress, what we are really looking for is how technology can be applied where it is needed most. In India it is needed most in the fields of farmers; in homes of our rural folk. It is needed most, to benefit the poorest, the most deprived in India. Our science and technology thrust must be in socially relevant areas. Wherever we have concentrated our efforts, we have made tremendous strides in science and technology. We are very lose to the forntline of development. At the same time, there are areas where our efforts have been diffused and we have not achieved what we should have achieved.[16]

Our idea and concept is not to change direction every year. It is the basic policy which has been developing from the freedom movement throughout our Independence. It is for continuing along this road that this budget gives us direction. So, those that are looking for a new direction, of course, will be disappointed. We have also done a number of things during the past two years which have perhaps made the budget a little less exciting. But that is a very deliberate thing.[17]

We are always in danger of getting too engrossed in the minutiae of development. Yes, statistics and indices are important, but we must look to the larger vision of India. India has mattered in the world. We have led in the world of ideas. Our major contribution has been to enduring values and standards, to the soul and the spirit of humankind. Our national task is to take India again to its rightful places of the front rank of human civilisation. Development is an essential tool in this endeavour, but the real challenge is the response to what lies beyond mere development and more growth. To that great task the nation is summoned in this fortieth year of our Independence.[18]

What have you done to the economy? In spite of a very good monsoon, perhaps the best monsoon for decades, inflation is running higher than ever before. Who is suffering? How did it happen? Last time, I pointed out to the Prime Minister that wheat and rice is costing too much. He said let them eat cement. you are in thid House. What has happened to the foreign exchange reserves? Tax collections are down. Where is the performance of this Government? Foreign exchange reserves are down between Rs. 3,000 crore to Rs, 4,000 crore. They were never so low before. And I am told they are depleting at the rate of Rs. 1.200 crore to Rs. 1,500 crore a month. You have got foreign exchange only for two or three months. You are going at the right time,

16. *Ibid.*
17. *Ibid.* 13 March 1987.
18. *Ibid.* 2 March 1988.

I do not know who is coming. Whoever is coming, is going to be in trouble with the economy you are leaving. Now the word is that you are going to do something that we have never done before. You are going to sell the gold of India....You are going to sell Rs. 2,000 crore worth of gold and this includes the gold that was collected during the chinese aggression. It was donated by the poorest, the weakest, from the villages. What is happening to the BoP?[19]

India's industrial policies are mired in confusion. For decades India's leaders shared a dislike for the use of the market, and imposed state controls over the private sector, promoted and protected the public sector, put a disproportionate share of resources into in dustrial rather than agrarian development emphasised an import substitution policy that encourged inefficiency and non-competitive industries, discouraged the growth of export-oriented industries, and restricted foreign investment.

India's politicians and intellectuals were proud of their country's commitment to self-reliance, and to a strategy of development that avoided the harshness of communism and the selfish materialism of capitalism. In the 1950s and '60s it was a strategy that won sympathy from many of India's friends aborad. Today, few believe that this is a workable strategy for the nineties. The collapse of command economies in the Soviet Union and eastern Europe, the effort to create market-oriented economies in these countries and in China, the extraordinary economic successes in east Asia, and the impressive growth rates of Indonesia, Malaysia and Thailand call for radical rethinking. To his credit, Rajiv Gandhi and his associates began in this direction, but their liberalisation policies proved to be slow and halfhearted. And now that the country is faced with deficits in the budget and in the balance of payments, the old protectionist instincts have returned. While former communist countries for foreign investment, the Indian Left clings to old slogans about multinational corporations. While Hungary, Poland and Czechoslovakia painfully seek to make their industries internationally competitive, the Indian government is restricting imports. And while governments else where are developing schemes for privatistation, the Indian government continues to run large, inefficient public enterprises and even manages hotels. It is not only an ideological commitment to socialism that inhibits reform. The system of discretionary controls provides financial benefits to India's politicians and bureaucrats. Politicians seeking votes and money, officials who take a cut, and anti-capitalist intellectuals all shares a common interest in avoiding, radical reform. V.P. Singh's promise to incre-

19. *Ibid.* 7 November 1990.

ase the number of OBCs in the administration and to elected bodies was an offer to share the spoils of office, not a promise of social justice for the poor. In one election after another India's parties have promised relief to the poor, but by almost any measure the poor have been neglected. Take just one example: education policy. Compared to other developing countries India has put more resources into higher education, and less into primary schools, and less into parimary schools. While other developing countries have insisted that all children attended school, India's Education Ministry and the state government (excepting Kerala) have taken the position that poor families have the right to keep their children at home. The result is that 60 per cent of all children who enter first grade drop out of school by the fifth standard. India is now the largest contributor to world illiteracy. Millions of children are in the labour force, depriving adults of employment, India's rural women remain illiterate. And yet no political party in India not even the parties of the Left, has launched an aggressive campaign for compulsory primary school education.[20]

The reform of the MRTP laws only raised the celing on total assets for exemption from the act, but did not relase the strictures against interconnected enterprises. As a result, they had less than a quarter of the desired was confined to the income tax, where they increased the income declared by over 150 per cent, but the much larger evasion that is taking place in excise duties was ignored although plans to tackle it by moving from excise duties to the value added tax had been prepared as far back as October 1985. Import liberalisation structure that had not been turned outwards and was content to produce for the domestic market alone. Rajiv Gandhi cannot be blamed for this. It is not the function of a Prime Minister to pursue every decision the government takes to ensure that it is correctly implemented. For that he must rely in his cabinet colleagues and the senior bureacracy who must in turn understand his worldview and share his goals. In his case neither of these conditions was fulfilled. His cabinet colleagues still treated the mixed economy as a religious incantation and the bureaucracy saw in liberalisation a threat to their power and self-importance. The incompleteness of Rajiv restruggles that ensued within the Congress and the government. In a vast and heterogeneous country like ours, such a profound change in thinking cannot be brought about overnight. Nor can it be dictated even by a Prime Minister backed by 401 members in the Lok Sabha.

But despite their incompleteness Rajiv Gandhi reforms started a process that cannot be reversed. As the policy makers will soon learn,

20. Myron Weiner. Old Thinking is the Problems, *The Time Of India*, 26 May 1991.

the double crisis caused by his liberalisation policies can only be resolved by completing the process of economic restructuring that he began and not by trying to go back to the autarchic, snails pace growth of the past. Rajiv may have left behind an economic crisis, but it was a benevolent crisis born out of growth, whose resolution will lead to still more growth. The challenge of completing the transformation that he began is his legacy to the country.[21]

Rajiv's liberalisation gave rise to unfettered consumerism and in this, entertainment electronics (colour television, audio and viedo cassete recorders, white goods such as washing machine microwaves ovens and colour photographs played a major part.

The story of the television industry was more of less on the same lines as that of computers where imports took place like nobody's business and TV sets were offered in price ranges that catered to the rich as well as the lower middle class. Not to forget the host of modern tow-wheelers manufactured with foreign collaboration. These two-whellers entered the market in the name of competition and could be seen neatly lined up in modern showrooms. All these items had a market and sold like hot cakes. For, it catered to a certain section of the population with the wherewithal to satiate their urge for such products, entertainment electronic items in particular. While the upper starts had the required funds for the purpose, others went in for such purchase on a demonstration effect, even if it be on bank finance at a higher interest. In the rural areas, while the landed gentry had the capacity for such purchases, it also percolated down to the landless to a certain extent, may be in the form of a black and white TV set. The growth and modernisation was lopsided for it is pitiable to see in the outskirts of metros (labour class slums) TV antennae sticking out of palmleaf thatched roof which may be leaking during the monsoons. Needless to say that exports to recover the foreign exchange spent on imports was minimal, and planned indigenisation through the phased manufacturing programme was essentially on paper. Besides, the QSS colour photography shops which have mushroomed everywhere (every colony can boast of a minimum of two to three) have no way of recovering the foreign exchange spent on imports of the expensive machines and cater to the interest and hobbies of a certain class. When the fault in the policies were realised, it was too late for when the import duties were raised to check the runway growth, the prospects of exports receded further while the demand in the domestic market was still thriving. Of course, the thriving demand for consumer durables led to a sharp rise

21. Prem Shanker Jha Rajiv's Economic legacy, *The Business and Political Observer,* 25 May 1991.

in the manufacturing growth rate to eight per cent with the subsector showing a rise of as much as 13-14 per cent. But this was not the growth pattern the country had wished for.

For the industry as a whole, he cut tax rates, increased the limit of MRTP companies of Rs 100 crore from Rs 20 crore, delicensed certain sectors sectors selectively (including computers and electronics) and fixed minimum economic sizes for with standing open competition. However, the essential fallacy lay in his not being able to halt the squandering of foreign exchange in non-essentials. In fact, to keep going, the country went in for short-term market borrowings from all available sources. In fact, Rajiv's economic policy lost track the moment he fell out with V.P. Singh and got surrounded by a self-seeking caucus. The main culprits were certain bureaucrats who, while realising that the economy was going astray, did previous little to sound warning signals and let it drift for feat of earning the wrath of the powers that-be. In fact, the persistent signals of a famous economist was given short shrift. And then started the decline. The image of the visionary was gone, self-seekers were at work to rake in profits from whatever avenues possible. Through bilateral aid packages for power projects even it spelt the death of the premier power unit in the public sector. Bitter critics note the present economic mess has its roots in Rajiv's policies. Besides, the sunrise industries are now in the midst of a recession and battling for survival.[22]

Sometimes back-when they were basking in their new-found friendship-Prime Minister Chandra Shekhar stated: 'What great sin has been committed if he (Rajiv Gandhi) accepted Rs 60 crore as commission? Is it such as catastrophe which will make or mar the country's future? "That the country's Prime Minister should condone larceny and graft at the highest level only reveals the depths to which political morality-and indeed public apathy has sunk. The ramifications are obvious. If a Prime Minister is permitted to pocket Rs 60 crore, then a secretary to the government can pocket Rs 60 lakhs, a policeman Rs 60,000 and a peon Rs 6,000 with impunity. In semi literate developing societies like ours, the values of leaders percolate down the line. If a prime minister can get away with making a private fortune-or at least is believed to have done so-then why not, goes the rationale, every private citizen. Corruption and graft have always existed in India at various levels. But their institutionalisation is catastrophic. If we intend condoning larceny from the public exchequer, the police and the judiciary would have no role. We might as well disland them. The Bofors issue dragged the country through a traumatic phase. Gandhi

22. Ashok Dasgupta. Rajivonomics. *The Sunday Mail,* 26 May 1991.

ıost his prime ministership due to his alleged involvement in the deal. V.P. Singh promised to uncover all facts within a fortnight of his assuing office. He failed do so. And now Cahndra Shekar asserts, that there is no sin, if Rajiv Gandhi did accept the commissions. What is a citizen to make out of this schizophrenic political environment? Is there anyone whom a citizen can trust any more? The truth about Bofors should see the light if only to vindicate the innocent and bring the really guilty to book. Whilst the rest of the world is forging ahead on the wheels of technology, we continue to wallow in the sludge and slush, created by politicians who have neither any conscience nor any shame left.[23]

Rajiv Gandhi pushed the momentum of economic development to a new high. The rate of economic growth had jumped up to an extraordinary 5.1 per cent during his stewardship and inflation and been restricted to below the double digit. Industrial production was also expanding fast. The percentage of people below the poverty line had declined from over fifty per cent to less than thirty per cent. Do we really have no remind ourselves how preciptious has been the economic decline in the last two years more so during these twelve months of agonising instability and economic brinksmanship? Rajiv Gandhi would have restored the economic momentum without which all talk of stability, employment and social justice is pure moonshine.[24]

Rajiv Gandhi believed that real strength of a country came from inside and its own sources. He was convinced that once a country embarked upon a new technological path and modernised its industry, its foreign policy outlook and perceptions would undergo a change to make the policy more productive in terms os acceptability. One of the areas that received immediate and a close attention from his after be assumed the Prime Ministership was the relations with other countries. The SAARC had just been started and he saw in this new group a tremendous potential for regional cooperation. He promoted this idea with sheet determination and never hesitated in making whatever concession needed to make the SARRC useful.[25]

The national spirit, which was once felt so deeply by all of us, seems to be fading away. The uncertain political situation caused by Mandal and Masjid controversies has disrupted schools, universities, factories and markets. Uncertainty about future came to the minds of even the educated, the competent and the confident. People have started viewing themselves as individuals and not as citizens of our proud nation.

23. Billo Aneja. The Guilty should be Punished. *The Independent,* 22 May 1991.
24. V.P. Dutt. The Assassination and After. *National Herald,* 29 May 1991.
25. K.V.S. Rama Sarma. Rajiv Gandhi. *National Herals,* 23 May 1991.

People are not feeling confident to make long-term investment which alone will ensure sustained growth and progress. This only reflects insecurity in the minds of people. Only productive use of capital will perpetuate prosperity and growth by full utilisation of our resources and manpower. Rising inflation, declining growth rate and the Balance of Payments crisis, in recent past, have not only created harships within the country and tarnished our image abroad, but it often makes us feel ashamed of ourselves. Inflation is of the order of 15 per cent to 16 percent, according to current consumer price index. The declaration of industrial production cannot go unnoticed. The major reduction in damand in the third and fourth quarters of the year, can be attributed to civic unrest, rising inflation and taxation overdose. The government raised more than Rs. 6,000 crore from the public in one single year. This additional collection is not used for increasing production, but is being wasted in non-developmental expenses of the government such as increased subsidies and waiving of loans, etc. We definitely require to review or tax structure. For increased revenue, base of taxation has to be increased by icreasing productivity and not the level of taxes. Instead of increasing burden on the same assesseesm it would be better to widen our tax-structure, to cover self-employed people, as well as well-to-do farmers. We have to promote a system that encourages greater tax compliance and reduces tax avoidance.[26] Our industrial output increased only 6 per cent as compared to 8.3 per cent last year. A number of industries, especially the consumer durables, are coming under the recession cloud. The infrastructure growth rate has been very disappointing. Power, petroleum and coal production increased by only 3.5 per cent during April-Dec. 1990, compared to 6-7 per cent in the corresponding period in 1989. The BoP crisis is indeed appalling. Our trade deficit in 1990-91 has been Rs 12,500 crore. India's ability to borrow from international market is declining. The inflow under Foreign currency Non-Resident Account Scheme was Rs. 1,916 crore, which is Rs 462 crore lower than last year. India's credit rating has fallen to 'BBB' rate. This is the lowest grading by standard and poor. The government requires to rework its industrial policy. In the formative years, the industrial policy reserved the 'commanding heights' of the economy for the public sectorn so that scarce resources could be directed into investments of strategice importance. This took care of core industries with heavy investments, low profit and long gestation period. But today the number of these public sector Undertaking has grown to 232 with an investment of rs 85,564 crore. The government today can overcomes its deficit problems very easily by privatising these

26. Asha Modi. Priorities for New Govt. *The Hindustan Times*, 27 May 1991.

public sector Undertakings. Adequate control can be retained by the government if only 49 per cent of the shares are sold to the public. At present there are 118 profitable public sector companies, showing a net profit of Rs 4,887 crore. The government that comes to poper has to be willing to take bold steps to save this country. We require to revive our spirit. The economically backward have to be lifted irrespective of caste or creed. Religion has to be isolated completely from politics. Code of conduct and morality has to be prescribed, for every office-bearer of the government. Perhaps it would be a good idea to insist on minimum qualification of either experience or education or both. Our policies have to be based on principles and our directions positive and clear. On the economic front the government has to change its basic policy. It would have to desist from additional taxation to bring down budget deficit. Instead it has to widen the tax-base; cut revenue expenditures reduce subsidies rather than dilute investment raise resources by diluting public sector holdings and making it more efficient; stimulate export by pressing on international standard and internatinal competition. Competition has to be encouraged by abolishing MRTP and licensing process. Protectionism as to be done away with. The saying is "when the going is tough, the gough get going". But in India, "when the going is tough, the tough go to the government". The governmetn should only govern and not indulge in business. Providing a sense of security and stability to every individual citizen should be the government's main tasks. Only a stable government and a secur nation of people can build India-a new India, strong and proud of itself.[27]

27. Ibid.

24
HIGH TECHNOLOGY

A critical appraisal of the economic policies of Rajiv Gandhi so soon after his brutal end is disconcerting. It reminds one of Mark Antony's speech. The intention, however, is not "inter the good......." but to make a sincere attempt in seeking where and how the "man with a vision" of modern India went wrong. Rajiv rode to power on the crest of a sympathy wave that blazed across. The country after his mother's assassination and which helped him bulldoze all opposition that came in his way. Such was the aura of "Mr. Clean" that even the semblance of the opposition in Parliament did not nurse a grudge against his position. For here at last was a man who would spare no efforts in clearing the Augean stables and bring fresh light in the dark corridors of power. Like a whiff of fresh air in the murky politics of the country that preceded him, Rajiv went about his task with clinical alacrity. His problem, however, was that though a man with a vision, he was myopic and saw no more than that what was directly on the runway. An airlines pilot by profession used to changing course at the press of a button-he mistook the vast country, with all its diversity, to be a larger cockpit which he flat would be able to leap frog into the 21st century by the mere use of some gadgets. Informatics, electronics and anything and everything to die with it was his first love and, unfortunately, he genuinely felt that these were enough ingredients to develop a modern India. Little did he realise that this would lead to modernization at the superficial level and not hit at the roots of the country's inherent problems of poverty, housing and unemployment. That is not to say that the country did not benefit at all. It was on account of his personal interest that computerization, a plan that had been lying in cold storage since 1975, was introduced in the Railways. This was followed by computerisation of the Income- Tax Department. All these made life much easier for officials and the common man. A national information center was set up to store all the economic data. Personal computers entered all government offices, so much so that senior officials in Central ministries were proud owners of the new gadgets. It is another matter that most PCs gathered dust. Egged on by the liberal policies of the government and a vast marketing waiting to be devoured, what used to be a nascent industry soon turned out to be a sunrise industry among many others. Computer units mushroomed all over the country for those who may have been selling peanuts earlier. They had also jumped on to the bandwagon.[1]

1. Ashok Das Gupta. Rajiveconomics. *The Sunday Mail,* 26 May 1991.

Nothing much was there to be done. Components and other peripheral imports had been put on open general licence at a concessional rate of duty to boost the industry for faster modermisation. A few screw-drivers were enough to assemble the finished product and market them as long as the going was good. Foreign companies also viewed India as a growing market for such products and tried up with the few serious entrepreneurs. Others were in it till the boom was on and had no intention of making any serious efforts of sustaining the large-scale capital-intensive imports through exports. It was only later that the Kelkar Committee pointed out that computers was one industry in which almost nil or negative value addition was taking place. In other words, importing the finished product would be much cheaper than buying components and assembling them in the country. Such a situation arose on account of the faulty policies pursued by the government. While imports were liberally allowed by all and sundry, no policy guidelines were drawn up for matching exports which literally led to the frittering away of precious foreign exchange to meet the demand in the domestic market and with no avenue to mop up the reserves spent. Entrepreneurs, on the other hand, argued that exports were not feasible owing to the high cost of production. For exports to be competitive, the duty on imports should be reduced to zero. This could not be done as not only would it appear partisan vis- a-vis imports by other industrial sectors but it would also lead to a fall in revenue through lower mop-up of indirect taxes. By hindsight, a better idea would perhaps have been to allow direct import of the end- product at a fixed rate of duty to meet the requirements of those who could afford it. In any case, driven to the wall in the present juncture, most of the units would have to close down as the clamp on imports imposed by the Reserve Bank of India (RBI) has rendered the industry into a fight of survival of the fittest. In the bargain, however, the loss of funds, owing to closures, would be that of the financial institutions and banks.[2]

Along with those who scoffed when Rajiv Gandhi repeatedly spoke about taking the country to the 21st century there were those who, impressed with his earnestness, began thinking seriously about how he was going to do it. The images thrown up by recurring talk about the leap to the next century were, among other things, those of modernised industry enriching the country with efficient and high quality production brought about with inputs of state-of-the-art technology. The magnitude of the tasks involved in turning such a vision to reality was not fully spelt out but the policy outlined and the successive steps taken during the years when Rajiv Gandhi was Prime Minister were indeed

2. *Ibid.*

remarkable for the trails that his Government was trying to blaze. The left-of-centre economic ideology which was shaping policy since Indira Gandhi had taken over as Prime Minister in 1966 was articulated in the policy directives for the curbing of the concentration of economic power and the pushing up of the public sector to commanding heights. It led to legislation typified by the Monopolies and Restrictive Trade Practices Act. The Government did not have any doubts at the time that it was going in the right direction and it was assured by its leftist supporters that this was how India could eventually become a "modern state" without the problems of acquisitive, exploitative capitalism. Indira Gandhi herself had lived long enough to see that this economic ideology was fast beginning to lose steam. While the public sector had become a perpetually loss-making leviathan, the shackles put on the private sector not merely precluded substantial production increases which were badly needed by the country. They also had the wholly unintended and undesirable result of making it possible for the private sector to maximise profits from restricted production and higher prices. The first steps towards liberalisation of the restrictive regime and making it more competitive were taken during the early 1980s before Indira Gandhi disappeared from the scene in 1984. The relatively high growth rate which was achieved by the Indian economy during the 1980s and repeatedly taken note of by the World Bank, the International Monetary Fund and other international agencies had undoubtedly been made possible by the policy of liberalisation pursued actively by Rajiv Gandhi's Government. The technology leap taken particularly by the international electronics industry was also making it obvious that India had just no choice but to jettison restrictive economic and industrial policies and becomes receptive and hospitable to technology and investment inflows. The new lingo which was beginning to invade the precincts of industry as well as government - software, compatibility, interface and the like- and the steady shedding of their ageing looks by industrial and government establishments with computer controls and terminals taking one are serving a purpose even if they are doing nothing more than infusing a whiff of change and freshness. The momentum imparted to the country's economic growth during at least the earlier half of Rajiv Gandhi's prime ministership will have to be sustained and accelerated in the years ahead. His strategy was not complete and there is some force in the criticism that an open door policy for attracting foreign capital could result in the foreign parties getting entrenched in the country without making any contribution to its economic development indiscriminate and unimaginative technology imports will demoralise indigenous research and development effort. Not the least important of the tasks is that of sustaining and accelerating food production, the expansion of opportunities and facilities for education and the rapid creation of jobs in productive sectors for wiping out the unemployment backlog and for the creation of more jobs. This challenge will have to be faced squarely by the government taking over when the trauma of the foul assassination at Sriperumbudur and the long drawn-out and jinxed mid-term poll melts away.[3]

The 21st century doesn't mean just computers. When we talk of technology although to an average person teachnology means computers and televisions and fancy data communication links and satellites, advanced technology also means genetic engineering, making seeds better, making them resistant to disease, making them more productive, seeing what else the farmer needs as back- up, tractors, implement, power, water, fertilizer. That too is technology. We have to give the best so that the farmer can perform his best.[4]

Despite his family's political background, Rajiv never showd any interest in history or any of the other arts subjects. He was average; some of his teachers even rated him as below average. But he did have a leaning towards the sciences.

Rajiv Gandhi understood what technology could do for a country like India. It is most ironical that the life of the man who wanted to take the country to the 21st century, has been cut short brutally nine years before he could see his dream year.

"I have no words to describe the tragedy. The manner in which it had happened is most shocking. I am trying to make sense of it," said a visibly stunned Sam Pitroda, Telecom Commission chief and a personal friend of the former prime minister.

Recalling his association with Rajiv, Pitroda said, "I saw in him a young, energetic and enthusiastic man who understood what I was trying to do."

He understood what technology meant. This got reflected in the initiatives taken by him in the telecom sector and technology missions. "Leaving aside politics, I enjoyed working with him and was impressed by the interest shown in technology matters," said Pitroda.

The news of Rajiv's assassination was taken with shock and disbelief in scientific and technological circles in the country. The science and technology initiatives taken during the Prime ministership of Rajiv Gandhi were widely appreciated, but unfortunately desired results could not be achieved for a variety of reasons.

3. *The Hindu*, 25 May 1991.
4. Rajiv Gandhi. *Children At His House*. New Delhi. 8 July 1985.

The initiatives taken by Rajiv Gandhi included launching of the technology missions to meet the needs of the society, an action plan to cleansing the Ganga, plan to regenerate wastelands and greater thrust to nuclear power generation. Besides this, Rajiv Gandhi continued the science policy adopted by his mother the late Indira Gandhi, envisaging greater self-reliance and use of science and technology for uplift of the poor.

The Central Ganga Authority and the National Wastelands Development Board were set up during Rajiv Gandhi's regime. Some of the technology missions launched, like the ones on drinking water and oilseeds made much headway and involved the country's scientific community, for the first time, in a big way in meeting basic needs of the masses.

Rajiv Gandhi had set a target of greening five million hectares of wastelands every year but the task could not be achieved. However, the interest taken by Rajiv in wasteland development, helped in bringing the subject of ecological protection into focus. At the international level, Rajiv Gandhi mooted the idea of establishing a Save Planet Fund at the Commonwealth summit to face the challenge of saving the earth's environment.

When Rajiv Gandhi was at the height of his popularity, when he had caught the imagination of the country with his slogans about the 21st century, Satyen Gangaram Pitroda was regarded as one of the men who were to lead this technological thrust. The Chairman of the Telecom Commission, who made some breakthroughs in indigenous telecom technology development, worked very closely with the former Prime Minister, on a broad range of technology- related matters. Pitroda talks about Rajiv Gandhi and his contributions.

One of my journalist friends woke me up on Wednesday night to tell me that Rajiv has been assassinated. It was a rude shock for me, who had the opportunity to work closely with him over the last several years. Rajiv had a modern mind, a vision for India. He knew technology and took intense interest in it. Never was he a passive participant in discussions on technology. He wanted to know the details and took pains to understand them. And he liked to see things presented precisely, accurately, and, of course, in diagrams and charts. There are times when he sat through hour long presentations on technology-related matters. Once when we had made a presentation for Gorbachov, Rajiv had a preview and suggested several modifications. Personally, I found that there was a level of communication between us which was difficult to establish with anyone else; we were on the same wavelength. He wasn't like many others, whose political decision-making didn't go beyond asking such things as: how exactly would this help poverty alleviation; have you thought about that? He could go much deeper. And understand that technology did have a large role to play in meeting basic human needs. He knew its role in raising productivity and efficiency, without which the nation cannot progress in the world. The results of this orientation towards technology are evident. In defence technology, the country made some of its great strides during his time-the scientists will tell you how he supported them, encouraged them. The Indian experiment in indigenous development of telecommunications technology wouldn't have been possible without his support.[5]

He also knew the importance of education. He once told me, "Sam, when you went to the USA, you had the same knowledge level as your classmates; Iam afraid the next generation of Indians will not have the same advantage since the tools they use in the schools will be so different. I want to avoid that; I want to give Indian children the same openings that others have". That was why he wanted to bring computers to schools. It's true that Rajiv may have had problems in communicating with senior leaders in his party. He was, perhaps, ahead of his time and there could have been a difference in perceptions. He was very well- organised, methodical and hardworking. It was a pleasure to see how he did even little things, the care he took about them. There were perhaps problems with the bureaucracy too, when he tried to cut through redtape. C-DoT, for example was allowed to be set up autonomously, with its own targets to be met. We may have overshot our deadlines but more important that, it helped Indian efforts at indigenous R&D tremendously. Contrary to what people think, as advisor to the Prime Minister on technology missions, I wasn't always advising him on the missions, giving copious reports and suggestions. That's not the way he worked. Once he discussed an idea and gave responsibility to someone, then he didn't talk about it. He took it for granted that the work would be done. At subsequent meetings, we talked about new things to be done. The stress was on planting new seeds for development, new ideas. As advisor on technology missions, I used to approach the prime minister's office only when I thiught a new policy decision was necessary, like in the case of oilseeds prices, and he always responded. Did it amount to an inability to see things through? No, I don't think so. There were so many things that needed to be done, what was important was making a beginning on different fronts, so that the seeds would grow eventually. And he always supported people when he knew they were being put under pressure unfa-

5. Sam Pitroda. Rajiv Gandhi-A Modern Mind. *The Economic Times*, 27 May 1991.

irly. A member of parliament once sent a letter to him making personal allegations against me. He sent me a copy. Later, he told me and a group of young scientists from C-DoT: "I know what you are going through; let me know if you need anything." That gave courage to them. Did I work closely with him on the political front? No, I didn't; what I did was act as a sounding board, alongwith others, for ideas in management techniques and things like that. That was not a political role. There was one instance, for example, where he asked me to see if I could improve the communication arrangements as Jawahar Bhavan. The assassination has, of course, changed things for me. I do not think there is another potential Prime Minister with whom I could have the same level of communication. I do not even have that kind of energy to build relationships any more. I'm going to take time off, think about things and decide what could be done now. The country is power without Rajiv Gandhi.[6]

The brutal assassination of Rajiv Gandhi came to me as a rude shock. When I first heard about it late last night, I just could not come round to accepting it. Many people say this cowardly act is a slap on the face of our democratic system. I don't share this view-I see it more as a test for our democracy. The sudden removal of Rajiv Gandhi from our national scene is a deep, personal loss to me. I held and continue to held him in very high personal regard and respect. I have always felt a deep sense of loyalty towards him, when he was in as well as out of power. He had a vision for a modern India and had an important role to play in its fulfillment. I first met Rajiv Gandhi along with his mother at Jamashedpur, shortly after the death of his brother Sanjay Gandhi in a plane crash in 1980. We had dinner together and I was struck by the man's politeness and sincerity. After that we did not meet for a few years. In 1985, when he took over as Prime Minister, I was very excited by the things he was saying, the freshness with which he was looking at economic and political issues. I felt here was a Prime Minister who was a man of our times. I then met him not to ask for anything but just to express my happiness and excitement at the new direction he was charting out for the country. I was once again struck by his decency, sincerity and forthrightness. I considered him a friend even though there was no close friendship between us. We did not have frequent meetings or even much direct interaction. Even though I was appointed by his government on the boards of a number of government organisations such as CSIR and Semiconductors Ltd or oversaw the preparation of some committee reports such as the one on project implementation. In fact, I read about my appointement as chairman of Air India in 1986 in the papers. Whenever I did meet him, I found that

6. *Ibid.*

he was a man with a capacity to listen and an ability to quickly grasp the main issues. He did not duck issues and answered hard questions. Often he would take notes in his interactions with various people. These would then be quickly followed up by the ministry concerned. Thus he brought about a new attitude in government. Of listening to people, exchanging ideas, accepting other people's views, debating issues. I think he made a major contribution here in making the government more open and responsive. One of his major contributions to the nation was in the economic sphere. He accelerated the pace of change towards liberalisation. He created a more open environment, greatly broadened the develop of controls and made access to domestic markets a lot easier for both foreign as well as Indian private enterprise. These were very brave decisions. His party was not necessarily in favour of doing this; the opposition too did not seem to be particularly supportive; the bureacuracy had its own fears of losing many of its powers. Many captains of industry also got worried and started running to Delhi to curb liberalisatin when it hurt them. Despite all this; and the fact that he was new to politics and governance, he never let go of the reins. Our image overseas improved considerably because of him and his politicies.[7]

The results of his ushering in an era of new economic policies are remarkable. I perceive a significant difference in our industry's product quality over the last five to six years. There can be no doubt that in manufacturing, process technology, and product finish, we are closer to world class products than we were in 1985. I do not think that liberalisation is responsible for our current BoP problems. Imports of capital goods or consumer products are very small in magnitude. One could not have expected our exports to rise very rapidly in a few years to cover our import bill. But exports did pick up and if we are to export more in the future the policies initiated by Rajiv Gandhi must be accelerated. I sincerely hope that whichever leader or political party comes to power next will also realise that India has to be open and global in orientation. In the next few months, the serious problems Indian business currently faces-of raw material imports, creditav ailability, etc-are likely to be aggravated. The postponement of elections also means the pushing back of the formation of a new government and budget making. Earlier, we had thought that the current economic crisis will blow over by june/july next and we could take care of our production runs in the interim with the help of inventories and in-the-pipeline inputs. But now I expect a very serious squeeze by june/july since no steps have been taken by anybody to tackle the now

7. Ratan Tata. Rajiv Had Vision for Modern India. *The Economic Times*, 23 May 1991

prolonged period of foreign exchange shortage. Thus there is all the more need for whoever comes to power next to make redoubled efforts to put the economy on the rails again. This may require some harsh policy measures. It is therefore. very important for all political parties to get together, bury their differences and stand united on firm policy measures that need to be taken.[8]

The economy is only clouding the picture further. India finds itself in a worse balance of payments situation than ever before. Growing current account deficits, culminating is a record $10bn deficit in the last financial year, have resulted in an outstanding debt of $70bn-$80bn. Foreign exchange reserves have run out and the sharp decline in India's credit worthiness abroad, following postponement of the February 1991 budget and the current climate of political uncertainty has closed the door to further commercial borrowing aboard. The risk of a default has risen as Indians living abroad begin to withdraw their foreign exchange deposit and US commercial banks cut back their short- term lending.

Whatever administration does emerge will be confronted with two immediate tests to its authority that will provide a barometer of political stability. The most immediate will be the need to prepare a budget on the basis of which negotiations for fresh borrowing can begin with the International Monetary Fund and the World Bank. The postponement of polling means a further delay in the formation of a new government, and hence in the preparation of a budget. This is bound to further undermine bankers' confidence in India's credit worthiness.

To obtain the substantial sums that India now needs from the IMFand the Bank-about $5bn-$7bn-will require both substantial cuts in the budget deficit and the launching of a programme of longer-term structural reforms. The combined package-including a reduction in subsidies, moves towards privatisation and allowing companies more freedom to shed labour-will be difficult to put through politically.

We have consolidated and reinforced our unity, integrity and democracy through our process of planning for development. Two basic principles have informed our system of planning: self- reliance and priority to the poor.

We understand self-reliance to mean paying our own way, standing on our own feet. As Panditji pithily put it:

"Nobody can bear our burdens for us; we have to bear them ourselves".

8. *Ibid.*

We hold ourselves responsible for our own development. We are not prepared to mortgage that responsibility to others. We are not prepared to put in jeopardy our hard-won independence more restrict our freedom of action. We are not prepared to abnegate our responsibility to build, on the basis of the quintessential values of our civilization and the vision of our founding fathers, an India which stands as an exemplar for the world. Therefore, nearly 93 per cent of the investment we have made in development over the last four decades has come from our own resources.

However, self-reliance, in our view, does not mean autarchy; it does not mean isolation from the international community or the global economy. That is why we have willingly sought-and given- economic and technical cooperation. We have, however, stressed that such cooperation can only be on terms compatible with our honour as a nation, our independence of the economies of the world. That is why we a affirm the need for an international economic order based on cooperation and domination. Panditji described this as:

"enlightened self-interest, realizing that if some parts of the world do not progress, re main backward, they have an adverse effect on the whole economy of the world and they tend to drag down those parts that are at present prosperous."[9]

The other key element in our planning has been priority to the poor. That too has helped hold the country together and place us in a position to fulfill our larger global responsibilities. I recall Panditji's words in the Lok Sabha in a speach made early in our experience of planned development. He said: We often go off at a tangent on grounds of provincialism, communalism, religion or caste. We have no emotional awareness of the unity of the country. Planning will help us in having an emotional awareness of our problems as a whole. It will help us to see the isolated 'problems in villages or districts or even provinces in their largest context". The poor constitute the vast majority of our country. They constitue the majority of every ethnic, linguistic and religious group in the country. Poverty cuts across every category. In making the poor the focus of our planning, and in ensuring that the poor of any one ethnic group are neither favoured nor discriminated against, we have pressed planning into the task of uniting the nation and given our people a common stake in political stability and economic progress. Poverty eradication is not merely a question of specific programmes. It is, above all, a political mindest. In his own inimitable way, Gandhiji called this the worship of *daridranarayana* as the highest form of worship. Panditji, in a rather more down to earth

9. *Rajiv Gandhi On Nehru and Indira.* New Delhi, 13 November 1989.

way made the poor the focus of all planned development. He made us understand that, whatever the specific task at hand, the emphasis on eradicating poverty in the shortest time possible has to permeate one's consciousness. Let me illustrate this proposition with regard to industrialization and technology as they affect poverty removal. Jawaharlal Nehru was "convinced that the rapid industrialization of India is essential to relieve the pressure on the land, to combat poverty and to raise standards of living, for defence, and a variety of other purposes." The short cut might have been to concentrate industrializaion where infrastructure was readily available. This we did not do. We spread it in two ways. One, by undertaking different types of industrialization ranging from cottage, village and small industry to more sophisticated larger units. Second, by extending industrialization to remote, backward areas through incentives and Governmental fiat. In particular, the public sector has played a notable part in opening out the hinterland, in bringing all of India within the purview of industrialization. We have thus avoided any unbridgeable chasm widening between industrial India and agricultural India, between rural India and urban India, between modern India and traditional India, between one part of India and any other part of India.[10]

Jawaharlal Nehru defined the role of science and technology in terms of the poor and the people at large. He said:

"It is science alone that can solve the problems of hunger and poverty, of insanitation, of illiteracy, of superstition and deadening custom and tradition, of vast resources running to waste, of a rich country inhabited by a starving people."

In the area of rural development, he began to solicit ways to increase people's participation, criticial and cynical of the bureaucracy as he always was. The Panchayati Raj bills were formulated to strengthen panchayats and the Jawahar Rozgar Yojana was announced, which for the first time money over the heads of the bureaucracy directly to village-level institutions. The entire effort, however, never got properly debated in India and was written off by the media as a vote-catching grimmick by an embattled Prime Minister. Rajiv was extremely proud of the change that he had himself made in the Environment Protection Act which empowered individuals to file cases against polluters. He would argue that only people can protect their environment and not the bureaucracy. Twice he told us that he was disappointed at the small number of cases filed by environmental groups against polluters. When the villagers of Bicchri near Udaipur complained to him that 60 wells had become balck because of pollution, he ordered the administration

10. *Ibid.*

to look into the mater, which then closed down the factory-about the only thing that has since happened to help the hapless villagers. Behind all this, Rajiv had a major weakness. While deeply suspicious of ways in which the government works and even while possessing an extremely open mind, he could not break out of the advice he received from his adviser-bureaucrats. This was because of his own lack of direct experience with and knowledge of the people. He, therefore, remained a prisoner of the bureaucracy despite all his keen desire for change. With experience, however, even this weakness would have disappered. And over time, the idiom, too, would have become more Indian. In his death, therefore, we lost an ardent and sincere environmentalist and leader who tried to push as hard as he could.[11]

The Green Revolution, which brought the prospect of progress to millions of our farmers, was in essence a revolution of science and technology, taking the results of the most sophisticated genetic sciences to the farmer tilling the soil. In the rain fed areas, we have a Technology Mission on oilseeds and edible oil as well as a National Project on pulses. A white Revolution-dairying and milk products-is now sweeping parts of the nation. In the hills, a horticultural revolution is in the making. In a similar vein, we have started a new initiative to harness technology to the service of the most pressing needs of the poor, such as immunization, drinking water, food control and the eradication of illiteracy. Mahatma Gandhi had stressed that democracy would be meaningful to the vast millions of our people only if it were based on village panchayats-the ancient village republics of India. In 1959, Jawaharlal Nehru launched Panchayati Raj in rural India as a great revolutionary measures to ststemically transform the Indian polity. What has happened to that dream? As I travel around the villages of India, I feel the seething tesnion of expectations beting totally at variance with reality and realistic possibilities. Because our young men and women have been brought up to look to governmental authority as the provender all things, good and bad, there is a kind of abnegation of responsibility for one's own development or the development of the local community to which one belongs. There is, therefore, little appreciation, in terms of resources mobilization and resources development, of what is required for the development process to proceed space. Unrealistic expectations are encouraged and then matched to a widening belief that development is a matter of establishing the right contacts and hoping that nepotism will bring results since the outcome does not appear to be related to merit. It is an explosive situation. The only way of preventing the explosion from the

11. Anil Agarwal and Sunita Narain. Green Politics. *The Economic Times,* 26 May 1991

taking plaçe is to end the present alienation of the individual citizen from the development process. Paternalistic planning must give way to participatory planning. Implementation from above must yield to implementation in cooperation with the people and their representatives. There must be representative institutions at the grassroots, entrusted with real powers and real responsibilities, for administration to be truly responsive to the people's felt needs and articulated aspirations.

In every village I visit, I see a glaring contrast between the vast sums of money being spent on development and the spectacle before out eyes on the ground. Much of the money, it seems, is being spent on the delivery mechanism rather than on the programmes. We must substantially augment the share of resources actually reaching the beneficiary. Our people are exploited at many levels, subjected to petty indignities, often denied a fair hearing, often denied justice. For almost all their problems, they have to turn to officialdom which, however benevolent, is no substitude for locally elected authority, representative of the people, accountable to the people, and responsive to their needs. The answer to these problems does not lie, indeed cannot lie, in making some change here or some adjustment there, some improvement here or some correction there. The system itself has to be changed.[12]

Union Minister for Commerce, Dr. Subramaniam Swamy described assassinated leader Rajiv Gandhi as the only Indian politican with a thoroughly organised "A true nationalist, he was a straight man with no pretention and guile, who etched India's name in the global map", Dr. Swamy said in an emotion choked voice.

He was speaking at a condolence meeting in New Delhi organised by the Delhi Parsi Anjuman. The meeting was attended by distinguished members of the Parsi community, some of whom had a personal friendship with Rajiv Gandhi.

At the beginning of the meeting, two Parsi clergies recited a hymn from Zorashtrian scripture. Later translated in English, it meant, that after the soul leaves the body it is surrounded by hundreds of millions of eternal light, just like a golden crown. The soul becomes like a new born baby heading for a new dimension. The it meets three angelic fingures, which cleans the soul and leads it to the bridge of judgement. At the bridge the soul meets a beautiful girl, who is the symbol fo good deeds. The motto is: Good deeds never die-and man shall become the mighty conquerer of death. The president of the Parsi Anjuman Retd Lt- Gen. Adi M. Sethna said the death of Rajiv Gandhi has cast a shadow of an unbelievable tragedy. Recounting meetings with Rajiv

12. Rajiv Gandhi. *On Nehru and India.* New Delhi, 13 November 1989.

Gandhi, Gen. Sethna said, "two years ago this handsome, lively bubbly youngman came to this Anjuman. He was so full of energy and enthusiasm." He added that Rajiv Gandhi's association with the Anjuman was never confined to a narow parochial sense.

Speaking about Rajiv Gandhi's characterstic traits, Dr. Swamy said that his slogan "*mera Bharat mahan*" was actually aimed at keeping the country together. A courageous man, who had never suffered any inhibitions Rajiv Gandhi was instrumental in fostering an atmosphere of modernity in the country, Dr. Swamy added.

I saw him on the morning after the defeat in the 1989 elections. He accepted responsibility and refused to blame anyone else. In the 15 months that followed, I worked with him closely and for long hours. Some times he would ask me to come first in the morning: sometimes I would be called late in the night after dinner and we would chat up to 1 or 2 am in the morning. He loved using his desk-top computer and every decision found its way into the data base. Rajiv was always thoughtful and kind. There was always coffee and soft drinks. If it was time for lunch or dinner, he would order soup or sandwiches. Often he would go in and fetch a box of chocolates. He knew he was weak on economic and was determined to correct this weakness. A few months ago, he set up a group of eminent persons to advise him on economic and national security matters. He was preparing for a second innings and was determined to score the century that he had missed in his first innings. The high point in recent weeks was the Congress election manifesto. His first term as Prime Minister was marked by a vision, largely technocratic and relying heavily on science and technology. In the 15 months that he took to prepare himself for the next term, this vision had been greatly tempered and reinforced by a new-found practical wisdom. Much of this is reflected in the last chapter of the Congress manifesto which contains a timebound programmed. We worked on this together for three full days. I told tim that only if he had the will to implement these promises should we put them into the manifesto. He assured me that he was determined to implement them. I am sure he would have done so and he would have ushered in a veritable revolution in the first 100 days in office. The manifesto and the time-bound programme are the legacy that Rajiv has left for the party and the nation.[13]

Rajiv Gandhi in his brief political career nevertheless left an indelible mark on the country's business and industrial environment. He inspired more confidence than any other contemporary leader not only among the business and industrial community at home but also among

13. P. Chidambaran. He Live Too Dangerously. *The Times Of India,* 26 May 1991.

those abroad who want to help India to come outof its present balance of payments problems. His death at this juncture, therefore, is a great blow to the process of economic revival of the country.

Had Rajiv Gandhi lived longer, he would have certainly contributed more to the progress of the country. But the path he has broken, the policies he has initiated and the direction he has given to the Indian economy cannot be rolled back. This is his legacy, which the nation will cherish for a long time to come.

25
FOREIGN POLICY OPTIONS

Between 1985 when Rajiv Gandhi leftCongress President office and now when a successor moves into the job, the international setting has undergone a sea change. Unfortunately, however, India's ability to rise to the new challenges and avail itself of opportunities stands greatly diminished for two reason. One is a dire economic crisis of the country's own making which makes the country dangerously vulnerable. Another is a precipitate decline in its standing because of the increasing fragility of its polity. The successor no matter who it is, will face a compelling need not only to find a whole set of new policy responses but also to obtain public endorsement for them. There was no need for Gandhi to do either because he carried on mostly along the lines already set by his mother. Only in Pakistan's case, he broke some new ground, and in some cases, China for example, managed to give an added momentum. In one notable instance, he undertook a creative reinterpretation of a long- established policy, namely that of keeping open India's nuclear option. It will be churlish not to give him credit for its ability to establish a rapport with his internatioal interlocutors and to gain popular esteem worldwide as an imaginative young leader manfully coping with the complex and difficult problems at home. This is at once evident from the line-up of 40 odd foreign luminaries at his funeral. They came not because protocol required their presence but presumable because they wanted to India take.[1]

After the collapse of the erstwhile socialist bloc led by the Soviet Union, Rajiv Gandhi had emerged as the most outstanding exponent of anti-imperialism. His role in the context of the Gulf crisis had proved that he was a fearless opponent of the politics of domination. He had boldly set out his opinion in this regard at the Belgrade Summit of the non-aligned. Then he was Prime Minister. That the subsequent defeat in elections had not cooled his ardour was clear from the stand he took on the way the US had manipulated the UN and the NAM. It would only have added to the desperation of the votaries of domino theory, particularly as he was fast on the comeback trail.

Rajiv Gandhi's violent death has put paid to the fallacy that foreign policy is a peripheral issue for the Indian people True, campaign speeches in Indian elections rarely touch upon foreign policy issues and when some major political parties devote no more than three

1. Dilip Mukerjee. Foreign Policy Options. *The Times of India,* 3 June 1991.

paragraphs in their manifestos to external affairs, it only serves to strengthen the assumption that for this country's 843 million people, what happens in the rest of the world does not matter. But if reports at the time of writing about Sri Lankan Tamil Tiger's involvement in the assissination turn out to be true, then Rajiv has fallen victim to his foreign policy. The threats that shadowed the former Prime Minister for most of his brief political career which spanned a decade always sprang from his domestic policies. And instead of lengthening, these shadows, as it turned out, all but disappeared as Rajiv's campaign style in the troubled northern states showed. What Indians overlooked as Rajiv went back to the people, casting aside the aloofness of high office, was that there was a Third World leader who internationalised India's prime ministership. Third World leaders who have similarly internationalised their office are legion. Men like Julius Nyerere and Gamal Abdel Nasser were, in fact, accused of devoting time to international issues at the cost of domestic affairs. But they, like Jawaharlal Nehru and Ahmed Sukarno, were leaders who were born out their countries struggles either for freedom or for an identity. Rajiv, on the other hand, was the first leader from among the developing countries to make the world a part of his political constiuency without a political legacy of his own to fall back on. During the fives years of his prime ministership, (1984-89) Rajiv visited 43 countries in all-visits ranging from a few hours to several days. He chose his destinations with care and some countries, like the US, the USSR and Japan, he visited more than more. Not all the visits were successful. Some of them, in fact, were plain ill-advised. Like the occassion when he went to Oman for the Sultanate's national day, which turned out to be little more and an assembly of Oriental potentates and leaders who received the Sultan's bounty either in plain aid or in the form of expatriate jobs for their nationals. To add insult to injury as it were, the Indian prime minister was made to sit along with heads of government, relegated as they were to a position of relative inconsequence, protocol-wise, behind the heads of state.[2]

But Rajiv was quick learner, as in this case, from the glee on the face of Gen-Zia-ul-Haq, the late Pakistani President, who not only had a pride of place as a head of state, but could also relate infinitely better to Oman's Sultan. When he went to other similarly unfamiliar destinations-Damascus, Budapest and Madrid being examples-during the remainder of his prime ministership, Rajiv was careful to ensure that India received adequate mileage from the visit. The most outstanding example, perhaps, of Rajiv working towards creating a personal rap

2. K.P. Nayar. Rajiv and the World,. The Economic Times, 26 May 1991.

port was a trip to Jordan in 1988. Jordan's Hashemite royal family has an 'attachment-in- law' to Pakistan, crown prince Hassan having married into a well- known Pakistani family. Besides King Hussein owes his life and his state to Gen Z ia-ul-Haq, who was stationed as the head of a Pakistani army unit in A man in 1970. When the Palestine Liberation Organisation all but seized power in Jordan, it was Gen Zia who led the massacre of the Palestinians in what history now knows as jordan's 'Block September'. However, by the time Rajiv ended his visit to Amman, he and Sonia Gandhi had cemented a bond with Hussein and his American-born Queen Noor, a bond that was to stand India in good stead during the evacuation of Indians from Kuwait and Iraq through Amman. During an altogether short span of one term as prime minister, Rajiv played a crucial role in setting up the Africa Fund-he pledged $40 million of the Fund's capital of $70 million-designed to set right imbalances of apartheid, initiated, along with like-minded leaders, the six- nation effort a peace' and disarmament and approached the creation of the G15 group of developing countries with missionary zeal. Rajiv reserved his most important foreign policy initiatives, though, to the areas of immediate concern to India, its neighbour hood. The ongoing work of the joint working group on the Sino-Indian border dispute is probably the best tribute to the former prime minister's role in steering Indian foreign policy. But foreign policy initiatives in India's neighbourhood also proved to be his undoing, as the suspected LTTE role in the murder indicates. India, caught up as this huge country was in the problems of Punjab and Kashmir, Mandir and Masjid, did not realise that its foreign policy had grown to a point where it claimed a price. Hardly anyone, perhaps including Rajiv, realised that a country which was prepared to send its troops to the Maldives or Sri Lanka and destabilise Nepal, would have to sheild its leaders from external theats in a way Washington shields its President. The lesson that the makers of India's foreign policy have to learn from last week's events is that they can no longer treat external relations in text book terms as they have been used to since the time of Jawaharlal Nehru.[3]

Regarding India's role in the world, Rajiv Gandhi had carried on with great distinction the tradition of the Indian National Congress and of Jawaharlal Nehru and Indira Gandhi to fully participate in world affairs in order to subserve the interests of India and other struggling countries and to secure a position in the councils of the world. Rajiv Gandhi left his imprint on many international issues on the quest for nuclear disarmament on relations with neighbours on the struggle in

3. *Ibid.*

Africa and on the non-aligned movement as well as in the area of relations with the Soviet Union and the United States. The galaxy of world leaders that came to attend his funeral was eloquent testamony of the mark that Rajiv had made in world affairs. The shame of the interregnum that followed the last elections when India fell from a high pedestal and became a non-entity is too patent to need eleboration. It is in all these areas and in the grim struggle against communalism and fanaticism that the Congress must carry on with Rajiv's legacy. It is a task that brooks no compromise and no complacency either. The country must immediately complete the electoral process so that the verdict of the people can be honoured and a government voted by the people be installed at the earliest. The proposal for a national government is misconceived and the brainchild of those who are afraid of the people's verdict. A national government is conceivable only in one situation when the country faces grave external threat and therefore the priority task comes to be that of meeting the threat with all political parties sinking their differences and coming together with the sole purpose of protecting the country's integrity. India faces no immediate threat of any external aggression. In the absence of such an imminent and present threat a national government of disparate elements would be even worse than the national confusion that we have had in the last two years. A coalition can be formed only of like-minded people with a certain minimum programme. A hotch-potch of clashing and conflicting ideologies and objectives would only breed greater cynicism and further damage the political system.[4]

India's policies, domestic and foreign are shaped by certain fundamental factors. What are these factors? Our geographical situation, our size, the diversity of our population, our history our innumerable collective experiences and memories, our struggle under Mahatma Gandhi's leadership against colonialism and, finally, the nature of the Indian state bequeath to us by Jawaharlal Nehru and his colleagues. Out of a colonial past India has emerged a strong and stable nation. We have had our share of crisess since independence attacks from across our borders, the assassination of our leaders, Mahatma Gandhi and Indira Gandhi, and secessionist and subversive movements. Each internal crisis, each external threat, has brought forth new focces of renewal. The Republic has emerged more united and stronger. Out democracy is vigorous, lively and noisy, as all great democracies are. It has sent down deep roots. Out is a politics of conciliation, not of confrontation. We solve problems through the ballot and across the table. Many of you will recall learned these in the mid- sixties predicting

4. V.P. Dutt; The Assassination and After, *National Herald*, 29 May 1991.

the imminent demise of India as a nation. India seems continually to baffle critics and disprove Cassandras. The main strength of the Indian people comes from their cultural heritage. The epic struggle for freedom gave it a new surge and direction, which led to the creation of a democratic nation state. The people participate extensively and decisively in the political process. They are today putting all their faith into building a new India. After Independence, our most important task was to build a new social and economic order. We set about changing the colonial framework, which had bred stagnation and poverty. We took up basic structural reforms and initiate the process of growth and development, based on modern science and technology. After three decades of development through planning our national economy has undergone a remarkable transformation. India's agriculture is acknowledged today as a success story. We have completed laying the foundations of self- reliance in industrialisation. These policies have been vindicated by the resilience and dynamism which our economy has shown in the past ten years in the face of an extremely difficult external environment. Many countries experience dislocation and disruption in the same period whereas the Indian economy has gone from strength to strength. The main objective of the planning process in India has throughout been the ending of mass poverty. We have still to cover a long distance but the change is there for everybody to see. Incomes and consumption levels of the poor have risen steadily. We have emphasised growth with social justice. We have not depended upon the trickle down theory of growth. We have launched special anti-poverty programmes which provide productive employment to the landless, small and marginal farmers, village artisans and women. Our very success in building a sound technological infrastructure now enables us to absorb and integrate advanced technology. We shall acquire whatever makes our economy modern and competitive. We are sreamlining both our adminstrative proceedures and our methods of training Human resource development is high on my list of priorities.[5]

The basic features of foreign policy are a logical outcome of our own experiences needs and aspirations. We have known the pain and humuliation of colonialism, as well as the joy of liberation. It is natural, therefore, that we have consitently stood with the oppressed peoples in their struggle to shape their own destinies in freedom. Rapid economic development is the overriding goal of our domestic economic policies. We are, therefore, in the forefront of the interna

5. Rajiv Gandhi *Address to the Council of Foreign Relations.* New York, 23 October 1985.

tional movement to create a more equitable world economic order, in which the developing countries will have a larger say. Knowing the importance of co-existence for our own national strength, we are for con-existence in the family of nations as well. Schooled in the Gandhi-Nehru ethos, we believe that there is a peaceful answer to every problem. India will not be a camp follower. We therefore affirm the principles of non-alignment, which allow all countries to retain true independence in their international relations. Non-alingment has been our response to the dangerous divisions that developed after the Second World War, it is rooted in our belief that the world is and has to be many hued. It is an assertion of our right to look at the world the way we see it. We do not think there is one and only one infallible path which all must folow. Non-alignment, however, is not a mere affirmation of an independent outlook. It carries an obligation to cooperate. It projects a new method of nations working together on the basis of natural respect and equality. It visualises a world order in which differences need not become permanent antagonisms. Inter-dependence is the core of the logic of non-alignment. May will recall the time when non- alignment, did not find acceptance in this country. You had leaders who knew what was right for us. To them Jawaharlal Nehru was a moral fumbler, consorting with communism. That view of non-alignment, fortunately, is now not so widespread in America. President Reagan's warm reference to non-alignment when we met in the White House earlier this year was most welcome. Even now, however, there is much unhappiness against India's supposed habit of voting against the US. If our voting pattern is analysed, it will be found that we have stood on principle and the merits of each issue. To refresh short memories it may be worth recalling our voting record on the Chinese representation in the UN and on the independence of so many colonial territories. We supported the right of the People's Republic of China even when our rdation with China were troubled. Cherishing Mahatma Gandhi's struggle against South African racism we cannot approve of a regime which swears by colour and crushes its people. We need make no apologies for the passion with which we abhor racism and oppose oppression. I am sure there are many in your country who, with hindsight, recognise the validity of our positions.[6]

"India values its friendship with the United States. The vision and eloquence of your founding fathers strirred us deeply. We welcome the world view of Presidents Wilson and Roosevelt and their role in establishing an international system. One of your President told my mother, 'The trouble about India is that you don't listen to US'. The

6. *Ibid.*

trouble with US is that we think for ourselves. But differences in perception should not come in the way of friendship between two democracies. America has helped our development efforts in many ways. We appreciate the assistance you gave us in the form of grain before we achieve self- suffiency. We have also benefited from a flow of technology from the US in several critical areas. We want America to recognise that it is natural for India to see the world from its own vantage point. Also to understand that one friendship need not be at the cost of another. We should like America's enormous intellectual vigour and material power to be used on behalf on world peace and development. India's close and friendly relations with the Soviet Union have developed on the basis that they do not require India to give up its foreign policy of non-alignment. They have been built on the foundations of mutual benefit, mutual respect and equality. The Societ Union has stood by us in times of national crisis. It has helped us in building our basic industries. The trade between us has worked to the advantage of both countries. And yet our relations with the Soviet Union have not come in the way of our developing friendly relations with other countries. Friendship and trust are not made overnight. They need to be nurtured over a period of time. Non-alignment cannot be judged by the yardstick of equidistance. The South Asian and Indian Ocean Region has its own tensions, suspicions and outside presences. Arrangements or regional cooperation could contribute significantly towards meeting scientific, cultural and developmental concerns. It is a recognition of this that is leading to the South Asian Association for Regional Cooperation Regional arrangements best succeed when there is no effort by the big powers to create constiuencies and interfere on strategic or other grounds. As you are aware, Sri Lanka is facing ethnic violence. We have been instrumental in bringing the parties together and have helped to establish a cease-fire and the commencement of a negotiating process, we should like normalcy to return to Sri Lanka so that all can live in safety, security, equality and honour and the over 1,00,000 refugees now in India can return with dignity.

We want close and friendly relations with Pakistan. We have proposed a comprehensive treaty of peace, friendship and cooperation. During the recent meeting of the Joint Commission of our two countries, we were willing to go great lengths to establish a good neighbourly relationship, not just between Governments but between our two peoples as well. The limitations were not of our making. Disarmament is imperative for human survival. Hanging over us is the cloud of nuclear death. The nuclear weapon States confront each other with destructive capabilities that stagger human imagination. Will manking maintain peace? Or will it be exterminated? Mankind has two options-the theory of deterrence, or peaceful coexistence. The theory of deterrance appears, at one level to be a modern version of the traditional doctrine of balance of power. But in fact it is qualitatively different. It does not ensure security at any acceptable level of stable balance. It does not ensure security by the threat of total annihilation. Escalation of destructive potential is built into this doctrine. There is no time when you can feel safe. The consequence is perpetual instability and fear. The big doctrine of mutually assured destruction has sired the little doctrine of limited good, little winnable nuclear wars. This is a dangerous illusion. There can be no limited nuclear wars. Technological advances and the location of missiles are reducing the identification decision and reaction time. It is becoming so short that the human thinking process is being eliminated. In Europe, where the missiles are face to face, the time between launch and strike is measured in minutes and seconds. Who will judge whether an alarm is false or real, correct or incorrect or assess whether the system has malfunctioned. In such a time-frame, what can statesmanship do. Is there an alternative, yes, peaceful coexistence-the acceptance that another nation has as much right to be on the planet as ourselves. As Indira Gandhi said: On this small planet of ours there is no room for permanent enmity and irreversible alienation. We have to live side-byside. International relations must be recognised gradually and surely on the basis of living and evolving together. Starting by finding areas of commonality and enlarging them, identifying the links and strengthening them. Disarmament especially nuclear disarmament is the first step towards creating an environment of peaceful coexistence. Disarmement must start with a freeze on present stocks, a halt to additions. It is urgent today to prevent the extension of the battle ground to outer space. Certain technologies are described as the ultimate answers to defence problems. There are no ultimate military answers. The non-aligned want disarmament because no nation will be spared. The basic responsibility for preserving global peace is that of the possessors of nuclear weapons. We welcome any search by them for peace. Constructive proposals deserve serious consideration The world's hopes and expectations are focused on the Reagan-Gorbachov meeting will they make it a turning point for peace. Ours is a very complex world. Science has placed at man's disposal the means to banish the ancient scourges of mankind hunger poverty, diseases as we have known for thousands of years has never been greater. But some nations continue to believe that what happened to the people of Hiroshima and Nagasaki cannot heppen to them. They think have a talisman against collective death. What are the answers? Where are the answers? How do we find them?[7]

The assassination of Rajiv Gandhi has certainly been the loss of a statesmen endowed with dynamism of vision, clarity of purpose and on top years for peace, not only for India but also for the entire humanity. He was first among a handful of champions of global peace and prosperity. Indeed, his contribution to numerous world for a has been unmatched and brilliant given his short stint of Prime Ministership of India from 1984 to 1989. Leaving aside the politics of pullovers, maligning and vulgarity at home. Rajiv Gandhi was a beacon of hopes for those millions who are fighting a struggle for independence in South Africa. He was undoubtedly the most shining star politician of the Third World which is always in dearth of versatile leaders. First in our vicinity Rajiv Gandhi took bold initiative to settle down the issue of Tamils in Sri Lanka. He signed an accord in 1987 with the then Sri Lankan President Mr. Jayewardane and the Liberation Tigers of Tamil Elam (LTTE). He genuinely wanted to free the millions of suffering Tamils from the scourage of violence. But it was LTTE volte face which forced him to send the Indian Peace Keeping Force (IPKF). Though there are many who blame him for military adventurism but it was his heart-felt desire to thrash out this problem. But the trecherous LTTE which is so far believed to be behind his assassination throttled his initiatives. With Pakistan, he had a cordial rapport with Benazir Bhutto and both of them wanted to sort out bialateral problems peacefully. With Bangladesh he was generous enough to resolve all water disputes partially and his time if he could have come in power all remaining problems could have been buried for ever. The South Asian Association for Regional Cooperation (SAARC) owes a lot to him for his keen interest in making it a strong economic and political forum to establish peace, stability and an era of cooperation in the Indian sub-continent. The Non-Aligned Movement (NAM) has truly lost its most effective exponent in Rajiv. He was behind the accelerated peace of NAM's struggle for political and economic justice for the Third world countries. Initiating a dialogue with the developed nations he was hopeful of establishing a "new economic order". The North-South dialogue which was losing its steam and teeth had got an unimpeachable loyalist in Rajiv, who helped mitigate the Third World debt crisis by compelling the IMF and World Bank to work out solutions. His pursuation led to formulation of Baker's plan by the US and other developed nations got interested in waiving off their loans particularly to poor countries.[8]

7. *Ibid.*
8. Shailai and Babita Malhotra. World After Rajiv. *National Herald*, 1 June 1991.

It is too severe a blow for Africa for which he had set-up "Africa Fund" to redeem poor nations from economic crisis. His contribution to Namibian independence through the United Nationas and NAM is unforgettable for every Namibian National. His efforts to make Namibian free eventually bore fruit and he had gone to participate in independence celebrations. South Africa has particularly lost a great activist of freedom. Rajiv was one of the brains behind sustenance of economic sanctions against apartheid in South Africa where the monolithic structure of racialism is tottering and giving way to justice and liberty today.[9]

When Rajiv Gandhi was alive, he could rarely ignore death, concerned though he was for safeguarding the interests of man and life. The occasion was the six nation summit on disarmament in January 1988, in Stockholm and my first with Prime Minister Rajiv Gandhi. The fight was delayed by over five hours because Khan Abdul Ghaffar Khan's death and necessitated a trip to Peshawar by an airforce plane. As the armed Pakhtoons escorted Rajiv through a maze of dust and smoke, one onlooker onserved: "Rajiv Gandhi has done what his Pakistani counterparts would notcoming over the moment he heard of Ghaffar Khan's demise. For all you know, they haven't woken up yet". Trivia such as this hardly affected Rajiv Gandhi, but it amused him no end. In front of the Khan's bier, however, he was sombre and looked as washed out as though one of his own had passed away. Back in Delhi he was back to his charming self, beaming as ministers and MPs lined up to shake his hand and bid him farewell. Disarmament was a subject close to his heart and he realised that even if the two superpowers kept a discreet distance from the meet, he had to drive home the priorities credibly and effectively-of peace and of the need of man to survive the prospects of a nuclear holocaust. Only a few days before, during his annual break he was reported to have saved a small whale. Like most of his ommissions and commissions this whipped up the expected controversy. Was it a whale or a dolphin, asked a national fortnightly. The excutive editor of the periodical repeated the question of the prime minister who had emerged at the makeshift media lounge in the aircraft in denims and a sports shirt, two hours after we had taken off for sweden. Before he could answer, a veteran of many such trips told the editor what he thought of him and his paper in so many worlds. As the quibbling got more and more strident, Gandhi who seemed to be enjoying every moment of the intermedia bashing put an arm around both of them and said that there were so many things to enjoy more than such meaningless arguments-like getting on with the drinks they

9. *Ibid.*

were nursing.[10]

He could also, if and when the occasion demanded, be delightfully evasive as I was to learn a little later Sharada Prasad, who was then his press advisor, had advised me that if I wanted an interview with the prime minister, I had to make an impression on him at the very outset by asking a question that he would find more than just "interesting". I asked Rajiv Gandhi what he, as a spokesman for peace and disarmament, would do if he was presented evidence that Pakistan had the bomb, sit back and talk of peace or get on with the task of emulating them. He pondered for a while and then flashed his traditional grin: "We shall see that they have done and, having made sure that they have done what we think they might have done we will do what needs to be done. I hope I have answer your question." He laughed and said "arms and the man" was an issue that should be taken up only in Sweden. Sharada Prasad had his thumbs Rajiv had a tremendous sense of humour. And he was particular about keeping his wife and children in good spirits, confided an airhostess who was looking after them. Typical of the kind of joke that he would reel off every now and then was the one on the Reagans. The butler askes the president whether he would like steak for dinner. Nancy asks him what else is on the menu. Vegetables, he answers. No, thank you, what I have with me is enough, she comments looking the way of the presidents Rajiv Gandhi, obviously, meant no offence to the Amreican president, for even he might have enjoyed this one. In stockholm, the Swedish reporters besieged the Indian prime minister with questions on Bofors. Even during the final press meet other heads of state were ignored and local journalists kept bothering Rajiv Gandhi for answers until Swedish prime minister Karlsoon said that they had come to the wrong press conference. This one was on disarmament, not Bofors, he said. I asked Karlsson, how much credibility he would attribute to a meet such as the one he was presiding over, from which other nuclear powers had stayed away. He was at pains to answer the question and Rajiv Gandhi for once, seemed both relieved and amused by the predicament the Swedish prime minister found himself in. The next morning, during the inauguration of a kindergarten on the outskirts of a the city Rajiv Gandhi entered with his encourage and a little after, spotting my, by then, not so unfamiliar face, he broke formalities, came to my corner, exchanged pleasantries and said that he thought I had asked meaningful questions of his Swedish counterpart and added that it would be a good idea if looked him up in Delhi. Then followed the amusing spectacle of some of his ministers introducing themselves to me. Quite clearly, they were

10. Utkal Chatterjee. In Search of Peace. *The Independent*, 24 May 1991.

their leader's men. Later, there was the usual press conference on board the aircraft that was also telecast by Doordarshan. Answering a question, he explained how concerned he was for man 'survival and progress and how his plans would see India through to the 21st century when every Indian would have reason to hold his head up in pride. Some paradox, that we did not allow him to survive and we hang our heads in shame today-on the verge of entering the 21st century.

If the US is more willing to accommodate India today than it has ever been before, this is largely because of waht Rajiv Gandhi achieved in his five-year tenure and what his successors have done to consolidate the gains. The continuity confirms that there is now a national consensus in this regard. The decision to permit refulling of US military aircraft en route to the Gulf was an entirely logical extension of this policy, and any conceivable Prime Minister would have acted as Chandra Shekhar did, though a wiser one would have sought to preempt the public outcry instead of trying to the hide the facts. While there is room for argument whether there is any significant conceptual difference between allowing overflights (as the previous government had done) and refuelling, the sheer politicking of bothe Rajiv Gandhi and V.P. Singh on the issue was a case of rank opportunism. The lesson to draw is that there is nothing any government can do if major parties as well as the political class prefer to duck hard choices, although the cost of their failure has to be borne by the underprivileged. As regartds Moscow, neither Rajiv Gandhi nor even V.P. Singh had to reckon with the momentous changes that have taken place in the past few months. New Delhi has not even begun to address its implications, not least because the past has no relevance in dealing with the challenges of today. However events in the Soviet Union unfold, India can no longer be sure of its support in tricky international situations, regardless of whether Gorbachov, for whose personal commitment to India Rajiv Gandhi deserves some credit, survics or not, the leadership in Moscow can be expected to take more sympathetic view than its counterparts in any other capital. Even so, India will have to make a very careful assessment of likely world reactions before engaging in actions like bread-bombing of Jaffna. India is, of course, hardly likely to do anything as egregious as what Saddam Hussein did to counter Kurdish disffection. It will, however, be dangerous to ignore human rights issues in copying with the secessionist challenge in Kashmir and Punjab. Here again, the past offers little guidance for the future. The next government will also have to contend with the reality that opinion-makers have yet to come to terms with the fact that the sovereign right of states in dealing with issues within their own borders are now increasingly subject to the limits set by international opinion- as in the case of north Iraq.[11]

Rajiv was particularly instrumental in neuclear disarmament. He stood by Gorbachov and wanted the Super Powers rivalry to end. He wanted a nuclear free world by 2010AD. For that the process had set in by many agreements between the US and the USSR. Who can forget his courageous and statesman like steps which he took during the recent Gulf crisis. Despite being in the opposition, he undertook a journey to Iran and Moscow for an early end of the Gulf war. His initiatives gave a new thrust to NAM also. Indeed his untimely demise has left a void in the international movement for "new economic order"and there is no leader of his stature who could fill this void. Sadly India's foreign policy has been left bereft of a gareat crusader who had given it a direction purpose and new thrust. Certainly Rajiv Gandhi's legacy is too much to be surpassed by anyone. And greatest tribute India and world can pay him is the establishment of a fair, just violence free and prosperous era which don't seem even in distant dream.[12]

The assassination at Sriperumbudur, near Madras, confirms finally, if confirmation was necessary, that India now tops the hit list in the New World Order. The emerging scenario over the erstwhile British Empire in South Asia itself is as follows:-[13]

(1) Segments of the US 7th Fleet and two warships of Her Majesty the Queen's Government are on the way to Bangladesh where nearly 20,000 Marines have landed over the past few weeks, who will continue to stay there, according to the Memorandum of understanding, as long as felt necessary by a client government, more than 90 per cent of whose development budget is funded from abroad.

(2) In spite of the high British stakes in the democratic opposition in Burma, headed by the daughter of the late Aung San, who was killed by the British, but whose daughter was carefully brought up in England, the military junta of Burma has managed to ingratiate itself to Anglo-American and Japanese capital by opening up Burma's natural resources to them over the last two years or so. One can expect that the demand for Mongoloid Indo- Burma Independent State comprising the north-east of India and northern Burma-the latter an old base of a section of the Kuomingtang rump, funded and armed by the Anglo-American block- will be properly promoted, funded and armed all the way from Manipur, Assam and Nagaland to northern and central Burma. The target, of course, is not merely India, but also the soft

11. Dilip Mukherjee, Foreign Policy Options. *The Times of India*, 3 June, 1991.
12. Shaili and Babita Malhotra. World After Rajiv,. National Herald, 1 June 1991.
13. Boudhayan Chattopadhyay. India Uder Slege *Patriot,. 30 May 1991.*

under- belly of China, inhabited by non-Han ethnic groups and minorities. There is the possible windfall also of the tremendous hydel potential of the Brahamputra, estimated to be equal to the total world production of electricity, crica 1970, as she goes through the seven steep falls before entering the Assam valley. Of course, the Brahamputra also creates problems of flooding down below in Bangladesh, and legitimately the "relief and rescue" operations of the Marines currently on in Bangladesh, may, in course of time, link up upstream along the Brahmaputra, Harvard studies on the water resources of Bangladesh lending a helping hand.

(3) The state of confrontation lending between the Nepali Congress and the major opposition, the Communist Party of Nepal (Marxist-Leninist) has already started showing symptoms of potential tensions with India on the issue of sharing of the hydel potential of the rivers of Nepal flowing into India, It should be remembered that, more than 60 per cent of the hydel potential of these rivers isinside Nepal. Till now, these rivers have been carrying the thin top soil of the Nepal vaileys into India without any quid pro quo, except for the floods in noryh Bihar. A coordinated programme of development of the hydel potential of the Brahamputra and the Nepal rivers, if conducted by the countries of the region, including China, would radically solve the energy problems of all these countries for the foreseeable future. It is to be expected, therefore, that the US Marines and the 7th Fleet would further extend the longivity as well as the terms of the Memorandum of Understanding with Begum Khaleda's Government, as attempts were made to further exacerbate the insurgency in the north-east and hopefully, also fan the potential of tensions between India and Nepal.

(4) There are forces inside India which can be suitably prompted to use the issue of Tibet to create serious problems between India and China. George Fernandes, like Barkis, is willing. It may be recalled that V.P.Singh, thanks perhaps to the company he kept, had managed to issue a statement after Rajiv Gandhi returned from China alleging that sell-out had been agreed to by Rajiv Gandhi. Of course, his leftist admirers don't like to be reminded of that "temporary" aberration.

(5) As even the British Labour Party has now veered round to the position of considering Kashmir to be disputed territory and Mr. Moynihan has given the verdict that neither Punjab nor Kashmir nor Tamilnadu need be considered part of India. Mr. Bush's New World Order continues to find Pakistan a major springboard for "pacifying", let us say, Punjab and Kashmir, the way northern Iraq is being "Pacified" for the Kurds by the US forces. There is the record fo previous such "pacification" campaigns in Malaysia and Vietnam. If the

SAARC countries cannot provide sufficient logistic support for relief and rescue operations of the victims of Bangladesh cyclone, and if with a little assistance from governments headed by Chandra Shekhar in Punjab and V.P. Singh, a la Jagmohan, in Kashmir, the Indian military and paramilitary forces are demonstrably unable to contain the "legitimate aspirations" of the people of Kashmir and the Punjab, surely, the United States, with the support of Pakistan, can respond to the fervent appeal of forces represented by, say, the Mann Akalis and the JKLF, to undertake the pacifying humanitarian missions under the wigns of B 52 bombers. The general dynamics have already spelt out the possible scenario.

(6) Colombo willing, the Trincomali port, with the LTTE bridge-heads of Tamilnadu, may be profitably utilised as simultaneous lines of action along out coast line in the east and the south.

(7) The Indian economy, in the meanwhile, has been sufficiently undermined to do a Latin American U-turn under the watchful and solicitous care of the IMF as the next loan with its conditionalities is eagerly sought after by the new Indian Government sans Rajiv Gandhi-with the BJP manifesto creating the suitable national climate among important segments of decision in the Indian administration, whose members, on retirement, can look forward to remunerative accommodation in the BJP.

Rajiv Gandhi lived a dangerous life while he worked ardently for peace at home and aborad.

His efforts for international peace and disarment set off a move to nominate him for Nobel Prize four years back. His last peace mission was an air dash to Moscow and Teheran in Feburary 1991 as a last-ditch effort to end the Gulf War. Rajiv Gandhi in his commitment to settle the Tamil problem despatched Indian troops to Sri Lanka-an unprecedented step. He also sent forces to the Maldives to crush a coup against President Abdul Gayoom in 1988. He signed an accord with President Junius Jayewardene to end the ethnic conflict. He survived two assassination attempts, one at home and the other in Colombo. He had a providential escape when a naval rating tried to hit him with a rifle butt as he was bout to leave the Sri Lankan capital for home. At a recent meeting with journalists, Rajiv Gandhi had said that though he and late

General Zia Ul Haq of Pakistan did not agree on many things, they pursued the process of normalisation of bilateral ties. He disclosed that India and Pakistan had come close to signing an agreement on the Siachin glacier issue. Unfortunately, Gen Zia's death in a plane crash left the task unfinished. Their initiative in 1985 to sign an agreement on non-attack of each other's nuclear facilities bore fruits last year. The two governments ratified the agreement after Rajiv Gandhi ceased to be the Prime Minister. Rajiv Gandhi turned his attention to environment at the United Nations well as the Belgrade Non-aligned summit in 1989. He proposed a planet protection fund which was adopted by the commonwealth heads of government meeting in Kuala Lumpur two months later. He was also instrumental in setting up the group of 15 Non-Alingned countries to promote south-south cooperation and activate the stailed north-south dialogue.. His successor, V.P. Singh attended the inaugural meeing of G-15 in the Malaysian capital in May 1990. Rajiv Gandhi visit to China in December 1988 was recognised an an event of major importance and historic significance. During his visit, the two countries besides signing agreements to promote cooperation in the fields of science and technology and civil aviation set up a joint working group to settle the boundary question. The group, at the foreign secretary level, is addressing the question of an overall boundary settlement. India's traditionally close relations with the Soviet Union were strengthened during his stewardship. Exchange of high-level visits added stmulus and provided greater content to India's bilateral economic and cultural ties with Moscow. The 1971 Indo-Soviet treaty for peace, friendship and cooperation was extened for five years in 1990.

Rajiv was sure that if the South Asian region was to develop in peace there should be no outside intereferncе and so when trouble crupted in Sri Lanka over the Tamil issue, he responded readily to a Colombo request to extend military half. It is a matter of judgement as to what extent the despatching of the Indian troops to Sri Lanka helped in checking the LTTE menance, But few would doubt that if India ha not agreed to Sri Lanka's request it would have opened the doors for external forces to sneak into the region. Similarly when the Maldivian Government faced a coup threat it was the Rajiv Government which acted with alacrity and saved the island republic from slipping into the hands of desperados. Rajiv Gandhi had not only maintained but improved upon the time-tested foreign policy dimensions of India, like its relations with the Soviet Union. At the same time, it paved the way for greater cooperation with the US and other western countries nor the first time in independent India's history. New Delhi was seen with much interest, respect and love in Bonn, London, Washington in the West as well as in Beijing, Tokyo and Hanoi in the East. India became the bridge that all the three blocs-capitalist, cummunist and nonaligned-could trust and depend upon. It was no small achievement for a man who was a fresher in the school of politics. He was soft and sophisticated, but firm and clear headed. He could have made a concession or two here and there and saved the Prime Minister's chair for himself and power for his party. He could have easily announced the acceptance of the Mandal Commission report on the eye of the elections and won the votes of the backward classes. Similarly he could have effortelessely manipulated the shilanyas and kept the Muslim vote in his pocket. But thinking of the votes while performing his job was not the style of Rajiv Gandhi. He was an honest man neck deep in a profession that seldom tolerated this quality. He was a visionary imbued with a missionary zeal to transform his motherland, unmindful of travails ahead. When he laid down his life at the political altar, he had made the supreme sacrifice refusing to dilute his vision of a glorious India and passing the mantle of his unfinished task to the youth of India.[14]

SAARC in the memorable words of a Sri Lankan journalist, is in irresistible invitation to sarcasm. A great deal of that commodity is in evidence as SAARC expert meet in New Delhi to examine the possibilities of economic cooperation between the coutries of South Asia. Much has been said about why the chances of turning SAARC into a full-fledged economic entity are so poor, notably because of mutual historical suspicions and the similarities in economic structures. But the winds of being left out in the cold as a result of the threatened breakdown of the international trading system and the emergence of rival trading blocs in other parts of the world should do more to alter attitudes and trading patterns within SAARC than commonsense has been able to achieve so far. The process of economic integration in Western Europe is expected to culminate in economic union in 1992. There are the moves for the formation of a pacific Rim trading bloc centred around Japan and the Bush Administration is trying to create a North American free trade zone extending from Canada to Mexico Quite apart from whether the emergence of such rival trading groups is desirable, these development have lent urgency to SAARC"S consideration of its own future. Is there scope to improve trade between SAARC countries with more or less similar exportables and similar levels of developments? According to a draft study before the current meeting of experts there are immediate and long-term opportunities to be grasped. It identifies "a large potential" in trade diversion from traditional sources to SAARC countries and in trade expansion by easing import restrictions. For this, mutual concessions will be required but as India's Foreign Secretary, Muchkund Dubey, points out, why shouldn't SAARC countries start by liberalising among themselves when they are going to have to liberalise vis-a-vis the rest of the world? Tarrif rates and non - tarrif barriers to trade are high expecially in

14. K.V.S. Rama Sarma. Rajiv Gandhi. *National Herald*, 23 May 1991.

Pakistan, India and Bangladesh. The advantages of geographical proximity have been neglected. Not only are land and inland water routes unavailable between the three large countries of the region but shipping freight structures are nothing short of absurd, it being cheaper to ship from Calcutta to Khulna, for instance.[15] Long-term proposals touch on joint trading strategies towards other blocs and restructureing of production bases to make use of comparative cost advantages. Opportunities for SAARC cooperation certainly exist; the political will required to seize them does not. However small strirrings within SAARC, even as a defensive reaction to global change, are reason to hope that the process of cooperation has begun.

In designing out policy vis-a-vis Pakistan, decision-makers on both sides of the border now resognise that war is no longer an affordable option for either country, given the imperative need to reduce fiscal deficits, India-like Pakistan-will have to cut back on defence spending in real terms. In fact, it is increasingly clear that both the fiscal deficit and the foreign exchange crunch stem to a large extent from the splurge during the 1980s on acquiring military muscle. According ot one widely used source of information, the rate of growth in expenditures (measured in constant dollar) was 3.6 per cent in first half of the 1980s and 5.5 per cent during the second half. It is during the second half that India emerged as the Third World's largest arms importer.[16]

The untimely demise of Rajiv Gandhi leaves a political vaccum both the country and the leadership of the Non-Aligned Movement (NAM). His life has been snuffed out at a time when the country and the world still needed him and when he himself had so much left to contribute to nation-building and the betterment of the developing nations. A symbol of the post-independence generation, Rajiv Gandhi stood for modernity and a forward-looking approach with a missionary zeal. More than at any other moment in the history of the NAM, without a visionary leader, its future seems dark and bleak. The Non-Aligned Movement from its inception, had oustanding leaders. The movement was the brainfhild of brilliant leaders like Jawaharlal Nehru, U.Nu. Sukarno, Nasser, Nkrumah and Tito, who were in touch with the pulse of their peoples. In fact any movement owes much to the leadership for its success. Able leadership imparts dynamism to its course through its vissicitudes and moulds its paradigm with the fast changing political landscape. Once the movement fails to respond to the stimuli of the exigencies of the world scenario, it loses its relevance and is edged out of the international agenda. The founders of NAM played a historical

15. *Indian Express*, 5 June 1991.
16. Diip Mukherjee, Foreign Policy, Options. *The Times of India*, 3 June 1991.

role in crying it out in the teeth of opposition from the two super powers. It was an era when Dulles had declared that "those who are not with us are against us". It was the towering stature of Nehru that sailed NAM through muddled waters of the cold war. Later on, under the second generation leadership, NAM got prominance when the mantle was donned by the late Mrs. Indira Gandhi. It was her perspicacity to perceive the economic challenges being faced by the developing countries, that the movement made a determined bid to establish New International Economic Order (NICO), South-South Cooperation, and to restructure the existing imbalances that were conducive to the perpetuation of neo-colonialism. After his mother, Rajiv Gandhi added a new dimension to the NAM by initiating innovative proposals to make it even more relevant. The Africa Fund, the Delhi Declaration by the six Nations Five Continent Initiative for Nuclear Disarmament, the Plannet Protection Fund, initiative for creation of G-15, group of the developing countries all testify to his creditable performance. In the recent Gulf crisis, he spared no effort in taking an individual initiative and had fruitful discussions with several heads-of state. It was his personal rapport with Jordan's King Hussein that stood India in good stead during the evacuation of Indians from Kuwait and Iraq through Amman.[17]

Under the present leadership of Yugoslavia, the movement is in a deep trough. Its preoccupation with its domestic crisis has meant that Belgrade has had no energy to focus on NAM. As long as a leader of the stature of Nehru or Rajiv is not at the helm, NAMs credibility stands to suffer. This indicates a black picture of NAM in the immediate future. It is in this part of the international arena that Rajiv will be most missed. That Rajiv Gandhi in his last phase of short-lived life was trying to mobilise the leaders of the developing countries with a view to mould the future of NAM on the basis of contemporary realities is abundantly clear. So attached to the NAM was he that even in one of his last interviews before his assassination, he spoke of need to make India's voice heard again more prominently on the international stage-NAM was one of the vehicles he wanted to use.[18]

The end of the cold war seems to have some what disoriented India, long a stalwart of the non-aligned movement (NAM), and it now seems unsure of the place it desires in any few world order, according to Strategic Survey 1990-91 published by the International Institute for Strategic Studies (IISS).

Led by technological sales, including the purchase of a Craysuper

17. Charan Singh Verma. NAM without Rajiv. *National Herald* 2 June 1991.
18. *Ibid.*

computer in December 1990, trade links with the US have greatly improved relations as a whole, the survey said. Nevertheless India remains suspicious of a world dominated by western military might, culture and free market. These concerns and contradictions were highlighted by the Persian Gulf crisis. Both the Indian government and the NAM waited until after the January 15, 1991, the United Nations deadline before launching a peace initiative. On January 19, Rajiv Gandhi critisised the government's lack of action saying, "We have lost the initiative and have been reduced to hapless spectators meakly following the lead given by others", the survey noted. However, until then Rajiv Gandhi had failed to provide his own plan or to use his party's influence with the minority government to prod it into action. The prime minister Chandra Shekhar, had in fact first authorised use of Indian airspace and airports during the early days of the Gulf war, but Rajiv Gandhi's condemnation of this breach of neutralism forced the government into an about turn. Nevertheless, India seemed content, even with its new membership of the Security Council, to float with the UN tide. The government (headed by Chandra Shekhar) ramains adrift. Electoral patience was showing every sign of wearing thin, as Rajiv Gandhi calculated the moment at which to withdraw his support from the ruling party. Even before he could do, so, however, Chandra Shekhar, tired of being branded a "puppet with no power" resigned on March 6, 1991. Yet it was stili too early to judge whether Rajiv Gandhi and a revitalised Congress would be the beneficiaries of the collapse in the elections set for May 1991. As the centre searched for a new and more permament coalition, the survey said, the forces of the Hindu right were hoping to capitalise on the continuing factional fighting, inefficiency and narrow self-interest which many of the electorate now take to be the halmark of Indian Political life. Many feared that they might succeed.

Rajiv Gandhi reached an agreement with President Jayewardene of Sri Lanka with a view to ending the Tamil insurgency in the island republic, carving out a reasonably autonomous Tamil area, satisfying the Indian as well as the Sri Lankan Tamils and simultaneously guaranteeing the integrity of Sri Lanka here Rajiv Gandhi had little choice as the people of Tamil Nadu were visibly disturbed by the treatment of Sri Lankan Tamils at the hands of the Sinhalese majority. The Gandhi Jayewardene settlement led to the 'induction of the Indian Peace Keeping Force' (IPKF) in the North and the East. The arrangement might well have succeede but for the fact that the new Sri Lankan Government of Mr. Premsdasa took serious exception to the accord and finally forced the IPKF out of the country, with the problem still unresolved. In Punjab and Sri Lanka alike, it was not the lack of an imaginativ epolicy or its judicious application which was at fault, but the complex nature of the problem and the change in circumstances that nullified the policy approach. Perhaps, Rajiv Gandhi's most significant impact was on economic thinking and policy making. By the time he took over the reins of administration, the command economy of India had taken deep root, with the bureacracy in full charge backed by political support. A complex system of centralised planning, extensive price controls, innumerable rules and regulations, a net work of licensing windows and a rigid mechanism for import and foreign exchange control had been firmly established over three decades.[19] Besides the bureaucracy, politicians of various hues had got oriented in the ways of the command economy they all knew only one method and one system-the administered and controlled system-and could not think of an alternative. As a critic recently said, the structure of official control extended over "what can be imported, who can import, the quantam of import, who can produce, what can be produced, and where to produce them, specifying also the amounts that can be produced, who can be employed and who declared redundant."

To turn now to China, the gains from Rajiv Gandhi's talks in Beijing in December 1988, as dramatised by the New Delhi's redeployment of substantial forces from the east to the west, are obvious enough. But it needs to be recalled that he as well as his party's stalwarts were debating, almost till the last minute, whether the gamble the visit involved was worth taking. With the initial breakthrough then made, it has been much easier for successors to move gradually ahead. It will be wise for the next government to continue the good work in the same quiet way, not taking majoriry initiatives on the emotive border issues to allow time for a change in elite perceptions in both countries about each other. In India's case, major parties have as yet done little to educate public opinion about the immense benefits of a appchement in terms of defence expenditure and India's relations with South Asian neighbours. Vis-a-vis these neighbours, India has predictably adopted a mixture of carrots and sticks all along but Rajiv Gandhi like his mother in her second term, was less diffident about using the stick than successors should now be because of the compulsions to shift to a less costly foreign policy. Both mother and son came to regard any attempt by a neighbour to gain external leverage in dealing with India as an affront, justifying the use of countervailing pressures-the arming of the LTTE being open example. This approach is not viable-as brought out by Nepal's acquisition of Chinese weapons to score a point in the aftermath of the Jaffna bread-bombing. Since all major powers recog-

19. A.M. Khusro, Rajiv Gandhi *Indian Express*, 5 June 1991.

nise India's regional primacy, they are themselves urging neighbours to resolve issues in dispute with India through a process of give and take. An outstanding example of this is the complete reversal of the US position on Kashmir. After having taken the lead in pressuring India for years to live up to its promise of a plebiscite, and having obtained a UN mandate for it,. Washington suddenly announced last year that it favoured as solution to the problem in terms of the Shimla agreement, thus endorsing New Delhi's stated position. China is being just as helpful now by taking the stand that all difference should be settled in a Panchsheel framework, meaning peaceful bilateral negotiations underpinned by respect for each country's sovereign equality.[20]

It is ironic and tragic that Rajivji, who always advocated peace and non-violence, should fall victim to violence," said Najma Heptulla, president of the Indo-Arab Society, and deputy Chairperson of Rajya Sabha, while paying tributes to the former prime minister, in New Delhi on June 4, 1991. She was chairing a condolence meeting of the society, founded in 1954 by the late Jawaharlal Nehru, and of which Rajiv Gandhi became a life member in 1983. The meeting was attended by envoys of several countries, including Tunisia, Egypt, Jordan, Pakistan, Qatar, Iraq, the PLO representative and senior diplomats and Congress MPs. Speaking on the occasion, Heptulla recalled Rajiv Gandhi's contribution as a world statesman. Particularly to the Arab cause. "He was an apostle of peace, and the presence of over 63 foreign delegations at his funeral shows it was not for a former Prime Minister or even a former MP, but they were all here to pay their respects to world leader", she said. "In his five years in office he made such an international impact, that his achievements will endure," said Natwar Singh, former minister of state for external affairs. Terming his assassination as tragic, he said, "he is irreplacable and the vacant place can never be filled". Natwar Singh said his major contribution was his initiative in improving ties with China, his desire to improve relations with Pakistan and his success with the non-aligned Movement, particularly at the Belgrade summit in 1989.

"We had presumed he will go on for another 30 years at least, the assassination has benumbed everyone. The one thing which we all will miss is his commitment to organisation and secularism," he said. Ali Muhsen Hamid, chief representative of the League of Arab Nations, in New Delhi also paid rich tributes to the former leader. His initiatives like his mother's before him, trying to find a solution to the West Asia problem will be remembered. "In his sad and untimely death the Arabs have lost a true friend", said Hamid.

20. Dilip Mukherjee, *Op. Cit.*

Finally successor governments will also have to take into account the fact that world opinion is beocming increasingly impatient with countries pursuing a policy of nuclear ambiguity. It is noteworthy that the destruction of Iraq's embryonic nuclear capabilities, which the US made into an objective without much concrete evidence about what Baghdad was up to, has now UN sanction, specifically endorsed by India. In any case, the number of near-nuclear nations has been cut by a third with Brazil and Argentina voluntarily giving up the option. It is to Rajiv Gandhi's credit that he made an effort to meet international concerns by proposing, at a special UN conference on disarmament in 1988, a plan for the complete elimination of nuclear weapons which required a commitment from nuclear aspirants to eschew them as well. Even more imaginative and courageous proposals will now be necessary.[21]

21. *Ibid.*

26
NEW CHALLENGES INDIA AFTER RAJIV

After the very sad and untimely demise of the Congress president, Rajiv Gandhi, the entire context and structure of future Indian politics has undergone a drastic transformation.

Since the passing of the mantle from Rajiv Gandhi to P.V. Narasimha Rao meant a general shift a look at the role of the youth in the party is called for. Rao can be trusted to take into confidence all the sections of the party in formulating and implementing party policies and programmes. Any effort on the part of any leader to ignore the overall party interests at this juncture would mean a real disaster to the party and to the nation. That would be a great disservice to themselves too. Now is the time for the Congress to establish viable and widely acceptable practices so that party functioning would become smooth as is the case in Japan, the US. France and Britain. It is also time that the party sets new forms in order to minimise, if not eliminate, inner-party frictions and problems.[1] The new phase in the history of the Congress poses new problems but the challenge has to be faced by the organisation which has inherited certain traditions and values. This will be in keeping with the Jawaharlal Nehru spirit.

The assassination of Rajiv Gandhi undoubtedly confronts India with its greatest challenge since Independence. The emotional shock of Indira Gandhi's death in 1984 was more intense-a woman prime-minister killed in office, who had been the country's head of government for 14 years. But the challenge now is greater than it was six years ago because India is a more fragile country. When Indira Gandhi was killed by Sikh extremists, the only significant threat to unity came form the separatist movement in Punjab. Not only faces threats to its unity from separatist insurgencies in two other border states-Kashmir and Assam. In other regions such as Tamil Nadu-where Rajiv Gandhi was killed-Maharashtra, Gujarat, Andhra Pradesh, and even parts of Bihar and Uttar Pradesh, there has been a welling up of regional sentiment against the arrogance and impotence of the central government. The problem of whether the union can hold together has never before been posed so acutely. As with regionalism, so with religion. The surge is strength of Hindu revivalism over the past year and the triumphal campaigiing during this election of the Bharatiya Janata Party (BJP) have undermined in unprecedented fashion India's secular tradition of a nation that embraced both Hindus and Muslims. The secular ideal-

1. K.V.S. Rama Sarma. In Keeping with Nehru Spirit. *National Herald*, 3 June 1991.

founded on the need to ensure communal harmony after Hindus and Muslims had massacred each other during the riots that accompanied partition and the birth of the Muslim state of Pakistan-is the most important legacy of the Nehru family. But in the life time of Jawaharlal Nehru, India's first Prime Minister and Rajiv's grandfather, there were already many in the Congress party who believed that India should have declared itself a Hindu state. Only Nehru himself had the authority to hold them at bay. Both Gandhi and Rajiv, while maintaining the secular vision, yielded ground.[2] Rajiv Gandhi, in particular allowed the foundation stone to be laid of the proposed Hindu temple at Ayodhya on a site that is part of a mosque. With that concession, the Hindu militant movements-the Vishwa Hindu Parishad and the Rashtriya Swayam-sevak-Sangh, which are closely connected with the BJP- realised that they had only to push harder for the door to open more. The women disappeared by different routes on May 21, 1991 Rajiv Gandhi and Mengistu Haile Mariam were contrasting figures on the international stage from start to finish. Mengistu, dictator of Ethiopia for 14 years, fled to Zimbabwe. Universally reviled, he nonetheless survives. Rajiv Gandhi, leader in the world's most challenging democracy, came to a Gandhi's end. These men, however, did have one deformity in common. Both were said to suffer from an inordinate love of power. Underlying some reactions to Gandhi's assassination was the sense that power corrupts, and somehow he'd courted this nemesis. There could not be a meaner understanding of what happened. The case of Rajiv Gandhi is more complex. He shows that power is as much a burden as a pleasure, the quest for it prompted by duty alongside all the fine anticipations of delight. Every country needs people who desire power. Power may corrupt a man, but a vacuum where power can assuredly corrupt and ruin a country. Gandhi was born to power but not designed to hold it. The dynasty was powerful, and in India, with its teeming, substantially illiterate electorate, the dynastic name was a rare source of coherence. All Gandhi's had a recognised identify. Rajiv, however, was not the intended inheritor. Only when his brother died in an air crash did he become involved in political power, alongside his famous mother. He appears to have had little desire for it, was not trained for it, would have preferred the life of professional gentleman that was originally available to him. When circumstance, in the shape of Indira Gandhi's own assassination, destroyed this expectation for ever it was his amateurishness as a political leader that first attracted attention. Also his explicit impatience with the corruption all around him. He was known as Mr. Clean. A year after suceeding his mother, he attacked

2. David Housego. Breaking point. *The Independent*, 27 May 1991.

his own Congress Party and the entire public life of India for its low standards of honesty and achievement.[3] It is true that this did not last. He himself became embroiled in charges concerning his family's venality. He was found to have misled Parliament over commission payments by the Swedish arms dealer, Bofors. He also became, in time a different sort of politician: more sophisticated, more devious, more steeped in the ways of survival in the byzantine system. Approaching the election that has now felled him, he showed a new political brutality of his own. But what is more interesting is that he fought it at all. He did not need to, was not always expected to. He could have retired from India altogether, to a place of safety from the myriad threats permanently levelled against his family. Not only did he choose to stay, he seems to have altered the persona he presented to the nation, away from the aloof grandee to the reckless presser of the flesh, protected from a thousand grasping hands by nothing more than a flak jacket. No doubt there was a certain greed in this. Power can indeed be delectable, and besides there was a defeat to be avenged. I prefer to reflect on the duty he was also acting out, the sacrifice he made. Power does naturally corrupt. All over Asia, financial corruption is part of the governing life. From relatively benign dictatorships like Indonesia, to thoroughly evil ones like China, power and peculation go together. In the larger world, not least our own continent, the alternative corruption-of hubris, of overmighty disdain-has an invariable tendency to engulf leaders who possess power for too long. The semblance of autocracy is a pleasure few leaders can resist. One cannot forget, all the same, the price it carries. This price can be extremely personal. Rajiv Gandhi is the latest in a line of men and women all over the world, form tranquil Sweden to turbulent Egypt or Manila or Los Angeles, who have placed themselves in leadership positions that identify them to someone or other as a suitable target for attack. Walking down whitehall, I am struck by how lightly we forget the spot form which, a few months ago, the British cabinet was almost wiped out by a mortar bomb. But the costs of power reach wider than personal security. To accept power, certainly in India, is to invite a life of incessant demands that can never be satisfied, of pressure which is the enemy of all personal peace. It is a summons to permanent failure, enlistment in a metier that can only disappoint. Power may fray the conscience. The holders of power need to be kept under attack. Counterpower is as valuable as power itself. Invigilation must do its best to get in the way of the ever-present tendency to corruption. Newspapers, oppositions, pressure-groups, operating in a system that protects freedom, including the freedom of political

3. Hugo Young. Careers of Power. *The Sunday Mail,* 26 May 1991.

leaders from death by violence, are vital protections. Whatever the system of government, it is desirable that power be made as difficult as possible for its holders to handle.[4]

But that only makes the point stronger. To assume responsibility responsibility in the world where these rules prevail is in some ways a selfless act. Those who do it should always be scrutinised but sometimes acquitted. They perform a necessary task for the world, even as they slake their private thirst. In Gandhi's case it would have been easier, and very likely as profitable in pecuniary terms, to have retreated to cultivate his garden in the south of Frances. Some critics, seeing the mess India has been in and the standards he had long since been obliged to compromise, say it would have been better for the world as well. This judgment is impossibly harsh. While a man may indeed be trained by the love of power, his desire for it does something else. It is the necessary, though not sufficient, condition for the survival of his society.[5]

I have watched, from abroad or from within India, every parliamentary election since 1952, and more state assembly elections than I care to remember. In two respects the present elections are special. The first is how central the issue of group identity has become. Indian voters have been told by political parties that they should vote their identity, that what matters is whether they are Hindus, or members of backward castes or scheduled castes, or belong to a particular linguistic community. Two major national parties, the Janata Dal and the BJP, have urged voters to assert their religious or caste identify, while in Kashmir, Punjab, Assam, Tamil Nadu and Andhra Pradesh, regional parties dominate the political scene. In previous elections candidates often sought to build caste, tribal, linguistic and religious vote banks, but never have political parties so blatantly made appeals to group identity. The second is that in this election many voters will have voted their fears rather than their hopes. Muslims are fearful that a victory for the BJP will mean their suboirnation. India's north Indian middle classes are fearful that reservations for the backward castes in education and employment will further narrow opportunities for their children. In Assam, Kashmir and Punjab minorities are fearful of the dominant community. Political parties have told voters that the election of their opponents will mean instability, violence, communalism, or national disintegration. In earlier elections it was hope rather than fear that was the predominated mood, certainly in Mrs. Gandhi's triumphant election in 1971 and again with the Janata victory in 1980. Rajiv Gandhi's

4. *Ibid.*
5. *Ibid.*

election in 1984 was marked by a mixture of fear and hope-with hope rising during the early months of his administration, when this young leader's government pursued a new economic policy and an accommodating stance towards Punjab and Assam.[6]

India's friends aborad have been distressed by still another feature of these elections: the reluctance of India's political leaders to take a fresh look at failed of irrelevant policies. None of the leading national figures-Rajiv Gandhi, L.K. Advani, V.P. Singh, or Chandra Shekhar-have seemed willing to do any new thinking.

The corrupting influence of electioneering is too well known to be repeated. But more disturbing than the vast funds of unaccounted money bandied about during the elections is the tendency of most political parties and candidates to turn over their campaign almost completely to the lumpens and the local mafia. In the metropolitan cities, goons, underworld dons and criminals brazenly participate in election campaigns. In fact, party bosses and candidates often seek the blessings of powerful dons and crime syndicates. If some political leaders stay away from such activity, most have not voiced disapproval of their lieutenants' shady dealings. A conscientious police officer would naturally be demoralised by such a scenario. A notorious underworld don was killed in a gang war in Bombay two years ago. Imagine the shock of a top-ranking police officer when he say scores of political leaders, coporations, legislators and social workers at the funeral. The don's henchmen, some of whom were affiliated to different political parties, organised a total bandh in the suburbs. A number of political leaders also demanded that a city street and a square be named after the criminal. Crime lords are the heroes of our new culture. Their influence is not confined to politics alone. Educational insiitutions seek their patronage, cultural and social organisations touch them for donations. Jobless lower middle-class youth find it more lucrative to enlist in an underworld gang than to earn a decent living. The philosophy of consumerism has already overwhelmed us. There is nothing immoral in earning money to improve one's lifestyle. But it is regrettable that social and political moral codes are frequently sneered at. Few talk of Gandhian austerity. The concept of sacrificing one's time and comforts for the underprivileged has been bulldozed by consumerism. In a society divided by daunting economic disparities, this tendency could create intense friction and violence[7].

Whipping up passions on casteist, communal and other divisive

6. Myron Weiner. Old Thinking is the Problem. *The Times of India* 26 May 1991.
7. Arun Sadhu. The Politics of Voilence. *The Times of India* 26 May 1991.

themes has already made this election one of the bloodiest in the country's history, the crowing shame being the murder of a political leader widely perceived to be on his come-back trail. Whether Gandhi fell victim to a hate campaign from within the party, a general atmosphere of murder and mayhem, or a wider conspiracy to subdue and dismember a debilitated nation is for the investigating authorities to establish. But nobody can deny that the resurgent cult of violence has claimed a prized head, and could take another if allowed to go unchecked. This makes it imperative that political leaders temper their pursuit of power and impart to the electioneering a level-headness which would prevent the deteriorating law and order situation from slipping inexorably out of hand. Democracy must be given a chance, as in that lies hope for the nation. Rajiv Gandhi's assassination is the third to traumatise the nation after Mahatma Gandhi's seven years ago. Unlike on the past occasions the use this time of a difficult-to-detect plastic explosive called RDX, reportedly of US military make clearly indicates the international ramifications. It brings home the point of how sophisticated is the armory of political assassins, and how much more onerous the task of protecting the VVIPS has become in less than a decade. Doubts on this score, if any, have long been cleared by the presence of imported weaponry and killings by terrorists in Punjab. Inevitably, the slaying of Rajiv Gandhi must change the whole pattern of VVIP security in the country, and cause their greater seclusion from those whose voice and will they seek to represent. This essentially sets in motion a new brand of politics, where in the security screens the leader form the followers; and aides and power-brokers determine what the leader should know directly and from whom, in the process arrogating to themselves a clout not legitimately theirs. If Rajiv Gandhi became a political victim of such a mode when he was in office, his tragic end threatens to cast the politics of the subcontinent in precisely the mould the masses despised and he tried to break out from. The people, however, may now have to accept remote contact with their leader, through video cassetters, which must perforce remain one-way.[8]

However, the evolution of the new process is not without pit- falls, nor can it guarantee against future political assassinations. For alienation of the electorate from the leader tends to engender among it a sense of neglect and discontent, particularly when his actions and decisions are not in consonance with popular sentiments. Only a leader with vision and foresight and a feel for the needs of the masses can act as a bulwark against degenerative tendencies in society. This variety of

8. *The Independent*, 28 May 1991.

leadership, alas, appears to be in short supply in the country as men of straw jockey for power using every means to divide and rule. Unless they display greater sagacity and actively work to promote tolerance and democratic values, the cult of violence will overtake the nation.

The Congress president's brutal end at a time when he was widely believed to be on a comeback trail has not only made a qualitative difference to that party's poll prospects but further vitiated the atmosphere of what threatens to be one of the bloodiest elections thus far. Heightened casteist and communal tensions, together with a brazen disregard for the rule of law, through a blatant use of money and muscle power have already confirmed the worst fears of election violence when during the first day of polling itself over 50 people lost their lives in various parts of the country. The brutal killing of Rajiv Gandhi has only added a more sinister dimension to this already surcharged ambience. All responsible political parties must therefore rally to rescue India's besieged democratic a system from mindless violence and hatred threatening to consume it. As a first step, political parties, especially the Congress, must resist the too-blatant temptation of exploiting the assassination in the hope to ride to victory on the crest of the "sympathy wave". People have been horrified by this murder and many of them at this juncture might want to give the Congress another chance to prove itself. However, the lesson of 1984 must not be forgotten when public passions following the assassination of Indira Gandhi were so whipped up that it resulted in the death of thousands of innocents. Political parties must, therefore, remember that passion once whipped up inevitably turns into frenzy, devoid of any rationality. True, the dastardly killing of a leader evokes sorrow and anger against the culprits. But there are enough lumpen elements always ready to exploit public ire to subserve their personal, selfish ends. At a time when the perpetrators of the crime remain unidentified and investigative agencies are engaged in the serious business of unravelling whether the LTTE or any similar terrorist agency singly committed this crime or it was part of a larger conspiracy, it is not right to hurl unsubstantiated allegations against political rivals. Violence in the wake of Rajiv Gandhi's assassination has been directed against political rivals. Given these circumstances, the difficult tasks of the Election Commission has been made more arduous. The fact that Rajiv Gandhi's assassination took place in Tamilnadu has exploded the myth that the South remained untouched by the pervasive criminalisation of politics in the North.[9] This has added to the responsibilities of the Election Commission since adequate deployment of paramilitary forces in the South,

9. *Patriot*, 30 May 1991.

especially to oversee the potentially explosive situation in Tamilnadu, would now have to be ensured. Chief Election Commissioner T.N. Seshan has thus far given the impression of wanting to be effective to ensure free elections, though his style of functioning has earned him a lot of flak. With some circumspection, Seshan can steer clear of any further controversies at this critical time. The death of Rajiv Gandhi is a national tragedy which must not be compounded by other excesses. The need of the hour undeniably is sobriety and caution on the part of all concerned.

Rajiv Gandhi spoke of continuity and change. The reference to continuity was misplaced unless he meant that he embodied it by virtue of being Indira Gandhi's son. He was serious about change. This meant a leap into the 21st century wholly on the strength of technology, borrowed as well as indigenously produced. If he was sensitive to the constraints and the risks, he did not show it. In fact, he imported Sam Pitroda from New York who convinced him that he (sam) could help him (Rajiv Gandhi) solve not only India's economic problems but shape the Congress into an efficient machine. Sam Pitroda symbolised the Rajiv approach as no one else-not Arun Nehru or Arun Singh or the PR men who made their fortune out of Rajiv Gandhi's search for the mirage of modernity. Machine is what Rajiv Gandhi could understand and machine is what Pitroda offered him and that too on the cheap, indigenously produced. I was not being original soon after the 1984 poll when I said at a public discussion at the India International Center that the people of India were looking for a king-emperor and had elected one in Rajiv Gandhi. The Economist of London, had described Indira Gandhi as queen-empress after India's military victory under her leadership over Pakistan and the establishment of Bangladesh as a sovereign nation in 1971. But implicit in what I said was also the foreboding that just as Indira Gandhi's glory did not last more than two years, Rajiv Gandhi would not last much longer unless he was exceptionally lucky and careful. He was not exceptionally lucky and he could not have been more maladroit in the choice of some of his ministerial colleagues and aides. Not only was V.P. Singh his choice as Finance Minister but was also allowed to appropriate the title of "Mr. Clean". Indira Gandhi would never have tolerated such a "misappropriation". The tragedy was built into the situation from the word go.' Soon after the elections, Rajiv Gandhi wrote me a letter which spoke of his natural friendliness; mind you, we had not met till then. He followed the letter with an invitation for a meeting with him. The meeting lasted for over two hours and the only subject of discussion was Punjab.[10]

10. Girilal Jain. A Fighter Nor A Deserter. *The Sunday Mail,* 26 May 1991.

From that discussion, it did not appear to me that he had informed himself adequately on the complexity of the Punjab problem, that he was fully aware of the bitter infighting among Akali leaders, the virtual impossibility of bringing major Akali factions together for a deal with the union government, their need to win back, if at all they could, the ground they had lost to the extremists through anti-government campaign well in advance of an election in the state and so on. Perhaps secret talks with Sant Longowal and his colleagues had not been initiated by then. Or else, be he would not have agreed to discuss with Swaran Singh the possibility of his once again acting as an intermedidiary between New Delhi and the Akalis. But by the time the meeting between them was arranged, Rajiv Gandhi was operating through other channels. He visibly lost interest in Swaran Singh within minutes of the beginning of the discussion. This is a long and completed story which obviously cannot be discussed in this piece. I have brought it up to make the point that only a basically good man unencumbered by experience and a knowledge of details could have approached to so vital a problem as Punjab in the manner Rajiv Gandhi did. He was inspired by goodwill and apparently he believed it would see him through the Punjab minefield. He came a cropper; that was unavoidable; it could easily have been predicted. That highlights another facet to Rajiv Gandhi's personality. Having adopted an approach which involved major concessions to the Akalis such as the transfer of Chandigarh to Punjab by a fixed date, he did not stick to it. If not he himself, his aids drove Chief Minister Surjit Singh Barnala, round the bend, obliged him to order the police into the Golden Temple when it was known that the militant leaders had already escaped and finally forced him out of office. If, however, one was looking for a single episode which highlights the theme of this piece, one would do well to get a copy of the speech Rajiv Gandhi delivered as president of the Congress at its centenary celebrations in Bombay in December 1986. He was, of course, sincere when he spoke of "power-brokers" in the party and of his determination on purge it off them. But this apparent sincerity was matched by blissful disregard of the reality that the Congress survived by virtue of its leaders role as "power-brokers", that politics in India, especially for a ruling party, inevitably involved mediation between the all- powerful bureaucracy and the people, particularly those in a position to help the party, that without such a mediation the economy would grind to a halt unless the system was overhauled to rid the bureaucracy of its enormous power and byzantine ways, and that weakening of the economy would provoke a political crisis of unmanageable proportions.[11]

11. *Ibid.*

It does not require special political acumen to recognise that by the middle of 1986, Rajiv Gandhi had lost the initiative to V.P. Singh. The Raja from Manda had run away with the emperor's "Mr. Clean" clock. I cannot say for sure whether Rajiv Gandhi was unaware of how his status was being undermined, or whether he was feeling helpless. But that is not particularly material. What is pertinent is the fact that with his well-advertised raids on leading business houses, V.P. Singh had placed himself in a position from where he could challenge Rajiv Gandhi if and when it become necessary or expedient. Imagine someone trying to do it so to Indira Gandhi and getting away with it.' Rajiv Gandhi could never again seize the initiative. He could shift V.P. Singh from the finance to the defence portfolio only admits a confrontation with Pakistan on the border in early 1986. Two points may be underscored in this connection. First, Rajiv Gandhi felt that V.P. Singh had to be allotted a protoflio which was as important as finance. Second, Rajiv Gandhi thought that he needed an opportunity like the one provided by the possibility of an armed conflict with Pakistan to make the change. I am in no position to say that by the time the Raja was shifted to defence, the stage had been set for the subsequent disclosures on the HDW submarine and Bofors gun deals. But I am told that this was indeed the case. Any way, the change placed the Raja in an excellent position to strike which is precisely what he did when he went public with his order for an inquiry into the HDW deal. A majority of people in India, as anywhere else in the world, admire the victor. They have nothing but contempt for the loser. And they are quick to spot a would be victor or a would-be loser. By the middle of 1987, public sympathy was clearly moving away from Rajiv Gandhi and towards V.P. Singh. It took another two- and-a half years for the issue to be clinched because elections were due only towards the end of 1989. But the outcome of the protracted conflict was at no stage seriously in doubt. Rajiv Gandhi's middle class constituency was quick to desert him partly because it was the Raja's constituency as well and party because, in addition to goodies, the latter offered it moral selfrighteousness as well. If we analyse Rajiv Gandhi's most important foreign policy decision to send Indian troops to Sri Lanka, we would discover the same story of an undue willingness to trust, disregard for details and failure to see through the game of the other side. It is as irrelevant to blame Jayewardene for leading Rajiv Gandhi into a trap as to blame V.P. Singh. As politicians they utilised the openings Rajiv Gandhi and circumstances offered them. So, as I reflect on Rajiv Gandhi's brief political career beginning truly with his mother's assassination on October 30, 1984, the first impression abides, a good man fallen among thieves. Neither expression, I may add by way of abundant caution, is used in a pejorative sense.[12]

Rajiv Gandhi's death itself injections fresh bitterness-though this has been kept somewhat out of the public eye. The BJP, led by L.K. Advani, is angry that the president and election commissioner decided-without consulting the political parties-on a lengthy postponement of the last two days of polling. An exit poll taken in Delhi during polling on May 20, 1991 showed the BJP was heading for a comfortable victory in the capital. The party obviously believes that the Delhi result reflects the pattern in the Hindi-speaking belt of the north. Gandhi's death-and the wave of sympathy that it could generate-have already changed the calculations for the remaining 306 seats of the 504 being contested. But the BJP fears that the Congress could now use the period left until polling to accentuate this advantage. The other area in which Gandhi's death could inject fresh bitterness is within the Congress party itself. The party was once a mirror of India's history since Independence-a "catch-all" party that embraced Hindus and Muslims, Indians from widely disparate castes and regions and which expressed the secular, modernising tradition that Nehru sought to establish. Over the past 10 years, the Congress has suffered from symptoms of decay and stagnation as the leadership lost contact with its local organisation. From a party of government, it has increasingly become a party of patronage and political spoils. Divisions have widened among its factional and regional barons. It has become much less successful in winning elections. This was the situation Rajiv Gandhi would have faced in the aftermath of the poll. If his party had won fewer than 200 seats in the new parliament-as many observers believed possible-he could have faced challenges to his leadership which might have led to his being ousted. In the aftermath of the election, he would in any case have found it difficult to control party rivalries. His widow-born an Italian but now an Indian citizen-will be under even more pressure from powerful party bosses, who will try to manipulate her. After Rajiv Gandhi's assassination, the break-up of the Congress party remain a real possibility.[13]

The morning after his death is very different from the aftermath of his mother's murder in 1984. If the edifice of India is to withstand the additional strains, a strong and stable government needs to emerge.

There are two ways in which this could be possible though at the moment the prospects look bleak. The firs[t] [c]ould be a political re-alignment in the wake of the election that [es]tablished an alliance of

12. *Ibid.*
13. David Housego. Breaking Point. *The Independent*, 27 May 1991.

secular parties against the Hindu revivalist movement. This would bring together the Congress, the Janata Dal of V.P. Singh (though probably without him) and Chandra Shekhar's breakway faction of the Janata Dal. Many in the Janata Dal are former members of the Congress party who have few policy differences with it. Such an alliance could expect support from the Communists, who are willing to back any party opposed to the BJP. Sonia Gandhi would now be one obvious candidate for the premiership-though it is hard to see the other parties accepting her leadership. Chandra Shekhar, who has proved to be a surprisingly successful prime minister, has also been in negotiation to head such a coalition. Though his party is likely to be virtually eliminated in the election, his personal stature is bound to have increased in the coming days while he continues to head the government and is exposed to world publicity. But opponents within the Congress party to his heading a new administration will want a prime minister to emerge from their own ranks. The second possibility is that Advani and the BJP are given a chance to form a government. This is what middle-class opinion in India-encouraged by the failures and opportunism of the existing parties-would increasingly like. But the BJP itself would prefer to wait until it has an absolute majority and has consolidate its position in the country. The chances of the BJP emerging as the single largest party have, however, considerably diminished with Rajiv Gandhi's death and the expected swing in sympathy to the Congress party.[14]

There cannot be an iota of doubt that the instinct for self- preservation prompted the group of men who formed part of Rajiv Gandhi's immediate entourage to rush to anoint his widow as president of the party. But the group also believed in good faith that the presence of a member of the Nehru-Gandhi family alone could keep the Congress in one piece and lead it to victory in the election. For better or for worse, it is the mystique of the family that has shaped the fortunes of the party and, by the same token, determined the fate of the nation. No one can say how it will fare in the future now that. Sonia Gandhi has steadfastly refused to play even a symbolic role in Congress affairs. Abruptly deprived of the psychological pro that the family provided even to its deteractors within its fold, the party has indeed entered a turbulent phase. But that is no reason to join the chorus of the customary prophets of India's doom. As it happens, the aftermath of Rajiv Gandhi's assassination has belied each one of their apocalyptic fears. Within hours of the tragedy, loud whispers about an impednging army coup, the imposition of a state of emergency, the indefinite postpone

14. *Ibid.*

ment of the elections and, not the least, bloodshed on a penisular scale echoed through the Capital. Not only did the fears not materialise but they also failed to numb the reflexes of an admittedly shaken and distraught nation. Thus, democratic governance, however cramped, was not jettisoned, Elections were postponed but not canceled. In a bizarre twist of events President R. Venkataraman did float the idea of a national government. That he should have done so in the midst of an election demonstrated scant regard for constitutional property and provoked unseemly specualtion about his motives. But barring the BJP all the other parties gave the idea short shrift. The BJP's ambivalent stand remains a mystery.[15]

The complexities of the Congress scenario apart, the emergence of the BJP as a new assertive force is a fact. Not that the Bharatiya Janata Party had not identified itself with the Hindu causes in the past, but the sort of radicalism it has exhibited in the past two years or so puts it on an entirely different political footing. The emergence of the BJP for that matter, might have pleased certain sections, though it has, understandably, alarmed other segments of Indian society. Equally disturbed are the contrast and left forces which include the Congress, the JD, the CPI, the CPM and socialists of different shades and hues. Since the anti-Congressism of the earlier years is no longer in vogue-more so now with the exit of Rajiv-the movement towards a new alignment is mainly directed against the BJP. Only a positive action plan can help the process of realignment. Anything negative or opportunistic is bound to be shortlived as has so often happened in the past. Viewed in a historical perspective, it is a fact that the Congress is the mother of all political parties in this country. And it is also a fact that the communists and the Muslim separatists were the first to come out of it. The Congress then had only one goal: independence of India. It was, therefore, reluctant to develop and ideology. Mahatma Gandhi gave it a simple programme for the uplift of the poor. And Nehru gave the party the rudiments of a foreign policy.

The communists and socialists, who alone were considered as 'intellectuals', did make a contribution to our understanding. But they left no comprehensive legacy of thought on Indian problems. Their's was a dogmatic ideology which believed that economics provided solutions to all problems. They neglected the political, social, psychological and religious dimensions of society. Worse, with their faith in internationalism, they did not feel it necessary to foster nationalism of a country which was yet to emerge as a nation.[16]

15. Dileep Padgaonkar. No Deluge After Rajiv. *The Times of India,* 29 May 1991.
16. Hari Jaising. The Polarisation Process. *The Business and Political Observer,* 1 June 1991.

It seems a heartless thing to say, but much of what has been writen about the murder of Rajiv Gandhi is pious falsehood. It is right to take one's hat off to a brave and well-meaning man, to join the grief of his family, and to abominate yet another political assassination-because, yes indeed, this sort of death does diminish us all. It is not right to go on to suggest, as so many have, that the killing of Rajiv Gandhi is probably the end of India, because he was somehow an indispensable man. That misunderstands both the durability and what is chiefly wrong with that unhappy country in 1991. Rajiv was indispensable, it is argued, because only someone with the name of Gandhi could hold the Congress Party together, and only the Congress Party can hold India together. The first part may be true. We shall soon see. But the second party is not true. It is, in fact, almost the opposite of the truth. To be sure, the bomb near Madras killed Rajiv Gandhi at an uncommonly bad moment, even by India's standards. The country has three secessionist wars going on at the same time. It is on the brink of a large economic crisis. Its majority Hindus and minority Muslims are glaring tensely at each other, as a Hindu-only party soars into the political sky to challenge the India for everybody's secularism of the past 40 years. And the Hindu majority is itself shaken by a violent new realignment of power among its component castes. It would be a brave man who said that India would certainly survive all this intact. Yet the hard fact is that much of what is now wrong with India is the fault of the Congress Party. To say that only the party can save India is therefore deeply implausible. In its nice, blurry-edged way, India is too much like the one party states of the old Communist world. Being India, of course, it has many different parties, and it runs genuinely free elections, and its press (but not its television) is vigorously free. But the Congress Party has been the Indian government for almost the whole of India's independent life, which is why by 1991 Congress shows the mark of the one-party beast.[17]

The party contains many men who are honest liberals in politics, and would honestly like to liberalise the rulebound, inward- looking, permit-ridden economy that Congress itself has created over the past 40 years. But the party also contains too many men who, because of its long near-monopoly of power, are by now hoplessly arrogant and corrupt.

These are the apparatchiks of India, and they are as deadly to the hope of change as are the apparatchiks of Russia. Their arrogance shows in Congress Party's frequent manipulation of state governments (which is one reason why some states want to get out of India), as well

17. Brian Beedham. Indian Politics. *The Times of India,* 29 May 1991.

as in the skill with which they outmaneuver their more liberal-minded colleagues in the central government. The corruption shows in the fact that Rajiv Gandhi, for all the good intentions with which the came to power, never got within a mile of breaking the network of bureaucracy, kickbacks and favour dispending that keeps the Indian economy moving at snail's pace. And it is partly because the economy is so snail-like that many Indians, despairing of a modern future, have turned to backward-looking alternatives like the Hindu revivalist party that is now doing so well. If India is to be saved, it must destroy the power of the self-serving apparatus that established itself during the years of Congress domination. That means breaking the party, at least in its present shape. The fact that Congress is indeed an all-India party, because it includes Hindus, Muslims and Sikhs, is now less important than the fact that it contains the same sort of reform-blocking forces that have frustrated Mikhail Gorbachov in the Soviet Communist Party. It is not hard to picture the realignment of politics that this would make possible. On one side would be the decent part of the old Congress Party, reunited perhaps with the defectors who have lately abandones it in despair, and reinforced by like- minded people from some of today's small parties-an alliance of Indians who want to have a modern capitalist economy but wish to balance that with a commitment to secular egalitarianism. On the other side would be a religious flavoured party of more conservative bent, but less chip-on-shoulder than today's Hindu revivalists because it would see that India was at last moving forward into the modern world. In its own Indian way, this new pair might be not unlike the politics of social democrats vs. Christian democrats in many European countries. Getting from here to there will not be easy. The next few years are going to be turbulent. But so they would have been even if Rajiv Gandhi's murder had not whacked the kaleidoscope into a different pattern.[18]

The decision by Sonia Gandhi to decline the presidentship of the Congress does not seem to have cooled the enthusiasm of some senior partyment. Several key members of the party are determined that the widow of the slain leader should lead the party, not only until the remaining part of the elections are over, but also beyond. Thus they not only want her to be the chief campaigner to garner the so-called sympathy vote, but also presumably to take over as prime minister in case the party wins an absolute majority. It is indicative of Sonia Gandhi's good sense that she has politely but firmly refused the offer which would have brought a lot of ridicule upon the party. Not many, except a few bigots, would have harped on her non - Indian origins or

18. *Ibid.*

her religion, but there is no getting away from the fact that she is a complete novice in politics. At least her husband, before he took over the mantle of party president and also the prime ministership after the tragic assassination of his mother, had a few years experience as a party functionary. But Sonia Gandhi's only apparent asset for the party is her acquired surname which her supporters feel will be enough to capture millions of votes. This desperation on the part of senior party men shows the straits to which the once great party has been reduced to, that in its moment of crisis it is incapable of finding a leader from within its ranks. The truth is that over the last two decades or so, the party has relied so much on a single family that no second line leadership has been built up. The Gandhis were more than just the presidents of the party. They provided a focal point to the vast organisation which has traditionally been riddled with petty factionalism. They kept the internecine fighting and the state bosses in check. This made for some discipline within the party but today, when there is no firm hand at the controls, the party machine appears to have collapsed. Behind the decision of a small but powerful coterie to bring in Sonia Gandhi is also the insecurity that they will be rendered completely marginal in the event of any other, stronger personality taking over as the party president. There are several Congressmen with no popular base of their own, who owe their entire political existence to Rajiv Gandhi. It is this group which acted with unseeming haste to announce Sonia Gandhi's election, even before she had been formally sounded out, let alone accepted.[19]

In thus trying to save their own skins, they have done the party a great disservice. The ghastly killing of Rajiv Gandhi who had shown that he was capable of keeping the party intact-has at the same time thrown up a new opportunity for the Congress. The party has a glorious tradition of nationalism and of throwing up stalwarts who have gone on to serve the country well. The party may still have within its ranks people of tremendous potential who could, given the time and the opportunity, emerge as leaders of national stature. Initially there will be turmoil in the party and undoubtedly all kinds of time-servers and petty chieftains will try to hijack the party and usurp its goodsill.[20] But if there is inner resilience and the will, the party will survive the crisis and come out of it stronger. The Congress still has in it the strength to be the key player on the Indian political scene, and its anticommunal and secular credentials are sorely needed at this critical juncture in the country's history. It will be a pity if shortsighted Congressmen allow

19. *The Independent,* 25 May 1991.
20. *Ibid.*

their own insecurities to prevent the party from fulfilling its destiny.

One of the biggest test comes from the growing strength of the separatist movements in the Punjab, Kashmir and Assam. The army and paramilitary forces are now badly overstretched in handling these insurgencies. Chandra Shekhar has opened the door to political negotiations. But these will be impossible to pursue without a government in Delhi that feels able to make concessions and to do so in the context of a review of the structure of the federation that allows greater autonomy to the states. As India's political and economic problems have intensified over the past two years, so the country has had to take a painful look at its place in the world. The Nehru view was of an India that was an important player on the world stage, whose policy of non-alignment made it a leader of the developing group of nations. This vision was inherited by Rajiv Gandhi who also sought to project India as a leading regional power with a military capability to match. Rajiv Gandhi's abortive attempt to mediate in the Gulf war by flying to Moscow virtually on the day of the American attack on Iraq showed how far ambitions and reality have got out of joint. Indians are beginning to realise that the country's political and economic weakness has lost them much respect in the world.[21] Rajiv Gandhi's death provides the opportunity for a new beginning. But the road will be long and hard.

The challenges Indian nation faces today, both internal and external, demand that we renew the spirit of patriotism and national awakening. Let us revive the real meaning of secularism and democracy in a new historical situation. From hamlets, slums, factories and fields, the Indian people should speak with one voice-We shall defend India's unity and freedom as we fought unitedly for it in the years gone by. But this will only be possible if we reawaken the sense of pride and cherish the legacy inherited by our nation. With confidence and determination we must complete the task of building a prosperious, economically independent and non-aligned India-the cause for which Rajiv Gandhi lived and died. In or out of power, Rajiv Gandhi's commitment was to the country and to the people. In the early years of his Prime Ministership, he was unsure of the ground in handling of political and economic affarirs. But he soon arrived at the perception that the removal of poverty and defence of the secular edifice were the primary tasks to be accomplished through pragmatism. This is how he emerged as one of the most popular leaders of the world in the eighties. Death comes inevitably to all. So it did with Rajiv Gandhi. But the situation was tragic. The country needed his leadership to grapple with the alarming developments that have taken palce in our country during the last two

21. David Housego. Breaking Point. *The Independent,* 27 May 1991.

years. Forces of international subversion like communalism, parochialism, casteism, regionalism and fanaticism have intensified their activities. That is why his death is a national tragedy.[22]

22. V.D. Chopra. National Tragedy. *Patriot,* 22 May 1991.

APPENDEXES

Appendix (i)

The following statement was adopted at a meeting attended by former PCC presidents, former president of the Youth Congress, Congress MPs, candiddates for the Lok Sabha election and editors of nationalist publications (The meeting was held at 141 South Avenue, residence of Mr. Ashok Gehlot, former president, Rajasthan PCC, on May 26, 1991):

The barbaric assassination of Mr. Rajiv Gandhi is a well planned assault on the values and ideals of the Indian national movement. It is part of a larger conspiracy aimed against the Indian nation state. At the present juncture, when the country is facing the threat of communal and casteist divisive forces, economic crisis and attack on democratic way of life, Mr. Rajiv Gandhi was the only hope for millions of Indians who were determined to defeat these menacing threats under his courageous leadership.

Mr. Rajiv Gandhi stood for the politics of consensus while the Janata Dal and its erstwhile communal ally, the Bharatiya Janata Party, and fundamentalists of all hues have stood for the politics of confrontation and hatred in their unabashed pursuit of power. It is this politics of hatred and violence which resulted in the brutal assassination of Mahatama Gandhi in 1948, of Mrs Indira Gandhi in 1984 and Mr Rajiv Gandhi now. It is unfortunate that these forces are glorifying Nathuram Godse today. The assasins of Mr Rajiv Gandhi have hoped that by felling the major obstacle in their path they would be able to realise their dark designs against the Indian nation state, but we are confident that the Indian people will see through the conspiracy and not let the sinister game succeed. We feel that the Congress leadership, deprived of wise guidance of Mr. Rajiv Gandhi bears of special responsibility at this critical juncture. Our party's role has become all the more important in view of the havoc caused by the Chandrashekhar government during its short tenure-a government which set spies on a leader who enabled them to come to power, a government which compromised the nation's dignity by altering our time-tested foreign policy without consulting other political parties, a government which encouraged the extremists and terrorists in Punjab and cleared the decks for the role of anti-national forces in that state and last but not the least, a government whose record in corruption is such that every honest and self-respecting Indian would hang his head in shame.

The country has to be pulled back from this brink of disaster. We are confident that the enemies of Indian nationalism will be defeated. We had seen the prophets of doom predicting disaster for the Congress and for India's democratic system in 1964 as well. As in the past, they will again be proved wrong. The sacrifices of the four generations of the Nehru-Gandhi family is our beacon lifht. It will ever inspire us. We are confident that the Indian National Congress has the leadership and the intrinsic strength to provide leadership to the country at this critical juncture.

We appeal to all Congressmen and to all secular-minded Indians to rise to the occasion and unitedly defeat these dark forces and strive for the glory of India.

SD/

President of PCC: Birendra Singh (Haryana), ex-presidents of PCC: Tariq Anwar (Bihar), Digvijay Singh (Madhya Pradesh), Ashok Gehlot (Rajasthan), Ahmed Patel (Gujarat).

Ex-president, Indian Youth Congress: Anand Sharma. MPs, ex-MPs, candidates for Lok Sabha: Suresh Kalmadi, Vilas Muttemwar, Udayan Sharma, Pratap Bhano Sharma, Narendra Budania, Jitendra Singh, Akbar Dumpy, Aslam Sher Khan, Suresh Pachauri, KV Thangabalu, Bhubaneshwar Kalita.

Office-bearers/MLA candidates: Ranjit Singh Judeo, Birdhi Chand Mochi, Jaswant Prasad, Rajiv Kumar Singh, Praveer Bagchi, Nizam Mohd, Banwari Lal Bairwa, S.N. Awasthy (Puttu Awasthy), Ashk Ali Tak.

Minister, Karnataka: K.J. George.

Editors: Shahid Siddiqui, Nai Dunia, Shubhabrata Bhattacharya, National Herald.

The undersigned members of the Tamil Nadu Congress Committee issued the following statement.

Mrs Sonia Gandhi is the only person who is acceptable to the Congressmen all over the country as president of the All India Congress. In the event of Mrs. Gandhi not accepting the presidentship immediately, she should be requested to reconsider her decision and, till the elections are over no president need be appointed, interim or otherwise.

Sd/-

K Ramamurthy, president, Tamil Nadu Congress Committee (I), G.K. Moopanar, former CLP leader, Mr M Palaniyandi, MP and former TNCC president, R Prabhu ex-MP, M Arunchalam, ex-MP and former union minister, P Chidambaram, ex-MP and former union minister, Rangarjan Kumaramangalam, ex-MP, whip, CPP, V Dhandayuthapani, ex-MP and general secretary, TNCC (I), D Yasodha, ex-MLA and general secretary, TNCC (I), Era anbarasu, ex-MP and secretary, Congress parliamentary party, A Jayamohan, ex-MP and general secretary, TNCC, (I) C K Kuppuswamy, ex-MP and vice-president, TNCC (I), R Jeevarathinam, ex-MP, K V Thangabalu, ex-MP and vice- president TNNC (I), N Dennis, ex-MP and vice-president, Jayanthi Natarajan, MP, Rajeshwaran, ex-MP, Vallal Peruman, ex-MP, Kumari Anandan, ex-MLA and former dy CLP leader, GPV Raju, DCC president, Maduari district.

Appendix (ii)

The following is the text of the statement issued by Mr. Vasant sathe, former union minister, in New Delhi on May 28, 1991:

The need of the hour in this worst period in our post- independence history is first for all Congressmen, old and young, who belong to this 106-year-old organisation, to rally once again under he Congress tri-colour, We must unite to save the hard-won independence and the unity of India as a ation. We have only to overcome our narrow, selfish ego and nothing else. Is this too big a sacrifice for e sake of our nation and coming generations? All who believe in Congress values must come together hout any pre-conditions or prejudices.

The second most important need is to eschew violence. Above all we must give up violence of thought language. We must stop the campaign of hatred and calling each other enemy or anti- national. all we have to sit together in the same Parliment and same House of the People with the common ate of serving the people of India.

w is the time to practice all noble principles of love, compassion and brotherhood preached by all r[illegible]ons and philosophies. Now is the time to live up to the precept of Bhagwad Gita:

"Advestha Srva Bhootanam, Maitrah Karunaevacha,

Nirmamo Nirahan Karo, Sukha Dukha Sama Schami"

History has shown us more than once that if we are divided by mutual hatred we have been enslaved by a handful of outsiders. Now it is not the armies that take over, it is economic imperialism that will enslave us.

Let us therefore rise to the occassion.

Sd/-

Vasant Sathe

Appendix (iii)

The following is the text of the statement issued by the All India Congress Committee in New Delhi on May 28, 1991:

The country is passing through a trauma after the assassination of Rajiv Gandhi. Taking advantage of the postponement of the second and third phases of the general election, a systematic attempt is being made to subvert the democratic process. Rumours of declaring emergency and further postponing elections denying the people their right to elect their own government are in the air. All these have a clear view to destabilise the country and to disintegrate the nation. The Congress is determined to defeat this evil design.

It is now clear there is a persistent design to destabilise the country. The pattern that emerges is one of divisive politics based on communalism and castesim. In the late 1940s, after independence, the Congress was in the process of establishing a stable government in the wake of the horrors of partition. But religious fanatics and their political mentors set off a chain of communal riots throughout the country. That destabilisation attempt culminated in the assassination of Mahatma Gandhi.

Again in the 1980s, the Congress was returned to power after the disastrous experience of the Janata Party government, Indira Gandhi set about restoring some balance to the government which had been distrupted by the factional rivalry of the Janata Party. Again the forces of destablisation became active. This time in Punjab and Assam, where secessionists launched a sustained attack on the unity and integrity of India. This attempt too ended in the brutal assassination of Indira Gandhi in 1984.

Rajiv Gandhi was elected by a landslide victory following her death. Things never looked better for India. When the complex issues threatening the unity and integrity of the country were settled amicably, the economy became vibrant and buoyant, international standing of the country reached new heights, the campaign began again. Slowly, insidiously the forces of destablisation began to palay upon India's religious and caste differences. And again the result was a dastardly assassination of Rajiv Gandhi.

Today, vested interests are spreading rumous of indefinite postponement of elections, declaring internal emergency with a view to destroy the democratic fabric of the nation. The Congress view these developments with concern. The forces of destabilisation are at work again, this time in an attempt to sow confusion in the minds of the people. And if per chance they succeed in implementing their nefarious designs, the Congress will stand with the people again to fight for their right to elect a representative government.

As always the burden of fighting for India's stability will be shouldered by the Congress. We are the Party that led the nation to Independence. Our heritage is rich with the sacrifices made by our leaders and ordinary workers to gain and preserve that freedom.

It is clear now that our call for stability was on target. Sadly its chief proponent Rajiv Gandhi has been assassinated. But the Congress is more determined than ever to fulfill its mission: To build a stable, united India. Like our felled leader, we are alert to the threat that has been posed to the basic democratic and secular sturcture of our nation. To preserve the unity and integrity of the country, secularism and democracy, the Congress will fight to the last drop of blood.

Appendix (iv)

The following is the text of the statement issued by Congress president P.V. Narasimha Rao in New Delhi on May 29, 1991.

I am greateful to the Congress Working Committee for electing me as President of the Indian National Congress. At this moment surcharged with grief and gratitude, my short response would be: I shall do my best, let us get on with the job together. I am sure that this is what the people want, what the thousands upon thousands of Congress workers want.

The sudden and tragic assassination of the leader of the nation, Rajiv Gandhi, just as he had reached the threshold of victory in the current election, has thrown India and India's democracy into a profound crisis. For the Indian National Congress this is an hour both of the deepest gloom and the greatest challenge.

As so often during its 106 years of existence, history has thrust upon the party of Mahatma Gandhi, Jawaharlal Nehru, Indira Gandhi and Rajiv Gandhi, the responsibility to keeep India and Indians together.

What India needs most of all now is a strong and stable government that can protect the unity of the present and nourish the vision of the future. It is only the Indian National Congress that can play this role today. No other party is in any position to do so, least of all the BJP, tainted as it is by communalism. The fundamental fact in India is that there can be no stability without secularism. BJP only means the institutionalisation of communal strife and hatred. As for the National Front, it simply does not have even the minimum number of credible candidates to make any sensible claim; it was an opportunist conglomeration that accepted casteism as its creed for political ends. It can not deliver the goods. It has already begun to crumble under the pressur of events. The Indian National Congress has shown that its ideological and institutional strength can lift it from the grief of the deepest tragedy to meet the greatest of challenges. Today, it feels proud of the example of Mrs Sonia Gandhi, and the personnel courage she has shown in this tragedy, as well as her deep commitment to the future of her Congress party and her India. We are grateful to Soniaji. This is a time when every member of the Congress must rise above himself or herself to serve our motherland with unity, dedication and sacrifice. Rajiv Gandhi fell to enemies within our nation and to their abetters and masters abroad. We will one day find out who assassinated Rajiv Gandhi-but we already know why he died: He laid down his life for India's unity and for the future of her youth and the poorest of her poor, for the oppressed minorities, downtrodden and outcast. Like his mother, he gave every drop of his blood to the motherland. We will not allow Rajiv Gandhi's dreams to die with him. The Indian National Congress will always strive to realise those dreams.

Sd/-

PV Narsimha Rao

Appendix (v)

The following is the text of the press release issued by the undersigned Congressmen in New Delhi on May 29, 1991:

The Congress is not merely a political party. It is a national movement. In its 106-year history, it has faced many challenges only to emerge stronger.

The heinous assassination of Rajiv Gandhi has left a terrible void. But, even in this moment of national grief, the need of the hour is to work to ensure the fullest implementation of the ideals for which he stood. Foremost among these was the nation's unity and integrity and the emergence of a strong and secular India.

In order to achieve these goals, the time has come for all secular, Left and democratic forces to close ranks and fight collectively to identify and isolate the forces of bigotry and hatred, which are trying to divide the country on narrow sectarian lines. We call upon the CWC to take the initiative to bring about unity in action, and appeal to the secular and democratic forces to rise above their narrow differences and join hands in the larger interest of the nation.

Rajiv Gandhi was a young leader. He brought to Indian politics the gleam of hope of millions of the youth of this country. He led the country's oldest political party but from a platform where the aspirations of the young found an effective voice.

The Congress Party, has a historic responsibility to lead the nation at this critical juncture. To preserve and strengthen the cherished values of the national movement and the ideology of the Congress Party, and to reflect the aspirations of the youth of this country, the Congress leadership must blend in itself the experience of age with the vitality of youth. The future of the Indian nation is at stake today. Obscurantist and divisive forces are set to implement their hidden agenda. Conspiracies are a foot. A vibrantly democratic and united Congress Party will deal a fitting blow to the faces of destruction and chaos.

Sd/-
Anand Sharma
Former Party spokesman, ex-president, IYC

Tariq Anwar
Ex-president, Bihar PCC

Y Raj Shekhar Reddy
Ex-president, Andhra PCC

Suresh Kalmadi
MP

Harish Rawat
Ex-MP

Appendix (vi)

The following is the text of the statement sent to Congress president PV Narsimha Rao by some former ambassadors, IAS, IFS and IPS offcers: professors and retired Services officess in New Delhi on June 3, 1991:

With the brutal assassination of Rajiv Gandhi, the country is faced with critical situation. The integrity, unity and independence of India are threatened both from within and without. The time has come when all like-minded people should join together to safeguard and uphold the secular fabric of our society against the poison of communalism, casteism, fanaticism and obscurantism.

The Congress party which led the movement for India's Independence is the largest political party in the country. Its hands must be strengthened. It is the most appropriate organisation for safeguarding the values which Mahatma Gandhi and Jawaharlal Nehru inspired us to believe in.

We had, so far, not belonged to any political party or organisation but in the new situation facing the country, we have decided to offer our support to the Congress party-not with an idea of asking for any favours or office of profit, but mainly for the purpose of mobilising public opinion and public support for the values and goals for which the Congress party stood and stands-a stable, secular, democratic society where fundamental rights of all citizens are respected and proctected. The need of the hour is to strengthen such forces and not to weaken them. We feel the time has come when we must make our voice headed through the most appropriate existing organised party-the Congress- instead of starting a new one. We hope that our decision will be welcomed by all patriotic Indians and our sentiments and motives appreciated.

Sd/-

Dr. JN Khosla, Mr. Kewal Singh, Mr. R Jaipal, Mrs Rukmini Menon, Mr. Menon, Mr R Goburdhan, Mr Pran Nacile, Mr G J Malik, Mr M A Rahman, Mr S L Kilam, Mr J N Dhamija, Mr T N Kaul, Mr A S Chib, Mr L M Bhatia, Mr A Dhar, Mr Ashwini Kumar and Mr B S Das; Prof Ravindra Kumar, Dr. S Z Qasim and Dr Kapila Vatsyyan; Mr Kamil Zaheer; Admiral A K Chatterjee, Vice-Admiral Narendra Bhalla, Commodore R Bhalla, Lt Gen H K Sibbal and Maj Gen Virandra Singh.